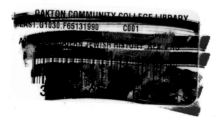

## STUDIES IN JEWISH HISTORY

Jehuda Reinharz, General Editor

THE JEWS OF PARIS AND THE "FINAL SOLUTION"
*Communal Response and Internal Conflicts, 1940–1944*
Jacques Adler

ATLAS OF MODERN JEWISH HISTORY
Evyatar Friesel

A SIGN AND A WITNESS
*2,000 Years of Hebrew Books and Illuminated Manuscripts*
Paperback edition (co-published with The New York Public Library)
Edited by Leonard Singer Gold

A CLASH OF HEROES
*Brandeis, Weizmann, and American Zionism*
Ben Halpern

THE MAKING OF CZECH JEWRY
*National Conflict and Jewish Society in Bohemia, 1870–1918*
Hillel J. Kieval

THE ROAD TO MODERN JEWISH POLITICS
*Political Tradition and Political Reconstruction in the Jewish Community of Tsarist Russia*
Eli Lederhendler

RESPONSE TO MODERNITY
*A History of the Reform Movement in Judaism*
Michael A. Meyer

CHAIM WEIZMANN
*The Making of a Zionist Leader,* paperback edition
Jehuda Reinharz

THE TRANSFORMATION OF GERMAN JEWRY: 1780–1840
David Sorkin

FOR WHOM DO I TOIL?
*Judah Leib Gordon and the Crisis of Russian Jewry*
Michael F. Stanislawski

UNWELCOME STRANGERS
*East European Jews in Imperial Germany*
Jack Wertheimer

WILHELM MARR
*The Patriarch of Antisemitism*
Moshe Zimmerman

OTHER VOLUMES ARE IN PREPARATION

(overleaf) *Detail of* Emigrants' Ship *by Lasar Segall (1891–1957)*

# ATLAS OF MODERN JEWISH HISTORY

Revised from the Hebrew Edition

EVYATAR FRIESEL



New York Oxford
Oxford University Press
1990

Oxford University Press

Oxford New York Toronto
Delhi Bombay Calcutta Madras Karachi
Petaling Jaya Singapore Hong Kong Tokyo
Nairobi Dar es Salaam Cape Town
Melbourne Auckland

and associated companies in

Berlin Ibadan



First published in the United States by Oxford University Press, Inc.,
200 Madison Avenue, New York, New York 10016



Library of Congress Cataloging-in-Publication Data

Friesel, Evyatar.
[Aṭlas Karṭa le-toldot 'Am Yiśra'el ba-zeman he-ḥadash. English]
Atlas of modern Jewish history/Evyatar Friesel. — Rev. from the Hebrew ed.
p. cm.
Rev. and translated ed. of: Aṭlas Karṭa le-toldot 'Am Yiśra'el ba-zeman he-ḥadash/Evyatar Friesel. 1983.
Bibliography:
Includes index.
ISBN 0-19-505393-1
1. Jews—History. 2. Jews—Civilization—Maps. 3. Jews—Migration—Maps. I. Title.
G1030.F6513 1989 <G&M>
912'.13058'924—dc19

88-675689

ISBN 0-19-505393-1

Printing (last digit): 9 8 7 6 5 4 3 2 1

*To Noa*

# PREFACE

This book, which attempts to present a comprehensive view of the development of modern Jewry through the medium of a historical atlas, is a revised and updated version of the Hebrew edition, published in 1983. The Hebrew edition aimed to fill a lacuna in modern Jewish historiography, and its success indicated that it would be worthwhile to bring the *Atlas of Modern Jewish History* to the attention of the English-speaking reader.

This atlas has both the advantages and the limitations of its medium. Obviously, much attention is given to the geographical dimension of Jewish history and to the demography of the Jewish people. But considering the characteristics of Jewish history, attention is also paid to economic, ideological, and religious developments. Graphics and diagrams are used extensively, since they are very useful in describing certain historical processes.

Scientific objectivity is the implicit condition of this work. Although making no judgments, the atlas is inspired by a point of view regarding Jews and Jewish history that influences evaluations about the diverse situations and developments in modern Jewish history. The Jews are treated here as a people, and the continuing existence of the Jewish people is viewed as a legitimate proposition. Jewish life is understood in comprehensive terms: Jews not only as a religious group, or as a national entity, or "only" as anything else, but as a people of multifaceted historical dimensions, able to adapt to changing historical and contemporary circumstances. Indeed, the adaptation to the ideological and political realities of the modern era, together with the retention of Jewish specificity, is here considered the cardinal development of modern Jewish history.

The atlas contains the most recent historical, geographical, and demographic data available. Unfortunately, for many places and periods, there are no exact (or even approximate) population figures. In some instances, data do not exist for Jewries that lived in periods that predated the practice of taking organized censuses; in others, it is because under conditions of discrimination or oppression, Jewish communities were wary of informing the authorities about their true numbers or their economic situation. And later, the principle of separation of church and state in many countries forbade censuses to include questions about religious affiliation. Nevertheless, through modern demographic methods, it is possible to obtain relatively satisfactory data. Sampling methods are now sophisticated enough to produce a convincing picture of the sociological and demographic conditions of most present-day Jewish communities.

The wide spectrum of themes discussed in this atlas made it imperative to seek assistance in a variety of fields in Jewish studies. It was my privilege to have been advised by a large group of specialists, and I am deeply grateful for their warm interest and unfailing readiness to cope with my many questions and sometimes bewildering requests. Sergio DellaPergola, an outstanding scholar in Jewish demography, deserves special mention; he was ever helpful, never impatient, and always superbly professional, and his contribution was decisive for the level of the present work. Also very helpful were Yosef Salmon and Michael Silber; their broad knowledge and discerning advice on a large number of themes were very much appreciated.

I am indebted to the following colleagues, who participated in the preparation of diverse geographical maps, thematic graphics, and diagrams relating to the history of the Jews in modern times: Michel Abitbol (Oriental Jews in international trade), Mordechai Altshuler (Soviet Union), Shalom Bar-Asher (northwestern Africa), Yaakov Barnai (Ottoman Empire), Israel Bartal (Russian Empire at the end of the nineteenth century and other related themes), Bronislaw Bloch (Warsaw), Mordechai Breuer (religious trends), Moshe Catane (France, seventeenth and eighteenth centuries), Stanley F. Chyet (United States), Shmuel A. Cygielman (Poland–Lithuania in the eighteenth century and other themes), Sergio DellaPergola (demographic developments, urban typology, urbanization, professional activities, Italy, France in the nineteenth and twentieth centuries, Great Britain, London, and other themes), Emanuel Etkes (diverse themes), Eliyahu Feldman (Rumania in the nineteenth and twentieth centuries), Nachum T. Gross (economic), Yisrael Gutman (Holocaust), Yaacov Hasdai (Hasidism in the eighteenth and nineteenth centuries), Michael Heymann (structure of the Zionist movement), Yosef Kaplan (Spanish–Portuguese Jews, seventeenth and eighteenth centuries), Erich Kulka (Auschwitz), Ezra Mendelsohn (Poland and the countries in East Central Europe between the world wars), Michael Meyer (the Reform movement, Jewish studies), Baruch Mevorach (Court Jews), Moshe Mishkinsky (Jewish socialism), Amnon Netzer (Iran), Marc L. Raphael (United States), Yosef Salmon (Jewish enlightenment, religious trends, Jewish nationalism, Zionism, Palestine in the nineteenth century, and other themes), Chaim Schatzker (youth movements), Uziel O. Schmelz (demographic developments, Prussia and Germany, nineteenth and twentieth centuries), Michael Silber (the beginnings of the Hasidic movement, Hapsburg Empire from the eighteenth to the twentieth century, Vienna, Budapest, Prague, religious trends), Shaul Stampfer (yeshivas in Eastern Europe), Zeev Tzahor (Palestine in the twentieth century, political parties), and Yosef Tobi (Yemen, Kurdistan, Iraq).

Thanks are due to friends and colleagues who advised me on questions related to the conceptualization of this atlas, or were helpful in other matters: Meir Bar-Asher, Robert Attal, Yehuda Bauer, Haim Beinart, Shmuel Ettinger ז"ל, Uri D. Herscher, Dov O. Kulka, Jacob Landau, Mordechai Nadav, Mayir Verete, Meir Wolff, Eliezer Yaffe, Benzion D. Yehoshua, and Paul Glikson ז"ל. Appreciation is due to the Division of Jewish Demography and Statistics at the Institute for Contemporary Jewry, Hebrew University of Jerusalem, for the use of its unequaled library resources; to the Lasar Segall Museum, São Paulo, Brazil, and to its director, Mauricio Segall, for the reproduction of the painting *Emigrants' Ship*; to Erich Kulka, for the aerial photographs of Auschwitz.

The English edition owes much to the interest and constant support of Jehuda Reinharz, whose help is acknowledged with gratitude. Barbara Ball was responsible for the preparation of the English edition; her talent, discernment, and dedication were decisive in its shaping. Moshe Kohn was very helpful in the editing of the English text. I am most appreciative of the imaginative work of Sarah Postavsky and Pirhya Cohen, who prepared the maps and diagrams of the Hebrew edition, and to the excellent team of cartography specialists of Carta, who worked on the present English edition.

It is with pleasure that I acknowledge the collaboration and support of Oxford University Press, New York: of Nancy Lane, the senior editor of history, and of Irene Pavitt, whose very professional editing and many suggestions are deeply appreciated. Last, but not least, Shay Hausman, Carta's managing director, was the essential executive hand leading us all. He bore the brunt of many of the difficulties involved in the preparation of the atlas, and did so with good spirits and unfailing good will.

For me, the preparation of an atlas on modern Jewish history was a most stimulating intellectual adventure. For much of the result, my collaborators, acknowledged earlier, deserve the credit. For all the shortcomings, I alone accept full responsibility.

Jerusalem
July 1989

E. F.

# CONTENTS

## IV. Muslim Countries



## V. European Jewry in the Interwar Years



## VI. European Jewry, 1940–1980s

## VII. The New Centers of Jewry



**Observations:**

Names of geographical regions or cities that were modified as a result of political changes were written according to the official name in the given period. Therefore, Lwów, Lemberg, and Lvov are the same city when under Polish, Austrian, or Russian domination, respectively. Pressburg became Bratislava when it passed from the Hapsburg Empire to Czechoslovakia.

Jewish names of localities in Eastern Europe are usually indicated in parentheses, especially when the name used by the Jews was significantly different from the official name.

In many demographic diagrams, the "median age" of the population was indicated. The median age is calculated by dividing the population into two equal parts, one younger and the other older.

Jews are included in the "total population," since their small numbers in a given population do not significantly change the data indicated.

# ATLAS OF MODERN JEWISH HISTORY

# Modern Times in Jewish History

The concept "modern times" embraces two distinct periods in Jewish history. One, from the seventeenth or eighteenth century until 1939, will here be called the "modern period." The other, from 1948 on, will be called the "contemporary period." Separating the two are those fateful years from 1939 to 1948 that changed the course of Jewish history.

The modern period did not begin at the same time for the various Jewish communities. The Spanish–Portuguese Jews living in Amsterdam and London were already "modern" in the early seventeenth century. For the majority of European Jews, different events in the late seventeenth and the eighteenth centuries marked the dawn of the modern period: the new direction of Jewish migration, from Eastern Europe westward; the effects of the partitions of Poland; the European Enlightenment; and the civic emancipation granted to Jews in the wake of the French Revolution. For the Jews in many Muslim countries and certain regions in Eastern Europe, modernity came only in the twentieth century.

For all Jews, wherever they lived, "modernization" meant basically the same thing: to cope with the new ideas and forms of social, cultural, and political life developing in the general society, and to adjust Judaism and Jewish society to them. This pattern—adapting to the general environment while maintaining Jewish identity—repeated a process that had occurred again and again in Jewish history. What made the modern situation more acute were the depth of the changes and the fateful implications, both positive and negative, that some of them had for the continuing existence of the Jewish people.

It was in Europe that most of the characteristics of Jewish "modern times" originated. And it was in Europe that most of the Jewish people were concentrated: more than 80 percent at the end of the nineteenth century. The largest Jewish communities were in Eastern Europe, most of them originating from historic Poland, the Poland before the partitions of the late eighteenth century. These communities retained many elements of the social and cultural distinctiveness of the old community (some to a lesser, some to a greater degree). The encounter between the traditional values and the new ideas circulating in the general European society produced a rich array of ideas and movements: the Jewish enlightenment (*haskalah*); different religious trends ranging from extreme Reform to ultra-Orthodoxy; the "Science of Judaism"; a flowering of Yiddish and Hebrew creativity; and the rise of Jewish nationalism, Jewish socialism, autonomism, and Zionism.

Almost all these new ideas and movements took hold also in Jewish communities in other parts of the world, such as the Americas and the Muslim countries, in each place being adapted to local conditions and needs. But it was in Europe that the drama of Jewish modernization was to be played out to a tragic denouement. Although the relationship between the general and the Jewish society in modern times offered many new opportunities, it spelled some awesome dangers. The growth of modern antisemitism and its terrible outcome, the Holocaust, revealed how perilous Jewish life in modern conditions could become.

The developments of the 1940s—the destruction of European Jewry and the re-creation of the Jewish state—closed one chapter in Jewish history and opened another. These two events were of opposite historical significance, although together they caused an upheaval in Jewish life of far-reaching consequences. In the tempest that swept the Jewish people during World War II, large, well-established communities were obliterated; many of those that survived could not recover from the internal demographic and spiritual havoc wrought by the Holocaust. And the events surrounding the establishment of the Jewish state shortly afterward shook the foundations of even older Jewish communities in Muslim countries and caused their ultimate dissolution.

The establishment of Israel led to the concentration there of Jews from all over the world. Two new centers—in Israel and in the United States—became the pillars of Jewish life. Substantive changes took place in the character of the Jewish people and in its relations with non-Jewish societies and countries. This process continued as the Jewish people moved toward the twenty-first century.

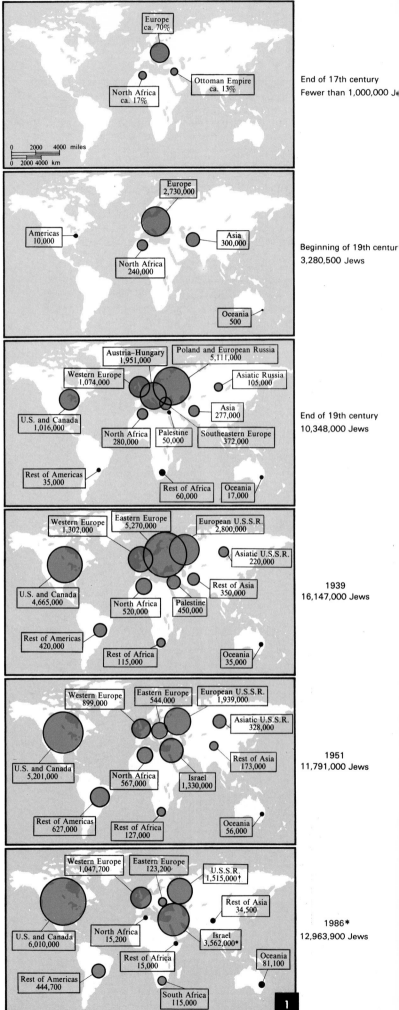

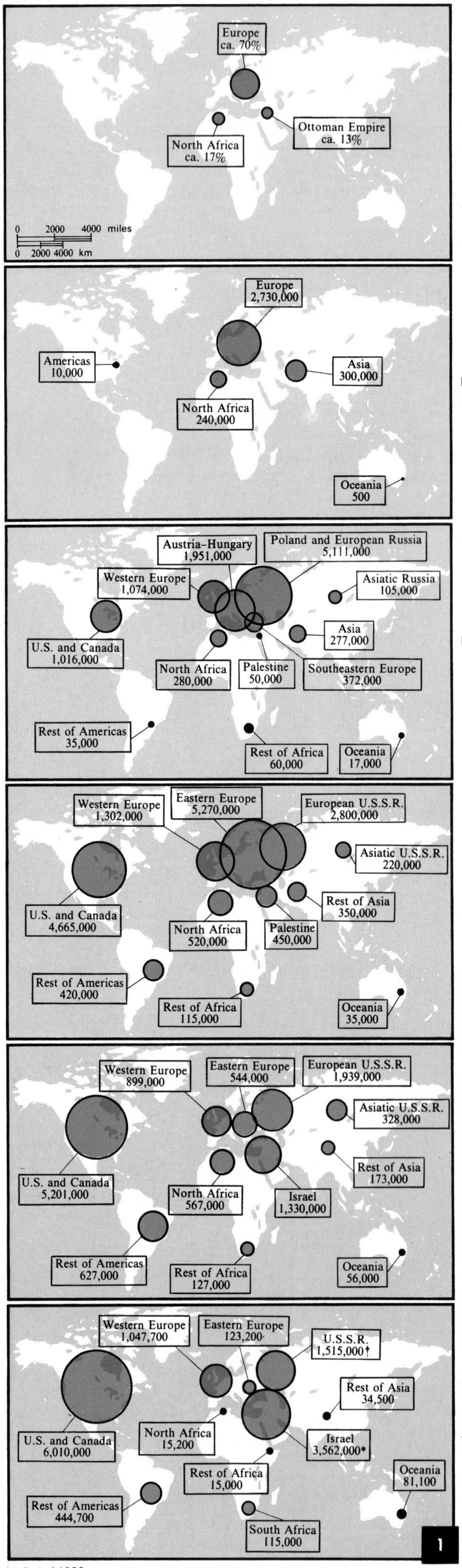


End of 17th century
Fewer than 1,000,000 J

Beginning of 19th centur
3,280,500 Jews

End of 19th century
10,348,000 Jews

1939
16,147,000 Jews

1951
11,791,000 Jews

1986*
12,963,900 Jews

* End of 1986
† Including Asian regions

## Jewish Centers:

Seventeenth Century to the 1980s

The Jewish people underwent significant demographic changes in the modern era. In the mid-seventeenth century the number of Jews had dropped to a low point in Jewish history: less than 1 million, concentrated mostly in Eastern Europe, with some living in the Ottoman Empire. A radical change occurred during the next 300 years; in 1939, the number of Jews had reached its highest point: more than 16 million, distributed all over the world.

The destruction of European Jewry during World War II and the creation of Israel in 1948 completely changed the demographic structure of the Jewish people. With the disappearance of most of the oldest centers of the Jewish people in Europe and the Muslim countries, the hubs of Jewish life now passed to the younger centers of Jewry, especially in the United States and Israel. In the last quarter of the twentieth century, 95 percent of all Jews were concentrated in nine countries: the United States, Israel, the Soviet Union, France, Great Britain, Canada, Argentina, South Africa, and Brazil. Sixty percent of all Diaspora Jews lived in the United States. Soviet Jewry, whose situation was complex, was still the second largest segment of the Jewish people in the Diaspora, numbering about 1,515,000 in 1986.

In the early 1980s, there were about 13 million Jews in the world, 10 percent more than in 1951. This seemed to be the numerical high point of the Jewish people in the second half of the twentieth century: internal demographic problems in Diaspora Jewry indicated that over the next generation, the number of Jews in the world might decrease, although there would be more Jews in Israel.

## Migratory Directions:

The Middle Ages to the Modern Period

From the end of the thirteenth century, Western Europe was gradually depleted of most of its Jews, as a result of their expulsion from England (1290), France (fourteenth century), Spain (1492), Portugal (1496–1497), most of the Italian peninsula (sixteenth century), and most of the German cities and principalities (sixteenth century). The bulk of these banished Jews migrated eastward, many settling in Poland. Others went from Spain and Portugal to North Africa and the eastern part of the Mediterranean basin, toward the Ottoman Empire.

Beginning in the late seventeenth century, Jewish migration changed direction. From Eastern Europe, Jews started moving westward, back to Central and Western Europe. The trend began in the wake of the pogroms in the Ukraine in 1648 and 1649 and the upheavals caused by the Russian–Swedish wars of 1648 to 1656. The westward migration resumed, eventually, during the great migration that started in the second half of the nineteenth century, bringing masses of Jews to the Americas. After World War II, other migratory patterns developed, reflecting the new Jewish situation.

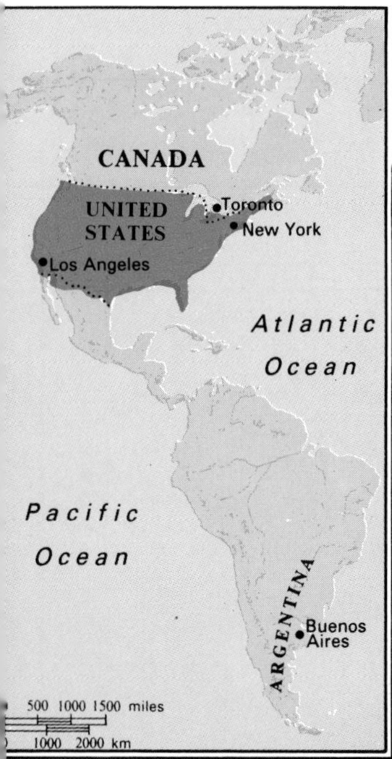


The United States: A Major Jewish Center After World War II

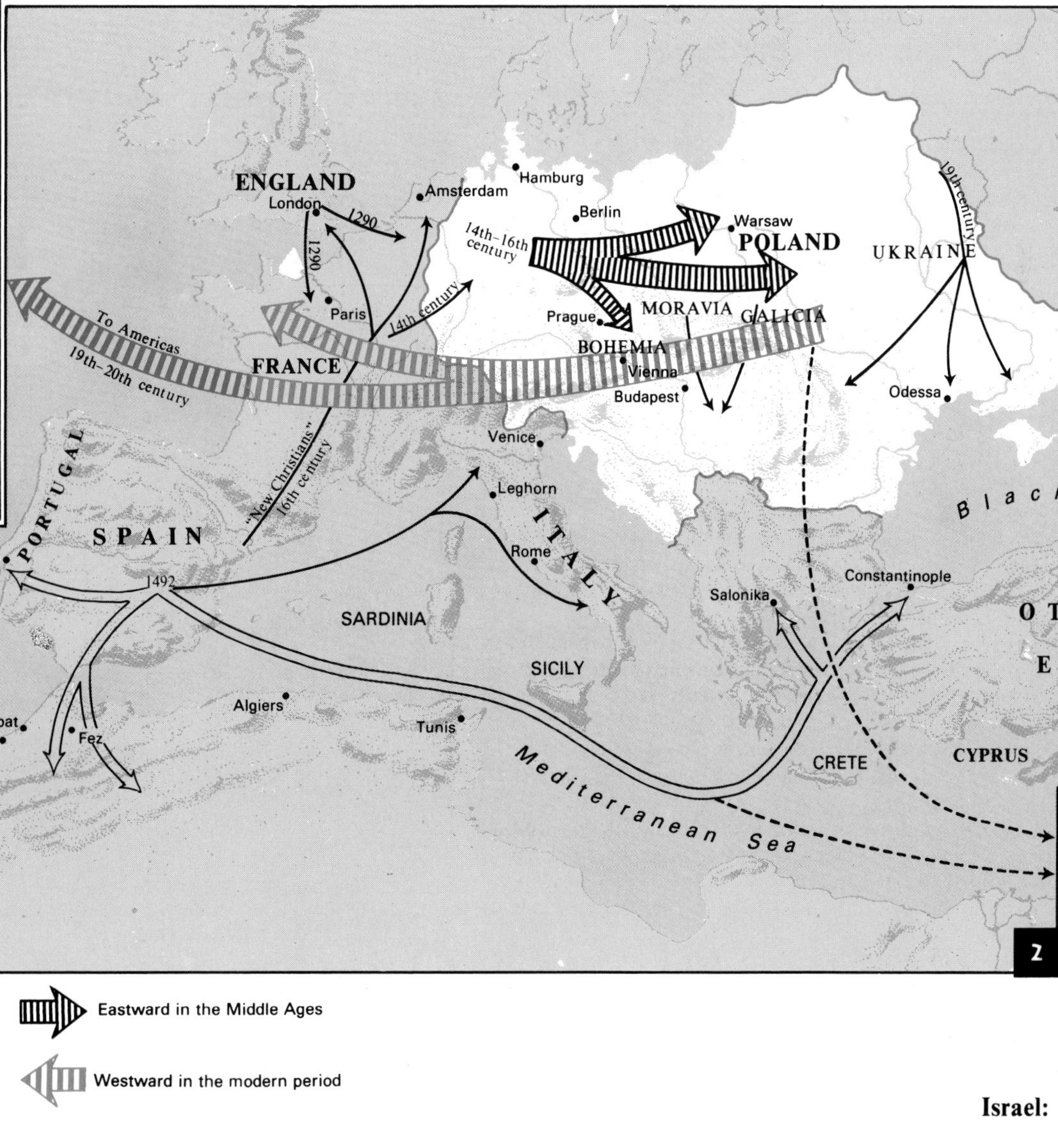


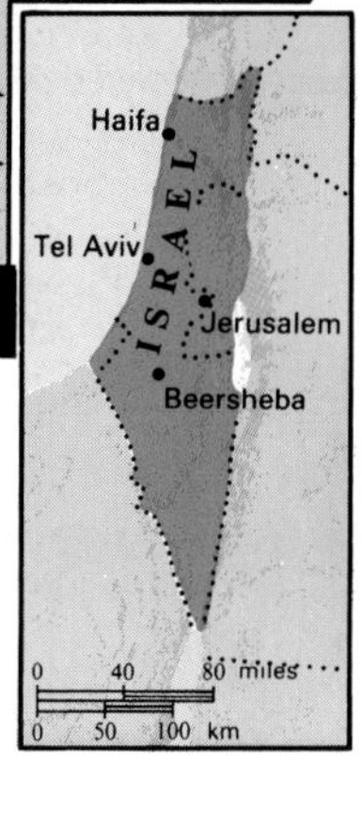


Israel: A Major Jewish Center After World War II

# Jewish Migrations:

Nineteenth and Twentieth Centuries

The migratory movement of the Jews in modern times showed two main patterns, which overlapped starting at some point in the nineteenth century: one extended from the mid-seventeenth century to the late nineteenth century; the other, from then until the present. In the first period, Jews migrated inside Europe, both between and within the different countries. The migration brought about the reconstitution of Jewish communities that had disappeared in earlier centuries, as well as the establishment of new ones. A trickle of Jewish immigrants crossed the Atlantic Ocean and founded the first Jewish communities in the Americas.

Three main factors may explain this new development of European Jewry. First, changes in European political and social philosophy beginning in the late seventeenth century improved the attitude of the general society toward the Jews and made possible their resettlement in countries from which they had been expelled in earlier centuries. Second, natural increase among Jews grew enormously; in the nineteenth century, it was much higher than among non-Jews, especially in Eastern Europe. Toward the end of the nineteenth century, there were about 7.5 million Jews in Eastern Europe, or 70 to 75 percent of the entire Jewish people. Third—connected with these two factors—Jews began emigrating in large numbers and settling all over the world. Before World War II, when the Jewish people reached its greatest size, established Jewish communities existed in Europe, the Americas, Africa, Palestine, and Oceania.

The mass emigration of Jews from Europe, which started in the 1870s, is one of the most important developments in modern Jewish history, since it completely changed the demographic structure of the Jewish people. Jewish emigration was part of the enormous migration of tens of millions of people from the Old World. But proportionately more Jews emigrated, relative both to the total number of Jews in Europe and to the percentage of non-Jews emigrating. Jewish emigration was also of a more conclusive character: it was family-oriented, with a high percentage of women and children and a very low percentage of people who later returned to the Old World. More than other emigrating groups, Jews burned the bridges connecting them to Europe. Furthermore, the growth of new Jewish centers as a result of the mass migration was to prove decisive after the Holocaust for the continuing existence of the Jewish people.

Jewish migration continued strongly in the late twentieth century. Between 1881 and 1939, an average of about 64,000 Jews immigrated yearly to different countries. From 1948 to 1982, the average was even higher, about 75,000 a year. But the countries of destination changed. Before World War II, almost all Jewish emigrants came from Europe, more than 90 percent of them from Eastern Europe. Their main destination was the Americas (83 percent), especially the United States (68 percent). After 1948, Israel became the main destination of Jewish emigrants (68 percent), and Europe again became the objective for many Jews (13 percent), most coming from African and Asian Muslim countries. In the 1960s, a new factor appeared on the map of Jewish migration: Jews leaving Israel. In the early 1980s, their number reached about 400,000, including children born after leaving Israel. Finally, during the 1960s and 1970s, almost 240,000 Jews were permitted to leave the Soviet Union, the majority (67 percent) settling in Israel.

## Jewish Migrations Within Europe

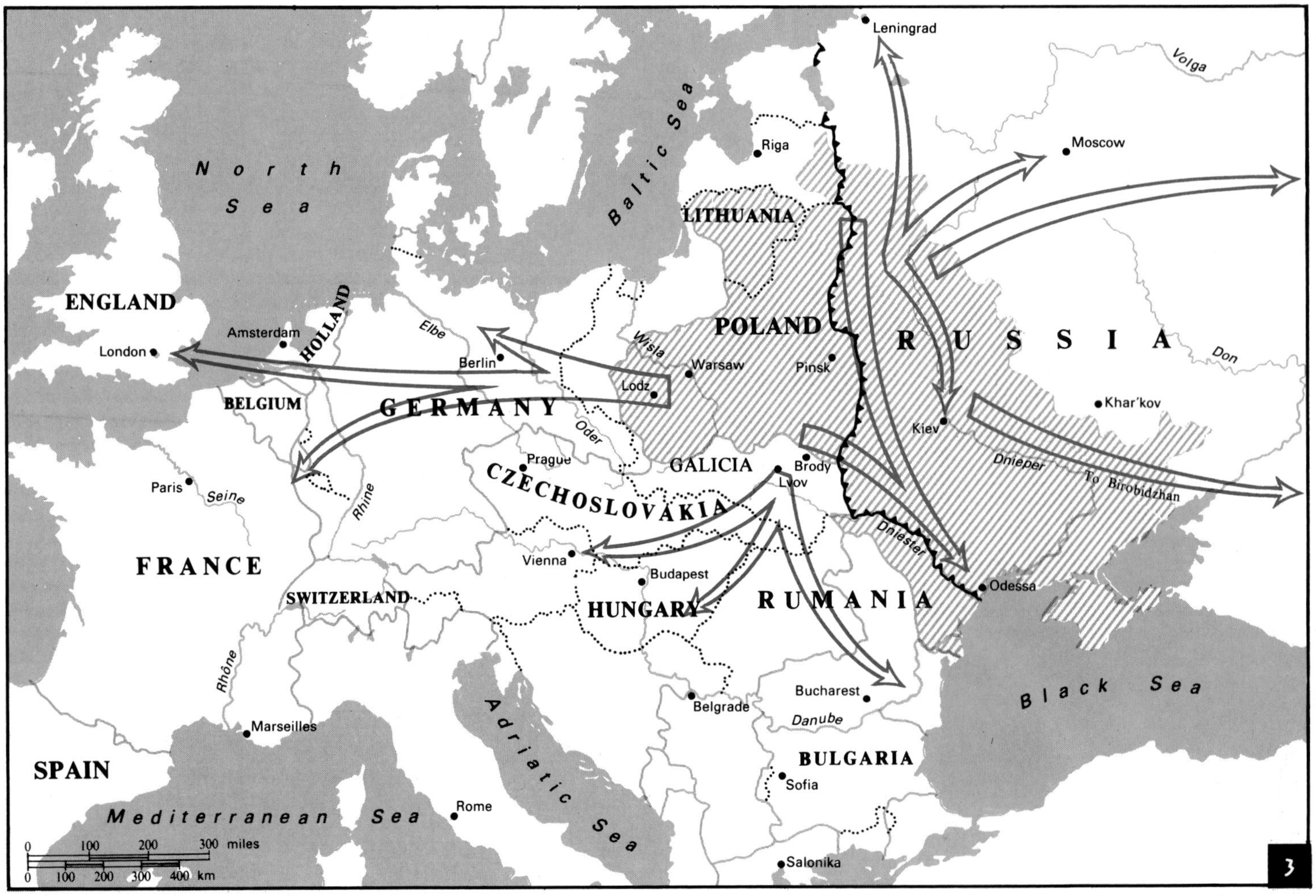


Borders on eve of World War I (1914)
Borders after World War I
Borders of U.S.S.R., 1921 (after Riga Treaty)
Pale of Settlement (abolished in 1917)

# Intercontinental Migrations of the Jews

## 1881 to 1939

Total Migration (100%)
3,715,000

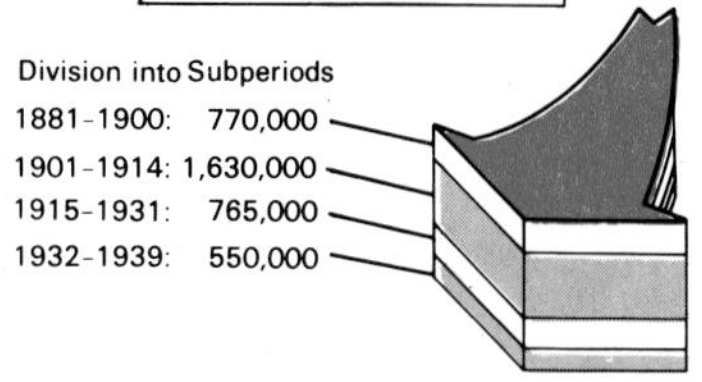


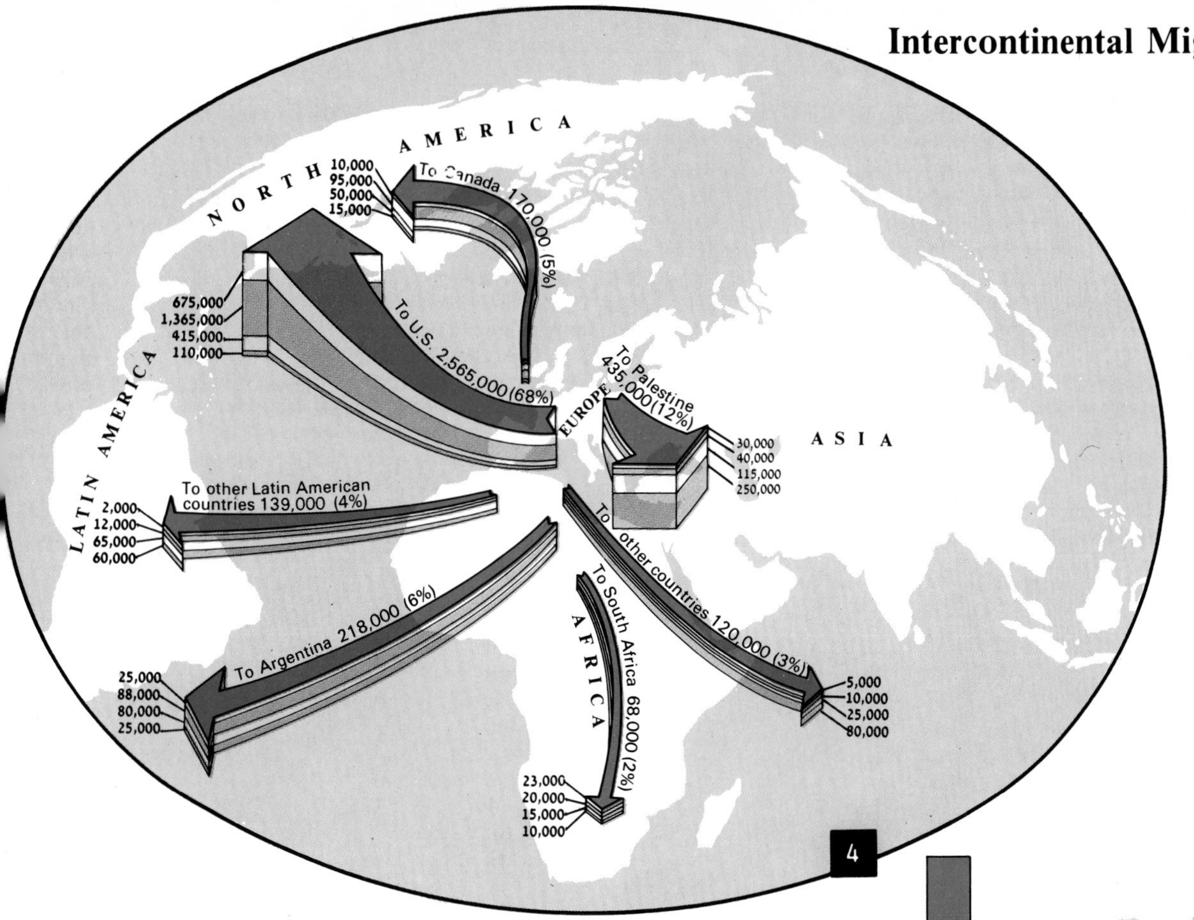


## 1940 to May 1948

Total Migration (100%)
300,000

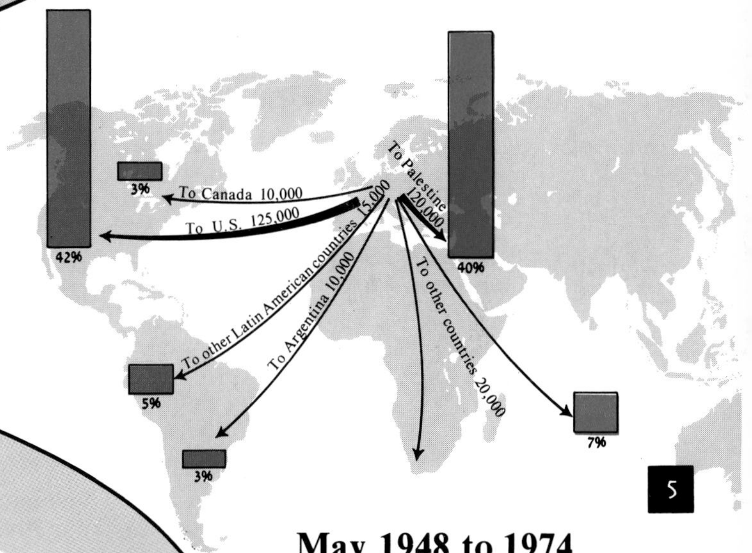


### Jewish Migrations: 1881–1982

| Country of Destination | No. of immigrants 1881-1974 | % | No. of immigrants 1975-1982 | % | **No. of immigrants 1881-1982** | % |
|---|---|---|---|---|---|---|
| Israel | 2,100,000 | 34 | 172,000 | 41 | **2,272,000** | **34** |
| United States | 2,950,000 | 47 | | | | |
| Canada | 275,000 | 4 | | | | |
| Argentina | 238,000 * | 4 | | | | |
| Other Latin American countries | 154,000 * | 2 | 243,000 | 59 | **4,428,000** | **66** |
| South Africa | 68,000 * | 1 | | | | |
| Western Europe | 285,000 † | 4 | | | | |
| Other countries | 225,000 | 4 | | | | |
| Total | 6,285,000 | 100 | 415,000 | 100 | **6,700,000** | **100** |

* To 1948
† After 1948

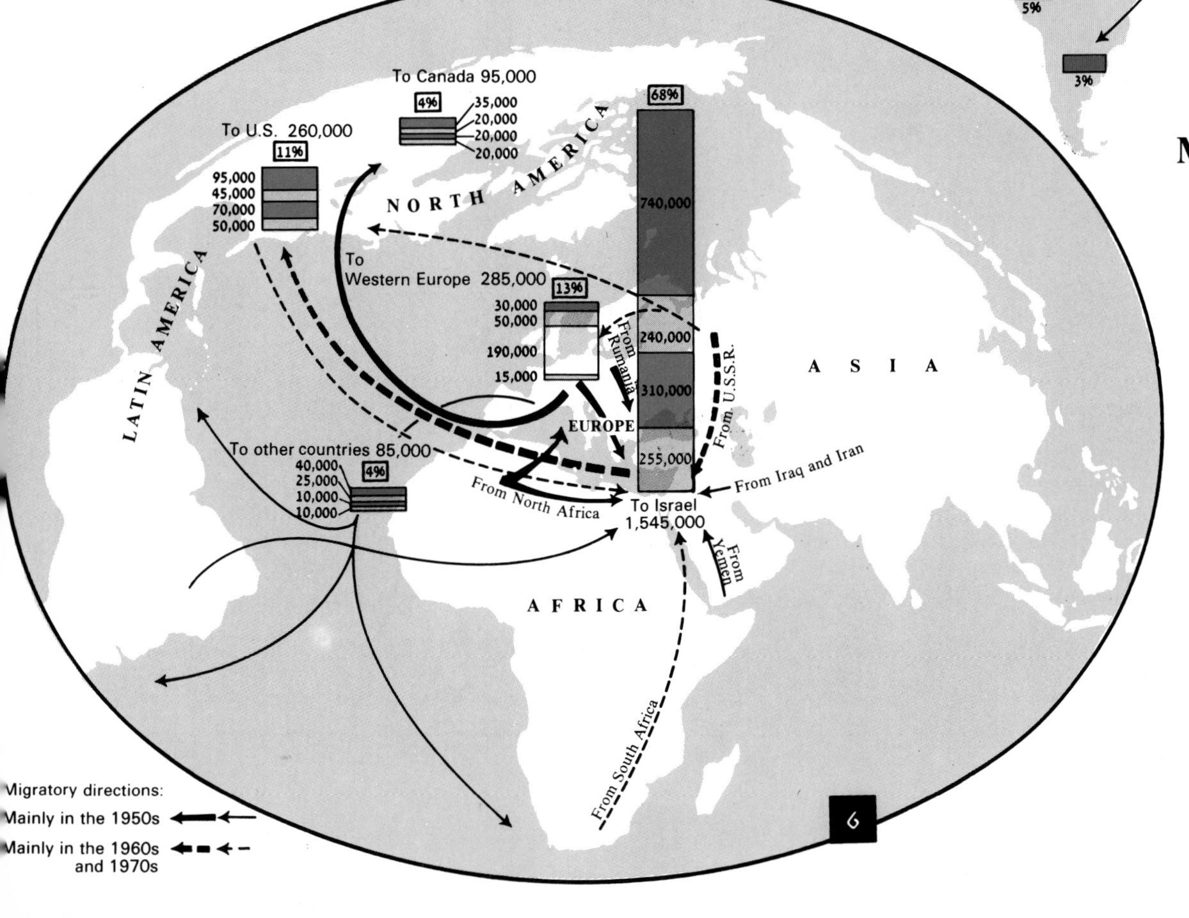


## May 1948 to 1974

Total Migration (100%)
2,270,000

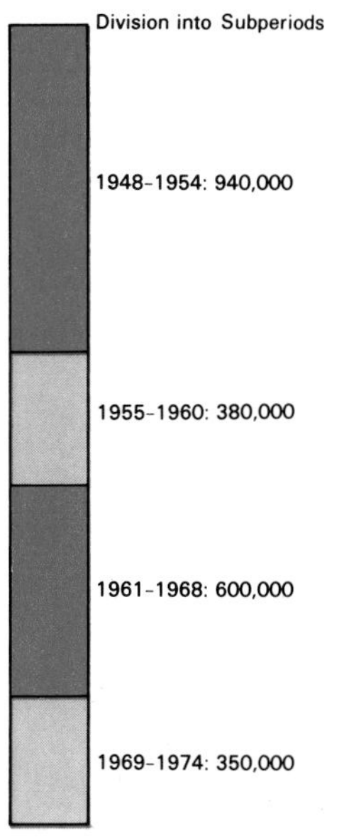

# Urbanization Among the Jews

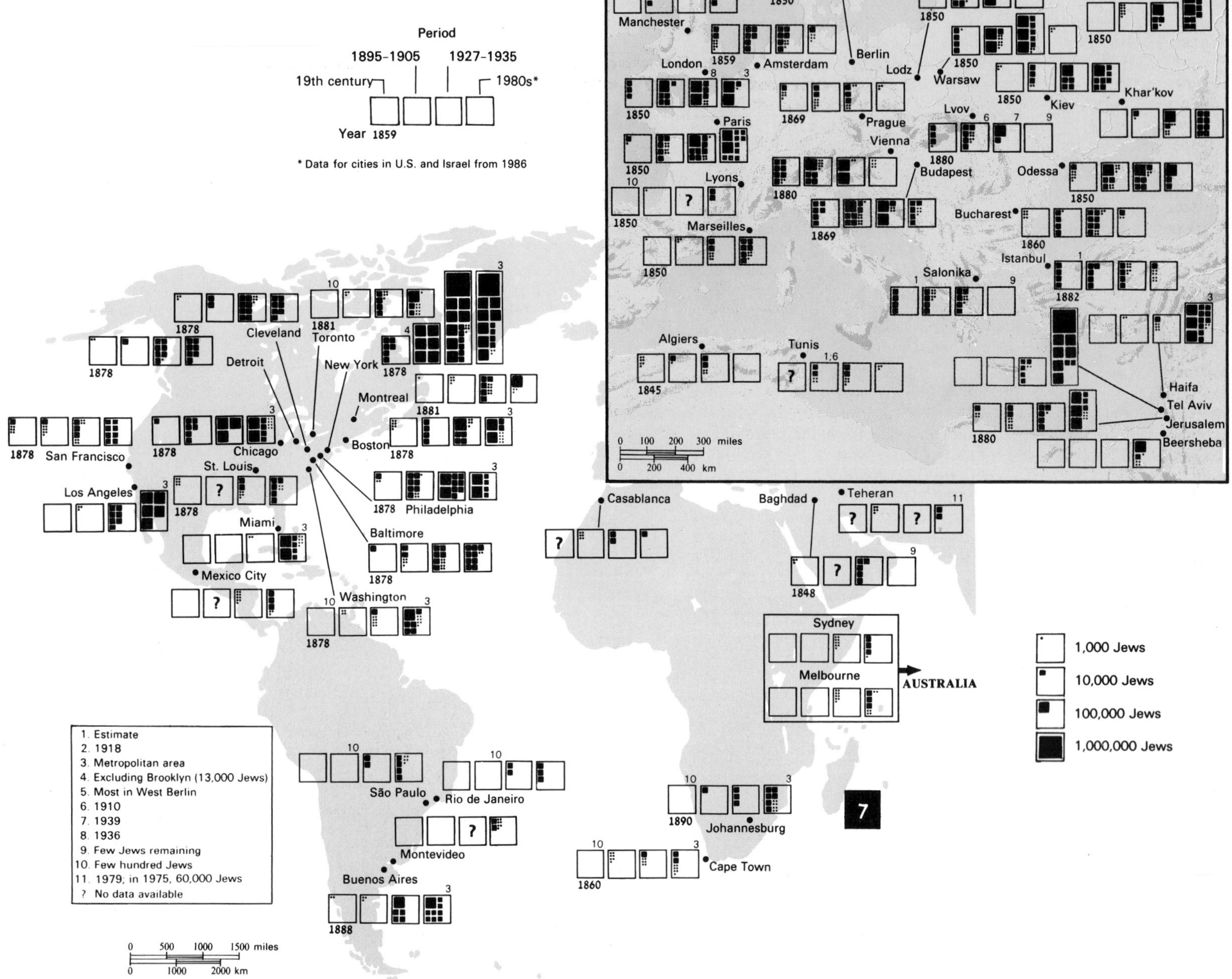


The urbanization of Jews in Europe was much more rapid than among non-Jews. In the 1930s, the proportion of Jews living in the cities was at least double that of non-Jews. One reason for this was that Jews had been an urban or a semiurban element in the villages or small towns of Eastern Europe, where most immigrating Jews originated. Indeed, in many places, the Jews had been the majority of the local population. They were organized in well-structured communities (*kehillot*) in which the *baalebatim* (literally, the "householders," referring to the more affluent family heads) led the community and its institutions.

Later, the concentration of Jews in large urban centers created new demographic and social realities. By the 1930s, New York City had about 2 million Jews, the largest urban concentration in Jewish history. In other metropolitan centers—like London, Paris, Moscow, Chicago, and, later, Los Angeles—the Jewish population totaled hundreds of thousands. But in spite of these huge numbers, the Jews were only a small percentage of the inhabitants of those cities. Even in New York, Jews were only about one-quarter of the city's population. Except in Israel, Jews in the twentieth century were minorities among the large urban populations in whose midst they lived.

Moving from their original locales in Europe to the larger urban centers, Jews brought with them their social traditions and institutions. The traditions survived, but many of the social structures collapsed under the new conditions. The new tenor of life, the uprootedness of the new Jewish population, and the promises of the modern city created new opportunities for the Jews, but also new problems to challenge their survival as a distinct group. No Jewish organizational structure with the authority of the *kehillah* of old was imaginable under modern conditions. The mobility of Jews in the huge metropolises, their various religious tendencies, and the cultural and civil openness of most of the new countries gave rise to congregations with varying orientations. Jewish integration into the general society produced many new Jewish cultural expressions, but also exacerbated the disruptive tendencies in Jewish life, such as assimilation, low fertility, and out-marriage.

Urbanization among Jews continued in the second half of the twentieth century. In the 1980s, 98 percent of all Jews lived in cities of more than 500,000 inhabitants. A common phenomenon was the concentration of the majority of Jews of a given country in one or two major cities: London, Paris, Montreal and Toronto, Budapest, Buenos Aires, Johannesburg and Cape Town. There was also the more recent tendency toward suburban concentration—still an urban trend—which started in the United States and was becoming popular among Jews in other countries.

There is not much demographic information about the Jews at the beginning of the nineteenth century, and assessments have yet to be made on a continental basis. Only toward the end of the nineteenth century did better demographic data become available, and even then we must still depend on estimates regarding many places in Asia, Africa, the Americas, and even in major European countries like France and England. Nevertheless, some demographic trends shown by Jews during the nineteenth century seem clear enough.

The most significant trend was the huge increase in the number of Jews, primarily in Eastern Europe. The general population of Europe grew considerably in the nineteenth century, but the increase among the Jews was even more rapid. The Jews were an estimated 1.4 percent of the European population during the first decades of the nineteenth century, but 2 percent at the end of the century. About 82 to 83 percent of all Jews lived in Europe in the nineteenth century. Fifty percent of the Jewish people was concentrated in the Russian Empire (Russia and Poland), and another 20 percent in the Hapsburg Empire (Austria–Hungary, from 1867). An important demographic development of those years was the rise of American Jewry. At the beginning of the nineteenth century, there were a few thousand Jews in the United States. By the end of the century, American Jewry numbered about 1 million, the result of the growing emigration of Jews from Europe, especially Eastern Europe, beginning in the second half of the century. Those emigrants settled in other parts of the world as well: in Central and Western Europe and, from the beginning of the twentieth century, in Argentina and South Africa. East European Jewry played a central role in the Jewish demographic changes in modern times.

Toward the end of the nineteenth century, there were indications that the large natural increase among the Jews had begun to slow down. The rate of natural increase of Jews fell in line with that of the general society, and in Western Europe was even lower. Another typical demographic tendency was the growing concentration of Jews in larger cities, in both Europe and the Americas. These two characteristics—a declining birth rate and urban concentration—were to continue in the twentieth century.

The percentage of Jews living in Muslim countries in Asia and Africa decreased in the nineteenth century. It was only toward the end of the century that the social and economic factors that had caused the demographic changes in Western Jewry began to have an impact in Muslim countries, where the Jews were among the first to be influenced by the modernizing trends. From the beginning of the twentieth century, the demographic characteristics of European Jewry during the nineteenth century—increasing birth rates and gradual urbanization—began to appear in Asian and African Jewries.

## The Jewish People:
Early Nineteenth Century

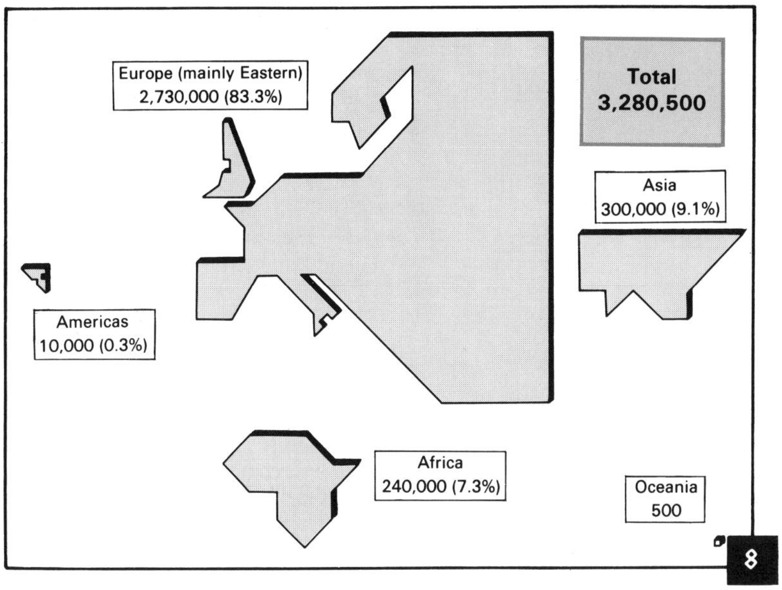


## The Jewish People:
Late Nineteenth Century

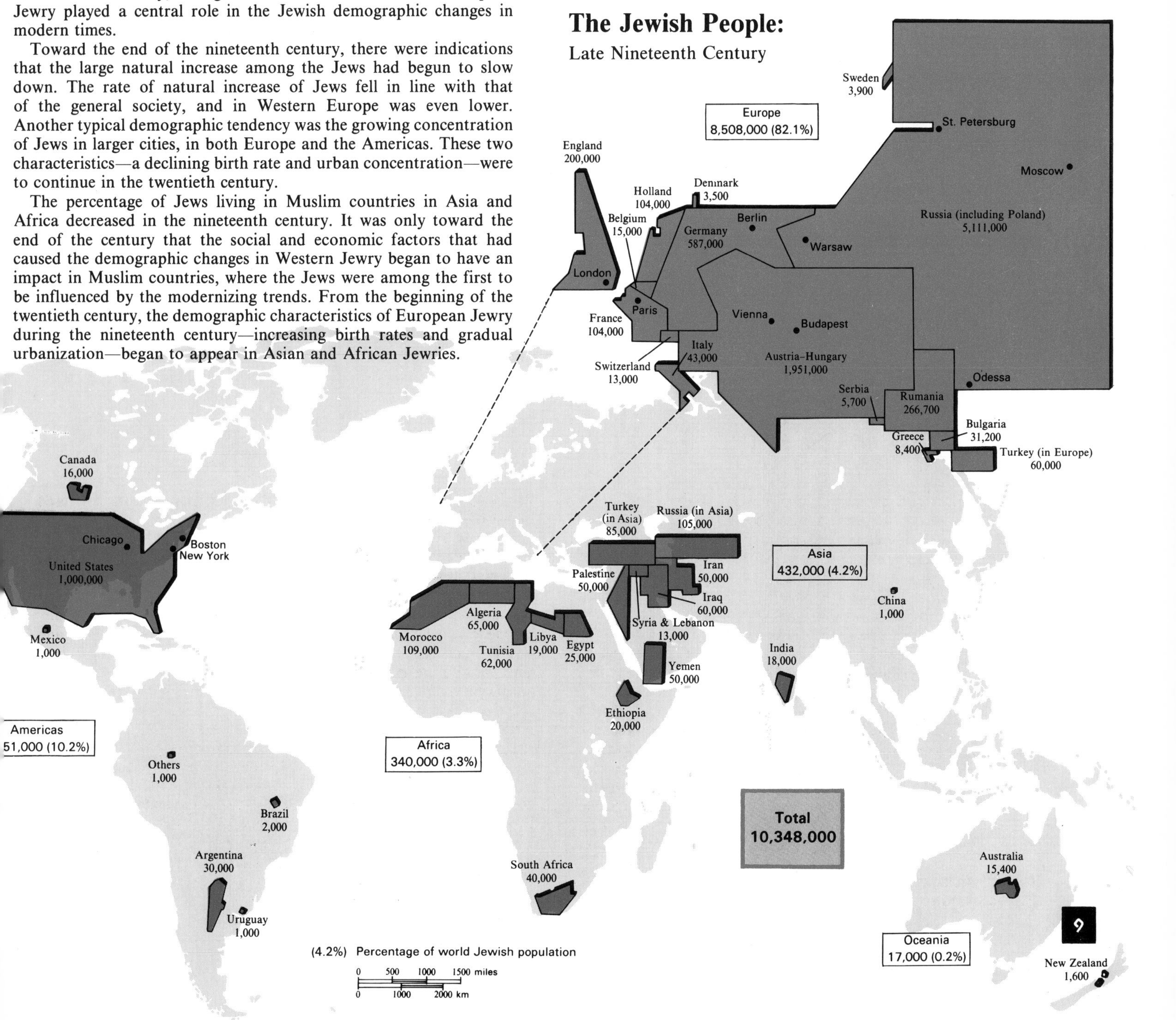

# The Jewish People on the Eve of World War II

The Jewish people reached a demographic high point in the late 1930s: more than 16 million Jews in the world, 90 percent of whom lived Europe and North America. The largest Jewish community was that in the United States, but 60 percent of all Jews still lived in Europe. The Jewish community in Palestine, which in 1939 consisted of only 3.6 percent of all Jews, was nevertheless the fifth biggest.

Never in Jewish history had such large and well-organized Jewish communities existed simultaneously in so many countries. This was one of the results of the migration of Jews in the preceding decades, which had created new Jewish communities in lands outside Europe and enlarged those in Central and Western Europe. But the signs of the impending catastrophe of the Jewish people were already discernible on the eve of World War II: three important Jewish communities in Europe—in Germany, Austria, and Czechoslovakia—were, under German domination, disintegrating.

The gradual urbanization of the Jewish people added another characteristic to its demographic situation. In 1939, more than 30 percent of all Jews lived in 22 communities of more than 100,000 Jewish inhabitants. Nevertheless, even the largest Jewish communities (New York, Warsaw) were minorities in their cities, 25 to 30 percent of the population. Most Jews lived in smaller communities, although also in major urban centers.

As a result of the demographic, cultural, and religious developments of the modern era, the Jews in the 1930s were highly diversified in differing, often opposing, religious and ideological positions. Furthermore, the integration of the Jews into different nations, and their acculturation to the ways of life of the societies in which they lived, produced significantly different types of Jews in various countries. For instance, Jews living in South America, Western Europe, North America, or Israel were inevitably influenced by different cultural attitudes and political conceptions. That process continued in later years.

The outbreak of World War II changed the Jewish situation and its characteristic trends. The year 1939 closed an era in Jewish history. The next decade was one of the most unsettling periods in Jewish annals.

## Jewish Population by Continents

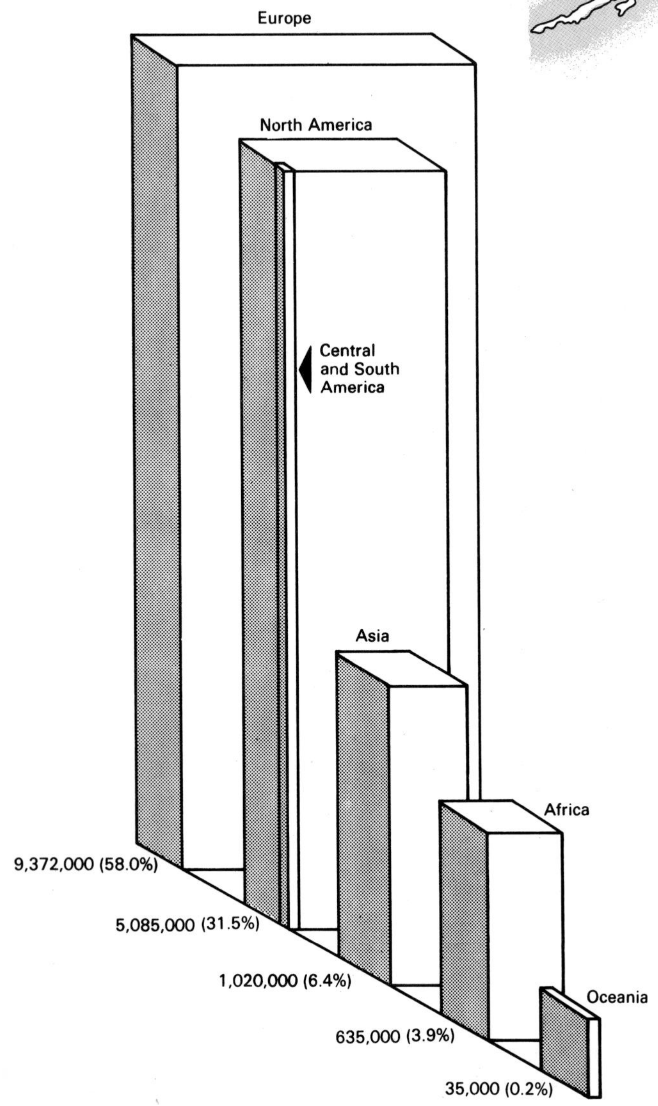


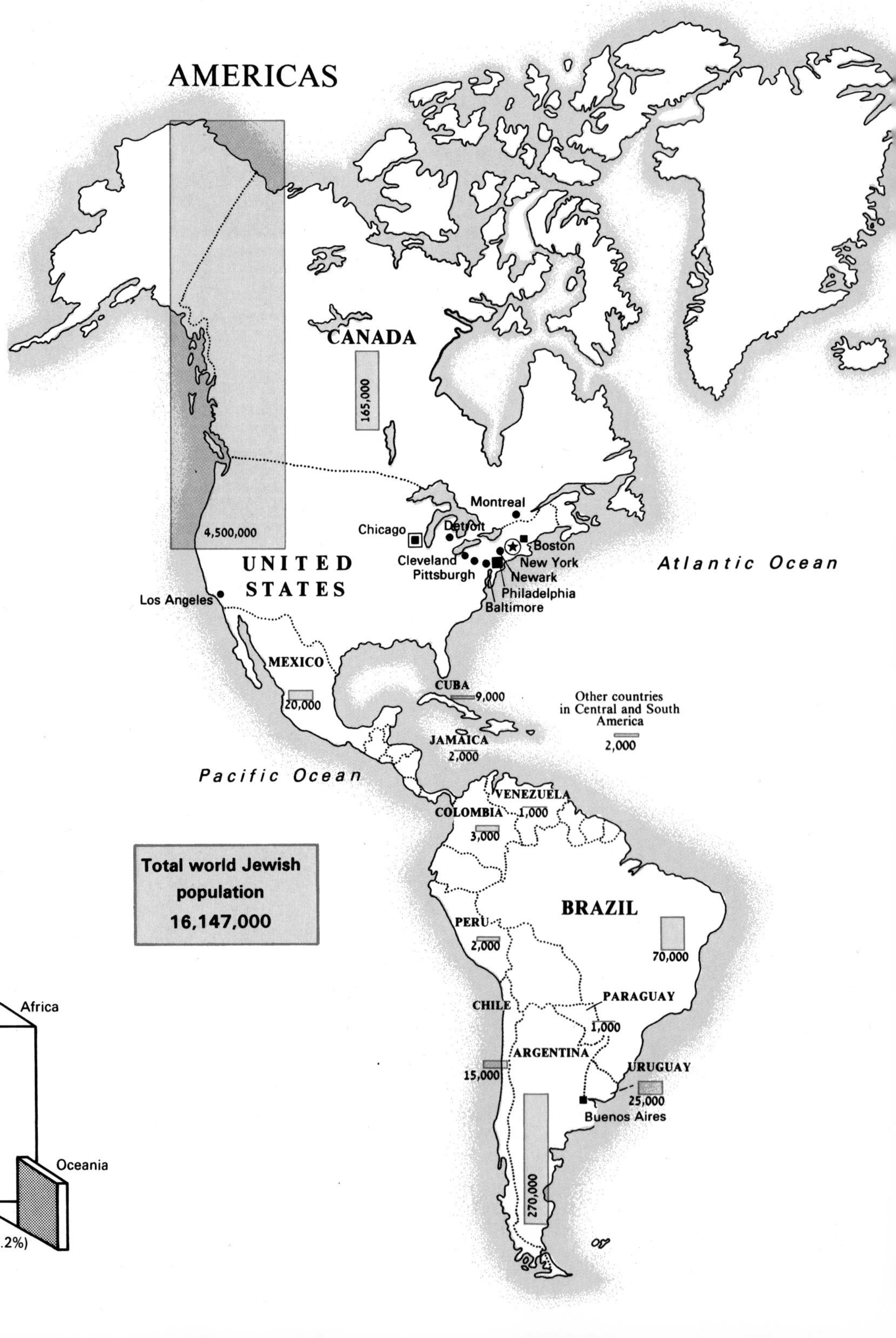

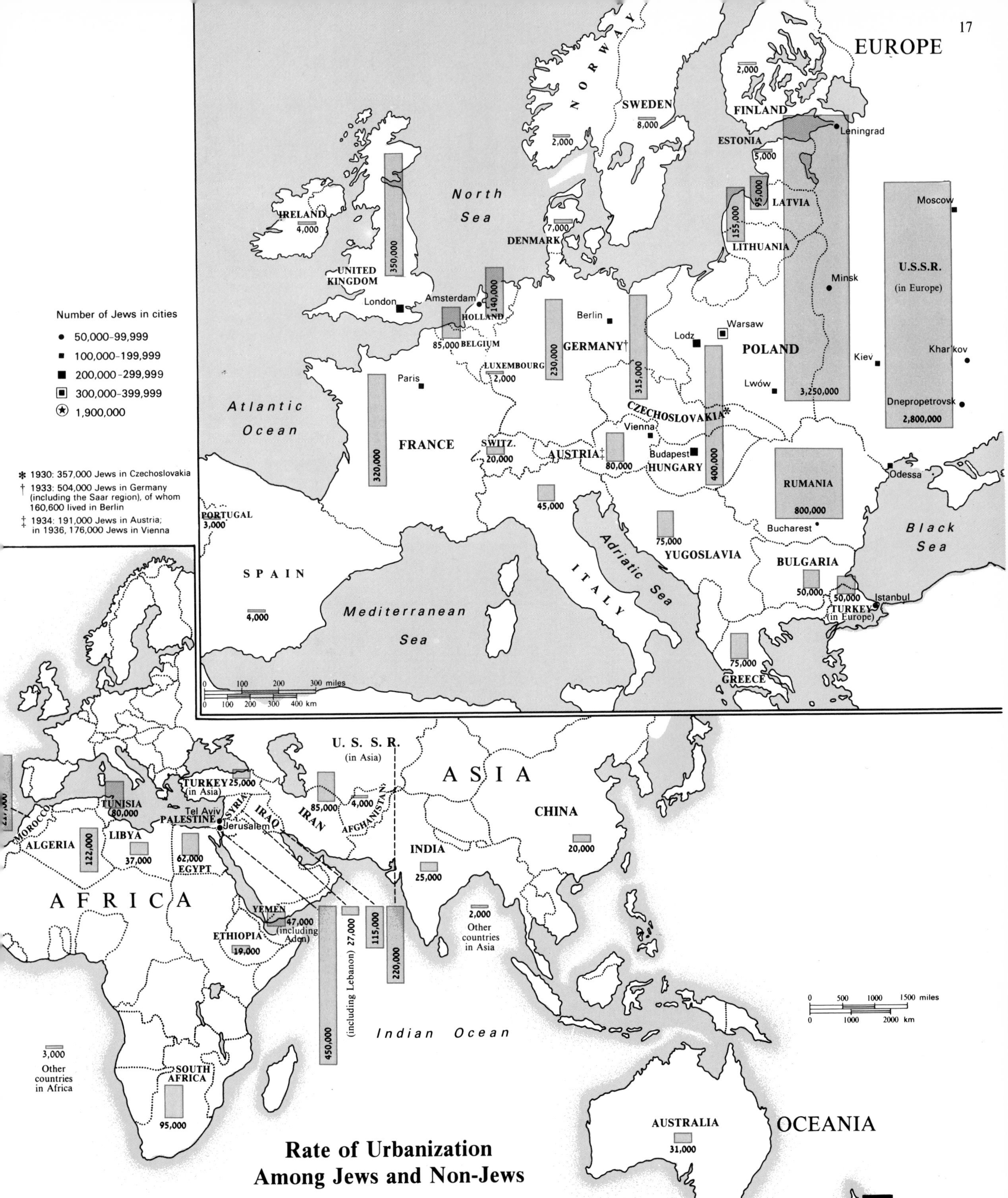
EUROPE
Number of Jews in cities
50,000-99,999
100,000-199,999
200,000-299,999
300,000-399,999
1,900,000
* 1930: 357,000 Jews in Czechoslovakia
† 1933: 504,000 Jews in Germany (including the Saar region), of whom 160,600 lived in Berlin
‡ 1934: 191,000 Jews in Austria; in 1936, 176,000 Jews in Vienna
NORWAY
2,000
SWEDEN
8,000
FINLAND
2,000
ESTONIA
5,000
Leningrad
LATVIA
95,000
LITHUANIA
155,000
North Sea
IRELAND
4,000
UNITED KINGDOM
350,000
London
DENMARK
7,000
Amsterdam
HOLLAND
140,000
85,000 BELGIUM
LUXEMBOURG
2,000
Berlin
GERMANY†
230,000
315,000
Warsaw
Lodz
POLAND
3,250,000
Lwów
Minsk
Kiev
Moscow
U.S.S.R.
(in Europe)
Khar'kov
Dnepropetrovsk
2,800,000
Paris
FRANCE
320,000
Atlantic Ocean
SWITZ.
20,000
AUSTRIA‡
80,000
Vienna
CZECHOSLOVAKIA*
400,000
Budapest
HUNGARY
RUMANIA
800,000
Odessa
Bucharest
Black Sea
PORTUGAL
3,000
SPAIN
4,000
45,000
Adriatic Sea
ITALY
75,000
YUGOSLAVIA
BULGARIA
50,000
50,000
Istanbul
TURKEY
(in Europe)
Mediterranean Sea
75,000
GREECE
0 100 200 300 miles
0 100 200 300 400 km
U. S. S. R.
(in Asia)
ASIA
TURKEY 25,000
(in Asia)
TUNISIA
80,000
MOROCCO
ALGERIA
122,000
LIBYA
37,000
PALESTINE
Tel Aviv
Jerusalem
SYRIA
IRAQ
IRAN
85,000
4,000
AFGHANISTAN
CHINA
20,000
INDIA
25,000
62,000
EGYPT
AFRICA
YEMEN
47,000
(including Aden)
ETHIOPIA
19,000
450,000
27,000
(including Lebanon)
115,000
220,000
2,000
Other countries in Asia
0 500 1000 1500 miles
0 1000 2000 km
Indian Ocean
3,000
Other countries in Africa
SOUTH AFRICA
95,000
AUSTRALIA
31,000
OCEANIA
10
NEW ZEALAND
4,000

## Rate of Urbanization Among Jews and Non-Jews

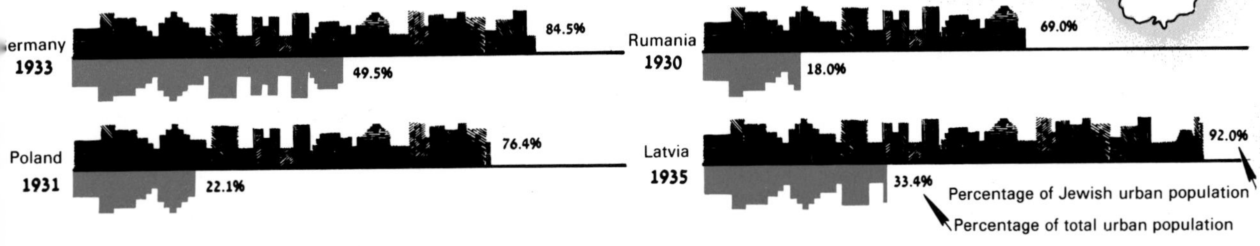
Germany
1933
84.5%
49.5%
Poland
1931
76.4%
22.1%
Rumania
1930
69.0%
18.0%
Latvia
1935
92.0%
33.4%
Percentage of Jewish urban population
Percentage of total urban population

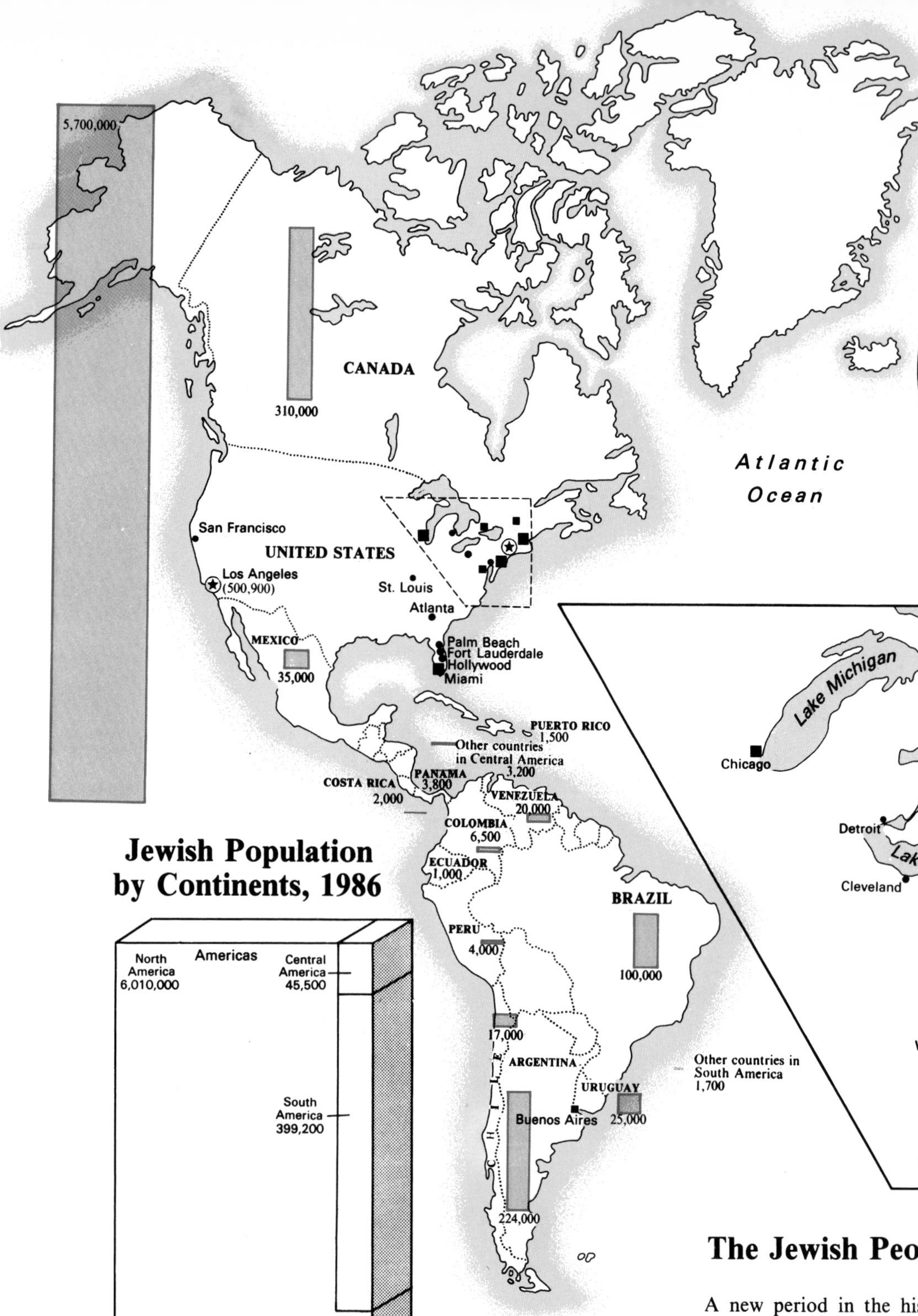


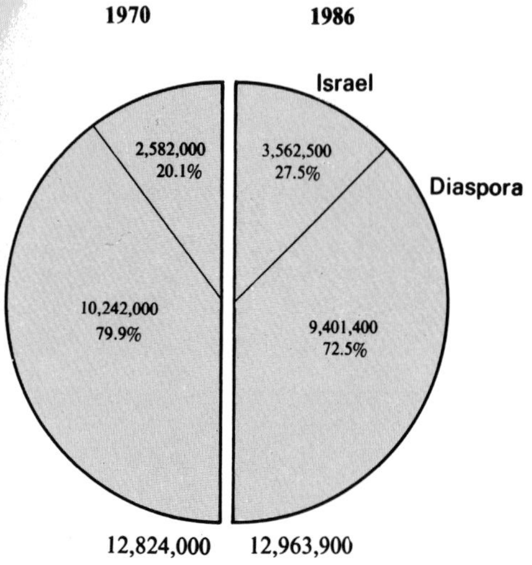


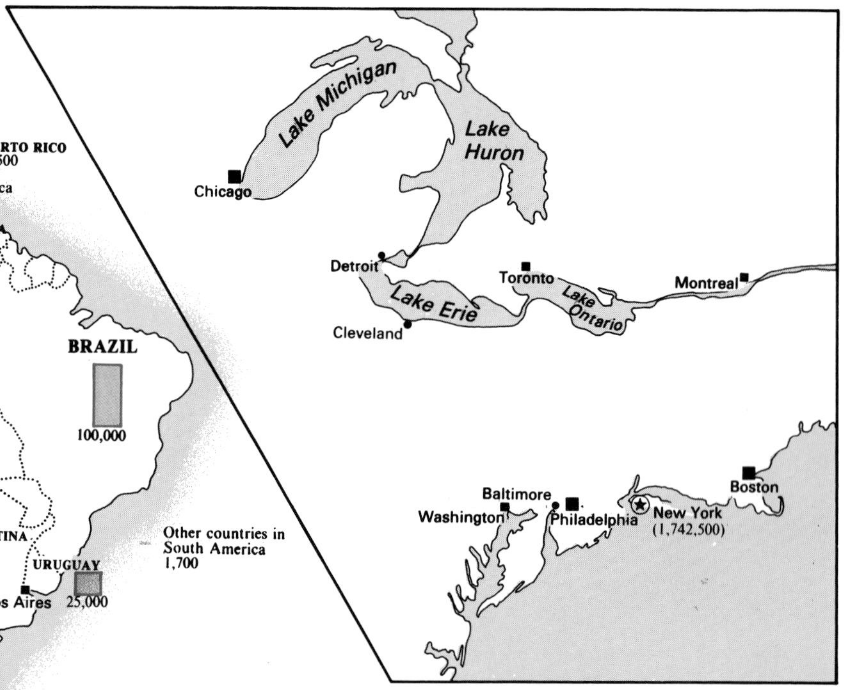


## Jewish Population by Continents, 1986

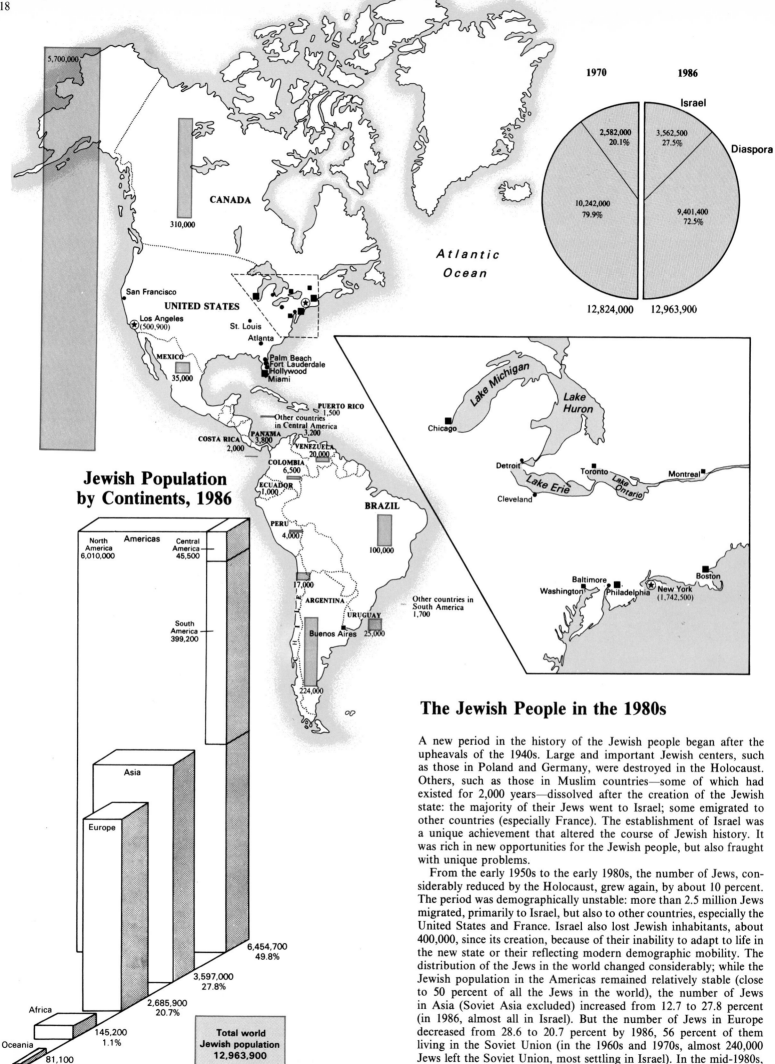

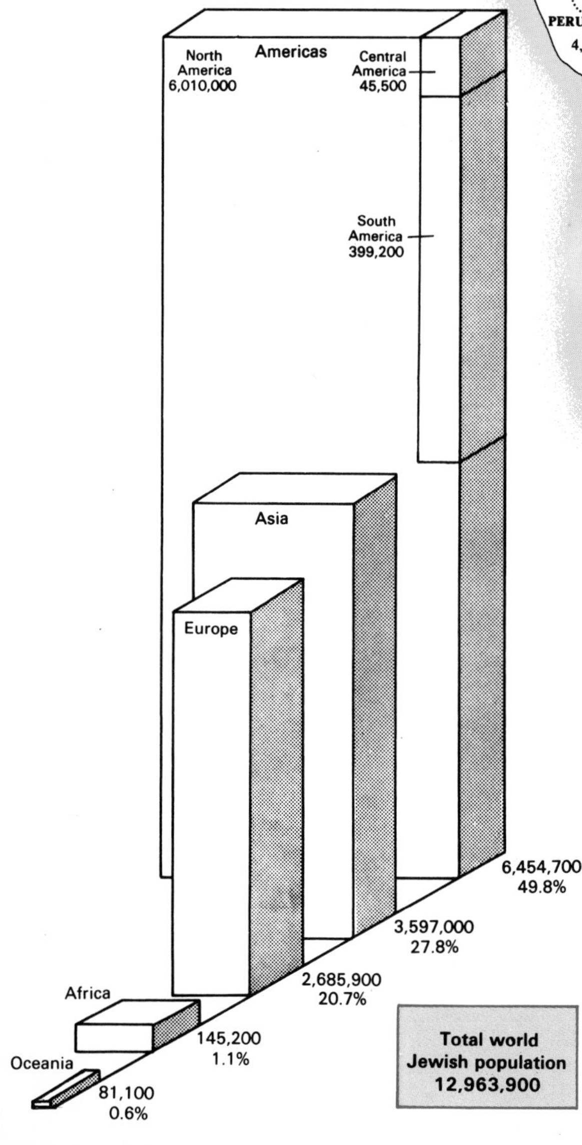


# The Jewish People in the 1980s

A new period in the history of the Jewish people began after the upheavals of the 1940s. Large and important Jewish centers, such as those in Poland and Germany, were destroyed in the Holocaust. Others, such as those in Muslim countries—some of which had existed for 2,000 years—dissolved after the creation of the Jewish state: the majority of their Jews went to Israel; some emigrated to other countries (especially France). The establishment of Israel was a unique achievement that altered the course of Jewish history. It was rich in new opportunities for the Jewish people, but also fraught with unique problems.

From the early 1950s to the early 1980s, the number of Jews, considerably reduced by the Holocaust, grew again, by about 10 percent. The period was demographically unstable: more than 2.5 million Jews migrated, primarily to Israel, but also to other countries, especially the United States and France. Israel also lost Jewish inhabitants, about 400,000, since its creation, because of their inability to adapt to life in the new state or their reflecting modern demographic mobility. The distribution of the Jews in the world changed considerably; while the Jewish population in the Americas remained relatively stable (close to 50 percent of all the Jews in the world), the number of Jews in Asia (Soviet Asia excluded) increased from 12.7 to 27.8 percent (in 1986, almost all in Israel). But the number of Jews in Europe decreased from 28.6 to 20.7 percent by 1986, 56 percent of them living in the Soviet Union (in the 1960s and 1970s, almost 240,000 Jews left the Soviet Union, most settling in Israel). In the mid-1980s,

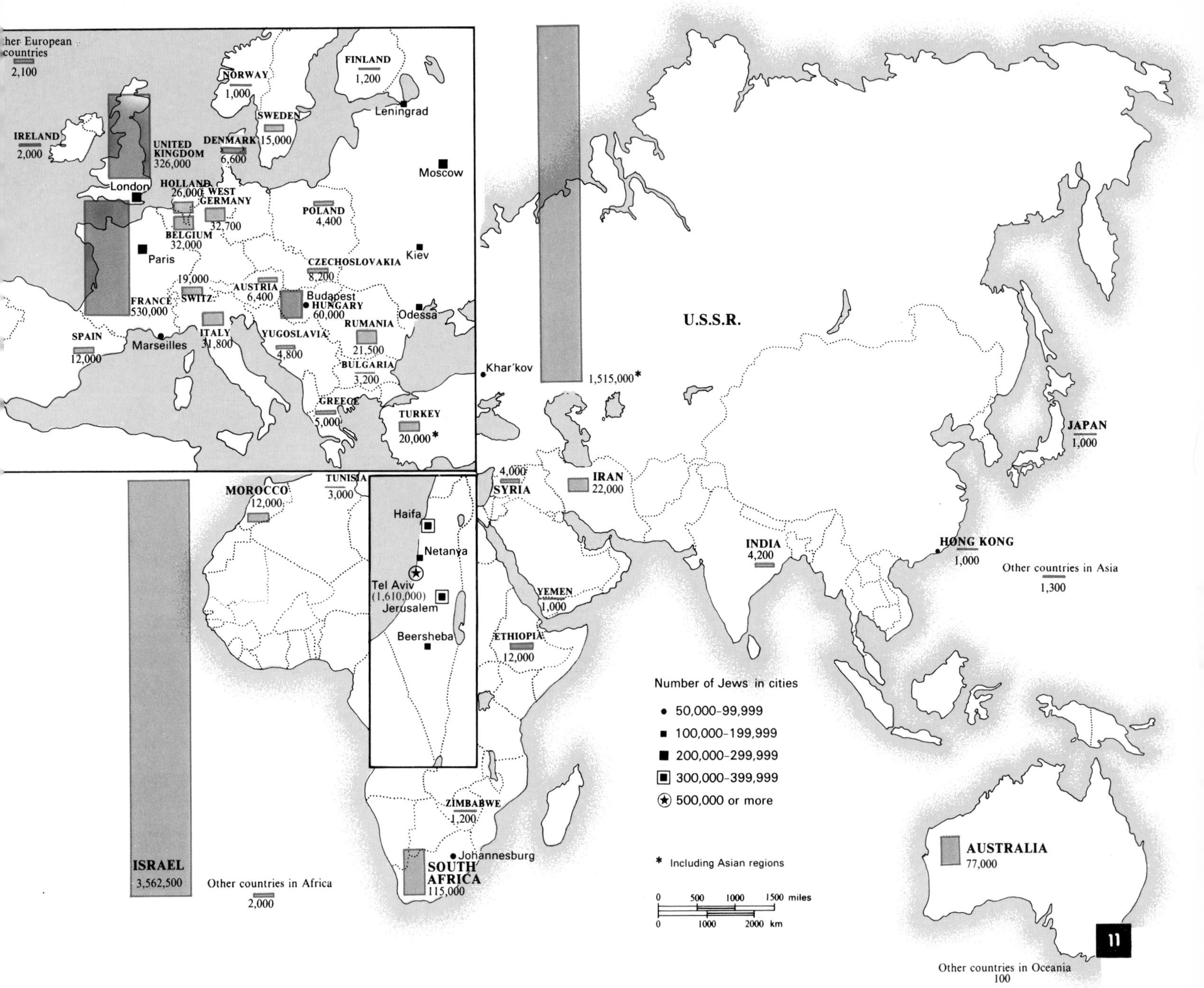


## Rate of Urbanization Among the Jews

| | 1900 | | 1925 | | 1975 | |
|---|---|---|---|---|---|---|
| Total Jewish population | 100% | 10,600,000 | 100% | 14,800,000 | 100% | 12,979,000 |
| Size of Jewish population in locality | | | | | | |
| 100,000 or more | 13.1% | 1,374,000 | 29.5% | 4,360,000 | 58.3% | 7,560,000 |
| 50,000-99,000 | 5.3% | 567,000 | 8.6% | 1,281,000 | 8.3% | 1,080,000 |
| 25,000-49,999 | 6.5% | 692,000 | 7.0% | 1,032,000 | 7.9% | 1,019,000 |
| 10,000-24,999 | 9.4% | 1,004,000 | 10.2% | 1,513,000 | 8.9% | 1,161,000 |
| Fewer than 10,000 | 65.7% | 6,963,000 | 44.7% | 6,614,000 | 16.6% | 2,159,000 |

71 percent of all Jews were concentrated in two major centers: the United States and Israel. Sociologically, the Jewish people presented a strange paradox: the bearer of an old and elaborate culture, it had become very young; its leading centers and communities were less than 100 years old. Indeed, many of the sociological and demographic problems afflicting the Jewish communities in the mid-1980s were typical of a new and not-quite-settled society.

Although in most countries, Jews lived on good terms with their non-Jewish compatriots, antisemitism did not disappear. It changed forms and produced new expressions, justifying the concept "contemporary antisemitism." Much of this new animosity focused on Zionism and the Jewish state, and its most active exponents were the Arab countries and the Soviet Union. Since contemporary antisemites made no distinction between Jews and Israelis, the problem weighed on the Jewish people as a whole.

One positive factor in the situation of the Jewish people in the second half of the twentieth century was the mutual support among its various segments, especially between the Jewish state and the Diaspora. When Israel was established in 1948, many thought (and suggested) that the Jewish people would (or should) split into two separate parts, developing in separate directions. Forty years later, this had not happened. On the contrary, identification and mutual interest among the different communities of the Jewish people had become even stronger than before.

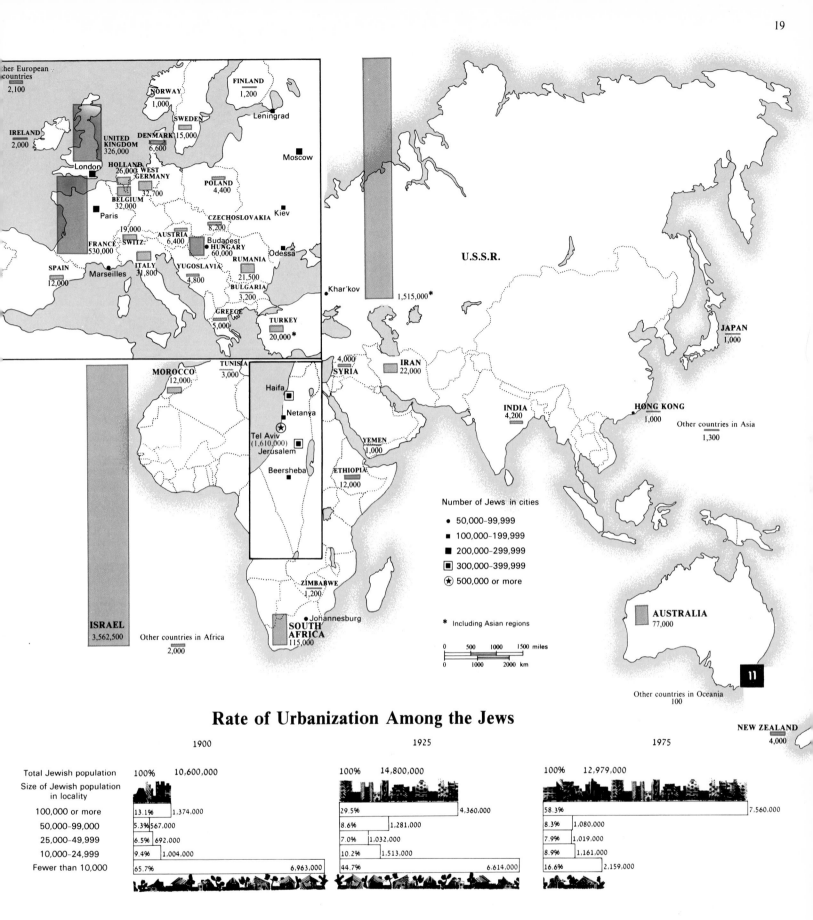

## Vital Statistics of the Jews and the Total Population

From the late eighteenth century to the end of the nineteenth century, the Jewish population in Europe (especially in Eastern Europe) was characterized by high birth rates and low death rates. The result was the great increase in the number of Jews in the modern period. Even where the birth rate of Jews was somewhat lower than that of the general population, lower infant mortality among the Jews resulted in a higher survival rate. The diagram clearly shows the significant difference between the two indicators when we compare Jews and non-Jews in countries like Hungary and Rumania, where the number of births was higher among non-Jews than among Jews, but mortality levels were significantly lower among the Jews. From 1850 to 1880, the annual increase among East European Jews was 1.7 percent (that is, 17 more births than deaths for every 1,000 persons). Such a proportion was enough to double the population in forty-one years, or to increase it fourfold in about eighty years. In Western Europe, on the contrary, in the nineteenth century, the ratio of births to deaths among Jews was lower than among non-Jews. Gradually, the natural increase slowed down also among East European Jewry, due to the declining birth rates. Between the two world wars, the natural increase of European Jews was only half that of non-Jews.

There were several reasons for this development. From the beginning of the twentieth century, the marriage age of Jewish women rose (also in Eastern Europe), which could have been a factor in the number of children born. The growing concentration of Jews in cities, especially in large cities, was another factor: the birth rate in cities was lower than that in small towns and villages, although in the twentieth century, the death rate, too, was lower, especially among newborns. Another reason for the decrease of births was the rise in the educational level of Jews, leading to widespread and more efficient family planning. Nevertheless, in Israel, where a great part of the Jewish population lived in cities, the birth rate was relatively high; indeed, it was among the highest in the developed countries, compared with that of non-Jews and certainly that of Diaspora Jews. This difference reflected specific values and attitudes of Israeli Jewish society.

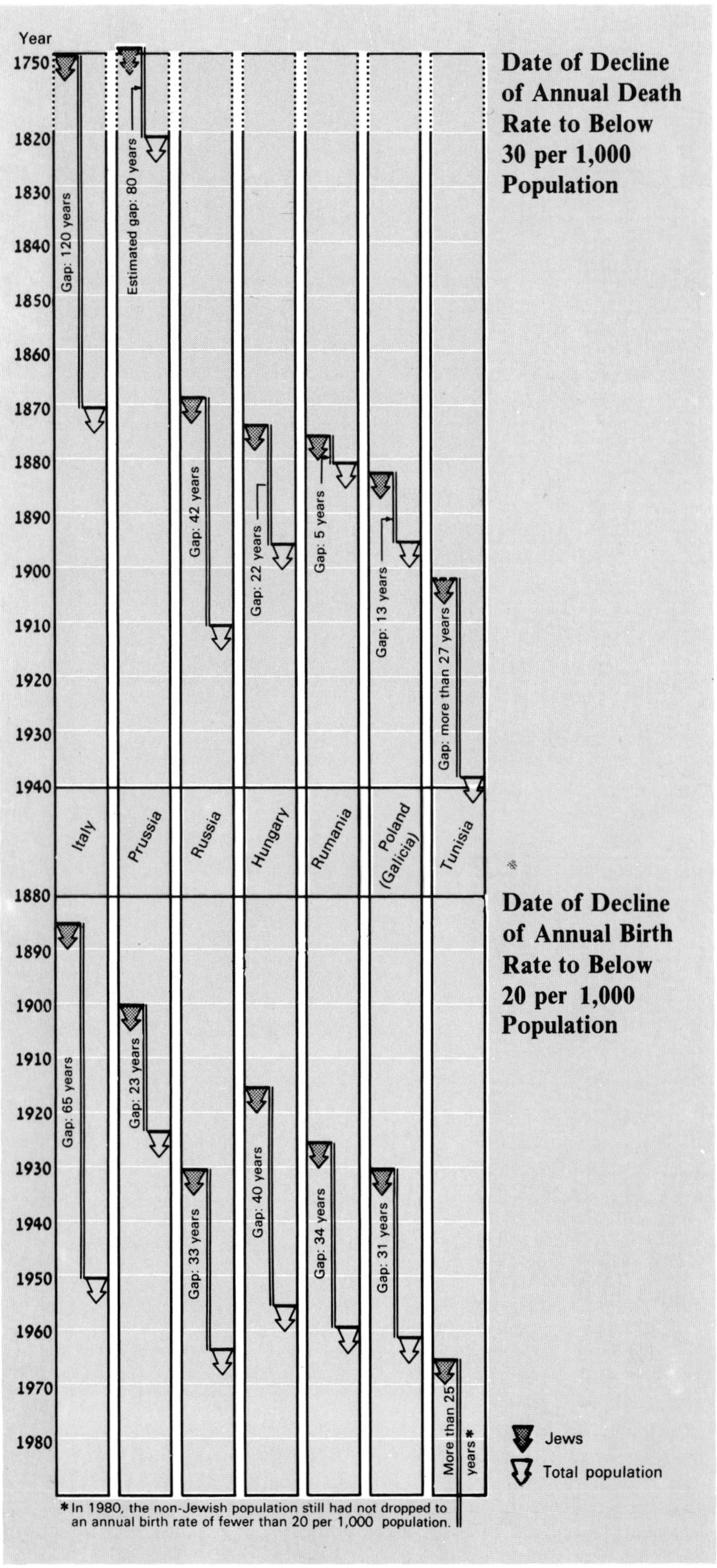


## Birth and Death Rates: Differences Between Jews and Non-Jews

The diagram shows the changes that occurred in given countries in the relative birth and death rates of Jews and non-Jews. As explained in the preceding note, the reduced death rate brought about the great increase in the Jewish population from the second half of the eighteenth century. In the diagram, we see the beginning of that process, which among Jews started long before it did among non-Jews. For instance, the annual death rate among Jews in Russia decreased to under 30 per 1,000 as early as 1868, forty-two years before it declined in the non-Jewish population.

If we examine the annual death rate of 15 per 1,000, we find again a significant difference, to the advantage of the Jewish population. In Italy, the Jewish death rate dropped to that level in 1905, twenty-five years before it fell in the non-Jewish population; in Prussia, in 1890 (twenty-two years); in Russia, 1905 (forty years); in Hungary, 1905 (thirty years); in Poland (Galicia), 1910 (twenty-three years); in Rumania, 1920 (twenty-eight years); and in Tunisia, 1946 (seventeen years).

A similar comparison of the data regarding births reveals an opposite tendency: almost without exception, the Jewish birth rate dropped below that of the general population much earlier. If we take the level of 35 annual births per 1,000, we see that in Italy, the Jews fell below it 195 years before the non-Jews (already in 1700!); in Prussia, sixty-five years (1840); in Hungary, sixteen years (1895); in Rumania, thirty-two years (1900); in Bulgaria, twenty years (1905); in Poland, fifteen years (1910); and in Tunisia, thirty-one years (1948). Only in Argentina was there no difference: among both Jews and non-Jews, it reached that level in 1920. The diagram shows also that even at a lower level, 20 annual births per 1,000 population, the Jewish rate dropped below the general rate much earlier; for instance, in the Soviet Union, it dropped thirty-three years earlier.

The data also indicate that the birth rate dropped much earlier in Western Europe than in Eastern Europe, with a considerable difference between Jews and non-Jews. The natural increase of a given population results from the combination of birth and death rates. In the case of the Jews, in many countries the lines crossed at some point in the twentieth century, as the death rate became higher than the birth rate—which meant that the balance between the two turned from positive to negative.

Births — Jews
Births — Total population*
Deaths — Jews
Deaths — Total population*
(per 1,000 population)
* In Israel, non-Jews

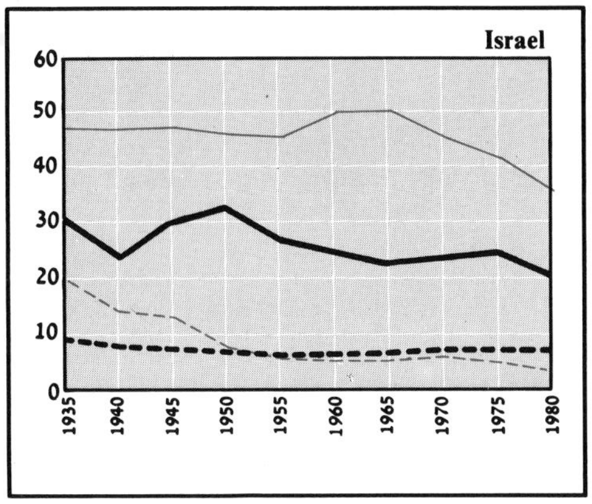


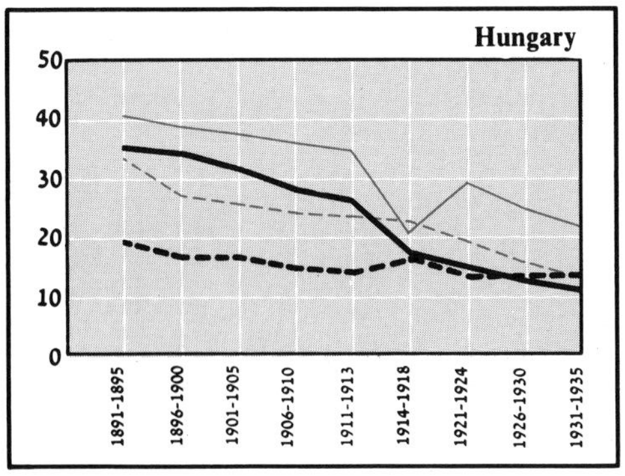


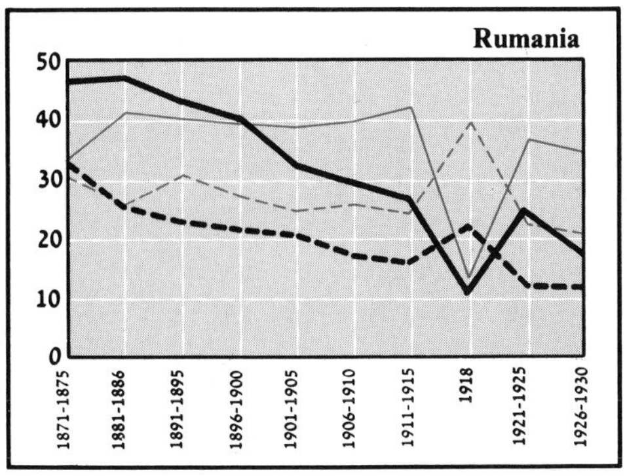


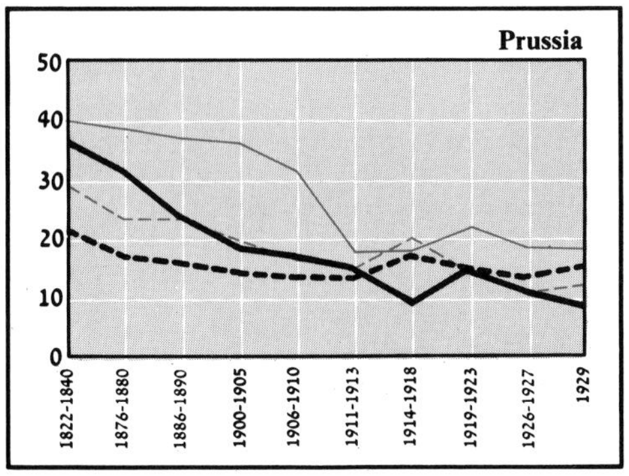


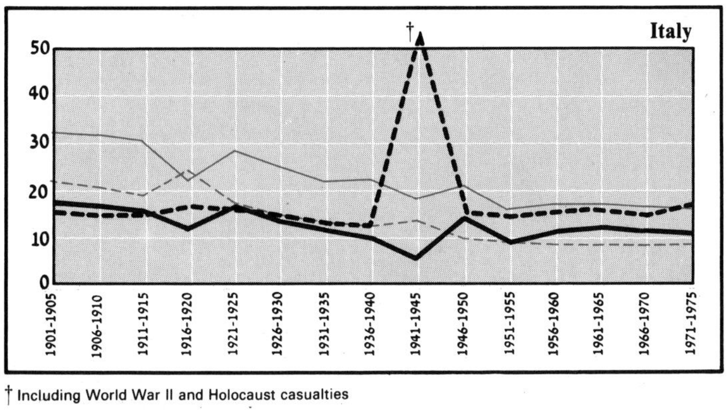


† Including World War II and Holocaust casualties

## Birth Rates Among Jews (per 1,000 population)

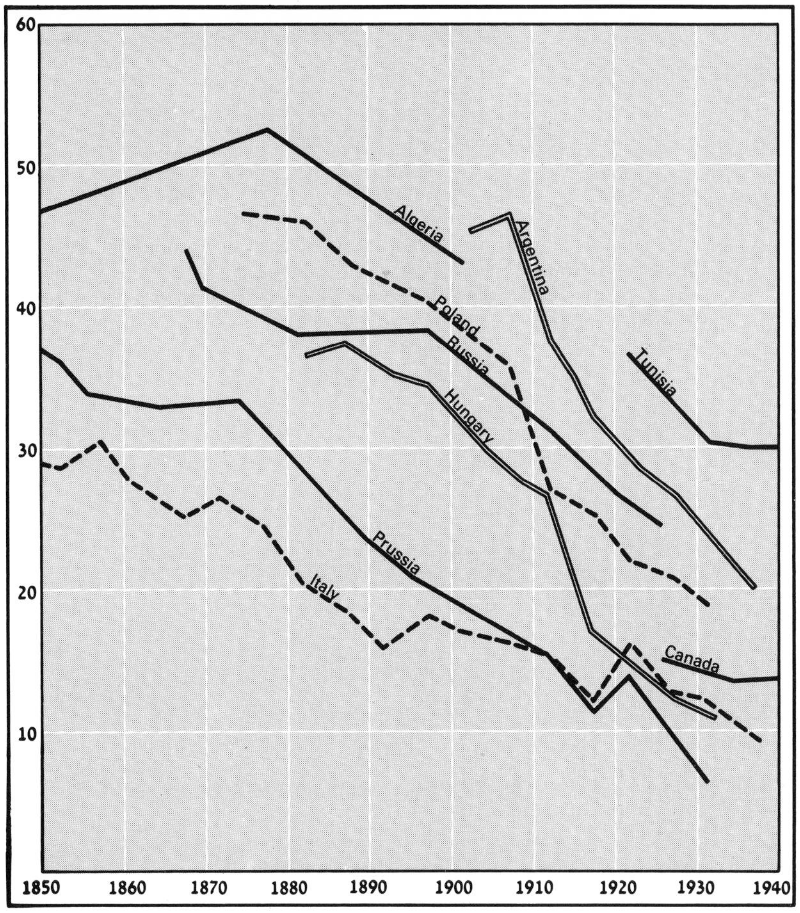


## Birth Rates Among Jews and Non-Jews

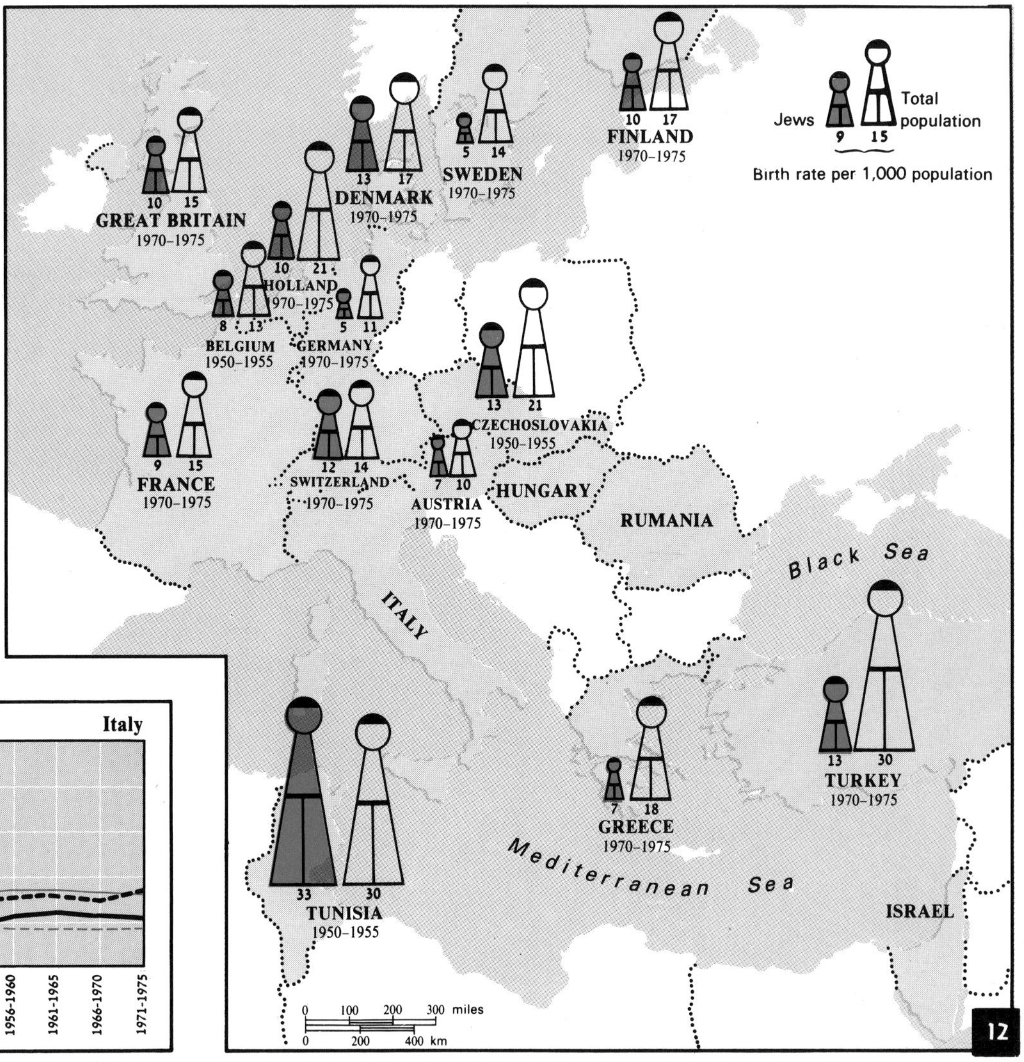

# Fertility of Jewish Women

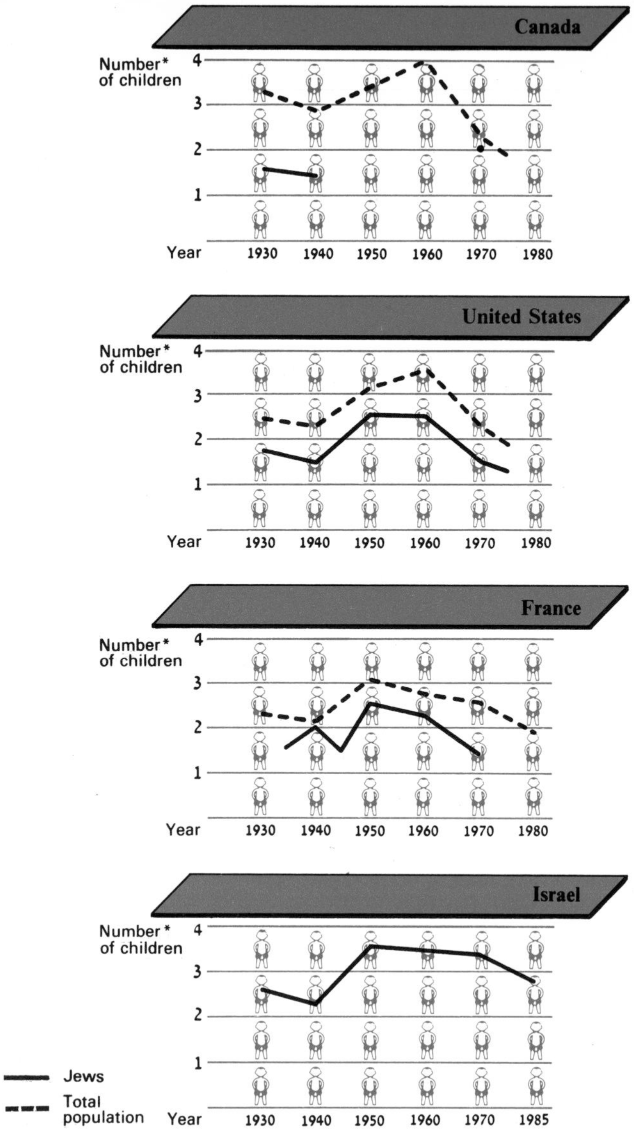


### TFR* of Jewish Women in Israel and France
(by continent of birth)

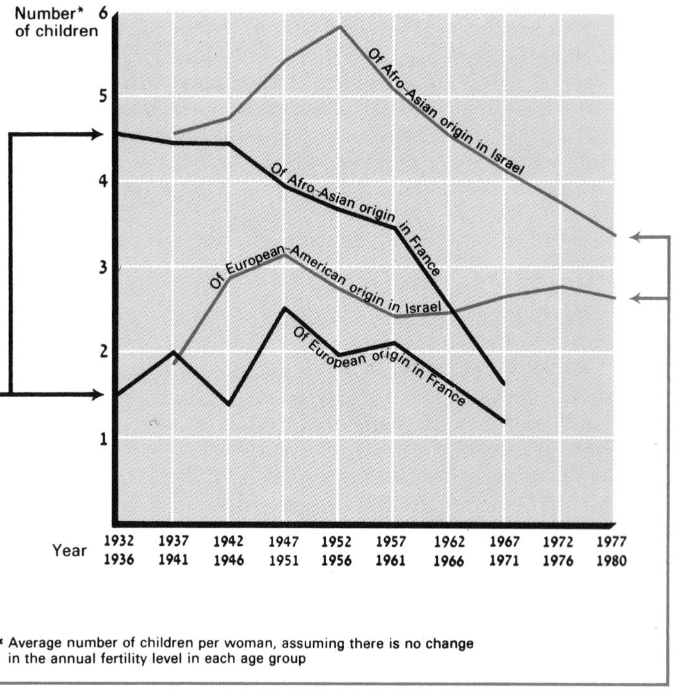


* Average number of children per woman, assuming there is no change in the annual fertility level in each age group

In the second half of the twentieth century, the birth rate among Jewish women in almost all Diaspora communities was very low. This resulted in the gradual aging of the Jewish communities and the increase of the median age (the age line dividing a population in two equal parts: one younger, and the other older). Both tendencies were apparent in most European Jewries by World War I, and among West European Jews by the end of the nineteenth century. Only among Jewish women in Muslim countries was fertility high.

The decrease in fertility among both European and American Jewish women was especially sharp between the two world wars. For instance, in the United States, the TFR (total fertility rate: the average number of children born to Jewish women, assuming that the fertility levels observed in a given year will remain constant) in 1930 was 1.7, compared with 2.4 among non-Jewish white women. In the late 1940s and the 1950s, there was a baby boom, which in the United States continued longer than in other countries. But the TFR fell again in about 1970, to 1.5 among Jewish women (2.2 among non-Jewish white women). In most countries, there was a symmetry in the rise and fall of the TFR of Jewish and non-Jewish women, the Jewish rate always being lower.

There was a significant difference between the fertility rates of Jewish women in Israel and in the Diaspora, clearly indicated in the diagram comparing the rates in France and Israel. In each country, Jewish women of different origins tended after some years to achieve similar fertility rates, which were much lower in France than in Israel. The French data are from the early 1970s, but the tendency seems to apply also to the 1980s. Furthermore, that negative tendency had been present for half a century. But the fertility rate among Jewish women in Israel was comparatively high and stable, reaching 2.8 in the early 1980s. It should be noted that the decline of the previously high TFR of Jewish women in Israel of Asian and African origin was accompanied by an increase in the fertility rate of women of European and American origin, and the difference between the two groups diminished: the ratio was 5.1 to 2.4 in 1960, and 3.2 to 2.8 in 1985. Of growing influence in the total picture were Israeli-born Jewish women of all backgrounds: their TFR was stable in the 1980s, at 2.8.

## Age Distribution of Jews (percent)

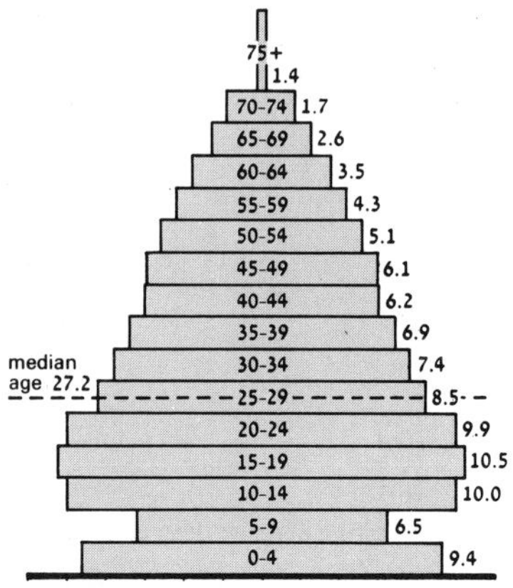


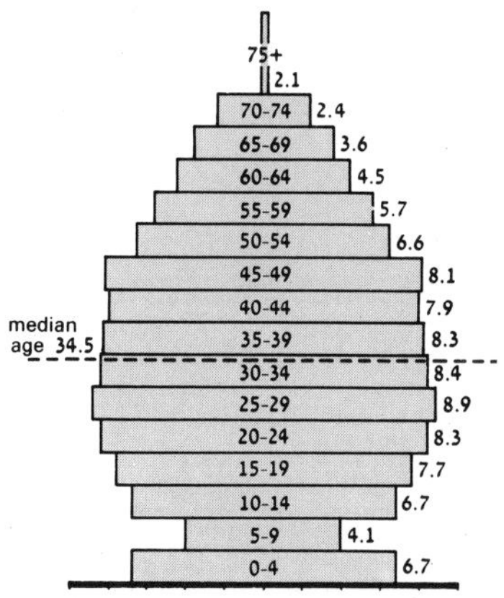


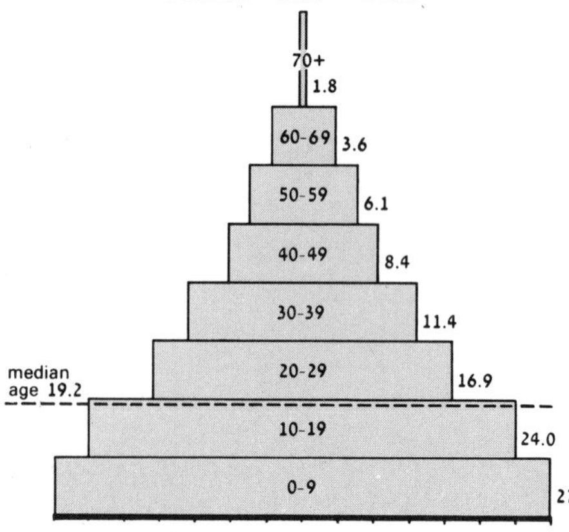

# The Distribution of Jewish Populations by Age Groups

The age pyramids show the demographic situation of different Jewries, and the influence of different levels of fertility and mortality. The resulting picture is a gradual aging of most Diaspora Jewries in the twentieth century, with the pyramid changing from the normal and "young" composition of the age pyramid of Polish Jewry in 1897, to the picture of Prussian Jewry in 1925 (concentration of most Jews in the middle, a narrow base of younger age groups, and broadening layers at the top), to the inverted pyramid of Rumanian Jewry in 1979. Rumania was the most extreme example of a Jewry with a very high median age: 57.3 years. But other European Jewries also had a very high median age: over 50 in Germany and Austria (Vienna) in the 1970s, 43.6 in the Netherlands in 1966, and 40.4 in Switzerland in 1980.

In the younger Jewish communities outside Europe, the situation was better, although there, too, the median age was rising, and always higher than that of the general population. The unfavorable age pyramid was probably the best indicator of the Jewish people's demographic problems in the second half of the twentieth century. The exception was the Jewish community in Israel. Its median age was much lower than that of other Jewries (27.6 in 1986), and one of the lowest among the more developed countries.

The projection of the age composition of the Jewish people for the beginning of the twenty-first century showed that if the tendencies of the mid-1980s continue, there would be a further aging of Diaspora Jewry and, to a more moderate degree, of Israeli Jewry.

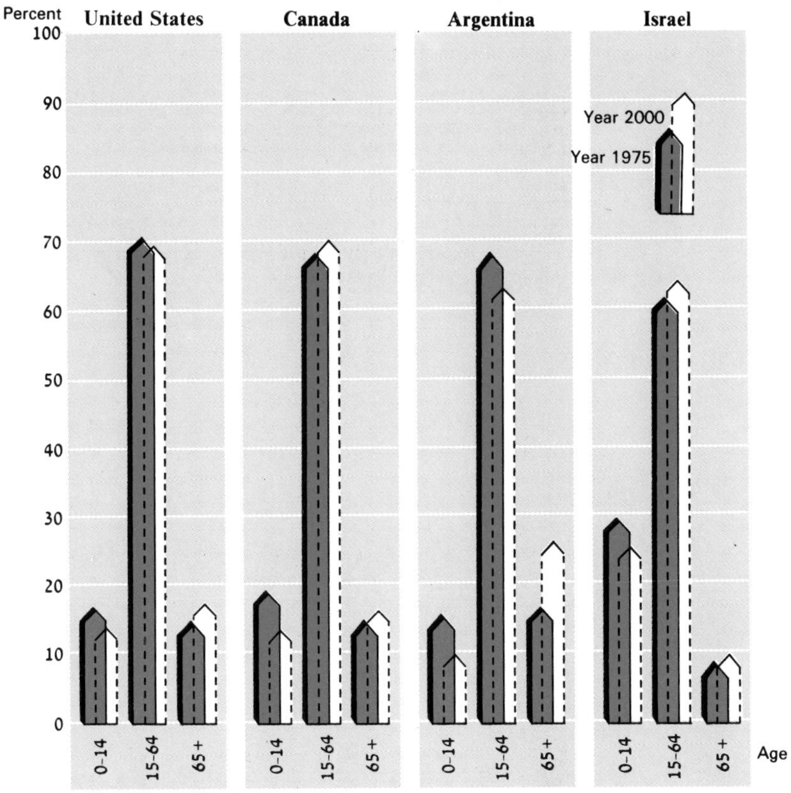


**Israel** 1986

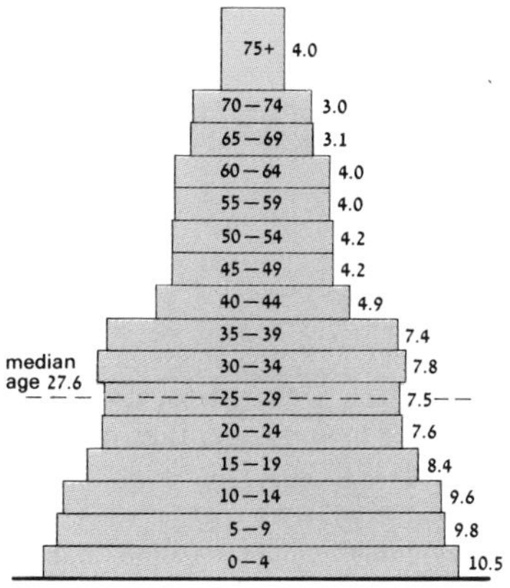


**Rumania** 1979

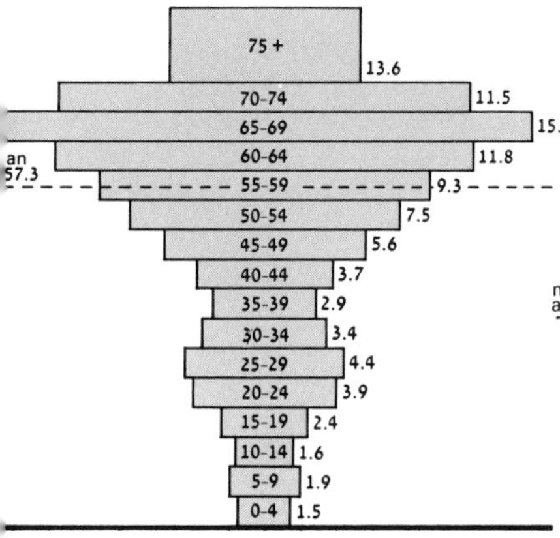


**Canada** 1981

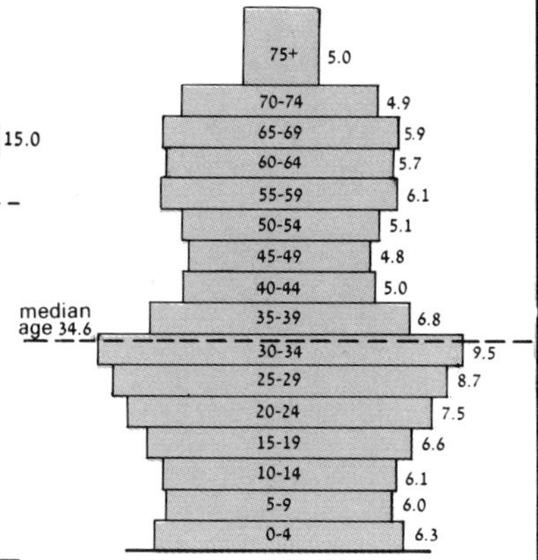


**Jewish and Non-Jewish Populations by Age Group in France and the United States**

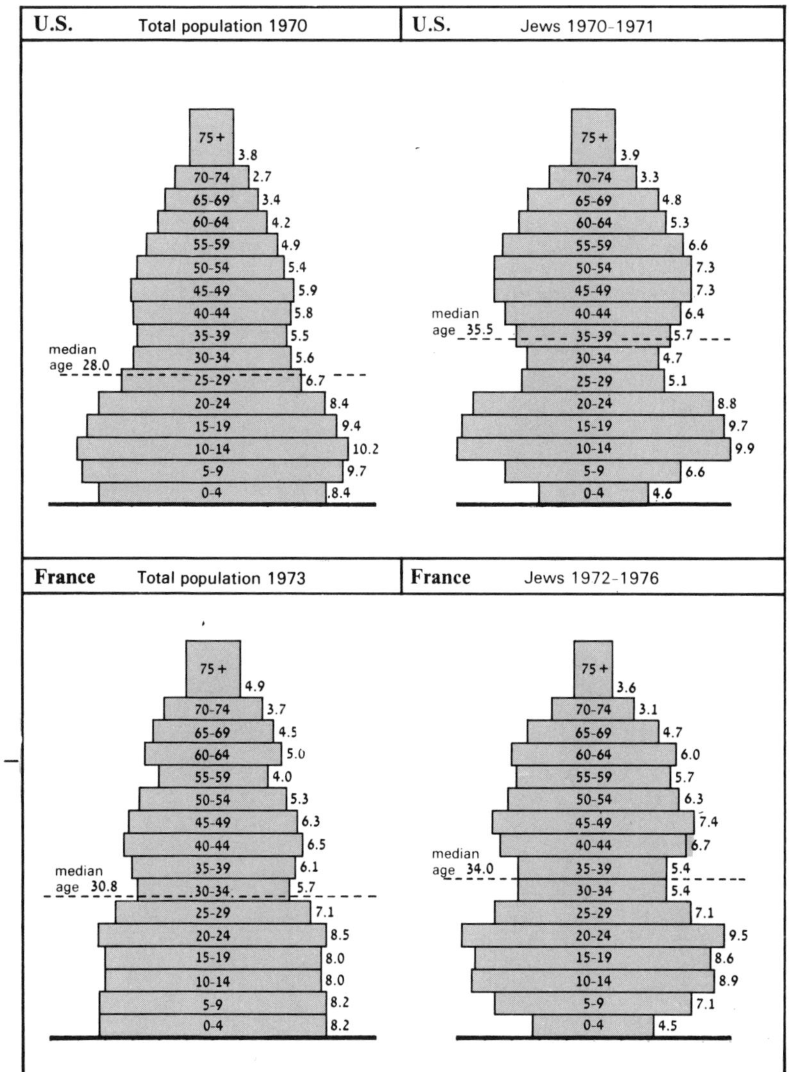

# Out-Marriage

The data on out-marriage are given in four forms: by couples; by individuals; cumulative data; and by period.

**Couples or Individuals:** If among 100 married couples, 50 consist of two Jewish partners and 50 include one non-Jewish partner, it means that 50 percent of the couples are out-married, or mixed. But if, with the same data, we calculate how many individual Jews out-married, then the 100 couples include 150 Jews, 50 of whom have non-Jewish (or non-Jewish-born) spouses; that is, 33.3 percent are out-married.

**Cumulative Data or By Period:** If we consider American Jewry, for example, out of *all* married couples (regardless of year of marriage) with at least one Jewish-born partner at the beginning of the 1970s, there were 12.5 percent mixed marriages. But if we consider only couples who married between 1965 and 1971, the number of mixed couples jumps to 34.8 percent. Among the 1965 to 1971 marriages, a further 10.3 percent were couples in which the non-Jewish partner had converted to Judaism, which brings the total of intermarried couples up to 45.1 percent.

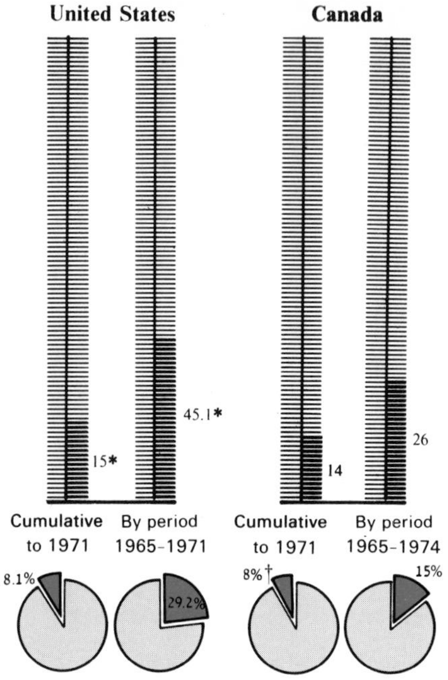


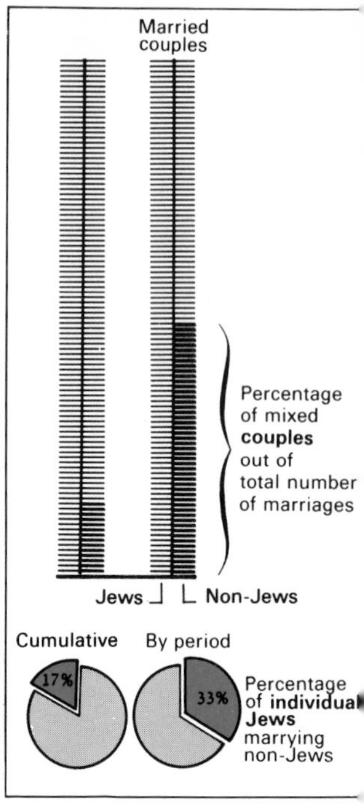


* Regardless of whether converted
† According to 1981 census: 9.7%
‡ 1981–1982: 47.6%

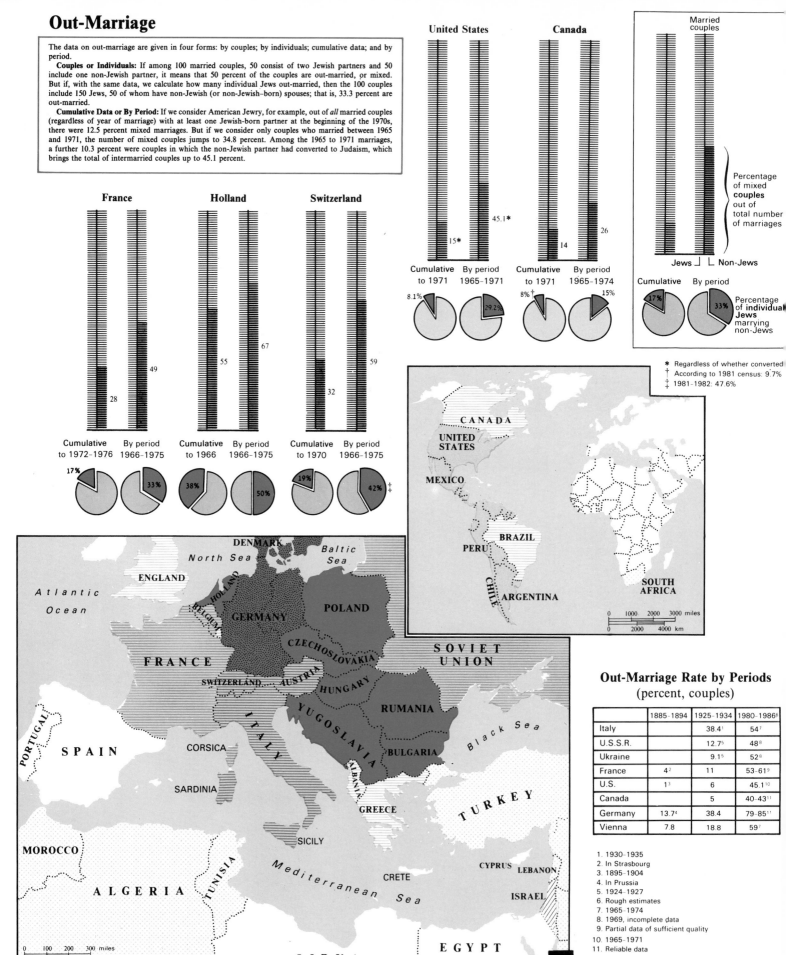

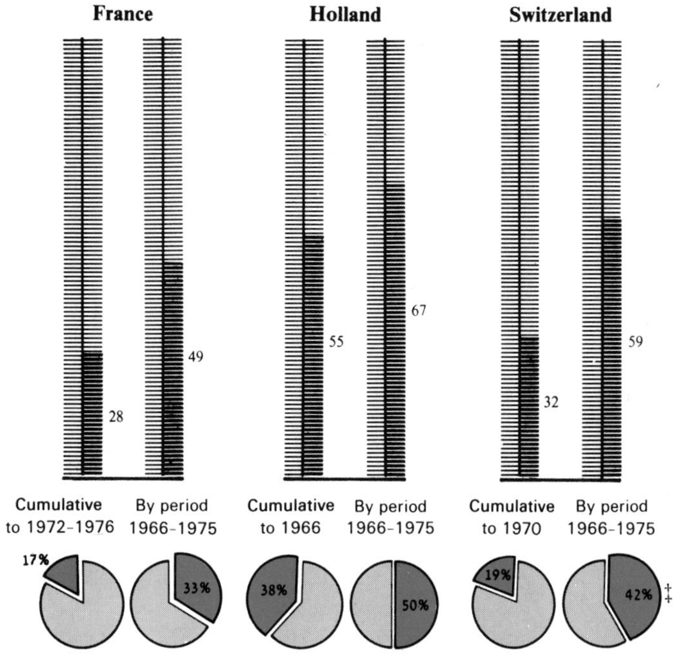


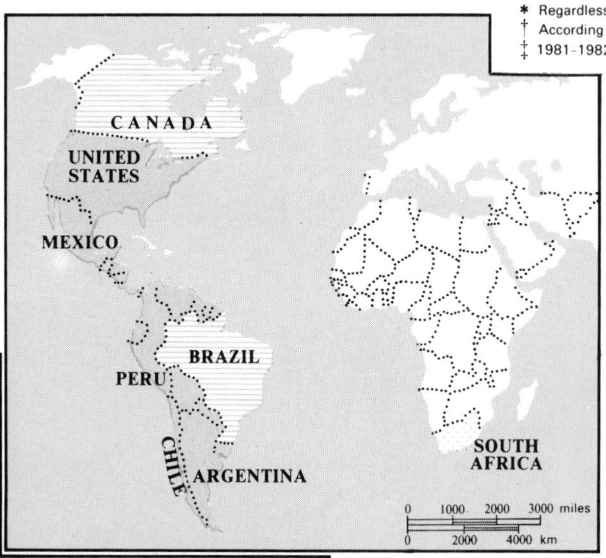


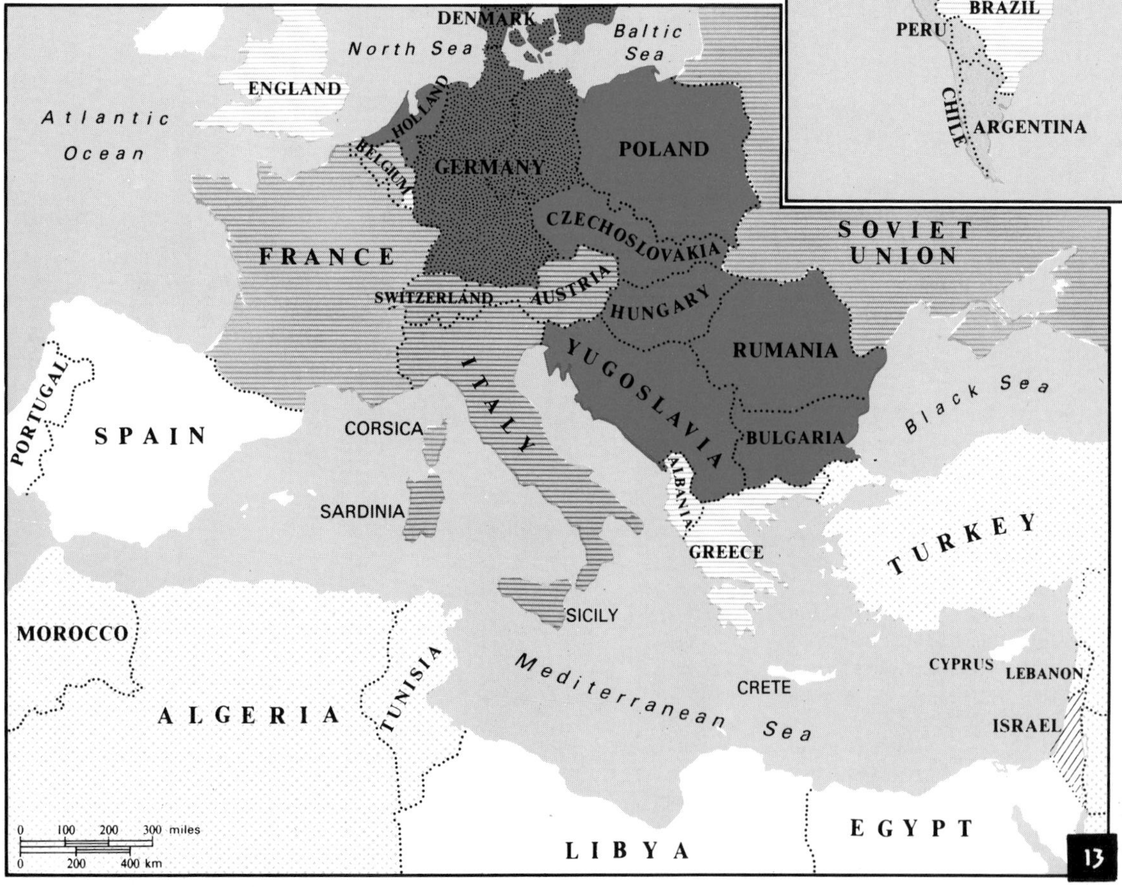


Percentage of mixed couples in the 1970s

0–1 | 5–24 | 25–34 | 35–44 | 45–54 | 55–64 | 65–74 | 75–84

No data available

## Out-Marriage Rate by Periods
(percent, couples)

| | 1885–1894 | 1925–1934 | 1980–1986[6] |
|---|---|---|---|
| Italy | | 38.4[1] | 54[7] |
| U.S.S.R. | | 12.7[5] | 48[8] |
| Ukraine | | 9.1[5] | 52[8] |
| France | 4[2] | 11 | 53–61[9] |
| U.S. | 1[3] | 6 | 45.1[10] |
| Canada | | 5 | 40–43[11] |
| Germany | 13.7[4] | 38.4 | 79–85[11] |
| Vienna | 7.8 | 18.8 | 59[7] |

1. 1930–1935
2. In Strasbourg
3. 1895–1904
4. In Prussia
5. 1924–1927
6. Rough estimates
7. 1965–1974
8. 1969, incomplete data
9. Partial data of sufficient quality
10. 1965–1971
11. Reliable data

# Out-Marriage of Jews:

Twentieth Century

Out-marriage of Jews is an essentially modern phenomenon. Although known in earlier times, out-marriages were few: religious, social, and cultural differences between Jewish and non-Jewish societies established barriers against mixed marriages, which were overcome only in exceptional cases.

Out-marriages became increasingly common in the nineteenth and twentieth centuries. They were a result of both the growing cultural and social integration of Jews in the general society, which often went hand in hand with the loss of Jewish identity, and the size of the modern urban Jewish population, which formed only a small minority of the large, general society. Jews living in smaller communities tended to out-marry more than Jews in larger Jewish communities.

Together with low or negative natural increase and assimilation, Jewish out-marriage is a critical component of the demographic and spiritual problems of contemporary Jewry. It reflects an insufficient level of Jewish conciousness and organized life. Families active in Jewish life usually have fewer cases of mixed marriages. The situation is especially acute in most European Jewish communities. The recent level of out-marriages there has been relatively high, mostly over 50 percent.

In the second half of the twentieth century, there was a clear increase in the percentage of out-marriages in most Jewries. In Canada, for example, the level of out-marriages per couple from 1965 to 1974 was 26 percent. It jumped to over 40 percent in the 1980s. For French Jewry, the percentages in the 1980s ranged from 53 to 61 (up from 11 percent between 1925 and 1934). In Italy, 38.4 percent of couples with at least one Jewish partner who married between 1930 and 1935 were mixed. From 1965 to 1974, the percentage rose to 54. The only exception was Israel. Because of the social organization and cultural conditions of Israeli Jewish society, the phenomenon of out-marriage was practically nonexistent.

There are behavioral differences between men and women regarding out-marriage: men out-marry more. Another question concerns the religion of children of out-marriages. Partial data indicate that in the second half of the twentieth century, only a minority of the children of out-marriages were educated as Jews. Only in the United States did a relatively significant proportion of such children grow up as Jews. In the United States, also, the non-Jewish partner converted to Judaism in about 25 percent of out-marriages.

# The Jewish People by the Year 2000: A Projection

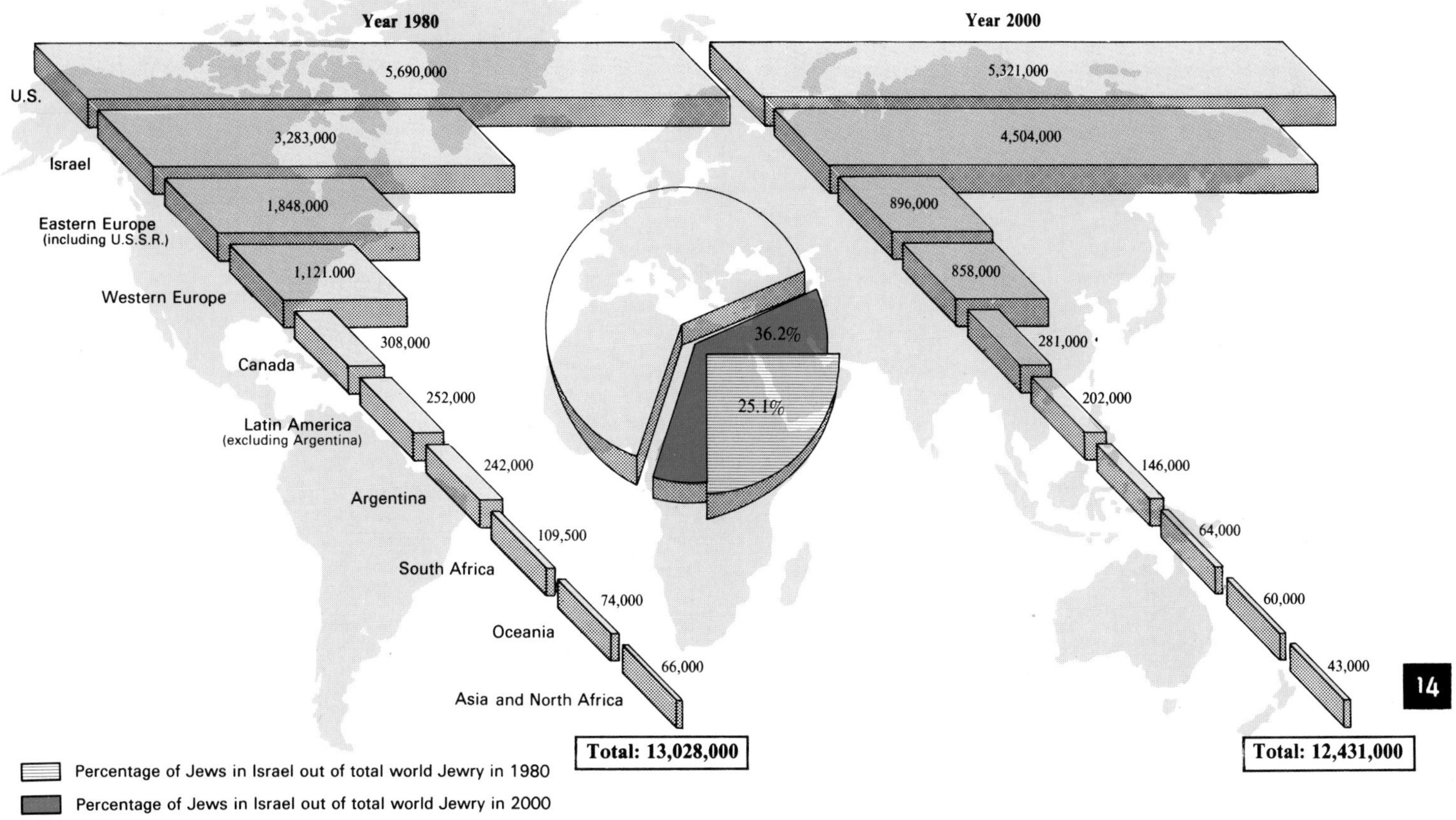


This projection, prepared in 1975, was based on factors and trends that it was assumed at the time would continue. To a large extent, this is indeed what has happened. The indications were that the number of Jews in the world would decrease by about 5 percent between 1980 and 2000, due mainly to the low fertility of Diaspora Jewry, and the consequent aging of the Jewish population. Out-marriage exacerbated the negative demographic situation. The problem was particularly acute in Europe: indications were that the decrease in the number of Jews in Europe in the period considered would reach about 40 percent, due especially to the decline in the number of Jews in Eastern Europe. Since these negative demographic factors did not exist among Israeli Jews, the distribution of the Jewish people between Israel and the Diaspora was also expected to undergo significant changes.

However, in the mid-1980s, it seemed probable that by the year 2000, the number of Jews in Israel would be about 300,000 fewer than projected, due to decreasing immigration from the Diaspora, especially from the Soviet Union. Consequently, and supposing that no further changes occurred, the proportion of Israeli Jews in world Jewry was expected to be about 33 percent by the year 2000. About 50 percent of all Jewish children under fifteen years of age would be living in Israel. North American Jewry would dwindle somewhat, although its proportion in Diaspora Jewry would increase. By the beginning of the twenty-first century, the Jewries of Israel and North America (which represented about 71 percent of all Jews in 1980) may account for over 80 percent of the Jewish people.

# The Spanish–Portuguese Jews in Europe and in the Americas:

Seventeenth and Eighteenth Centuries

The Spanish–Portuguese Jews (Sephardim) were among the harbingers of the modern era in Jewish history. Some were descendants of the Jews expelled from Spain (1492) and Portugal (1496–1497). Most, however, were "New Christians"—Jews who had been forced to convert in those countries, continued to observe Judaism secretly, and returned to open Jewish life when circumstances allowed. They then created new Jewish communities, some of which became very important.

The New Christians who left Spain and Portugal during the sixteenth century (frequently because of the Inquisition) settled mainly in northern Italy, the Netherlands, and southern France. During the next century, many moved northward, still to the Netherlands, and from there to northern Germany (Hamburg, Altona), England, and even North and South America. Some settled (without establishing communities) in Central and Eastern Europe.

The great center of Sephardic Jewry was Amsterdam. In the seventeenth century, Amsterdam was a city of intense economic and cultural life, with a relatively tolerant religious atmosphere. The Jewish community in Amsterdam, which began to organize itself at the end of the sixteenth century, was very small (in modern terms)—between 2,500 and 5,000 Jews, or 1 to 2 percent of the city's population. Other Spanish–Portuguese communities of the seventeenth century were not larger: 500 Jews lived in London; 3,000 lived in Leghorn, one of the oldest communities. Important communities existed in Venice, Bordeaux (recognized by the authorities only in the 1720s), and Hamburg. The Amsterdam community was the economic and cultural center for the whole Sephardic dispersion, and its spiritual influence was felt far beyond Jewish circles. Its cultural creativity, influenced by the fecund amalgamation of Jewish and non-Jewish spiritual elements, was highly original and expressed itself in important religious and philosophical works. One important center of Amsterdam Jewry's religious activity was the Etz Haim Yeshiva. The influence of the European Spanish–Portuguese Jews declined in the late eighteenth century, due to their gradual assimilation into the general society.

Ashkenazic Jews began to settle in Amsterdam at the end of the seventeenth century, their number rising to about 10,000 in the eighteenth century. The relations between them and the older, patrician strata of Sephardim were mostly strained.

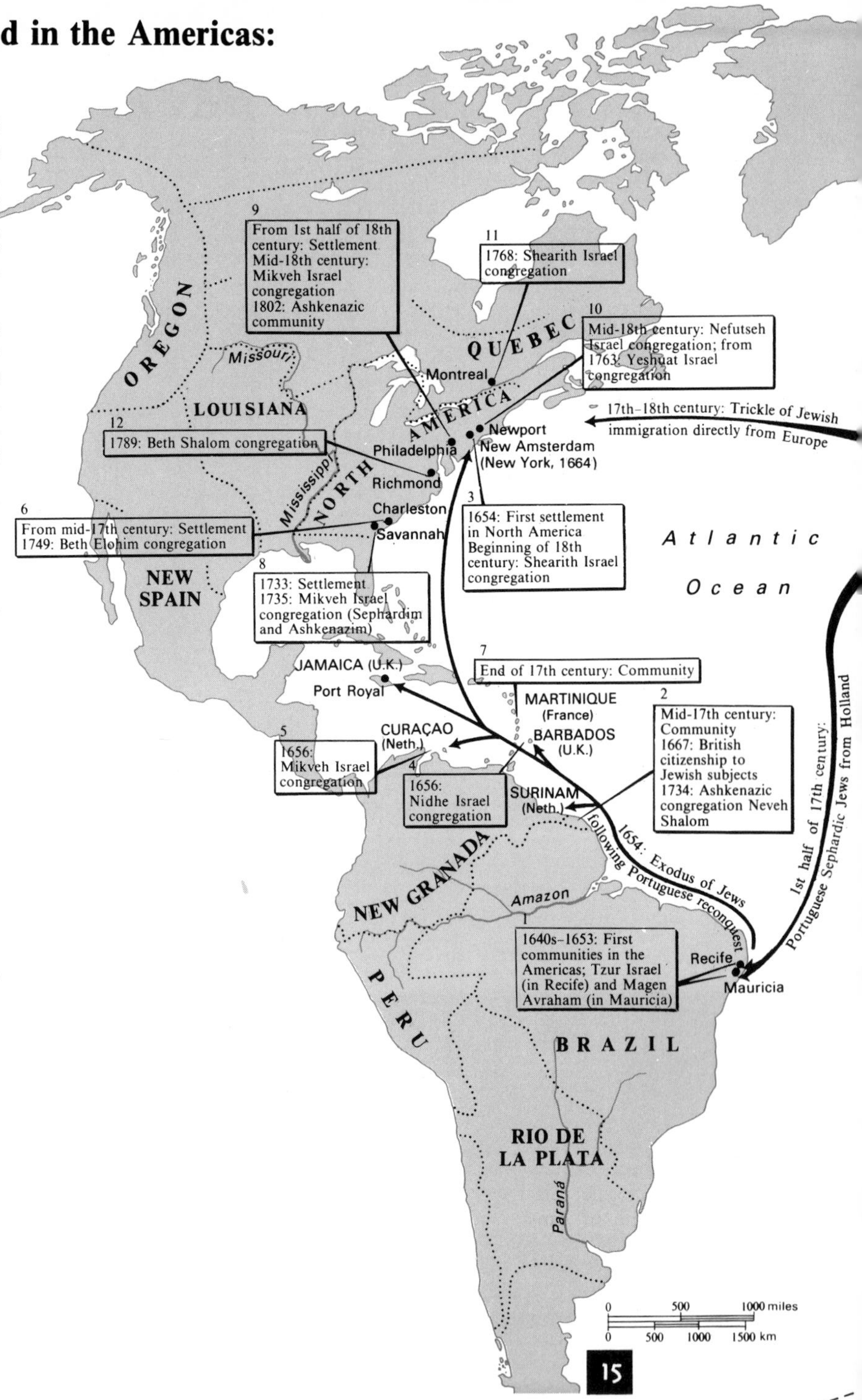


# The Beginning of Jewish Settlement in the Americas

"New Christians" traveled to the Americas as early as the sixteenth century. In the 1630s, Spanish–Portuguese Jews from Amsterdam arrived in the Portuguese colony of Recife, in northeastern Brazil, then under Dutch domination. They established two communities, the first in the New World. With the expulsion of the Dutch from Recife in 1653, the Jews also left. Some of them went northward, to Dutch or English settlements: Surinam, Curaçao, Jamaica, Barbados, and New Amsterdam, which in 1664 came under English domination and changed its name to New York. Other Jews, mostly Spanish–Portuguese, migrated from England and Holland in the seventeenth and eighteenth centuries and established about a dozen communities in North America. Ashkenazic Jews started arriving in the eighteenth century.

The legal situation of the Jews in the English and Dutch colonies was much better than in Europe. European rulers wished to attract settlers to the New World, and various laws in the seventeenth and eighteenth centuries (the law regarding Surinam in 1665, and the Plantation Act of 1740) guaranteed the Jews broad social and civil rights. With American independence in 1776, the Jews there became full and equal citizens of the republic. Their social and economic situation was satisfactory, too. The number of Jews in the Americas remained small: no more than about 3,000 at the end of the eighteenth century, two-thirds of them in North America, which also became the main destination of Jewish immigration: in about 1820, some 15,000 Jews lived in North America.

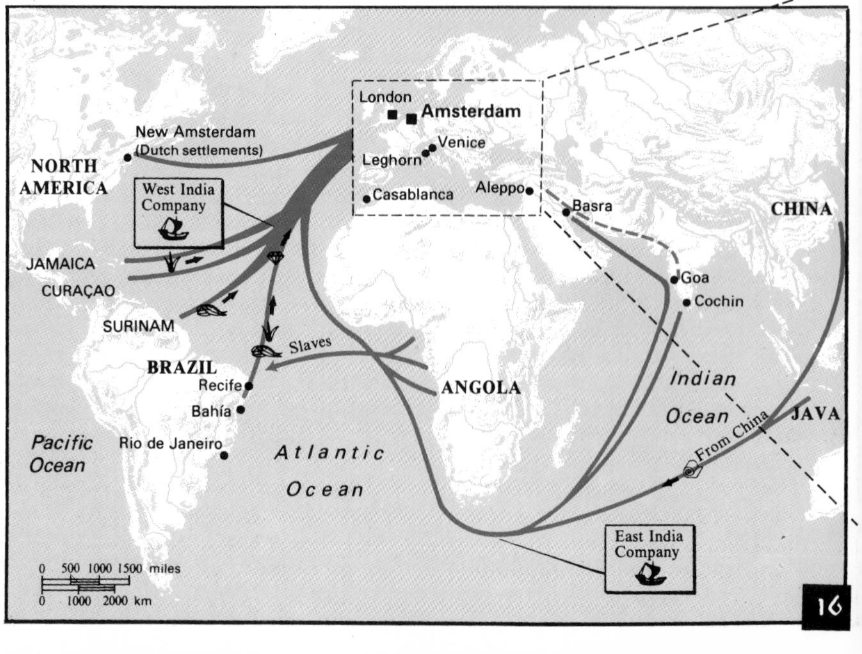

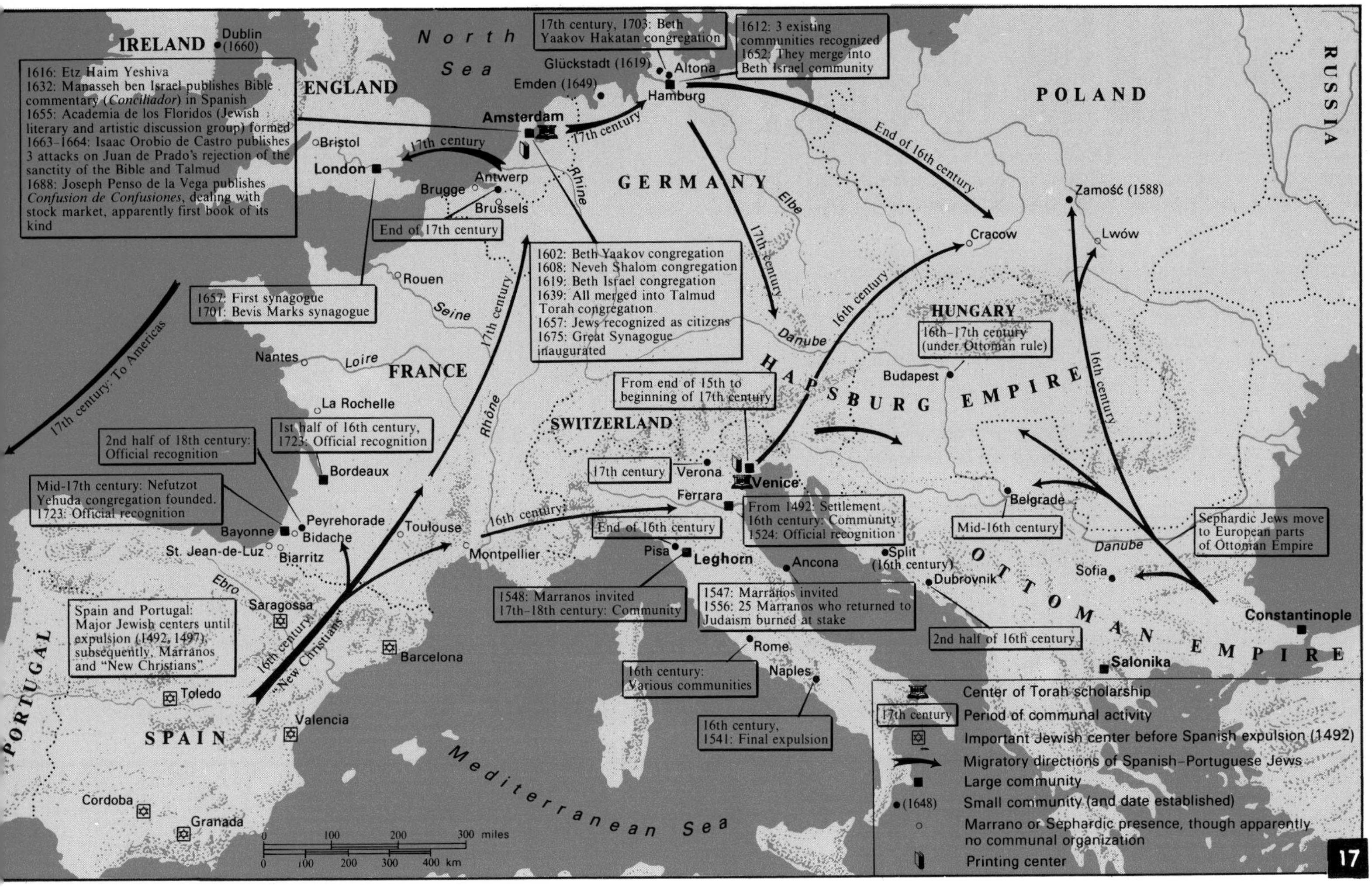


## Economic Activities:

### Seventeenth and Eighteenth Centuries

Spanish–Portuguese Jews were influential in international commerce in the seventeenth and eighteenth centuries. Their experience, financial means, and international family connections enabled them to build a network of economic relations that spanned the entire known world. Operating out of Amsterdam, London, Hamburg, Leghorn, and other commercial centers, these Jewish entrepreneurs carried commodities from and to the Mediterranean countries, Africa, the Americas, India, and even China. In many of these places, they were represented by family members or Sephardic acquaintances. Sugar, tobacco, silk, and precious stones were among the main products that the Spanish–Portuguese Jewish merchants imported into Europe. They were also involved in the printing industry in Europe, producing books with both Latin and Hebrew characters. They participated in two large commercial concerns: the East India Company, active in India and Asia in general; and the West India Company, active in the Western Hemisphere. They also played a role in the development of the modern banking system.

The Sephardic Jews did not act independently, but as part of the economic life of the centers where they lived. They were far from being among the most important merchants in places like London or Amsterdam. In general, they belonged to the more prosperous segment of the population, but many Christian merchants were much richer. Jews were usually forced to take greater business risks, and the competition from the Christian guilds of merchants and craftsmen gradually drove them from dealing in many profitable goods, such as sugar and silk. Only in one field, precious stones, have Jews, mainly of Ashkenazic stock, maintained a leading presence throughout the modern era.

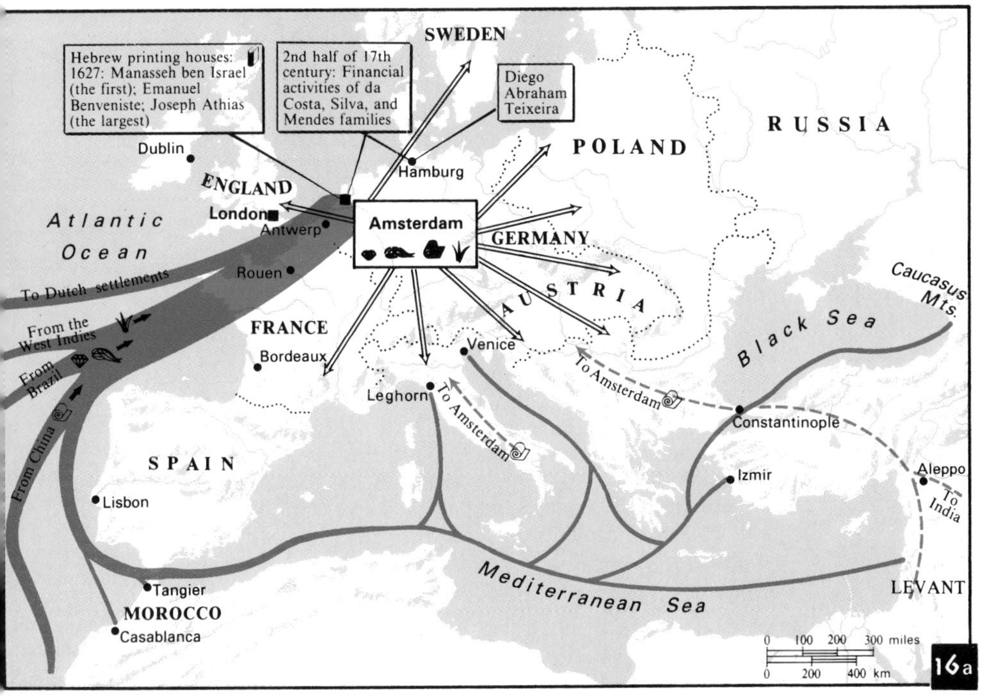


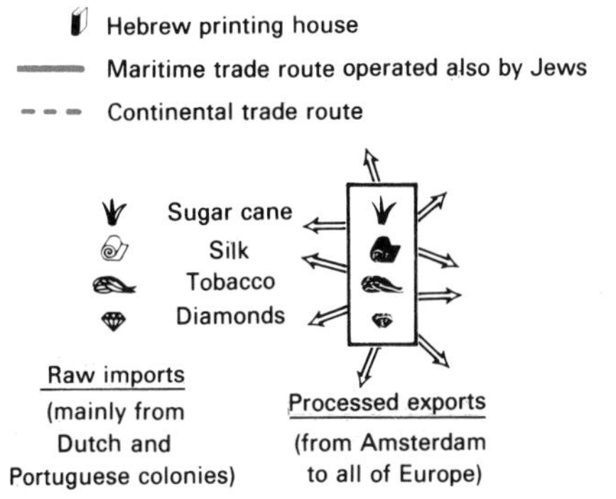

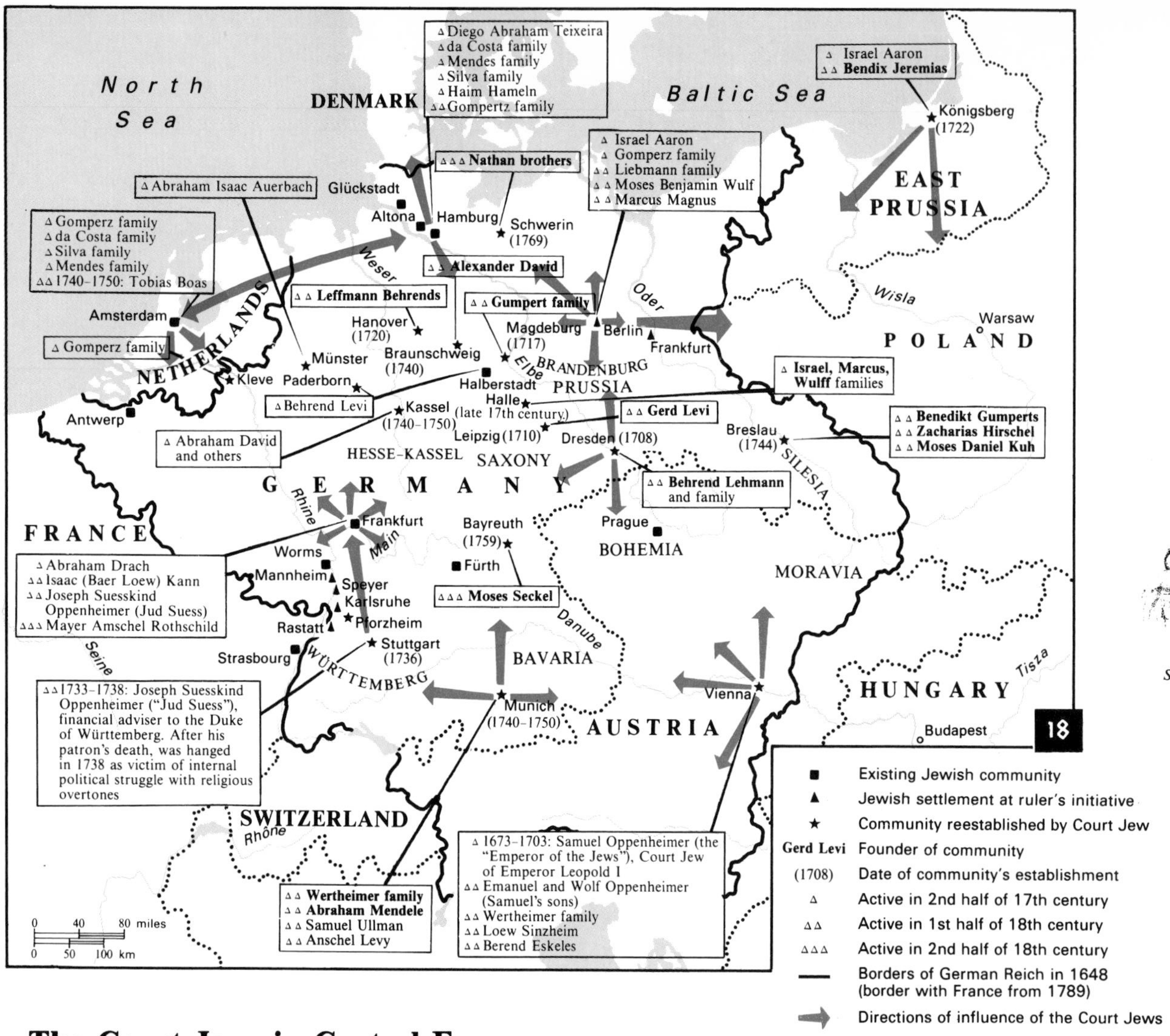

*Samuel Oppenheimer, Court Jew in Vienna*

# The Court Jews in Central Europe:

## Seventeenth and Eighteenth Centuries

Few Jews lived in Central Europe at the beginning of the seventeenth century. Most had been expelled in the fifteenth and sixteenth centuries and had moved eastward, to the large Polish kingdom. From the mid-seventeenth century, new social and political conditions in Europe made possible the gradual return of the Jews. In Western Europe after the Reformation, religion began to lose its influence on political and intellectual life, and the first indications of what was later known as the "secular" society began to appear, generating, among other things, greater tolerance toward Jews. The Jews' position was also enhanced by such developments as the rise in Western Europe of the absolute state and the economic system related to it, mercantilism. The ambitions of the new absolute ruler, his growing financial needs, and the tensions between him and the social classes in his land whose rights he was trying to curtail combined to make possible and necessary the appearance of some new element in the ruler's court who would be loyal to him and could satisfy his various needs. That task was fulfilled by a specific Jewish type, the Court Jew (*Hofjude*). From the ruler's point of view, the Court Jew offered the great advantage of being dependent on him and neutral in the struggle between the ruler and the three social groups disputing his growing power in the state: the nobles, the cities, and the clergy.

The Court Jew helped the ruler obtain money, organized supplies for his army (now under the ruler's command, and no longer mobilized through the feudal-type services of the nobles), executed diplomatic services, and supplied the court with the luxury articles that were such an important sign of status in that era. Indeed, so important were the tasks of Court Jews that from the mid-seventeenth to the late eighteenth century, there was virtually no king or ruling noble in Central Europe who did not employ at least one Court Jew. Court Jews were especially prominent in such important states as Prussia, Bavaria, Saxony, and Württemberg.

The Court Jews did not act alone, but were helped by family members and other Jews, collaborated with one another and with Sephardic merchants in Hamburg and Amsterdam, and maintained close relations with wealthy Jews in Eastern Europe.

The activities of the Court Jew were a fascinating mixture of great opportunities and equally great dangers. He could rise to enormous riches and great political influence, or lose everything, including his freedom and even his life. The most rewarding and dangerous of his tasks was supplying the ruler's army. This was a time of ceaseless wars, and the Court Jew depended on their outcome, on the outcome of court intrigues, and on the whims of his royal protector. The difficult life of the Court Jew was well exemplified by the well-known Samuel Oppenheimer, Court Jew of Emperor Leopold I of Austria. For thirty years (1673–1703), Oppenheimer organized and financed the supply system of the emperor's armies; he knew periods of enormous wealth and utter despondency, and he died penniless. His fate taught other Court Jews to avoid dealing in military supplies.

One important result of the existence of so many Court Jews and of the Jews who served them was the return of Jews to places from which they had been expelled in earlier centuries. Many new communities were established by Court Jews or by rulers interested in the presence of Jews for economic reasons.

The institution of Court Jew was transitory, and toward the end of the eighteenth century, his services were no longer needed or were performed by others. The gradual development of state bureaucracies and the better organization of the European armies rendered many of the Court Jew's tasks superfluous. However, the new atmosphere of greater religious tolerance during the Age of Enlightenment in Europe, together with the expanding economic opportunities brought about by the Industrial Revolution, not only made it possible for Jews who had returned to Central and Western Europe to remain and prosper, but also attracted a growing number of Jewish immigrants from Eastern Europe. The Court Jews entered new economic fields; for instance, some of them established private banks, several of which were to play major financial roles in the nineteenth century.

# The Jews in Poland and Lithuania Before the Eighteenth-Century Partitions

In the mid-eighteenth century, shortly before the partitions of the Polish state, more than two-thirds of all Jews in the world lived in that large kingdom, which extended from the Baltic Sea and Silesia in the west to the Dnieper River and the Ukrainian steppe in the east. The origins of Polish Jewry go back to the Middle Ages. Its beginnings were at times difficult, but by the eighteenth century, it had built a firm position for itself in the kingdom and was well organized in hundreds of small and large communities. Polish Jews engaged in a variety of economic activities, had a rich cultural and religious life, and were well served by a large degree of internal autonomy.

Considering the conditions in Poland in the seventeenth and eighteenth centuries, Polish Jewry of that time had a mainly "urban" character. More than 70 percent of the Jews lived in cities or small towns, in many of which they were the majority of the population. Even the Jews who lived in villages were not serfs or peasants, but renters of mills, producers of alcoholic beverages, owners of inns, or administrators of the estates of the largely absent Polish nobles.

In 1580, a general Jewish authority, the Council of the Lands (*Vaad Haaratzot*), was established. Its purpose was to represent the Jews before the Polish rulers, especially regarding the payment of the poll taxes to the king. These taxes were collected internally, according to a system agreed on by the members of the council. The council (or the regional councils) also dealt with internal Jewish matters, such as regulations for the nomination of rabbis and religious-court judges (*dayanim*), communal elections, resolution of quarrels between communities or between individuals and communities, and communal authorizations for book printings. The original council had representatives from Great Poland (main community, Poznań), Little Poland (main community, Cracow), Reissen (or Ruthenia; main community, Lwów), and Lithuania—thus the common name Council of the Four Lands. In 1623, the Lithuanian communities established their own council. There were additional changes in the number of lands, circuits (*glilot*), and communities represented in the councils, and in the extent of the influence of each of these bodies.

In Poland in the mid-seventeenth century, after the rebellions and wars that took their toll in the Jewish communities as well, Polish Jewry reorganized itself, and the period that followed was one of relative prosperity and population increase. But the inability of the Polish state to solve its own social and political problems and the gradual decline of the central authority also weakened the authority of the Jewish central institutions. Tensions developed between the Jewish communities and the Christian population of the cities. Sources of income disappeared; the centralized collection of taxes became impossible; and many communities sank deeply into debt. In the end, the authorities decreed the dissolution of the councils—of Poland in 1764, and of Lithuania in 1765.

**The Partitions of Poland**

The internal weakness of the Polish–Lithuanian kingdom and its growing internal anarchy awakened the ambitions of the neighboring countries, whose more developed centralist and absolute regimes were served by armies organized according to modern principles. Poland's neighbors (Prussia, Austria, and Russia) decided to conquer and partition Poland and Lithuania. In 1772, 1793, and 1795 (Austria did not participate in the second partition), they divided the Polish kingdom among them. Independent Poland disappeared until 1919.

The partitions opened a new period for Polish Jewry, whose life had followed the autonomous communal pattern characteristic of the Middle Ages. Polish Jewry now found itself living in states whose political systems were, or strove to be, of the absolute type and, as such, very different from that of the semifeudal Polish state. The subsequent development of each part of Polish Jewry was influenced by the very different economic, social, and political conditions of each of the states to which the Jews now belonged. Meanwhile, Polish Jewry continued to grow in number; at the beginning of the nineteenth century, there were about 1.25 million Jews living in the territories of former Poland, about 70 percent of all the Jews in the world.

**The Russian Empire and the Jews**

There were very few Jews in Russia before the partitions of Poland. Since the late Middle Ages, Jews (the "enemies of Christ") had not been admitted into the principality of Moscow, the nucleus of the future empire—an example of Jew-hatred without Jews. The annexation of the Polish and Lithuanian territories, with their large and well-rooted Jewish populations, forced the Russian authorities to deal with what gradually came to be regarded as the "Jewish problem." In the 1780s and 1790s, during the reign of Catherine II, the Jews of the annexed territories received the status of city dwellers and merchants, and the first steps were taken to establish a territorial sphere where they could live—the beginning of what later developed into the Pale of Settlement. From 1794, the Jews in Belorussia and the Ukraine had to pay a double poll tax, and their settlement in the eastern part of the empire was limited. However, Catherine II also decided that the Jews should continue to maintain their autonomous internal administration in the form of their communities (the *kahal*), and for the next generation, the Russian authorities virtually did not interfere with the internal life of the Jews.

In 1815, after the end of the Napoleonic wars and as a result of the new political arrangements approved by the Treaty of Vienna, Russia acquired most of the Grand Duchy of Warsaw, thus significantly enlarging its Polish holdings. An autonomous kingdom of Poland (known as Congress Poland) was now established as part of the Russian Empire and ruled by the czar. The special status of Poland was reflected in its large Jewish population, whose situation was somewhat better than that in the western provinces of Russia (which had also belonged to Poland before the partitions).

In spite of the regional differences, the large and growing Polish–Russian Jewry was, to a large extent, characterized by internal Jewish cohesiveness. In the later nineteenth century, it would become a source of the emigration movement that would spread throughout the world and establish new Jewish communities, and the cradle of most ideological and spiritual movements in modern Jewry.

## Partitions of Poland

### First Partition, 1772

### Second Partition, 1793

### Third Partition, 1795*

—— Polish border, 1772

* After 1815, the borders of Poland, now part of the Russian Empire, were those on map 21, page 32.

# Jewish Population in the Provinces (*Województwo*), 1760s

## Jews in the Crown Lands (Poland)

| | Province | Number of Jews |
|---|---|---|
| 1 | Belz | 16,400 |
| 2 | Braclaw | 20,300 |
| 3 | Brześć Kujawski | 1,300 |
| 4 | Chelm | 9,800 |
| 5 | Chelmno | 600 |
| 6 | Cracow | 19,300 |
| 7 | Gdańsk | 2,700 |
| 8 | Gniezno | 6,500 |
| 9 | Inflanty* | 3,000 |
| 10 | Inowroclaw | 2,500 |
| 11 | Kalisz | 6,500 |
| 12 | Kiev | 22,400 |
| 13 | Leczyca | 2,900 |
| 14 | Lublin | 20,100 |
| 15 | Malbork | 100 |
| 16 | Masovia | 10,700 |
| 17 | Plock | 4,000 |
| 18 | Podlasie | 19,000 |
| 19 | Podolia | 38,400 |
| 20 | Poznań | 19,900 |
| 21 | Rawa | 5,300 |
| 22 | Ruthenia | 100,100 |
| 23 | Sandomierz | 43,000 |
| 24 | Sieradz | 7,900 |
| 25 | Volhynia | 50,800 |
| | **Total** | **433,500** |

* (Livonia)

## Jews in the Grand Duchy of Lithuania

| | Province | Number of Jews |
|---|---|---|
| 26 | Brześć Litewski | 22,000 |
| 27 | Minsk | 13,400 |
| 28 | Mścislaw | 2,600 |
| 29 | Nowogródek | 21,100 |
| 30 | Polock | 6,700 |
| 31 | Troki | 33,700 |
| 32 | Vitebsk | 12,000 |
| 33 | Wilno | 27,000 |
| 34 | Żmudź | 15,800 |
| | **Total** | **154,300** |

**Total number of Jews in the Polish-Lithuanian Kingdom 587,800**

The data are based on censuses conducted (in Poland in 1764 and in the Grand Duchy of Lithuania in 1765) according to the royal administrative division and not according to the Jewish lands. The censuses were based on the number of Jews liable for the poll tax, and it may be assumed that the number of Jews was about 20% greater than officially declared. Furthermore, these data did not include children below the age of one year, who composed, on the average, 5.6% of the Jewish population.

# Poland and Lithuania:
Eighteenth Century

1623: Land Council of
Lithuania separates from
Council of Four Lands

Dünaburg • Dryssa • *Dvina*

Polock
(Polotsk)

Vitebsk

niewiez

**U T**

Lady
(Lyady)

Orsza

Szklów

Mścislaw
(Mstislav)

**RUSSIAN EMPIRE**

Wilno
(Vilna)
(4,000)

Troki

Smorgon

Borisov

Mohylew
(Mogilev)

Olkieniki

**V I L N A**

Oszmiana

**G R O D N O**

Radun

Lida

Minsk

Bychów

**G R A N D    D U C H Y    O F**

Sozh

**N O W O G R O D E K**

Nowogródek

Mir

Nieświez

Bobruisk

Czeczersk

**B E L O R U S S I A    M I N S K**

Wolpa

Niemen

Szczara

Kleck
(Kletsk)

Sluck
(Slutsk)

Ptycz

*Berezyna*

*Dnieper*

Homel

Ikowysk

Zelwa

Slonim

Lachowicze

**B L A C K    R U T H E N I A**

Sluch

Pruzana

Sielce

**L I T H U A N I A**

Motol

Lachwa

Turów

**P I N S K**

Mozyr

Khoyniki

Chomsk

Oginski Canal

*Jasiolda*

Janów
Poleski

Dawidgródek

Brahin

Drohiczyn

Pinsk-
Karlin

Goryń

Stolyń

*Prypet*

Kobryń

Dnieper-Bug Canal

Styr'

**P I N S K**

**P O L E S I E**

*Dnieper*

Wysock
(Visotsk)

**P O L E S I E**

Owrucz

Czarnobyl
(Chernobyl)

tycze

Zamość–Chelm region
(Nine Communities),
administrative unit in
early 18th century

Vladimirets

Olewsk

*Teterev*

Czartorysk

Stepań

Kolki

**V O L H Y N I A**

Radomyśl

Kiev

Luboml

Kovel

Turzysk

Deraznia

vice

Wlodzimierz
(Ludmir)

Lokachi

**V O L H Y N I A**

Tuczyn

Olyka

Miedzyrzecz
(Mezhirech)

Korostyszów

Brusilov

**U K**

Hrubieszów

Luck
(Lutsk)

Rowne

Annopol

Zytomierz
(Zhitomir)

Tyszowce
(Tishvitz)

Horochów

Sluch

Kanów

asczów

Dubno

Ostróg

Shepetovka

Polonne
(Polonnoye)

Cudnów

Pavolotch

Biala Cerkiew

szów
ski

Belz

Bereszteczko

Zaslav

Berdyczów
(Berdichev)

**R A**

Uhnów

**B E L Z**

Brody
(7,200)

Krzemieniec

Lubar

Wolodarka

*Dnieper*

Zólkiew
(Zholkva)

Jampol

Sieniawa

Tetiev

Smiela

Lwów
(6,200)

Gliniany

Zloczów

Zbarazh

**P O D O L I A**

Lipowiec

Sokolowka

**I N E**

Szczerzec

Przemyslany

Tarnopol

Ploskirov

Miedzybóz

Vinnitsa

Il'intsy

**R U T H E N I A**

Komarno

Chodorów

Brzezany

Grzymalów

Latyczów

Satanów

**P O D O L I A**

Bar

Brailów

Niemirów

Humań
(Uman)

Drohobycz

Rohatyn

Podhajce

Husiatyn

Krasno

Braclaw
(Bratslav)

Stryj

Halicz

Buczacz

Czortków

Szarogród

Tulczyn

Tomashpol

**R E I S S E N**

Bolechów

Stanislawów

Tyśmienica

Kamieniec Podolski

*Seret*

Mohylew Podolski
(Mogilev)

Ataki

*Boh*

Dolina

Bohorodczany

Horodenka

Zaleszczyki

*Dniester*

**20**

Nadwórna

Kolomyja

Zablotów

*Prut*

Raszków

**P O K U C I E**

Kutów

**O T T O M A N    E M P I R E**

0    20    40    60 miles

0        40        80 km

# The Jews in the Russian Empire:

## Late Nineteenth Century

More than 5 million Jews—about 50 percent of the Jewish people—lived in the Russian Empire (Poland included) at the end of the nineteenth century. More than 90 percent lived in the Pale of Settlement, which in its final form (1835) included fifteen provinces in western Russia and the ten provinces that formed the kingdom of Poland, incorporated into the empire in 1815. The kingdom had its own administrative status, and only in 1868 were the Jews permitted to pass freely from the Polish to the Russian region. Several other limitations existed in the Pale: Jews were forbidden to live in certain cities or, in part of the nineteenth century, along the empire's western frontier. At the end of the nineteenth century, the Jews made up about 11 percent of the Pale's population, but 36 percent of its urban population (about 50 percent, if Poland is excluded).

Complex relations developed between the Russian government and the large Jewish population, so different in religion and culture from the empire's other populations, and possessing a well-rooted tradition of autonomy. The government's policy was expressed in a long series of edicts, the most significant being the 1804 Jewish Statute of Alexander I and the May Laws (or Temporary Laws) of 1882.

The basic intention of the 1804 edict was to integrate the Jews gradually into Russian society in the social, cultural, and economic spheres—that is, to bring about their "Russianization." The Russian czars tried to attain that goal by various means: by exerting pressure (Nicholas I, 1825–1855); by granting rights (Alexander II, 1855–1881); or by combining the two (Alexander I, 1801–1825). The regime of Nicholas I was particularly harsh; among many other steps, special military duties were forced on the Jews (1827, the cantonist system), and the Jewish communal structure (the *kahal*) was abolished in 1844.

The May Laws, or Temporary Laws, of 1882 marked a radical change in the government's policy toward Russian Jewry. They reflected new ideological trends in Russian governmental circles, such as the growing influence of pan-Slavic and anti-Western attitudes, combined with disillusionment over the results of the efforts to Russianize the Jews. The official position was now to discourage the integration of the Jews into Russian society, to keep them apart, and to encourage their emigration from the country (reigns of Alexander III, 1881–1894, and Nicholas II, 1894–1917). A difficult period began for Russian Jewry, a time of discrimination and several waves of pogroms, which continued until the revolution of 1917.

During the nineteenth century, Russian–Polish Jewry underwent gradual cultural modernization, which became pronounced beginning in the reign of Alexander II. New concepts about Jewish life, together with the pressures faced by the Jews in Russia, spurred Jewish intellectuals to seek new ways for Russian Jewry. The emigration movement—to other parts of Europe or overseas—gradually grew to enormous proportions. New ideological movements arose, such as socialism and Zionism. All these trends expressed the deep dissatisfaction of Jews with the conditions in which they lived.

The data show that at least in Poland (and perhaps also in Russia), the number of Jews continued to grow, in spite of emigration and the first signs of a decline in the natural increase. Approximately 1.3 million Jews lived in Poland at the end of the nineteenth century (14 percent of the whole population), and close to 2 million in 1913 (15 percent of the population). World War I and its consequences were to alter radically the political and demographic conditions of the Jews in both Russia and Poland.

### Occupations of Jews, 1897

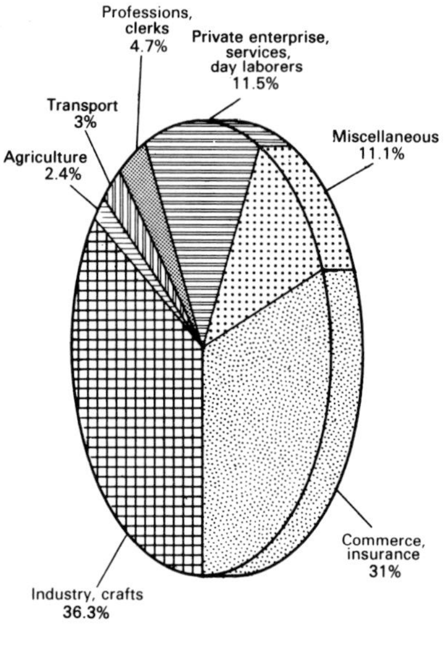

# Jewish Population in the Pale of Settlement, 1897

| Percentage of Jews in locality | Jews in localities of this percentage | 1,000–4,999 | 5,000–9,999 | 10,000–24,999 | 25,000–64,999 | 95,000 and more* |
|---|---|---|---|---|---|---|
| Number of localities | | 851 localities | 118 localities | 33 localities | 13 localities | 3 localities |
| 90–100 | 88,300 in 47 localities (2.1%) | 46 | 1 | | | |
| 80–90 | 131,500 in 52 localities (3.2%) | 48 | 4 | | | |
| 70–80 | 404,700 in 114 localities (9.8%) | 98 | 12 | 3 | 1 (h) | |
| 60–70 | 584,300 in 157 localities (14.1%) | 130 | 22 | 3 | 2 (g, n) | |
| 50–60 | 797,400 in 214 localities (19.3%) | 174 | 32 | 6 | 2 (f, j) | |
| 40–50 | 792,200 in 170 localities (19.1%) | 134 | 24 | 7 | 5 (d, e, k, m, o) | |
| 30–40 | 815,700 in 106 localities (19.7%) | 87 | 8 | 6 | 2 (i, p) | 3 (a, b, c) |
| 20–30 | 214,200 in 65 localities (5.2%) | 55 | 6 | 4 | | |
| 10–20 | 170,400 in 51 localities (4.1%) | 42 | 8 | | 1 (l) | |
| 0–10 | 139,000 in 42 localities (3.4%) | 37 | 1 | 4 | | |
| Total number of Jews | Total 4,137,700 Jews† (100%) | 1,866,800 | 821,200 | 492,000 | 501,000 | 456,700 |
| Jewish population in percent | | 45.1% | 19.8% | 11.9% | 12.1% | 11.1% |

* No localities with 65,000–95,000 Jews

† The Jewish population of localities with at least 1,000 Jews constitutes 79.3% of the total Jewish population in Russia and Poland.

**Large Jewish communities**

a. Warsaw
b. Odessa
c. Lodz
d. Vilna
e. Kishinev
f. Minsk
g. Bialystok
h. Berdichev
i. Yekaterinoslav
j. Vitebsk
k. Dolinsk
l. Kiev
m. Zhitomir
n. Brest Litovsk
o. Kremenchug
p. Kovno

## Demographic Characteristics of the Pale, 1897

| | Non-Jews: Percentage in cities | Non-Jews: Percentage in other places | Jews: Percentage in cities | Jews: Percentage in other places | Cities: Non-Jews | Cities: Jews | Other places: Non-Jews | Other places: Jews |
|---|---|---|---|---|---|---|---|---|
| Whole Pale of Settlement | 10.6 | 89.4 | 48.8 | 51.2 | 62.3% | 37.7% | 93.0 | 7.0 |
| Poland | 16.6 | 83.4 | 61.6 | 38.4 | 62.3 | 37.7 | 93.0 | 7.0 |
| Lithuania | 7.4 | 92.6 | 42.7 | 57.3 | 50.0 | 50.0 | 90.3 | 9.7 |
| Belorussia | 5.7 | 94.3 | 44.8 | 55.2 | 44.8 | 55.2 | 91.6 | 8.4 |
| Ukraine | 6.8 | 93.2 | 35.3 | 64.7 | 64.1 | 35.9 | 93.0 | 7.0 |
| New Russia | 16.8 | 83.2 | 68.6 | 31.4 | 73.9 | 26.1 | 96.8 | 3.2 |
| Bessarabia | 10.8 | 89.2 | 48.0 | 52.0 | 62.6 | 37.4 | 92.8 | 7.2 |

# The Jews in Odessa

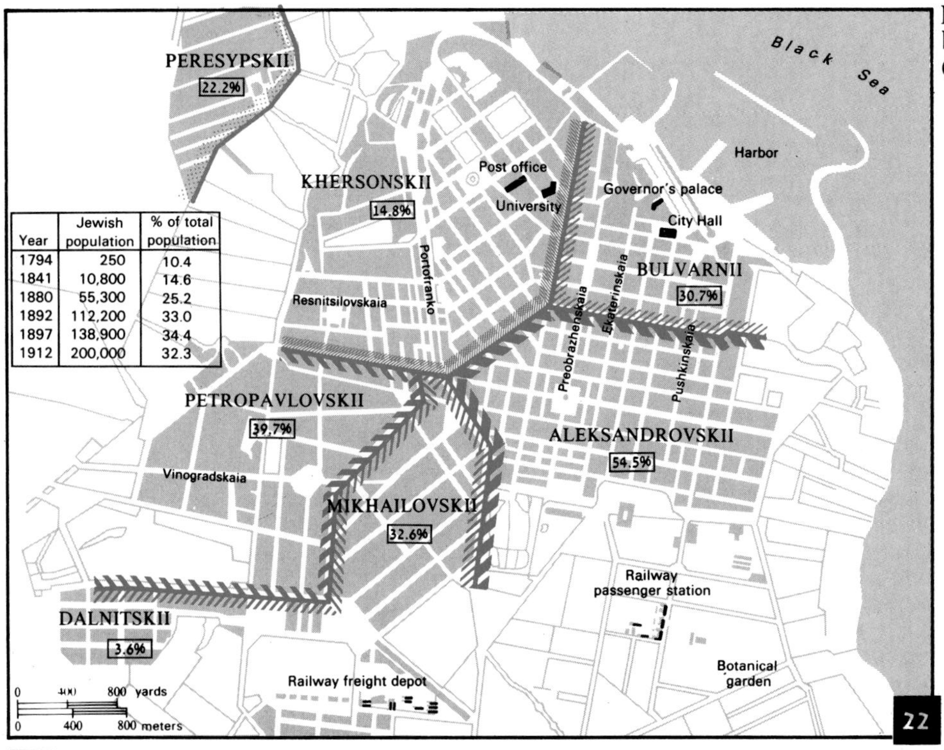


| Year | Jewish population | % of total population |
|---|---|---|
| 1794 | 250 | 10.4 |
| 1841 | 10,800 | 14.6 |
| 1880 | 55,300 | 25.2 |
| 1892 | 112,200 | 33.0 |
| 1897 | 138,900 | 34.4 |
| 1912 | 200,000 | 32.3 |

54.5% Percentage of Jews in quarters' total population, 1897

## Division of Jews by the City's Quarters, 1897

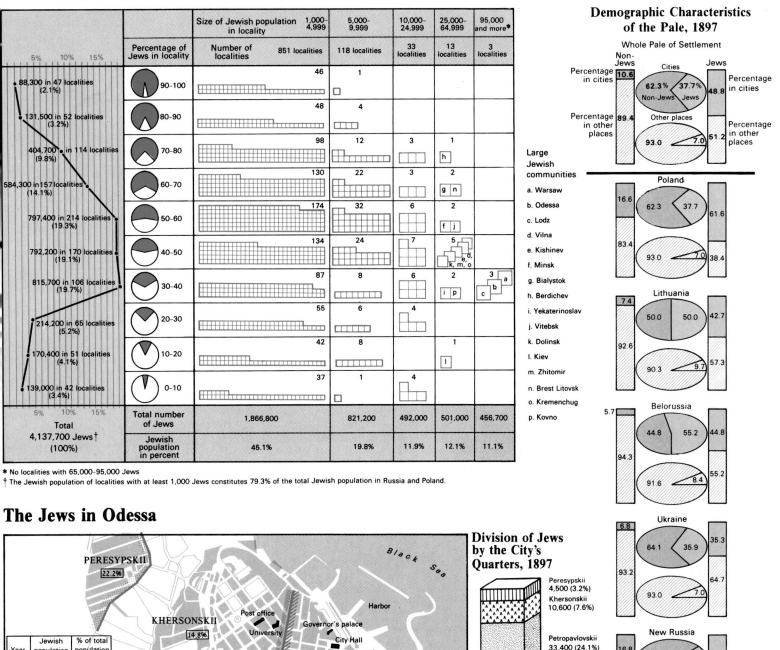

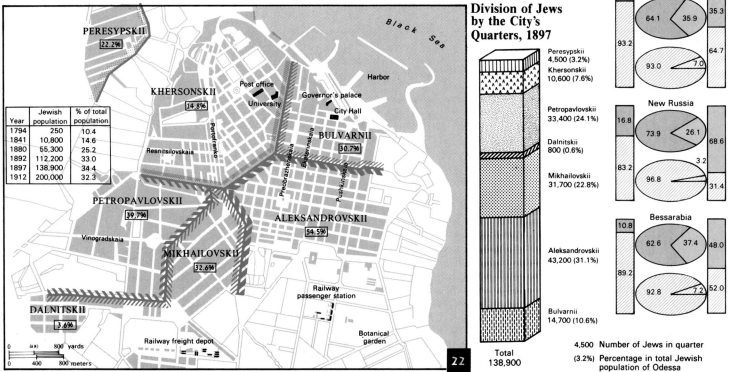

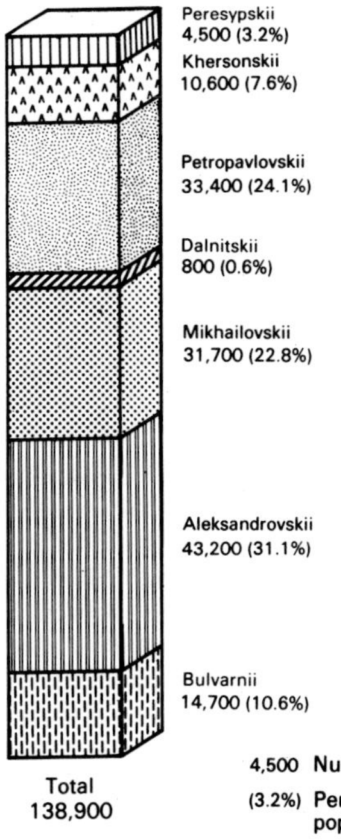


4,500 Number of Jews in quarter

(3.2%) Percentage in total Jewish population of Odessa

After Warsaw, Odessa was the largest Jewish center in the Russian Empire. The city was conquered from the Turks only in 1789. The Russian authorities, interested in its development, opened the city to Jewish settlement, together with southern Russia in general. Many of the new Jewish inhabitants came from Galicia.

Odessa became an important port and thriving economic center, with an international population. The Jews lived in all parts of the town, and they prospered, being represented in all economic fields. Because of the city's liberal atmosphere in both the Jewish and the general society, Odessa became a vibrant intellectual center, the meeting place for Jewish writers, maskilim, Jewish socialists, Jewish nationalists, Zionists, and journalists, expressing themselves in Yiddish, Hebrew, and Russian. Odessa's spiritual influence was felt by Jews throughout Russia.

# The Jews in the Hapsburg Empir

Late Eighteenth Centu

Border of Hapsburg Empire in 1918
(excluding areas of Italy, mainly Lombardy and Tuscany, and Belgium and part of Galicia, which were part of the empire at various times during the 18th and 19th centuries)
Border between Hungary and other parts of the empire
Border of Bohemia, Moravia, Galicia, and Hungary
Border between the other lands
500–1,000 Jews, or smaller but important communities
1,000–2,000 Jews
2,000–5,000 Jews
5,000–10,000 Jews
*Toleranzpatent* (edict of rights) of Joseph II and date

# Jewish Population of the Empire:

Mid-Eighteenth Century to 1830

| Period | Mid-18th century | 1787–1790 | 1830 |
|---|---|---|---|
| Number of Jews throughout empire | 251,700 | 333,700 | 608,100 |
| Bohemia — number of Jews in region | 29,100 | 43,800 | 67,300 |
| Bohemia — percentage of total population | 1.5 | 1.6 | 1.7 |
| Moravia (including Silesia) — number of Jews in region | 20,300 | 28,300 | 32,200 |
| Moravia (including Silesia) — percentage of total population | 2.3 | 1.8 | 1.6 |
| Galicia (including Bukovina) (estimate) — number of Jews in region | 187,000 | 178,100 | 249,900 |
| Galicia (including Bukovina) (estimate) — percentage of total population | 6.0-7.0 | 5.6 | 5.5 |
| Hungary — number of Jews in region | 14,800 | 83,000 | 245,000 |
| Hungary — percentage of total population | 0.5 | 1.0 | 2.2 |
| Austria (mainly Vienna) — number of Jews in region | 500 | 500 | 3,000 |
| Other areas — number of Jews in region | | | 10,700 |

Legend
Up to 1,000 · 10,000 · 100,000 — Absolute numbers
1.6 — Percentage of total population

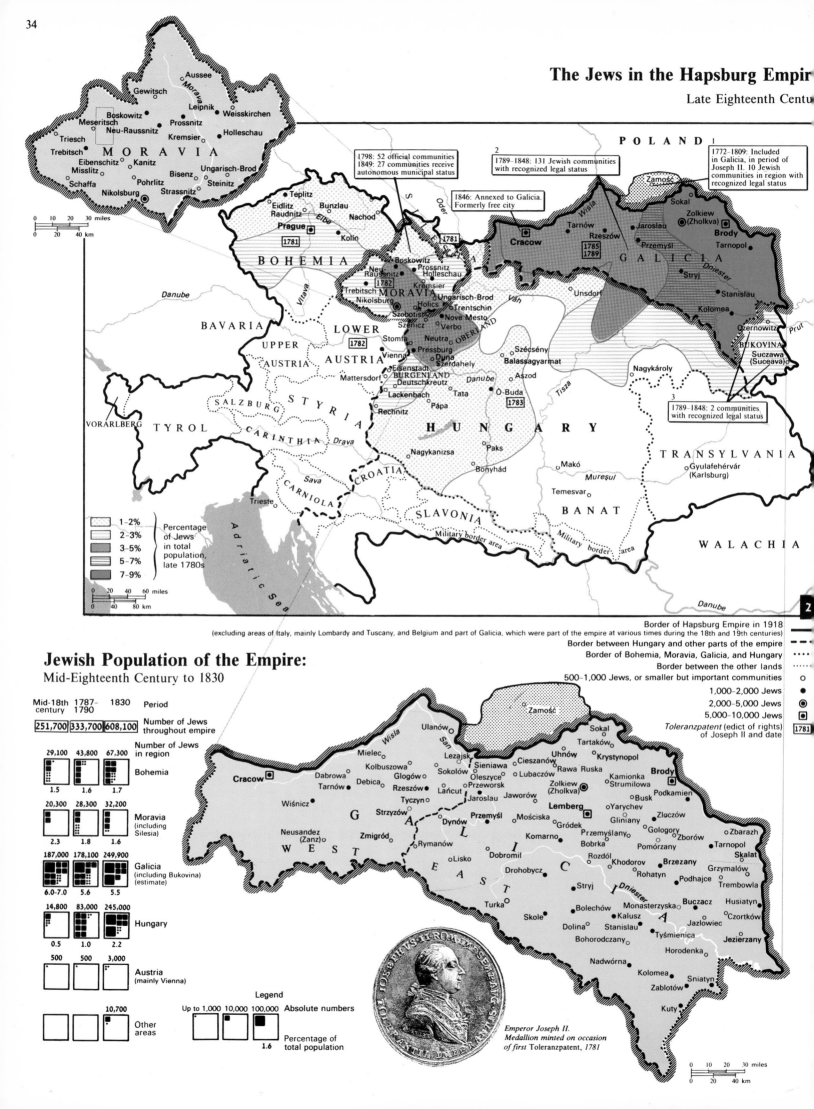

*Emperor Joseph II. Medallion minted on occasion of first* Toleranzpatent, *1781*

The Hapsburg Empire, with Austria at its center, was a major European power in the eighteenth and nineteenth centuries. The empire was a conglomeration of countries and peoples, each with its own culture and language, and each maintaining many of its own customs and laws. Consequently, the position of the Jews varied from land to land, and in some cases was rooted in relations established in the Middle Ages. Restrictions were in force regarding the settlement of Jews in the "German lands" of the empire (Upper Austria, Lower Austria, Vorarlberg, Tyrol, Styria, Carinthia, Carniola). Their presence was forbidden in Croatia, Slavonia, and the militarized border region in southern Hungary. In Transylvania and Banat, in southern Hungary, the Jews could (in theory) live in only one town in each region, and their presence was forbidden in certain parts of Hungary. A small Jewish community lived in the capital, Vienna, subject to many restrictions. Furthermore, Jews were not permitted in the "free cities" of the empire, cities with their own charters of rights. In Moravia, the Jews were not permitted to live in the villages.

The Jews could live (in some instances, under certain restrictions) in Bohemia, in some cities in Moravia, and in most parts of the Hungarian lands reconquered from the Turks in the seventeenth century. The largest number of Jews lived in Galicia, which had been annexed to the Hapsburg Empire only in 1772 (as a result of the first partition of Poland) and was not subject to the limitations imposed on other parts of the empire. In the 1780s, about one-half of the Jews of the empire lived in Galicia, one-quarter in the lands belonging to the Bohemian Crown (Bohemia, Moravia, and Silesia), and one-quarter in the Hungarian lands, most of them immigrants from Galicia and Moravia. In the eighteenth and nineteenth centuries, the Jewish population in Galicia increased significantly. Emigration from there was a major factor in the development of Jewish settlements in other parts of the Hapsburg Empire and in some provinces of the Russian Empire: 70,000 to 150,000 Jews left Galicia between 1765 and 1830; over 50 percent settled in Hungary, the others going to Bukovina, Moldavia, Bessarabia, southern Russia, and parts of central (Congress) Poland, formed in 1815 as part of the Russian Empire. Most of the Jewish population in Galicia and Moravia lived in small towns, although there were also some major communities in cities. In Hungary and Bohemia, there was a larger percentage of Jews living in villages.

**The Jewish Policies of Joseph II (1781–1790)**

Joseph II, a ruler of the enlightened absolute type, promulgated several decrees (*Toleranzpatenten*) between 1781 and 1789. These were a combination of concessions and restrictions aimed at "improving" (according to the emperor's concepts) the ways of life, the cultural level, and the economic activities of the Jews. General schools for the Jewish population were established in many communities. In 1785, most of the rights of the communities as autonomous bodies were abolished, especially regarding their juridical powers. Some communities were recognized as religious bodies: 141 communities in Galicia (including 10 in Zamość province), 52 in Moravia, 1 in Bohemia (Prague), and 2 in Bukovina. In 1788, it was decided to enlist the Jews into the army. Furthermore, restrictions were imposed on Jewish estate-renting in Galicia, to remove the Jews from the rural population and concentrate them in the towns. It was decided in 1783 to open the "free cities" in Hungary to the Jews, but they still were not permitted to live in the German lands of the empire. The various edicts put heavy pressure on the Jews in Galicia, about 50,000 of whom lived in villages. The economic regulations and the enlistment into the army were among the factors that impelled many Jews to migrate to Hungary and other countries.

After the death of Joseph II in 1790, many of his decrees were disregarded, except in Bohemia and Moravia, where the central government had more influence.

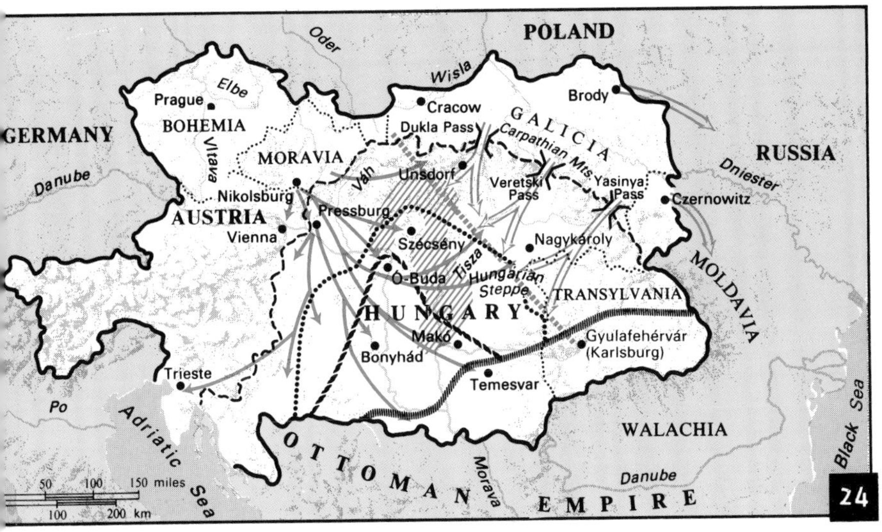


Area barred to Jewish residence
Migration of Jews from Galicia and Moravia
Line separating Galician immigration from Moravian immigration
Border of Ottoman expansion in 17th century
Border of northward penetration of Sephardic Jews in 18th century in wake of Ottoman conquests
Border of northernmost penetration of Sephardic Jews

## The Beginnings of Hungarian Jewry:

### Eighteenth Century

The reconquest of Hungary from the Turks in the seventeenth century opened that large country, relatively unencumbered by legal restrictions, to Jewish settlement. In the eighteenth century, a significant number of Jews arrived from two main directions: from Moravia, to the northwest, between 30,000 and 35,000 Jews, about half its Jewish population, migrated to Hungary in the early eighteenth century; and from Galicia, to the northeast, about 25,000 Jews migrated during the 1770s and another 50,000 in the mid-nineteenth century.

Legal restrictions and natural obstacles (the Carpathian Mountains in north-central Hungary) divided the two streams of immigrants. Later, the mountain barrier also influenced the development of Hungarian Jewry into two cultural types: one East European (of Galician origin) and the other Central European (of Moravian origin). Each type developed its own relationship with the general society as well as its own patterns of Jewish cultural and religious life.

## Rural and Urban Jews in the Period of Joseph II, 1781 to 1790

**Occupations of Jews**

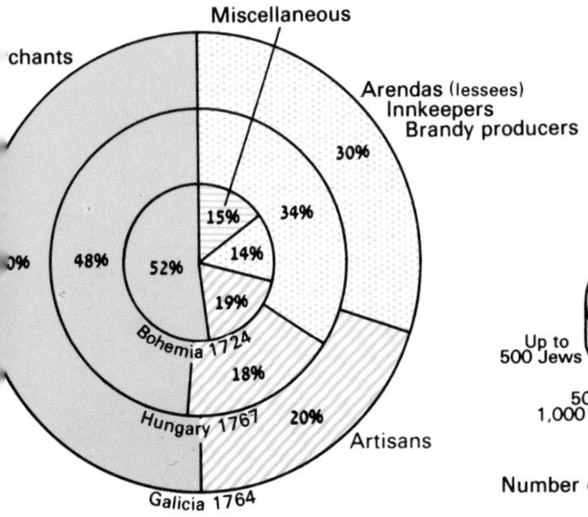


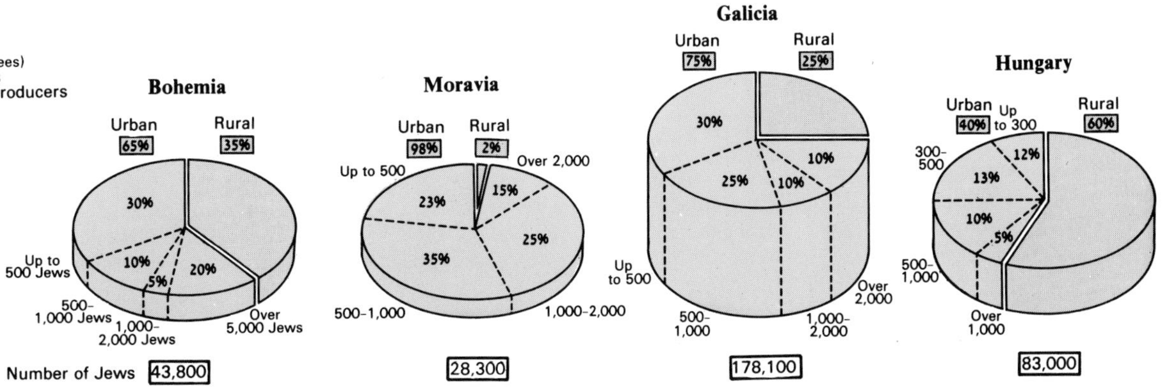

# The Jews in Austria–Hungary: Early Twentieth Century

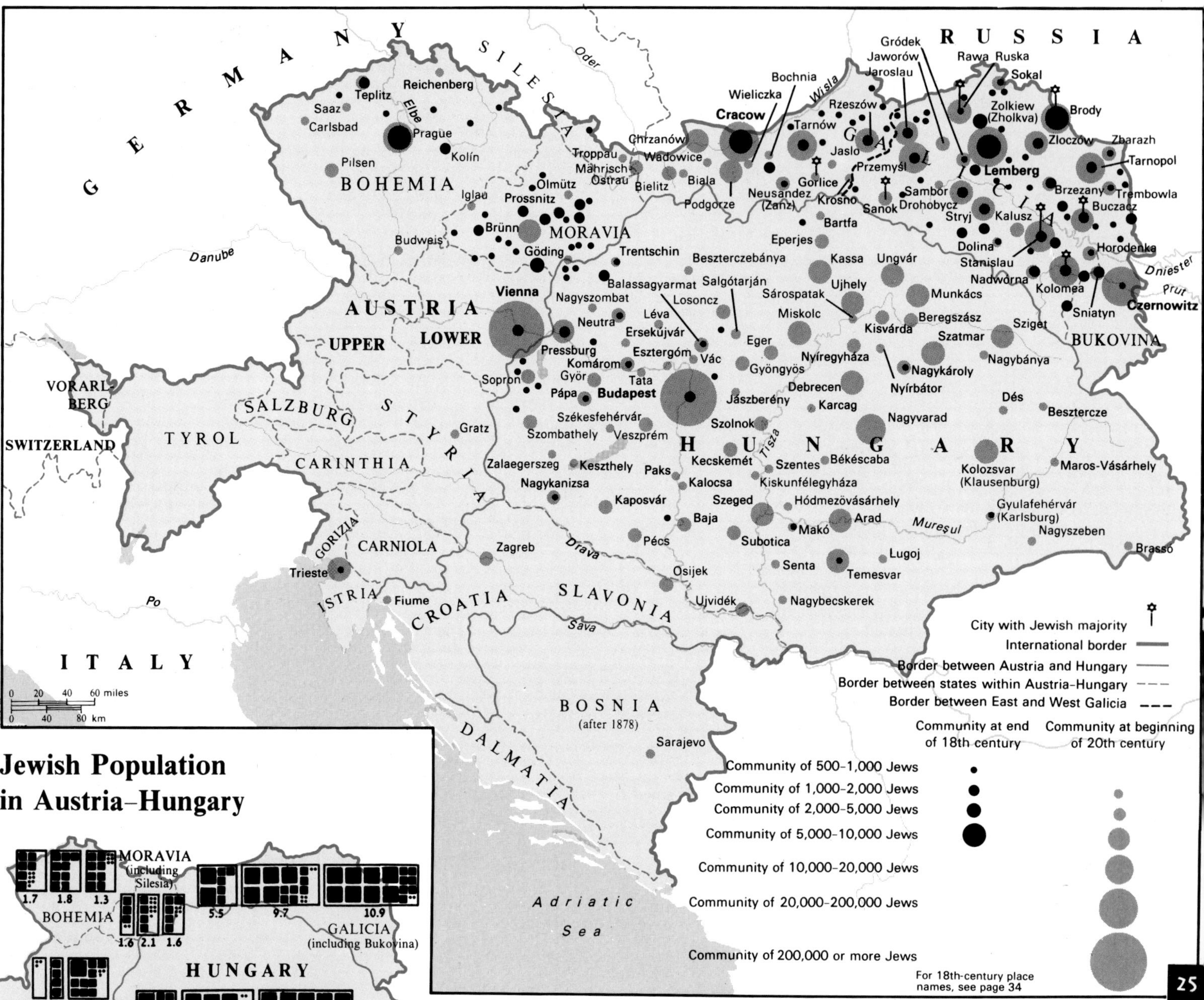


## Jewish Population in Austria–Hungary

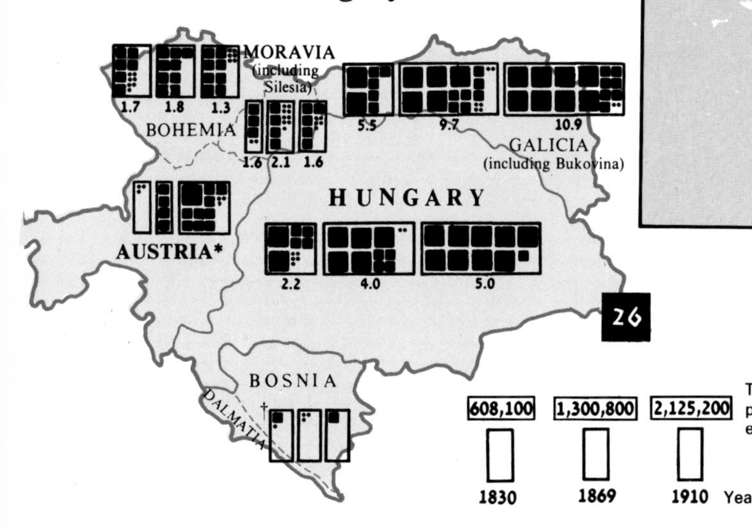


* Most Austrian Jews lived in Vienna: about 65% in 1830 and 1869, and 91% in 1910

† Includes about 7,000 Jews in the Italian regions assigned to the Kingdom of Sardinia in 1859 to 1869

In 1867, the Hapsburg Empire was reorganized politically: the Austro-Hungarian monarchy was established, ruled by the Hapsburg dynasty. All subjects were granted full civil and political rights, and all the restrictions regarding the Jews were abolished. The number of Jews continued to grow in the nineteenth century, especially in Hungary and Galicia. Many Jews settled in cities, which until the mid-nineteenth century had been closed to them (until 1840 in Hungary, and until 1848 in the rest of the empire). In the early twentieth century, Vienna and Budapest were among the largest Jewish centers in Europe.

In Galicia, there were demographic and cultural differences between the Jews of the larger, eastern part (east of the San River), where 75 percent of them lived, and those of the western part. In 1910, the Jews made up 31.2 percent of the population in the eleven largest cities in western Galicia (but only 8 percent of the total population), and 38.5 percent of the inhabitants of the nineteen largest cities in eastern Galicia (12.3 percent of the total population). The occupational structure of the Jews throughout the monarchy reflected their urban character: a small percentage in farming (although higher in Galicia than in other European countries), and more in commerce.

Until the 1890s, natural increase among the Jews remained higher than among other religious groups in the empire. This changed between 1890 and 1900, and in a relatively short period, natural increase of the Jews fell below that of other groups. In addition, from the end of the nineteenth century, Jews began to emigrate in growing numbers from Austria–Hungary (especially Galicia) to Western Europe or overseas. Both trends brought the increase of the Jewish population in Austria–Hungary to a halt. Although the number of Jews in Galicia grew from 686,600 in 1880 to 871,900 in 1910, their proportion in the total population fell from 11.5 to 10.9 percent. In contrast, neighboring Polish Jewry (under Russian rule) continued to increase until World War I, both absolutely and relative to the general population.

## Natural Increase

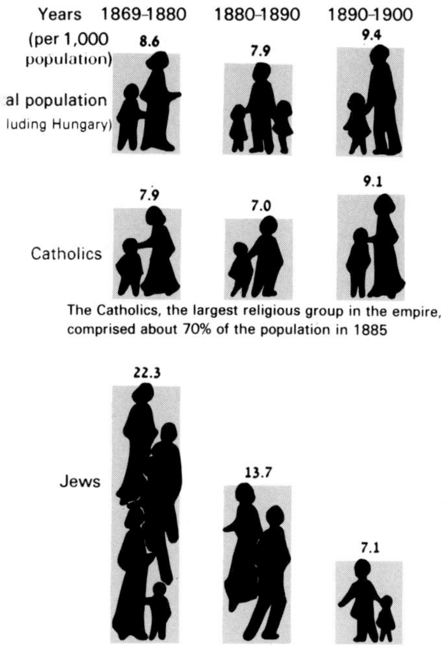


The Catholics, the largest religious group in the empire, comprised about 70% of the population in 1885

In 1890, the Jews (about 4.8% of the population) had the largest natural increase among the religious groups in the empire

## Occupations (percent)

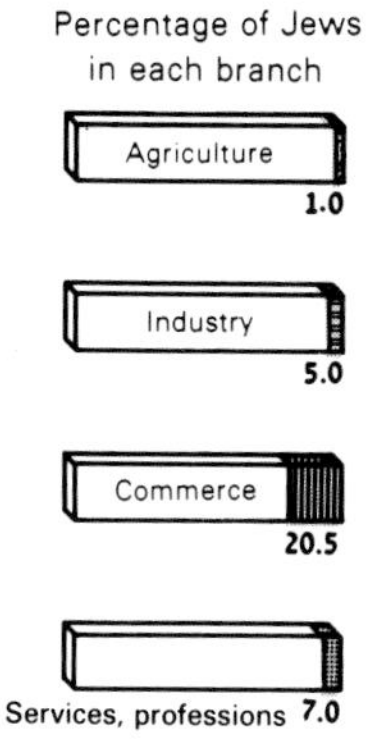


### Entire Empire, 1900
(excluding Hungary)

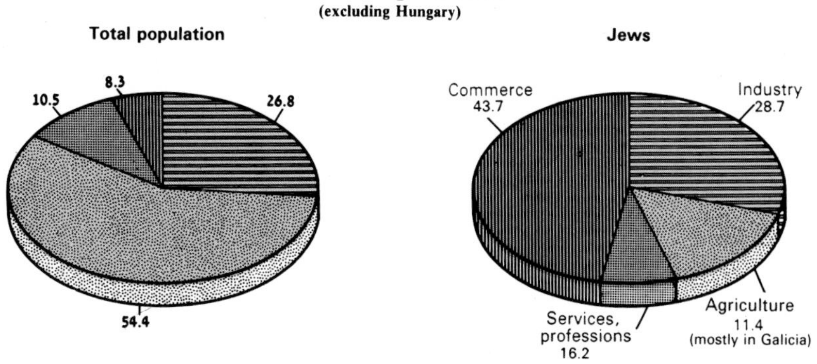


### Hungary, 1910

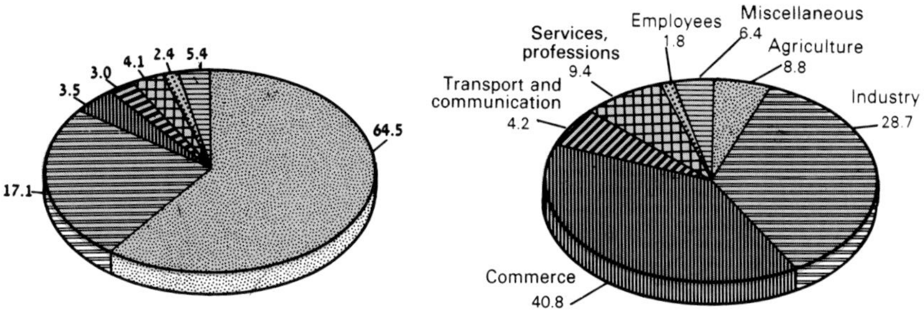


### Galicia, 1900

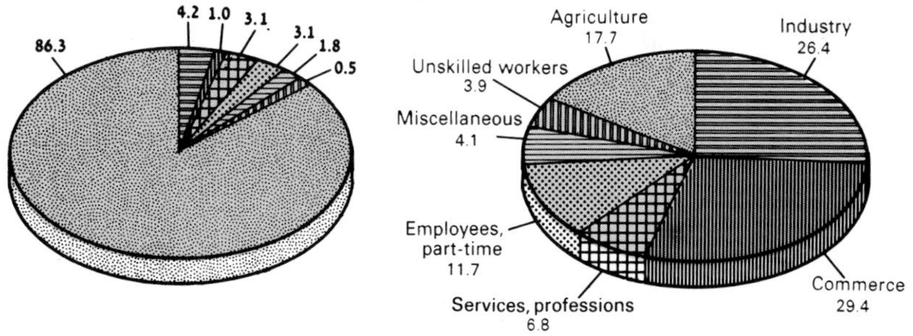


## National Groups in Austria–Hungary

By the turn of the twentieth century, Austro-Hungarian Jewry was the second largest Jewry in Europe. It was not a homogeneous community. Each historical group—Hungarian Jews, Galician Jews, Moravian Jews, Bohemian Jews—preserved its identity. Moreover, the growing national tensions in the empire and the increasing integration of the Jews into the general societies in which they lived forced them to define themselves vis-à-vis the different national groups. The reform of 1867 gave the Hungarians broad political rights. Other peoples (Poles, Ruthenians, Czechs) were recognized as nationalities but were not granted political rights. The Jews were defined only as a religious group, and in many places they had to side with one or another of the national groups. Consequently, Jews often acknowledged that they, too, were a nationality and should seek recognition as such.

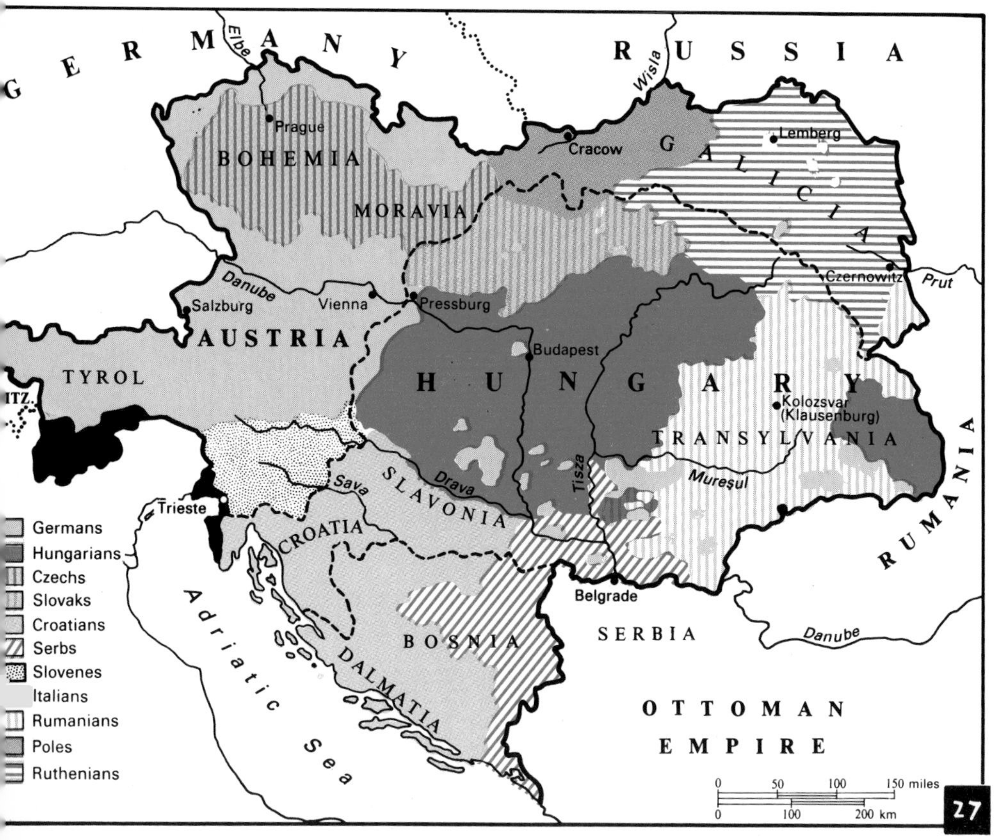


## Population Division by Age Group, 1890 (percent)

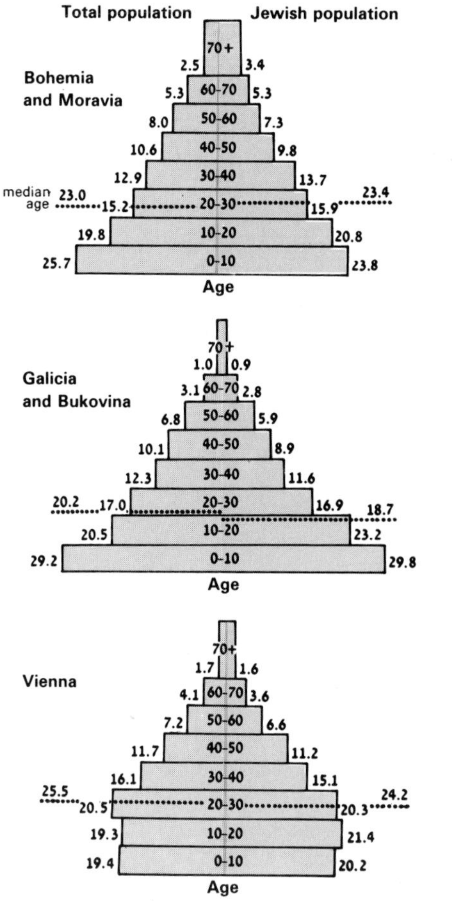

# Jewish Neighborhoods in European Cities

Most European cities were established in the early Middle Ages (or earlier) beside waterways and were surrounded by walls, beyond which lay broad expanses of land. When at the end of the eighteenth century, and especially during the nineteenth century, the cities started to grow, the open spaces beyond the walls were gradually developed.

Usually, the Jewish neighborhood or ghetto was built close to the city walls, inside or outside. When the old city was built on a river, the Jews often settled on the other side of it (Budapest, Vienna). In some instances, the Jews moved during the Middle Ages from one side of the river to the side closer to the city walls (Rome, Paris).

In another typical pattern, in cities where Jews arrived in significant numbers only in the nineteenth century, they settled close to the railroad station (Berlin) or the port (London). Poor living conditions in the original Jewish quarter impelled the more prosperous Jews to move to better neighborhoods. Usually, their place was filled by Jewish newcomers. In the second half of the nineteenth century, the Jews began to settle in neighborhoods just being built or in older parts of the cities where they had never lived before, often forming new Jewish concentrations.

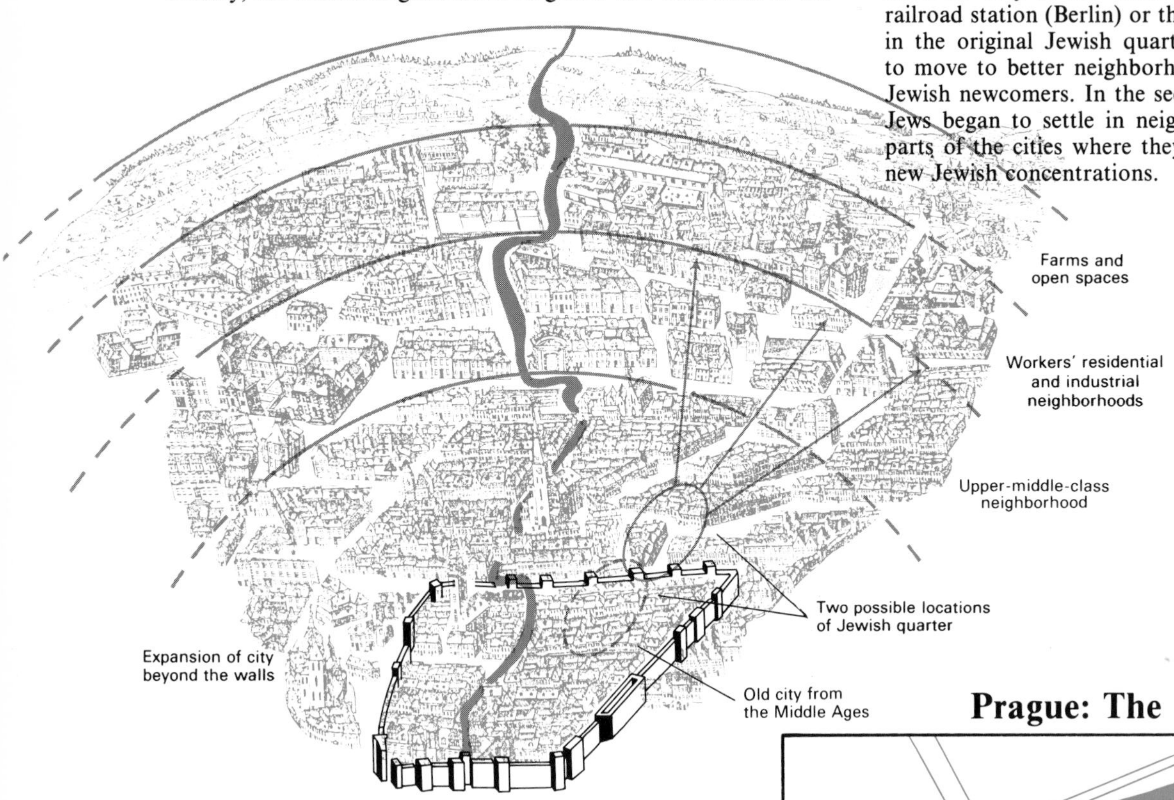


**Model of Jewish Population Expansion**

## The Jews in Prague

Jews lived continuously in Prague since the Middle Ages. In the seventeenth century, it was the largest Ashkenazic community in Europe. The Prague ghetto (established in the thirteenth century)—with its synagogues and Jewish institutions, its rabbis and scholars—was the backdrop of many stories and legends. Until 1859, Jews were confined to the ghetto; afterward, they were permitted to live throughout the city.

In the second half of the nineteenth century, Prague's Jewish population grew, but the number of Jews in the ghetto diminished. Nevertheless, Prague Jewry grew less than the other well-known Jewish communities in Europe. At its peak, in 1930, there were about 35,000 Jews in Prague. Most had come from Bohemia; in the 1930s, about one-half of Bohemian Jewry lived in Prague.

From the beginning of the twentieth century, Prague Jewry manifested negative demographic tendencies: a low birth rate, an aging population, and a relatively high rate of out-marriage. These trends reflected more sharply the situation of Bohemian Jewry in general.

Following the German occupation of Czechoslovakia in 1938, many Jews were brought to Prague from the countryside. In 1939, there were more than 50,000 Jews in the city. Most were sent during the war to concentration and extermination camps. The Germans did not destroy Prague's historic Jewish buildings, though, because they intended to transform them into a museum of Judaica.

Only about 3,400 Jews remained in Prague in 1950. In the late 1970s, about 3,000 Jews lived in the city.

**Prague: The Old City and Jewish Ghetto**

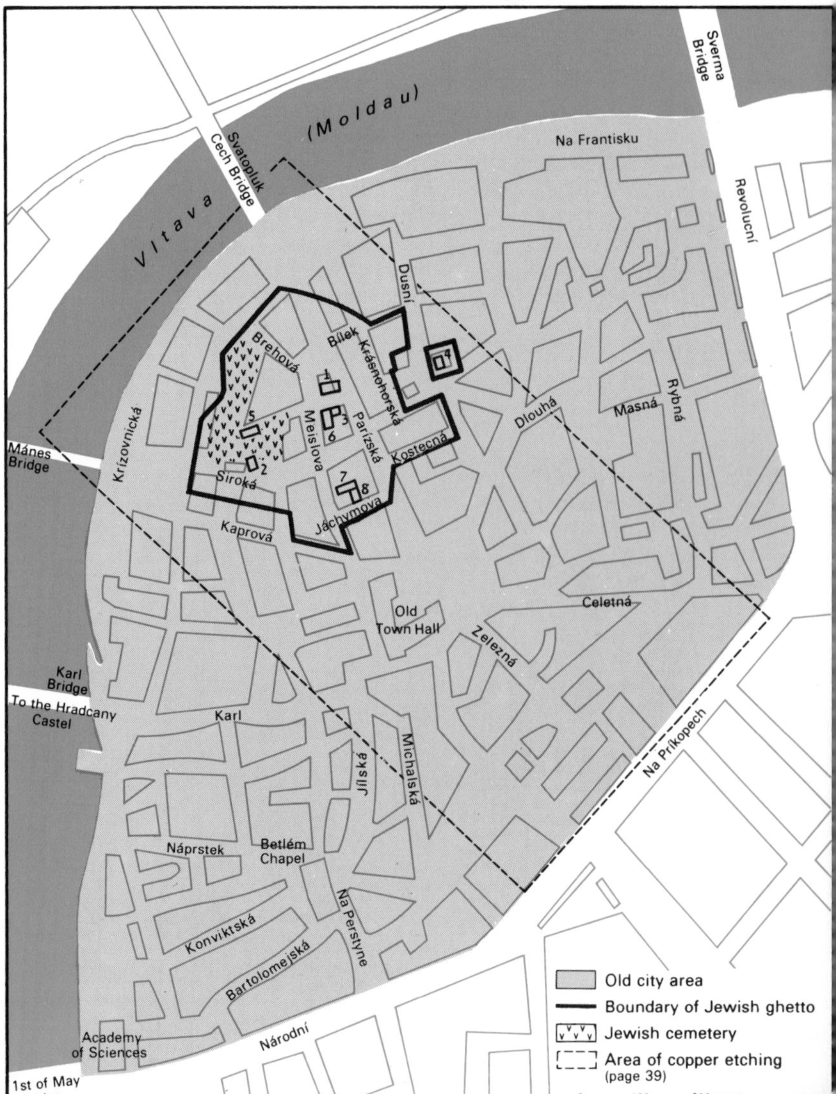


1. Altneuschul synagogue, built at end of 13th century (still in use)
2. Pinkas synagogue, built in 1st half of 16th century
3. High synagogue, built in 2nd half of 16th century
4. Sephardic synagogue (formerly Altschul), built in early 17th century Reconstructed in 1866. Today, State Jewish Museum
5. Klaus synagogue, built at end of 17th century
6. Jewish Town Hall. Reconstructed in 1765. Today, seat of Jewish community institutions
7. Meisel synagogue. Reconstructed in 1885 to 1913
8. Bet Sefer ha-Torah. Today, State Jewish Museum
9. Offices of Jewish and Zionist institutions

# Areas of Jewish Settlement in Prague

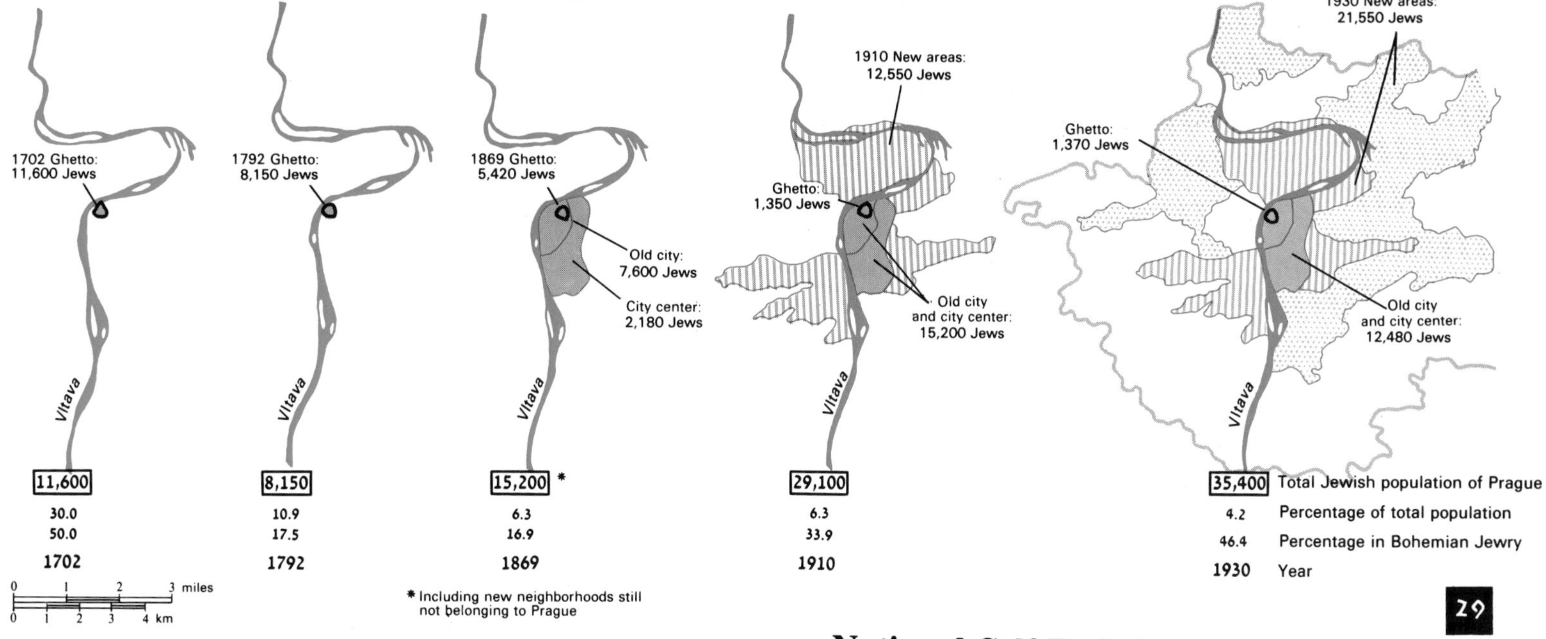


# National Self-Definition Among the Prague Jews

In 1890, 73.8 percent of Prague Jews declared themselves German. Ten years later, under the influence of the growing Czech national consciousness, 55.4 percent declared themselves as Czech nationals, a figure that remained quite stable (in 1930, it was 54.8 percent). The number of "Germans" decreased, especially after 1921, when the Jews had the option of defining themselves as being of Jewish nationality. In 1921, 20.1 percent of Prague Jews did so; in 1930, 27 percent.

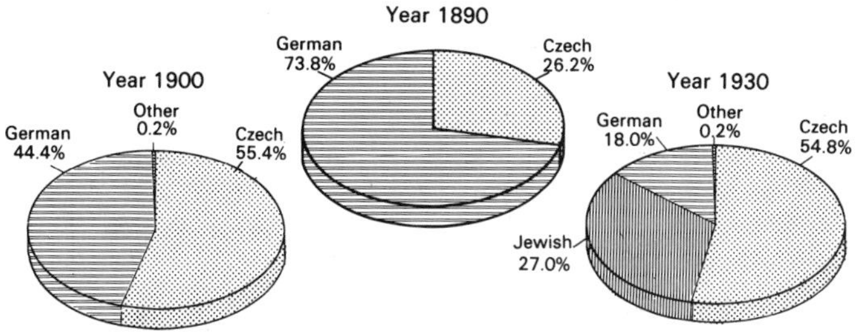


# The Jewish Ghetto in Prague

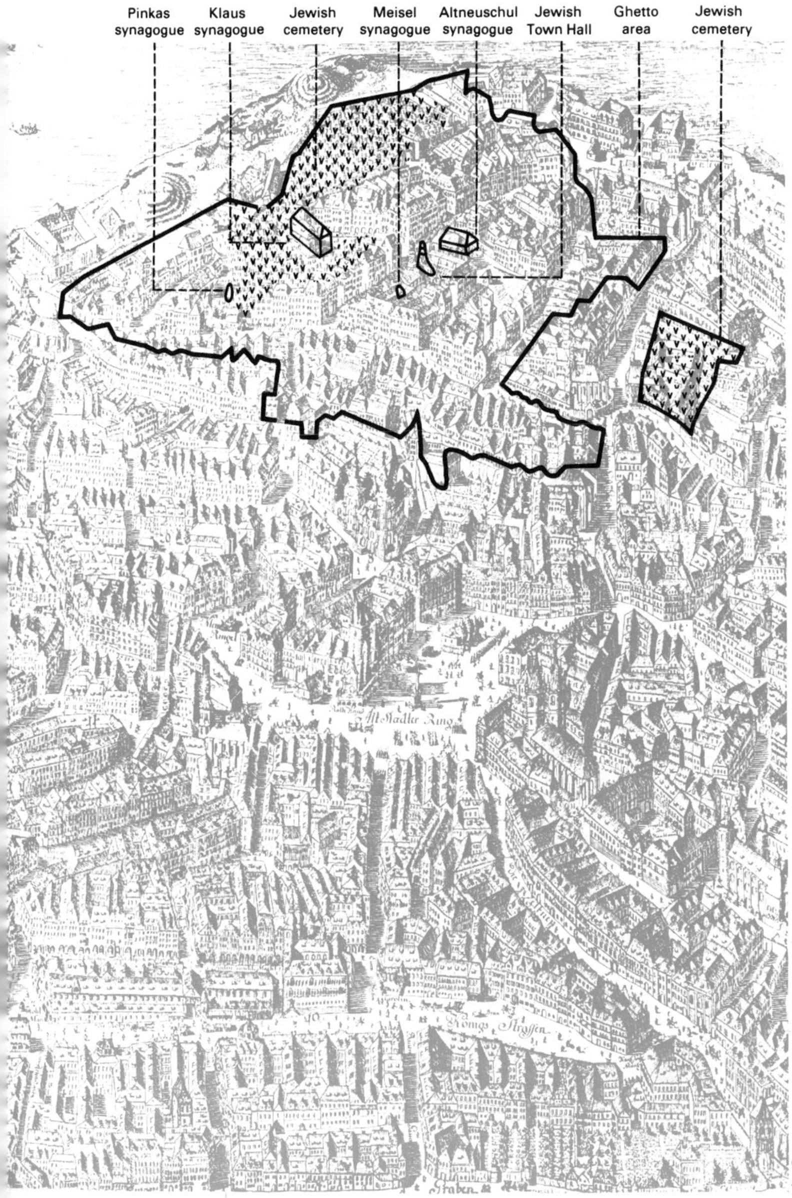


*Copper etching of Prague by Daniel Joseph Huber (1769)*

# Percentage of Jews in Total Population by Neighborhoods, 1930

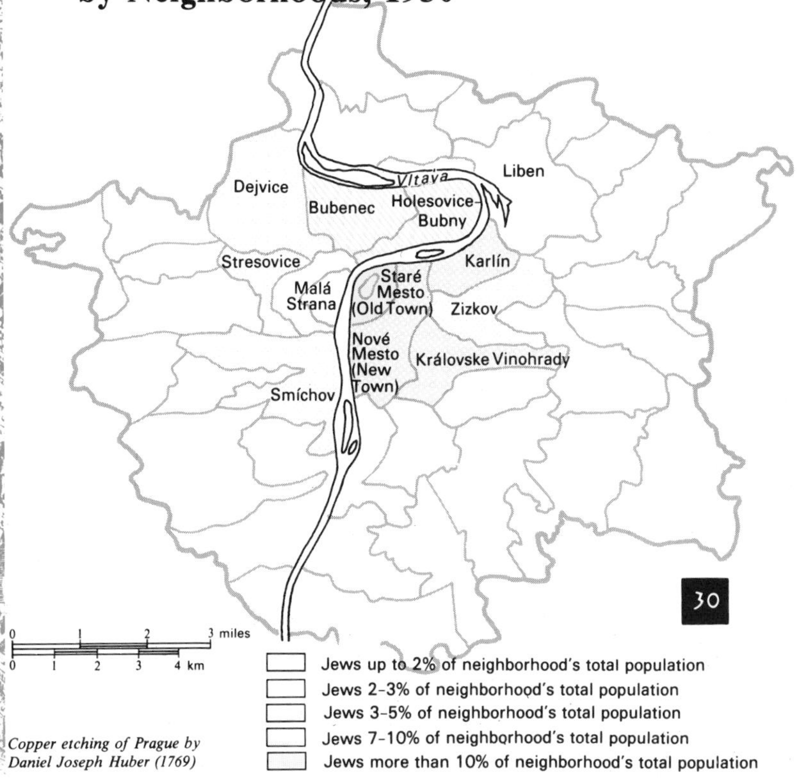

# The Jews in Budapest

## Occupational Composition of the Jews, 1890

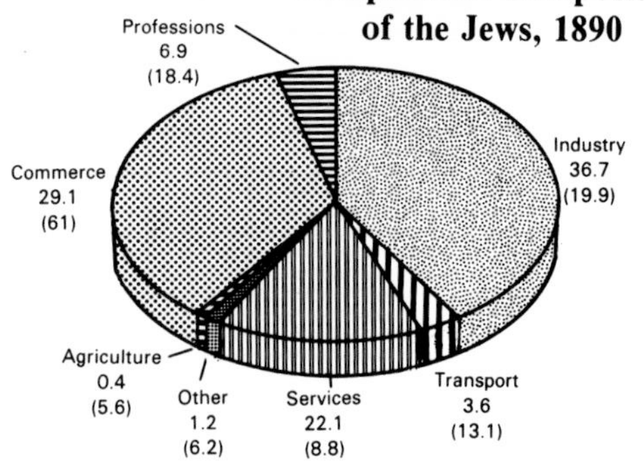


3.6 Percentage of Jews in sector out of total Jewish population

(13.1) Percentage of Jews out of total number in sector

| Neighborhood and number | 1890 | 1930 |
|---|---|---|
| (1) Tabán Krisztinaváros | 1.9 | 0.8 |
| (2) Viziváros | 1.3 | 2.7 |
| (3) Ó Buda | 4.1 | 2.7 |
| (4) Belváros | 3.7 | 2.3 |
| (5) Lipotváros | 11.8 | 12.0 |
| (6) Terezváros | 30.2 | 19.2 |
| (7) Erzsébetváros | 31.0 | 27.6 |
| (8) Józsefváros | 11.8 | 14.8 |
| (9) Ferenczváros | 3.2 | 5.9 |
| (10) City's suburbs | 1.0 | 12.0 |
| Total | 100 | 100 |

## Jewish Population by Neighborhood (percent)

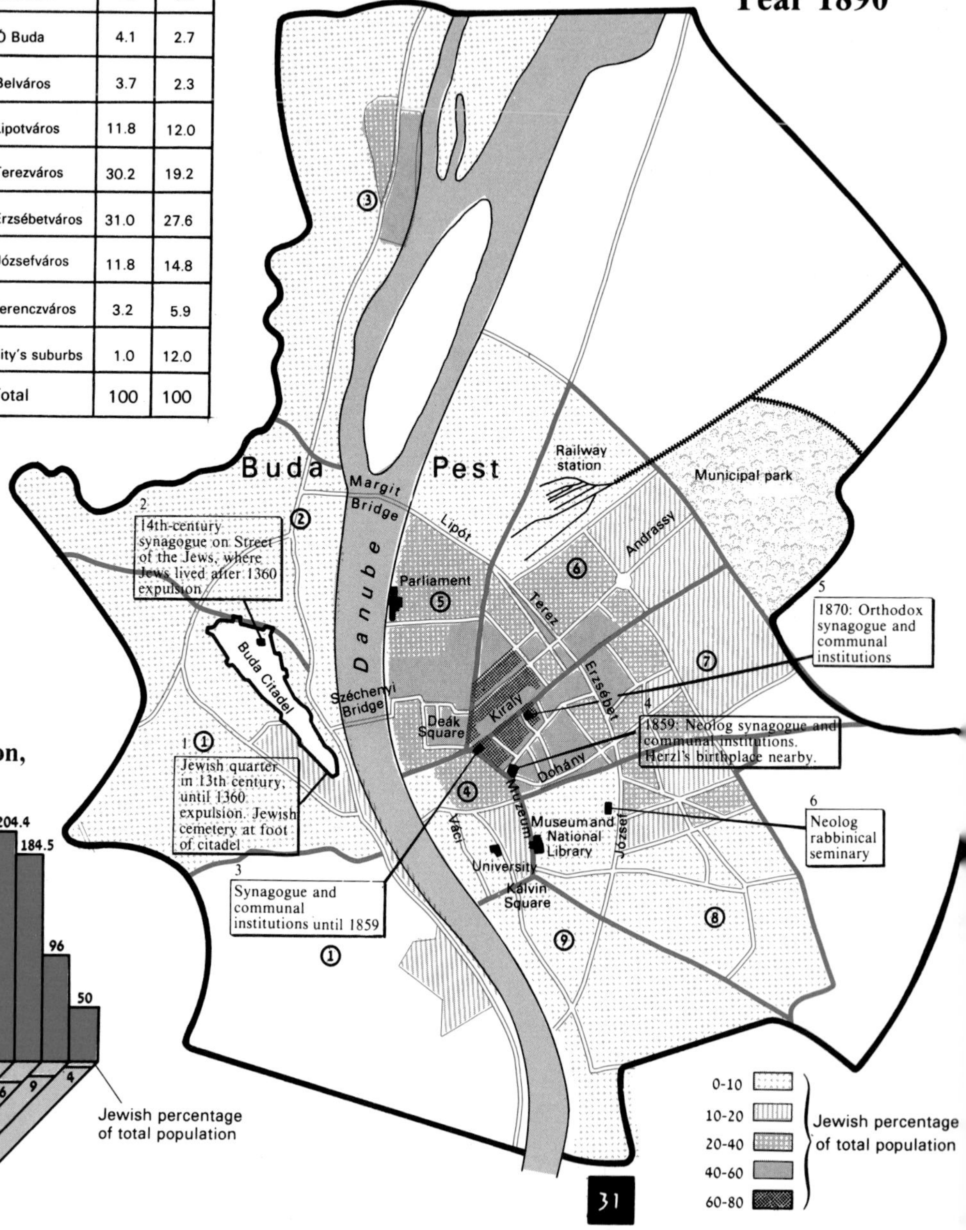


## Age Distribution of Jews

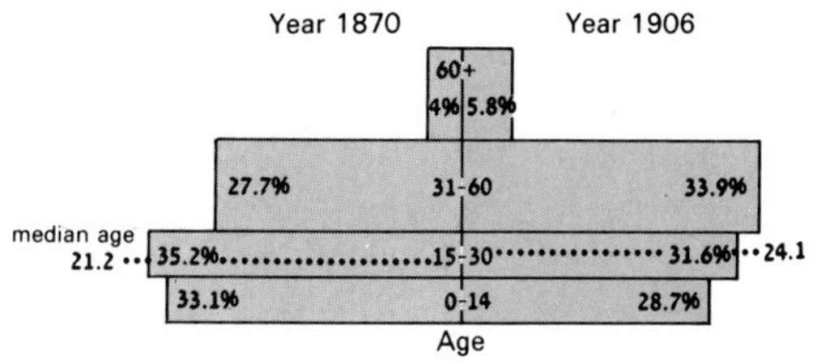


## Division of Jews, by Spoken Language

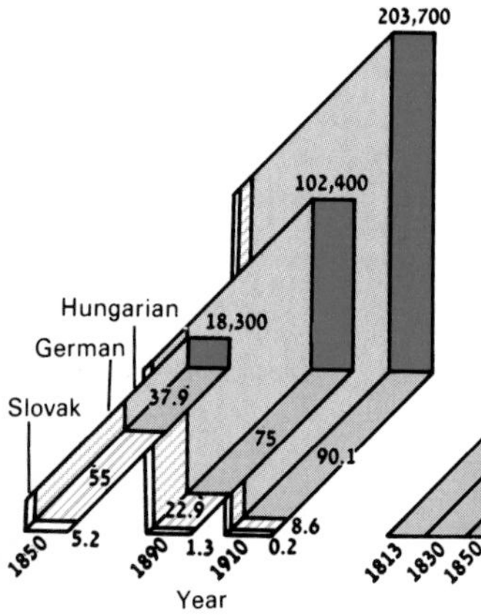


## Jewish Population, by Year

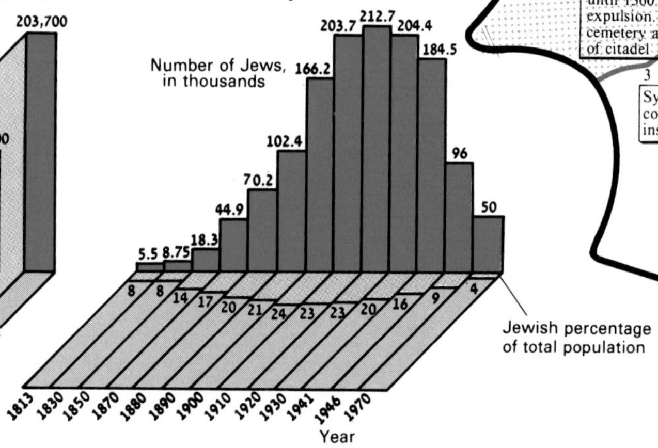


## The Jews of Budapest by Place of Birth, 1910

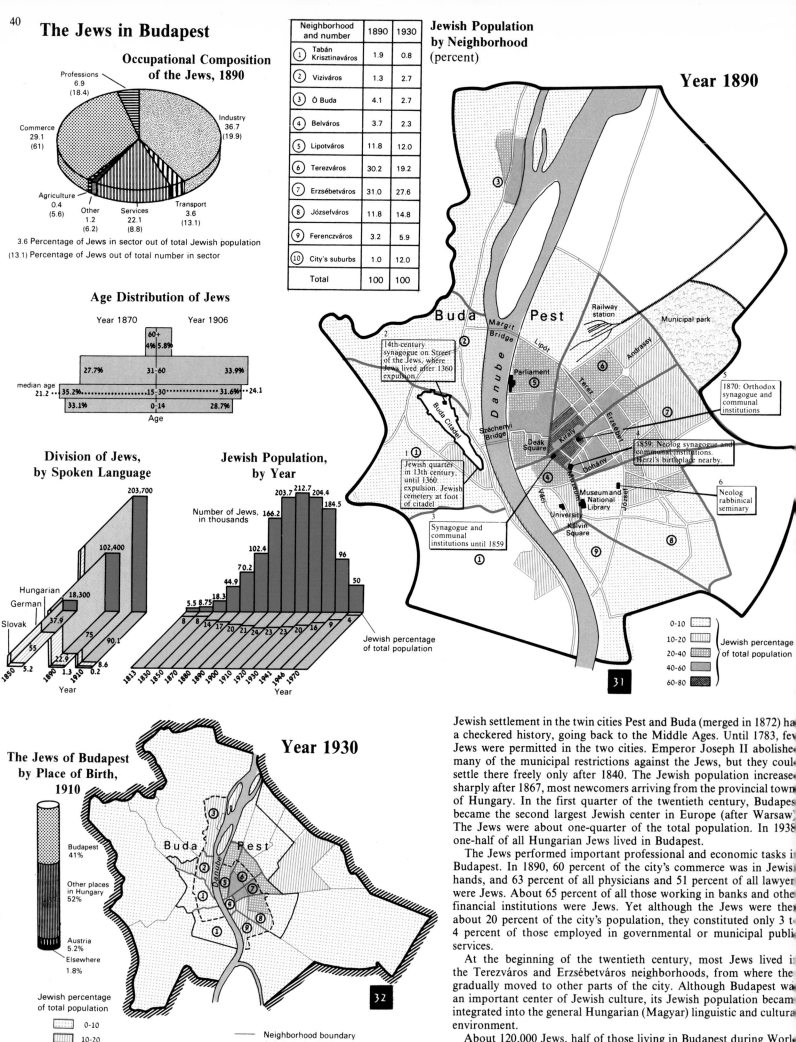

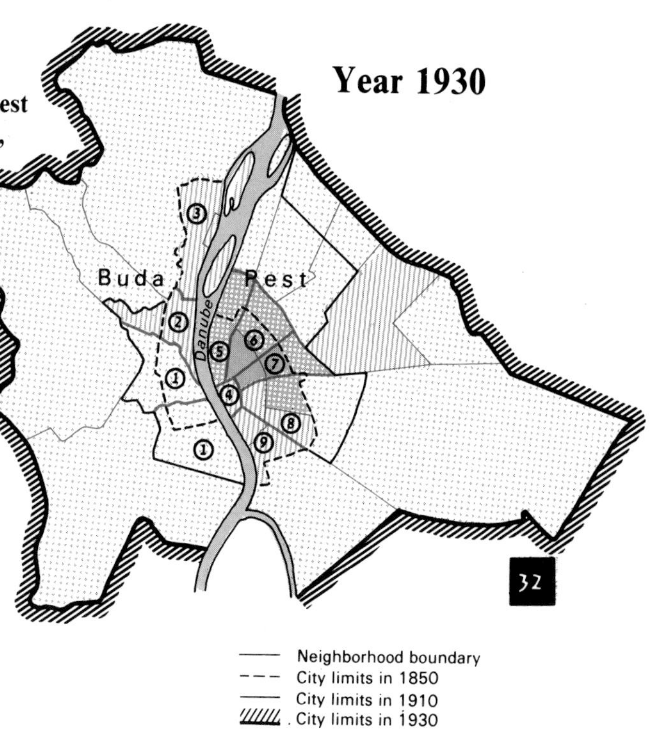


Jewish settlement in the twin cities Pest and Buda (merged in 1872) had a checkered history, going back to the Middle Ages. Until 1783, few Jews were permitted in the two cities. Emperor Joseph II abolished many of the municipal restrictions against the Jews, but they could settle there freely only after 1840. The Jewish population increased sharply after 1867, most newcomers arriving from the provincial towns of Hungary. In the first quarter of the twentieth century, Budapest became the second largest Jewish center in Europe (after Warsaw). The Jews were about one-quarter of the total population. In 1938 one-half of all Hungarian Jews lived in Budapest.

The Jews performed important professional and economic tasks in Budapest. In 1890, 60 percent of the city's commerce was in Jewish hands, and 63 percent of all physicians and 51 percent of all lawyers were Jews. About 65 percent of all those working in banks and other financial institutions were Jews. Yet although the Jews were then about 20 percent of the city's population, they constituted only 3 to 4 percent of those employed in governmental or municipal public services.

At the beginning of the twentieth century, most Jews lived in the Terezváros and Erzsébetváros neighborhoods, from where they gradually moved to other parts of the city. Although Budapest was an important center of Jewish culture, its Jewish population became integrated into the general Hungarian (Magyar) linguistic and cultural environment.

About 120,000 Jews, half of those living in Budapest during World War II, perished in the Holocaust. In the late 1980s, about 55,000 Jews, or 90 percent of all Jews in Hungary, lived in the city.

### Jewish Population, by Quarters (percent)

| Name of quarter and number | | 1880 | 1910 |
|---|---|---|---|
| 1 | Innere Stadt | 17.1 | 6.2 |
| 2 | Leopoldstadt | 48.3 | 32.5 |
| 3 | Landstrasse | 7.5 | 5.7 |
| 4 | Wieden | 2.7 | 2.2 |
| 5 | Margareten | 2.6 | 2.1 |
| 6 | Mariahilf | 4.3 | 4.7 |
| 7 | Neubau | 4.2 | 4.6 |
| 8 | Josefstadt | 2.3 | 2.7 |
| 9 | Alsergrund | 9.5 | 12.4 |
| 10 | Favoriten | 1.5 | 1.9 |
| 11 | Simmering | | 0.3 |
| 12 | Meidling | | 1.1 |
| 13 | Hietzing | | 1.9 |
| 14 | Rudolfsheim | | 2.1 |
| 15 | Fünfhaus | | 1.4 |
| 16 | Ottakring | | 2.6 |
| 17 | Hernals | | 2.0 |
| 18 | Währing | | 2.3 |
| 19 | Döbling | | 2.2 |
| 20 | Brigittenau | | 8.1 |
| 21 | Floridsdorf | | 1.0 |
| Total | | 100 | 100 |

### Year 1910

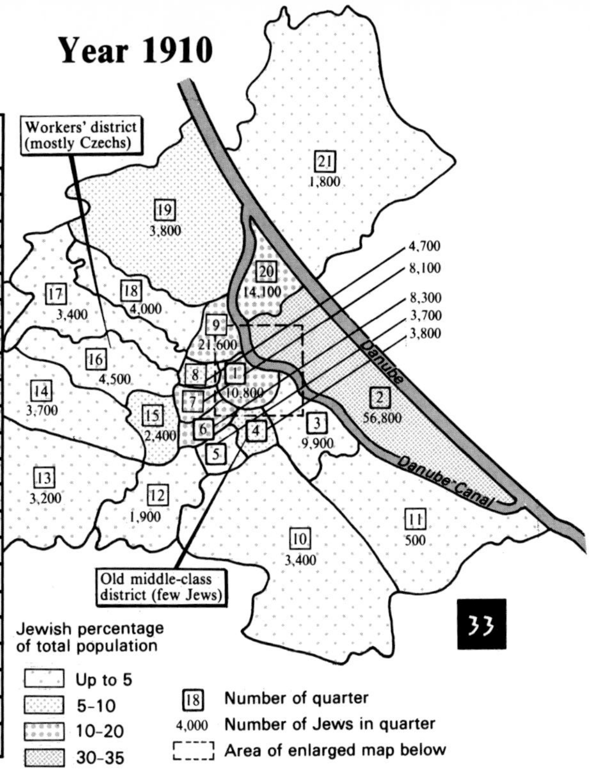


### Occupations of Jews, 1880

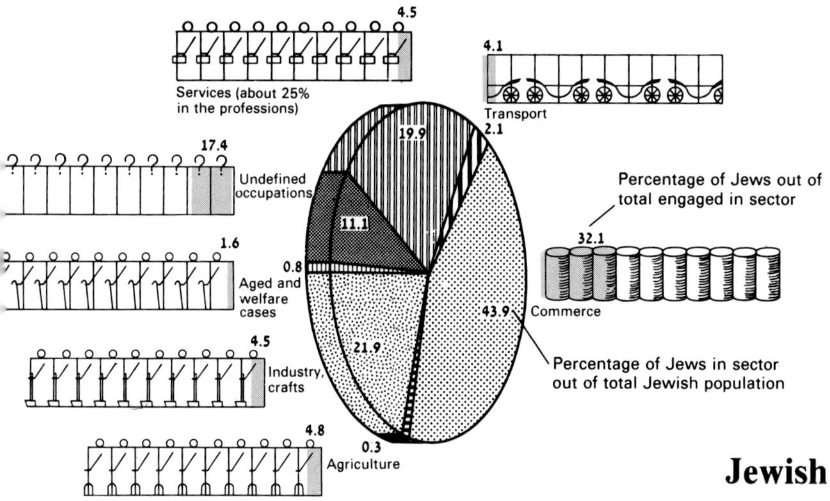


### Division of Viennese Jews, by Place of Origin

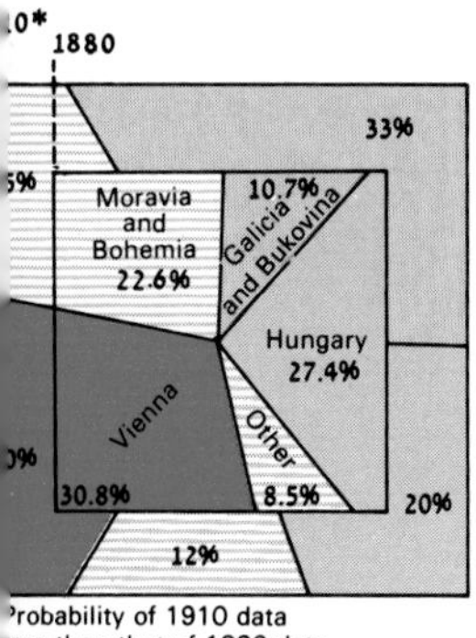


Probability of 1910 data less than that of 1880 data

### Growth of Jewish Population in Vienna

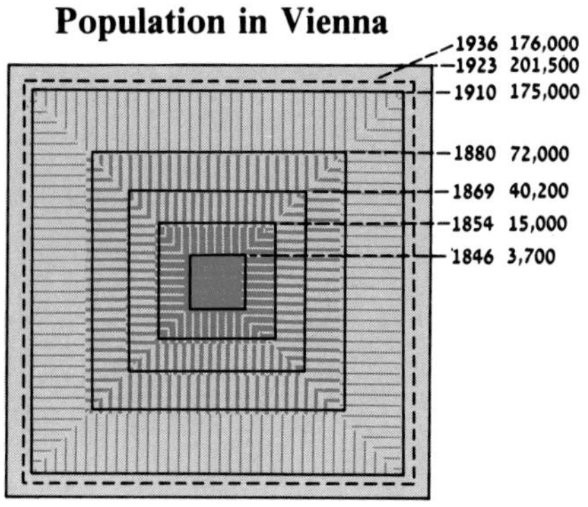


# The Jews in Vienna

In the seventeenth century, the Jewish community of Vienna was among the largest in Europe. Then, in 1670, the Jews were expelled by order of Emperor Leopold I. Until 1848, only a few very rich Jewish families, some of them ennobled, lived in Vienna; other Jews were admitted for short periods, and still others lived there illegally. They totaled between 2,000 and 4,000. The ban on the Jews was lifted after the 1848 revolution, and a large influx of them followed, especially after 1867. From the 1880s until the early twentieth century, Vienna attracted a considerable number of Galician Jews. The city became the third largest Jewish center in Europe, after Warsaw and Budapest.

One-third of Vienna's Jews lived in the Leopoldstadt quarter. Those who prospered gradually moved to the neighboring quarters, especially the First Quarter (the old city, or Innere Stadt) and the Ninth Quarter (Alsergrund). Present in all occupations, the Jews excelled in medicine and law: in 1880, about 30 percent of Vienna's physicians and some 30 percent of its lawyers were Jews, and later their proportion increased, even though they were only 7 to 10 percent of the population. The Jews were prominent in the city's commercial and financial sectors and played a significant role in its cultural and scientific life—in the theater, literature, and journalism. Since Vienna was a meeting place of West European and East European Jewish influences, all the ideological and spiritual trends in modern Jewish life coexisted (or competed) in the city: *haskalah*, religious reform, Hasidism, and Jewish socialism. Vienna was the home of Theodor Herzl, and there the Zionist movement was born and took its first steps.

Relations between the Jews and the general population were usually tense. Vienna was the center of a very active antisemitic movement. It was the only European capital where an antisemitic party acquired the political leadership of the city: the Christian-Socialist Party, led by Karl Lueger, who became mayor of Vienna in 1896.

After World War I, when Austria's size was drastically reduced, about 90 percent of Austrian Jews lived in the capital. Germany's annexation of Austria in 1938 marked the beginning of the end of Vienna Jewry. Their property was confiscated; they were forced to emigrate; and those who remained were later sent to concentration and extermination camps.

There were about 6,000 Jews in Vienna in the mid-1980s, mostly elderly people. In the second half of the twentieth century, Vienna became a place of refuge or passage for Jewish emigrants from various East European countries, such as those who left Hungary after the 1956 revolution, and emigrants from the Soviet Union in the 1970s.

## Jewish Institutions in Central Vienna

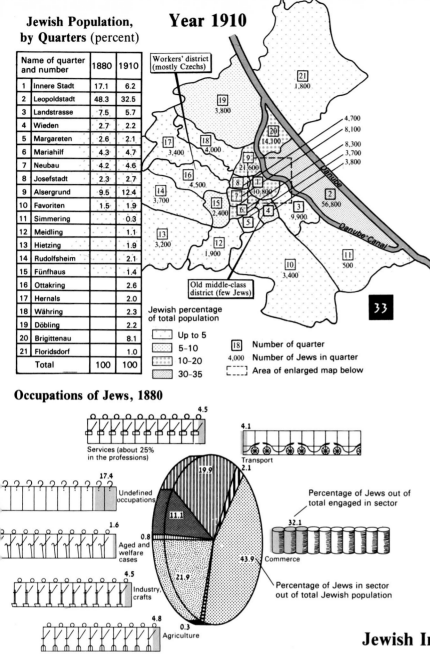

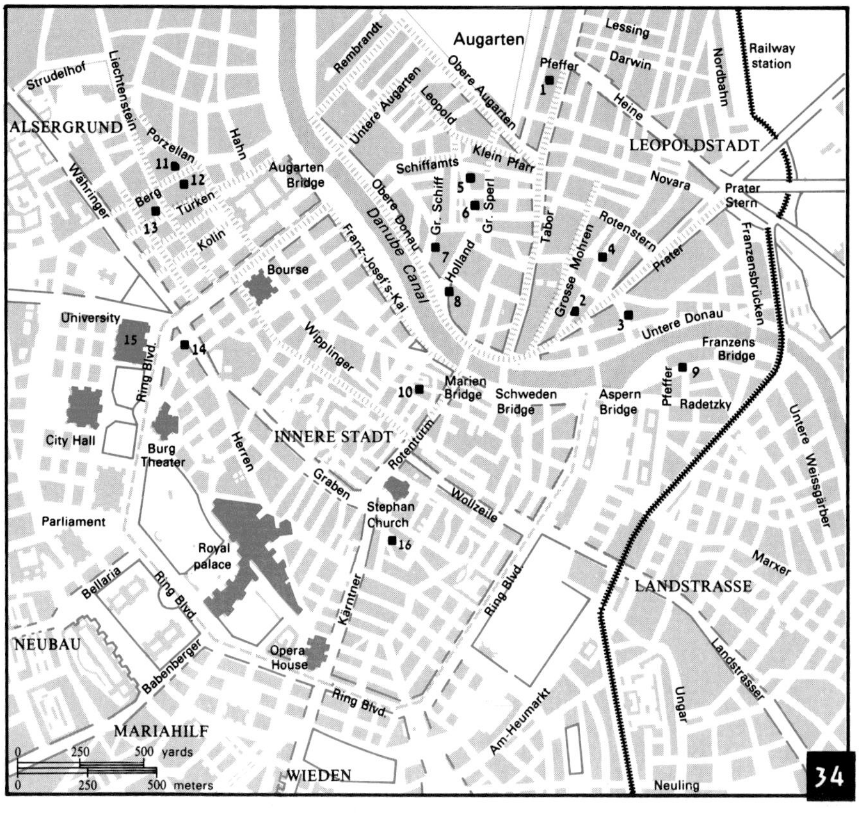


**Jewish institutions**

1. House of Sigmund Freud (1870s and 1880s)
2. Editorial office of *Die Neuzeit*, next to Herzl's home (1870s)
3. Reform Beth Hamidrash synagogue
4. Turkish synagogue
5. Polish Beth Israel synagogue (from 1893)
6. Juedischer Volksverein
7. Schiffschul synagogue
8. Polish synagogue
9. Hasidic synagogue
10. Reform synagogue (1825) and communal institutions
11. House of Sigmund Freud (20th century)
12. Oesterreichisch-Israelitische Union
13. Zionist Bureau, editorial office of *Die Welt*, Herzl's home (beginning of 20th century)
14. Juedischer Turnverein
15. Kadimah student's society
16. Allianz

Street with high concentration of Jewish residents

City limits in Middle Ages; from mid-19th century, Ring Boulevard

# The Jews in France:

## Eighteenth and Nineteenth Centuries

In the second half of the eighteenth century, 30,000 to 40,000 Jews lived in France; the expulsion decrees of the fourteenth century were still in effect; and only Jews who had arrived later in special circumstances or who lived in territories later added to France were permitted to stay. This was the case with the "New Christians," who had settled mainly in Bordeaux and Bayonne in the sixteenth century, or in the Comtat Venaissin region and in Avignon in Provence, which had belonged to the pope—altogether, about 3,000 Jews, most of them merchants, who were well integrated into the general society and well off economically. The main Jewish settlement was in eastern France, in Alsace–Lorraine, which had become French under the Treaty of Westphalia (1648) and other treaties. These Jews were of Ashkenazic stock, supporting themselves by lending money and peddling, and living in a tenuous relationship with the general population. A few hundred Jews lived in Paris illegally.

Long debates about the civil status of the Jews took place in the wake of the French Revolution. Among the revolutionaries, there were doubts about whether the Declaration of the Rights of Man and of the Citizen, approved in August 1789, applied to the Jews. The first debate on the question took place in December 1789. The Sephardic Jews of Provence were recognized as full citizens in January 1790. But the debate continued regarding the Jews of Alsace–Lorraine, who were not granted full citizenship until September 1791.

Napoleon Bonaparte, emperor from 1804 to 1815, sought to ensure the civil integration of the Jews in France and to formalize their position, like that of all other religious groups, in the framework of the state and under its supervision. With that aim in mind, Napoleon acted in two directions. First, in July 1806, the Assembly of Jewish Notables convened. More than 100 elected delegates from France and northern Italy (then under French domination) participated. The Jewish delegates were asked to answer twelve questions dealing with various aspects of Jewish life and religion, economic activities, and the position of the Jews vis-à-vis other citizens and the state. The answers, formulated by the delegates with great care, achieved a balance between loyalty to the state and adherence to the obligations of Jewish religious law (*Halakhah*). The answers were approved by Napoleon, who then convened a second body, a Sanhedrin, made up of seventy-one rabbis and lay leaders. At its meeting in Paris in February 1807, the Sanhedrin endorsed the recommendations of the Assembly of Jewish Notables and declared them to be binding on all French Jews.

Second, in March 1808, Napoleon issued a decree deferring for ten years all debts owed to Jews by people in Alsace–Lorraine and laying down certain restrictions on the economic activity of Jews.

An additional step was the establishment in 1808 of the consistory system, organizing all Jewish communities within an official frame attached to the French Ministry of Religions. Every French district (*département*) or group of districts organized a consistory, and all consistories were under the authority of the Central Consistory in Paris. The whole system was under official control. Its tasks were mainly religious, although it also dealt with educational and social-welfare matters. Originally, thirteen regional consistories were established, but over the years the system underwent several modifications, reflecting also the territorial changes of France. The law of separation of church and state, approved in 1905, abolished the system's official status, although part of its authority continued, as a matter of tradition.

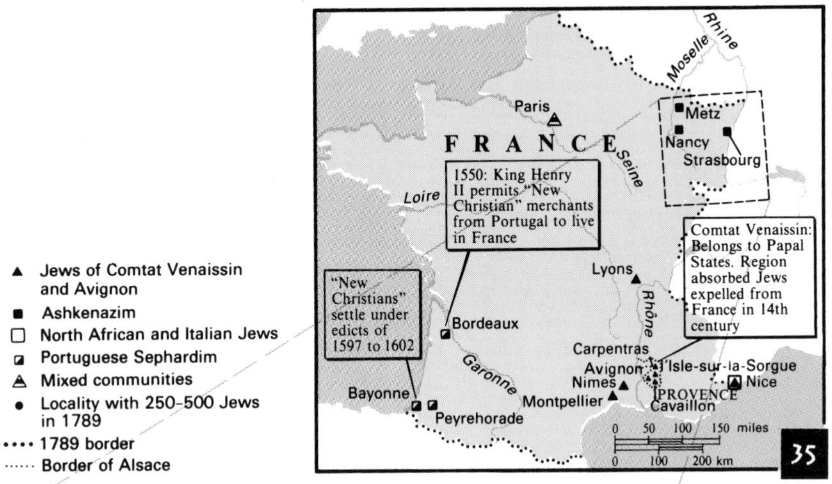


## The Jews in Alsace–Lorraine: Late Eighteenth Century

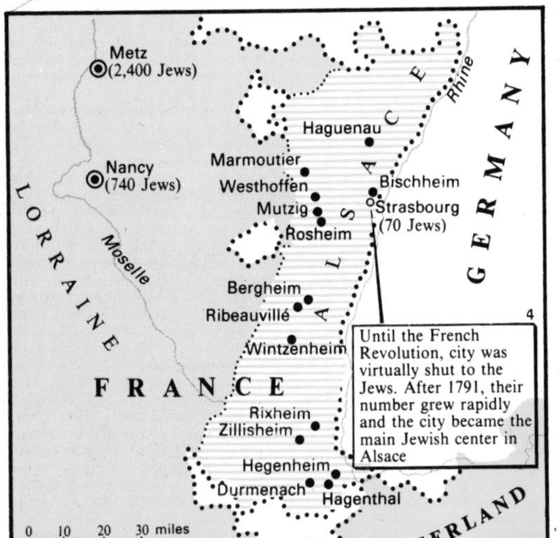

*Joseph David Sinzheim, the first chief rabbi of the Central Consistory of Jews in France*

*Seal of the Assembly of Jewish Notables in Paris (1806–1807)*

## The Consistories: Nineteenth Century

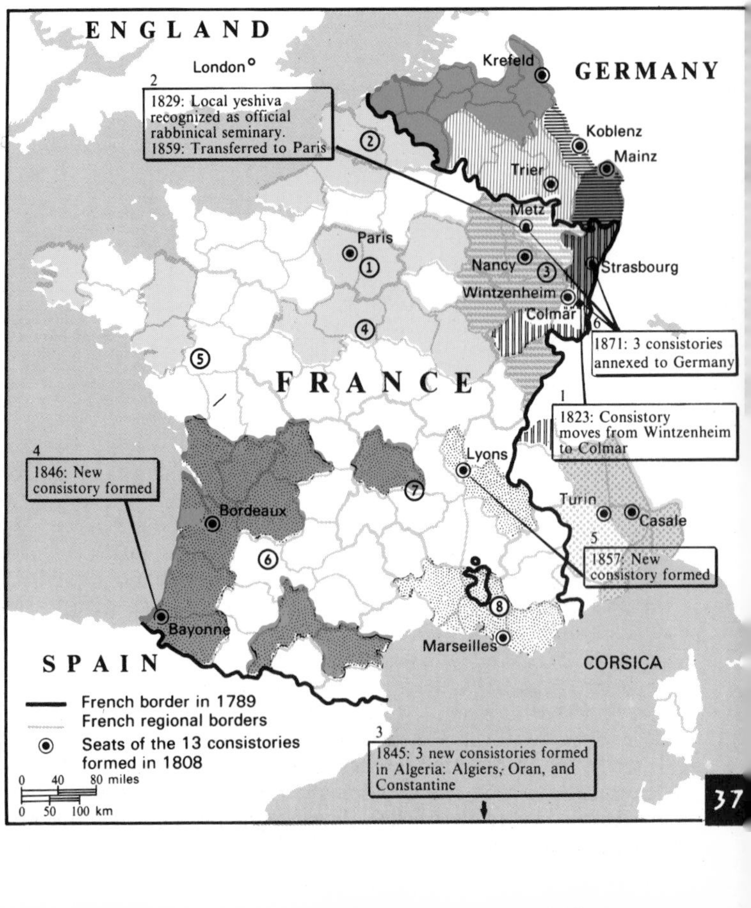


| Total Jewish population in France in 1808: 47,200 |
|---|
| ① Paris and suburbs: 3,000 Jews |
| ② North: 200 Jews |
| ③ East: 37,100 Jews |
| ④ Paris basin: 500 Jews |
| ⑤ West: 100 Jews |
| ⑥ Southwest: 3,500 Jews |
| ⑦ Southeast: 200 Jews |
| ⑧ Mediterranean littoral: 2,600 Jews |

# ewish Entrepreneurs:
## ineteenth and Twentieth Centuries

*Schocken department store in Chemnitz. Designed by architect Eric Mendelsohn*

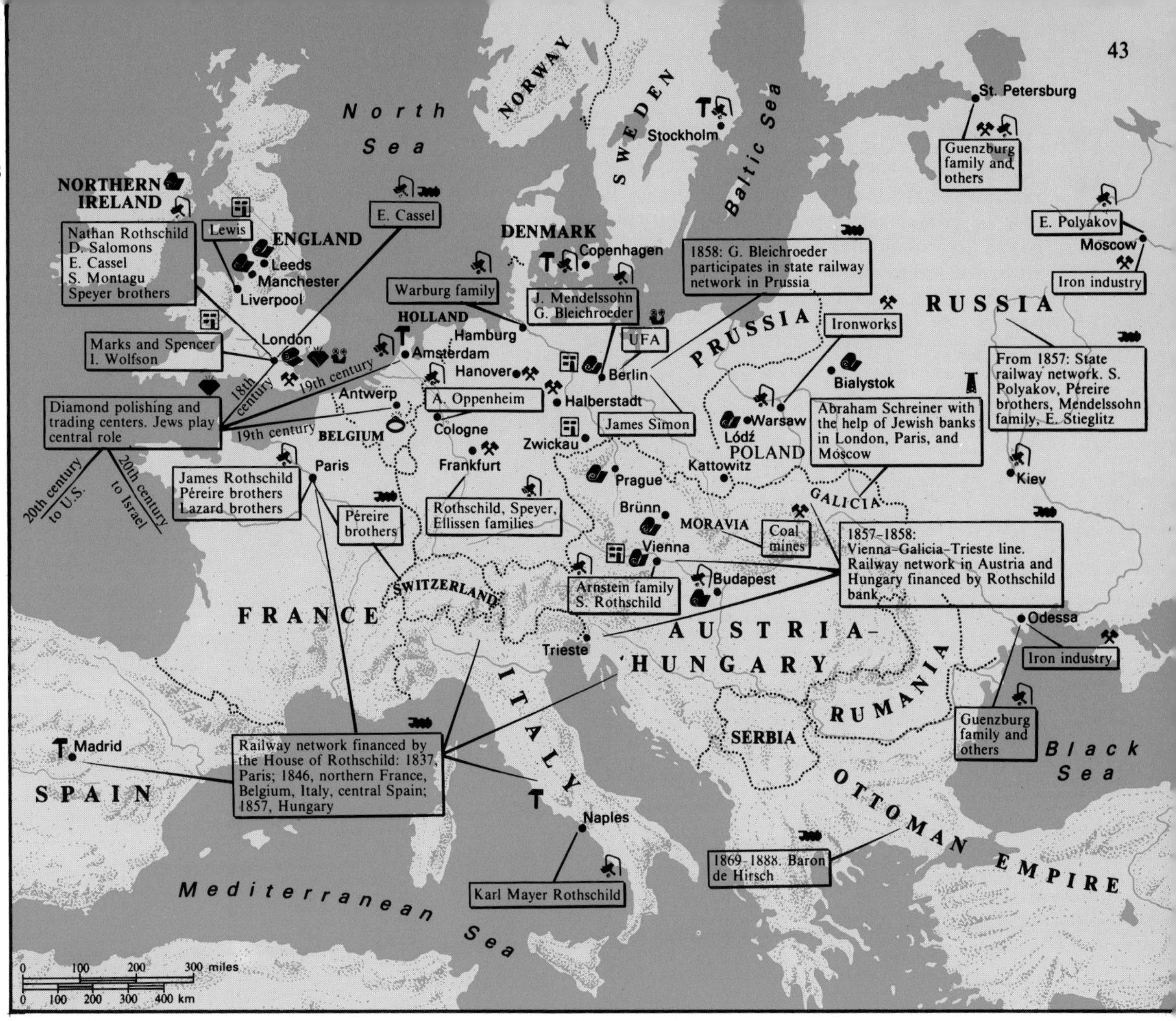


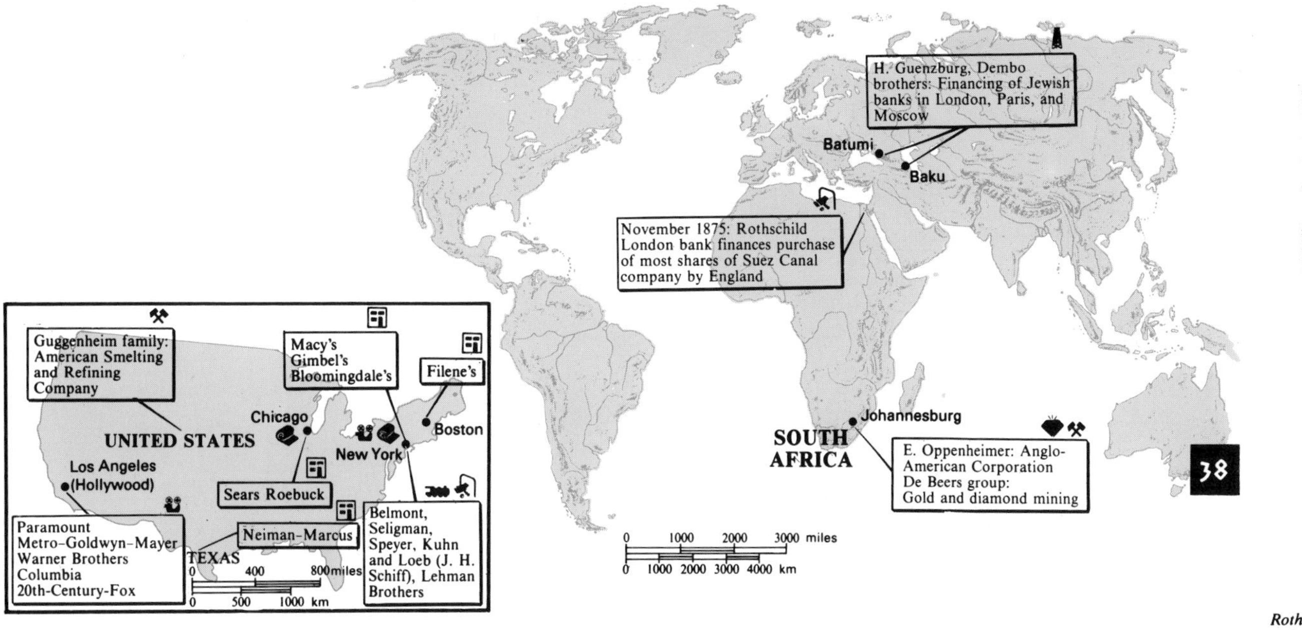


38

*Rothschild home in Frankfurt-on-the-Main, 16th century*

The intensive development of modern Europe (and later of the United States) created economic opportunities for the Jews. Jews were among the entrepreneurs active in the expanding commerce. The earliest modern Jewish entrepreneurs were the Spanish–Portuguese Jews of Amsterdam and London in the seventeenth century, whose economic activities embraced the entire known world. A later type was the Court Jews of Central Europe in the eighteenth century, who established a broad network of business connections, often with Jews in other countries. In the nineteenth century, Court Jews, their descendants, and other Jews also went into banking. Prominent among them were the Rothschilds, who started in Frankfurt and eventually established bank branches and other banking connections in Germany, France, Italy, England, the Hapsburg Empire, and even Russia. Characteristically, Jewish entrepreneurs and bankers entered new economic fields, to avoid the competition of the guilds of craftsmen or merchants, which often forbade Jewish participation in established occupations. Jews were active (and sometimes important) in the sugar industry and trade, the development of the railroad system in Europe (and later in the United States), and the nascent petroleum industry. Jews were also prominent in the diamond industry and trade from the seventeenth century on.

Another field in which Jews pioneered was the garment industry, especially in the United States. In the twentieth century, Jews played a major role in the establishment of large department stores, including some famous chains in Europe and the United States. They were also prominent in communications and entertainment: journalism, the theater, the film industry, radio, and, later, television.

Notwithstanding this wide range of activities, the Jews were only one factor, and with few exceptions not the most important one, in the economic development of the Western world in modern times.

# Professions of the Jews:

## Nineteenth and Twentieth Centuries

In the nineteenth and twentieth centuries, the Jews were predominantly middle-class city dwellers, a fact reflected in their occupational structure. A comparison between widely disparate locales or countries shows that a higher percentage of Jews than non-Jews were gainfully employed in commerce, crafts, and light industry.

In spite of the far-reaching demographic changes in the period under consideration (migrations, the birth of new large Jewish centers in Western Europe and the Americas, the transformation of the Jews from hamlet dwellers to denizens of metropolises), Jews remained an urban element in their new environments, just as they had been in their East European hamlets. Consequently, many basic characteristics of the occupational and social structure of Jewish society remained unchanged under modern conditions.

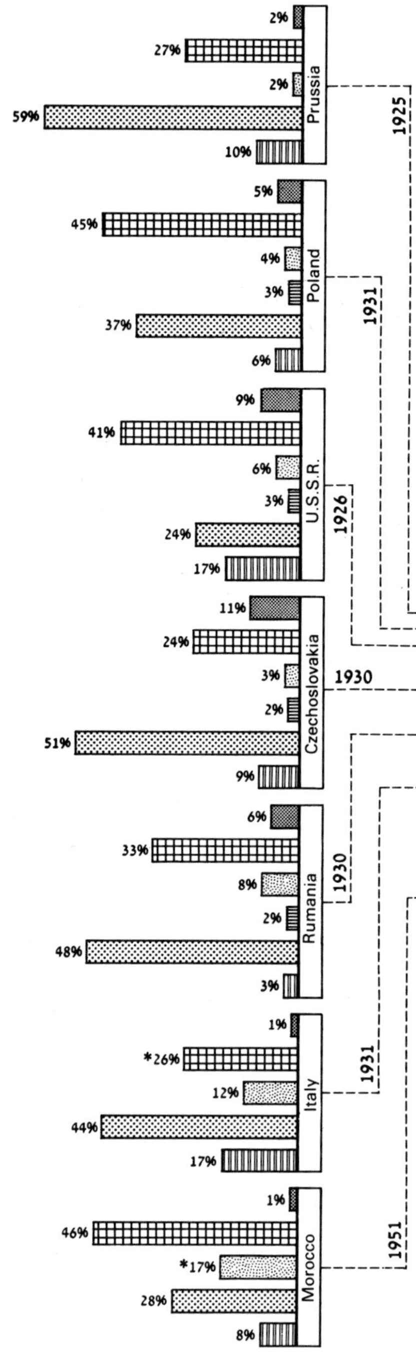


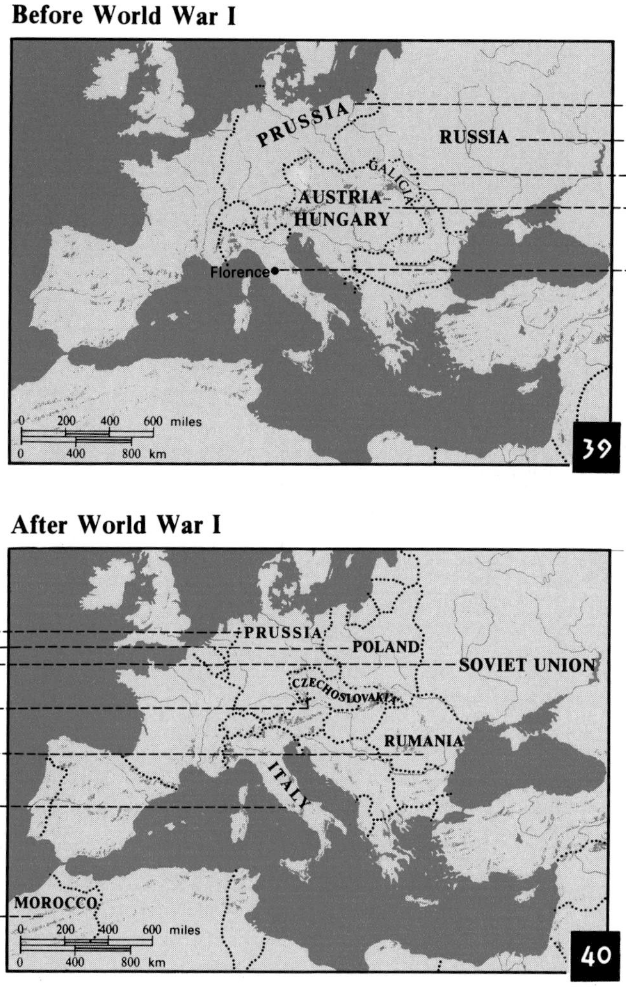


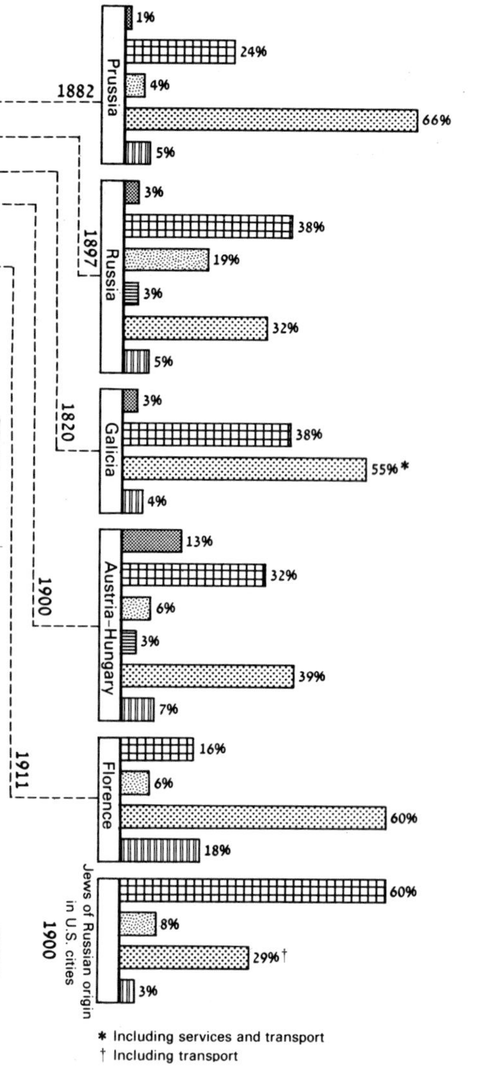


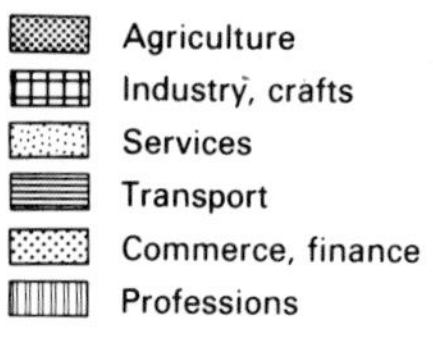


## Percentage of Jews in Selected Professions

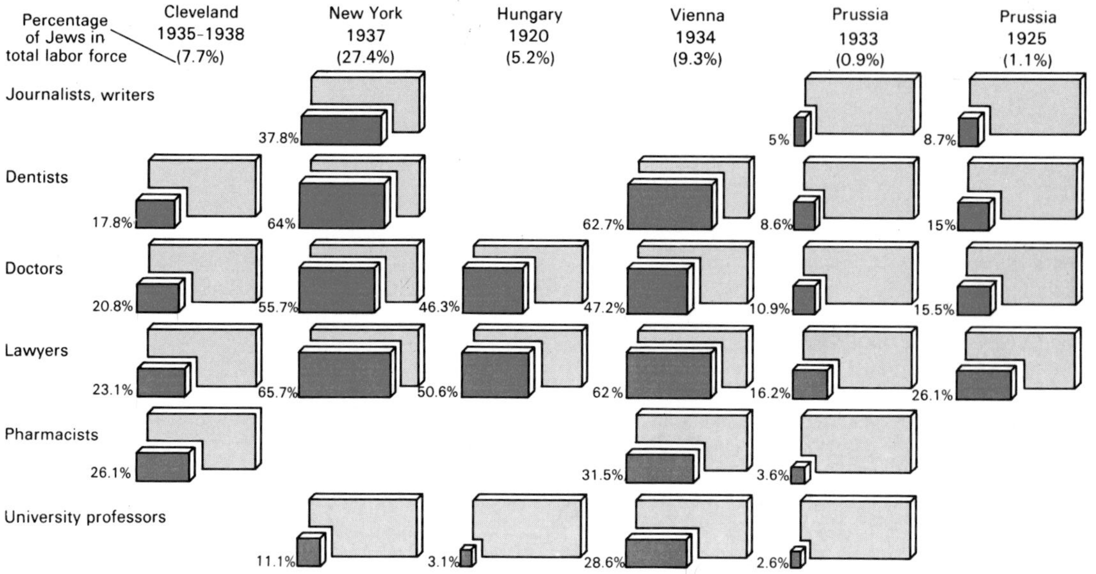

# The Labor Force: Jews and Non-Jews

(excluding agriculture)

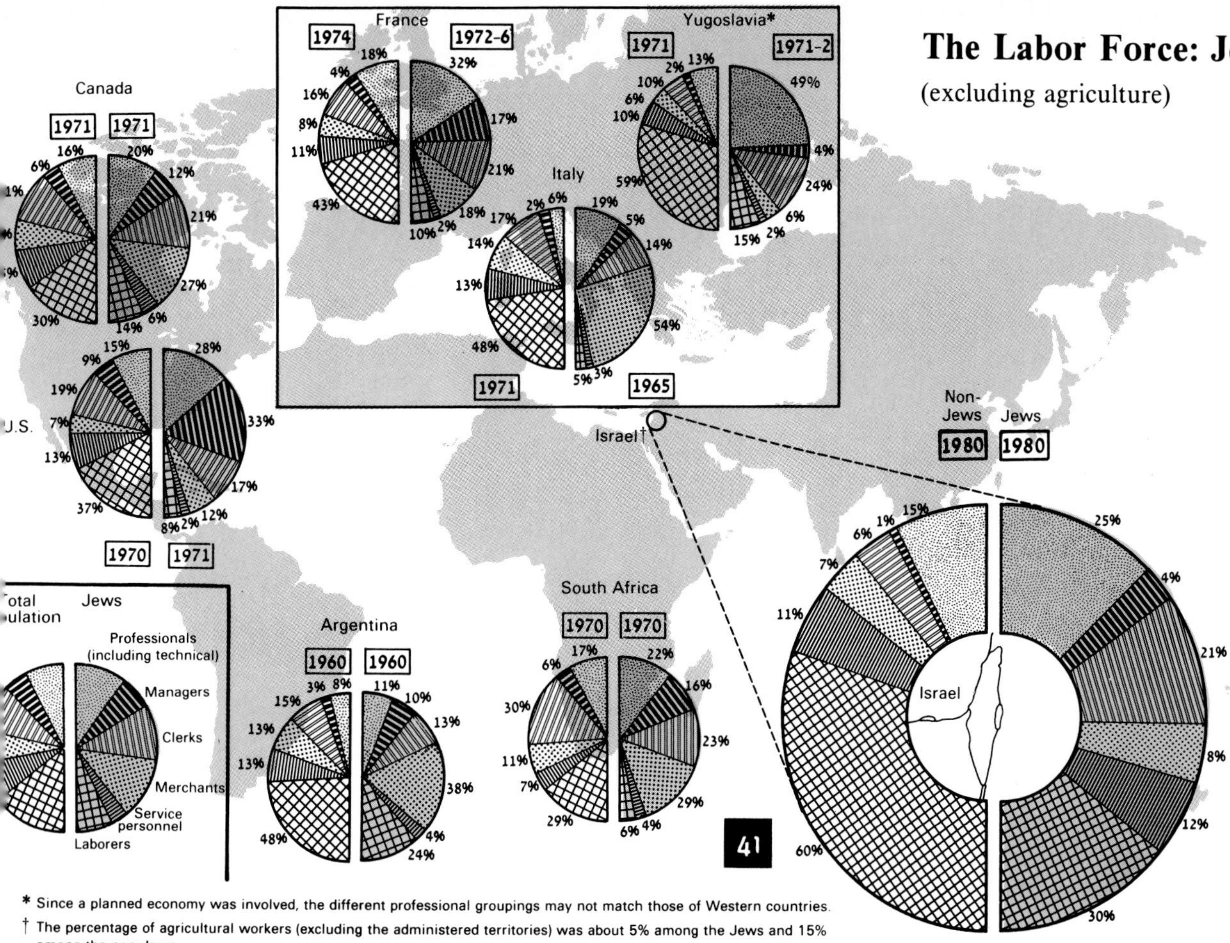


## The Jewish Labor Force in Israel by Place of Origin, 1980

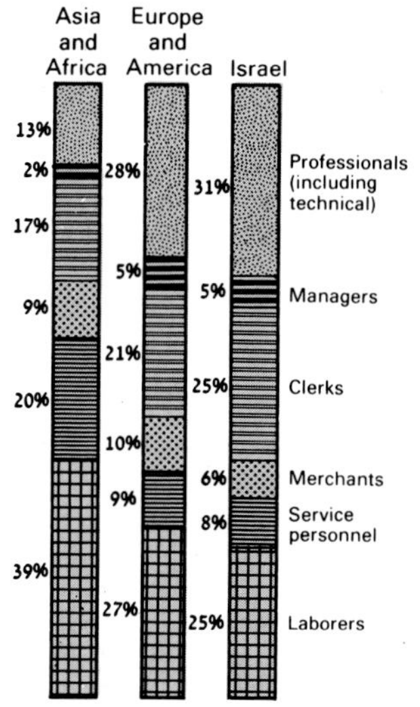


* Since a planned economy was involved, the different professional groupings may not match those of Western countries.

† The percentage of agricultural workers (excluding the administered territories) was about 5% among the Jews and 15% among the non-Jews.

# The Jews in Agriculture

The number of Jews in agriculture in modern times remained very small: only 1 to 2 percent of all Jewish wage earners before World War II. In the past 100 years, various Jewish organizations and movements have tried to attract Jews to farming, as part of the effort to bring about the "productivization" of Jewish society: the Am Olam movement, directed to the United States; the Alliance Israélite Universelle; and especially the Jewish Colonization Association (ICA), founded in 1891. But the Jewish farm colonies established in the United States, Argentina, Brazil, and other countries failed after one or two generations.

In some parts of Europe (Galicia, Czechoslovakia, southern Russia) in the early twentieth century, between 9 and 13 percent of the Jewish breadwinners worked in agriculture, although some did so only in related occupations (administration, transport). This class of Jews disappeared during the Holocaust. Outside Europe, there was a significant percentage of agricultural workers among the mountain Jews of Kurdistan (Iraq).

Jewish agriculture in Palestine is a separate story. The creation of a class of Jewish farmers in Palestine was a central aim of Zionist ideology that found expression in new social forms: the kibbutz, the *moshav*, and others. In the second half of the twentieth century, Israel was the only country with a Jewish farming class.

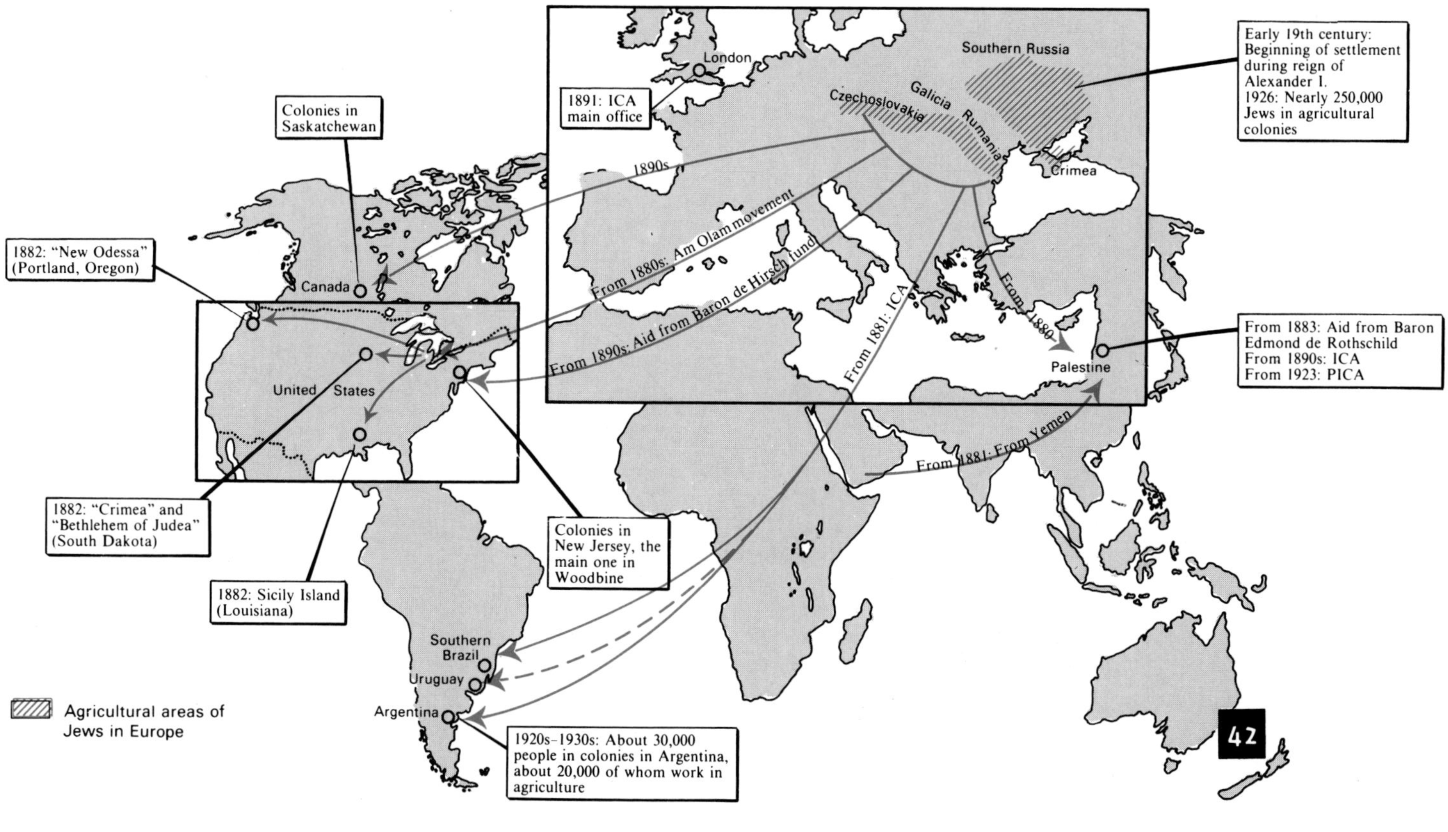

## Rights that Evolved Gradually

**England**

| | |
|---|---|
| 1655 | Conference convened by Cromwell to discuss return of Jews to England reaches no decision |
| 1656 | Antonio Robles, English-born merchant, recognized as Jew. **Precedent for recognition of Jewish presence in England** |
| 1753 | Jewish Bill. Parliament permits small number of (foreign-born) Jews to acquire citizenship. Public protest leads to annulment of law the same year |
| Late 18th–early 19th century | Extensive rights *de facto* |
| 1858 | Jews Bill. Parliament permits small number of (foreign-born) Jews to acquire citizenship. Public protest leads to annulment of law the same year |

**Netherlands**

| | |
|---|---|
| 1597–1603 | Marranos begin to organize as Jewish community |
| 1616 | First discussion of conditions of Jewish settlement. No decision; presence of Jews accepted *de facto* |
| July 13, 1657 | States General of the Netherlands recognizes Jews as subjects |
| 17th–18th century | Gradual broadening of Jews' rights |
| September 9, 1796 | After establishment of Republic of Batavia (1815–1831, monarchy), equal rights to Jews |

## Absence of Full or Equal Rights

**Russian Empire**

| | |
|---|---|
| 1791–1835 | Consolidation of Pale of Settlement |
| 1804 | Jewish Statute of Alexander I. Various rights and restrictions |
| 1825–1855 | Reign of Nicholas I. Pressure on Jews intensified |
| 1855–1865 | Reign of Alexander II (first part). Rights broadened |
| 1882 | May Laws. Increasing restriction of Jewish rights |
| April 2, 1917 | **Following February Revolution, equal rights** |

**Rumania**

| | |
|---|---|
| 1859 | With founding of Rumanian state, Jews denied civil rights |
| 1879 | Most Jews classified as aliens, to deprive them of equal rights |

## Rights from the Outset, Without a Special Decision

**United States**

| | |
|---|---|
| 1740 | British Plantation Act. Full rights to aliens, including Jews. Are exempted from Christian Oath |
| December 16, 1785 | Virginia passes Statute of Religious Freedom |
| September 17, 1789 | Constitution |
| November 3, 1791 | First Amendment of Constitution |

Rights from the outset also in Canada, South Africa, and South America

## Rights Based on Law or Constitution

**France**

| | |
|---|---|
| July 10, 1784 | Louis XVI issues edict to Alsace Jews. Body tax abolished and various rights granted |
| August 26, 1789 | Declaration of the Rights of Man and the Citizen |
| January 28, 1790 | National Assembly grants equal rights to Spanish-Portuguese Jews and Jews of Avignon and vicinity |
| September 3, 1791 | French Constitution. Freedom of worship, civil rights |
| September 28, 1791 | **Equal civil rights to all Jews** |
| June 4, 1814 | Monarchy restored. New constitution. Temporary preference to Catholicism. In fact, full rights to Jews |
| 1905 | Separation of church and state |

**Prussia and Germany**

| | |
|---|---|
| 1730–1750 | Combination of rights and restrictions in spirit of absolutism |
| March 11, 1812 | Hardenberg laws. Many civil rights to Jews, valid only in areas under Prussian rule |
| December 5, 1848 | Revolution. Civil rights, though curtailed in 1850s |
| 1869–1871 | **Constitution, with establishment of German Empire** |

**Hapsburg Empire**

| | |
|---|---|
| 18th century | In light of differences between the lands of the empire, different laws regarding Jews |
| 1782–1789 | *Toleranzpatenten* of Joseph II. Combination of duties and rights in spirit of enlightened absolutism |
| 1848 | Revolution. Civil rights, though curtailed in 1850s |
| December 21, 1867 | **Constitution of Austro-Hungarian monarchy** |

Rights based on law or constitution

Rights that evolved gradually

Absence of full or equal rights

Rights from the outset, without a special decision

Constitution granting equal rights to all citizens regardless of religion, with date

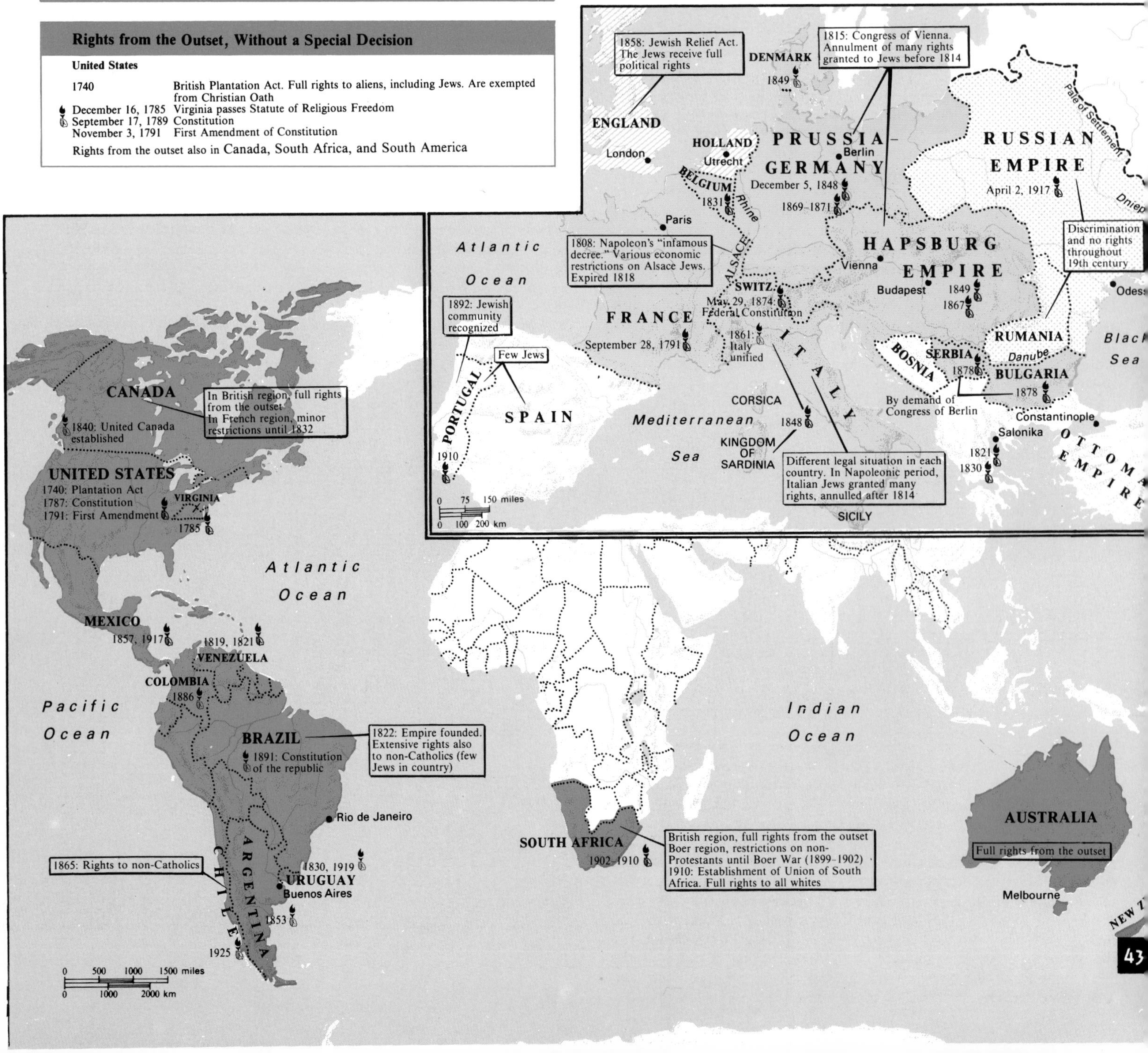

# The Legal Situation of the Jews Until World War I

New social and political concepts that developed in Europe in modern times changed the legal position of the Jews, in each country according to a pattern of its own. Until the rise of the absolute states in the seventeenth and eighteenth centuries, the Jews were regarded as a foreign people in the European countries or cities, and their presence was based on and regulated by a legal contract ("privilege") between them and the local ruler. The ruler's interest in the Jews was economic; the attitude of the general society was strongly influenced by the historical tensions between non-Jews and Jews. Under the absolute rulers, the legal situation of the Jews changed: from foreigners, they became subjects. Their new status involved some rights and many duties, since it was thought that the Jews had to be "improved." The absolute ruler considered it his right and duty to intervene in the life of the Jewish community (as he did in the lives of his other subjects), in order to move it in the "desirable" direction.

In Western and Central Europe (but not in Eastern Europe), absolutism gradually gave way to regimes and systems inspired by the French Revolution, which also had a far-reaching influence on the situation of the Jews. The French National Assembly decided in 1791 that Jews should be granted citizenship with full civil and political rights. But in many countries, this so-called Jewish emancipation involved an implicit or explicit accord between non-Jews and Jews: in exchange for their new rights, Jews were supposed to relinquish much (or most) of their distinctiveness, such as their separate group existence. These conditions were not specifically mentioned in the emancipation laws, but were clearly expressed in the discussions related to them. During the debate on the Jews in the French National Assembly, in December 1789, Count Clermont-Tonnerre formulated it thus: "Everything must be refused to the Jews as a nation but everything must be granted to them as individuals; they must be citizens." These and similar statements expressed the uneasiness and doubt about the new status of the Jews and set conditions for their full integration into the general society. The conditions were not and could not be clearly defined and were interpreted differently by each ideological sector of the general society. Together, however, these conditions and interpretations placed a question mark on the Jews' position and cast a shadow on the whole process that was to prove fateful, with the development of modern antisemitism. That ambivalence in the new situation of the Jews, that combination of many new possibilities with as many problems attached to them, became one of the main characteristics of the modernization of European Jewry.

Nevertheless, the granting of citizenship rights to the Jews by the French National Assembly was a landmark in modern Jewish history: it put the Jews on an equal footing with all other French citizens and provided a model that sooner or later was followed by most other West European countries. For the Jews, it set a goal and a challenge that deeply influenced the subsequent internal development of Jewish society, in each country according to local conditions. But in many of the countries where Jews gained civil and political rights, an undeniable gap remained between theory and practice, and the new laws were unable to persuade non-Jews to overcome their deep-rooted prejudices. And in several countries, there was a semiofficial (or tacit) preference for the religion of the majority group.

In Eastern Europe after World War I, a positive approach was adopted (or imposed) regarding the cultural and national rights of minority groups (including the Jews), opening new possibilities for Jewish life and self-definition in the countries of that region.

Although the development of American Jewry showed European influences, the legal situation of American Jews was quite different from that of European Jews. No separate discussion took place in the United States about the legal rights of the Jews. The Plantation Act of 1740 granted full civil rights to Jews and members of other religious groups who had been living in the British colonies in America for at least seven years. The law, characteristic of the mercantilist age, aimed to attract settlers to the undeveloped and uncolonized Crown lands in the New World, and it established a basis for the legal equality of the Jews in America long before the colonies declared and won their independence. Consequently, in the United States there was never a "Jewish emancipation" as it evolved in Europe, with all the attendant problems and conditions. Some laws discriminating against Jews existed in several American states, but they were rescinded during the nineteenth century.

The situation in the Latin American countries (most became independent in the nineteenth century) was not much different from that in the United States, although Roman Catholicism was recognized in most South American states as the predominant or official religion. Jews also enjoyed full equality in other nations established in the nineteenth and twentieth centuries—for example, Australia, Canada, and South Africa.

# The Legal Situation of the Jews in Muslim Countries

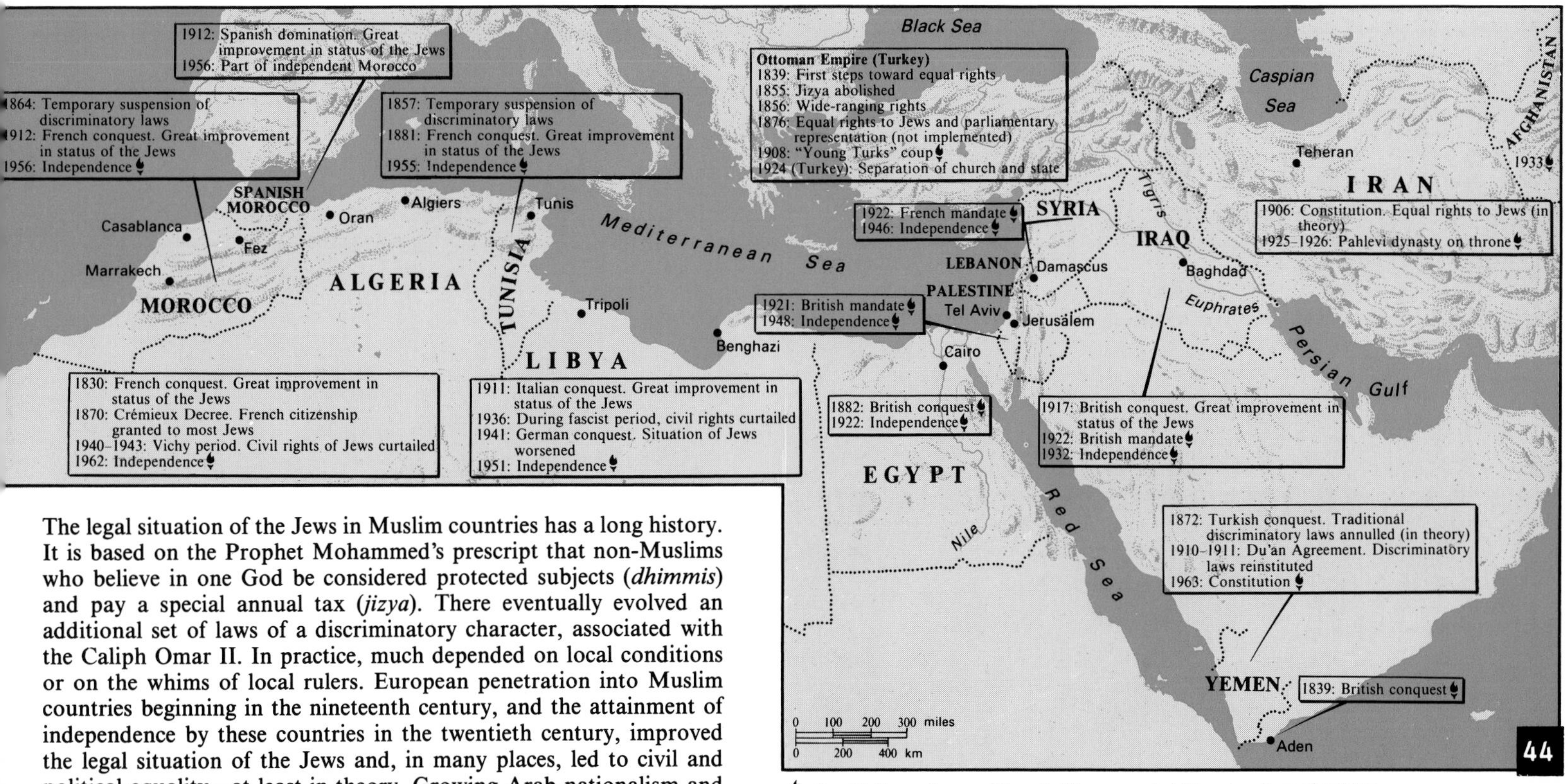


Constitution or law granting all citizens equal rights, regardless of religion

The legal situation of the Jews in Muslim countries has a long history. It is based on the Prophet Mohammed's prescript that non-Muslims who believe in one God be considered protected subjects (*dhimmis*) and pay a special annual tax (*jizya*). There eventually evolved an additional set of laws of a discriminatory character, associated with the Caliph Omar II. In practice, much depended on local conditions or on the whims of local rulers. European penetration into Muslim countries beginning in the nineteenth century, and the attainment of independence by these countries in the twentieth century, improved the legal situation of the Jews and, in many places, led to civil and political equality—at least in theory. Growing Arab nationalism and the worsening Arab–Zionist conflict undermined the position of the Jews in most Muslim countries around the mid-twentieth century and was one of the reasons for their emigration.

# Jewish Enlightenment (*Haskalah*) in Europe:

## Eighteenth and Nineteenth Centuries

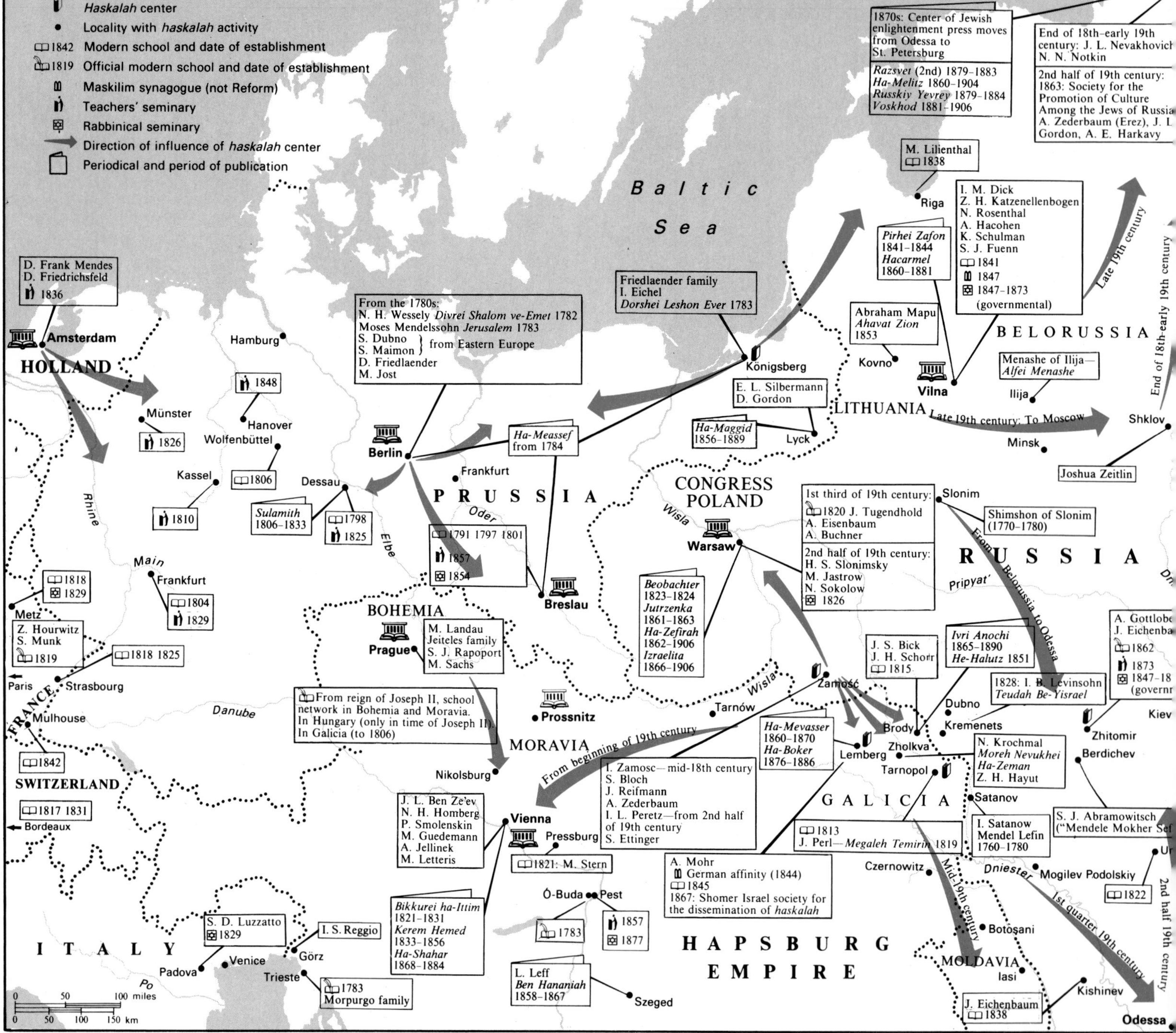


### Late Nineteenth Century Influences

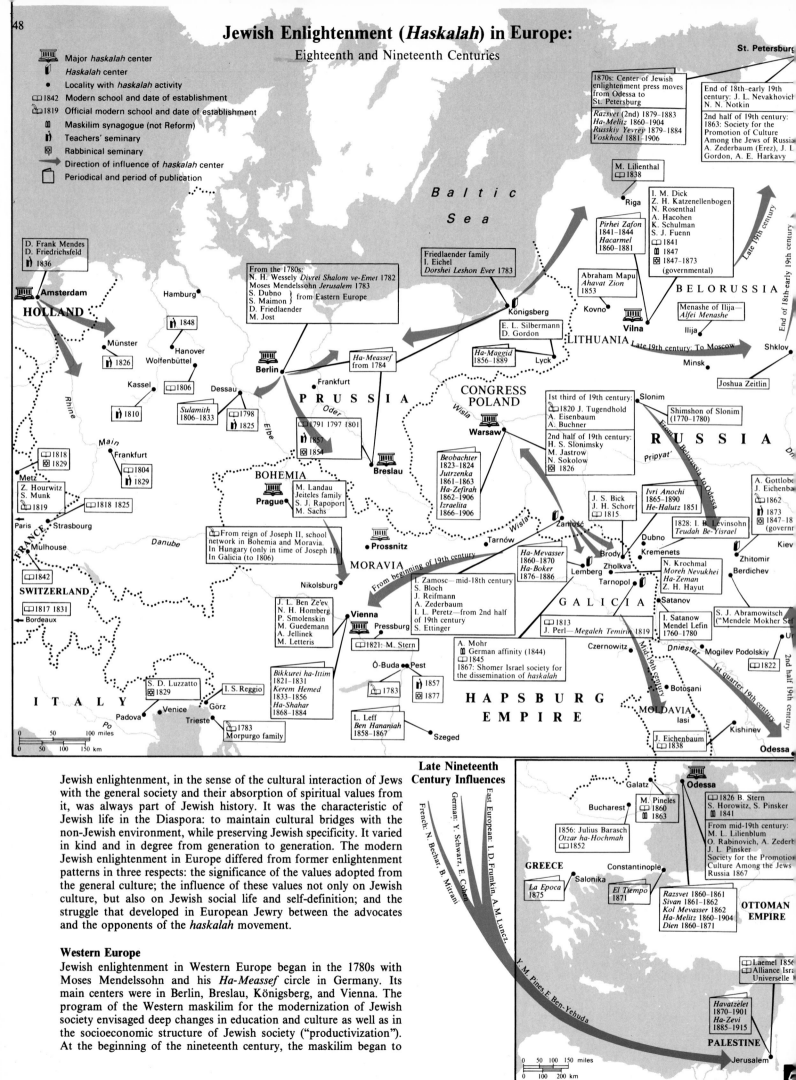

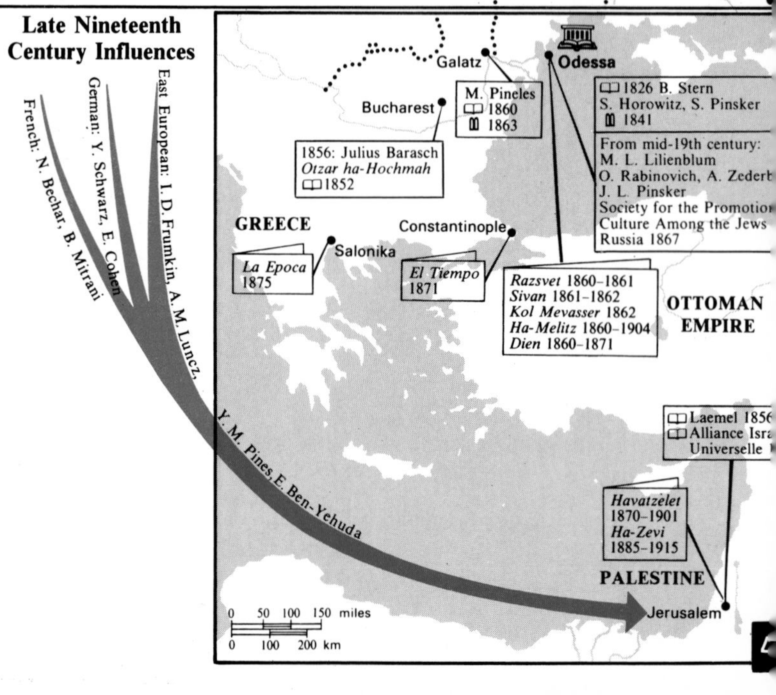


Jewish enlightenment, in the sense of the cultural interaction of Jews with the general society and their absorption of spiritual values from it, was always part of Jewish history. It was the characteristic of Jewish life in the Diaspora: to maintain cultural bridges with the non-Jewish environment, while preserving Jewish specificity. It varied in kind and in degree from generation to generation. The modern Jewish enlightenment in Europe differed from former enlightenment patterns in three respects: the significance of the values adopted from the general culture; the influence of these values not only on Jewish culture, but also on Jewish social life and self-definition; and the struggle that developed in European Jewry between the advocates and the opponents of the *haskalah* movement.

**Western Europe**

Jewish enlightenment in Western Europe began in the 1780s with Moses Mendelssohn and his *Ha-Meassef* circle in Germany. Its main centers were in Berlin, Breslau, Königsberg, and Vienna. The program of the Western maskilim for the modernization of Jewish society envisaged deep changes in education and culture as well as in the socioeconomic structure of Jewish society ("productivization"). At the beginning of the nineteenth century, the maskilim began to focus their efforts on reforming traditional religious practices and beliefs. A fierce struggle broke out between the Western maskilim and the proponents of classical Judaism, especially (but not only) over religious changes, which led to a deep and lasting breach.

West European *haskalah* was inspired by its own vision of the place of Jews and Judaism in modern society, and by its hopes for Jewish social and cultural "emancipation." But since the number of Jews in Western Europe was small and their communal structures were relatively weak, many of them lost their identification with Judaism as a result of the influence of modernizing trends.

The founding of the Association for the Culture and Science of Judaism (the Kulturverein), which was active in Berlin from 1819 to 1824, may be regarded as the final activity of Western *haskalah* as a separate tendency. From then on, *haskalah* was active as a basis for or part of other trends and movements in Western and Central Europe, such as the "Science of Judaism" and the Reform movement.

### Eastern Europe

Small circles of maskilim began to appear in Belorussia in the mid-eighteenth century. New groups were formed toward the end of the century in Galicia, Lithuania, Bohemia and Moravia, St. Petersburg, and Warsaw. By the early nineteenth century, several distinct types of East European *haskalah* were apparent: the Galician, the Lithuanian, and the Polish. Important centers of Jewish enlightenment gradually emerged: Zamość, Warsaw (Poland), Brody, Tarnopol, Lemberg (Lwów [Galicia]), Odessa, St. Petersburg, and Vilna (Russian Empire). Circles of maskilim, each with its own characteristics, appeared in Vienna and Prague (Hapsburg Empire), influenced by both Western and Eastern Jewish enlightenment.

At first, East European maskilim met with little opposition from the other segments of Jewish society, since their main interests were cultural and scientific. But by the end of the eighteenth century, they began to turn their attention to the social improvement of Jewish society, a matter raised by the authorities as well, first in the Hapsburg Empire, and then in czarist Russia. By the 1820s, the maskilim were working to modernize Jewish society and severely criticizing its ways of life. These efforts led to a confrontation with the more traditional sector of East European Jewry, composed of both Hasidim and Mitnagdim, who together still made up a huge majority. The struggle intensified from the middle of the century, partly as a result of pressure from the authorities, who tried by various means to force modernization on the Jewish masses and to undermine the traditional structure of Jewish society. However, the mounting tendencies toward assimilation among the Jewries of Western Europe undergoing modernization only strengthened the traditionalists' opposition to Jewish enlightenment.

The maskilim, who often collaborated with the authorities, began to create their own institutions, such as schools and synagogues. Their numbers and influence increased greatly during the relatively liberal reign of Czar Alexander II (1855–1881). Many were attracted by the schools that the authorities established for Jewish children beginning in the 1840s, both because of their growing interest in modernization and because of the exemption from military service offered to Jews who acquired a general education. The publication of Jewish newspapers (another expression of *haskalah*) in German, Hebrew, Yiddish, and Russian contributed greatly to the movement's expansion. From the 1860s, new organizations were formed for the propagation of *haskalah*. Additional centers of *haskalah* were the rabbinical seminaries established with governmental support in Warsaw (1826), Vilna, and Zhitomir (1847–1873). The official rabbinate (*mitaam*) was also a tool of the enlightenment. All these enterprises combined to give the East European *haskalah* movement a framework within which to function.

Since East European Jewry was sizable, concentrated in strong Jewish centers, spiritually very active, and relatively secluded from the general population, most maskilim sought to implement their new ideas *inside* Jewish society, not *outside* it, as those in Western Europe had done. East European *haskalah* grew in different directions, and its proponents adopted a wide range of attitudes to the problems of Jewish life. But even the later maskilim, who supported religious reforms, had reservations about the West European brand of Jewish reform, which defined Jews and Judaism on a very narrow religious basis. Most major cultural or social initiatives inspired by ideas rooted in East European *haskalah* aimed to preserve Jewish group life and to develop it, even if according to the new ideological approaches gradually being formulated.

Three main ideological trends emerged under the influence of East European *haskalah* in the last quarter of the nineteenth century. One, similar to the West European pattern, favored a high level of social and cultural integration into the general society. This position was expressed by the associations for the propagation of *haskalah*, and even more so by the circles that issued Jewish publications written in Russian, such as *Dien* (Odessa, 1869–1871) and the important *Voskhod* (St. Petersburg, 1881–1906). The second trend, partly influenced by the first, turned to Jewish nationalism in its different forms. This approach involved important authors who wrote in Hebrew and Hebrew-language publications, such as *Ha-Shahar*, *Ha-Maggid*, *Ha-Melitz*, and *Ha-Zefirah*, as well as Russian-language newspapers. Two significant cultural enterprises of these circles were the transformation of Hebrew into a living language and the fostering of Yiddish. The third current turned to socialism. Its beginnings were already apparent in the 1870s, and it reached its fullest expression with the creation of the Jewish socialist party, the Bund, in 1897.

A different kind of *haskalah* developed in Palestine beginning in the second half of the nineteenth century. It was a combination of East European, German, and French elements, brought to the country by immigrant Jews. In the new Jewish centers in North and South America the *haskalah* was part of Jewish life, since conditions of modernity already prevailed there. Consequently, the kind of confrontation between Jewish modernism and traditionalism that had been so important in shaping Jewish life in the Old World did not occur in the New.

## Tendencies in Jewish Enlightenment (*Haskalah*)

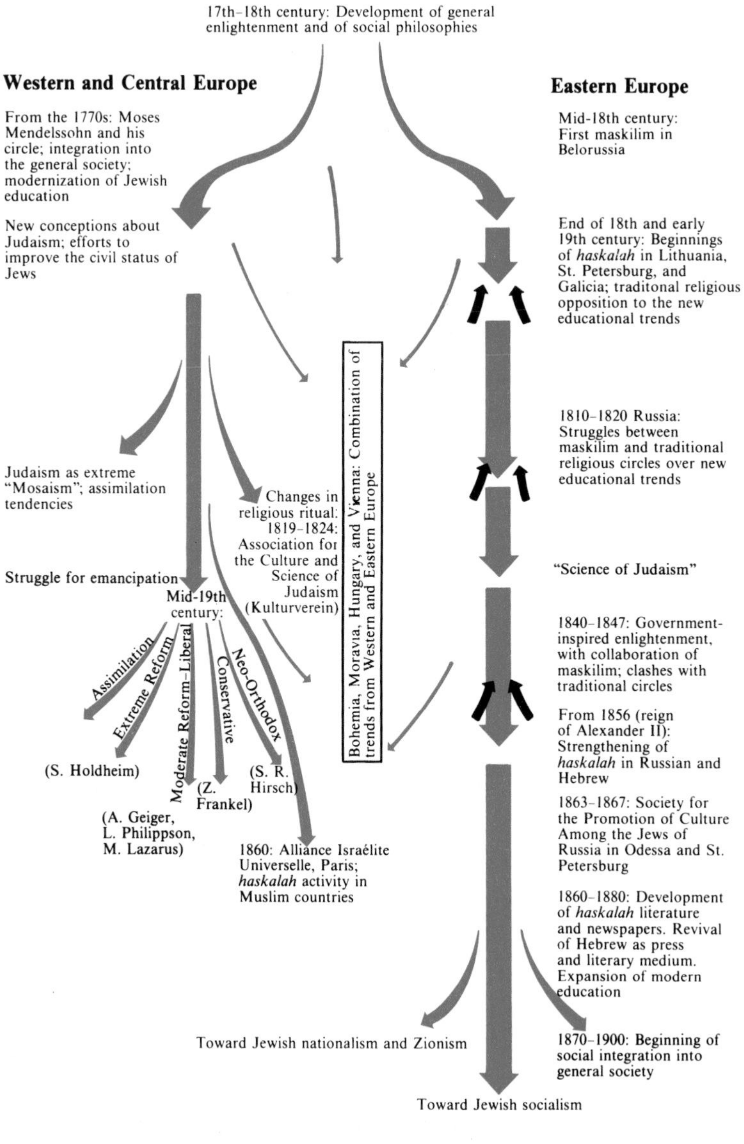
17th–18th century: Development of general enlightenment and of social philosophies
Western and Central Europe
Eastern Europe
From the 1770s: Moses Mendelssohn and his circle; integration into the general society; modernization of Jewish education
New conceptions about Judaism; efforts to improve the civil status of Jews
Mid-18th century: First maskilim in Belorussia
End of 18th and early 19th century: Beginnings of haskalah in Lithuania, St. Petersburg, and Galicia; traditonal religious opposition to the new educational trends
Bohemia, Moravia, Hungary, and Vienna: Combination of trends from Western and Eastern Europe
1810–1820 Russia: Struggles between maskilim and traditional religious circles over new educational trends
Judaism as extreme "Mosaism"; assimilation tendencies
Changes in religious ritual: 1819–1824: Association for the Culture and Science of Judaism (Kulturverein)
Struggle for emancipation
Mid-19th century:
"Science of Judaism"
Assimilation
Extreme Reform
Moderate Reform–Liberal
Conservative
Neo-Orthodox
(S. Holdheim)
(A. Geiger, L. Philippson, M. Lazarus)
(Z. Frankel)
(S. R. Hirsch)
1860: Alliance Israélite Universelle, Paris; haskalah activity in Muslim countries
1840–1847: Government-inspired enlightenment, with collaboration of maskilim; clashes with traditional circles
From 1856 (reign of Alexander II): Strengthening of haskalah in Russian and Hebrew
1863–1867: Society for the Promotion of Culture Among the Jews of Russia in Odessa and St. Petersburg
1860–1880: Development of haskalah literature and newspapers. Revival of Hebrew as press and literary medium. Expansion of modern education
Toward Jewish nationalism and Zionism
1870–1900: Beginning of social integration into general society
Toward Jewish socialism

## Sabbateanism, Frankism, and Early Hasidism

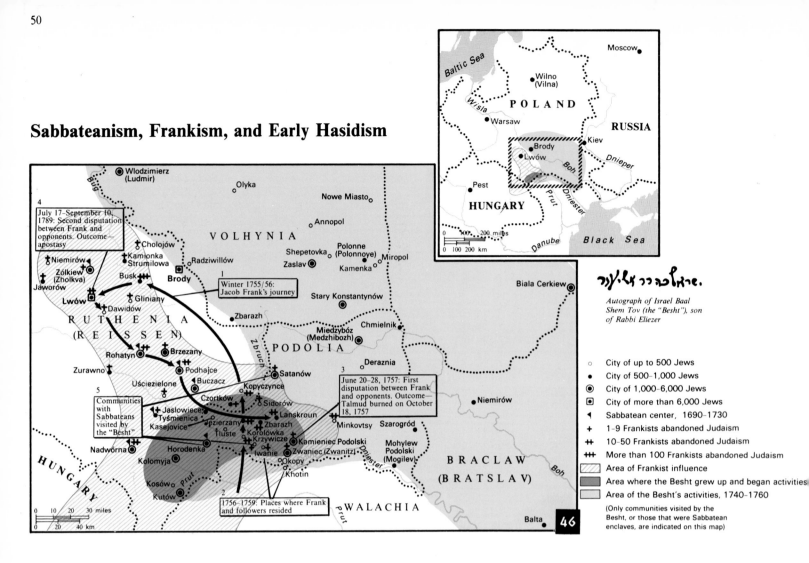

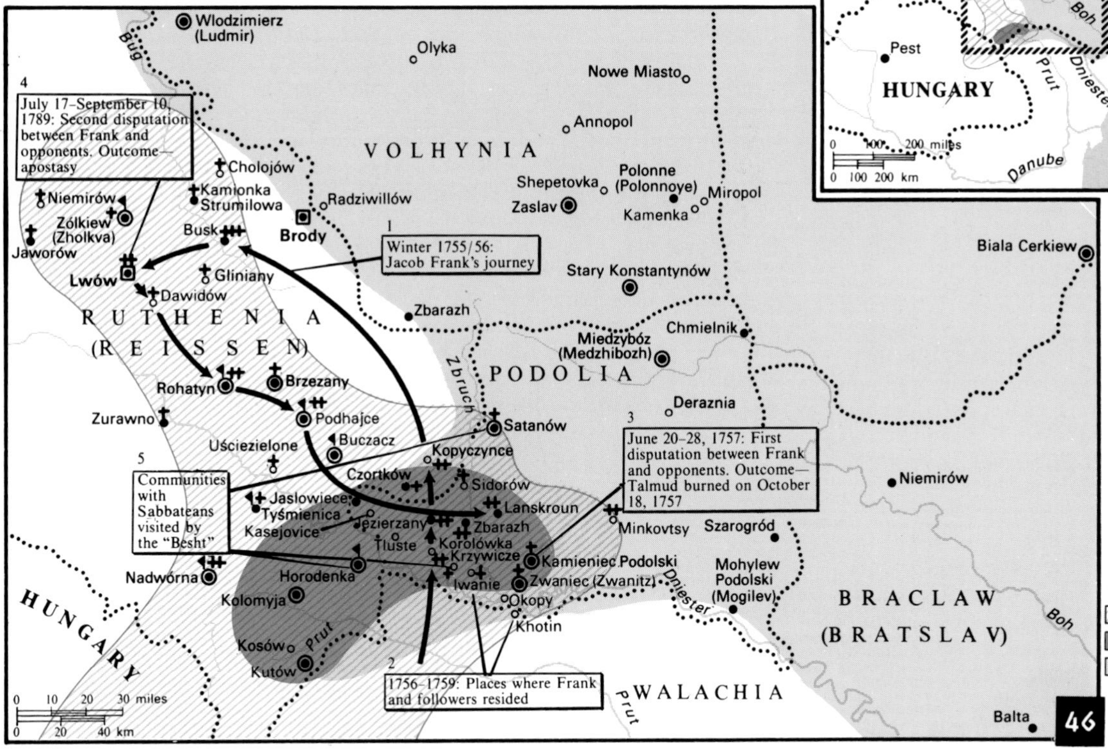


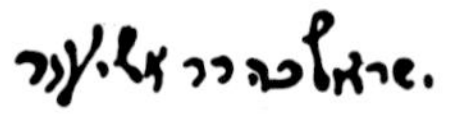

*Autograph of Israel Baal Shem Tov (the "Besht"), son of Rabbi Eliezer*

- ○ City of up to 500 Jews
- ● City of 500–1,000 Jews
- ◉ City of 1,000–6,000 Jews
- ▣ City of more than 6,000 Jews
- ◂ Sabbatean center, 1690–1730
- + 1–9 Frankists abandoned Judaism
- ++ 10–50 Frankists abandoned Judaism
- +++ More than 100 Frankists abandoned Judaism
- Area of Frankist influence
- Area where the Besht grew up and began activities
- Area of the Besht's activities, 1740–1760

(Only communities visited by the Besht, or those that were Sabbatean enclaves, are indicated on this map)

Two streams of mysticism were evident among the Jews in southeastern Poland in the early eighteenth century: Sabbateanism and Hasidism. Sabbateanism, a religious movement whose members believed that Sabbetai Zevi was the Messiah, had been strong in the second half of the seventeenth century but later declined. Hasidism arose toward the mid-eighteenth century and became one of the most influential movements in modern Jewish history. At first glance, the geographical proximity of the centers of the two might suggest mutual influence. Jacob Frank led a sect that continued the Sabbatean tradition, and in the winter of 1755 visited Jewish communities in Poland that apparently were Sabbatean centers. His appearances generated local religious tensions and heated discussions between his critics and his supporters. About 500 of the latter converted to Christianity in 1759 and 1760.

A closer examination of the geographical data, however, raises doubts about a relationship between the two streams. It is true that Rabbi Israel Baal Shem Tov (the "Besht"), the creator of Hasidism, was born and grew up in a region where there apparently were Sabbatean influences (west of the River Zbruch, near the River Prut). Around 1740, however, he began to propagate his new ideas in Medzhibozh (Miedzybóz) and other areas that were free of those influences. This analysis is based mainly on the writings of Rabbi Jacob Emden, the list of the Sabbateans who converted in Lwów in 1759 (which includes their places of residence), and the book *Shivhei Habesht*.

## Hasidism: Beginnings and Expansion

Hasidism, a movement of religious renewal, appeared in Poland in the mid-eighteenth century. Scholars, cabalists, and common folk banded together in groups led by a *zaddik* or *admor*. The *zaddik*, a new type in Jewish religious leadership, was an essential figure in the development of Hasidism. Typically, he was a mystic (*mekubbal*, or cabalist) dedicated to a personal life of holiness, who now agreed to lead a sect of followers. The *zaddik* was believed to connect the higher spheres of holiness with the lower spheres of daily life, as explained in the kabbalah (Jewish mysticism).

The founder of the Hasidic movement was Rabbi Israel Baal Shem Tov (the "Besht," 1700–1760), who became known in Podolia from about 1735. His most important successor was Rabbi Dov Baer (the "Great Maggid"), who led the Hasidic movement from 1760 to 1772 from Mezhirech (Miedzyrzecz), a small town in Volhynia. After his death, his many followers dispersed over the country, and the movement gradually split into many Hasidic courts, led by a descendant or disciple of the Besht or the Great Maggid.

The expansion of Hasidism brought it into conflict with sectors of the Jewish population opposing its views—the Mitnagdim (opponents), who tried to stop its expansion and even to excommunicate the Hasidim. The best-known leader of the Mitnagdim was Rabbi Elijah (the "Gaon of Vilna"). Nevertheless, Hasidism continued to grow, and since its adherents upheld religious law (*Halakhah* and mitzvoth) and did not attempt to change the traditional structure of the Jewish community, a total schism between the factions was avoided. The growth of Hasidism was aided by the fact that the Polish state was disintegrating at the time; the weakness of the Polish central government also weakened the established Jewish institutions and their possible reaction against the new current. Later, the rise of the Jewish enlightenment drew the Mitnagdim and Hasidim together to combat what they considered a common threat.

By the end of the eighteenth century, Hasidism had become a substantial movement, large sectors of the Jewish population in central Poland, Galicia, parts of the Ukraine, and even some parts of Lithuania having accepted it.

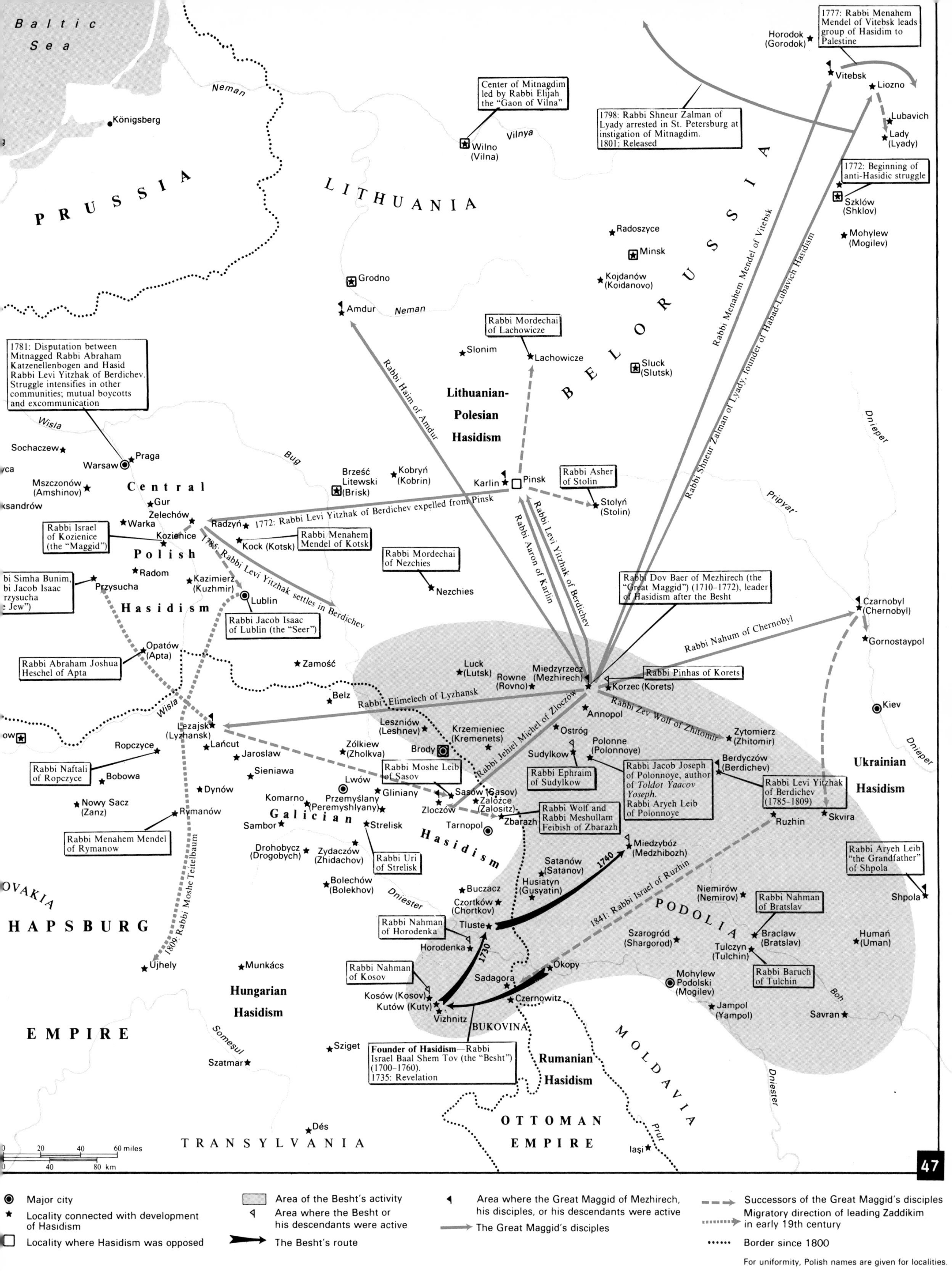
Baltic Sea
PRUSSIA
LITHUANIA
BELORUSSIA
Neman
Vilnya
Königsberg
Center of Mitnagdim led by Rabbi Elijah the "Gaon of Vilna"
Wilno (Vilna)
Horodok (Gorodok)
1777: Rabbi Menahem Mendel of Vitebsk leads group of Hasidim to Palestine
Vitebsk
Liozno
Lubavich
Lady (Lyady)
1798: Rabbi Shneur Zalman of Lyady arrested in St. Petersburg at instigation of Mitnagdim. 1801: Released
1772: Beginning of anti-Hasidic struggle
Szklów (Shklov)
Mohylew (Mogilev)
Radoszyce
Minsk
Kojdanów (Koidanovo)
Grodno
Amdur
Neman
Rabbi Mordechai of Lachowicze
Lachowicze
Slonim
Sluck (Slutsk)
Rabbi Menahem Mendel of Vitebsk
Rabbi Shneur Zalman of Lyady, founder of Habad-Lubavich Hasidism
Rabbi Haim of Amdur
Lithuanian-Polesian Hasidism
1781: Disputation between Mitnagged Rabbi Abraham Katzenellenbogen and Hasid Rabbi Levi Yitzhak of Berdichev. Struggle intensifies in other communities; mutual boycotts and excommunication
Wisla
Sochaczew
Warsaw
Praga
Mszczonów (Amshinov)
Aleksandrów
Central Polish Hasidism
Gur
Zelechów
Warka
Kozienice
Rabbi Israel of Kozienice (the "Maggid")
Radom
Bug
Brześć Litewski (Brisk)
Kobryń (Kobrin)
Karlin
Pinsk
Rabbi Asher of Stolin
Stolyń (Stolin)
1772: Rabbi Levi Yitzhak of Berdichev expelled from Pinsk
Radzyń
Kock (Kotsk)
Rabbi Menahem Mendel of Kotsk
Pripyat'
Dnieper
1785: Rabbi Levi Yitzhak settles in Berdichev
Rabbi Aaron of Karlin
Rabbi Levi Yitzhak of Berdichev
Rabbi Mordechai of Nezchies
Nezchies
Rabbi Simha Bunim, Rabbi Jacob Isaac of Przysucha ("the Jew")
Przysucha
Kazimierz (Kuzhmir)
Lublin
Rabbi Jacob Isaac of Lublin (the "Seer")
Rabbi Dov Baer of Mezhirech (the "Great Maggid") (1710–1772), leader of Hasidism after the Besht
Czarnobyl (Chernobyl)
Rabbi Nahum of Chernobyl
Gornostaypol
Opatów (Apta)
Rabbi Abraham Joshua Heschel of Apta
Zamość
Luck (Lutsk)
Rowne (Rovno)
Miedzyrzecz (Mezhirech)
Rabbi Pinhas of Korets
Korzec (Korets)
Kiev
Belz
Rabbi Elimelech of Lyzhansk
Lezajsk (Lyzhansk)
Lańcut
Jaroslaw
Sieniawa
Ropczyce
Rabbi Naftali of Ropczyce
Bobowa
Dynów
Nowy Sacz (Zanz)
Rymanów
Rabbi Menahem Mendel of Rymanow
1809: Rabbi Moshe Teitelbaum
Lesznioẃ (Leshnev)
Krzemieniec (Kremenets)
Zólkiew (Zholkva)
Brody
Rabbi Moshe Leib of Sasov
Lwów
Gliniany
Przemyślany (Peremyshlyany)
Komarno
Sasów (Sasov)
Zalóźce (Zalositz)
Zloczów
Rabbi Jehiel Michel of Zloczow
Annopol
Ostróg
Rabbi Zev Wolf of Zhitomir
Zytomierz (Zhitomir)
Sudylków
Polonne (Polonnoye)
Rabbi Ephraim of Sudylkow
Rabbi Jacob Joseph of Polonnoye, author of Toldot Yaacov Yoseph. Rabbi Aryeh Leib of Polonnoye
Berdyczów (Berdichev)
Rabbi Levi Yitzhak of Berdichev (1785–1809)
Ukrainian Hasidism
Dnieper
Skvira
Ruzhin
Rabbi Wolf and Rabbi Meshullam Feibish of Zbarazh
Zbarazh
Tarnopol
Galician Hasidism
Sambor
Strelisk
Rabbi Uri of Strelisk
Drohobycz (Drogobych)
Zydaczów (Zhidachov)
Bolechów (Bolekhov)
Miedzybóz (Medzhibozh)
1740
Satanów (Satanov)
Husiatyn (Gusyatin)
Buczacz
Czortków (Chortkov)
Dniester
1841: Rabbi Israel of Ruzhin
Rabbi Aryeh Leib "the Grandfather" of Shpola
Shpola
Niemirów (Nemirov)
Rabbi Nahman of Bratslav
PODOLIA
Braclaw (Bratslav)
Tulczyn (Tulchin)
Rabbi Baruch of Tulchin
Szargoród (Shargorod)
Humań (Uman)
Rabbi Nahman of Horodenka
Tluste
Horodenka
1730
Okopy
Sadagora
Czernowitz
Rabbi Nahman of Kosov
Kosów (Kosov)
Kutów (Kuty)
Vizhnitz
BUKOVINA
Mohylew Podolski (Mogilev)
Jampol (Yampol)
Savran
Boh
OVAKIA
HAPSBURG EMPIRE
Ujhely
Munkács
Hungarian Hasidism
Somesul
Sziget
Szatmar
Founder of Hasidism—Rabbi Israel Baal Shem Tov (the "Besht") (1700–1760). 1735: Revelation
Rumanian Hasidism
MOLDAVIA
Dniester
Prut
OTTOMAN EMPIRE
TRANSYLVANIA
Dés
Iaşi
0 20 40 60 miles
0 40 80 km
Major city
Locality connected with development of Hasidism
Locality where Hasidism was opposed
Area of the Besht's activity
Area where the Besht or his descendants were active
The Besht's route
Area where the Great Maggid of Mezhirech, his disciples, or his descendants were active
The Great Maggid's disciples
Successors of the Great Maggid's disciples
Migratory direction of leading Zaddikim in early 19th century
Border since 1800
For uniformity, Polish names are given for localities.

# Religious Tendencies in Modern Judaism

The process of religious transformation in modern Jewry generated one of the great internal spiritual struggles in Jewish history, with important social and even political overtones and consequences.

Until the end of the eighteenth century, Jews were mostly "traditional" in outlook and way of life and accepted the strict religious practices and beliefs of Jewish religious law (*Halakhah*) as God's command handed to Moses at Mount Sinai. This was true even of those small segments of the Jewish people that were already "modern" and relatively well adapted to the societies in which they lived, such as the Spanish-Portuguese Jews of Amsterdam and London. Furthermore, on the eve of the modern period, East European Jewry underwent a profound religious revival of a "traditional" character in the form of Hasidism combined with the opposition (*hitnagdut*) it evoked. The two together invigorated traditional Jewish religious life and strengthened it against the challenges of the modern era, which were posed by the Jewish enlightenment and one of its major consequences, the "acculturation" of Jewish society.

From the early nineteenth century, different segments of Jewish society in Western Europe became estranged from Jewish religious matters. Other groups criticized the beliefs and life ways of classical Judaism. They developed new concepts about the practice and principles of Judaism, which led to the Reform movement. Both the trend toward religious indifference and the efforts to introduce religious changes drew a fierce reaction from the defenders of classical Judaism.

Acculturation, meaning the gradual integration into the social and cultural life of the general society, was a central theme in the religious quest of nineteenth-century Jewry. It began among West European Jews in the late eighteenth century (in some instances, even earlier), advanced gradually through Central Europe during the nineteenth century, and later touched a growing part of East European Jewry.

Acculturation presented Jewish society with a wide gamut of new and intellectual questions that evoked the most diverse responses. Since modern European culture had strong secular overtones, one consequence of acculturation was the slackening adherence to the precepts of classical Judaism or a critical attitude toward them. In Western Europe, some—although relatively few—Jews were able to combine their cultural integration into the general society with strict religious practice. But the majority accepted the idea that the Jewish religion should be reformed. Large sectors of East European Jewry, however, reacted differently. Set in their traditional ways, deeply attached to classical Judaism, and relatively isolated from the surrounding non-Jewish society, they were wary of the new influences and tended to reject them, fearing that they would lead to changes in the *Halakhah* and mitzvoth (religious duties). The tradition-minded response to the challenges of acculturation expressed itself in a new religious attitude, Orthodoxy. This produced several currents, which varied with time and place: in Western Europe, it produced Orthodoxy and neo-Orthodoxy; in Eastern Europe, *Haredut*; and in Hungary, ultra-Orthodoxy. What they had in common was the uncompromising observance of Jewish religious law and the total rejection of any reforms in Judaism.

Viewed historically, the retreat from the extreme religious way of life was but one feature of Jewish society undergoing modernization. At the beginning of the twentieth century, most East European Jews still lived according to the *Halakhah*; in Western Europe, the Reform position already had the upper hand, while many other Jews had become indifferent to religious matters. Later, the growing influence of secularization further weakened the religious life of Jewish society. This tendency was even sharper among Jews who emigrated from Europe: their traditional Jewish institutions, religious and other, lost influence in their adopted countries. In the Soviet Union, the regime's antireligious ideology made the practice of all religion difficult. Finally, the Holocaust destroyed the main centers of classical Judaism in Europe.

In Palestine, and later in Israel, religious life developed a logic of its own. The emergence of an autonomous Jewish society, which later won political independence, made the question of the character of that society a matter of principle. The different currents in classical Judaism were impelled to participate in the public and political life of the country—not only to safeguard their interests, but also to promote their own conception of Jewish life. After a period of uncertainty and defensiveness, Orthodox Jewry gained self-assurance and became very active in Israeli public life, while other religious positions continued to struggle to gain recognition.

### The Reform Movement

The Reform movement aimed to adapt the forms of classical Jewish ritual and to explain the concepts of Judaism, according to the forms and ideas absorbed from the general society. It introduced changes in Jewish ritual from the beginning of the nineteenth century, first in German-speaking countries, then in other places in Europe, and later in the United States. From the 1830s, new conceptions about the character of Judaism were presented, and gradually the Reform position in modern Jewry was formulated. The movement's thinkers and leading figures (Abraham Geiger, Samuel Holdheim, Isaac Mayer Wise, and others) did not consider religious law (*Halakhah* and mitzvoth) to be binding and immutable. They distinguished between what they considered to be the essence and the forms of Judaism. Their intention was, as stated by Abraham Geiger in his younger years, to free the spirit, the eternal ideas, of Judaism from the "petrified" forms in which it had been imprisoned. They hoped that their proposed changes would remold the Jewish religion and bring it into harmony with the concepts of a modern and progressive general society. Judaism, according to most of the reformers, should be limited to the realm of religion, while in the civil and cultural domains, the Jews should live as loyal and integrated citizens of their respective countries.

In its more developed form, the Reform trend in Europe was known as the Liberal movement; only its more extreme sector, which was limited in size, called itself "Reform." In the United States, the movement became large and significant during the last two decades of the nineteenth century and adopted the name "Reform." The American movement was usually more extreme than its European counterpart.

In order to unify their positions regarding the envisaged changes in Jewish ritual and belief, the Reform rabbis in Germany convened assemblies of rabbis (1844, 1845, 1846) and later meetings of rabbis and lay leaders (the Synods, 1869, 1871). No agreement was reached in those discussions, as the gap between the moderate and the radical attitudes on many precepts of Judaism was apparently too wide to bridge. In Hungary, the supporters of the Reform movement adopted the name "Neology." The reforms it introduced were on the whole moderate. In Eastern Europe, the Reform movement did not become popular, and the proposed changes dealt more with ritual than with religious conception. In the Jewries of the Muslim countries, there never was a Reform movement. In the United States, the radical Pittsburgh Platform of 1885 provided a basis for most of the developing Reform congregations.

Toward the end of the nineteenth century, Liberal and Reform Jews started taking positions also on Jewish issues that were not of a purely religious nature, such as the expanding Zionist movement, which they fiercely opposed.

### The Historical-Positivist Approach

The proponents of the historical-positivist approach, who lived mostly in Central and Western Europe, stood between the Orthodox and the Reform movements, although somewhat closer to the former. They considered the *Halakhah* to be an imposing religious historical creation. Most believed that it was rooted in divine revelation, but had undergone transformations in the course of Jewish history. Indeed, many regarded revelation as a continuing process, and not as a unique, one-time event. The outstanding representative of the historical-positivist approach was Zacharias Frankel, who from 1854 headed the Juedisch-Theologisches Seminar in Breslau. The advocates of historical positivism proposed moderate reforms, but they had difficulty establishing clear criteria for them. They insisted on belief in the *Halakhah*, but the pressures of modernization frequently pushed them to a middle position between Orthodoxy and Reform. Many maintain that the historical-positivist position, as developed in Germany, later influenced the Conservative movement in the United States.

### West European Orthodoxy

West European Orthodox Jews (like Liberal Jews) accepted the definition of Judaism as being a religion only, but their attitude toward Jewish religion was comprehensive. Most were close to the position of Moses Mendelssohn, one of the main figures of the Jewish enlightenment, who in his treatise *Jerusalem* (1783) asserted that Judaism was divine legislation revealed to the Jewish people by

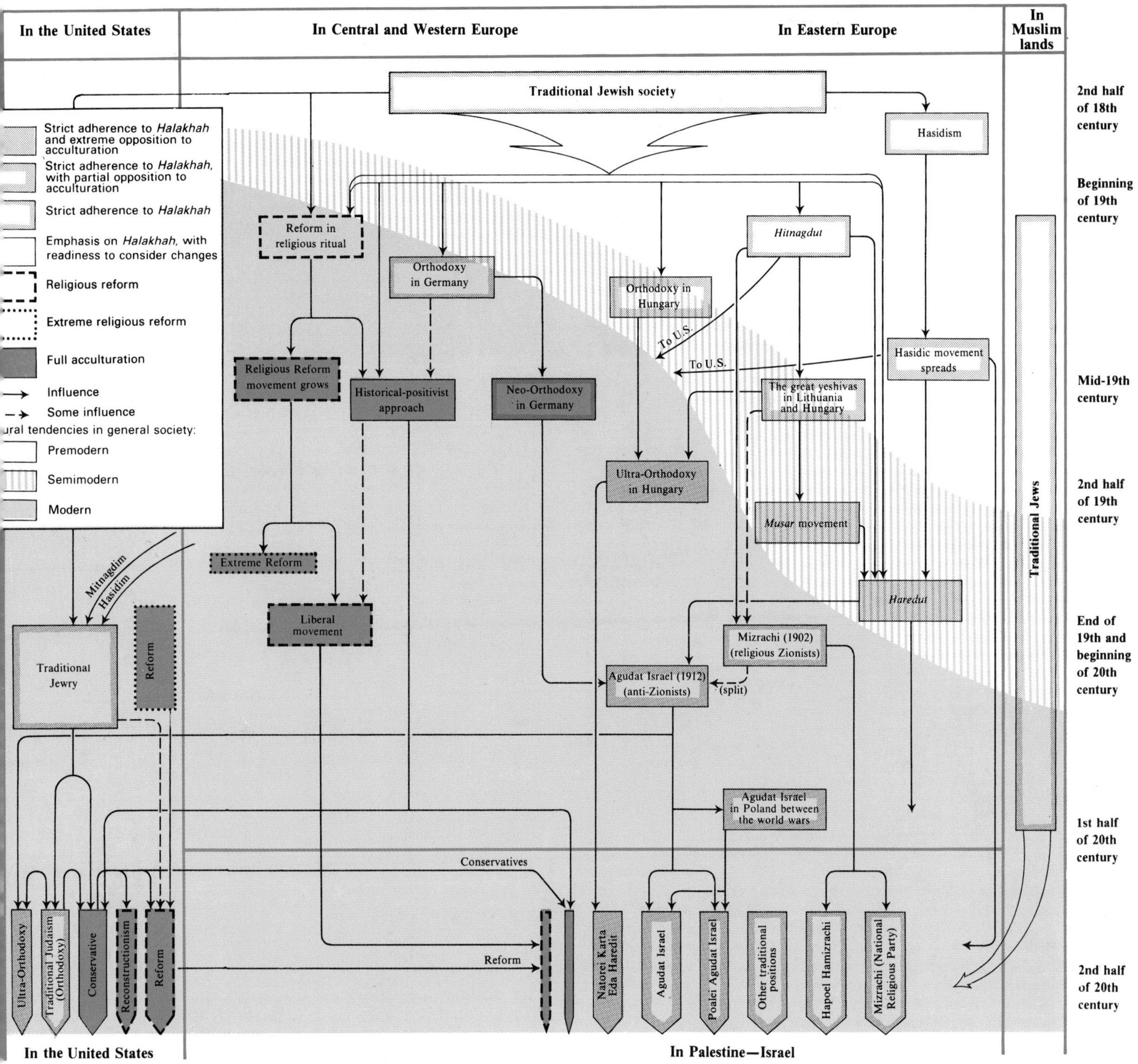


God at Mount Sinai and therefore binding, eternal, and irrevocable, both in its principles and in its laws. However, almost all West European Orthodox Jews accepted the principle of the separation of church (religion in general) and state, and regarded their duties as citizens as no less binding than their duties as Jews. It should be noted that among many Orthodox Jews in Western Europe (and later in America), religious practice often diverged from religious principle, objective conditions making full observance of all the details of classical Judaism exceedingly difficult.

A serious confrontation between the Orthodox and the Liberal (Reform) currents took place in Germany. In the nineteenth century, most Jewish communities in Germany, which originally had held the classical position, became Liberal. Synagogues that introduced organ playing during the religious service, for example, often lost the Orthodox members of their congregations.

## Neo-Orthodoxy in Germany

The leading figure of what came to be known in the second half of the nineteenth century as neo-Orthodoxy was Samson Raphael Hirsch, rabbi of the Orthodox segment of the Jewish community in Frankfurt-on-the-Main. Hirsch formulated the principle of *Torah im derech eretz*, meaning the Jewish classical observant position combined with full participation in general German cultural life. Hirsch and his followers were extreme on both counts: they were equally scrupulous in the total observance of *Halakhah* and mitzvoth, in the performance of their civic duties as German citizens, and in their participation in German culture. They organized their own communities (Secession Laws of 1876 and 1878), in which they isolated themselves in order to follow their own Jewish way of life. But not all those associated with neo-Orthodoxy agreed with the separatist tendencies of the Frankfurt group. For instance, Rabbi Azriel Hildesheimer, who served the neo-Orthodox community of Berlin (Adath Israel) and in 1873 founded an Orthodox rabbinical seminary there, was more open-minded about working with other Jewish institutions, and later became interested in the Hibbat Zion movement.

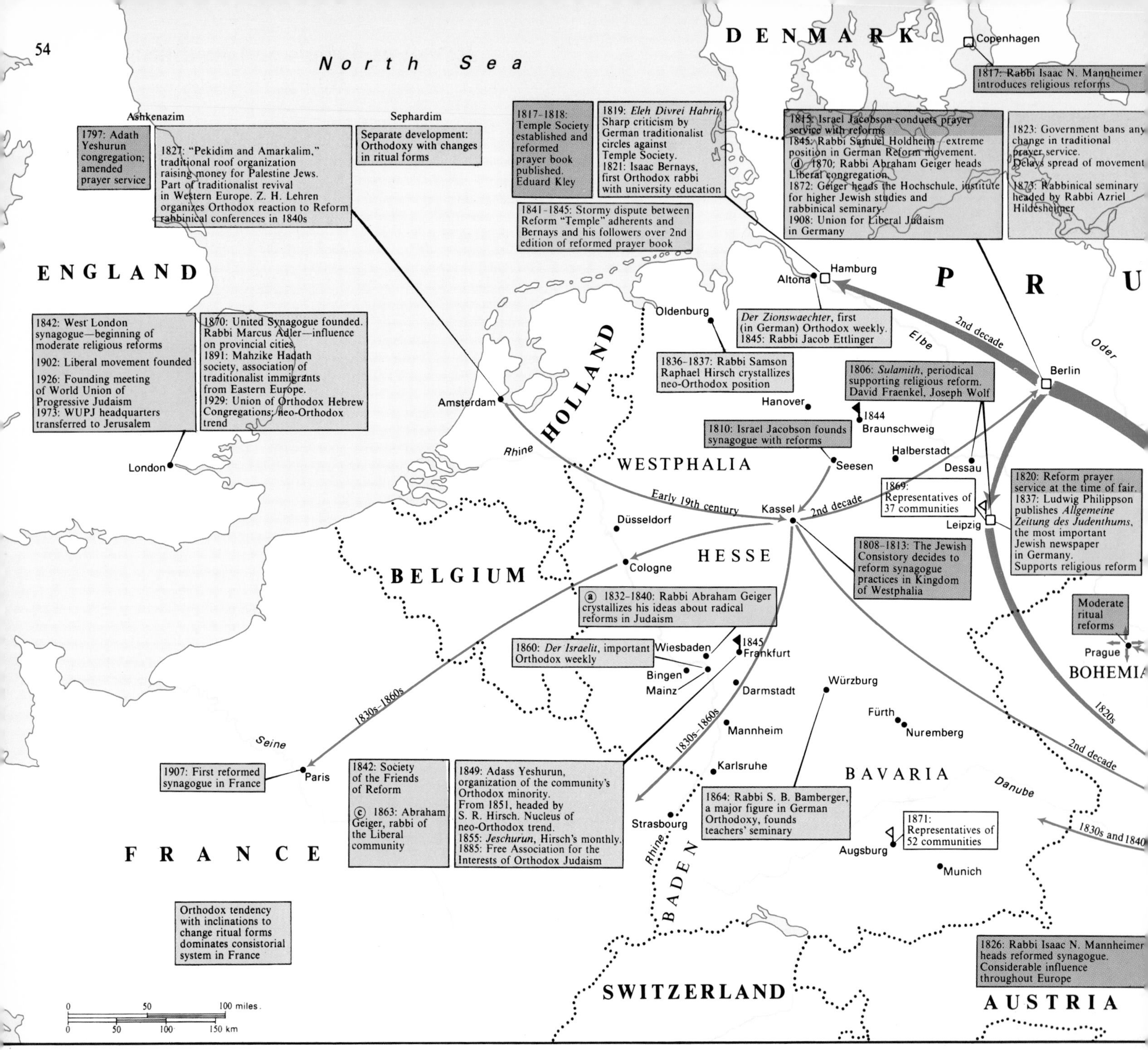
North Sea
DENMARK
Copenhagen
1817: Rabbi Isaac N. Mannheimer introduces religious reforms
Ashkenazim
Sephardim
1797: Adath Yeshurun congregation; amended prayer service
1827: "Pekidim and Amarkalim," traditional roof organization raising money for Palestine Jews. Part of traditionalist revival in Western Europe. Z. H. Lehren organizes Orthodox reaction to Reform rabbinical conferences in 1840s
Separate development: Orthodoxy with changes in ritual forms
1817–1818: Temple Society established and reformed prayer book published. Eduard Kley
1819: Eleh Divrei Habrit. Sharp criticism by German traditionalist circles against Temple Society. 1821: Isaac Bernays, first Orthodox rabbi with university education
1815: Israel Jacobson conducts prayer service with reforms 1845: Rabbi Samuel Holdheim extreme position in German Reform movement. ⓓ 1870: Rabbi Abraham Geiger heads Liberal congregation. 1872: Geiger heads the Hochschule, institute for higher Jewish studies and rabbinical seminary. 1908: Union for Liberal Judaism in Germany
1823: Government bans any change in traditional prayer service. Delays spread of movement
1873: Rabbinical seminary headed by Rabbi Azriel Hildesheimer
1841–1845: Stormy dispute between Reform "Temple" adherents and Bernays and his followers over 2nd edition of reformed prayer book
ENGLAND
Hamburg
Altona
PRU
Der Zionswaechter, first (in German) Orthodox weekly. 1845: Rabbi Jacob Ettlinger
Oldenburg
1842: West London synagogue—beginning of moderate religious reforms
1902: Liberal movement founded
1926: Founding meeting of World Union of Progressive Judaism 1973: WUPJ headquarters transferred to Jerusalem
1870: United Synagogue founded. Rabbi Marcus Adler—influence on provincial cities. 1891: Mahzike Hadath society, association of traditionalist immigrants from Eastern Europe. 1929: Union of Orthodox Hebrew Congregations; neo-Orthodox trend
HOLLAND
1836–1837: Rabbi Samson Raphael Hirsch crystallizes neo-Orthodox position
1806: Sulamith, periodical supporting religious reform. David Fraenkel, Joseph Wolf
2nd decade
Elbe
Oder
Berlin
Amsterdam
Hanover
1844
Braunschweig
1810: Israel Jacobson founds synagogue with reforms
Halberstadt
Rhine
London
WESTPHALIA
Seesen
Dessau
1869: Representatives of 37 communities
1820: Reform prayer service at the time of fair. 1837: Ludwig Philippson publishes Allgemeine Zeitung des Judenthums, the most important Jewish newspaper in Germany. Supports religious reform
Early 19th century
Kassel
2nd decade
Leipzig
Düsseldorf
1808–1813: The Jewish Consistory decides to reform synagogue practices in Kingdom of Westphalia
HESSE
Cologne
BELGIUM
ⓐ 1832–1840: Rabbi Abraham Geiger crystallizes his ideas about radical reforms in Judaism
Moderate ritual reforms
Prague
BOHEMIA
1860: Der Israelit, important Orthodox weekly
Wiesbaden
1845
Frankfurt
Bingen
Mainz
Darmstadt
Würzburg
1830s–1860s
Fürth
Nuremberg
1820s
Mannheim
Seine
1830s–1860s
2nd decade
Karlsruhe
BAVARIA
Danube
1907: First reformed synagogue in France
Paris
1842: Society of the Friends of Reform
ⓒ 1863: Abraham Geiger, rabbi of the Liberal community
1849: Adass Yeshurun, organization of the community's Orthodox minority. From 1851, headed by S. R. Hirsch. Nucleus of neo-Orthodox trend. 1855: Jeschurun, Hirsch's monthly. 1885: Free Association for the Interests of Orthodox Judaism
1864: Rabbi S. B. Bamberger, a major figure in German Orthodoxy, founds teachers' seminary
Strasbourg
1871: Representatives of 52 communities
Augsburg
1830s and 1840s
FRANCE
Rhine
BADEN
Munich
Orthodox tendency with inclinations to change ritual forms dominates consistorial system in France
1826: Rabbi Isaac N. Mannheimer heads reformed synagogue. Considerable influence throughout Europe
SWITZERLAND
AUSTRIA
0 50 100 miles
0 50 100 150 km

### Ultra-Orthodoxy in Hungary

The confrontation between reformers and defenders of classical Judaism in Hungary was particularly bitter. The latter developed a position that, because of its extremism, has been called ultra-Orthodoxy. Rabbi Moses Sofer ("Hatam Sofer"), yeshiva head in Pressburg, Hungary, from 1806 to 1839, laid the foundations of ultra-Orthodoxy by interpreting a passage in the Talmud, *Hehadash assur min ha-Torah* (New is forbidden by the Torah), as meaning that any innovation, merely by virtue of being an innovation, is forbidden—not only in religious practice, but in all aspects of life. Some of his disciples were even more extreme (decisions of the Michalovce Orthodox convention, 1865). The ultra-Orthodox secluded themselves in their own separate communities, opposed any form of general culture, and avoided any contact with Jewish groups that did not adopt their position. But their principles were not accepted by the majority of Hungarian Orthodox rabbis, and their influence was limited mainly to the northeastern part of the country.

The religious split inside Hungarian Jewry was officially recognized after the General Jewish Congress, held in Budapest from the end of 1868, whose aim had been to create an overall Jewish organization. Under pressure of the ultra-Orthodox, the Orthodox also rejected collaboration with the reformers, the Neologists. In the following years, Hungarian Jewry remained divided into three main camps: the Neologists, the Orthodox (including the ultra-Orthodox), and the Status Quo Ante communities, which remained loyal to classical Judaism but were ostracized by the Orthodox. Some of the ultra-Orthodox settled in Jerusalem, where they formed a small and extremist faction in the Orthodox community, the Natorei Karta. Another faction emigrated to the United States in the wake of World War II and, led by Rabbi Joel Teitelbaum (the "Satmar Rebbe"), attained a certain influence, notwithstanding its small size.

### Religious Zionism

The issue of Zionism also split religious Jewry. The neo-Orthodox, the ultra-Orthodox, Agudat Israel, and, on the opposite religious side, the Reform and Liberal movements vehemently opposed Zionism, each on its own grounds. But broad segments of traditional Jewry very enthusiastically adopted the Zionist idea. Important rabbis were among the leaders and activists of the Hibbat Zion movement. Later, the World Zionist Organization was one of the few modern Jewish institutions in which religious and nonreligious Jews coexisted and worked together in spite of the deep differences between them regarding the character of the Jewish society that Zionism aimed to create in Palestine.

In 1902, the Mizrachi organization was established, representing the classical religious position in the Zionist movement. Mizrachi quickly became a worldwide organization with hundreds of branches.

# Religious Trends and Institutions Among European Jews

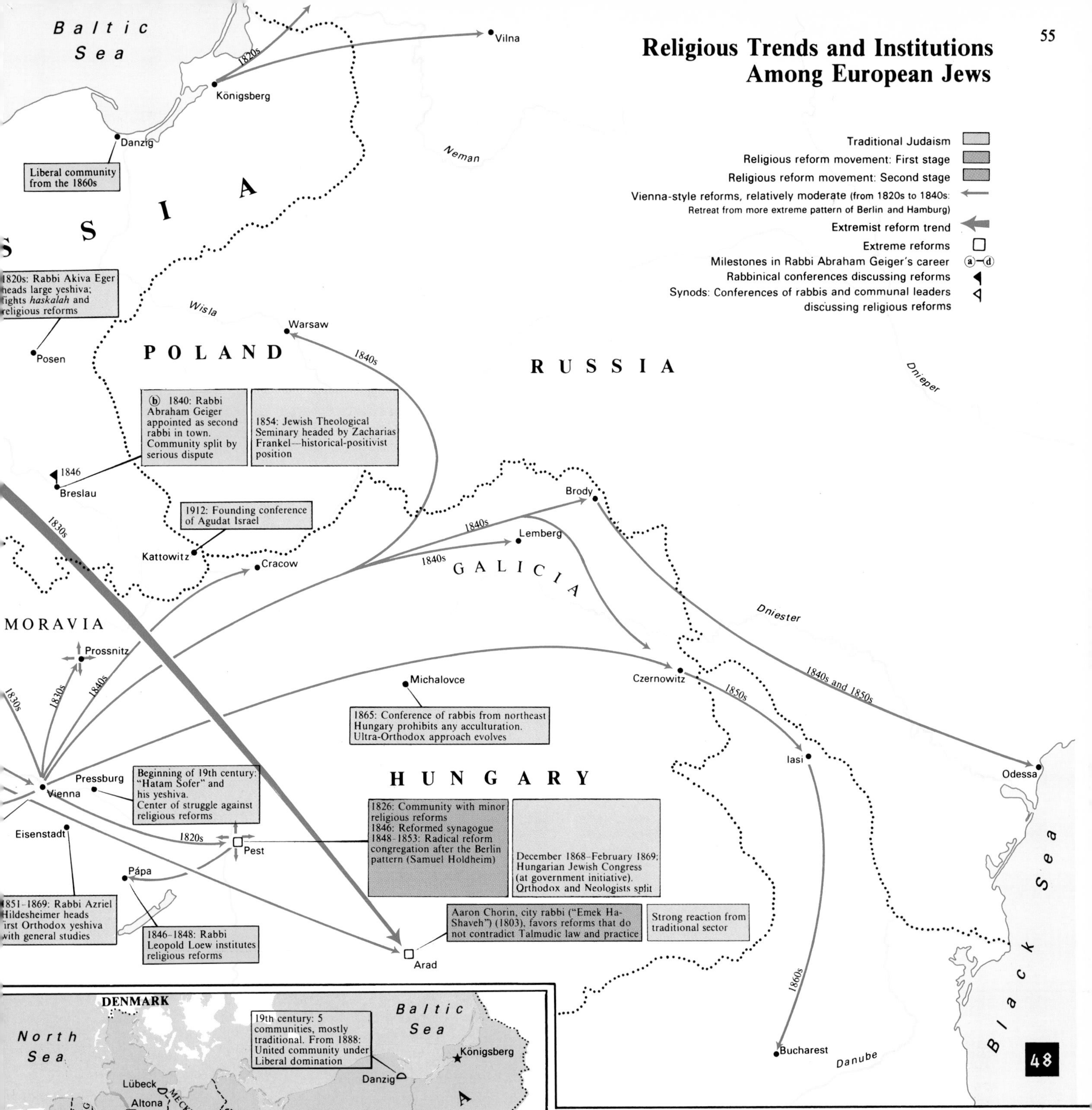

## Secessionist and Unified Communities in Germany

In most German states, only one Jewish community was permitted in each locale, and membership in it was compulsory. The Secessionist Law passed in Prussia (1876) and Hesse (1878) made possible the formation of separate communities, the secessionist communities, most of which were Orthodox. In some places, Liberal and Orthodox Jews agreed to form unified communities, in which the majority (in general, the Liberals) permitted the minority group to maintain its own institutions. In several cities—including Frankfurt, Berlin, and Cologne—unified and secessionist communities existed side by side, and Orthodox Jews belonged to either. Toward the end of the nineteenth century, a third type of religious congregation appeared in many larger cities, that of the new immigrants from Eastern Europe. They were mostly Orthodox, but did not fit in well in the older German Orthodox congregations.

## Orthodoxy (*Haredut*) in Eastern Europe

From the early nineteenth century on, the leadership of classical East European Judaism was well aware that new spiritual trends developing among Jews, such as the *haskalah* (Jewish enlightenment), ran counter to the traditional Jewish ways of life. But only toward the end of the century did it become clear that those new trends, which had meanwhile grown and assumed many different forms and expressions, posed a danger to classical Judaism. The response to this challenge was resistance, which expressed itself in the formation of the Russian–Polish brand of Orthodoxy, or *Haredut*, in which Mitnagdim and Hasidim collaborated.

The main forum of public activity of the *Haredim* was Agudat Israel, founded in 1912, with the participation of German neo-Orthodoxy. Its initial aim was to combat the growing Zionist movement. After World War I, Agudat Israel's main center of activity was in Poland, where it also participated in the public life of Polish Jewry, to protect the interests of its adherents.

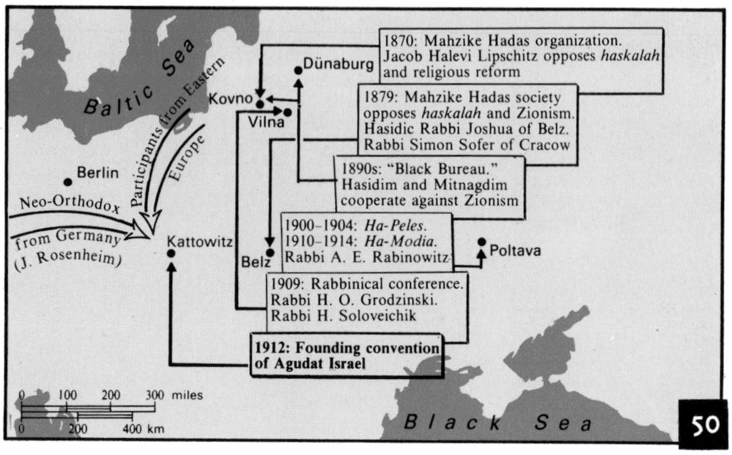


## The Great Yeshivas in Eastern Europe and the *Musar* Movement

*Rabbi Jonathan Eyebeschuetz*

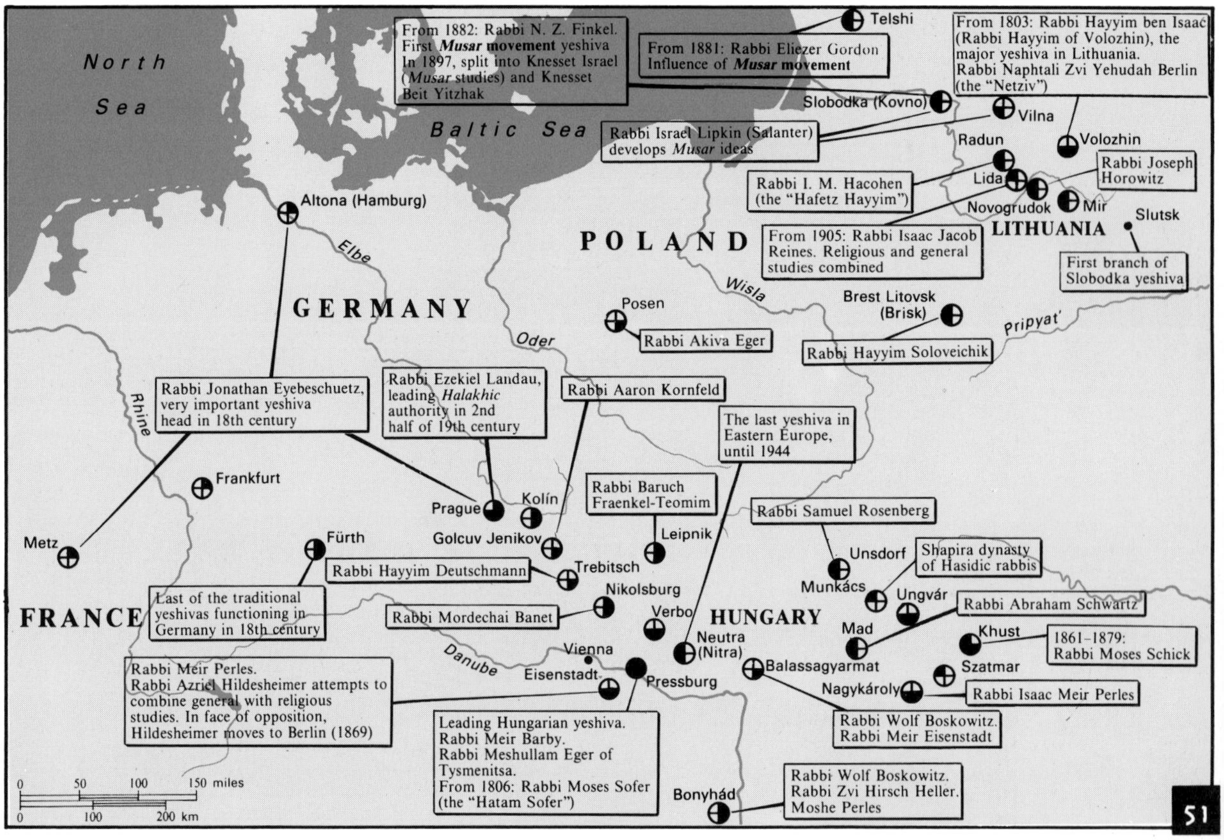


Period of activity:
- 18th century
- First half of 19th century
- Second half of 19th century
- First half of 20th century

Until the second half of the seventeenth century, the most important yeshivas were in Eastern Europe. Then they declined, and from the late seventeenth to the beginning of the nineteenth century, important centers of religious learning were established in Bohemia, Moravia, and several German-speaking countries. These yeshivas were dependent on the local communities, and were usually headed by the local rabbi. Outstanding among these heads of yeshivas was Rabbi Jonathan Eybeschuetz, who taught in Prague, Metz, and Altona. The students came from all over Europe, and they were exposed to the different spiritual trends of the time, such as Sabbateanism, on the one hand, and *haskalah*, on the other. In the nineteenth century, the "great yeshivas" were created in Eastern Europe.

### The Lithuanian Yeshivas

In 1803, Rabbi Hayyim ben Isaac (Volozhiner) established a yeshiva in Volozhin that soon became the outstanding academy of its kind in Lithuania. The yeshiva (later named Etz Hayyim) differed from others in at least two respects. It was independent of the local community, being supported by contributions from all over Lithuania and beyond. And it accepted only long-term students, most of whom came from outside Volozhin. Other yeshivas were established in Lithuania on similar principles, but none became as famous as Etz Hayyim.

The *Musar* movement developed out of the great yeshivas in the second half of the nineteenth century, under the inspiration of Rabbi Israel Lipkin of Salant, commonly known as Rabbi Israel Salanter. The movement stressed pietism and ethical-moral conduct, combined with formal religious studies. It reflected the spiritual restlessness characteristic of East European Jewry at the time, but it was an inner-directed trend that paid little attention to the non-Jewish environment and concentrated on traditional Jewish issues.

Toward the end of the nineteenth century, Rabbi Israel's influence gave rise to yeshivas of a new type, the *Musar* yeshivas. Existing yeshivas, too, adopted many of his ideas. The *Musar* yeshivas had a considerable influence on the religious life of East European Jewry.

### The Hungarian Yeshivas

Of far-reaching importance was the institution founded in Pressburg in 1807 by Rabbi Moses Sofer (the "Hatam Sofer"). In 1857, the authorities recognized it as a rabbinical seminary, thus qualifying its students for exemption from military service. In 1866, that exemption was extended to students at other Hungarian yeshivas.

The Pressburg yeshiva inculcated in its students total and unquestioning adherence to classical Judaism, and, together with related yeshivas, it played an important role in the struggle against the Reform movement in Hungary. After World War I, parts of Hungary were incorporated into other countries. Pressburg, in the Slovakian "Oberland," became part of Czechoslovakia (and was renamed Bratislava). The eastern part of the country was turned over to Rumania. The original yeshiva continued to function, and several new ones were established in a now smaller Hungary.

# The Hasidic Movement:

## Nineteenth Century

The political changes in Eastern Europe influenced the development of Hasidism during the nineteenth century. The partitions of Poland (where the movement originated) in the second half of the eighteenth century divided its Jewish population (and Hasidism) between Russia, Prussia, and Austria. In the nineteenth century, the movement spread to Hungary, Rumania, Palestine, and, later (to a smaller extent), the new centers of Jewish immigration in Western Europe and North America.

The structure of the Hasidic movement underwent changes in two main directions: first, the Hasidic leaders dispersed as the sons and grandsons of the founders themselves became heads of Hasidic groups; second, there arose large, new, and powerful Hasidic dynasties, whose influence extended far beyond the areas of their leaders' residence.

The major Hasidic centers in Europe were destroyed in the Holocaust. Hasidic leaders and followers who survived created new centers in the United States and Israel.

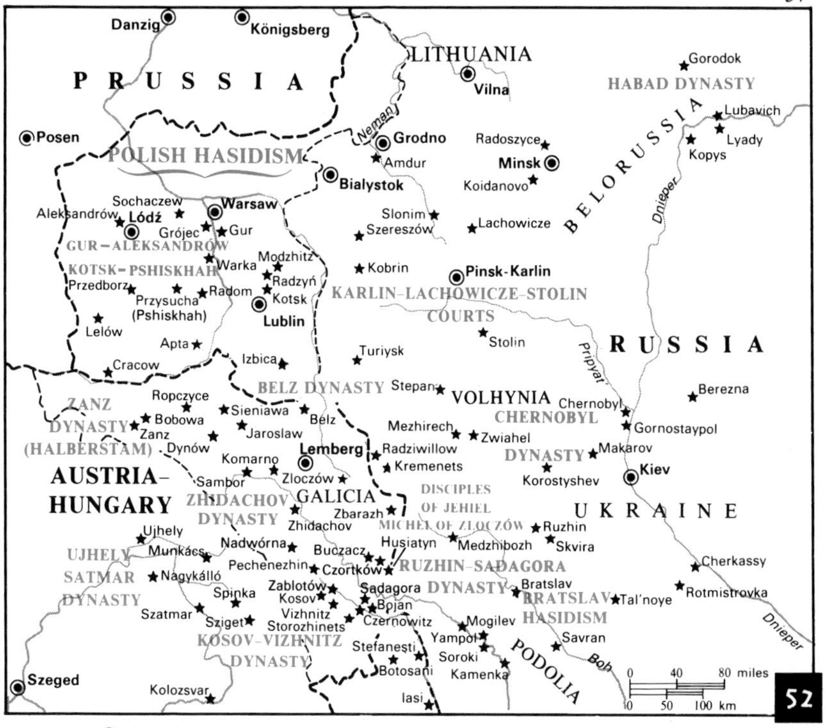


◉ Main city
★ Locality linked to Hasidism
– – Borders in mid-19th century
— — Borders of Poland and Galicia

# Reform and Conservative Congregations:

## Early Twentieth Century

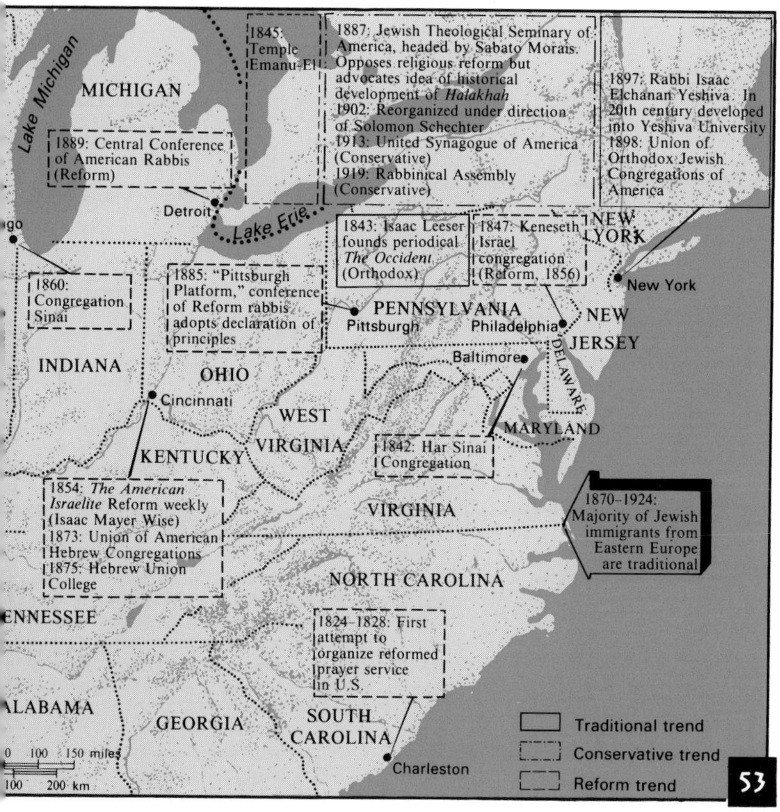


# The Religious Organization of American Jewry

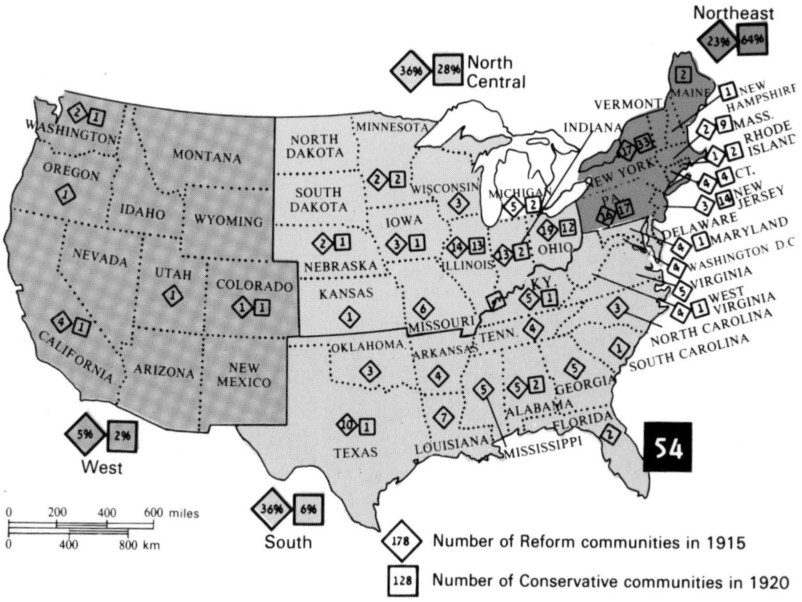


The few Jewish communities in North America in the eighteenth century were tradition-minded, although their members were not fully observant. From the mid-nineteenth century on, Jewish immigrants brought with them the ideas about ritual and religion being debated in Europe. In the American environment, these ideas developed along new lines, resulting in the different American Jewish religious currents.

The Reform movement developed during the period of the German Jewish immigration (the second half of the nineteenth century) and was the first to establish its own institutions (rabbinical seminary, union of congregations, and organization of rabbis). In 1885 at the Pittsburgh Convention, the Reform leaders (Isaac Mayer Wise and his colleagues) elaborated the principles of the American Reform movement, which was extreme in its position, adopting far-reaching religious innovations and, later, becoming anti-Zionist.

The large mass immigration from Eastern Europe brought mostly Orthodox Jews to the United States. But under the impact of American conditions, Orthodoxy lost most of the public overtones that characterized it in Eastern Europe. At the beginning of the twentieth century, a new religious movement was established, the Conservative trend. As formulated by Solomon Schechter, Conservative Judaism was traditional and strictly observant, but geared to the English language and the American way of life. It had a certain affinity with the European historical-positivist position.

Over the years, as American Jewry underwent deep changes, so did the different religious positions in its midst. There was a general trend away from Orthodoxy and toward more flexible religious positions, and second- and third-generation Jews became Reform, Conservative, or religiously indifferent. The religious trends themselves also changed. The Reform movement gradually became less radical, developing a new interest in tradition and, over the years, a more positive attitude toward Zionism. The Orthodox trend split in several directions, and many of its members were impelled to compromise regarding many mitzvoth, such as traveling on the Sabbath. The Conservative movement was caught in the middle, although it aspired to create an original position. One offshoot of it was the Reconstructionist movement, created in the 1930s and 1940s by Mordecai M. Kaplan.

Hasidic leaders who arrived in the United States before and after World War II established Hasidic courts and yeshivas there, and strengthened the classical Orthodox camp.

# Modern Antisemitism: Ideological Sources

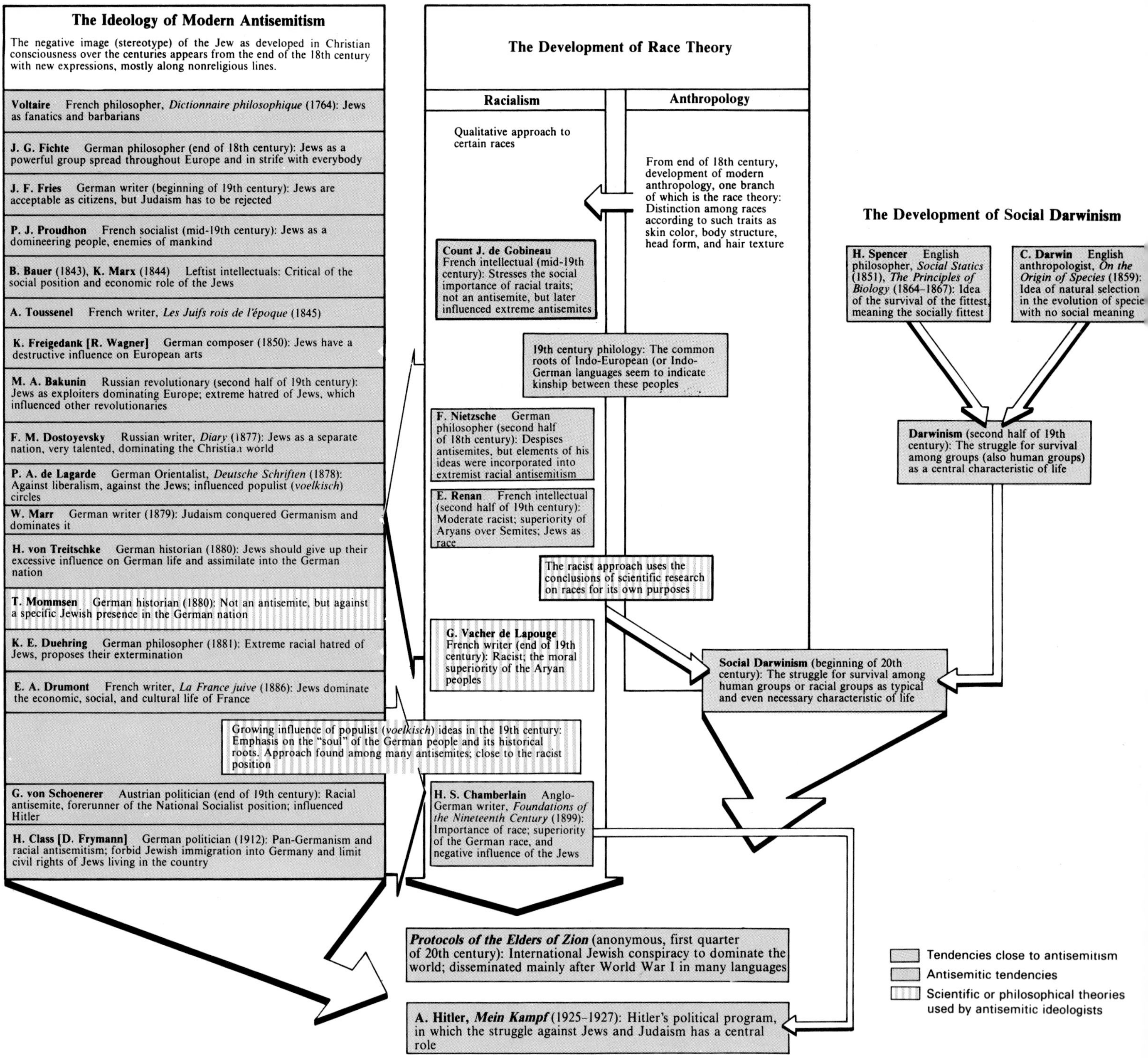
The Ideology of Modern Antisemitism
The negative image (stereotype) of the Jew as developed in Christian consciousness over the centuries appears from the end of the 18th century with new expressions, mostly along nonreligious lines.
Voltaire French philosopher, Dictionnaire philosophique (1764): Jews as fanatics and barbarians
J. G. Fichte German philosopher (end of 18th century): Jews as a powerful group spread throughout Europe and in strife with everybody
J. F. Fries German writer (beginning of 19th century): Jews are acceptable as citizens, but Judaism has to be rejected
P. J. Proudhon French socialist (mid-19th century): Jews as a domineering people, enemies of mankind
B. Bauer (1843), K. Marx (1844) Leftist intellectuals: Critical of the social position and economic role of the Jews
A. Toussenel French writer, Les Juifs rois de l'époque (1845)
K. Freigedank [R. Wagner] German composer (1850): Jews have a destructive influence on European arts
M. A. Bakunin Russian revolutionary (second half of 19th century): Jews as exploiters dominating Europe; extreme hatred of Jews, which influenced other revolutionaries
F. M. Dostoyevsky Russian writer, Diary (1877): Jews as a separate nation, very talented, dominating the Christian world
P. A. de Lagarde German Orientalist, Deutsche Schriften (1878): Against liberalism, against the Jews; influenced populist (voelkisch) circles
W. Marr German writer (1879): Judaism conquered Germanism and dominates it
H. von Treitschke German historian (1880): Jews should give up their excessive influence on German life and assimilate into the German nation
T. Mommsen German historian (1880): Not an antisemite, but against a specific Jewish presence in the German nation
K. E. Duehring German philosopher (1881): Extreme racial hatred of Jews, proposes their extermination
E. A. Drumont French writer, La France juive (1886): Jews dominate the economic, social, and cultural life of France
Growing influence of populist (voelkisch) ideas in the 19th century: Emphasis on the "soul" of the German people and its historical roots. Approach found among many antisemites; close to the racist position
G. von Schoenerer Austrian politician (end of 19th century): Racial antisemite, forerunner of the National Socialist position; influenced Hitler
H. Class [D. Frymann] German politician (1912): Pan-Germanism and racial antisemitism; forbid Jewish immigration into Germany and limit civil rights of Jews living in the country
The Development of Race Theory
Racialism
Anthropology
Qualitative approach to certain races
From end of 18th century, development of modern anthropology, one branch of which is the race theory: Distinction among races according to such traits as skin color, body structure, head form, and hair texture
Count J. de Gobineau French intellectual (mid-19th century): Stresses the social importance of racial traits; not an antisemite, but later influenced extreme antisemites
19th century philology: The common roots of Indo-European (or Indo-German languages seem to indicate kinship between these peoples
F. Nietzsche German philosopher (second half of 18th century): Despises antisemites, but elements of his ideas were incorporated into extremist racial antisemitism
E. Renan French intellectual (second half of 19th century): Moderate racist; superiority of Aryans over Semites; Jews as race
The racist approach uses the conclusions of scientific research on races for its own purposes
G. Vacher de Lapouge French writer (end of 19th century): Racist; the moral superiority of the Aryan peoples
H. S. Chamberlain Anglo-German writer, Foundations of the Nineteenth Century (1899): Importance of race; superiority of the German race, and negative influence of the Jews
The Development of Social Darwinism
H. Spencer English philosopher, Social Statics (1851), The Principles of Biology (1864–1867): Idea of the survival of the fittest, meaning the socially fittest
C. Darwin English anthropologist, On the Origin of Species (1859): Idea of natural selection in the evolution of specie with no social meaning
Darwinism (second half of 19th century): The struggle for survival among groups (also human groups) as a central characteristic of life
Social Darwinism (beginning of 20th century): The struggle for survival among human groups or racial groups as typical and even necessary characteristic of life
Protocols of the Elders of Zion (anonymous, first quarter of 20th century): International Jewish conspiracy to dominate the world; disseminated mainly after World War I in many languages
A. Hitler, Mein Kampf (1925–1927): Hitler's political program, in which the struggle against Jews and Judaism has a central role
Tendencies close to antisemitism
Antisemitic tendencies
Scientific or philosophical theories used by antisemitic ideologists

One of the great hopes of nineteenth-century Jewry was that the strengthening of liberal trends in the general society would banish the age-old hatred of the Jews. Indeed, certain developments during the 1860s and early 1870s in France, England, Germany, Austria-Hungary, and even Russia seemed to bear out this hope. But from the end of the 1870s, changes occurred in the attitude of large sectors of European society to the Jews, and the old tensions between non-Jews and Jews reappeared. A review of the century from 1850 to 1945 reveals a fateful symmetry between the progress that the Jews in Europe made toward civil equality and the growing animosity of the general society toward them: the better the civil status of the Jews, the more threatening the antisemitic manifestations erupting in the very society that was recognizing them as full citizens.

New expressions of animosity against Jews now appeared—"modern" antisemitism—although the older forms continued to exist among certain segments of the population. Modern antisemitism had many carriers: social groups pushed aside by modern development, especially in the larger cities; urban dwellers who in the late nineteenth century acquired full political rights but remained economically deprived; the lower middle class, which feared absorption into the proletariat; and intellectuals trying to understand and explain the transformations that modern society was undergoing. These and other groups resented the new Jewish presence in modern society: Jews were now full citizens, quite successful culturally and economically, yet somehow they seemed to be different, keeping to themselves and enjoying all the advantages of modern society without fulfilling all the conditions implicit in their new rights. The resentment of the antisemites was fed by populist ideas tinged with romantic and nationalistic overtones. New racial and social theories influenced public opinion. Most of these had little to do with the Jews: Social Darwinism, race anthropology, or the social conditions in the new large cities had no intrinsic antisemitic significance. Under the influence of the old anti-Jewish hatred, however, they became the components of modern antisemitism. The traditional negative stereotype of the Jew remained unchanged, although it now assumed new expressions. The classical image of the base, cringing Jew was replaced by one of the mighty, aggressive, domineering Jew. It was now said that a historical struggle existed between the Jews and the Germans (Marr, 1879) or between Judaism and Christianity (Dostoyevsky, 1877), in which the Jews had the upper hand. It was said that the Jews dominated the German stock exchanges and its press (Treitschke, 1880) and French finances (Drumont, 1886). Racial theory, which became popular in the late nineteenth century, was used to maintain that there were basic differences between the Jewish race and the Aryan race, the latter being represented in its purest form by the Germanic peoples (Chamberlain, 1899). Close to this line of thought was the belief in the existence of an international Jewish conspiracy to take over the world. This canard was spread throughout Europe before and especially after World War I, receiving its most elaborate exposition in the book *The Protocols of the Learned Elders of Zion.*

Whereas in the older kind of antisemitism religious beliefs had played a central role, modern antisemitism was secular in its views and its solutions to the Jewish threat. Some of these solutions were "moderate": the total integration of the Jews into the general society, meaning also renunciation of their specific group characteristics (Treitschke, 1880). The more extreme attitude advocated curtailing the civil rights of the Jews and halting Jewish immigration from Eastern Europe (Class, 1912). The most extreme approach declared that there was no possibility of integrating the Jews and that, in any event, such a step was highly dangerous for German society, and therefore the best solution was the "elimination" of the Jews (Duehring, 1881; Hitler, 1919).

Antisemitic agitation reached a peak in the last two decades of the nineteenth century, and subsided early in the twentieth. But it did not disappear, and the new antisemitic ideas gradually insinuated themselves into the general anti-Jewish feeling of many segments of the general population, capable of flaring up again under the right conditions.

The emergence of modern antisemitism was a bitter disappointment to those sectors of Jewish society that had integrated culturally and socially into the general society. They had trouble coping with the new phenomenon, because its irrational and intolerant character was so out of tune with the liberal and enlightened principles that were part of the ideological basis for Jewish acculturation. Only gradually did they create organizations aimed (among other things) at combating antisemitism by means of the law and of publicity, such as the Centralverein in Germany (1893) or the Anti-Defamation League of B'nai B'rith in the United States (1913). But these measures could not halt the growth of modern antisemitism or change its character. The more extreme trends prevailed and brought about the near extermination of European Jewry by the Germans (with the active or passive participation of other European peoples) during World War II.

Antisemitism did not disappear in the second half of the twentieth century, although it changed many of its slogans. The emergence of the Jewish state, the continuing Arab–Israeli conflict, and the perpetuation of historical anti-Jewish attitudes created new expressions of contemporary antisemitism. Although the Zionist movement and the state of Israel served as central themes in this new version, the antisemites of the late twentieth century made little distinction between Jews in Israel and Jews elsewhere. The tension between Jews and non-Jews seemed to be a persistent phenomenon, its forms changing according to circumstances.

## Antisemitic Parties and Organizations in Europe:

Late Nineteenth and Early Twentieth Centuries

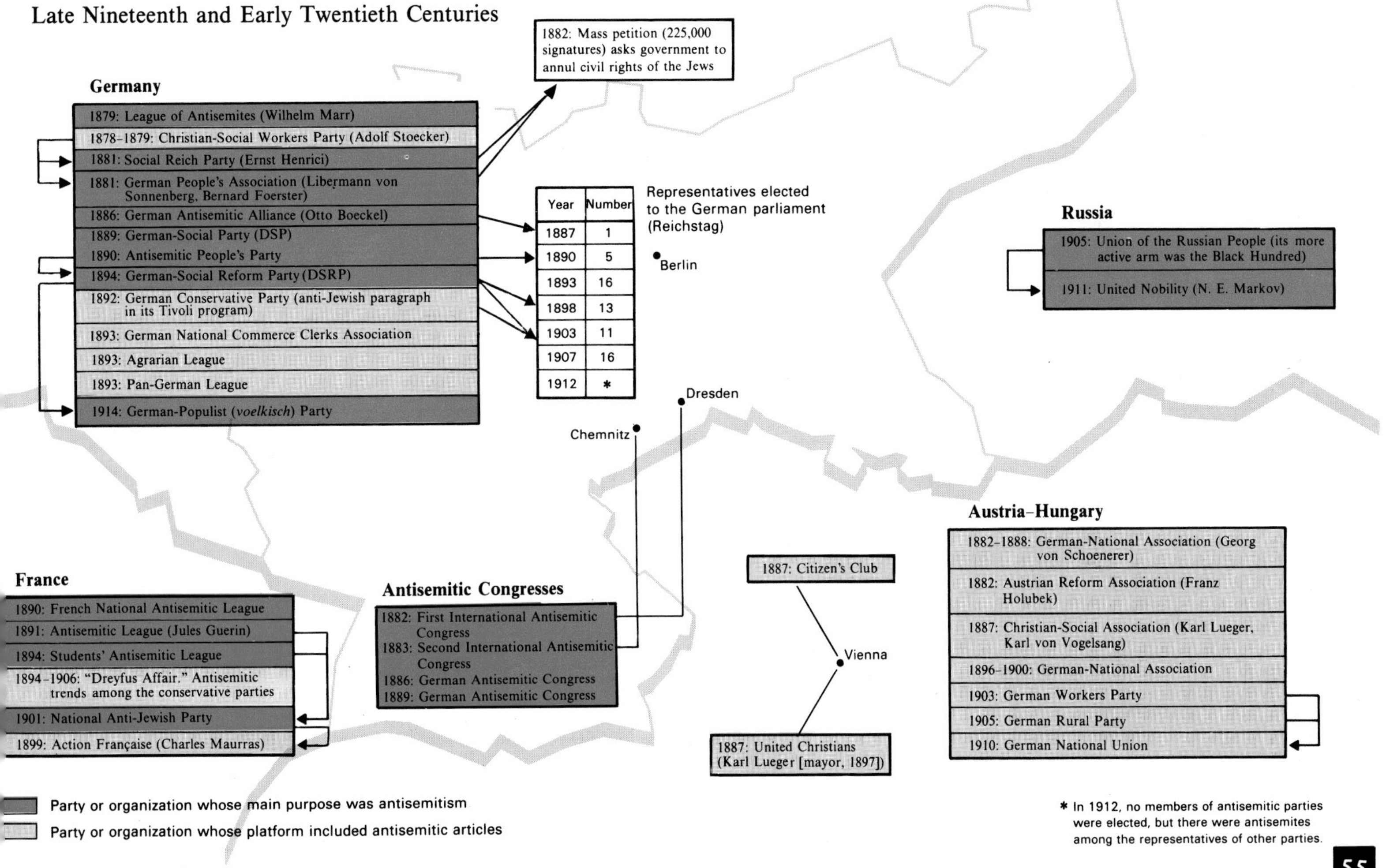

1882: Mass petition (225,000 signatures) asks government to annul civil rights of the Jews
Germany
1879: League of Antisemites (Wilhelm Marr)
1878–1879: Christian-Social Workers Party (Adolf Stoecker)
1881: Social Reich Party (Ernst Henrici)
1881: German People's Association (Libermann von Sonnenberg, Bernard Foerster)
1886: German Antisemitic Alliance (Otto Boeckel)
1889: German-Social Party (DSP)
1890: Antisemitic People's Party
1894: German-Social Reform Party (DSRP)
1892: German Conservative Party (anti-Jewish paragraph in its Tivoli program)
1893: German National Commerce Clerks Association
1893: Agrarian League
1893: Pan-German League
1914: German-Populist (voelkisch) Party
Year
Number
1887
1
1890
5
1893
16
1898
13
1903
11
1907
16
1912
*
Representatives elected to the German parliament (Reichstag)
Berlin
Dresden
Chemnitz
Russia
1905: Union of the Russian People (its more active arm was the Black Hundred)
1911: United Nobility (N. E. Markov)
Austria–Hungary
1882–1888: German-National Association (Georg von Schoenerer)
1882: Austrian Reform Association (Franz Holubek)
1887: Christian-Social Association (Karl Lueger, Karl von Vogelsang)
1896–1900: German-National Association
1903: German Workers Party
1905: German Rural Party
1910: German National Union
1887: Citizen's Club
Vienna
1887: United Christians (Karl Lueger [mayor, 1897])
France
1890: French National Antisemitic League
1891: Antisemitic League (Jules Guerin)
1894: Students' Antisemitic League
1894–1906: "Dreyfus Affair." Antisemitic trends among the conservative parties
1901: National Anti-Jewish Party
1899: Action Française (Charles Maurras)
Antisemitic Congresses
1882: First International Antisemitic Congress
1883: Second International Antisemitic Congress
1886: German Antisemitic Congress
1889: German Antisemitic Congress
Party or organization whose main purpose was antisemitism
Party or organization whose platform included antisemitic articles
* In 1912, no members of antisemitic parties were elected, but there were antisemites among the representatives of other parties.

55

The new ideology of antisemitism found diverse public, political, and organizational expressions in different European countries. Antisemitic congresses were held in Germany in the 1880s, antisemitic parties were formed in Germany and Austria–Hungary, and antisemitic planks were included in the political platforms of existing parties even if antisemitism was not their main political aim (the Conservative Party in Germany, 1892).

The May Laws against the Jews promulgated in Russia in 1882 indicated a new and much more negative attitude by the government toward its large Jewish population and helped to create the conditions that led to the anti-Jewish riots in later years. The Dreyfus Affair in France (from 1894) injected antisemitism into the discussion of the political problems of the Third Republic, causing a sharp increase in antisemitism among all strata of the French population. French antisemites did not organize into separate parties, but were active in the existing right-wing parties.

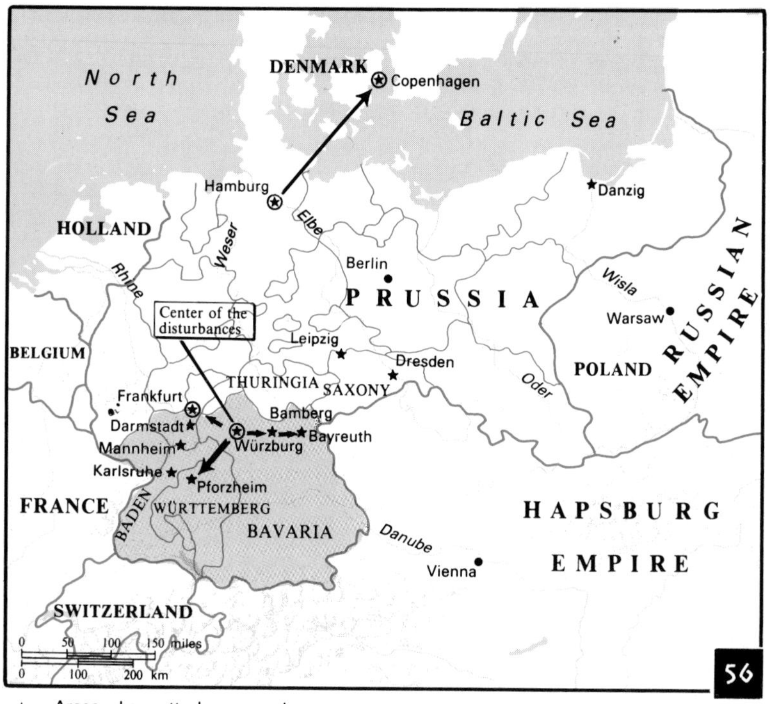


★ Areas where attacks occurred

⊛ Areas where attacks caused great damage

▭ Main area of ferment

## The "Hep-Hep" Disturbances, 1819

The violent expression of anti-Jewish feeling gradually intensified from the nineteenth to the twentieth century.

In 1819, a wave of riots, called the "Hep-Hep" disturbances, erupted against Jews in Germany and Denmark. The first incidents occurred in southern Germany, and from there they spread to the north and west. Jews were attacked in several large cities—Frankfurt, Hamburg, Copenhagen—and in small towns and villages in Baden, Württemberg, and Bavaria, where they had been living for many generations. The main reasons for the incidents were traditional anti-Jewish hatred and economic tensions. Much damage was done to Jewish property, but few Jews were physically attacked. Almost without exception, the authorities took steps against the assailants and order was quickly restored. Nevertheless, the "Hep-Hep" incidents deeply affected the Jews and caused many of those who had been hopeful about Jewish acculturation in German society to reevaluate their situation. An indirect outcome of the incidents was the formation of the Gesellschaft zur Foerderung der Wissenschaft des Judentums (Society for the Advancement of Jewish Scholarship) in 1819, which over the years generated a new cultural trend in Jewry on the road to modernization.

*Sketch of "Hep-Hep" disturbances of 1819, printed in Frankfurt at that time.*

## Anti-Jewish Riots During the Revolutions of 1848

Serious anti-Jewish riots erupted in many of the countries swept by the 1848 revolutions, from Alsace in France to Hungary. The riots were not related to the revolutions and their aims or to Jewish participation in them in several important cities, such as Berlin and Vienna. They were a product of the general situation of upheaval, and the rioters were mainly farmers, apprentices, and members of the lower middle class. The authorities and the social groups active in the revolutions—the middle class and the intellectuals—acted forcefully to stop the riots.

The riots of 1848 were a source of bitter disillusionment for the Jews, especially those who had supported the revolutions. Many concluded that it was more realistic to seek a better future elsewhere and migrated to the United States, where they were part of the immigrant group that came to be known as "the '48ers."

★ Anti-Jewish attacks ⊛ Serious anti-Jewish attacks ▭ March–April Period of disturbances

## Anti-Jewish Riots in Russia, 1881–1906

An additional chapter in the increasingly bloody story of anti-Jewish violence unfolded in Russia in the last half of the nineteenth century. Serious anti-Jewish riots broke out in Odessa in 1871 (on a smaller scale, also earlier). In 1881, after the assassination of Czar Alexander II, a wave of anti-Jewish riots swept southern Russia. A result of the old antagonism between non-Jews and Jews, this violence reflected the general unrest following the czar's death. There is no evidence that the authorities had a hand in the riots, but the railway network being built in southern Russia facilitated the movement of the rioters from place to place. The attacks spread to Poland and the Baltic states, continuing until 1884.

A much more murderous wave of riots swept the Pale of Settlement between 1903 and 1906. Although the government may not have encouraged the incidents, persons or groups connected with the authorities organized or planned the attacks, and soldiers or policemen participated. From Kishinev in 1903 to Siedlce in 1906, thousands of Jews were killed or wounded and Jewish life in Russia was seriously disrupted. The mass emigration of Jews from Russia and Poland to Western Europe and across the ocean to America during these years attested to the panic that had seized the Jewish communities.

In the late nineteenth and early twentieth centuries, anti-Jewish riots occurred also in some Muslim countries. They were generally connected with the tensions arising from the domination of these countries by European powers and the internal upheaval caused by the gradual process of modernization. In Algeria, where the Jews acquired French citizenship in 1870 (Crémieux Decree), they were sporadically attacked until the beginning of the twentieth century. The French occupation of Morocco in 1912 generated severe riots against the Jews of Fez.

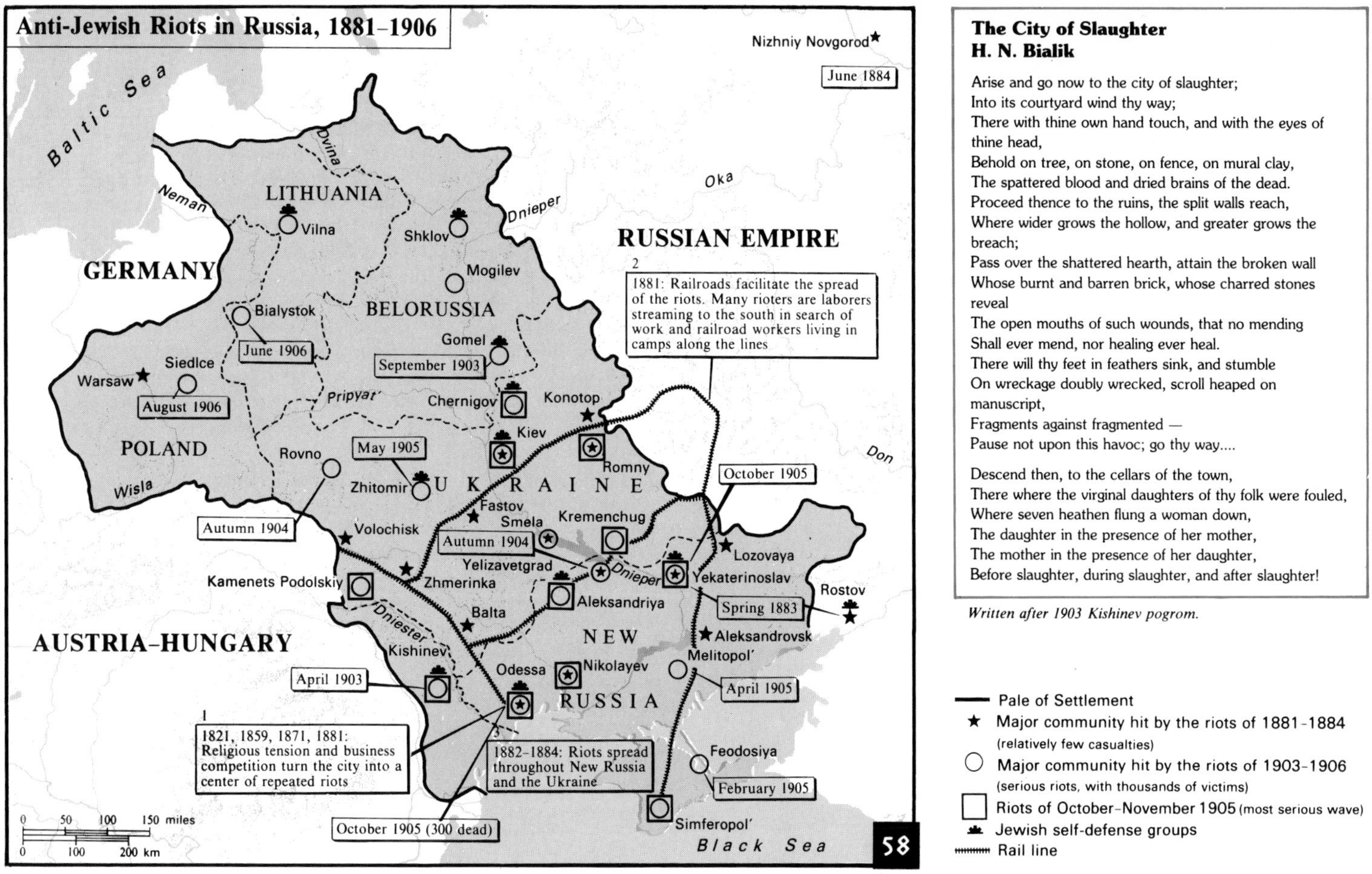


**The City of Slaughter**
**H. N. Bialik**

Arise and go now to the city of slaughter;
Into its courtyard wind thy way;
There with thine own hand touch, and with the eyes of thine head,
Behold on tree, on stone, on fence, on mural clay,
The spattered blood and dried brains of the dead.
Proceed thence to the ruins, the split walls reach,
Where wider grows the hollow, and greater grows the breach;
Pass over the shattered hearth, attain the broken wall
Whose burnt and barren brick, whose charred stones reveal
The open mouths of such wounds, that no mending
Shall ever mend, nor healing ever heal.
There will thy feet in feathers sink, and stumble
On wreckage doubly wrecked, scroll heaped on manuscript,
Fragments against fragmented —
Pause not upon this havoc; go thy way....

Descend then, to the cellars of the town,
There where the virginal daughters of thy folk were fouled,
Where seven heathen flung a woman down,
The daughter in the presence of her mother,
The mother in the presence of her daughter,
Before slaughter, during slaughter, and after slaughter!

*Written after 1903 Kishinev pogrom.*

# Blood Libels:

## Nineteenth and Twentieth Centuries

The blood libel—the accusation that Jews use Christian blood, especially that of children, for various ritual purposes, such as the preparation of matzot (unleavened bread for Passover)—was one of the most terrible superstitions to develop in the Middle Ages. The fact that the blood libel continued into the modern period showed how deeply hatred of Jews was ingrained in popular culture. Although in modern times, blood libels happened mostly in the more backward parts of Europe, their influence was widely felt, since they were the subject of trials that received extensive newspaper coverage.

Antisemitic groups everywhere exploited the blood libels for their own purposes, even when they did not believe in them. Several blood libels were of particular significance in modern times.

### The Damascus Affair

In February 1840, a French monk and his Muslim servant disappeared in Damascus, and the local Jews were accused of murdering them to use their blood. Through collaboration between the French consul in Damascus and the Turkish governor, several Jewish notables were imprisoned and tortured. Two died and the others "confessed," but since they were unable to produce the corpses, the tortures continued. Leading Jewish figures, including Adolphe Crémieux in France and Moses Montefiore in England, asked their governments to intercede on behalf of the Damascus Jews, who were finally freed.

### The Beilis Affair

Menahem Mendel Beilis was accused in March 1913 of killing a Christian boy near Kiev, Russia. Various antisemitic leaders and organizations demanded a blood-libel trial. The trial, held in Kiev in 1913, attracted international attention. A jury acquitted Beilis.

### The Leo Frank Affair

Blood-libel accusations were heard even in the United States, although rarely. In April 1913, Leo Frank of Atlanta, Georgia, was accused of killing a fourteen-year-old girl. In an atmosphere charged with prejudice, in which Frank's Jewishness featured prominently, he was tried, convicted, and sentenced to death. When the governor of Georgia commuted his sentence to a life term, an incensed mob took Frank from jail and lynched him.

In 1928, a little Christian girl vanished in Massena, New York, a few days before Yom Kippur. The police were questioning the local rabbi about the alleged Jewish custom of using the blood of Christian children for ritual purposes, and a mob was preparing a lynching, when the girl was found in the nearby woods, unharmed.

Jewish organizations and individuals reacted vigorously against the resurgent blood libel, taking steps to persuade the authorities and the public that such accusations were utterly false.

# Judaic Studies:

## Nineteenth and Twentieth Centuries

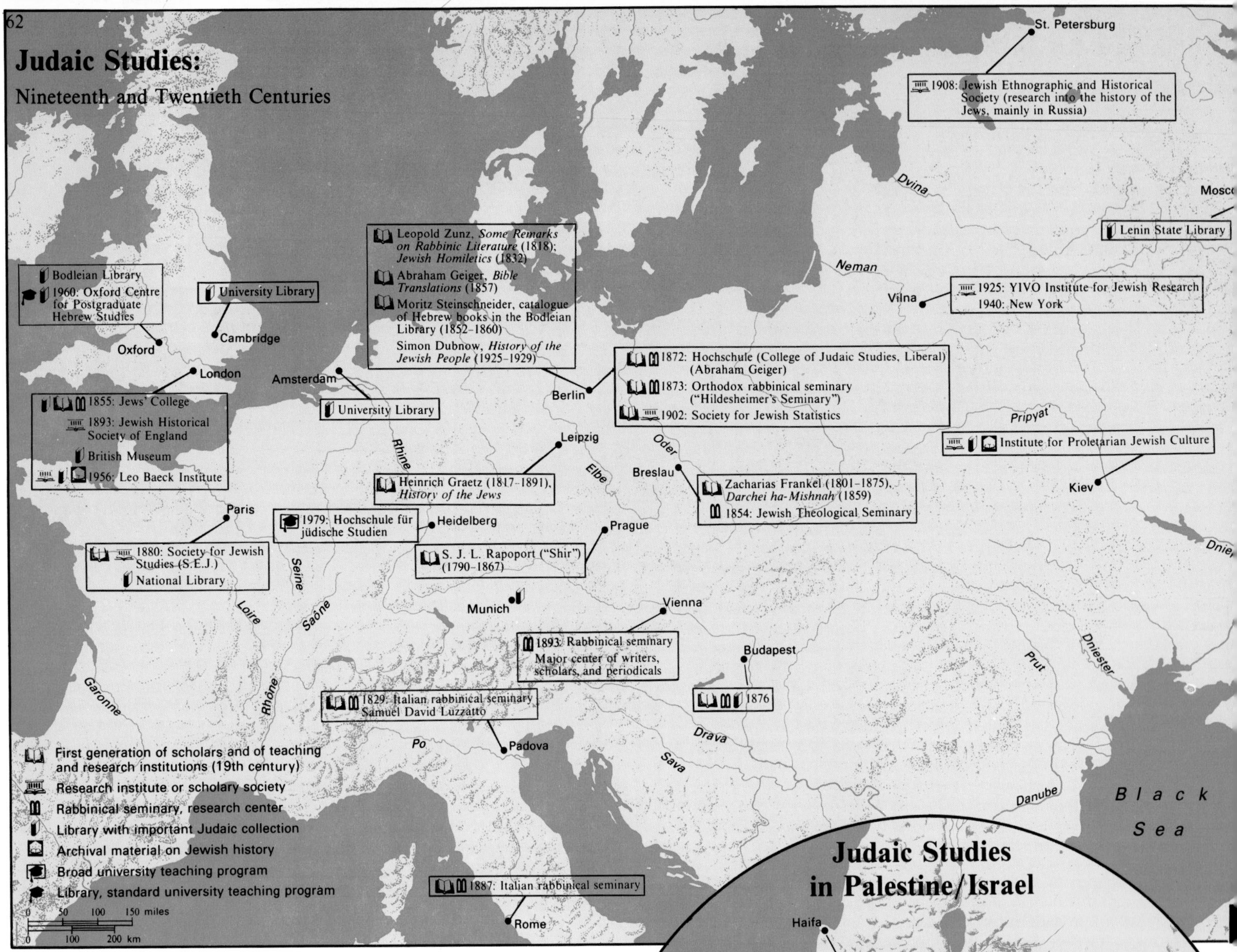


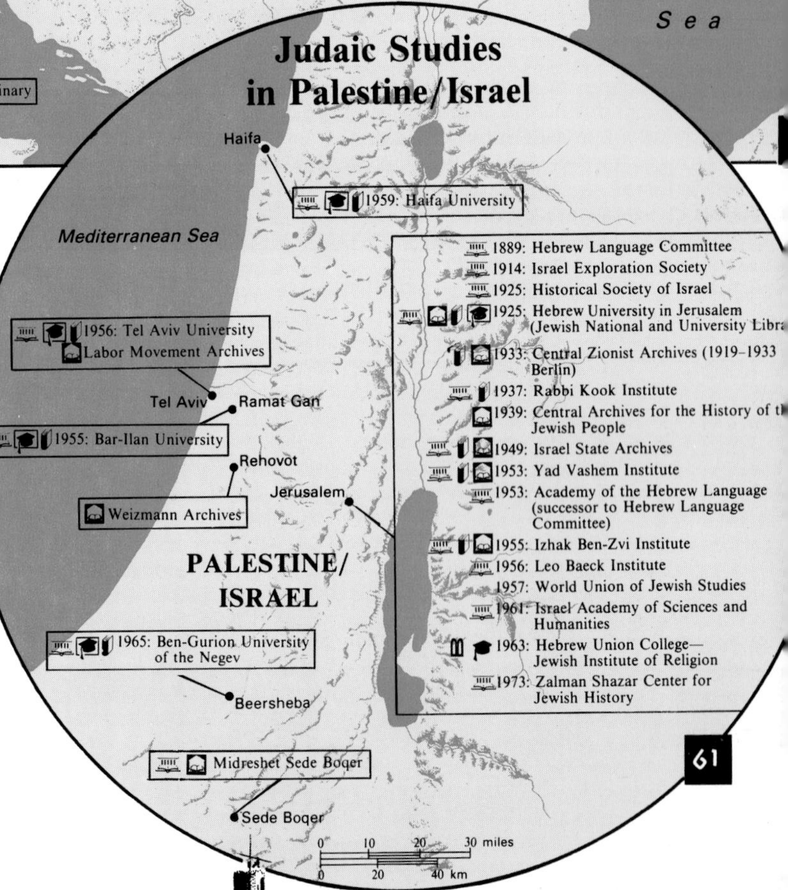


61

The "Science of Judaism" (*Wissenschaft des Judenthums*) was an outgrowth of the Jewish enlightenment. The scholars engaged in it aimed to examine the cultural and spiritual creations of Judaism, using the scientific methods and tools developed in Europe since the eighteenth century. A major definer of its aims was Leopold Zunz, who in 1818 drew up a plan dividing the scientific study of Judaism according to different themes. He and other scholars of his time (Zacharias Frankel, Samuel David Luzzatto, Solomon Rapoport, Abraham Geiger) established the gradual division of the Science of Judaism into various fields, including history, literature, philology, and philosophy.

The attitude to the Science of Judaism varied over the years. The first generation of scholars, especially those from Western and Central Europe, were inclined to regard their work as no different from the study of any past culture—such as ancient Greek or Roman culture—whose spiritual creativity had ended. They tried to show that Judaism, like other great classical cultures, was part of and had helped to shape Western civilization. This provided an additional argument in support of Jewish integration into modern European society: the spiritual contribution of the Jewish people. Different aims for the Science of Judaism were formulated from the second half of the nineteenth century by a new generation of Jewish scholars, who regarded the study and research of Judaism as an expression of a living, developing culture.

The progress of Jewish studies led to the creation of institutions of higher learning, scientific journals, and societies of scholars. In the late twentieth century, the different branches of Jewish studies were included in the curricula of universities around the world, especially in the United States and Israel. The results of the scientific labors of hundreds of scholars were published in many languages. Archives and a large and ever-growing body of literature were the source material for the continuing work in the Science of Judaism.

*The new Hebrew University campus on Mt. Sco*

# Judaic Studies in North America

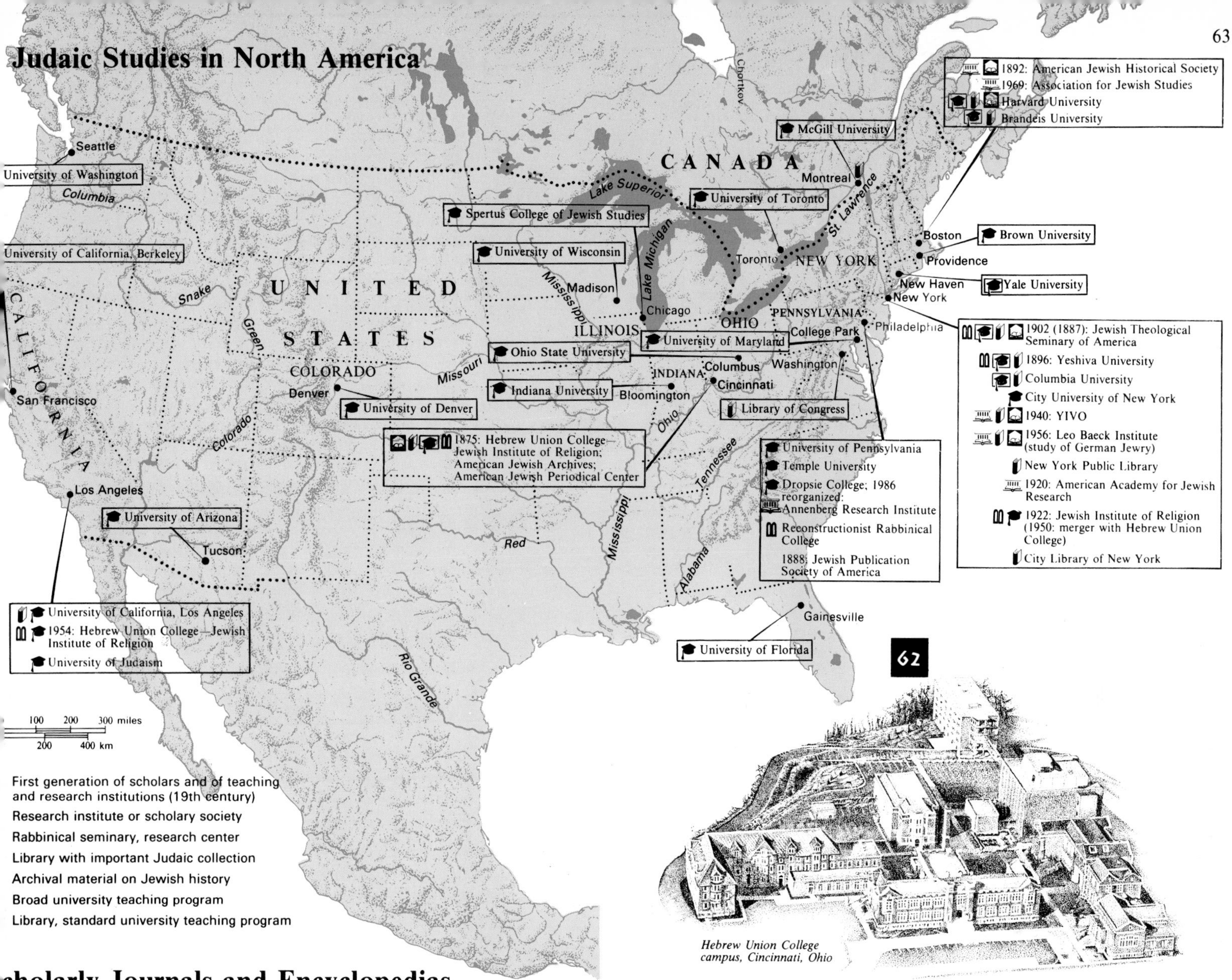
CANADA
UNITED STATES
CALIFORNIA
COLORADO
ILLINOIS
INDIANA
OHIO
PENNSYLVANIA
NEW YORK
Seattle
University of Washington
Columbia
University of California, Berkeley
Snake
Green
San Francisco
Colorado
Los Angeles
University of California, Los Angeles
1954: Hebrew Union College—Jewish Institute of Religion
University of Judaism
University of Arizona
Tucson
Rio Grande
Red
Denver
University of Denver
Missouri
Spertus College of Jewish Studies
University of Wisconsin
Madison
Mississippi
Lake Michigan
Lake Superior
Chicago
Ohio State University
Columbus
Indiana University
Bloomington
Cincinnati
Ohio
1875: Hebrew Union College—Jewish Institute of Religion; American Jewish Archives; American Jewish Periodical Center
Tennessee
Alabama
University of Maryland
College Park
Washington
Library of Congress
Philadelphia
University of Pennsylvania
Temple University
Dropsie College; 1986 reorganized: Annenberg Research Institute
Reconstructionist Rabbinical College
1888: Jewish Publication Society of America
Gainesville
University of Florida
Toronto
University of Toronto
Montreal
McGill University
St. Lawrence
Chortkov
Boston
Brown University
Providence
New Haven
Yale University
New York
1892: American Jewish Historical Society
1969: Association for Jewish Studies
Harvard University
Brandeis University
1902 (1887): Jewish Theological Seminary of America
1896: Yeshiva University
Columbia University
City University of New York
1940: YIVO
1956: Leo Baeck Institute (study of German Jewry)
New York Public Library
1920: American Academy for Jewish Research
1922: Jewish Institute of Religion (1950: merger with Hebrew Union College)
City Library of New York
100 200 300 miles
200 400 km
First generation of scholars and of teaching and research institutions (19th century)
Research institute or scholary society
Rabbinical seminary, research center
Library with important Judaic collection
Archival material on Jewish history
Broad university teaching program
Library, standard university teaching program
62

*Hebrew Union College campus, Cincinnati, Ohio*

# cholarly Journals and Encyclopedias

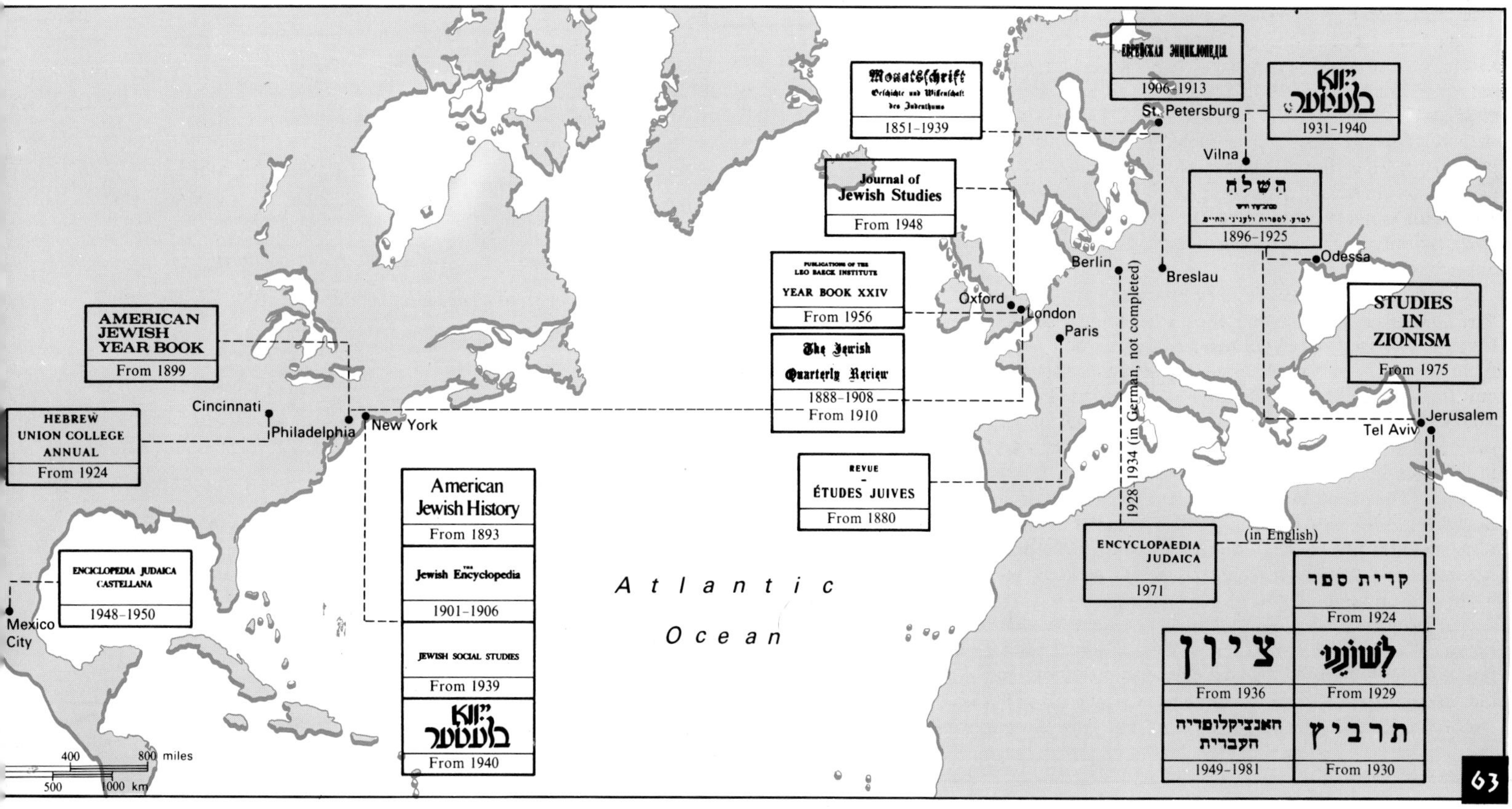
Monatsschrift für Geschichte und Wissenschaft des Judenthums
1851–1939
1906–1913
St. Petersburg
1931–1940
Vilna
1896–1925
Odessa
Journal of Jewish Studies
From 1948
Publications of the Leo Baeck Institute
YEAR BOOK XXIV
From 1956
The Jewish Quarterly Review
1888–1908
From 1910
Oxford
London
Paris
Berlin
Breslau
1928–1934 (in German, not completed)
STUDIES IN ZIONISM
From 1975
Jerusalem
Tel Aviv
REVUE ÉTUDES JUIVES
From 1880
ENCYCLOPAEDIA JUDAICA
1971
(in English)
From 1924
From 1936
From 1929
1949–1981
From 1930
AMERICAN JEWISH YEAR BOOK
From 1899
Cincinnati
Philadelphia
New York
HEBREW UNION COLLEGE ANNUAL
From 1924
American Jewish History
From 1893
The Jewish Encyclopedia
1901–1906
JEWISH SOCIAL STUDIES
From 1939
From 1940
ENCICLOPEDIA JUDAICA CASTELLANA
1948–1950
Mexico City
Atlantic Ocean
400 800 miles
500 1000 km
63

# Languages of the Jews

A specific language is a main characteristic of a human group with its own historical consciousness and continuity. The Jewish people carried to its Diasporas two closely related languages: Hebrew and Aramaic. Over the centuries, the Jews also adopted (and adapted) the local languages of different countries, infusing into them Hebrew or Aramaic words or sentence structures, writing them in Hebrew characters, and taking them along to new Diasporas. The resultant variety of "Jewish languages" makes their definition difficult, but in general they can be defined as the languages used by Jews in particular places, but differing up to a point from the vernaculars from which they evolved. Clear-cut examples are Yiddish and Ladino. Each was adopted in one country (Germany and Spain, respectively, in the Middle Ages) and taken by wandering Jews to other places, where they differed from the local tongues, although they were slightly influenced by them. They were the main languages of the Jews, both for daily use and for literary expression, and were written in Hebrew characters. The Judeo-Arabic language (in its various dialects) had many of the same characteristics.

Another type of language spoken by smaller Jewish groups were local dialects, generally residues of older tongues. These had certain unique elements, but they can hardly be considered "Jewish languages." Among them were remnants of Judeo-Greek, spoken by Jews on some Aegean islands, and the *Haketia* dialect (a mixture of old Castilian, Hebrew, and Arabic), used in parts of northern Morocco.

With the gradual modernization of the Jewish people and their acculturation to the general society, most Jewish languages fell into disuse, becoming the second tongue of fewer and fewer Jews. Yiddish underwent a different process: at the beginning of the modernization of Jewish society, there was a most interesting flowering of Yiddish, first in Eastern Europe, and then, from there, among the Jewish immigrants in the United States and in other major centers of Jewish life—London, Paris, Montreal, and Buenos Aires, for example. Besides being the spoken language, Yiddish was the language of newspapers, belles-lettres, theater, and Jewish political groups. In the years between the two world wars, it was either the first or the second language of about two-thirds of the Jewish people. Later, the Holocaust and the sociological changes in the new Jewish settlements sent Yiddish into a sharp decline.

Another impressive development was the renaissance of the Hebrew language. Although the use of Hebrew had shrunk drastically, it had never ceased, even for everyday purposes. The Enlightenment produced a renewed interest in Hebrew among both Jews and non-Jews. The Zionist movement set as one of its major objectives the use of Hebrew as the spoken language of the Jewish people. The two main centers of the evolution of modern Hebrew were Eastern Europe and Palestine. In Eastern Europe, the development was primarily literary, while Yiddish remained the main spoken language. In Palestine, Hebrew provided the necessary link among Jews of different origins even before the Zionist enterprise got under way, and it later became the spoken language of the Jewish population and the second language of the non-Jewish population. From the mid-twentieth century, efforts have been made to establish Hebrew as the Jewish language of Diaspora Jewry.

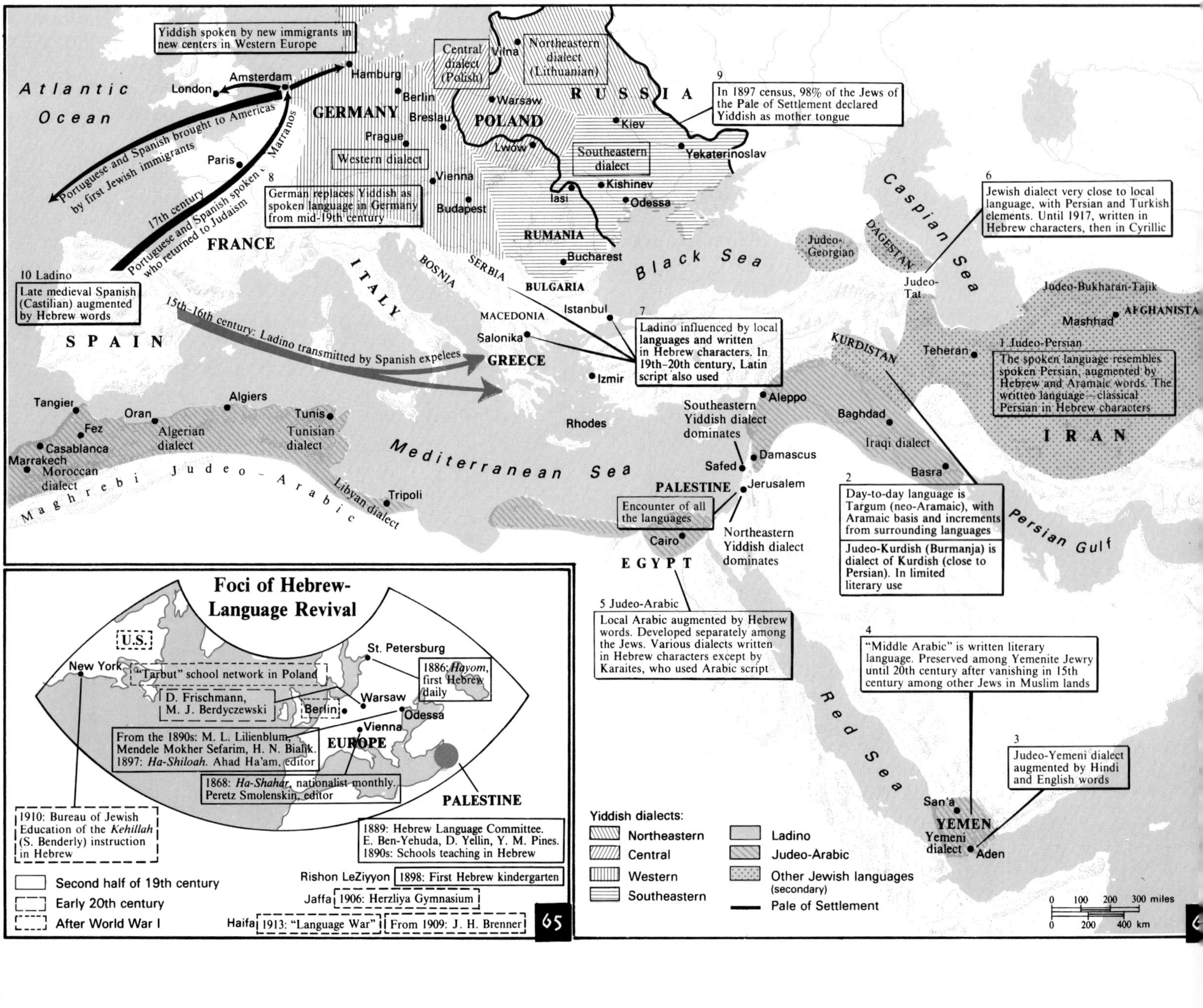

# The Jewish Press

culation of Jewish Newspapers and Periodicals, 1970

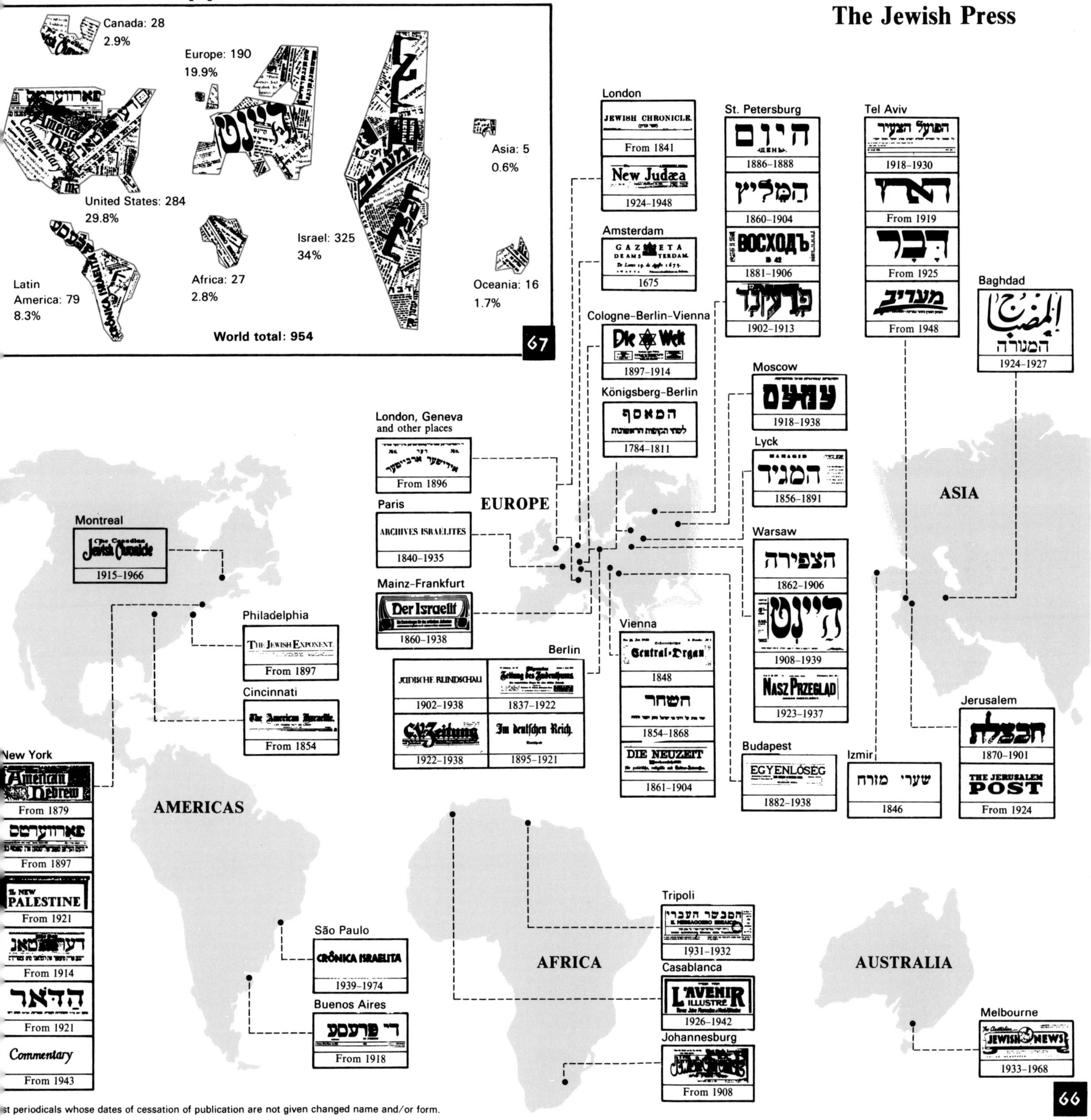



st periodicals whose dates of cessation of publication are not given changed name and/or form.

Jewish newspapers were published in most of the languages of the lands in which Jews lived, as well as in most of the Jewish tongues. They began to appear in the second half of the seventeenth century (*Gazeta de Amsterdam*, in Ladino, 1675), but the first Jewish daily appeared only at the end of the nineteenth century (*Hayom*, in Hebrew, St. Petersburg, 1886). For the Jews in Western Europe and later in the Americas, the Jewish newspaper was usually the "second newspaper," a weekly read in addition to the general daily newspaper. Especially important were the *Allgemeine Zeitung des Judenthums* (Germany, 1837–1922) and the *Jewish Chronicle* (London, founded in 1841). In Eastern Europe, Jewish newspapers (in Yiddish or Hebrew) were often the "first newspaper" of the Jewish public. Both types existed in the United States, at least during the first part of the twentieth century. In 1916, the daily *Forverts* (in Yiddish, New York) reached a circulation of 200,000 copies.

All types of journalism were represented among the Jewish newspapers, from the popular press (*Haynt*, in Yiddish, Warsaw, 1908–1939) to high-caliber scholarly journals. Most Jewish political and ideological currents published their own periodicals, such as the Zionist *Die Welt* (in German, 1897–1914), the socialist *Der Yiddisher Arbeiter* (in Yiddish, end of nineteenth century), and *The American Israelite* (founded in 1854), which for many years was the unofficial organ of the American Reform movement. Some publications walked a fine line between Jewish and general concerns, such as *Commentary* (New York, founded in 1945).

Jewish journalism reflected the multifaceted cultural character of the majority of modern Jewry, integrated into the general society while retaining a measure of Jewish identity—to which the Jewish newspapers themselves attested. Until 1929, more than 5,000 Jewish journals had appeared throughout the world, although some were short-lived. In the 1970s, about 950 Jewish journals were published. Naturally, the major center of the Jewish press through the 1980s was Israel, and the major language, Hebrew.

# Civil-Rights and Welfare Organization

## Late Nineteenth and Early Twentieth Centuries

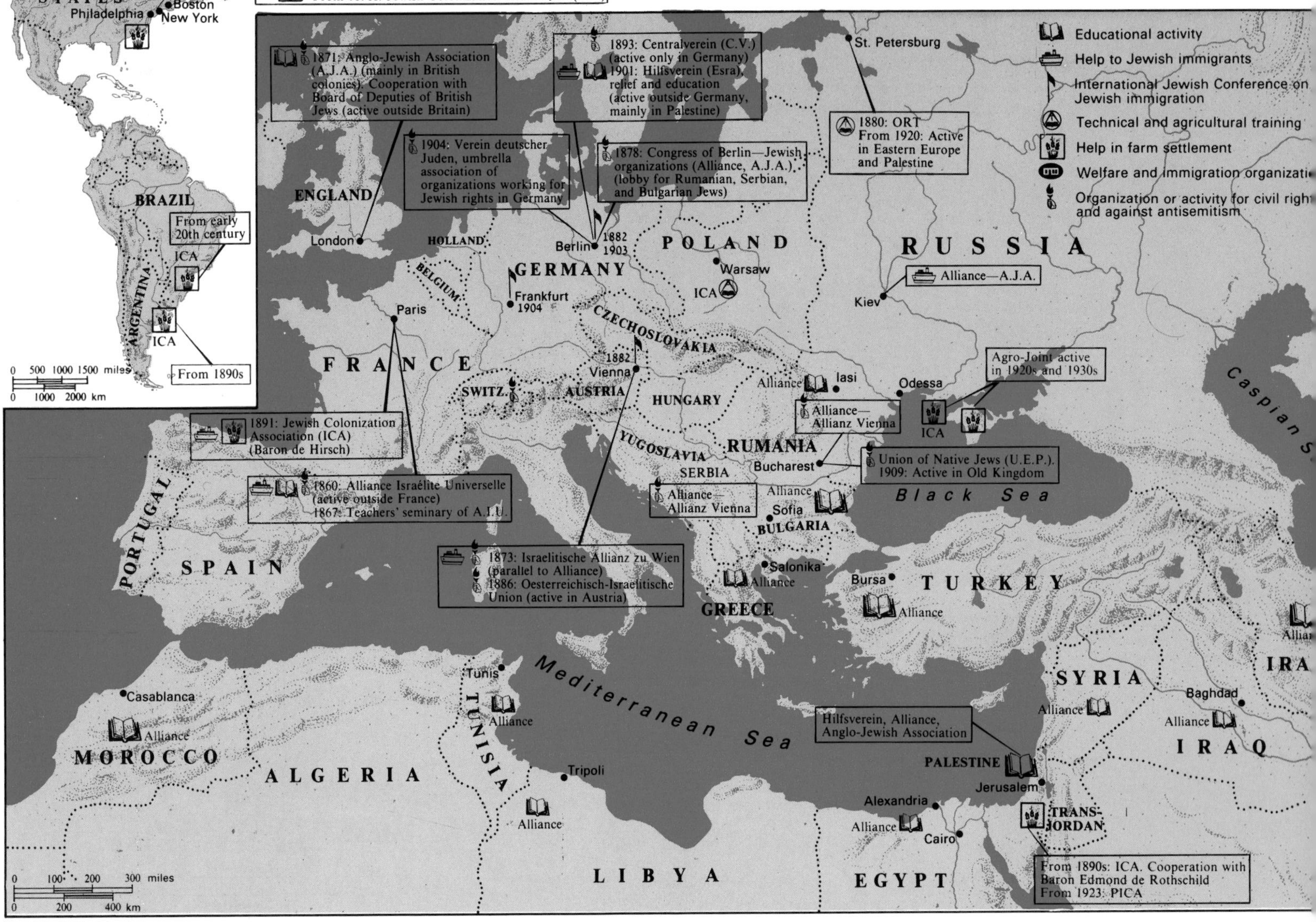


Post World War I borders

New organizational forms, reflecting the cultural and social integration of the Jews in Western and Central Europe, appeared in the second half of the nineteenth century. Some of the new organizations worked for civil rights for Jews. Linked to that was another aim: fostering educational enterprises for the Jews.

The first and prototypal association of the new kind was the Alliance Israélite Universelle (Paris, 1860). It was founded in the wake of several anti-Jewish incidents, chiefly the Damascus Affair (1840) and the Mortara case (1858). There was a certain ambivalence in the activity of the Alliance and similar organizations: they represented a segment of Jewish society already well integrated into the general environment, and no longer defining itself as Jewish in the traditional sense. At the same time, those Jews evinced a new interest in and a sense of responsibility for Jews and Jewish matters.

The leadership of most of these organizations was oligarchic: small groups of well-established notables who preferred to act quietly behind the scenes. The organizations were no longer local, as most had been in earlier times, but of national or even international scope. They differed somewhat in their concerns and operations. The Alliance Israélite Universelle promoted both civil rights and education—religious and general (in French)—for the Jews, the educational aspect becoming predominant toward the end of the nineteenth century. The German Centralverein (1893) and the American Jewish Committee (1906) were not involved in education. The German Hilfsverein (1901) worked primarily for education (in German). The Centralverein operated only in Germany; the Alliance Israélite Universelle, the Anglo-Jewish Association, and the Hilfsverein operated mostly outside the countries in which they were based. The American Jewish Committee was active abroad as well as in the United States.

As Jewish migration mounted in the 1880s and the needs of the Jewish immigrants grew, the Jewish civil-rights organizations became active in this sphere, too, collaborating with Jewish welfare and colonization associations. The latter were another new form of Jewish organization, of which the most important were the Jewish Colonization Association (ICA, 1891), the Hebrew Immigrant Aid Society (HIAS, 1909), and the powerful American Jewish Joint Distribution Committee (1914). Outstanding Jewish figures headed various organizations; men like Baron Maurice de Hirsch, Jacob H. Schiff, Louis Marshall, and Baron Edmond de Rothschild were typical. The achievements of these associations were enormous. In critical circumstances, such as war or persecution of Jews, some took steps to protect the threatened communities, while others mobilized funds on their behalf.

Together, these associations were typical of a phase of modern Jewish organizational history, in which the integration of the Jews into general society was considered the central goal. A later phase was the development of organizations and parties like the socialist Bund and the Zionist movement, based on divergent ideological conceptions about modern Jewish life and, as mass movements, very different in their organizational structures. The relations between these and the civil-rights and welfare organizations were usually strained; nevertheless, in certain circumstances they cooperated with one another.

# The Roots of Jewish Nationalism:

## Late Nineteenth Century

The gradual integration of certain sectors of the Jewish people into the general society had contradictory results. One group reduced the Jewish component of its self-definition to a minimum, or even lost it and assimilated. Another sector began considering its Jewishness in the light of new ideas absorbed from the general culture, but emphasized the Jewish component. From the latter trend emerged, after some elaboration, Jewish nationalism—a very complex interplay of Jewish and general ideological influences, with various ramifications.

Among the general influences were the unification of Italy and of Germany, and the national awakening of peoples in the Balkans and Austria–Hungary, all of which caused the Jews to think about themselves in national terms. East European Jewish intellectuals were led in that direction by reflections about the vagueness of Jewish self-definition in the conditions of modern European society: neither the traditional position nor the new Jewish attitudes in Western Europe seemed to offer satisfactory answers. Another factor was the historical attachment of the Jews to the land of Israel, now sharpened by the growing attention of the European powers to the Holy Land. Some Jewish notables, such as Moses Montefiore, began to take an interest in Palestine and in the situation of the Jews there, without considering Jewish immigration to Palestine or nationalistic conceptions about modern Jewry.

The various ideological components—questions about the specific character of the Jewish people, reflections about the relation between modern Jewry and nationalism, interest in Palestine and in the Jewish community there—often appeared independently, totally unrelated to one another. The first proto-Zionists (David Alkalai, Zvi Hirsch Kalischer, David Luria) and the men interested in the Jews of Palestine (Charles Netter of the Alliance Israélite Universelle, Moses Montefiore), for example, could not have been farther apart ideologically. Others asked why a national definition of the Jewish people should apply only to the past and not also to the present and future. But the very perception of the Jewish people in national terms was a complex proposition. Some sought a spiritual definition of Jewish nationality (Heinrich Graetz, Samuel David Luzzatto); others proposed a political definition (David Gordon, Eliezer Ben-Yehuda). Jewish national, or quasi-national, ideas began appearing also in mystical, social, or spiritual formulations.

That difficult and widespread process of ideological elaboration continued unabated in the last quarter of the nineteenth century. It received further impetus from the continuing acculturation of large segments of East European Jewish society, the growing influence of European ideologies, and the emergence of new and threatening patterns of antisemitism. The outcome of these ideological labors were four social and political trends: the Hibbat Zion movement, which began in the 1880s and led in the late 1890s to the Zionist movement; Jewish socialism; Jewish autonomism; and Jewish territorialism.

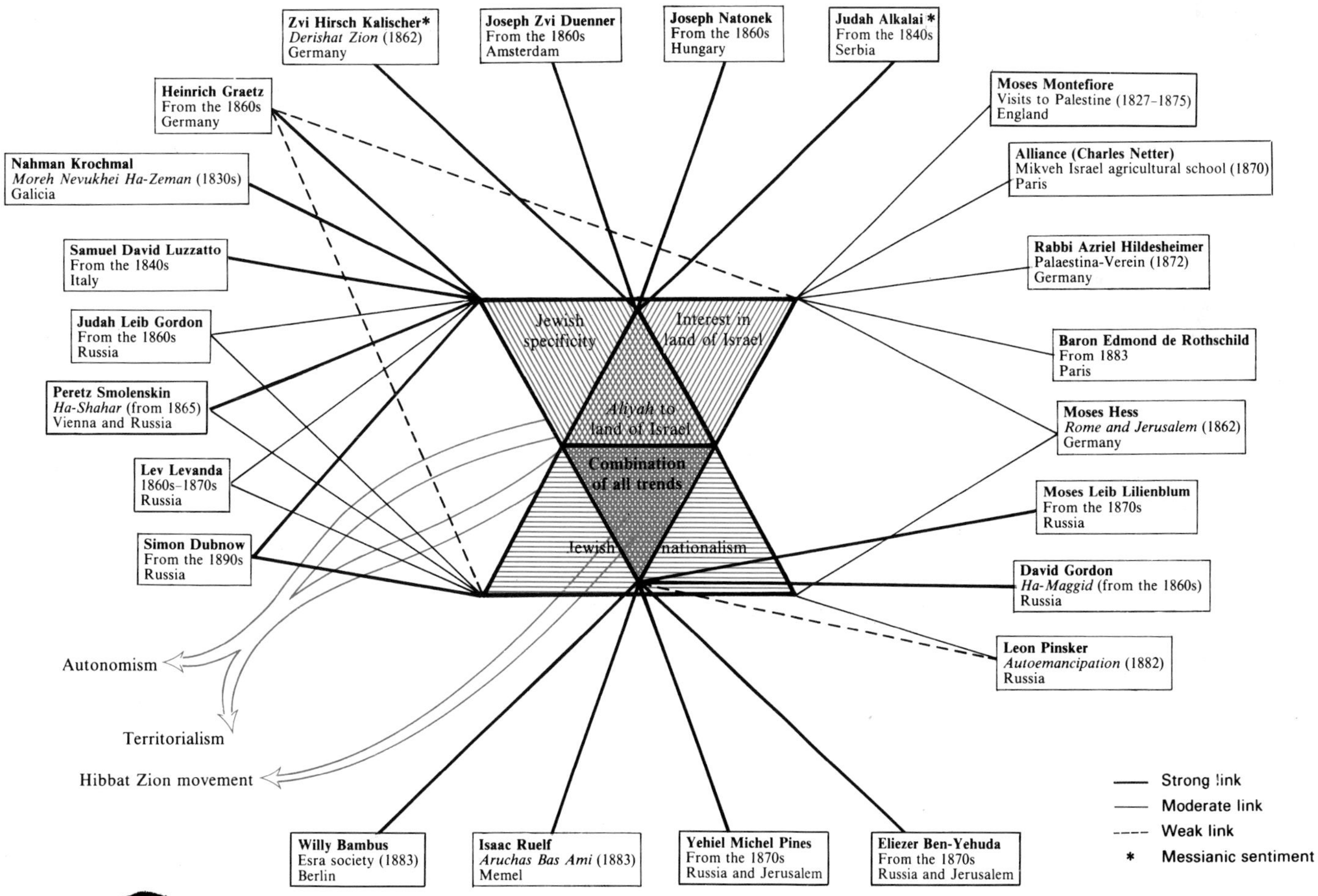

*Rabbi Zvi Hirsch Kalischer*

*Rabbi Azriel Hildesheimer*

*Leon Pinsker*

# Jewish Nationalism: Ideological and Organizational Tendencies

From the end of the nineteenth century, four main nationalist trends developed in European Jewish society: Zionism, socialism, autonomism, and territorialism. These tendencies existed separately or in different combinations, such as socialist Zionism and socialist territorialism.

The trends spawned a bewildering array of movements and parties, usually centered in Eastern Europe, although they appeared also in Western Europe and in the countries of Jewish immigration, especially the United States. They were further distinguished by their positive or negative position regarding the continued existence of the Jews amid other peoples. The Jewish socialists and autonomists belonged to the "positivists"; Zionists and territorialists (with their socialist offshoots), to the "negativists." In spite of the differences among the many parties, trends, and movements, they shared a deep dissatisfaction with the prevailing relationship between the Jewish and the general society and a desire to change that relationship, according to their respective conceptions.

Jewish socialists believed that the transformation of the capitalist economic and social structure of general society would solve the Jewish problem. The Zionists thought that the problems of modern Jewry would be solved through the creation of an independent Jewish home in Palestine. The territorialists sought to direct part of the Jewish people—especially those emigrating from Europe—to some underdeveloped region where Jews would be a majority, perhaps even with a state of their own. The autonomists strove for broad rights, including national rights, in the countries where the Jews were already established, especially in Eastern Europe.

All these programs marked a new phase in the interpretation of the relationship between Jews and non-Jews. Whereas the "integrationist" segments of European Jewry had hoped to attain full civil and political rights for the Jews in the countries in which they lived, the new organizations wanted more: the recognition of the specificity of the Jews as a group with well-defined characteristics, even national ones.

The boundaries between the different trends were not always clear. Obviously, some of the envisaged solutions were not mutually exclusive. The different movements split, split again, and recombined. However, real hostility, bitter and uncompromising, expressing itself in long and fierce struggles, existed between the Bund—the main Jewish socialist organization—and the Zionist movement.

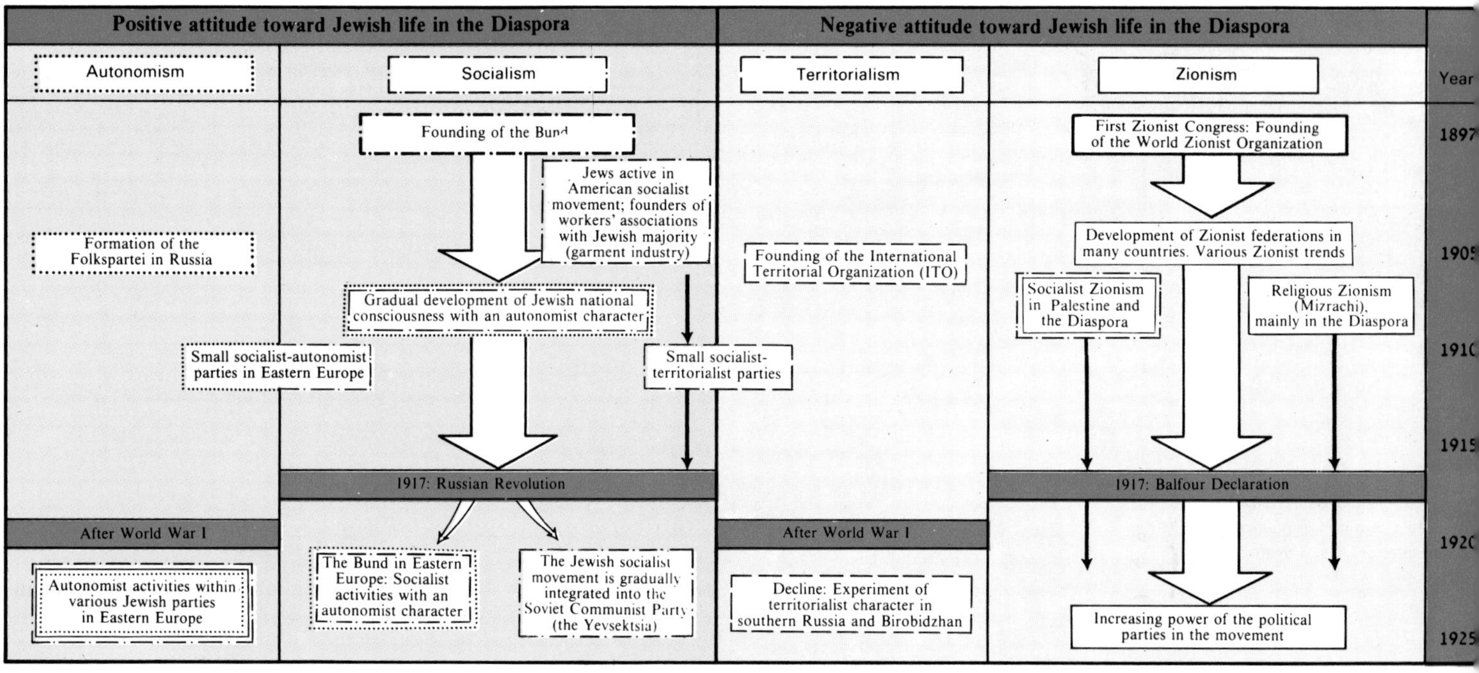


# Jewish Socialism: The Bund

In Central and Western Europe, Jews with socialist leanings did not form separate political organizations, but became active in the general socialist parties. In Eastern Europe (and in some major centers of Jewish immigration), Jewish socialism developed as an independent movement. Its foremost example was the Bund.

At the beginning of the twentieth century, the Bund (League of the Jewish Workers in Lithuania, Poland, and Russia, 1897) was the best-organized Jewish association in the Pale of Settlement. Its members were also among the founders and outstanding activists of the general Russian Socialist Party. Other Jewish socialist groups in the Pale were the Poalei Zion (Labor Zionists) and some smaller groups of territorialist or autonomist orientation.

The center of the Jewish socialist movement was in Lithuania, in Vilna and its vicinity. From there, it spread to Poland and then to the Ukraine (southern Russia). The ideological orientation of the Bund was Marxist, directed toward the revolution of the international working class, and only hesitantly did it formulate a Jewish national-cultural program. The fourth convention of the Bund, held in 1904, decided that the concept of "nationality" applied also to the Jewish masses. This development was influenced by both the strengthening of the national idea in other sectors of East European Jewry and the nationalistic tendencies that appeared in the general socialist movement, especially in Poland and Austria-Hungary. The Bund maintained that the Russian social-democratic movement should be reorganized on a federative basis, joining together the major national groups of the Russian working class. This approach was rejected by the party's centralist-minded leadership, headed by Lenin, who also opposed the definition of the Jews as a national group. As a result of these differences, the Bund withdrew from the Russian Social Democratic Party in 1903, returning in 1906, after a compromise had been worked out guaranteeing it virtual autonomy inside the Russian movement.

Relations between the Bund and other Jewish groups were usually strained. The Bund stressed the class differences in Jewish society, totally opposed all religious tendencies, and was usually wary about participating in activities of a Jewish communal character. Nevertheless, it campaigned vigorously for the rights of Jewish workers, and during the anti-Jewish riots in Russia in the early twentieth century, it was very active in organizing its members in self-defense groups.

After the Bolshevik Revolution in Russia in 1917, the Bund split. Its pro-Communist faction merged with the Soviet Communist Party, with many Bund members becoming active in the Yevsektsia—the Jewish section of the Communist Party. The Bund's social-democratic faction gradually disappeared. The Bund continued to be active in other East European countries, especially Poland, where it became a recognized Jewish political party. During World War II, Bund members played an important role in the underground. The extermination of Polish Jewry brought about the end of the Bund in Europe.

In the United States, to which many Bundists migrated in the early twentieth century, the Bund did not organize as a separate political party; rather, its members became active in existing professional, social, and political organizations with a leftist orientation.

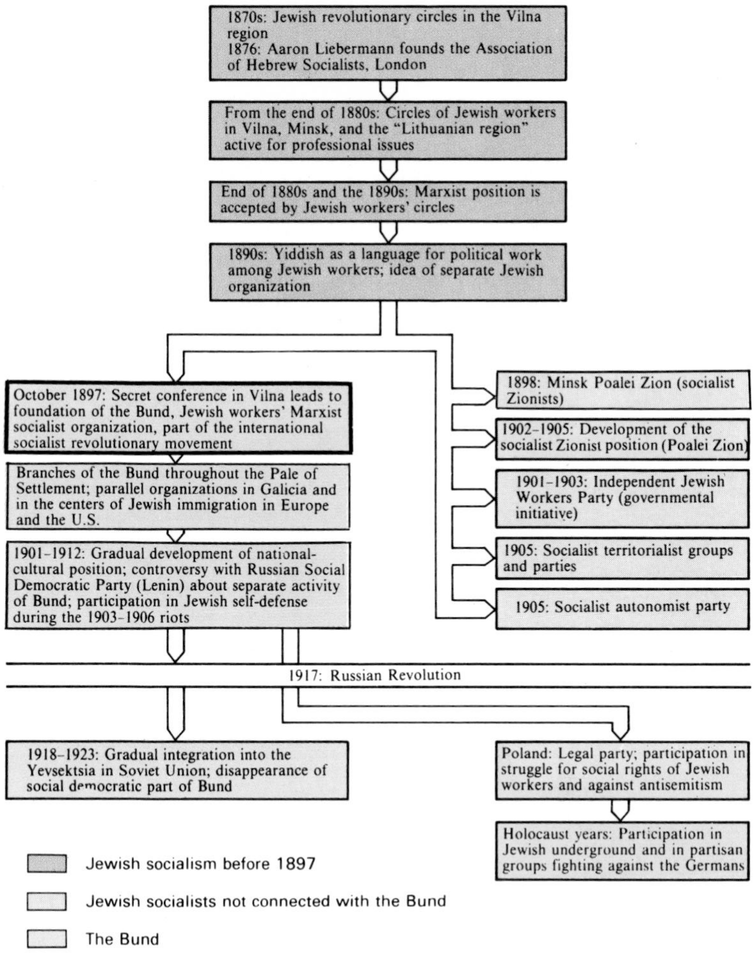
1870s: Jewish revolutionary circles in the Vilna region
1876: Aaron Liebermann founds the Association of Hebrew Socialists, London
From the end of 1880s: Circles of Jewish workers in Vilna, Minsk, and the "Lithuanian region" active for professional issues
End of 1880s and the 1890s: Marxist position is accepted by Jewish workers' circles
1890s: Yiddish as a language for political work among Jewish workers; idea of separate Jewish organization
October 1897: Secret conference in Vilna leads to foundation of the Bund, Jewish workers' Marxist socialist organization, part of the international socialist revolutionary movement
Branches of the Bund throughout the Pale of Settlement; parallel organizations in Galicia and in the centers of Jewish immigration in Europe and the U.S.
1901–1912: Gradual development of national-cultural position; controversy with Russian Social Democratic Party (Lenin) about separate activity of Bund; participation in Jewish self-defense during the 1903–1906 riots
1898: Minsk Poalei Zion (socialist Zionists)
1902–1905: Development of the socialist Zionist position (Poalei Zion)
1901–1903: Independent Jewish Workers Party (governmental initiative)
1905: Socialist territorialist groups and parties
1905: Socialist autonomist party
1917: Russian Revolution
1918–1923: Gradual integration into the Yevsektsia in Soviet Union; disappearance of social democratic part of Bund
Poland: Legal party; participation in struggle for social rights of Jewish workers and against antisemitism
Holocaust years: Participation in Jewish underground and in partisan groups fighting against the Germans
Jewish socialism before 1897
Jewish socialists not connected with the Bund
The Bund

# he Rise of the Bund and Its pread in the Pale of Settlement

St. Petersburg
Baltic Sea
Novgorod
Pskov
Stage I: Rise of the Jewish socialist movement and of the Bund. Main center from the 1890s to World War I
Libau
Riga
Moscow
Kovno
Vilna
Vitebsk
Smolensk
PRUSSIA
Suwalki
LITHUANIAN REGION
Main center of the Independent Jewish Workers' Party. 1898: Beginnings of Poalei Zion
Wisla
Grodno
Minsk
Mogilev
Lomza
Plock
BELORUSSIA
Orël
Warsaw
LITHUANIA
alicz
Lódź
POLAND
Kursk
Radom
Lublin
UKRAINE
Khar'kov
Cracow
Zhitomir
Kiev
Poltava
Lemberg
AUSTRIA-HUNGARY
Yekaterinoslav
Don
Budapest
Mainly after the Kishinev pogroms (1903)
BESSARABIA
Balta
NEW RUSSIA
Kishinev
Dnieper
Kherson
Odessa
Main center of Bund growth
Center of Bund growth
First
Second
Third
Fourth
Stages of expansion
Pale of Settlement
Feodosiya
0 100 200 300 miles
0 100 200 300 400 km
69

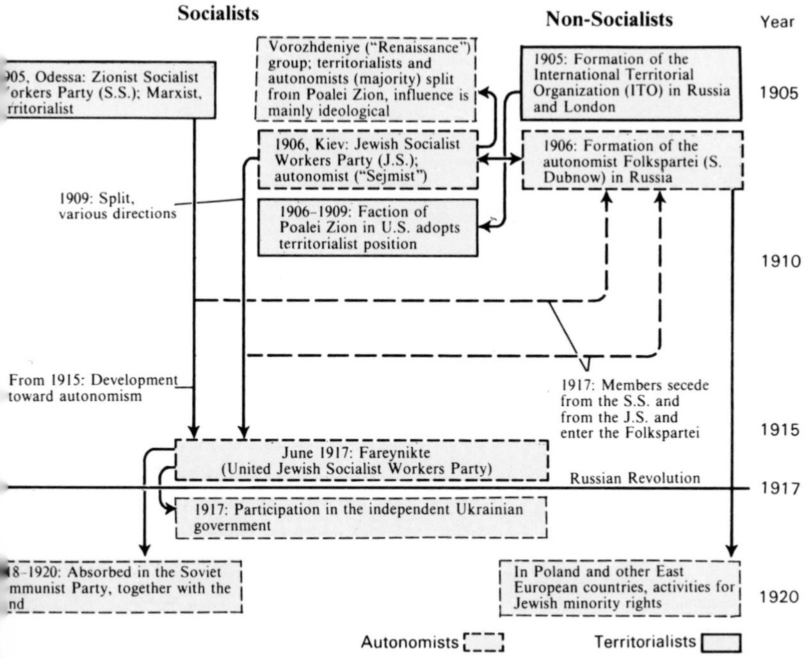
Socialists
Non-Socialists
Year
05, Odessa: Zionist Socialist orkers Party (S.S.); Marxist, rritorialist
Vorozhdeniye ("Renaissance") group; territorialists and autonomists (majority) split from Poalei Zion, influence is mainly ideological
1905: Formation of the International Territorial Organization (ITO) in Russia and London
1905
1906, Kiev: Jewish Socialist Workers Party (J.S.); autonomist ("Sejmist")
1906: Formation of the autonomist Folkspartei (S. Dubnow) in Russia
1909: Split, various directions
1906–1909: Faction of Poalei Zion in U.S. adopts territorialist position
1910
From 1915: Development toward autonomism
1917: Members secede from the S.S. and from the J.S. and enter the Folkspartei
1915
June 1917: Fareynikte (United Jewish Socialist Workers Party)
Russian Revolution
1917
1917: Participation in the independent Ukrainian government
8–1920: Absorbed in the Soviet mmunist Party, together with the nd
In Poland and other East European countries, activities for Jewish minority rights
1920
Autonomists
Territorialists

## Autonomist and Territorialist Organizations and Parties

In the first decades of the twentieth century, several small parties and groups, with an autonomous or territorialist orientation, were active among East European Jews. Their significance lay in the broad ideological spectrum they represented in Jewish society rather than in whatever political weight they may have carried. Territorialism, which was influenced by some components of Zionist ideology, aimed to settle the Jews as a majority in an underdeveloped region where they might be able to live with a significant measure of autonomy, or perhaps even establish a state of their own. Autonomism sought to attain for the Jews recognition as a national minority in their countries of residence (especially in Eastern Europe), with the right to develop and administer their own cultural, educational, and religious life. Both these positions had socialist and nonsocialist ramifications.

The International Territorial Organization (ITO) was the best-known group in this category. It was created after the Seventh Zionist Congress, held in 1905, by a group of former Zionists, mostly Russians but also some West Europeans, who invited the Anglo-Jewish writer Israel Zangwill to head the new organization. The Folkspartei (Jewish People's Party) was based on the ideas of the historian Simon Dubnow. Organized in Russia in 1906 and in other East European countries (especially Poland) after World War I, it was the most important of the autonomist and territorialist organizations, the only one still active between the world wars. The Folkspartei played an important role in the development of Yiddish educational and cultural institutions. It had a difficult existence, however, squeezed as it was between the more extreme trends in East European Jewry. All told, the autonomist position was very influential; most of the political trends and parties in East European Jewry accepted many of its elements, incorporating them into their own programs. In various forms, some autonomist ideas were adopted by the Jewries outside Europe, where their impact continued to be felt.

## Zionism: Ideological Components

Few movements in modern Jewish (or even modern general) history were as ideologically complex as the Zionist movement. The Zionist idea had three indispensable components: yearning for Zion (that is, the historical attachment of the Jewish people to the land of Israel), nationalism (that is, the influence of European national and civil concepts), and antisemitism. Combined in a certain way, these components produced an additional idea that became characteristic of Zionism: negation of Galut (*Sh'lilat Hagalut*), the rejection, on both pragmatic and ideological grounds, of the idea of continued Jewish group existence in non-Jewish societies.

A broad array of positions developed inside the Zionist movement, based on these elements and their various constellations. In addition, local conditions inevitably influenced the conceptions of the regional Zionist organizations. The later Zionist parties—such as socialist Zionism or religious Zionism—added their own ideological perspectives to the basic components of the Zionist idea, enriching it, but also making it more complex. A trenchant debate started at the beginning of the twentieth century between religious and nonreligious Zionists as to the cultural content of the Zionist program. Religious Zionists (and religious Jews in general, many of whom were anti-Zionists) believed that the Jewish society in Palestine should live according to the *Halakhah* (Jewish religious law). This discussion continued through the 1980s in other forms.

Containing so many ideological elements, the Zionist movement was an arena for conflicting trends. But the existence of common goals established a basis for joint action. The "Uganda Scheme" (1903) ended by emphasizing Palestine, the historical land of Israel, as the sole objective of Zionist endeavors. The Helsingfors Conference of the Russian Zionist movement (December 1906) adopted the principle of work in and for the Diaspora communities (*Gegenwartsarbeit*) as one of the means to attain the Zionist ends. In the first decade of the twentieth century, three political and cultural trends became active in the movement, each stressing a different aspect of Zionist activity. "Synthetic Zionism," formulated toward the end of the decade, brought these trends together.

The Zionist program generated more dissension inside modern Jewry than existed between Jews and non-Jews, and it was the subject of heated debates. It was fiercely opposed by the Jewish socialists, the Orthodox, and those segments of Jewish society committed to integration into the general society. Yet the struggle for Jewish statehood in 1947 and 1948 united almost all ideological sectors of the Jewish people.

*Ahad Ha'am*
*(Asher Hirsch Ginsberg)*

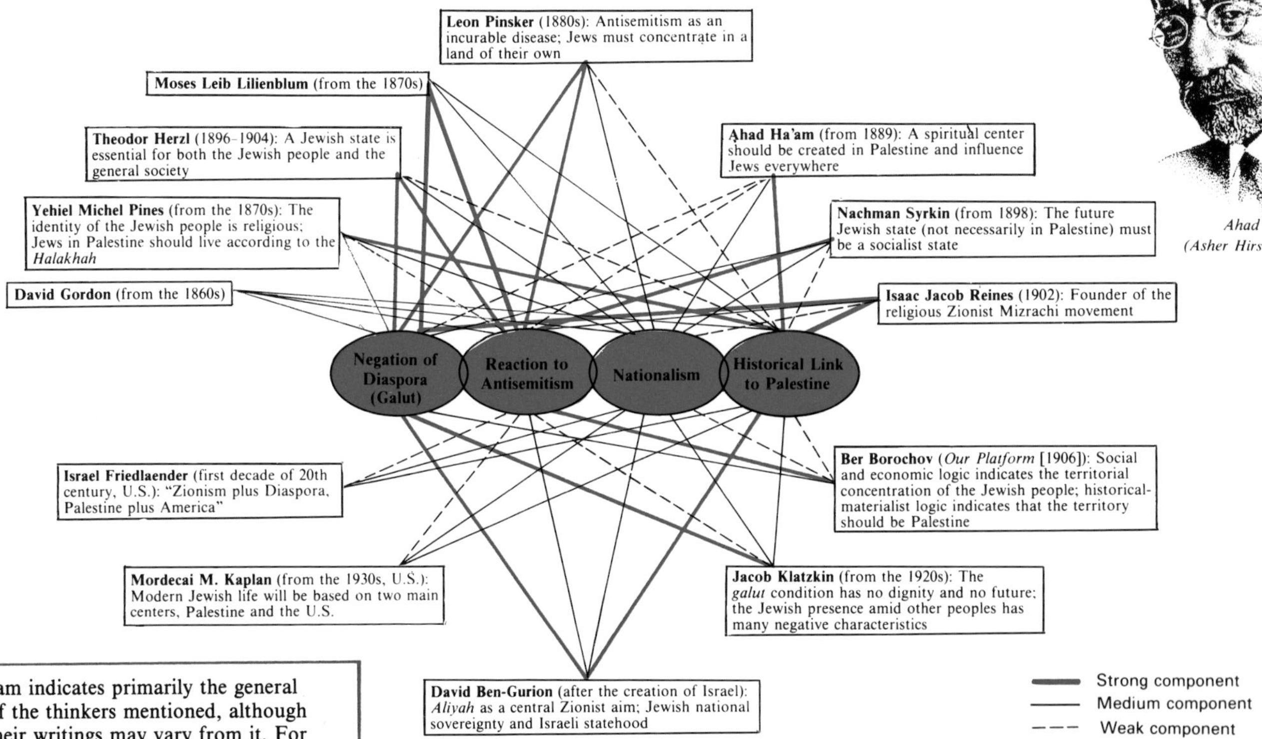
Leon Pinsker (1880s): Antisemitism as an incurable disease; Jews must concentrate in a land of their own
Moses Leib Lilienblum (from the 1870s)
Theodor Herzl (1896–1904): A Jewish state is essential for both the Jewish people and the general society
Ahad Ha'am (from 1889): A spiritual center should be created in Palestine and influence Jews everywhere
Yehiel Michel Pines (from the 1870s): The identity of the Jewish people is religious; Jews in Palestine should live according to the Halakhah
Nachman Syrkin (from 1898): The future Jewish state (not necessarily in Palestine) must be a socialist state
David Gordon (from the 1860s)
Isaac Jacob Reines (1902): Founder of the religious Zionist Mizrachi movement
Negation of Diaspora (Galut)
Reaction to Antisemitism
Nationalism
Historical Link to Palestine
Ber Borochov (Our Platform [1906]): Social and economic logic indicates the territorial concentration of the Jewish people; historical-materialist logic indicates that the territory should be Palestine
Israel Friedlaender (first decade of 20th century, U.S.): "Zionism plus Diaspora, Palestine plus America"
Mordecai M. Kaplan (from the 1930s, U.S.): Modern Jewish life will be based on two main centers, Palestine and the U.S.
Jacob Klatzkin (from the 1920s): The galut condition has no dignity and no future; the Jewish presence amid other peoples has many negative characteristics
David Ben-Gurion (after the creation of Israel): Aliyah as a central Zionist aim; Jewish national sovereignty and Israeli statehood
Strong component
Medium component
Weak component

The diagram indicates primarily the general position of the thinkers mentioned, although some of their writings may vary from it. For instance, in Herzl's *The Jewish State* (1896) and in Pinsker's *Autoemancipation* (1882), there was little or no mention of Palestine. But the same element is indicated as weak in Borochov's *Our Platform* (1906), although in his general position, the attachment to Palestine was stronger.

## The Beginning of the Zionist Movement

Organized Zionism began in the 1880s with the Hibbat Zion movement, whose practical achievements were modest. The First Zionist Congress, convened by Theodor Herzl at Basel in 1897, ushered in a new era. The congress approved the Zionist (Basel) Program, and founded the World Zionist Organization. From 1901, the congress met every two years. Branches of the World Zionist Organization were organized around the world.

Until World War I, the settlement of Jews in Palestine faced many difficulties, yet it continued to grow at a small but steady pace. The invasion of Palestine by Great Britain during World War I led to the Balfour Declaration (November 2, 1917). The declaration, which reflected a complex mixture of British interests and sentiments, created a great political opportunity for the Zionists. The Zionist Commission, led by Chaim Weizmann, which went to Palestine in March 1918; the San Remo Conference, held in April 1920; and the British Mandate on Palestine (approved by the League of Nations in July 1922) were some of the first political steps taken toward the creation of a Jewish national home in Palestine. Parallel to this, Jewish immigration into Palestine resumed, and the Zionist Executive began development work in the country. In 1914, there had been about 85,000 Jews in Palestine. During the war, about 30,000 left the country or died. By 1922, the Jewish population again numbered about 85,000, still only 11.1 percent of the population.

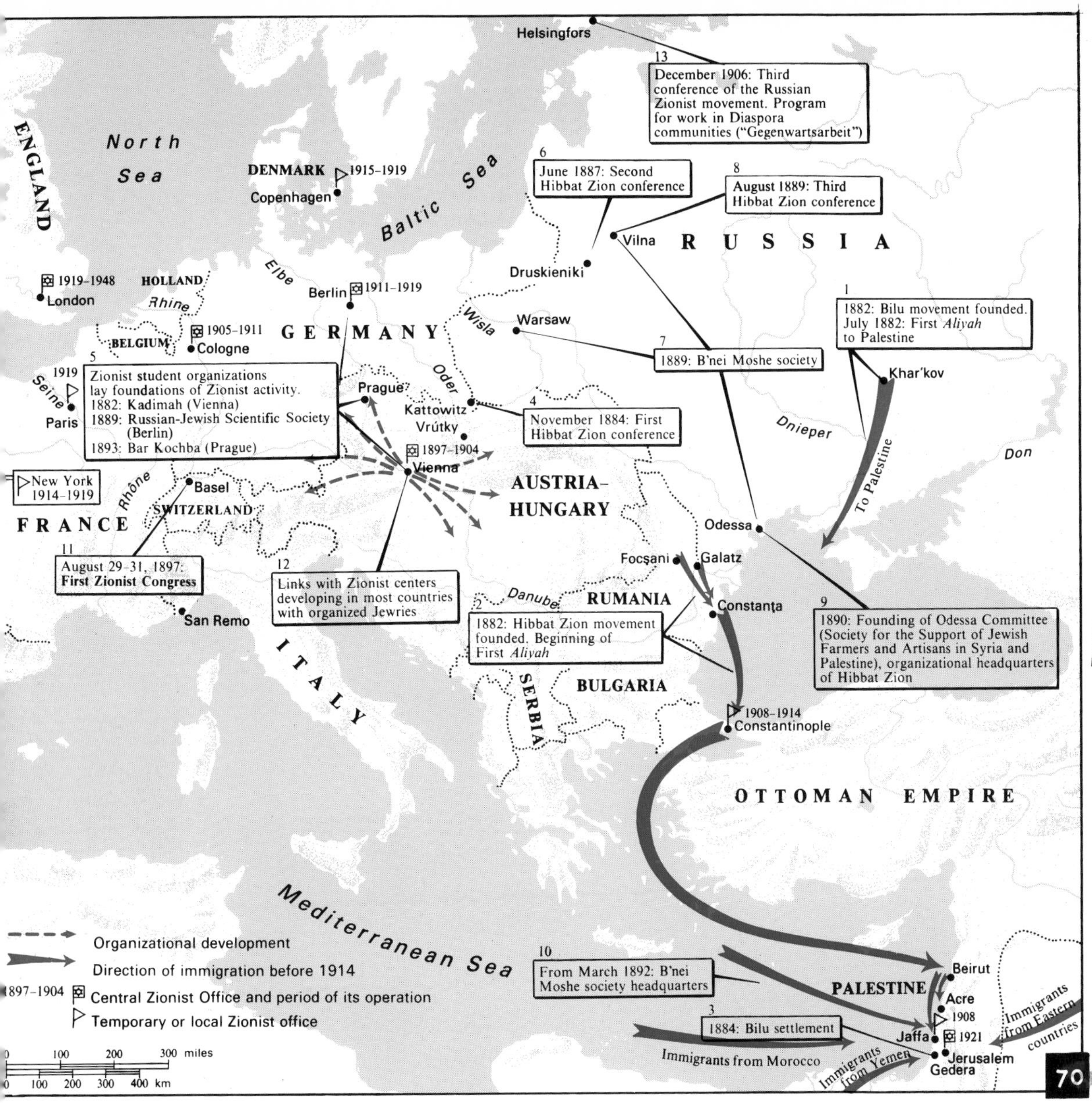


## Zionism and Palestine

- 1897: First Zionist Congress. World Zionist Organization founded
- 1897–1904: "The political period." Effort to obtain Charter
- 1901: Fifth Zionist Congress. Debate over religious and secular culture and its place in the Zionist undertaking
- 1903: Sixth Zionist Congress. Uganda Scheme. In reaction, strengthening of Palestine-directed tendency
- 1903–1909: Debate between practical and political Zionists about course of Zionist activity
- December 1906: Helsingfors Conference. Diaspora work accepted as part of Zionist program
- 1907–1911: Crystallization of synthetic trend in Zionist activity, combining political, practical, and Zionist activities
- 1908: Zionist Office in Jaffa
- 1917: Balfour Declaration
- 1917–1918: British conquer Palestine
- 1920: Civil administration headed by High Commissioner Herbert Samuel
- 1922: British Mandate over Palestine confirmed
- 1922: Transjordan separated from Palestine

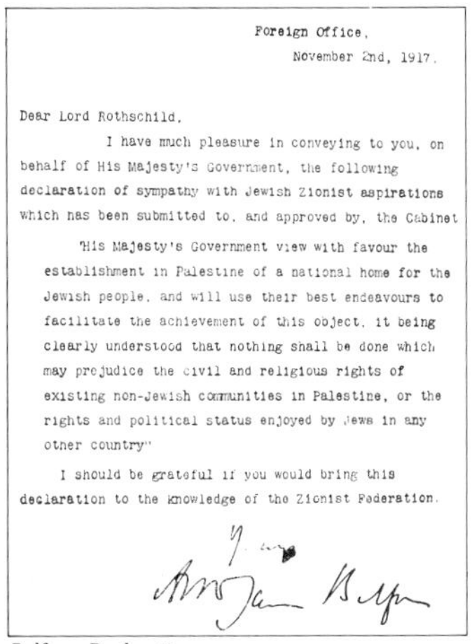

Foreign Office,
November 2nd, 1917.

Dear Lord Rothschild,

I have much pleasure in conveying to you, on behalf of His Majesty's Government, the following declaration of sympathy with Jewish Zionist aspirations which has been submitted to, and approved by, the Cabinet

"His Majesty's Government view with favour the establishment in Palestine of a national home for the Jewish people, and will use their best endeavours to facilitate the achievement of this object, it being clearly understood that nothing shall be done which may prejudice the civil and religious rights of existing non-Jewish communities in Palestine, or the rights and political status enjoyed by Jews in any other country"

I should be grateful if you would bring this declaration to the knowledge of the Zionist Federation.

*Balfour Declaration*

## Socialist Zionism

The socialist Zionist approach was formulated in Eastern Europe from the end of the nineteenth century. Inspired by ideas from Jewish sources and modern socialist theory, socialist Zionism aimed to create in Palestine a Jewish society based on principles of social and economic justice. The movement, which was to play a crucial role in the developments that led to the establishment of Israel, was torn between opposing currents: Zionism, territorialism, and autonomism; Marxist and non-Marxist socialism; and, after the Russian Revolution of 1917, the challenge of Communism. All these trends were also present on the organizational level, expressed by numerous splits in or mergers between the various socialist Zionist groups.

The most important representative of the socialist Zionist trend at the beginning of the twentieth century was the Poalei Zion movement, which was relatively well organized (a world union was established in 1907) and had a Marxist orientation. Another party was Tzeirei Zion, which appeared during the first Russian revolution (1904–1905). The latter was stronger in Palestine (under the name Hapoel Hatzair) than in the Diaspora. Poalei Zion and Tzeirei Zion diverged on various political issues. In the long run, the different factions and parties in the socialist Zionist camp tended on the whole toward collaboration and unification. A large sector of the Palestine branches of Hapoel Hatzair and Poalei Zion united in 1930 to form Mapai (Eretz Israel Workers Party). Their Diaspora factions united in 1932 to form the World Union (Ihud Olami). The ascendancy of the party in Palestine over that in the Diaspora was already evident at that time.

Another socialist Zionist organization that became active in the early 1920s was Hashomer Hatzair, which began as a youth movement in the Diaspora and later developed in Palestine.

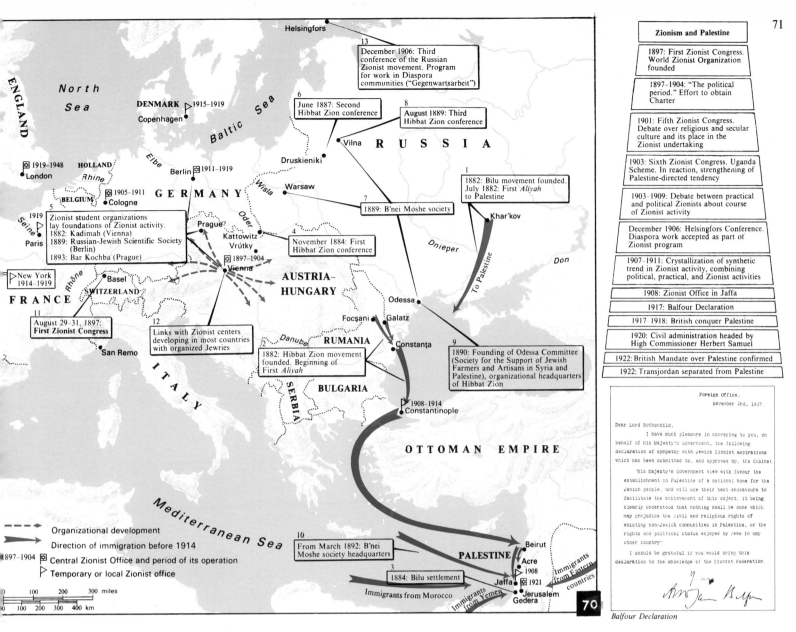

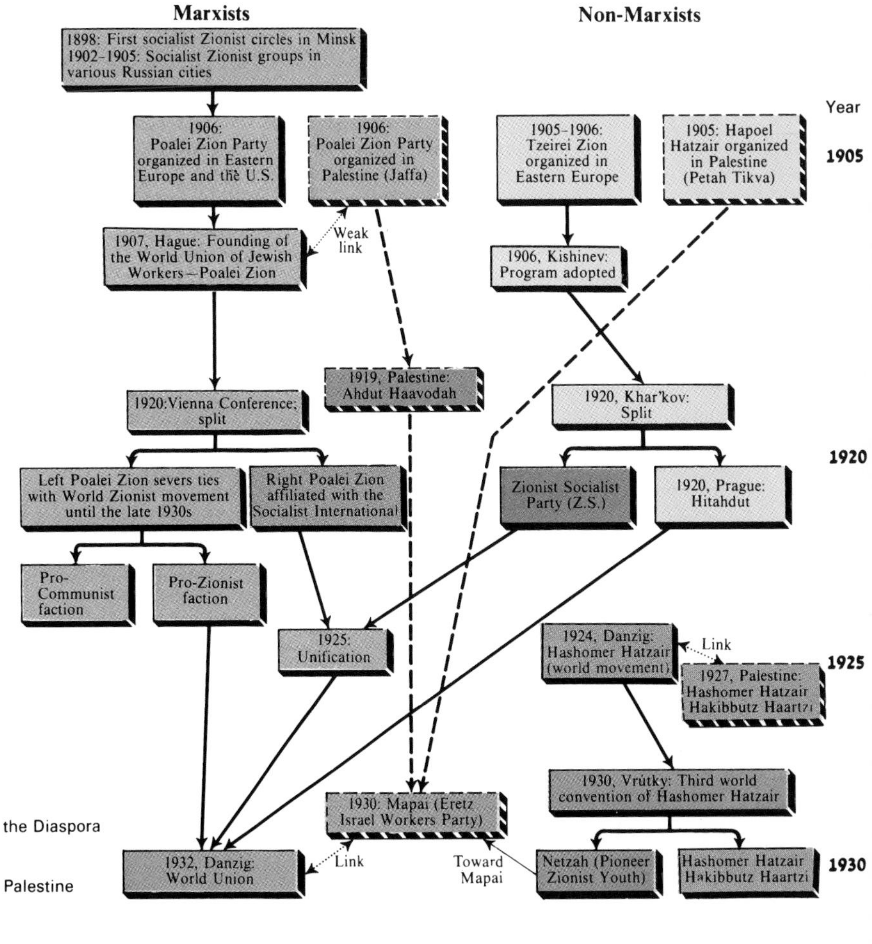


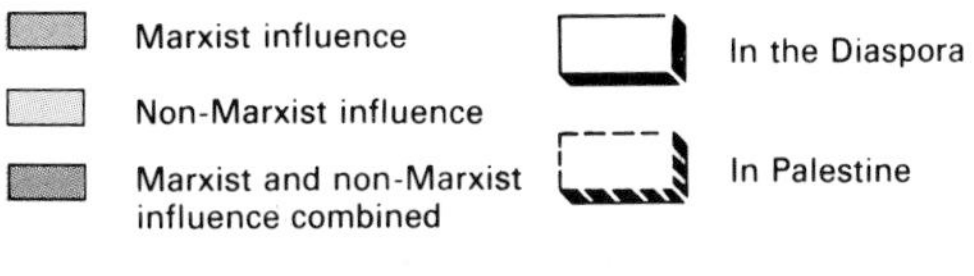

# The Structure of the World Zionist Organization, 1929

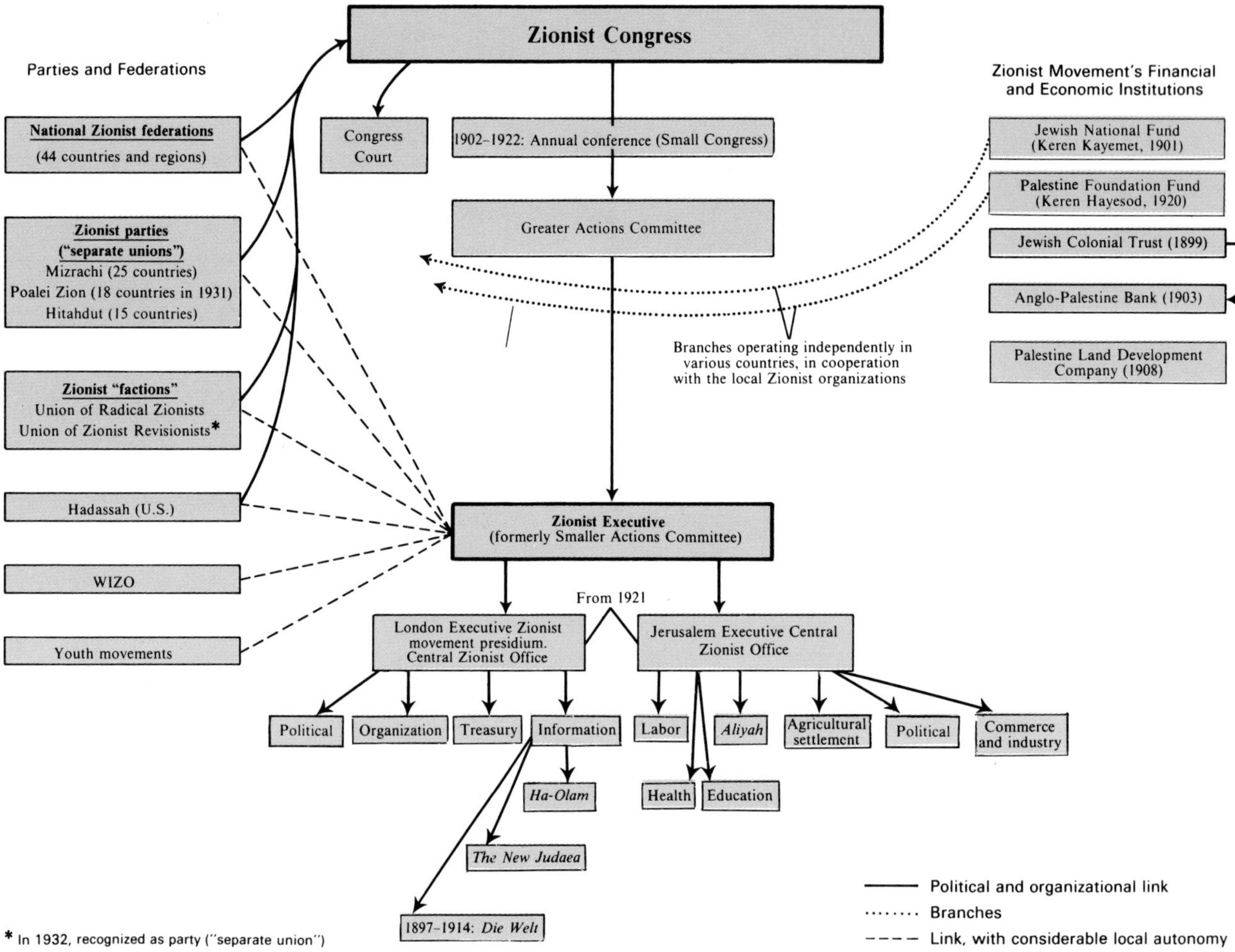


* In 1932, recognized as party ("separate union")

The Zionist movement functioned through a number of parallel or interrelated bodies that together composed the World Zionist Organization. Its supreme organ was the Zionist Congress, which generally met every two years. Its delegates, elected from all over the world, formed a large Jewish parliament whose interest was inevitably drawn also to issues beyond Zionism. The Zionist Congress adopted resolutions of an organizational and political character and elected the president of the Zionist movement (Chaim Weizmann, for most of the years between 1920 and 1946). It also chose the bodies that led the movement between the convening of congresses: the Greater Actions Committee (today called the Zionist General Council), which met between one and three times a year and had thirty to forty members; and the Zionist Executive (formerly, the Inner or Smaller Actions Committee), which during the 1920s had from ten to thirteen members and led the movement in its day-to-day activities. The Executive was served by the Central Zionist Office, which was divided into departments. Until 1920, both bodies were variously based in Vienna, Cologne, or Berlin. Thereafter, the Executive and the Central Office each had sections in both London and Jerusalem. Although during the 1920s and 1930s the seat of the movement's political leadership was in London, the tasks and powers of the Jerusalem-based Zionist Executive gradually increased.

The Zionist Executive acted in different countries or regions through Zionist federations. In 1929, there were forty-four such federations, each with its own organizational structure, central administration, local branches, annual or biennial conventions, and bodies for financial affairs, propaganda, education, youth, and the like. Besides the federations, which were organized on a geographical basis, there were the ideological Zionist parties ("separate unions")—such as Mizrachi, Poalei Zion, and the Revisionists—each of which also had world headquarters. In the 1920s and 1930s, the party structure in the Zionist movement gradually grew stronger (especially in Europe), while many of the federations lost support. Other important Zionist associations were the women's organizations; in the 1930s, the Women's International Zionist Organization (WIZO) functioned in dozens of countries, and the well-organized Hadassah was active in the United States. There were also the Zionist youth movements, organized on a worldwide basis. In the early 1930s, there were seven such groups, most of them connected with the Hehalutz movement, which prepared many of their members for pioneering *aliyah* to Palestine, where they became members of kibbutzim.

An important organizational development was the formation in 1929 of the (enlarged) Jewish Agency, which brought together Zionists and non-Zionists interested in the creation of a Jewish national home in Palestine. As it turned out, the success of the Jewish Agency was more one of principle than of practice; it expressed the idea that the development of Palestine was the concern of the whole Jewish people, and not only of the Zionist movement. In practice, the work for and in Palestine remained mainly in the hands of the World Zionist Organization and its affiliated bodies.

The Zionist enterprise in Palestine was financed by several agencies, the most important of which were the Jewish National Fund (Keren Kayemet le-Israel), dedicated to land redemption in Palestine, and the Palestine Foundation Fund (Keren Hayesod), dedicated to Zionist development projects. Both functioned in close cooperation with local Zionist bodies, but non-Zionists were prominent in the Keren Hayesod.

In many countries, especially in Eastern Europe, the Zionists were among the most active element in Jewish public life. Their activities were supported by a large Zionist press. About 200 periodicals were published in 1931 by the various Zionist bodies, and another 50 Jewish magazines or newspapers supported Zionism.

After the creation of the state of Israel, the World Zionist Organization underwent important internal changes. New statutes, adopted in 1960, opened the door to participation in the Zionist movement of Jewish organizations that accepted the Zionist program, such as the Jewish Reform movement in the United States.

# The Political Composition of Zionist Congresses, 1921–1939

Two main tendencies characterized the development of the Zionist movement: the gradual growth of the party system, and the increasing power of the leftist parties. At the Twelfth Zionist Congress, held in 1921, the General Zionists (politically unaligned) had 73 percent of the delegates, and Labor, 8 percent. At the Twenty-first Congress, convened in 1939, Labor had 42.5 percent of the delegates, and the General Zionists, only 32.4 percent. The General Zionists had meanwhile become affiliated; the politicization of the movement in the 1920s and 1930s had compelled them to define themselves politically. By 1935, they were represented by two parties (A and B), speaking for the Jewish middle class, with its characteristic social and economic positions. The B group, also called Progressives, supported Chaim Weizmann. The Labor representation consisted of a broad array of ideological positions, all of which were leftist-oriented (Poalei Zion–Hitahdut, Hashomer Hatzair, and, from 1938, Left Poalei Zion), that outside the Zionist Congress acted independently. The most important representation of religious Zionism was Mizrachi, although many religious Zionists voted for other Zionist parties. Another important Zionist party was the Revisionists, organized in 1925, which was mostly middle class and extremely nationalistic. In 1935, the Revisionists left the World Zionist Organization and founded the New Zionist Organization, which existed independently until 1946.

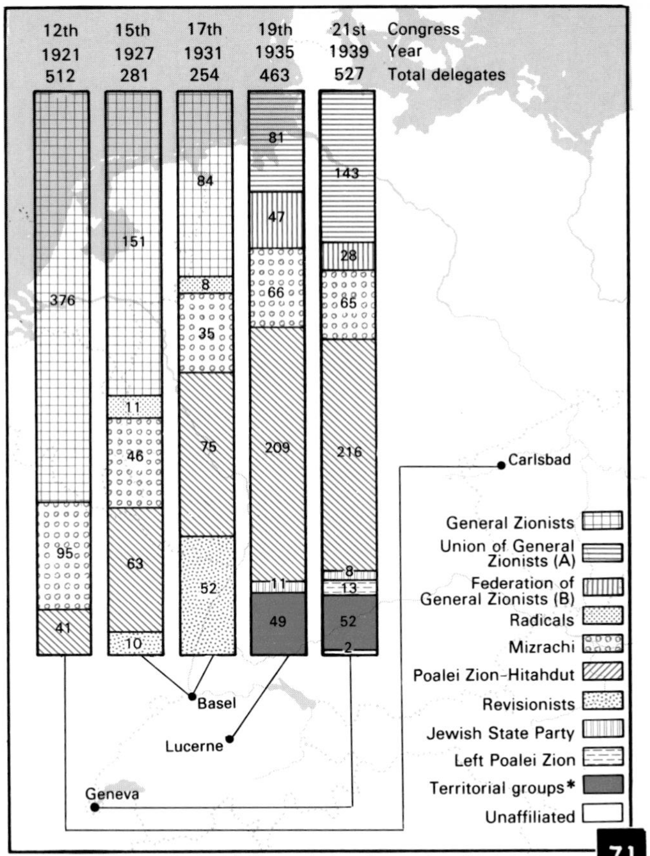


* Delegates from countries (mainly Germany) where it was not possible to hold elections for the Zionist Congress

# The Zionist Movement by Countries, 1931

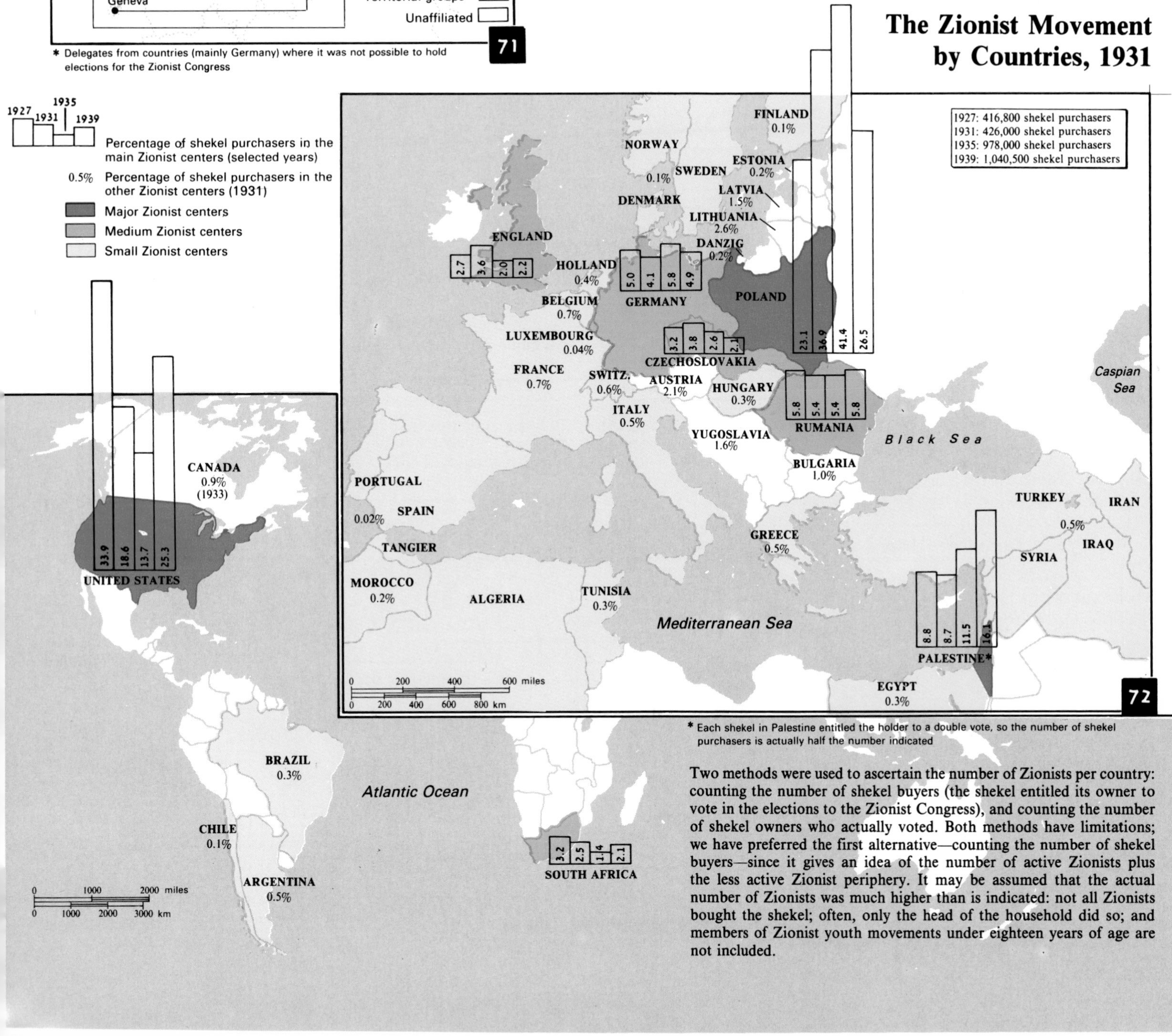


* Each shekel in Palestine entitled the holder to a double vote, so the number of shekel purchasers is actually half the number indicated

Two methods were used to ascertain the number of Zionists per country: counting the number of shekel buyers (the shekel entitled its owner to vote in the elections to the Zionist Congress), and counting the number of shekel owners who actually voted. Both methods have limitations; we have preferred the first alternative—counting the number of shekel buyers—since it gives an idea of the number of active Zionists plus the less active Zionist periphery. It may be assumed that the actual number of Zionists was much higher than is indicated: not all Zionists bought the shekel; often, only the head of the household did so; and members of Zionist youth movements under eighteen years of age are not included.

# Jewish Student Organizations and Youth Movements

Several very interesting social functions in modern Jewish life (especially in Europe) were fulfilled by the younger strata of Jewish society, organized in youth movements and student organizations. A significant number of the future Jewish leaders belonged to these groups. The Zionist and pioneer youth movements played important roles in the building of the Jewish national home in Palestine.

There were basic conceptual differences between the Jewish student organizations, which appeared in Europe from the last decade of the nineteenth century, and the youth movements, which appeared from the beginning of the twentieth century. Both represented a part of society that was critical of the Establishment and dissatisfied with the situation of modern Jewry in general society. Each group, however, developed its own ideological expression and form of organized action.

### Youth Movements

The Jewish youth movements were divided into two quite diverse branches. The first developed in Western Europe, especially in Germany. The main movements there were Blau-Weiss (before World War I), Jung-juedischer Wanderbund (JJWB), Kameraden, and what later became Habonim–Noar Halutzi (after World War I). The Jewish youth associations were influenced by the classic German youth movement (the Wandervogel), which aimed to create a new type of person through spiritual development in a unique social framework. The Jewish organizations added their own objectives: to foster Jewish consciousness and attachment to Jewish values. That internal development gradually brought most of their members to Zionism.

The other branch of the Jewish youth movement, whose center was in Eastern Europe (although it also appeared in Western Europe and in some Muslim countries), produced a new type between the two world wars, the Zionist youth movement. Its aims were better defined than those of the classic youth movement, and to some extent it managed to avoid the inevitable fate of youth movements: to disappear as its members reached adulthood, or to become a section of a political party. An outstanding example of a Zionist youth movement was Hashomer Hatzair. It began in Vienna as a group of young scouts, according to the classic pattern, and developed strongly in Eastern Europe; later, it adopted Zionism, socialism, and pioneering ideals; established kibbutzim in Palestine from the mid-1920s that combined to form an independent kibbutz federation (Hakibbutz Haartzi); and eventually founded a political party—all the while maintaining the youth movement as a structure for the younger generation.

The Zionist youth movements reflected the political divisions within the Zionist movement: rightist (Betar), leftist, or religious with a leftist orientation. The leftist-orientated movements, which based themselves on a pioneering life style (*halutziut*), became large and influential. They emphasized personal implementation (*hagshamah*) of their ideals, in which settlement in Palestine occupied a prime place. The attainment of this goal, together with the other basic ideals of the classic youth movement, had not only a spiritual and personal significance, but also a profound impact on the shape of the Jewish society and body politic developing in the land of Israel.

The Hehalutz (Pioneer) movement provided an umbrella organization for Zionist youth on their way to Palestine, where they became the spearheads of the Zionist enterprise. The pioneer youth movements were instrumental in the development of the different kibbutz federations in Palestine.

Branches of the Zionist youth movements were established in most Jewish communities around the world. Young Judea, the youth movement of the Zionist Organization of America, founded in the first decade of the twentieth century, was typical of the American youth movements: it was active in Zionist education, but lacked the dimension of social rebellion characteristic of the European youth movements. Although it supported *aliyah*, it did not oblige its members to settle in Palestine.

The Bund, the Jewish Socialist Party in Eastern Europe, created its own youth movement, which belonged in the category of associations that were youth sections of political parties.

## The Rise and Development of the Jewish Youth Movements in Europe

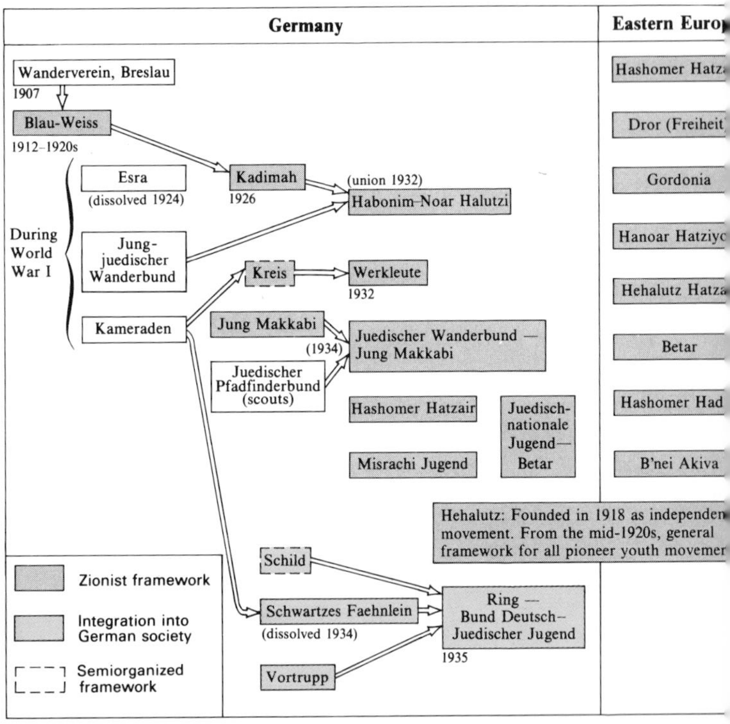


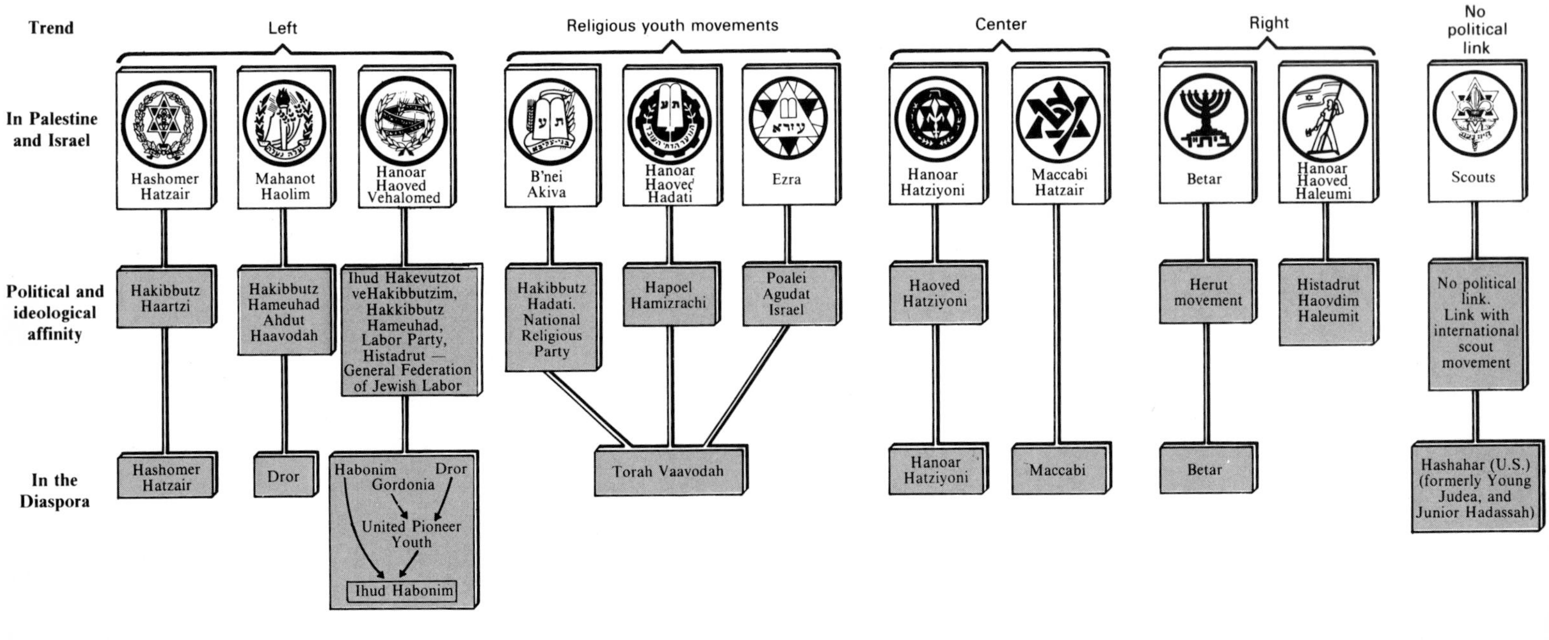

# Jewish Student Organizations in Europe

The creation of separate organizations of Jewish students in Europe was a clear expression of the tensions between non-Jewish and Jewish students at European universities, especially in Germany; German student associations were hotbeds of antisemitism. But the desire of Jews to associate with one another to achieve goals advantageous to Jews was also a factor in the formation of the Jewish associations. Jewish student organizations also sprang up in the United States, for reasons somewhat different from those in Europe, although in the first decades of the twentieth century discrimination against Jews was not uncommon at American universities.

Another development was the associations of Jewish students from Eastern Europe at many West European universities from the last years of the nineteenth century. Because of discriminatory laws in Russia, many young Jews were forced to seek university education in the West. There they founded associations that had a very dynamic intellectual life.

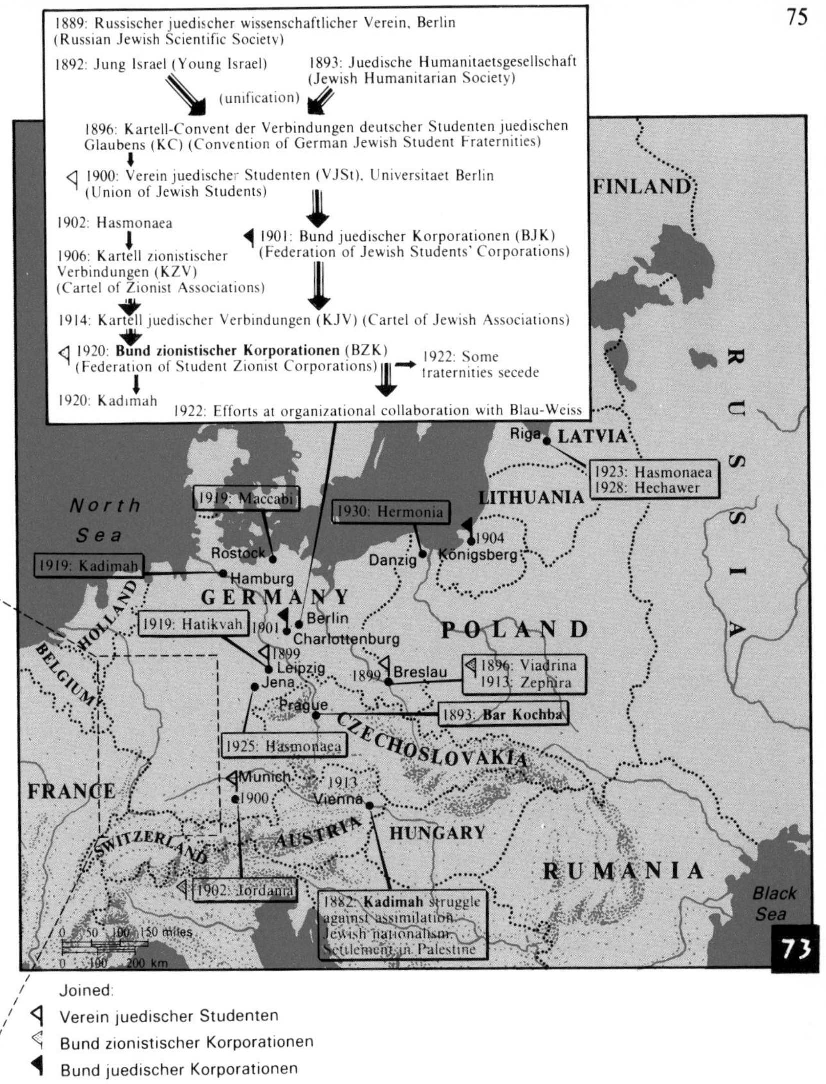


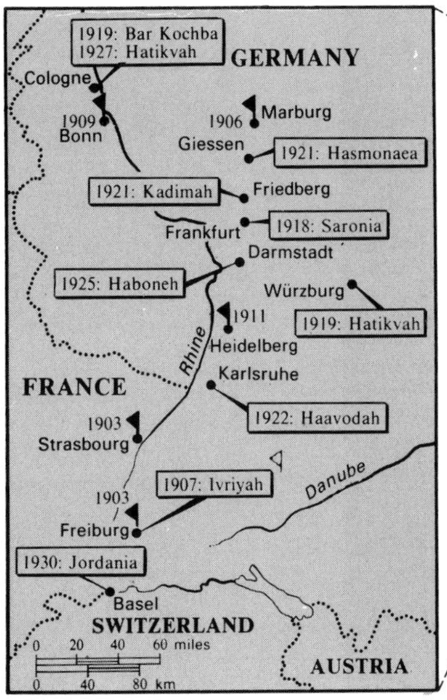


AVUKAH

# Jewish Student Organizations in the United States

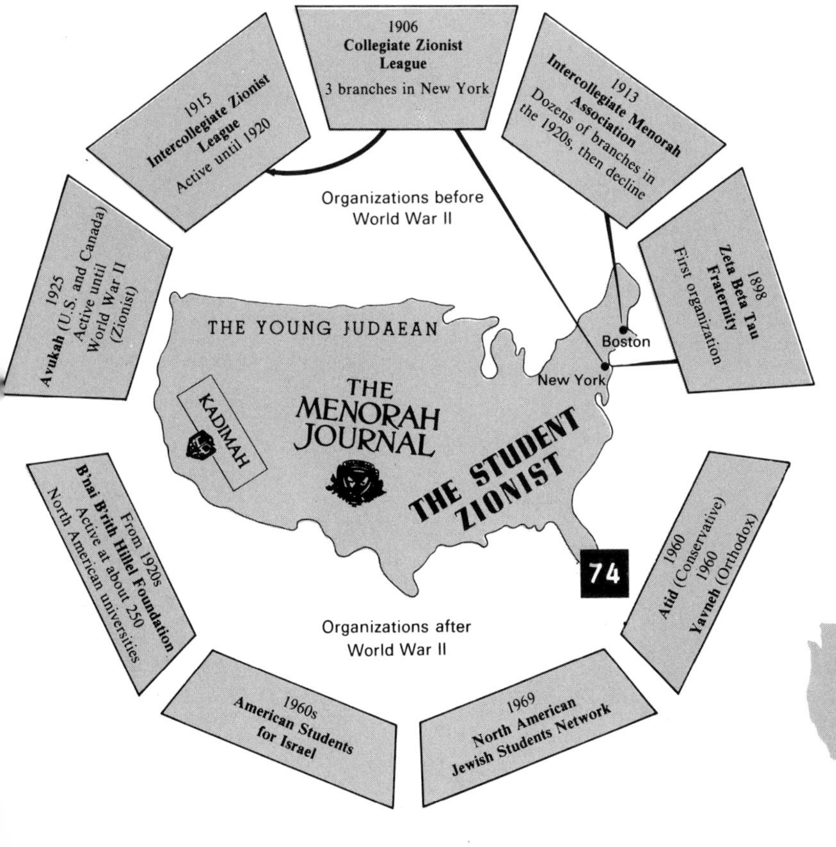


# Percentage of Jewish Students in Total Population

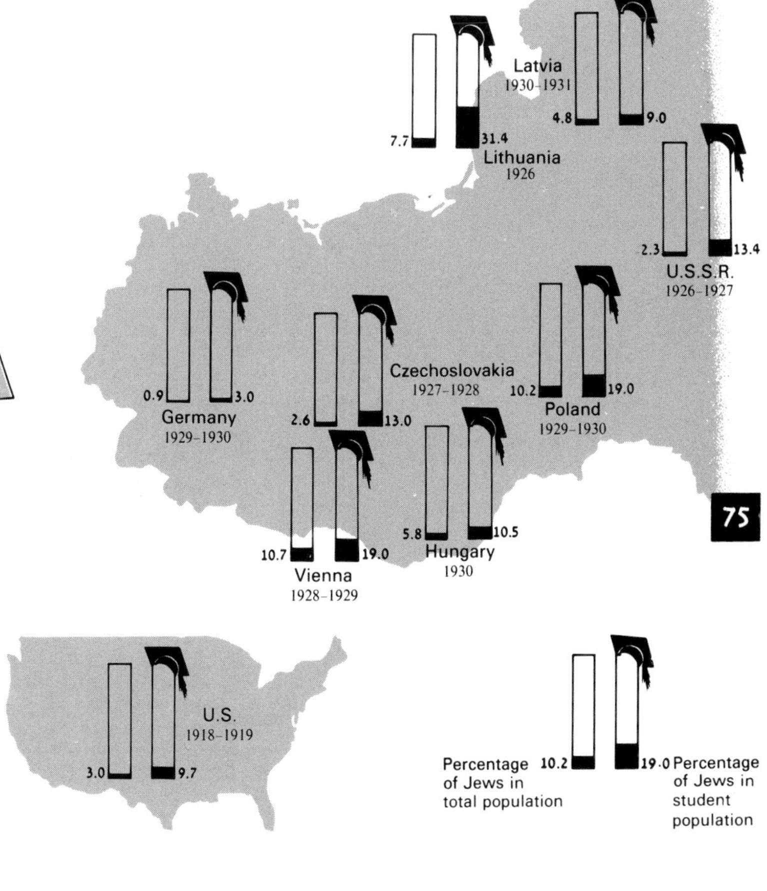

# The Jews in Muslim Countries

In the nineteenth and twentieth centuries, an important segment of the Jewish people lived in Muslim countries, in a broad belt extending from Morocco in the west to Afghanistan in the east, and including about a dozen countries in North Africa and the Middle East.

These Jewries evolved very differently from one another. Tradition has it that the Jews lived in Yemen in southern Arabia and in Morocco in North Africa since the Second Temple period, and perhaps even earlier. Other communities, such as those in Turkey and Greece, underwent radical transformations in the fifteenth and sixteenth centuries, with the arrival of the Jewish refugees from Spain and Portugal, who imposed their culture, language, and customs on the older Jewish society, the Romaniots. Another group was Egyptian Jewry: Jews had been in Egypt since times immemorial; but relatively few lived there in the eighteenth and nineteenth centuries, and new communities arose in the nineteenth century.

In spite of these differences, several important characteristics linked almost all Jewish communities in Muslim lands. Their life in these countries and their situation within Islamic society were based on two common legal foundations: (1) the principle established by the Prophet Mohammed that non-Muslims believing in one God (such as Jews and Christians) were protected subjects (*dhimmi*), although they had to pay a special annual tax (*jizya*); and (2) a set of discriminatory laws adopted in the time of the Caliph Omar II (717–719). These laws reflected a harsher attitude of Muslim society to the Jews. Their implementation, however, varied greatly, depending on which religious trend was dominant in a given time and place.

Most of these Jewish communities were also affected by the rise of the Ottoman Empire in the fifteenth century. The Turks came to dominate all the countries from northwestern Africa to the Middle East, conquering a large segment of southeastern Europe as well, and imposing a certain degree of unity in their empire. The decline of the Ottoman Empire, which began in the second half of the sixteenth century, was reflected in the conditions of its subjects, including the Jews. The "modernization" that began in Europe in the sixteenth and seventeenth centuries reached the Ottoman Empire only in the second half of the nineteenth century.

The third important factor in the development of the Jewries in Muslim lands was the growing European presence in the nineteenth and twentieth centuries. Many Muslim countries became European colonies—from the French conquest of Algeria in 1830 to the British occupation of Iraq in World War I. The situation of the Jews improved immensely under the colonial or semicolonial European regimes. They adapted quickly to the cultural and political changes that swept the Muslim countries from the mid-nineteenth century, and participated in the economic development associated with the European presence. The process was facilitated by another characteristic of most of the Jewries in Muslim countries: their urban or semiurban character. Even in countries where a large number of Jews lived in villages or small towns—such as Morocco, Yemen, and Kurdistan—the Jews' occupational structure was more urban than was that of the general population. The trend toward urbanization among these Jews, once modernization started in the Muslim countries, had interesting similarities to the behavior of the Jewish communities in Eastern Europe.

Finally, all the Jewries in Muslim countries faced a common crisis caused by the establishment of Israel. A combination of external pressures (strong hostility by the general population) and internal aspirations (the yearning for Zion component in their Jewish consciousness) brought about the dissolution of most of these Jewish communities. Most of the Jews migrated to Israel; many settled in Europe or North America. It is estimated that in 1948, more than 900,000 Jews lived in Muslim countries. In the 1980s, only 5 to 10 percent remained. In the second half of the twentieth century, the Jewries of the Muslim countries and of the Christian West, who had been separated for centuries, met and were reuniting in Israel and several other countries.

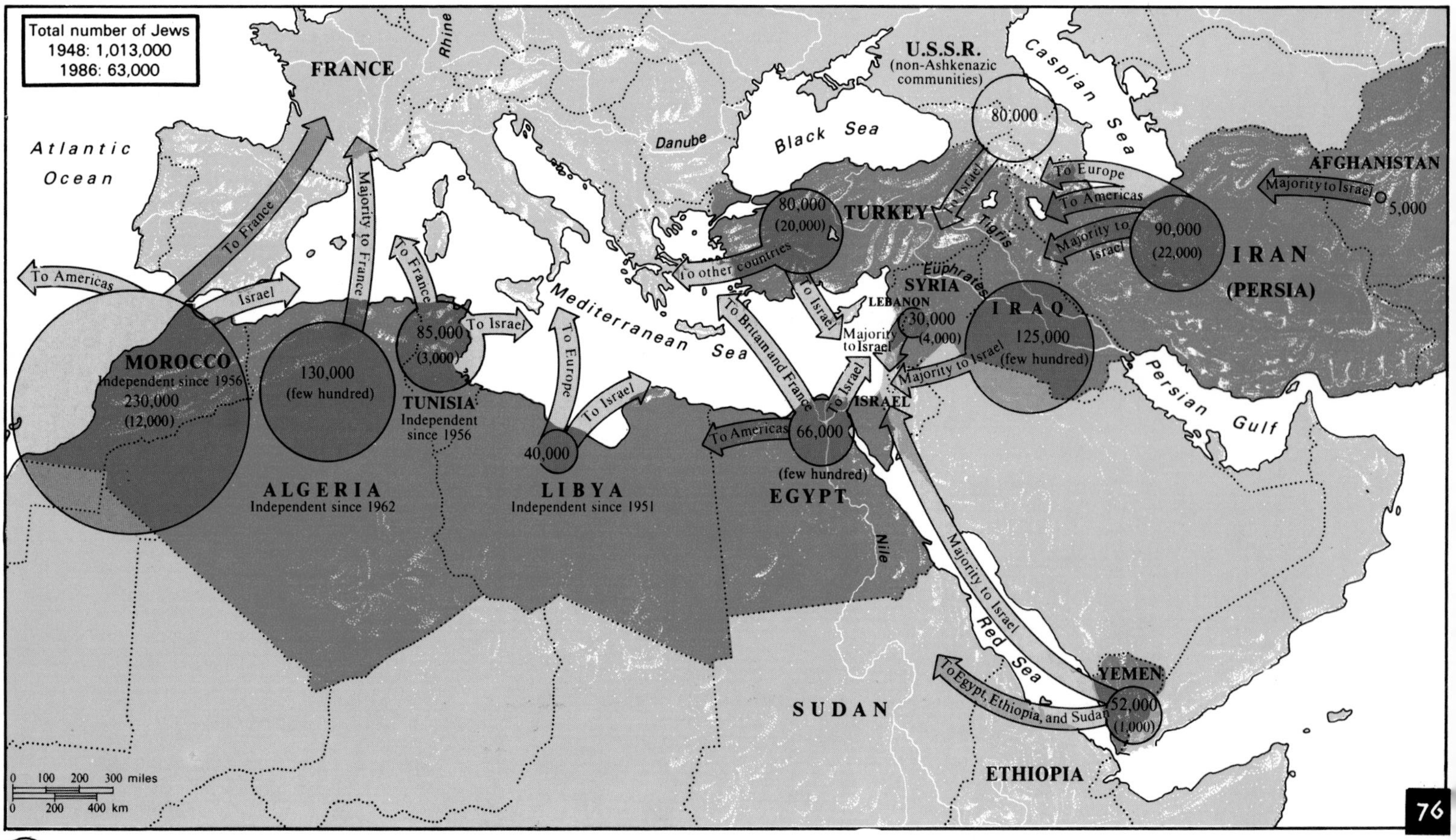


40,000 Number of Jews in 1948

(22,000) Estimated number of Jews remaining in 1986

Muslim country with Jewish population

For civil rights of Jews in Muslim countries, see page 47

# The Jews in Morocco

The largest Jewish community in the Muslim lands in the twentieth century was in Morocco. It is estimated that early in the century, about 100,000 Jews lived there, increasing in the 1940s to between 200,000 and 250,000 (including those in the Tangier international zone).

Jews had lived in Morocco for many centuries. They apparently arrived in Roman times, and, with occasional setbacks, their organized existence continued until the mid-twentieth century. In the modern period, Moroccan Jewry comprised three distinct groups: city dwellers along the Atlantic coast; villagers in the south or interior; and mountain dwellers, alongside the Berber population. The city dwellers were divided into the autochthonous Jews and the "newer" Sephardic Jews, descendants of refugees who had come from Spain and Portugal in the late Middle Ages.

Until the French conquest in 1912, Jewish life in Morocco was regulated by the traditional Muslim pattern: the Jews were protected subjects of the local ruler, and they paid special taxes. In the nineteenth century, their situation varied: those living in cities, where the power of the Moroccan sultan was effective, were well protected. Those living farther away were frequent victims of persecution, which occupied European Jewish public opinion. In 1864, Moses Montefiore visited Morocco and persuaded the sultan to revoke anti-Jewish laws. But later, under pressure from Muslim clergymen and local rulers, the sultan changed his mind.

The situation of the Jews improved considerably with the establishment of the French protectorate over Morocco in 1912. The following decades were a period of peace and prosperity for the Jewish community (although only in 1956 did the Jews become full citizens), and Moroccan Jewry underwent radical internal changes. Many villagers settled in the coastal cities. Toward the middle of the century, about half of the country's Jews lived in several larger cities, especially Casablanca. The Jews in Morocco, like those in Algeria and Tunisia, were deeply influenced by French culture, a process spurred by the Alliance Israélite Universelle school system. In 1948, there were more than fifty Alliance schools in Morocco.

After 1948, Moroccan Jewry began to emigrate—the majority to Israel, some to France, some to other European countries or North America. By 1962, 160,000 Jews remained in Morocco; in 1986, there were only 12,000, most of them in Casablanca.

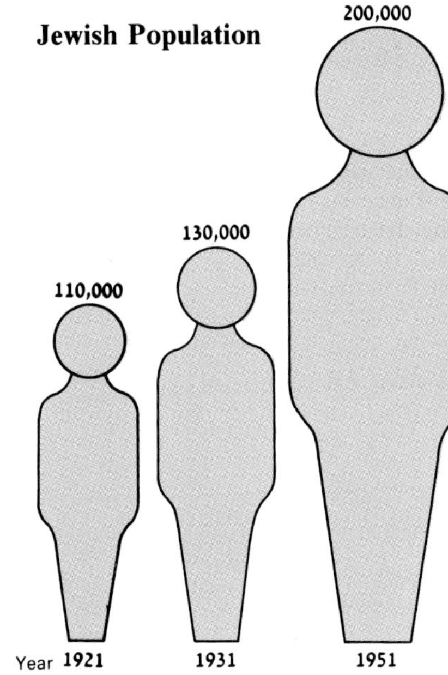


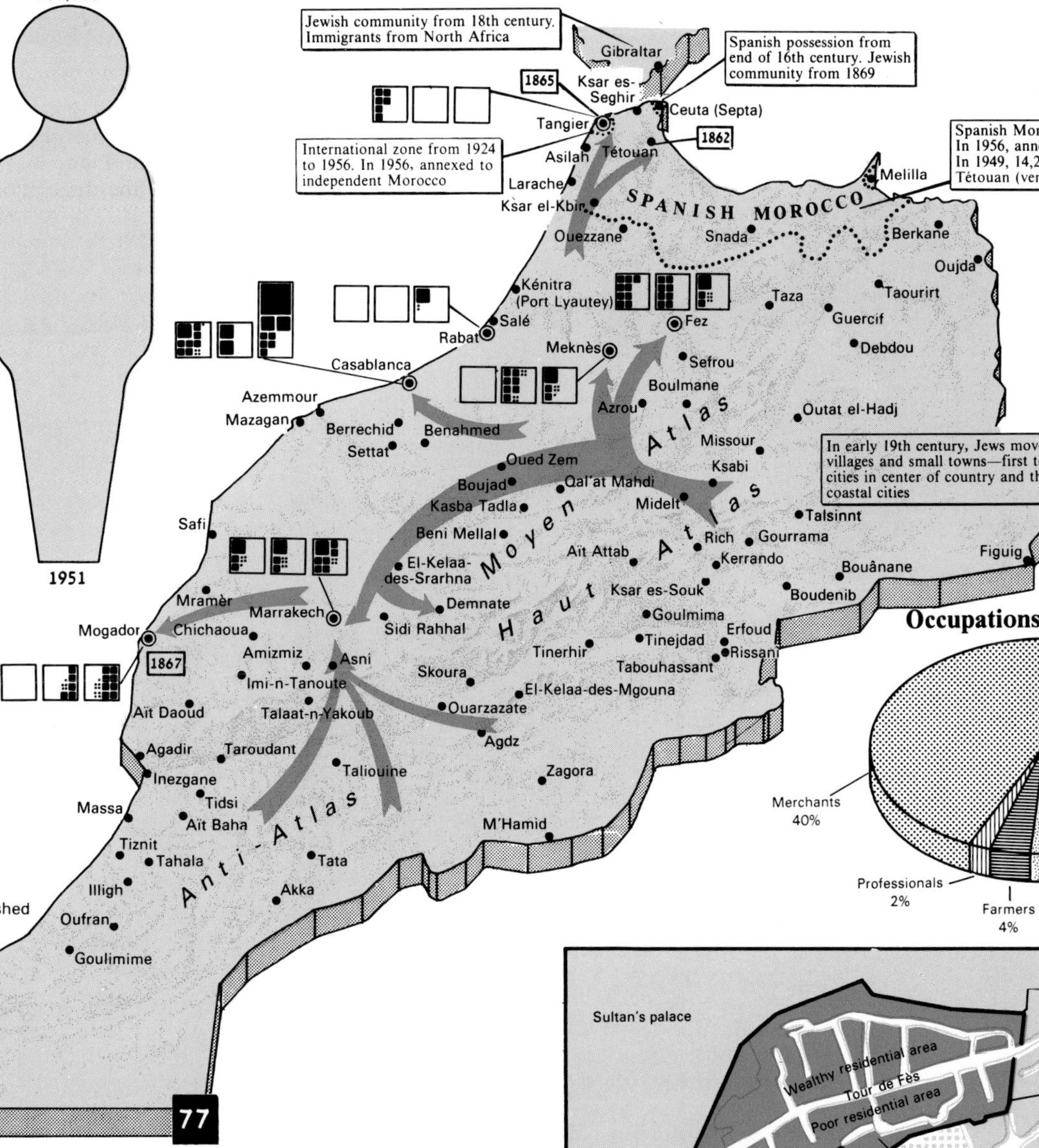


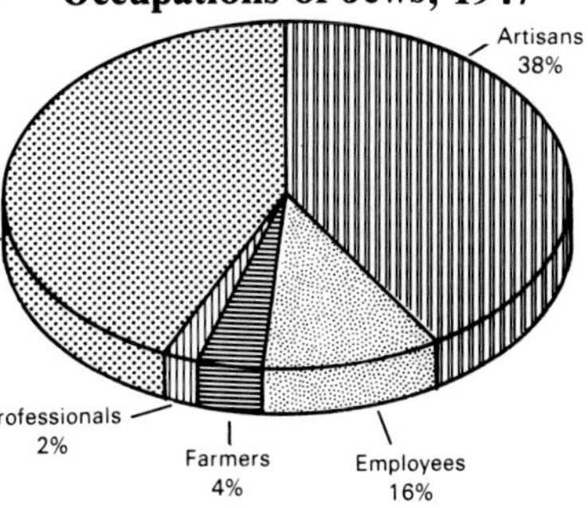


## The Jewish Quarter (*Mellah*) of Fez

The *mellah* of Fez was in the New City, close to the sultan's palace. It was a small, very crowded neighborhood, which in 1912 contained about 12,000 Jews. It consisted of two parts divided by a main street. The more affluent Jews lived in the northwestern part, higher and close to the palace; the poorer Jews lived in the southern, lower part. A large section of the *mellah* was burned down in 1912, when the Muslim population rioted against the French occupiers.

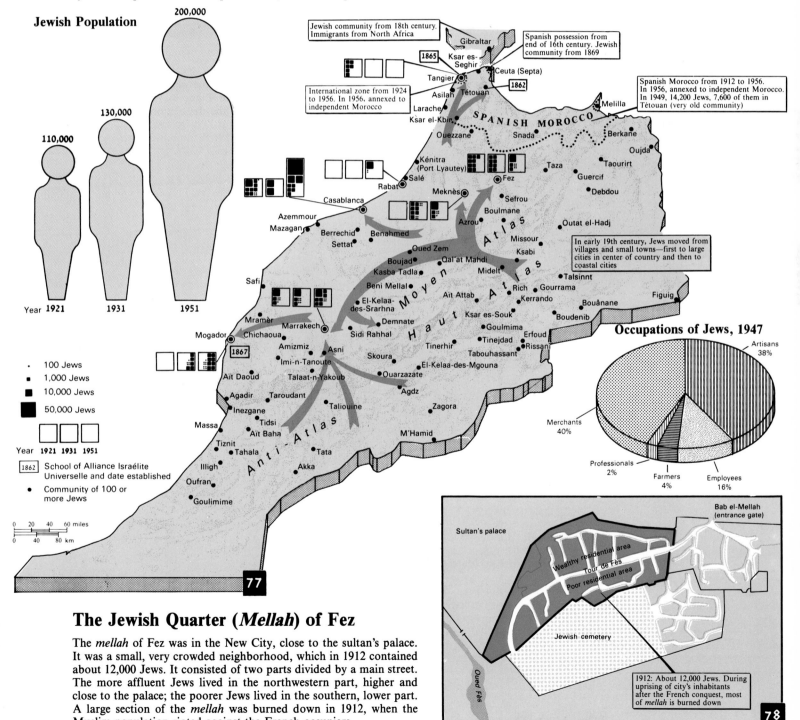

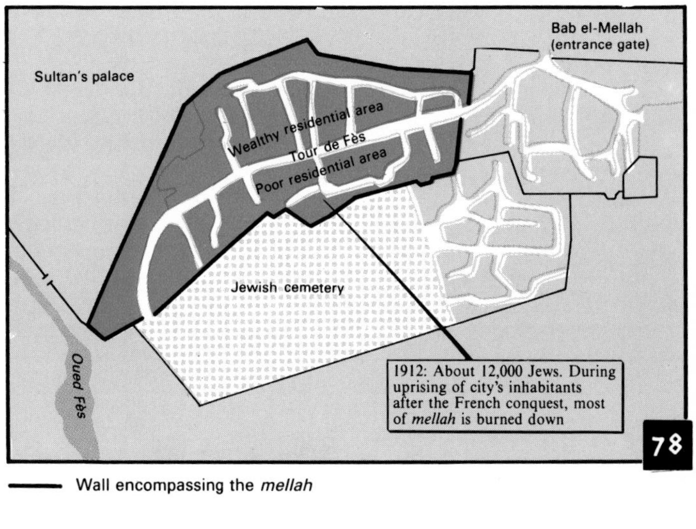

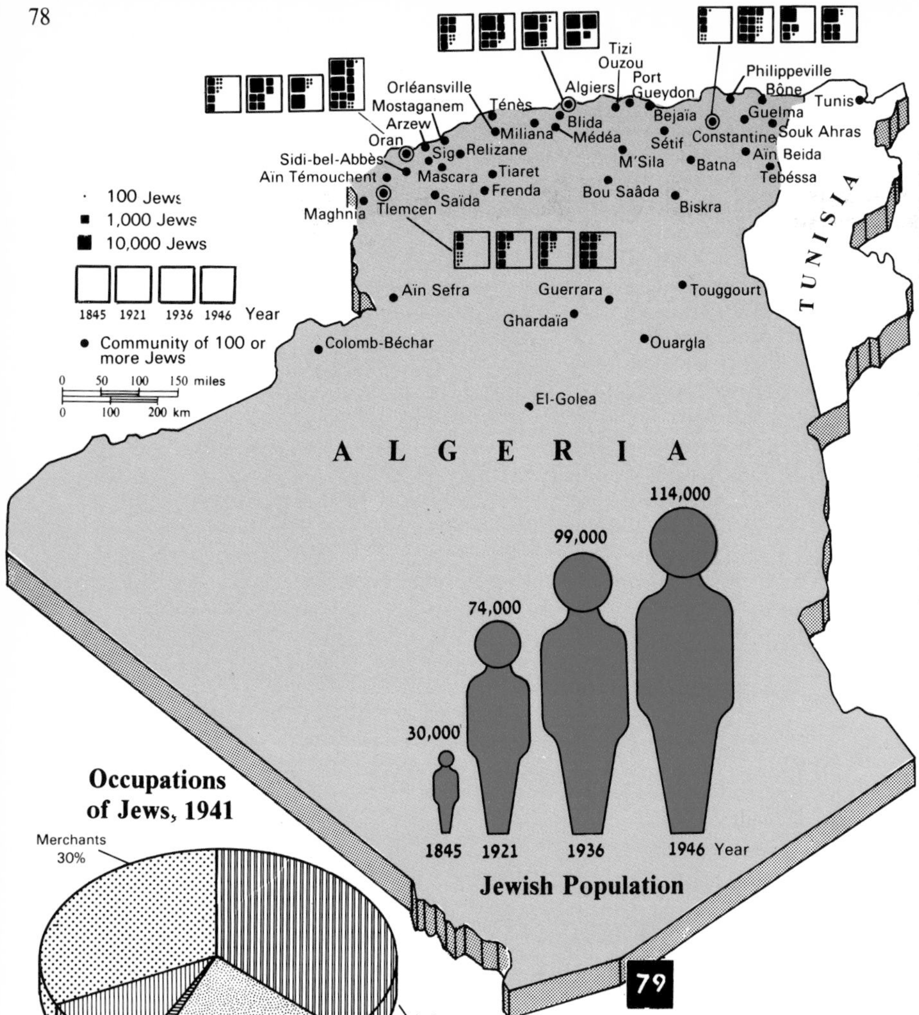


## Occupations of Jews, 1941

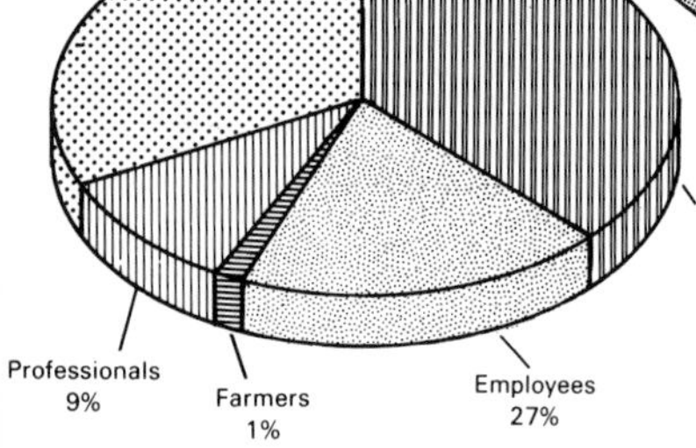


# The Jews in Algeria

Jews lived in Algeria from time immemorial. In the nineteenth century most were concentrated in several large and well-organized communities on the Mediterranean coast: Algiers, Constantine, Tlemcen and others. The communities were led by a *mukadam* (the Jewish elder, or *sheikh al-Yahud*), who had broad powers. The Spanish–Portuguese Jews had their own communal organization. Relations with the Muslim population were relatively good.

The French conquest of Algeria in 1830 brought many benefits for the Jews. Their civil situation improved, becoming the best of any Jewry in the Muslim world. In 1870, the Crémieux Decree granted French citizenship to the Jews in the major coastal cities. This aroused resentment among the Muslim and French (Christian) inhabitants leading to riots and antisemitic incidents, which later subsided.

The authorities established for the organization of the Jewish communities the consistorial system that existed in France. Three consistories were formed—in Algiers, Constantine, and Oran—connected with the Central Consistory in Paris and the French administration in Algiers. The Jews underwent a rapid and rather extreme process of French acculturation. The richer families sent their sons to study at universities in France. On their return to Algeria, they eventually occupied leading positions in the Algerian administration and in the professions.

Algerian Jewry underwent difficult times during World War II when the French Vichy regime revoked the Crémieux Decree. After the struggle for Algerian independence (1956–1962), the Jews concluded that their future in the new state was doubtful. Most (in 1955 they numbered 130,000 to 140,000) emigrated to France; some went to Israel and other countries. In the 1980s, a few hundred Jews remained in Algeria.

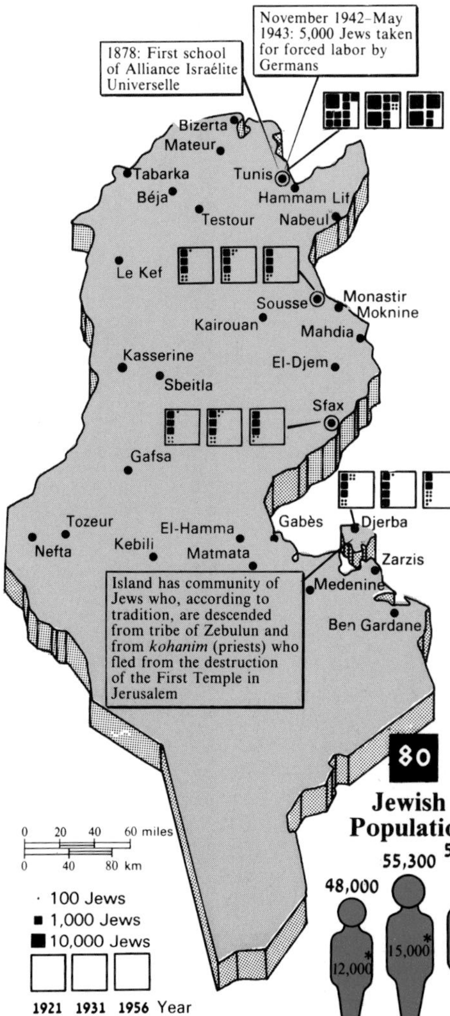


## Synagogues in Tunis's Jewish Quarter

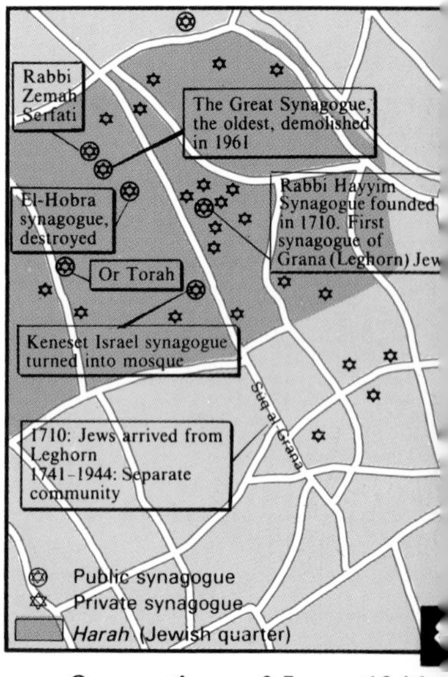


## Jewish Population

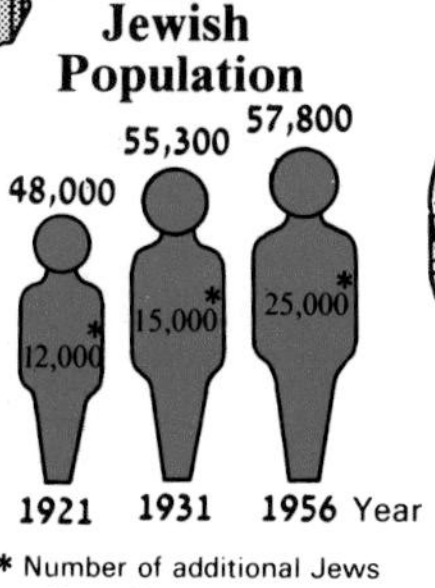


## Occupations of Jews, 1946

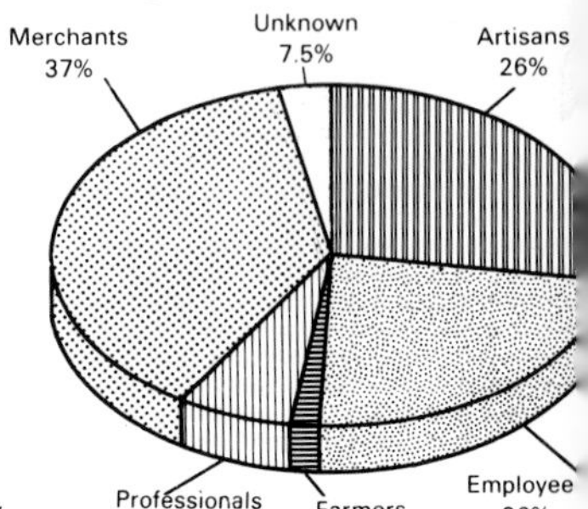


# The Jews in Tunisia

In the nineteenth and twentieth centuries, Tunisian Jewry consisted of two separately organized groups: authocthonous Jews (Touansa) and Spanish–Portuguese Jews (Grana), some of whom had come from Italy. The two communities were at odds with each other, which caused problems within Tunisian Jewry and in its relations with the Muslim authorities. An ancient and highly interesting community, the subject of many legends, lived on the island of Djerba.

More than half the country's Jews lived in the capital, Tunis. They worked chiefly in commerce and the crafts. Some larger Jewish merchants were active in the country's international commerce, especially with France and Italy.

In 1881, Tunisia became a French protectorate. The Jewish community was reorganized in one unified frame, the Tunisian Jewish Welfare Fund, in which the various bodies participated. It dealt with both religious and social matters. Tunisian Jewry came under the influence of the French language and culture. Many young Jews went to France to study, and later occupied important positions in the professions.

During World War II, Tunisia was under German military occupation from 1942 to 1943, very difficult years for the Jews. Tunisia became independent in 1956, and the Jews were granted the civil rights enjoyed by the rest of the population. Until 1967, the Tunisian government took a relatively moderate position regarding the Arab–Israeli conflict. Nevertheless, most Jews left the country in the 1950s and 1960s, mainly for France and Israel. In 1986, about 3,000 Jews remained in Tunisia, mainly in the capital.

## The Jews in Libya

Jews are believed to have lived in Libya since the Second Temple period. In modern times, Libyan Jewry was relatively small—about 25,000 in 1931. Two-thirds lived in Tripoli, where they made up 20 percent of the population. Benghazi was the second largest community. Amruz (near Tripoli) also had an important community, and there were several smaller communities in towns along or near the Mediterranean coast. Libyan Jews were cohesively organized according to traditional patterns, and their relations with their Muslim neighbors were relatively good. In 1911, the Italians conquered Libya, their domination continuing until 1943, when the British took it. The situation of Libyan Jews had been good under the Italians, but deteriorated on the eve of and during World War II, when Italy allied itself with Germany and the country was a major arena of the military operations in North Africa.

After 1948, almost all of Libya's Jews migrated to Israel, most in 1948 and 1951, and the rest later.

## The Jews in Egypt

Jews lived in Egypt almost as long as in Palestine, although there were different and noncontinuous Jewish settlements. In the seventeenth and eighteenth centuries, most Egyptian Jews were concentrated in two large and well-organized communities, Alexandria and Cairo, in such smaller ones as Rosetta, Mansura, and Damietta; and in several villages. Their total number was small: in the early nineteenth century, there were 5,000 to 7,000 Jews, including about 1,200 Karaites.

A small segment of the Jewish population consisted of veteran, well-established settlers, usually Ottoman citizens. In the eighteenth century, European Jewish merchants settled in Alexandria, mostly under the protection of the Capitulations (as subjects of foreign powers). In the 1820s, Jews from Greece and the Greek islands arrived, followed later in the century by more Jews from Greece and some from Italy, Iraq, and even Morocco. There was also a significant immigration of Ashkenazic Jews from Eastern and Central Europe. Many of these newcomers settled in Alexandria, Egypt's gateway to Europe and a city of cosmopolitan character and very active economic life.

Under Mohammed Ali (1805–1848), Egypt opened to European modernizing influences. The more affluent part of the population began to adopt European customs and languages. The Jews, too, accepted the Europeanizing trend. When Great Britain took over Egypt in 1882, the Jews' legal status was made equal to that of the rest of the population. Many Jews prospered.

The Jewish population was concentrated in the cities. In the late nineteenth century, most breadwinners were in commercial occupations—from clerks to middle-size or large merchants. The European origin or cultural tendencies of the Jews eased their way toward professions connected with Egypt's growing commercial contact with Europe. Many also acquired higher education, in Egypt or abroad, and Jews gradually became prominent in the professions.

In the nineteenth century, the Cairo and Alexandria communities dominated the country's Jewish social and religious life, with the support of the authorities. Newcomers had to struggle to establish their own synagogues. In 1854, Italian Jews in Alexandria created their own communal organization. In 1865, an Ashkenazic community was established in Cairo, over the opposition of the incumbent Jewish leadership. Over the years, the diversity of Egyptian Jewry expressed itself also in the separate Jewish institutions that each group created.

The relatively good situation of Egyptian Jewry continued until the mid-twentieth century. After the establishment of Israel, most Jews gradually left Egypt, emigrating to Israel and France, as well as to Latin America, the United States, and other countries. In the mid-1980s, only a few hundred Jews lived in Egypt, mostly in Cairo and Alexandria.

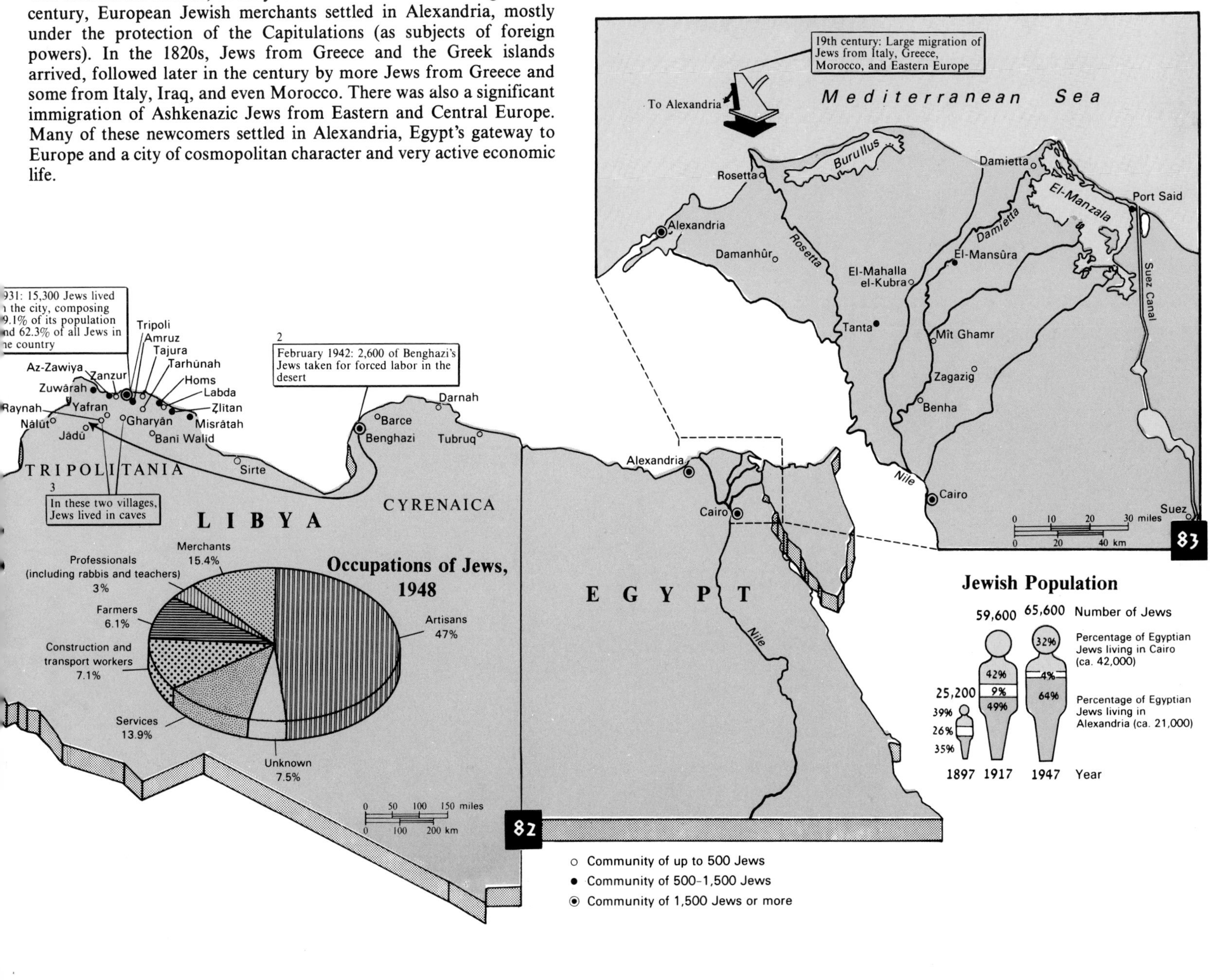

# The Jews in the Ottoman Empire and Turkey

The Ottoman Empire underwent many political changes in the nineteenth and twentieth centuries that gradually reduced its size. Greece became independent in 1830 (although its northern part, with the great Jewish center in Salonika, became part of Greece only in 1913). Between 1859 and 1878, the empire lost Walachia and Moldavia (which formed Rumania), Bosnia (to Austria–Hungary), Serbia, and Bulgaria. Great Britain conquered Egypt in 1882, and Italy took over Libya and Rhodes in 1911 and 1912. As a result of World War I, the Turks had to yield large parts of the Middle East (the Arabian Peninsula, Iraq, Syria, Lebanon, and Palestine). The Ottoman Empire was dissolved, and the core that remained became modern Turkey.

Large and varied Jewish communities lived in the lands that had been under Ottoman domination. The Jewish population usually consisted of groups that had settled in a particular place over the centuries. There was usually a small older stratum, the Romaniots (or Gregos), which was augmented by a large influx of Jewish refugees from Spain and Portugal in the sixteenth century. The Sephardim strongly influenced Jewish life and culture during the succeeding centuries. In Palestine and in several other places in the empire, there were also Ashkenazic Jews. Constantinople was an important center of the Karaite sect. An interesting community, with specific characteristics, lived in Rhodes. In general, the particular conditions in the different parts of the empire were a factor in the shaping of the local Jewish communities.

On the whole, the legal situation of the Jews in the empire was good. However, local traditions regarding relations between Jews and non-Jews, and the whims of the local ruler, affected the status of each community. As "non-believers" (Islamically speaking), Jews paid a special tax (*jizya*, or *haradj*), were protected subjects (*dhimmi*), had internal autonomy, were unhindered in their economic activities, and could, in principle, travel freely. Social reforms in the empire in the nineteenth century (the *tansimat*) bestowed new civil rights on Muslim subjects and, as a result of pressure by the European powers, also on non-Muslims. The *hakham-bashi* (head *hakham*, or chief rabbi) of Constantinople was recognized by the authorities as the official religious leader of the Jews of the empire, with a considerable voice in the nomination of rabbis (*hakhamim*) in the larger provincial communities. Two commissions were established in each community, one for religious and one for social matters, and together with the *hakhamim* they administered the life of the Jewish general community (*millet*, or nation).

The growing European cultural influence left its mark. A specific type of *haskalah* (Jewish enlightenment) developed among the Jews of the major Ottoman centers, especially Constantinople and Salonika. One of its results was the flowering of Ladino, which began to be used in newspapers and books.

The Jews acquired full civil rights in the new Turkish state created by Mustafa Kemal (Atatürk) in the early 1920s. Most Jews now lived in the larger cities. In 1927, half of Turkey's 81,500 Jews lived in Istanbul (Constantinople). In the 1920s and 1930s, many Jews emigrated, mainly to the Americas.

After 1948, 30,000 to 40,000 Jews emigrated to Israel. Emigration to other countries continued as well. In 1986, about 20,000 Jews lived in Turkey, mostly in Istanbul and Izmir.

### Syria and Lebanon

Syria and Lebanon became separate French mandates after World War I, and independent countries after World War II. Only 15,000 Jews lived in Syria in the 1940s, but the two main communities, Aleppo and Damascus, were old and well established. Most Jews left Syria after 1948, for Israel or other countries. In the 1980s, a few thousand remained, and their situation was precarious. About 4,000 Jews lived in Lebanon in the 1940s, mainly in Beirut. In the 1950s, the Jews in Lebanon were better off than in other Arab countries, but in the 1960s most Jews emigrated, only a few remaining in the 1980s.

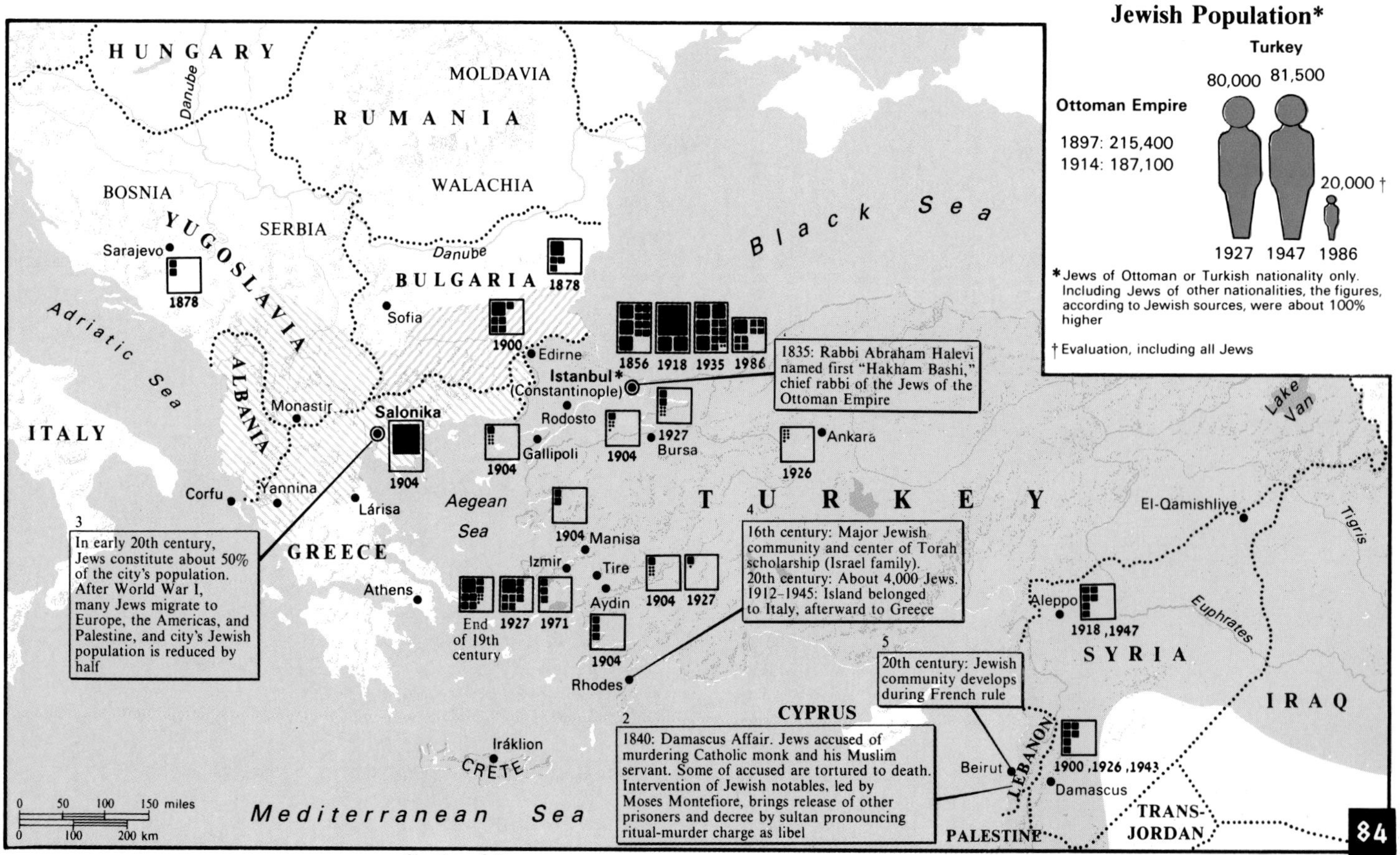


*Jews of Ottoman or Turkish nationality only. Including Jews of other nationalities, the figures, according to Jewish sources, were about 100% higher

† Evaluation, including all Jews

······ Post-World War I border
Ottoman Empire after 1878
Joined to Bulgaria after 1885
Joined to other countries in 1912–1913

Number of Jews
· 100
▪ 1,000
■ 10,000
■ 50,000

1927 and 1935 data based on censuses. Other data are estimates

*Census data indicated 19,200 Jews of Ottoman nationality in 1878, and 22,400 in 1886

## The Jews in Constantinople (Istanbul)

Jews lived in Constantinople continuously since antiquity. Their status and conditions were affected by the changing character of the city over the centuries, from Christian–Byzantine to Muslim–Turkish times. There was no permanent Jewish quarter, and in different periods the Jews moved from one part of the city to another, although they settled for longer periods on the southern shore of the Golden Horn.

The long presence of the Jews in Constantinople was reflected in their internal organization. There was an older group of Romaniots, the remnants of the first Jewish settlers. A large number of Jews exiled from Spain and Portugal arrived in the sixteenth century. They prospered in Constantinople, attaining important positions in public life, and created a new Jewish type and culture in the Ottoman Empire. Additional Jewish settlers came in later centuries, including, in the eighteenth century, Ashkenazic Jews. The various Jewish groups did not organize in a common framework, but maintained separate communities, according to their origins. Severe fires in the seventeenth and eighteenth centuries destroyed large sections of the Jewish neighborhoods, which led the diverse groups to seek greater cooperation with one another.

The sixteenth and seventeenth centuries marked a high point in the development and influence of Constantinople Jewry. In the nineteenth century, the Jews were strongly influenced by the gradual penetration of European culture. In 1864, the authorities reorganized the minority groups (*millets*, or nations), including the Jews. The post of *hakham-bashi* (chief rabbi) was created in 1835, with broad powers over the religious and internal life of the Jewish communities in the empire. This strengthened the position of Constantinople Jewry. In the late nineteenth century, 40,000 to 50,000 Jews lived in the city, and perhaps even more in the early twentieth century, but their number decreased after World War I. With the establishment of the Turkish republic, Jews became full citizens, and their economic and professional situation improved. Nevertheless, many emigrated, mostly to Europe, America, and, after 1948, Israel. About 50,000 Jews lived in the city in 1948; 30,000 in 1970; and about 18,000 in 1986.

1740: After fire in the ancient Jewish quarter in the Golden Horn, Jews settle in Muslim quarters, especially Galata, Ortaköy, and Üsküdar

- ⋰ Quarter with concentration of Jewish families

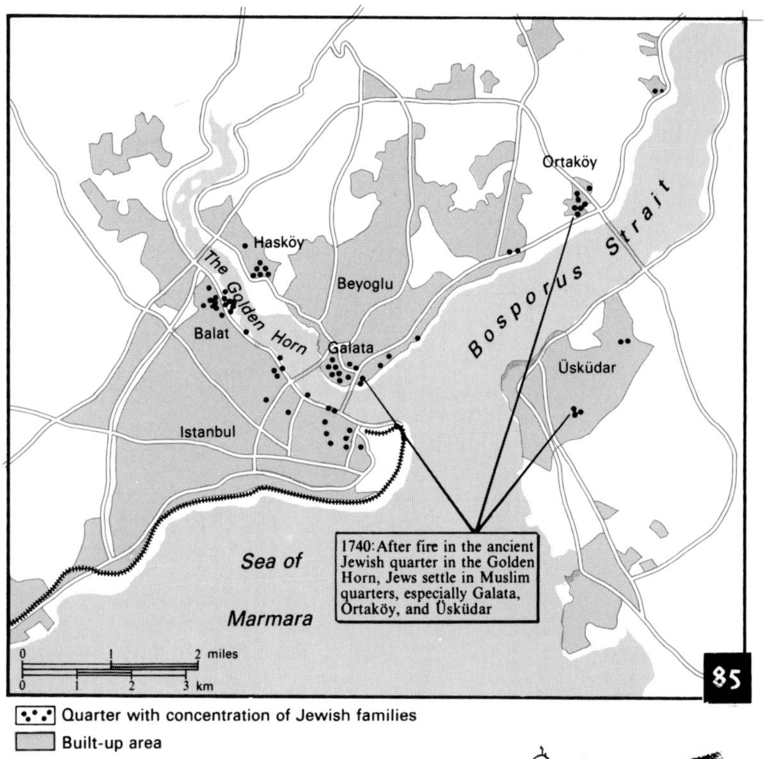

*Gate of Etz Hayyim synagogue in Ortaköy, Istanbul. Synagogue burned down in 1934 and was rebuilt*

## The Jews in Salonika

August 18, 1917: Large parts of the city destroyed by fire, including most Jewish neighborhoods

- ▨ Built-up area
- --- Area destroyed in 1917 fire

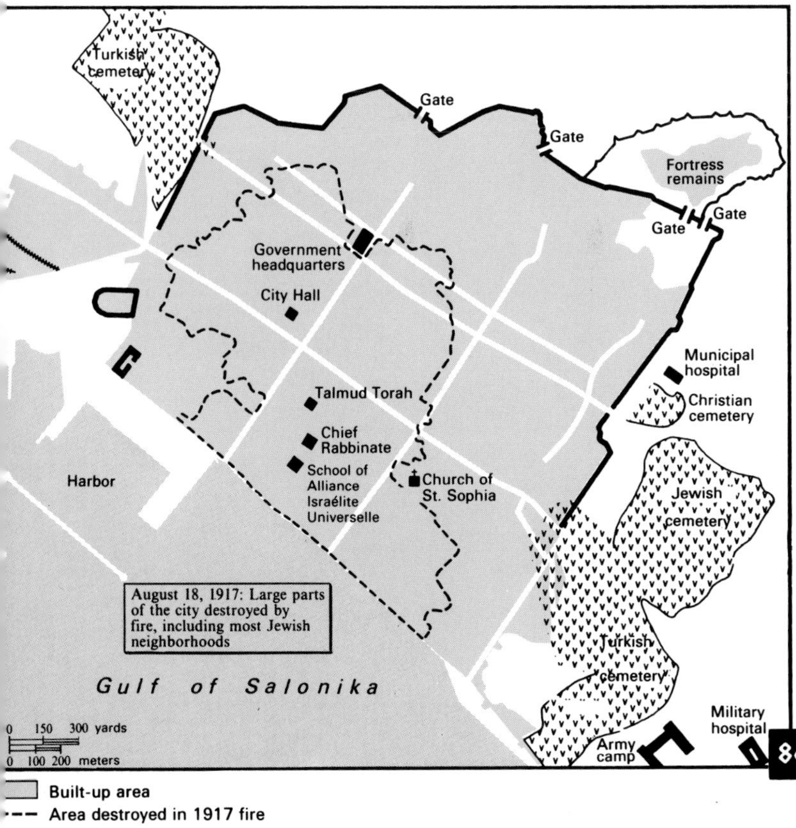


Until the ninteenth century, the Jewish communities of Salonika and Constantinople were the two largest in the world. In Salonika, the Jews were able to create a much more unified community than in Constantinople. In the early twentieth century, there were more than 50,000 Jews in the city, about half of Salonika's total population. There was also a large community of "Doenmeh," descendants of seventeenth-century followers of the false messiah Sabbetai Zevi who had become Muslims without renouncing Judaism, which they interpreted according to new principles. Most of the Jews were Sephardim, descendants of Spanish–Portuguese Jews who had arrived in the sixteenth century. Salonika became a major religious and spiritual center of Sephardic Jewry, known for its rabbis and sages. In the nineteenth century, Salonika also became a center of Jewish enlightenment (*haskalah*). A small but very influential element were the Francos—European Jewish merchants from Central and Western Europe, who were important transmitters of modern ideas.

The occupational structure of Salonika Jewry was particularly interesting; Jews were in all the occupations: manual laborers, stevedores (the large Salonika port was said to have closed down on the Sabbath and other Jewish holy days), artisans, as well as large merchants, professionals, and bankers. A group of Jewish intellectuals and Doenmeh belonged to the Young Turk revolutionaries in the first decade of the century. In 1913, the city was handed over to Greece.

Large fires in the city in 1890 and 1917 destroyed the Jewish neighborhoods and ruined their inhabitants. After World War I, many Jews left Salonika, while Christian Greeks settled in the city. The portion of Jews in the total population decreased in the interwar years to 25 percent, but Salonika remained an important Jewish center.

The end of the Jewish community came in the summer of 1943. The German conquerors sent most of the 40,000 to 50,000 Jews living in Salonika (including many previously deported there from other places) to death camps in Poland. In the mid-1980s, only a few Jews remained in Salonika.

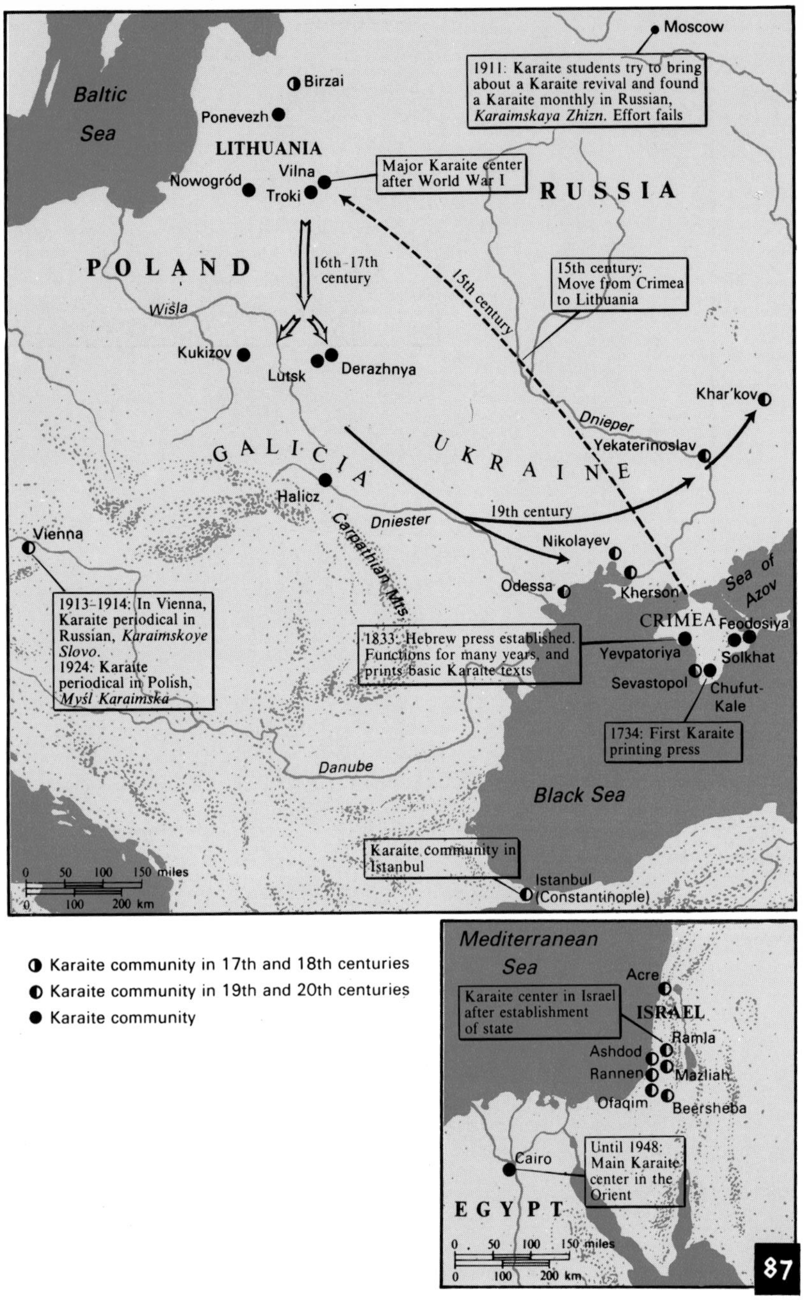


# The Karaites

The Karaite sect dates to the eighth century. Karaism opposed the mainstream Talmudic–rabbinic tradition, rejecting the "Oral Law" and adhering to a fundamentalist, literal reading of the written text of the Bible.

In modern times, most Karaites lived in Russia (Lithuania and the Crimea), Poland, Egypt, and Palestine. In the eighteenth century, when the Russian Empire absorbed Lithuania, the Karaites were recognized as a separate religious sect; the same happened in 1840 regarding the Crimean Karaites. At the end of the nineteenth century, there were about 13,000 Karaites in Russia, mostly in the Crimea. The Karaites spoke a variety of languages: an Arabic dialect in Iraq and Egypt, a Turkish dialect in Constantinople, and Crimean-Tataric in the Crimea.

In the twentieth century, their number decreased to about 12,000 (1930). Most lived in the Soviet Union, and the rest in Poland (Vilna became a Karaite center), Turkey, Iraq, Egypt, and Palestine. During World War II, the Germans granted a Karaite request for recognition as an independent religious group. Nevertheless, their centers in Europe were destroyed.

Most Karaites from Muslim countries emigrated to Israel after the establishment of the state. The largest concentration of them settled in Ramla, which became the seat of their leading institutions: a synagogue, a yeshiva, and a religious court; unlike the Muslim or Druse religious courts, however, the Karaite one did not have state sanction. Smaller Karaite communities were established in other Israeli localities.

In Israel, they are defined as "Karaite Jews." Since the Karaites strictly obey the biblical prohibition against "counting the people," there are no exact data about their number. Estimates range from 10,000 to 18,000, most in Israel, and the rest in the United States, Canada, France, and Turkey.

*Beta Esrael synagogue*

# The Ethiopian Jews

The Jews of Ethiopia (generally called Falashas; they call themselves Beta Esrael, or "House of Israel") consider themselves descendants of King Solomon and the Queen of Sheba. Modern researchers think that they are black tribes that adopted the Jewish religion in the Middle Ages. Their holy books are the Bible and part of the Apocrypha. They did not know the Mishnah or the Talmud.

It seems that until the seventeenth century, they were a largely autonomous community, even independent at times. They retained their identity even when subjected to persecutions instigated by Christian missionaries. "Pro-Falasha Committees" were organized among European Jews in the twentieth century, to help the Ethiopian Jews.

Their number in the early twentieth century is estimated to have been 50,000. They lived in northern Ethiopia, near the Sudanese border, in or around the city of Gondar. They worked in agriculture and crafts. Their language was Amharic, the official language of Ethiopia, but they read the Bible in Ge'ez, the classical holy language of the Ethiopian church. They were organized in communities led by religious leaders.

The Jewish Agency established contact with the Ethiopian Jews before the creation of the state of Israel. In 1969, they numbered 25,000 to 30,000. Their situation deteriorated considerably in the 1960s and 1970s, due to the political situation in Ethiopia, and efforts were made to rescue them. In the mid-1980s, a large portion of Ethiopian Jewry arrived in Israel.

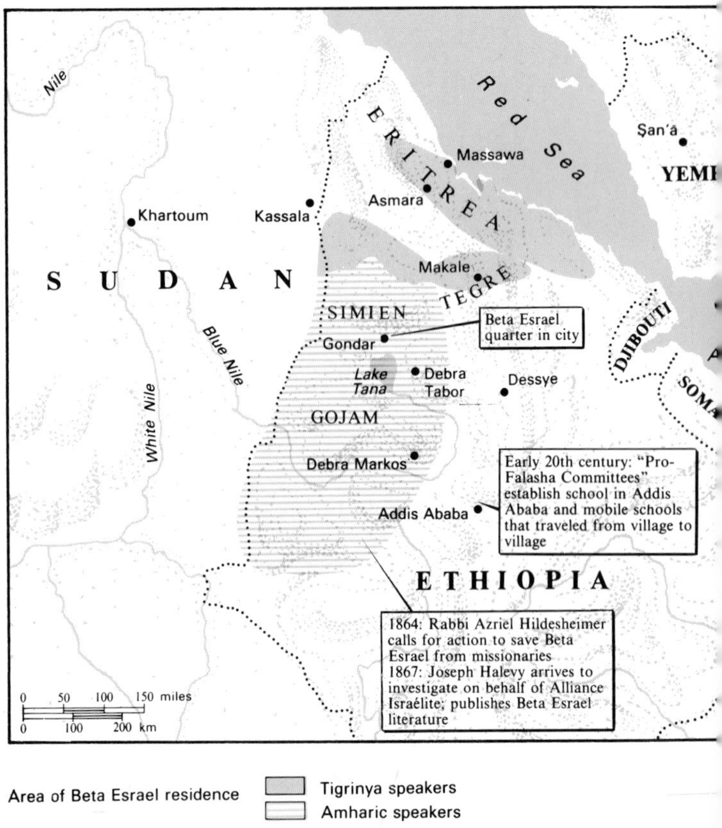

# The Jews in Iraq

Iraq became part of the Ottoman Empire in 1638. Jews (referred to in Hebrew as Babylonian Jews) had lived in the country since the dawn of Jewish history. In the modern period, they were divided in two groups: the inhabitants of the lowlands (living mainly in the capital, Baghdad), and the mountain Jews of Kurdistan. They were defined as a minority (*millet*), and although their situation depended considerably on the whims of the local ruler (the pasha), it was usually better than that of the Jews in most other Muslim countries and that of the Christian *millet*. Conditions improved further starting in 1839, with the implementation of the social reforms (*tanzimat*) in the Ottoman Empire. The special poll tax (*jizya*) was abolished in 1855, and new rights were gradually granted. With the British conquest of Iraq in 1917, the Jews acquired civil rights equal to those of the Muslims. After Iraq achieved independence in 1932, Jews became full citizens of the new state. Parts of the community integrated into the cultural and political life of the general society and underwent "Iraqization." But their situation was ambivalent: first signs of discrimination began to appear, reflecting nationalistic and anti-European tendencies in Iraqi society. In mid-1941, there were severe riots against the Jews in Baghdad and other parts of the country. Hundreds of Jews were killed.

In the twentieth century, more than two-thirds of Iraqi Jewry lived in Baghdad, which was the spiritual center for all Jews who lived east of Damascus. Its leading position had been established in the nineteenth century, in the days of Rabbi Joseph Haim (1833/5–1909), the community's leading religious figure from 1859. While the religious authority was in the hands of the rabbi, the community was headed by the sheikh (or *nasi*), usually a rich Jew who was well connected with the authorities and had the power to veto communal appointments. Baghdad Jewry was a community primarily of merchants, some very important, whose activities extended over the whole country and beyond.

Iraqi Jewry had always maintained contact with Palestine. In the twentieth century, immigration to Palestine increased, and by 1948, about 11,000 Iraqi Jews already lived in the country. The creation of Israel caused severe tension between the Jews and the general Iraqi population. An agreement was reached in 1950 that enabled all the Jews to emigrate from Iraq to Israel. Almost the entire community of about 120,000, including the Kurdish Jews, left in a short time in what is known as "Operation Ezra and Nehemiah." Most went to Israel; others, to Europe and the United States. By the end of 1951, about 6,000 Jews remained in Iraq, and in the mid-1980s, their number had diminished to about 200.

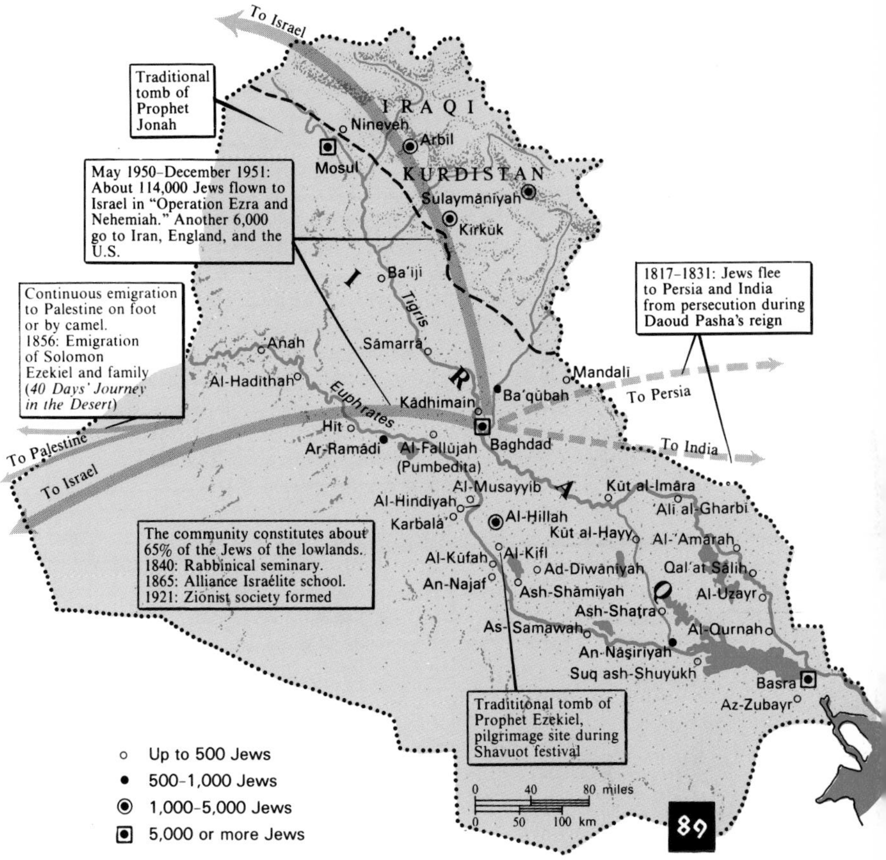


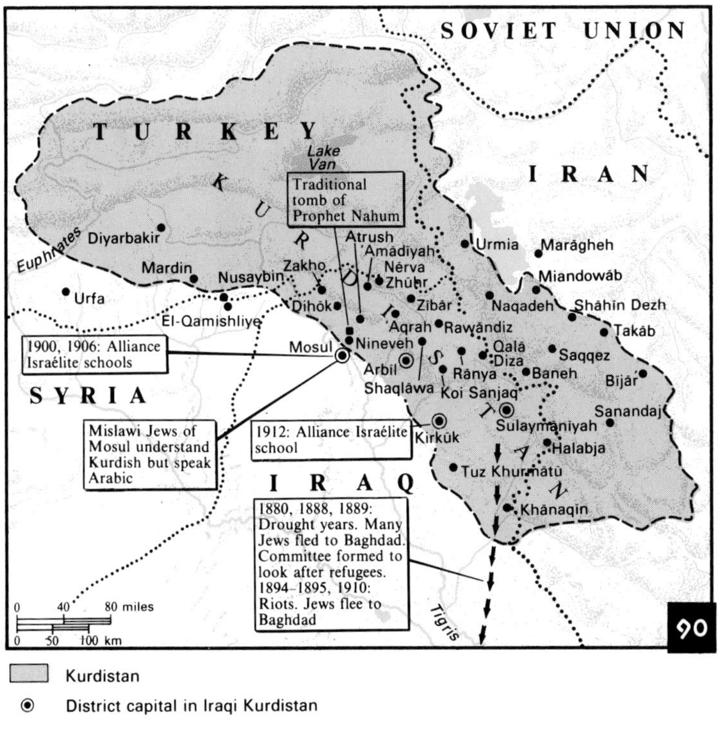


# The Jews in Kurdistan

The majority of Kurdish Jewry lived in the mountain region of northern Iraq. They constituted a well-defined group among Middle Eastern Jewry, with their own Jewish culture and traditions, very different from those of the Jews in the Iraqi lowlands, and much older. In the twentieth century, there were 15,000 to 20,000 Kurdish Jews living in about 150 small mountain villages in Iraq and about 50 villages in northeastern Iran, southeastern Turkey, and Syria—the other areas into which Kurdistan extends. They lived in greater hardship than the Jews of the Iraqi lowlands. The rule of the local Kurdish chieftain (the *aga*), to which they were subject, was often oppressive. The portion of Kurdish Jews in agriculture was higher than that of other Jewries, but many were virtually serfs. Other Kurdish Jews were artisans or small tradesmen. They spoke Judeo-Kurdish, an Aramaic dialect used also by other minorities of the region, as well as Kurdish, an Indo-European language akin to Persian.

The political changes in Iraq in the 1930s and 1940s made the situation of Kurdish Jews increasingly difficult. Riots against the Jews in the lowlands spread to the mountains. Many Kurdish Jews began to emigrate to Palestine, to which the community had a longstanding attachment, and when Israel was established it already had a sizable Kurdish community. Most Kurdish Jews—from Iraq and the neighboring countries—went to Israel in "Operation Ezra and Nehemiah."

# The Jews in Iran

The Jewish communities in Persia (renamed Iran in 1935) were among the oldest in Jewish history. In the early nineteenth century, when Persia dominated Afghanistan in the east and regions in Central Asia in the north, it had about 50,000 Jews. When those lands were later lost, the number of Jews in Persia fell to about 25,000. It rose again to 50,000 in the twentieth century, reaching a peak on the eve of the creation of Israel—about 90,000, including 13,000 Jews in Iranian Kurdistan. On the eve of Israel's establishment, 20,000 to 30,000 Iranian Jews were living in Palestine. More came later, but in 1975 there were still about 80,000 Jews in Iran. The Jews were a tiny part of the total population: 0.5 percent at the beginning of the century, and 0.2 percent in the 1970s.

The legal situation of the Jews conformed to the traditional Muslim pattern: protected subjects, who had to pay the poll tax (*jizya*), and from time to time were subjected to discriminatory regulations. There were occasional persecutions, such as under the Safawid dynasty (1502–1736), which tried to convert the Jews. Legislation in 1906 broadened the civil rights of the non-Muslim minorities, including the Jews. The *jizya*, however, was abolished only in 1926—much later than in other Muslim countries—after Reza Shah Pahlevi rose to power, and equal rights were granted to all the country's inhabitants.

The Jews were scattered throughout Iran, living mainly in cities. In the early twentieth century, the largest Jewish center was Shiraz and its vicinity—although only 10 to 15 percent of all Persian Jews lived there. In the coming years, the Jewish population gradually became concentrated in several larger centers, especially the capital, Teheran: about 30 percent of the country's Jews in 1948, and about 75 percent in 1975, when more than 90 percent were living in three major centers. Parallel to the concentration in cities, Iranian Jewry was influenced by modern European manners and concepts, and integrated into the country's social and cultural life.

The occupations of the Jews reflected their urban character. Until the early twentieth century, they were mainly small tradesmen and craftsmen. Later they branched out into new fields: as professionals, merchants (some of them very large), real-estate agents, and the like.

Like other Middle Eastern Jewish communities, Iranian Jewry had a twin leadership, religious (the *mullah*, or rabbi) and secular (the *kadkhuda*). The *kadkhuda* was responsible for the collection of the *jizya* and the community's relations with the authorities. The *mullah* acted also as religious judge, teacher, and *shohet* (ritual slaughterer). Sometimes the same prestigious figure occupied both offices, bearing the title *nasi*. Sometimes the *nasi* served with a council of elders, the "eyes of the community." In the second half of the twentieth century, most matters regarding Iranian Jewry were dealt with by the Organization of Teheran Jews, which aimed to represent all the country's Jews.

After 1948, part of Iranian Jewry migrated to Israel. The Islamic revolution in 1979 completely changed the internal life of the Jewish community. The new regime regarded all Jews as Zionists, and most Jewish institutions were forced to cease operations. Several leading Jewish figures, including the former head of the Teheran community, were executed. Most Jews managed to leave the country, settling mainly in Europe, America, and Israel. In 1986, about 22,000 Jews remained in Iran, the majority in Teheran.

# The Jews in Afghanistan

Although there are documents from the early Middle Ages mentioning Jews in Afghanistan, most Afghan Jews in the modern period were of Persian origin. They lived mainly in the western part of the country, in Harat (about 2,000 Jews in the mid-nineteeth century) and Balkh (about 100 Jews in the early twentieth century). In 1948, there were about 4,000 Jews in the country. Laws enacted in 1933 granted the Jews equal rights.

Afghan Jews were mostly traders, many of them in the international commerce between Persia, Bukhara (until the Russian Revolution), and India. They had close social and economic relations with the Jewish community of Meshed, in northeastern Persia.

Most Jews left Afghanistan in 1951 and 1952, the majority emigrating to Israel, and others to Europe and America.

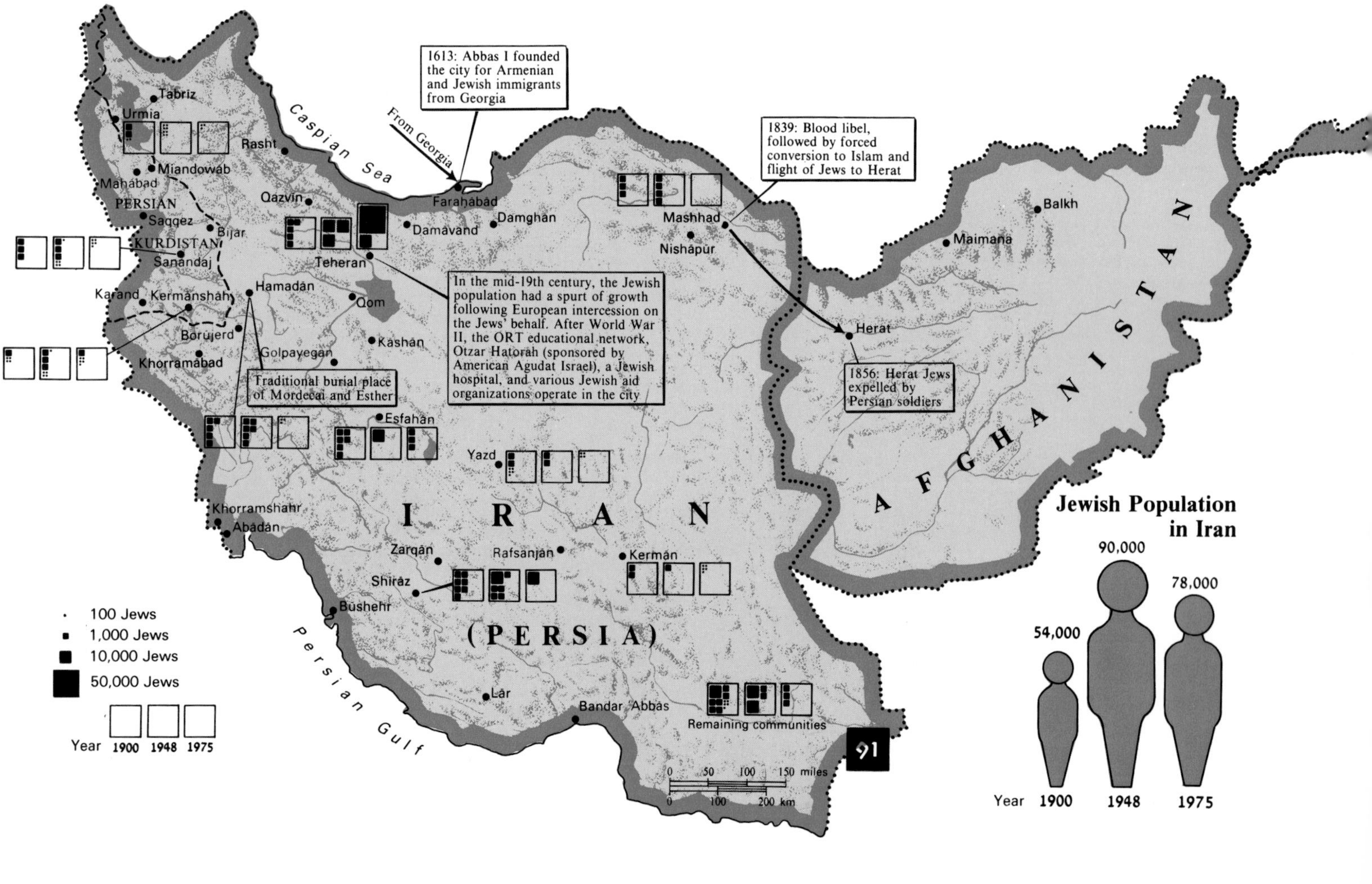

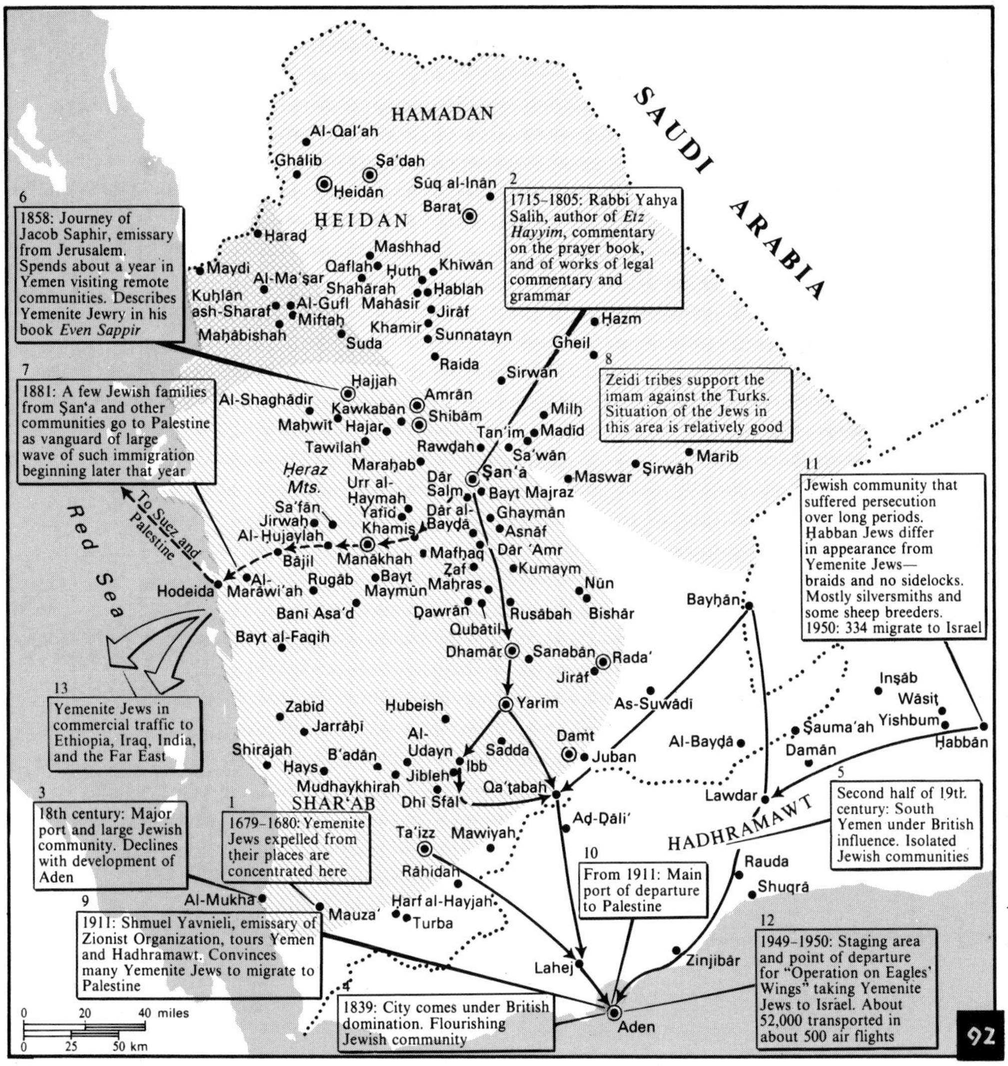

*Final page of 15th-century Ṣan'a Bible*

# The Jews in Yemen

As in many other countries, Jews had been living in Yemen for centuries; legends place them there even before the Second Temple period. In the nineteenth and twentieth centuries, they were in hundreds of communities thoughout Yemen, some of them very small. The largest was in Ṣan'ā, the capital, where 5,000 to 10,000 Jews lived in the early twentieth century, making up 5 to 10 percent of its population.

Most Yemenite Jews were concentrated in three regions: the central plateau, in and around Ṣan'ā; the south, the Shar'ab region; and the north, the Ḥeidān–ash-Sham region, where the main community lived in Ṣa'dah. Two additional, smaller Jewish settlements were in Ḥabbān and its environs and in Aden, Arabia's important southwestern port, under British domination from 1839. In each region, the Jews had their distinct dialect (in both Hebrew and Arabic), dress, customs, occupations, and pattern of relations with the local populations.

As was usual in the Muslim lands, the Jews were, in principle, protected subjects, paying the *jizya* and practicing their own religion and customs. In fact, however, they were subjected to many discriminatory regulations: the prohibitions on building houses higher than those of their Muslim neighbors and on riding horses. But there were no restrictions on their occupations, and they were permitted to own real estate and businesses. The Jews were frequent victims of Yemen's internal troubles, such as the protracted struggles between the central ruler (the imam) and the local chieftains, or between both of these and the Ottoman overlords. The seventeenth century was a particularly troubled one. The Sabbatean movement (1667) swept Yemenite Jewry, which incensed the Yemeni rulers. In 1679, many Jews were exiled briefly to the remote southern city of Mauza. New restrictive laws were imposed on the Jews in the eighteenth and nineteenth centuries: Ṣan'ā's synagogues were closed for thirty years (1762–1792); Jews were forced to do menial cleaning jobs; and the community had to deliver Jewish orphans for conversion. These regulations were enforced mainly in the central and southern regions, where the imam's authority was more effective. In the north and east, where the tribal heads were powerful, the situation of the Jews was sometimes easier. The best place for Jews was Aden, under the British.

After the Ottoman reconquest of Yemen in the second half of the nineteenth century, most restrictions against the Jews were abolished. But Ottoman power did not extend equally over the whole country; it was effective only in the central plateau and along the Red Sea coast. In other parts of Yemen, especially in the north and east, the local tribes remained semi-independent; toward the end of the nineteenth century, they rebelled against the Turks. In 1905, Imam Yahya occupied the capital, Ṣan'ā, holding it for some months. He reinstituted the traditional laws regarding the Jews. They were reaffirmed in 1911, when an agreement was reached between the imam and the Turks, giving the imam control over the country's internal affairs.

Yemen's Jews were not centrally organized. Each community had full local responsibility. The local leadership was divided between the *mori* (rabbi) and the *haakil* (or sheikh, head, *nasī*). The *mori* was responsible for the community's internal affairs; the *haakil* dealt with matters between the community and the local rulers. Since his position was recognized by the authorities, his standing was higher than the *mori*'s.

Most Yemenite Jews were craftsmen (few Yemeni Muslims worked in crafts) or small businessmen. A few Jews became large merchants, some even on an international scale, and had connections with India, Iraq, and Ethiopia. Many Jews owned land, although the farming was done by Muslims.

Yemenite Jews began to emigrate from the country in the early nineteenth century, establishing communities in India, Egypt, Ethiopia, and Sudan. In 1881, they began to emigrate to Palestine in growing numbers. It is estimated that in early 1948, about 52,000 Jews lived in Yemen, and tens of thousands of Yemenite Jews were already in Palestine. Most of the others migrated to Israel after its establishment. In 1986, about 1,000 Jews were living in Yemen.

# The Jews in India

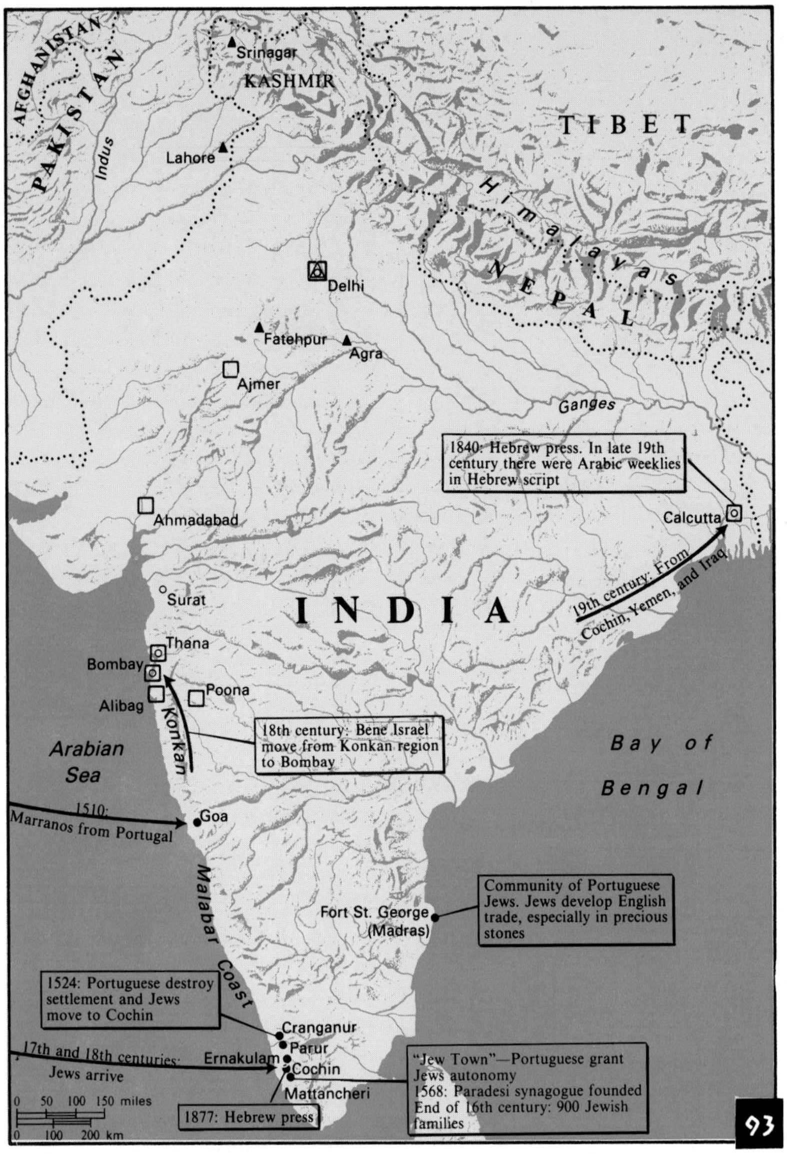


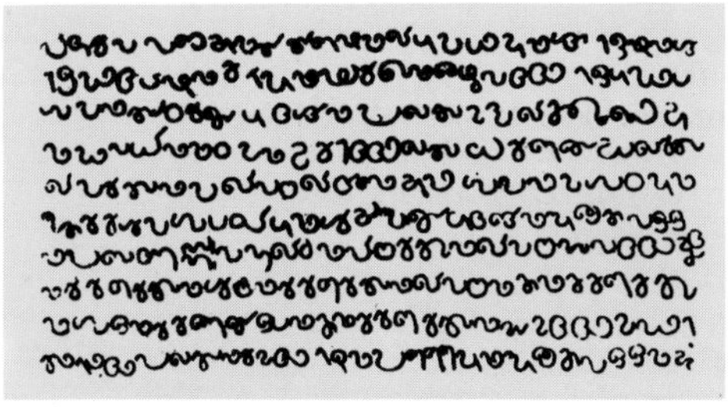

*Tamil inscription on copper plate in which Hindu ruler of Malabar grants privileges to Cochin Jews*

The Jews in India historically consisted of three groups. Two of them, Bene Israel and Cochin Jews, had lived in the country since ancient times; there is no documentary information about their origins. The third group was composed of Jews who had emigrated from various countries since the sixteenth century.

The Cochin Jews lived on the Malabar Coast, in southwestern India. The Bene Israel lived in villages in the Konkan region, south of Bombay. In the second half of the eighteenth century, they began to move to Bombay, and only then was contact established between the two groups. The Cochin Jews guided the Bene Israel in Jewish matters. The European Jews who arrived in the sixteenth century were mostly Spanish–Portuguese, but they also included Ashkenazim. They settled in the towns along the Malabar Coast. Some mixed with the Cochin Jews, creating yet another Jewish group. Additional Jewish settlers migrated from Yemen, Persia, and Iraq. At the end of the eighteenth century and especially during the nineteenth century, hundreds of Iraqi Jews, mostly from Basra and Baghdad (and therefore designated "Baghdadis"), came to India. They settled mostly in Bombay and Calcutta, where they formed their own communities. The Baghdadis were large-scale merchants, with international connections (the Sassoon, Kedoorie, Gabai, and Yehuda families), who traded throughout Asia.

The situation of the Jews in India was good. Under Dutch domination in Cochin (1663–1795), the Jews enjoyed the same rights as Jews in Holland. After the British conquest of India in the 1770s, their situation remained unchanged. Nevertheless, the rigid caste system in Hindu society kept the Jews isolated in their own social stratum. In the twentieth century, in Israel, questions arose regarding the religious status of the two older groups of Indian Jews (especially the Bene Israel), since they observed only part of the *Halakhah*. Most of the problems were solved.

There were about 7,000 Bene Israel in 1880. In the early twentieth century, there were 3,500 Jews in Cochin. In 1948, there were 28,000 Jews in India, more than half of whom were Bene Israel, and the others mainly Baghdadis and Cochin Jews. From the 1950s, many Jews left the country, emigrating to Israel, Australia, the United States, and Canada. About 10,000 Jews remained in India in 1970, and only about 4,200 in 1986.

# The Jews in the Far East

Jewish traders visited the Far East in the Middle Ages and established commercial relations in different countries, but did not settle there. Jews settled in China in the nineteenth century, in the wake of the European penetration, mainly in Hong Kong, Shanghai, and Tientsin. Most of these Jews were British citizens, from India or Iraq. In 1937, there were about 10,000 Jews in China, many of them refugees from Europe. From 1938 to 1941, 18,000 to 20,000 Jews fled from Europe to Shanghai, then under Japanese domination. In the 1940s, their number rose to between 25,000 and 30,000. In 1948, after the Communist victory in China, most Jews left the country. They emigrated to Israel, the United States, or the Soviet Union. Several hundred Jews remained in Hong Kong.

In the mid-1980s, there were about 1,000 Jews in Japan (mainly in Tokyo and Yokohama), about 1,000 Jews in Hong Kong, and a few hundred in Singapore, Thailand, and the Philippines. Most of them had arrived in these countries in the second half of the twentieth century from Europe, Israel, and elsewhere.

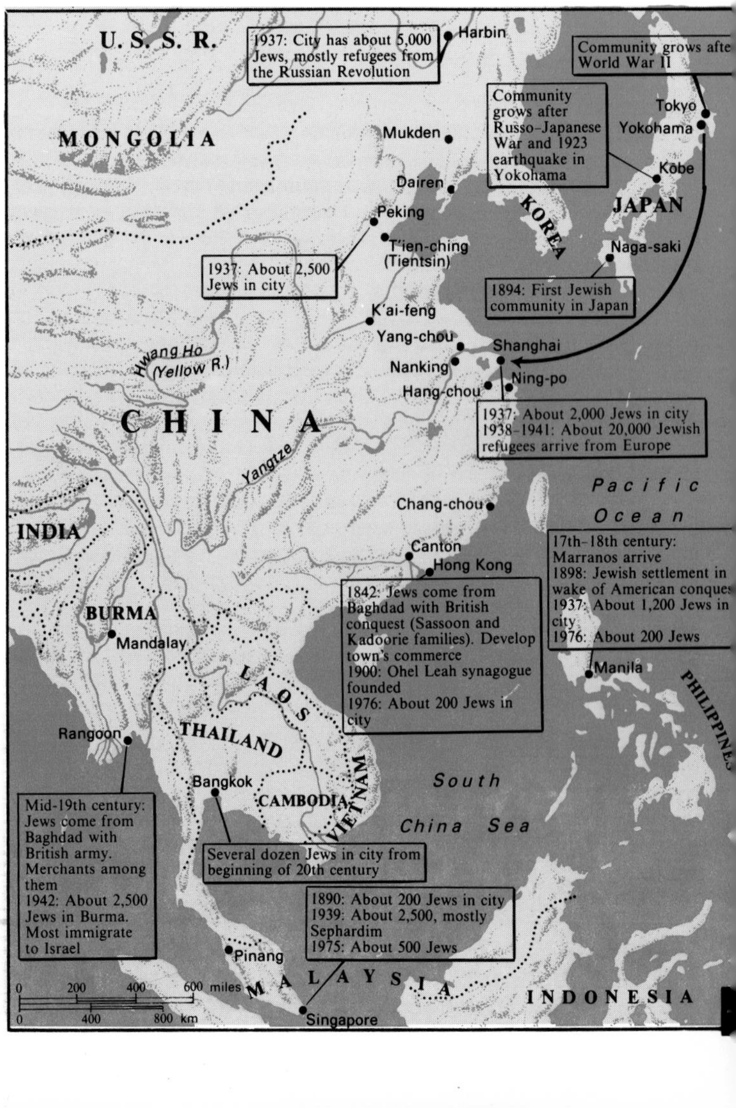

# Oriental Jews in International Trade

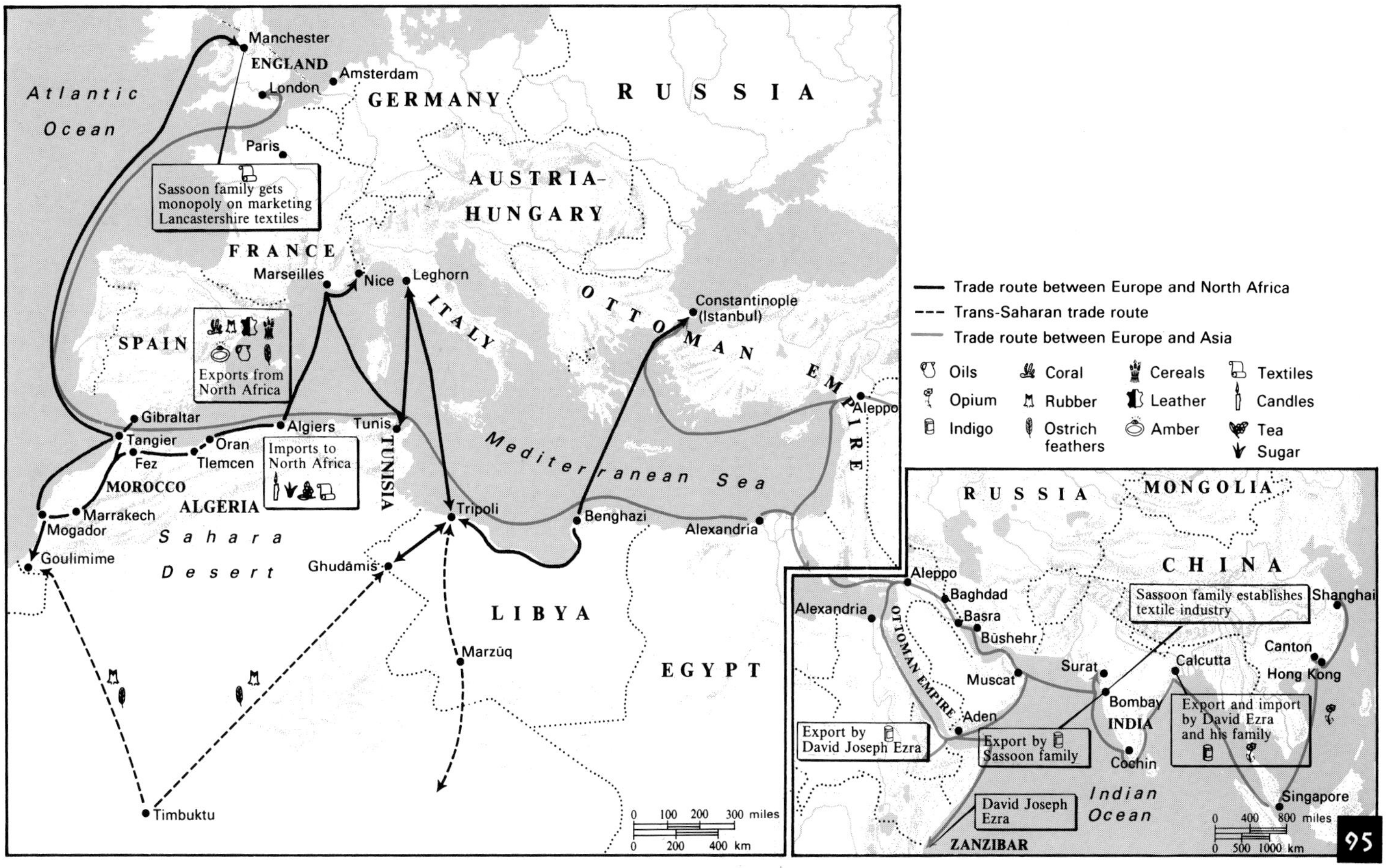


In the nineteenth century, two extensive networks of commercial relations developed from several Jewish centers in Muslim countries; they eventually spanned half the globe, from England to China through the Mediterranean Sea. This was made possible by the improvement of communications, greater safety on the intercontinental routes, the presence of the colonial powers (as economic and defense factors), and the initiative of several large Jewish families that sent representatives to establish branches in different countries. There was a striking similarity between the economic activities of the great Jewish merchant houses in the Orient and those of the Spanish–Portuguese Jews of Amsterdam two centuries earlier.

The economic activities of the Oriental Jews developed along two apparently unconnected networks: one extended through North Africa and the western Mediterranean region; the other, from Syria and Iraq, through the Persian Gulf and the Indian Ocean, to China.

In the North African network, the Jews were active either as independent traders or as commercial agents for local chieftains and Muslim rulers who regarded the Jews as buffers against European penetration. Their business dealings with Leghorn, Marseilles, Gibraltar, and Manchester covered the import and export of a wide range of commodities: they imported textiles, candles, sugar, and tea (which had become very popular in Morocco); they exported cereals, oils, leather, amber, coral, rubber, and ostrich feathers (the last two on caravans crossing the Sahara, in which the Jews also traveled). One of their major problems was how to compete with the European merchants, who enjoyed the support of their governments. But their good relations with the local rulers ensured them success, and in the end the European businessmen (and the consuls behind them) cooperated with the Jewish merchants instead of competing with them. The Jewish traders also bought shares in enterprises related to their business, such as the Paquet company (maritime transport) and the Péreire bank, which consequently expanded its operations in North Africa.

The importance of the Jewish merchants was reflected in their social standing. In Tunisia and Algeria, the Muslim authorities appointed the most important Jewish businessmen as heads (*mukadam, ka'id*) of the local Jewish communities; in Morocco, the great Jewish merchants were given the title *tudjar a-sultan* (the king's trader), which carried with it special privileges, such as exemption from the *jizya.*

The Asiatic network differed from the North African one in that it was based on the initiative of members of several families who, unsupported by local rulers and starting from humble beginnings, built up veritable commercial empires. Two examples are David Sassoon and David Joseph Ezra.

David Sassoon, the son of a Baghdad merchant, settled in the early nineteenth century in Basra, on Iraq's Persian Gulf shore. Later, he moved to Bombay. With his brother and several Jewish partners, he began to export indigo to Europe, especially to Britain—from where he exported textiles to the Orient. The Sassoons invested their earnings in textile mills in Bombay and opened commercial branches along the Indian Ocean, passing through Calcutta to China, Singapore, and Hong Kong. In the second half of the nineteenth century, the family extended its operations to Aden, in southern Arabia, and to Egypt; in partnership with Yemenite Jewish merchants, even got to Ethiopia. At the end of the nineteenth century, the Sassoon family transferred its business headquarters to London.

David Joseph Ezra was born in Aleppo, Syria, moved to Baghdad and Basra, and later to Calcutta. In 1820, he began, like the Sassoons, to trade in indigo. In the second half of the nineteenth century, he became one of the largest exporters of opium from China. The opium was sent to Europe through stations along the Persian Gulf and the Baghdad–Istanbul route that were controlled by members of his family or other Jewish partners. The Ezra family developed close relations with the rulers of the Muscat principality. Acting as the rulers' commercial agents, the Ezras established business relations with Zanzibar, on Africa's eastern coast.

# The Jews in East Central Europe in the Interwar Years

Eastern Europe underwent far-reaching political changes in the wake of World War I. The Austro-Hungarian Empire was dissolved, and the considerably reduced Austrian state (whose Jewish population was concentrated in the capital, Vienna) belonged culturally to Western Europe. Large parts of the former Russian Empire became independent countries.

About 8 million Jews, half of the Jewish people, lived in Eastern Europe in the interwar period. Politically, they were divided into two groups: one in the Soviet Union, and the other in East Central Europe. The large Jewish group in the Soviet Union found itself in conditions very different from those of other European Jewries, as a result of the Russian Revolution. In the southern part of East Central Europe (the Balkans), several Jewish communities bore the mark of their particular history, influenced by the former Turkish presence in part of the region and by their unique ethnic composition, including Sephardim.

About 5 million Jews lived in seven countries of East Central Europe, from Estonia in the north to Rumania in the south. Most of those countries became politically independent after World War I, or gained territory (Rumania) or lost it (Hungary). The Jewries of Central Europe were one of the most vital segments of the Jewish people, with well-established religious and cultural traditions, social characteristics that distinguished them from the general populations, and a very high level of Jewish consciousness. In most countries (the main exception being Czechoslovakia), relations between Jews and non-Jews were not good, and they deteriorated in the 1930s. This was partly a continuation of former tensions. In addition, political conditions in most of the new states were unstable, and the economic situation was difficult. Many new states contained large national minorities, including Jews, who did not live peacefully either with one another or with the majority group. The influence of the Nazi regime in Germany beginning in 1933 exacerbated the already deteriorating situation of the Jews in almost all the East Central European countries. The development of East Central European Jewry had a tragic dimension, presaging the impending disaster of World War II.

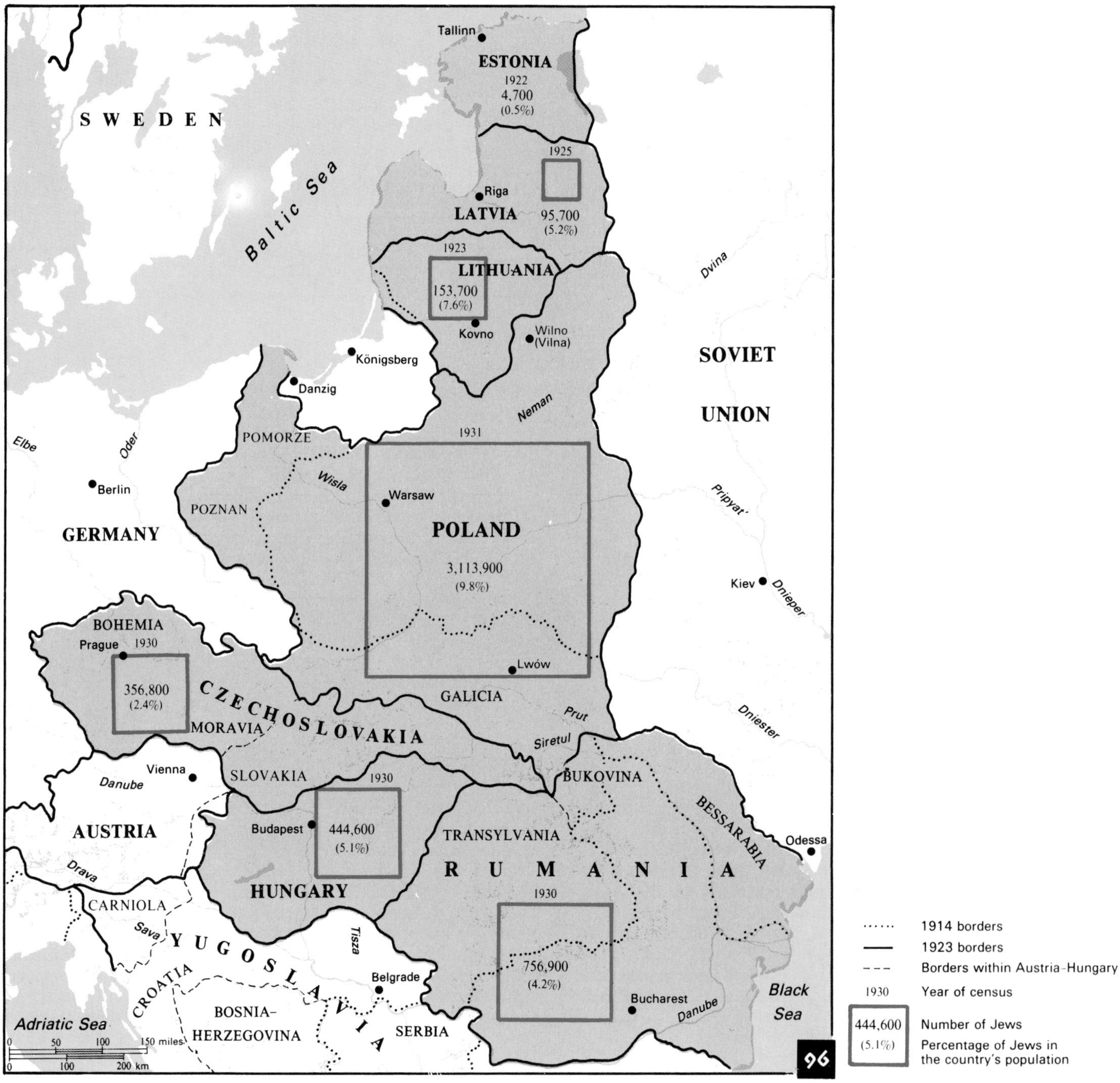

## Cultural Subgroups Among the Jews in East Central Europe

With regard to the dominant non-Jewish cultural orientation, the Jews of East Central Europe may be divided into six major groups: German, Russian, Polish, Czech, Hungarian, and Rumanian. The political borders of the new East European states and the cultural borders of these subgroups did not coincide. Indeed, some states—such as Poland, Czechoslovakia, and Rumania—contained more than one subgroup, while in some regions, several cultural influences existed side by side—German and Russian in the Baltic countries, Hungarian and German in Transylvania. Nor was this situation static; since the national problem was of foremost importance in most of the new countries, several governments (dominated by the majority national group) vigorously sought to propagate their own national culture, especially their language. Sometimes the Jews, too, vacillated between different cultures—for example, between the Czech and the German orientation in Czechoslovakia. The national question added a dimension to the complex situation of the Jews in the East Central European countries, and to their troubled relations with the non-Jewish populations.

Culture:
German
Russian
Polish
Czech
Hungarian
Rumanian

...... 1914 borders
—— 1923 borders

According to the main non-Jewish language spoken at the beginning of the interwar period

## "Western European" and "Eastern European" Types of Jewries in East Central Europe

Two models of Jewish communal life existed in interwar East Central Europe, distinguished by economic structure, religious affiliation, demographic pattern, political behavior, and the extent and character of acculturation. The West European model was typical of communities in Bohemia, Moravia, ,and Hungary. The East European model was found in Galicia, central Poland, Polish Lithuania, independent Lithuania, Bukovina, Sub-Carpathian Ruthenia, Bessarabia, and Latgalia (southern Latvia). Some regions, such as Slovakia and Moldavia, had a mixed type.

The West European model was usually urbanized and middle class. The Jews abandoned Yiddish for the local vernacular and could be considered acculturated, and Reform Judaism of one kind or another was practiced in those communities. There was a low birth rate and a significant out-marriage rate. The patterns of Jewish behavior were quite similar to those of German, French, and English Jewries.

The East European type was also largely urban, but the communities had preserved the old-style *shtetl.* The Jews usually belonged to the lower middle and working classes, had a relatively low level of acculturation, spoke Yiddish, were Orthodox, had large families, were a large percentage of the total population, and rarely out-married. Acculturation often led to modern nationalism rather than to the politics of integration. Jewish identification was religious (meaning Orthodox) and/or national (in many instances secular national).

There were clear differences in the public and political behavior of the two groups. It was the Jews of the East European type who developed the diverse Jewish ideological positions, such as autonomism, Zionism, Jewish socialism, and Hebrew and Yiddish education and culture, and who established the political parties to implement these ideas. Among the Jewish communities of the West European type, autonomous Jewish culture and politics were much less in evidence.

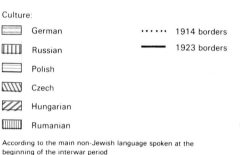

East European-type Jewry
West European-type Jewry
Mixed-type Jewry

# The Jews in Eastern Europe After World War I

Most of the states carved out of Eastern Europe and the Balkans after the dissolution of the Russian and Austro-Hungarian empires were multinational. The Paris Peace Conference (1919) established the principle that the rights of minorities should be protected. The issue was much debated between the representatives of the victorious Entente powers and of the new states. The latter stressed that civil rights also guaranteed national rights, while the representatives of the national groups (including the Jews) demanded explicit recognition of their national status in addition to civil rights.

## Pogroms in Russia and Poland, 1917–1921

April 21, 1919: Polish occupation army attacks Jews
Passover 1919: Attacks on Jews
April 5, 1919: 35 members of Tzeirei Zion executed by Polish army on charge of belonging to Communist underground
November 22, 1918: Polish army massacres Jews
December 1918–March 1921: Hundreds of pogroms. About 60,000 killed; tens of thousands wounded
Summer 1919: Grigoryev and Makhno pogroms. 40 communities destroyed; 6,000 Jews killed
Dvina
Vitebsk
Smolensk
Kaluga
Tula
Wilno (Vilna)
Lida
Minsk
Mogilev
Orël
BELORUSSIA
Kursk
Don
Pinsk
POLAND
Ovrich January 1919
Route of Denikin's army
Kiev
Zhitomir
Fastov
UKRAINE
January, February 1919
Berdichev January 1919
Boguslav
Lwów
Proskurov February 15, 1919
Tetiyev
Lysyanka
Dnieper
Nemirov
Brailov June 5, 1919
Bratslav
Novomirgorod May 1919
Yekaterinoslav
Uman'
Kamenets-Podolskiy
Tulchin
Bershad'
NEW RUSSIA
BESSARABIA
Dniester
Prut
Balta
Yuzhnyy Bug
RUMANIA
Kishinev
Kherson
Pale of Settlement (until 1917)
Petlyura pogroms (until mid-1919)
Denikin pogroms (from 2nd half of 1919)
Main pogrom region
Black Sea
0 50 100 150 miles
0 100 200 km
99

## Jewish Delegations at the Paris Peace Conference, 1919

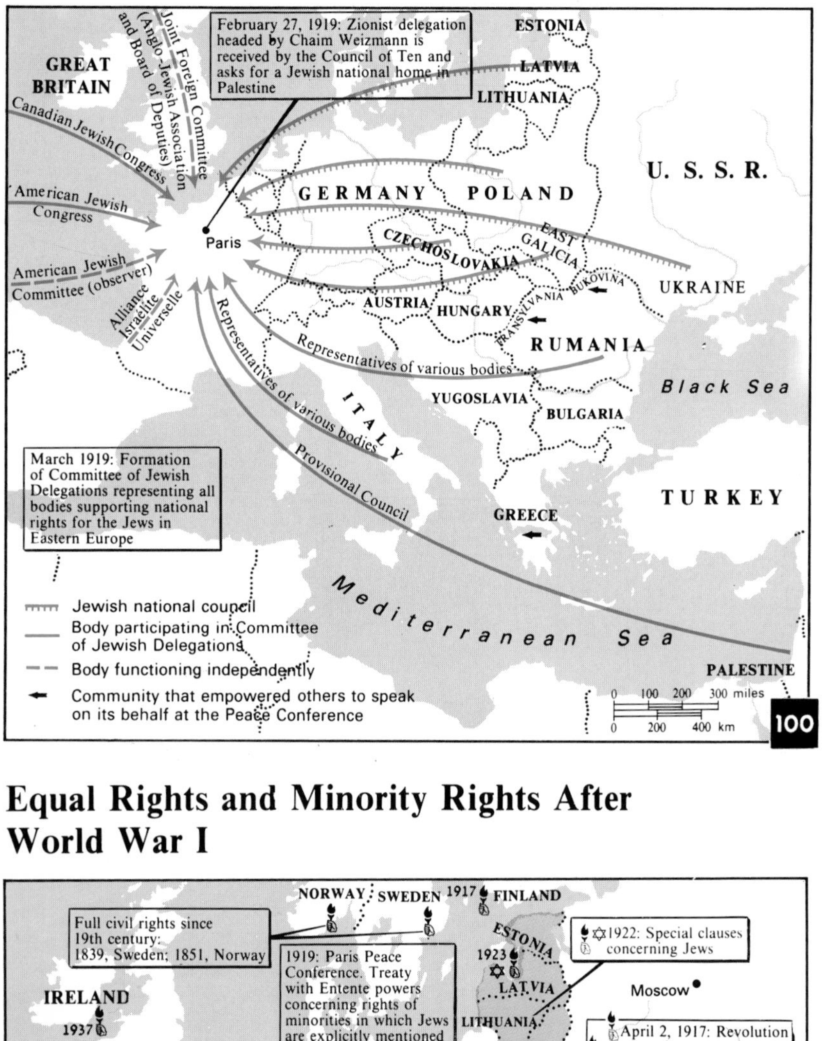
February 27, 1919: Zionist delegation headed by Chaim Weizmann is received by the Council of Ten and asks for a Jewish national home in Palestine
Joint Foreign Committee (Anglo-Jewish Association and Board of Deputies)
GREAT BRITAIN
ESTONIA
LATVIA
LITHUANIA
Canadian Jewish Congress
American Jewish Congress
American Jewish Committee (observer)
Alliance Israélite Universelle
U. S. S. R.
GERMANY
POLAND
Paris
CZECHOSLOVAKIA
EAST GALICIA
BUKOVINA
TRANSYLVANIA
UKRAINE
AUSTRIA
HUNGARY
RUMANIA
Representatives of various bodies
Black Sea
YUGOSLAVIA
BULGARIA
ITALY
March 1919: Formation of Committee of Jewish Delegations representing all bodies supporting national rights for the Jews in Eastern Europe
Provisional Council
TURKEY
GREECE
Mediterranean Sea
PALESTINE
Jewish national council
Body participating in Committee of Jewish Delegations
Body functioning independently
Community that empowered others to speak on its behalf at the Peace Conference
0 100 200 300 miles
0 200 400 km
100

## Equal Rights and Minority Rights After World War I

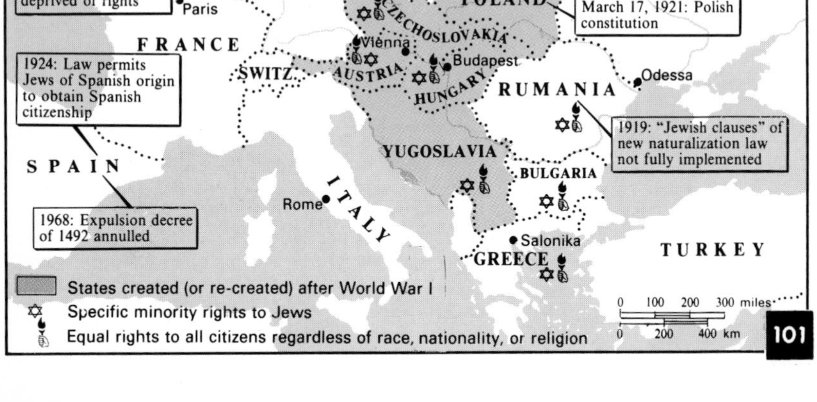
NORWAY
SWEDEN
1917
FINLAND
Full civil rights since 19th century: 1839, Sweden; 1851, Norway
1919: Paris Peace Conference. Treaty with Entente powers concerning rights of minorities in which Jews are explicitly mentioned
ESTONIA
1923
1922: Special clauses concerning Jews
IRELAND
1937
LATVIA
LITHUANIA
Moscow
April 2, 1917: Revolution
December 5, 1936: New constitution
London
Berlin
1919: Weimar Republic constitution 1933: Jews gradually deprived of rights
GERMANY
Warsaw
Paris
Kiev
U. S. S. R.
POLAND
March 17, 1921: Polish constitution
FRANCE
CZECHOSLOVAKIA
Vienna
Budapest
SWITZ.
AUSTRIA
HUNGARY
Odessa
1924: Law permits Jews of Spanish origin to obtain Spanish citizenship
RUMANIA
1919: "Jewish clauses" of new naturalization law not fully implemented
YUGOSLAVIA
SPAIN
BULGARIA
ITALY
Rome
1968: Expulsion decree of 1492 annulled
Salonika
GREECE
TURKEY
States created (or re-created) after World War I
Specific minority rights to Jews
Equal rights to all citizens regardless of race, nationality, or religion
0 100 200 300 miles
0 200 400 km
101

The Jews were one of the largest minority groups in several of the new states. Jewish delegates from these countries, as well as from Jewish organizations in Western Europe and America, went to Paris to lobby for Jewish rights in the new states. They disagreed among themselves about whether the Jews should content themselves with full civil rights or insist on recognition as a national group. On March 28, 1919, the Committee of Jewish Delegations to the Peace Conference was formed, comprising those seeking national recognition for East European Jews: the delegates of the East European Jewish national councils and the American Jewish Congress. Those who did not support the quest for national rights acted separately: the Joint Foreign Committee (representing part of British Jewry), the Alliance Israélite Universelle, and members of the American Jewish Committee. The Zionists, who were the driving force behind the Committee of Jewish Delegations, also appeared separately before the peace conference's Council of Ten, on February 27, 1919. Led by Chaim Weizmann, they presented the case for a Jewish national home in Palestine.

The treaty with Poland, approved on June 28, 1919, was the most important document to come out of the conference on the minorities question. Several articles guaranteed the rights of the minorities living in Poland, but no mention was made of *national* rights. The treaty also included two "Jewish" clauses (numbers 10 and 11), which guaranteed the Jews control over their schools and recognized Saturday as the Jewish day of rest. Similar treaties were signed with the other new or restructured states. In practice, few of the new states fully upheld the Jewish minority clauses. During the 1930s, growing internal problems in most East European states and the influence of the German Nazi regime worsened the general situation of the East European Jewries.

While negotiations were going on in Paris, the situation of the Jews in the lands bordering Poland and the Soviet Union deteriorated. The political uncertainty during the establishment of the Soviet and Polish states, and the internal struggle between the Red Russians and their opponents (White Russians and other groups), led to civil war in a region densely inhabited by Jews, in Galicia and in the former Pale of Settlement. The Jewish population suffered terribly from the soldiers' violence. The forceful intervention of the new Soviet regime improved the situation in the territories under its control. This did not apply to other armies, such as the Poles in the north and the bands led by Simon Petlyura and other chieftains in the Ukraine, who killed tens of thousands and destroyed hundreds of communities. The pogroms that erupted between 1917 and 1921 were the worst anti-Jewish outbreaks since the Cossacks' rebellion in 1648 and 1649.

# Jewish Civil and Political Organizations in the Interwar Years

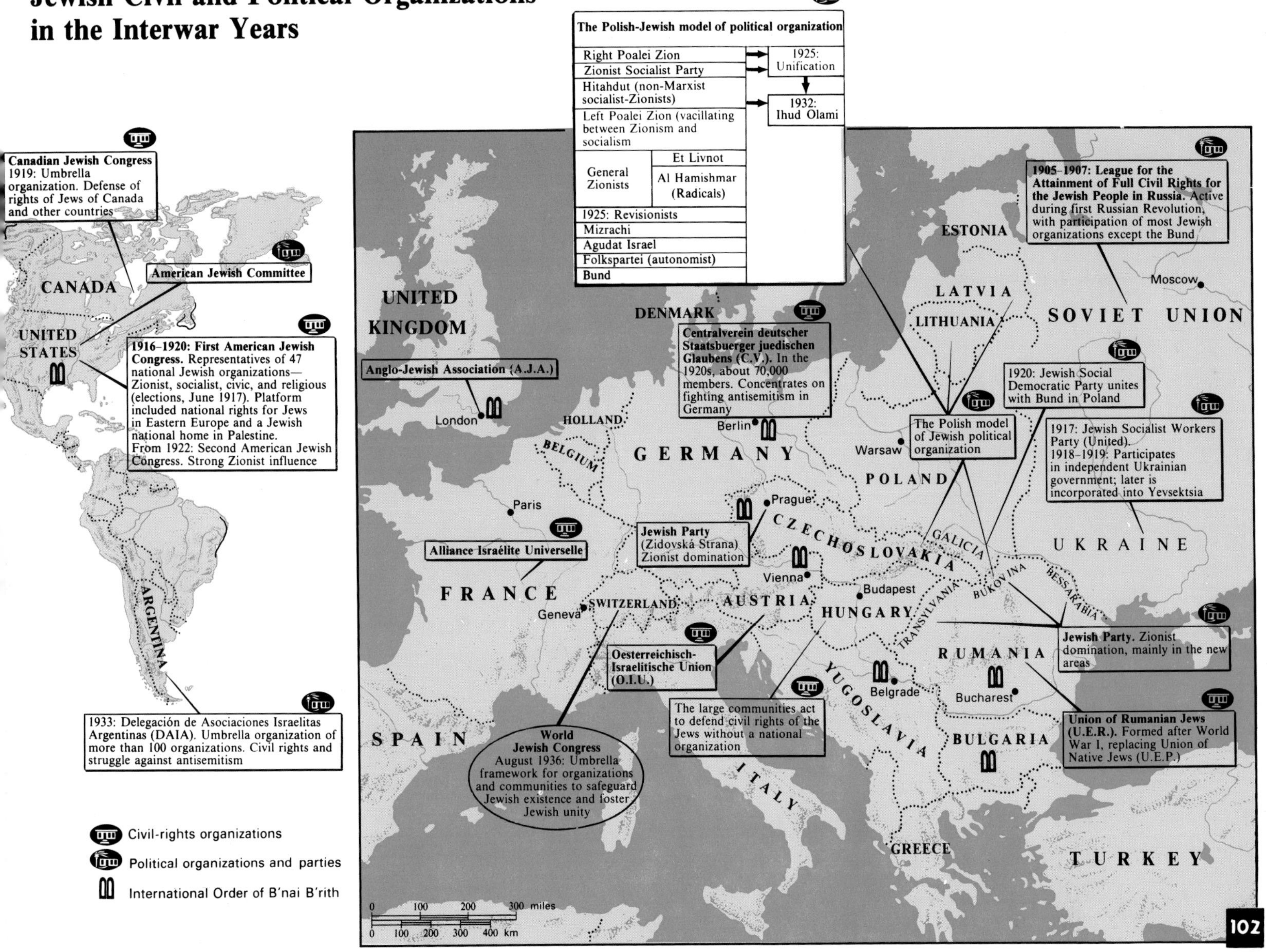
The Polish-Jewish model of political organization
Right Poalei Zion
Zionist Socialist Party
1925: Unification
Hitahdut (non-Marxist socialist-Zionists)
Left Poalei Zion (vacillating between Zionism and socialism
1932: Ihud Olami
General Zionists
Et Livnot
Al Hamishmar (Radicals)
1925: Revisionists
Mizrachi
Agudat Israel
Folkspartei (autonomist)
Bund
Canadian Jewish Congress 1919: Umbrella organization. Defense of rights of Jews of Canada and other countries
CANADA
American Jewish Committee
UNITED STATES
1916–1920: First American Jewish Congress. Representatives of 47 national Jewish organizations—Zionist, socialist, civic, and religious (elections, June 1917). Platform included national rights for Jews in Eastern Europe and a Jewish national home in Palestine. From 1922: Second American Jewish Congress. Strong Zionist influence
ARGENTINA
1933: Delegación de Asociaciones Israelitas Argentinas (DAIA). Umbrella organization of more than 100 organizations. Civil rights and struggle against antisemitism
Civil-rights organizations
Political organizations and parties
International Order of B'nai B'rith
UNITED KINGDOM
Anglo-Jewish Association (A.J.A.)
London
HOLLAND
BELGIUM
Paris
Alliance Israélite Universelle
FRANCE
Geneva
SWITZERLAND
SPAIN
World Jewish Congress August 1936: Umbrella framework for organizations and communities to safeguard Jewish existence and foster Jewish unity
DENMARK
Centralverein deutscher Staatsbuerger juedischen Glaubens (C.V.). In the 1920s, about 70,000 members. Concentrates on fighting antisemitism in Germany
Berlin
GERMANY
Prague
Jewish Party (Zidovská Strana) Zionist domination
CZECHOSLOVAKIA
Vienna
AUSTRIA
Oesterreichisch-Israelitische Union (O.I.U.)
The large communities act to defend civil rights of the Jews without a national organization
ITALY
Budapest
HUNGARY
TRANSYLVANIA
YUGOSLAVIA
Belgrade
Bucharest
RUMANIA
BULGARIA
GREECE
TURKEY
ESTONIA
LATVIA
LITHUANIA
Warsaw
POLAND
The Polish model of Jewish political organization
GALICIA
BUKOVINA
BESSARABIA
1905–1907: League for the Attainment of Full Civil Rights for the Jewish People in Russia. Active during first Russian Revolution, with participation of most Jewish organizations except the Bund
Moscow
SOVIET UNION
1920: Jewish Social Democratic Party unites with Bund in Poland
1917: Jewish Socialist Workers Party (United). 1918–1919: Participates in independent Ukrainian government; later is incorporated into Yevsektsia
UKRAINE
Jewish Party. Zionist domination, mainly in the new areas
Union of Rumanian Jews (U.E.R.). Formed after World War I, replacing Union of Native Jews (U.E.P.)
0 100 200 300 miles
0 100 200 300 400 km
102

Changing concepts about Jewish society and Jewish rights gave birth in the first quarter of the twentieth century to new patterns of civic and political action and to new forms of Jewish organization.

Three main types of organizations were active among the Jews in the interwar years. One was the "civil-rights" association, such as the Alliance Israélite Universelle in France and the American Jewish Committee, whose concepts had been formulated in the second half of the nineteenth century. They felt that the Jews were entitled to full civil and political equality in the countries in which they lived, and they worked to ensure this. Another type was also concerned with civil rights, but it developed new ideas or new organizational structures. A particularly interesting example was the first American Jewish Congress (1916–1920). Its structure was democratic, with almost all the trends in American Jewry represented in it. One of its aims was to gain for the East European Jews recognition as national minorities in their countries of residence. The Centralverein, the important German Jewish civil-rights organization, created a broad democratic structure, which developed in a semipolitical direction. Another association of a civil and political nature was the League for the Attainment of Full Civil Rights for the Jewish People, established in Russia during the first revolution, in 1905.

The third type of organization was the Jewish political party. Parties were founded in various East European countries with the purpose of attaining civil and national rights for the Jews. They attained their fullest fruition in Poland, the largest Jewish center in interwar Europe. The various Jewish parties in Poland—Zionist, religious, socialist, autonomist—vied with one another (and sometimes also collaborated) on three electoral levels: the Polish parliament (Sejm), the city councils, and the Jewish *kehillot* (community councils). The Zionists had a slight electoral edge, which, however, they usually failed to take advantage of because of their internal political differences. Other strong parties were Agudat Israel (Orthodox) and the Bund (socialist). Unlike in Russia before the Bolshevik Revolution, the Bund operated in Poland as a legal party. It also did much for the development of Jewish culture and education in Yiddish, and acted forcefully against Polish antisemitism. The Zionists, a central factor in the struggle for Jewish rights in Poland, were no less active in the work for the establishment of a Jewish national home in Palestine. The Zionist youth movements in Poland were the strongest in Europe.

Other East European Jewries (in Lithuania, Latvia, Czechoslovakia, Rumania) developed political structures similar to the Polish one, although on a smaller scale. As in Poland, the Jews in most of these countries were divided in different ethnic and cultural groups, which also affected the positions they took on public issues.

The overall picture of the Jewish organizational and political activities in the interwar years indicated a tendency in modern Jewish society (or in a significant part of it) to broaden the patterns of Jewish self-definition that had been shaped in the nineteenth century. In the delicate balance between general and Jewish life, there was a tendency to give more weight to the Jewish dimension and to act according to new concepts with different civil and/or political means. That development came to its fullest expression in the East European Jewries, but in diverse and more moderate forms it could be found also among Western Jewries (in Europe and America), even when they espoused the principle of Jewish political, social, and cultural integration into the general society.

# The Jews in Poland, 1921–1931

About 3 million Jews lived in Poland in the interwar years, making it the largest Jewish community outside the United States. The Jews made up about 10 percent of the Polish population, but about 30 percent of all city dwellers.

The treaty signed by Poland on June 28, 1919, gave the Jews full Polish citizenship and guaranteed specific Jewish interests (religion, language, education). In practice, however, the attitude of the authorities was at least suspicious, and became increasingly negative. Antisemitic traditions and efforts to "Polonize" the state found expression in a variety of limitations imposed on the Jews. The difficult economic situation and the growing power of right-wing political groups increased the pressure on the Jewish population.

Although the conditions in Poland spurred many Jews to emigrate, the interwar years were a period of cultural and educational blossoming and intense public and political activity. Communal institutions were established, including an impressive Jewish school system in which instruction was mostly in Yiddish or Hebrew.

Jewish life in Poland came to an end in World War II. More than 90 percent of Polish Jews were exterminated in the Holocaust. One of the most important communities in the history of the Jewish people disappeared.

## Historical Subgroups in Polish Jewry

## The Jewish Population in the Provinces (*Województwo*)

| Province | 1921 Number of Jews | 1921 % of total population | 1921 % of urban population | 1931 Number of Jews | 1931 % of total population | 1931 % of urban population |
|---|---|---|---|---|---|---|
| Warsaw (city) | 310,300 | 33.1 | 33.1 | 352,700 | 30.1 | 30.1 |
| Warsaw (province) | 203,400 | 9.6 | 34.3 | 219,100 | 8.7 | 29.7 |
| Łódź | 327,000 | 14.5 | 33.5 | 378,500 | 14.4 | 31.2 |
| Kielce | 300,500 | 11.9 | 33.9 | 317,000 | 10.8 | 30.2 |
| Lublin | 287,600 | 13.8 | 48.2 | 314,400 | 12.7 | 43.7 |
| Bialystok | 194,100 | 15.0 | 46.2 | 197,400 | 12.0 | 38.4 |
| Wilno | 91,800[1] | 9.4 | — | 110,800 | 8.7 | 29.2 |
| Nowogródek | 74,500 | 9.1 | 45.5 | 82,900 | 7.8 | 42.6 |
| Polesie | 110,600 | 13.0 | 56.5 | 114,000 | 10.1 | 49.2 |
| Volhynia | 164,700 | 11.3 | 58.9 | 207,800 | 10.0 | 49.1 |
| Poznań | 10,400 | 0.5 | 1.4 | 7,200 | 0.3 | 0.8 |
| Pomorze | 2,900 | 0.3 | 1.0 | 3,400 | 0.3 | 0.9 |
| Silesia | 16,700[1] | 1.5 | — | 18,900 | 1.5 | 3.9 |
| Kraków | 152,900 | 7.7 | 25.1 | 173,600 | 7.6 | 24.8 |
| Lwów | 313,200 | 11.6 | 35.3 | 342,400 | 11.0 | 33.2 |
| Stanislawów | 141,500 | 10.5 | 37.0 | 139,700 | 9.4 | 34.8 |
| Tarnopol | 129,000 | 9.0 | 37.1 | 134,100 | 8.4 | 34.7 |
| Total Poland | 2,845,300[2] | 10.5 | 31.4[3] | 3,113,900[4] | 9.8 | 27.2 |

1. Parts of the Wilno and Silesia provinces were not covered by the 1921 census because Polis suzerainty over them had still been decided. They were inclu in the above data on the basis the 1919 census.
2. The total includes 14,200 Jew who served in the Polish army.
3. There may be a slight deviatio either direction.
4. In 1939, there were an estima 3,250,000 Jews in Poland.

## Urbanization of Polish Jewry*

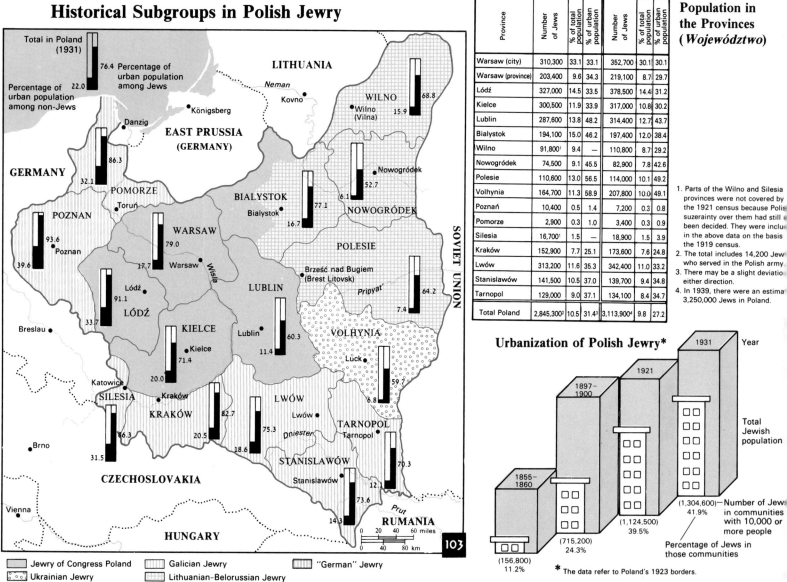

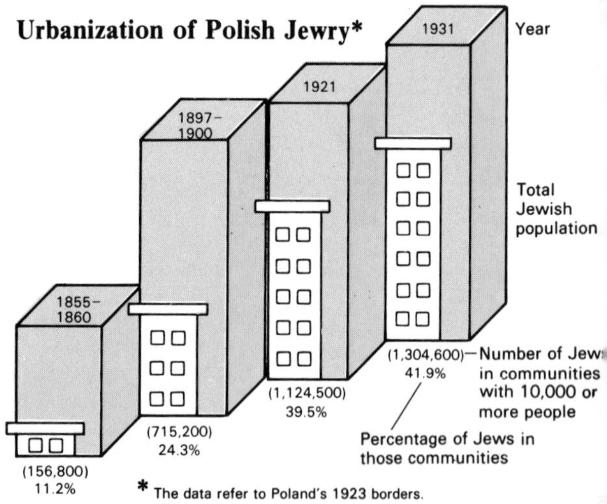


* The data refer to Poland's 1923 borders.

The Polish state, reborn in 1919, was multinational. One-third of its population consisted of minorities: Ukrainians, Jews, White Russians, and Germans. The Jews, the second largest national group in Poland, belonged to five different historical subgroups.

### Congress (Central) Poland Jewry

In the nineteenth century, Central Poland, although under Russian domination, was the heart of ethnic Poland. Some Jews in the larger cities were influenced by the dominant Polish culture, although the Hasidic movement was very strong in Central Poland.

### Galician Jewry

Until the end of World War I, Galicia belonged to the Austro-Hungarian Empire, where Jews had enjoyed full civil rights since 1867. In the interwar years, the Polish cultural influence became stronger than the former German one. Jewish enlightenment had deep roots in Galicia, but the opposing Hasidic movement was also very influential.

### Belorussian and Lithuanian Jewry

Both Belorussia and Lithuania, which had been parts of the Russian Empire, were divided after World War I among four countries: the Soviet Union, Poland, Lithuania, and Latvia. In Poland, the area involved was called *kresy*, the borderlands, whose Jews were less open to external influences than were those of Congress Poland and Galicia. Besides Yiddish, they spoke Russian rather than Polish. The Lithuanian region, with its well-known major city, Wilno (Vilna), was a strong center of *haskalah* and of opposition to the Hasidic movement. From the late nineteenth century, Jewish national movements developed here, both the socialist Bund and Zionism.

### Ukrainian Jewry

Until World War I, the province of Volhynia was part of the Russian Ukraine. In the view of the Poles, it, too, belonged to the *kresy*. As in the Lithuanian region, the Jewish intelligentsia was oriented to Russian rather than to Polish culture. Yet the Ukrainian Jews there were a distinct group.

### "German" Jewry

Upper Silesia, Poznań (Posen) and Pomorze (Pomerania) belonged to Germany until the end of World War I, and the Jews there leaned toward German culture. Few Jews remained in these provinces in the interwar period.

# Occupations of Jews and Non-Jews, 1931

The differences between the economic structures of the Jews and non-Jews were reflected in both their occupational and their social structures: among non-Jews, there was a preponderance of salaried laborers; among Jews, the majority were self-employed—mostly artisans, coachmen, and small merchants. The Jews were a mainly urban population, occupied in commerce, crafts, and light industry, with only a minority working in agriculture.

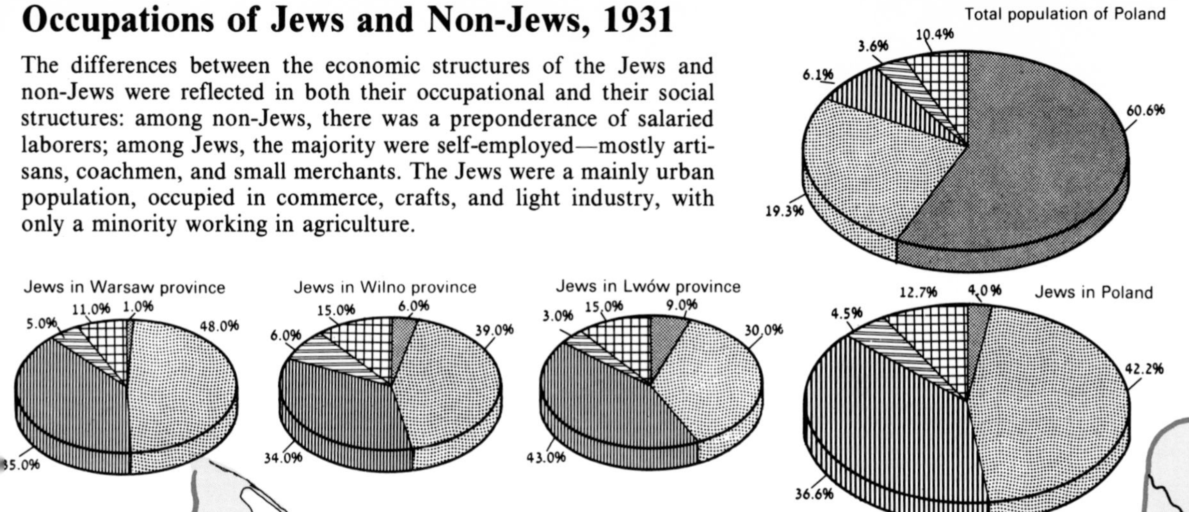


# Jewish Communities in Poland, 1921

## Social Division of the Labor Force in Poland, 1931

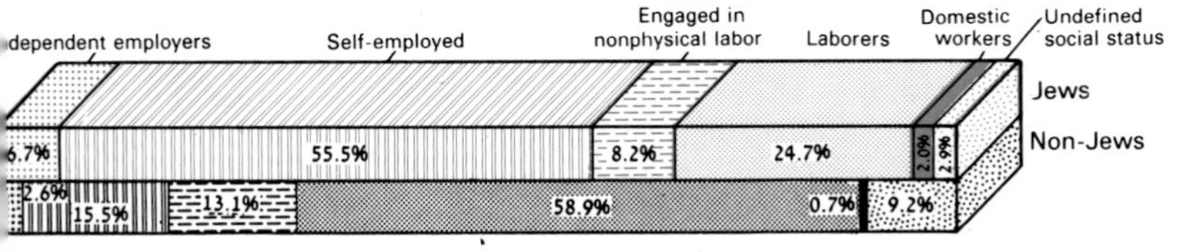

# The Jews in Warsaw

Until the late eighteenth century, Jews were not permitted to settle in Warsaw, although a few thousand had special permits to live there. After the partitions of Poland, the city came under Prussian domination (1796–1807), and in spite of continuing restrictions, the number of Jews grew to about 7,700. Most concentrated in the Marywil neighborhood (later called Theater Square) and the nearby streets. During the time of the Warsaw Duchy (1807–1815), most Jews were forced to move to the southern and southwestern parts of the city. They settled around Marszalkowska, Krolewska, and Twarda streets, up to the southern border of Jerozolimska Boulevard. In the mid-nineteenth century, the Jews were again forced to move to the northern part of the city. In 1862, the Jews in Congress

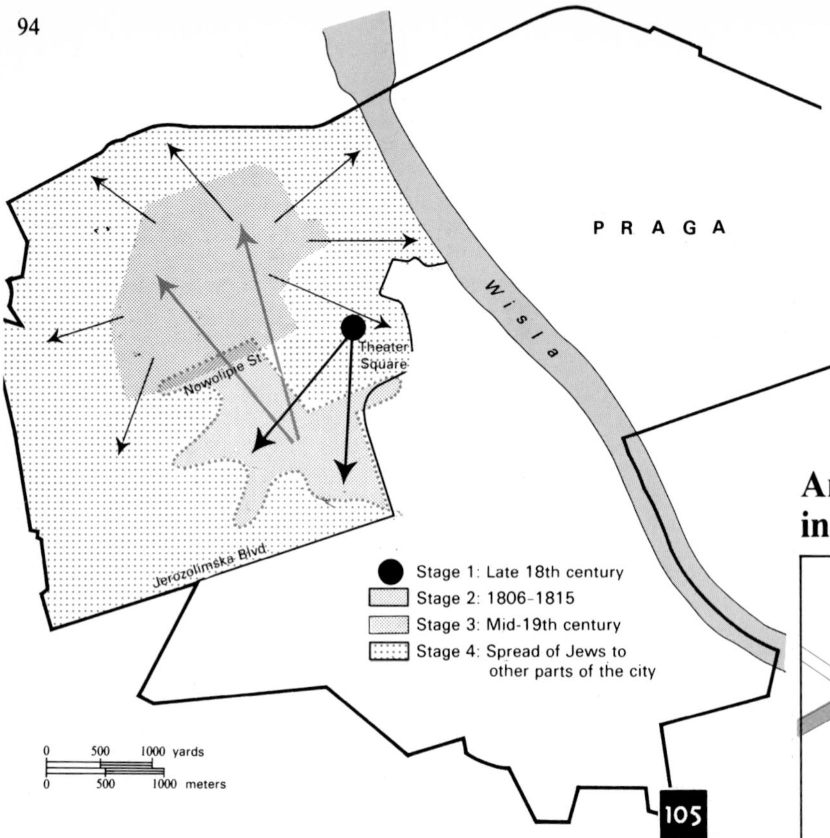


## The Jewish Population in Warsaw's Districts, 1938

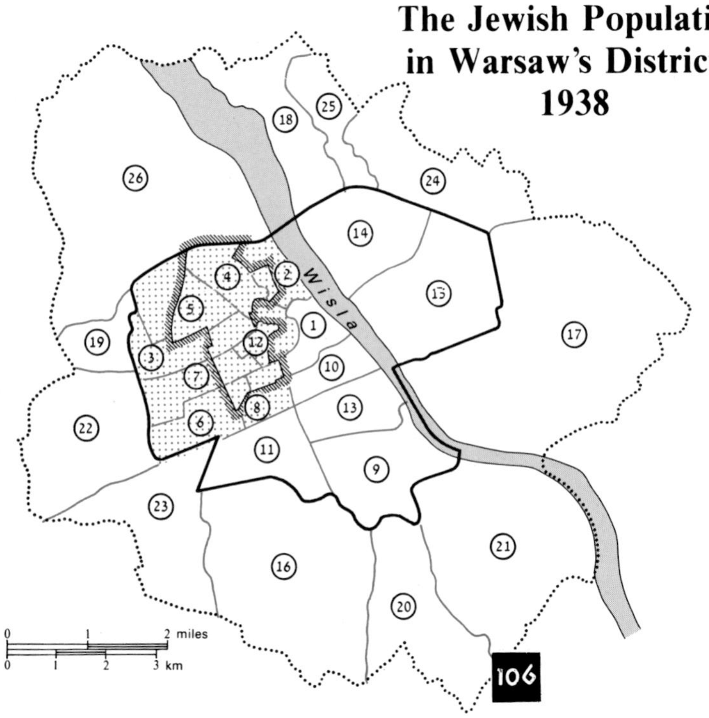


—— Warsaw until 1916
........ Warsaw after 1916
Area with over 25% Jews
Area of high Jewish concentration
—— District (commissariat) border
(18) District number

| District | Number of Jews, 1938 | % in total population |
|---|---|---|
| 1. Krak. Przedm. | 3,100 | 7.9 |
| 2. Stare Miasto | 18,400 | 37.4 |
| 3. Leszno | 54,400 | 57.5 |
| 4. Muranów | 57,900 | 90.5 |
| 5. Powazki | 72,300 | 76.2 |
| 6. Towarowy | 18,700 | 27.0 |
| 7. Mirówski | 37,800 | 38.3 |
| 8. Grzybowski | 36,700 | 53.0 |
| 9. Ujazdowski | 2,100 | 5.5 |
| 10. Ordynackie | 3,900 | 8.8 |
| 11. Koszyki | 5,800 | 8.1 |
| 12. Ratuszowy | 12,700 | 44.8 |
| 13. Solec | 5,200 | 9.0 |
| 14-15. Central Praga | 21,700 | 18.2 |
| 16-26. Suburbs | 17,800 | 5.4 |
| Total | 368,500 | 29.1 |

## Area of High Jewish Concentration in Warsaw, 1938

District (commissariat) border
Subdistrict border
Area of high Jewish concentratic
14,600 Number of Jews in district (within area of high Jewish concentrat
(67.5%) Percentage of Jews in total popu

Percentage of Jews in total population
50–69
70–79
80–91

| | 1922 | | | 1931 | | | 1938 | | |
|---|---|---|---|---|---|---|---|---|---|
| | Number | % in population | % of Jews | Number | % in population | % of Jews | Number | % in population | % of Jews |
| High Jewish concentration* | | | | 236,100 | 74.1 | 66.9 | 250,200 | 76.4 | 67.9 |
| Significant Jewish concentration (2 8, 12) | 268,000 | 53.7 | 83.3 | 294,500 | 51.6 | 83.5 | 308,800 | 54.3 | 83.8 |
| Central Warsaw and Central Praga (1 15) | 310,000 | 37.5 | 96.3 | 336,700 | 36.4 | 95.5 | 350,700 | 38.1 | 95.2 |
| Suburbs (16 26) | 12,000 | 9.3 | 3.7 | 16,000 | 6.8 | 4.5 | 17,800 | 5.4 | 4.8 |
| Total (1 26) | 322,000 | 33.7 | 100 | 352,700 | 30.1 | 100 | 368,500 | 29.1 | 100 |

*District 4 and part of districts 2 to 8 and 12

In 1897, there were 210,500 Jews in Warsaw (33.7% of total population), and in 1913, 317,900 Jews (37.6%).

Poland were granted the same rights as the rest of the population, and could now live freely in Warsaw. The city's Jewish population grew rapidly, reaching 337,000 in 1914, and expanded around the old nucleus, especially southward. Warsaw's Jewish community became the largest in Europe and, unlike in other cities with large Jewish populations, remained concentrated in the central part of the city, relatively few Jews settling beyond it. There they made up about 37 percent of the total population, a percentage that remained stable in the interwar period. In some neighborhoods, as many as 90 percent of the inhabitants were Jews.

Warsaw was a major center of Jewish culture and public life. All parties and movements active in modern Jewry organized, met, and struggled in Warsaw: Zionists and assimilationists, socialists and capitalists, Hasidim and Mitnagdim, religious and secular Jews.

Warsaw Jewry was destroyed during World War II. In the mid-1980s, about 3,000 Jews lived in the city, most of them elderly.

* * *

# The Jews in the Baltic States in the Interwar Years

## ban and Rural Population in Lithuania and Latvia

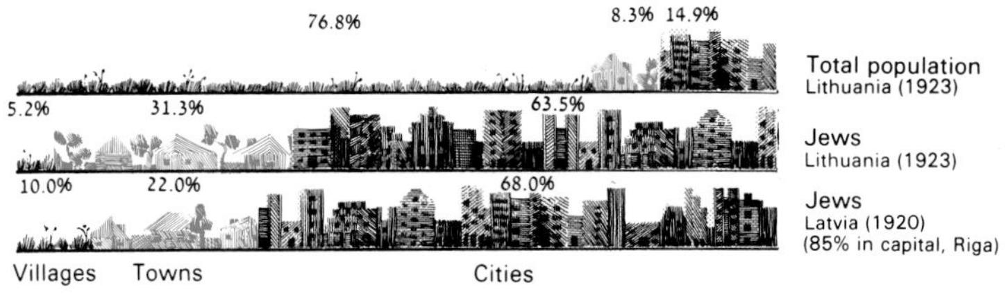


## rcentage of Jews in Urban and Rural pulation of Lithuania, 1923

## pulation in Lithuania by Age Group, 1923

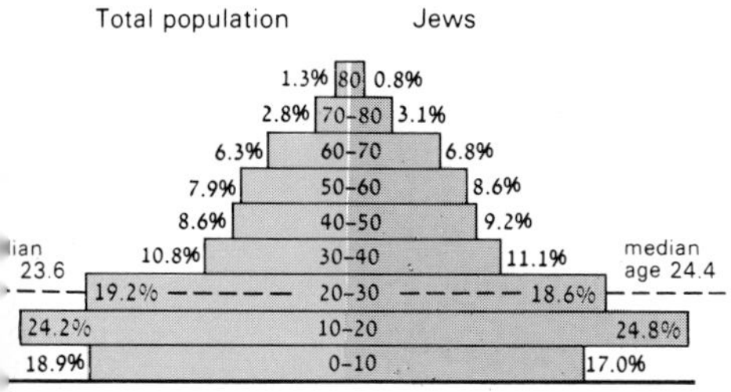


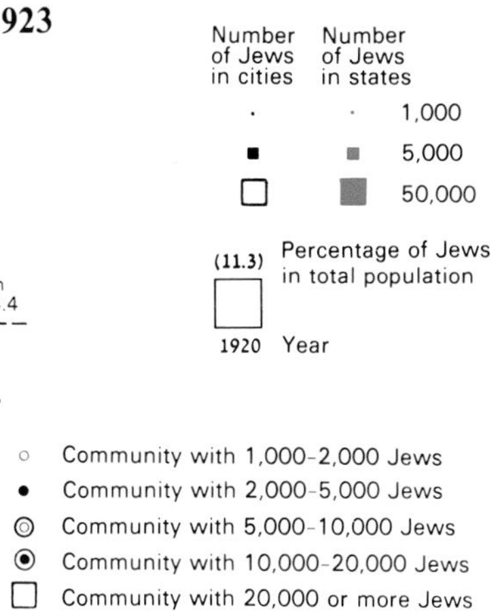


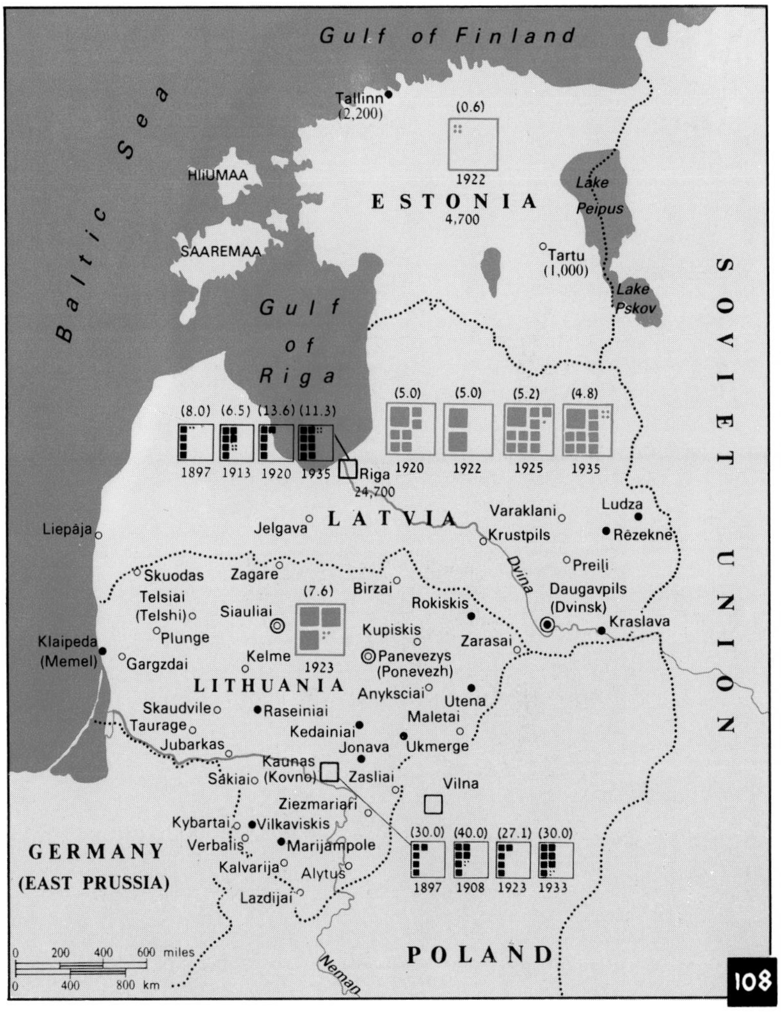


### Lithuania

A large and well-established Jewish community lived in historical Lithuania. After World War I, the country was divided between Poland and the Soviet Union, and only the northwestern part became independent. Vilna, the foremost Jewish center of old Lithuania, became part of Poland.

The Jews acquired extensive national and cultural rights in the new state, and the government included a minister for Jewish affairs. The *kehillot* (community councils) had official recognition; Jews controlled their own education and culture; Jewish parties organized on the Polish pattern and participated in the general political life.

In 1926, there was a right-wing revolution in Lithuania, and all democratic institutions were abolished. The policy toward the Jews changed completely, and strong antisemitic trends developed. Economic pressure was exerted against the Jews, aimed at reducing their numbers in various occupations.

Lithuania was occupied by the Germans in 1941. During the war, 90 percent of the Lithuanian Jews were exterminated.

### Latvia

About 100,000 Jews lived in Latvia in the interwar period, enjoying relatively good conditions until 1934. Their rights as citizens and as a minority were recognized, and they organized their own communal institutions and schools, formed parties, and elected representatives to parliament. Latvian Jews came under various cultural influences, which found expression in the languages used in the Jewish schools: Russian, German, Yiddish, or Hebrew. Economically, they were better off than the Jews in neighboring countries. They concentrated in the cities; in 1935, about half of all Latvian Jews lived in the capital, Riga.

After a fascist revolution in Latvia in 1934, all autonomous institutions were abolished. Jews were now defined as a religious group only. Antisemitism surged in the late 1930s. Latvia was conquered by the Russians in 1939, and by the Germans in 1941. The Germans, with the help of part of the non-Jewish population, killed about 90 percent of the Latvian Jews.

### Estonia

Fewer than 5,000 Jews lived in Estonia in the interwar years, half of them in the capital, Tallinn. Their legal situation was among the best in East European Jewry. They had full civil rights and were recognized as a national minority. Although Estonia, too, was conquered by the Germans in World War II, 60 percent of its Jews escaped to the Soviet Union. Most of those who remained were exterminated by the Germans.

# The Jews in Czechoslovakia in the Interwar Years

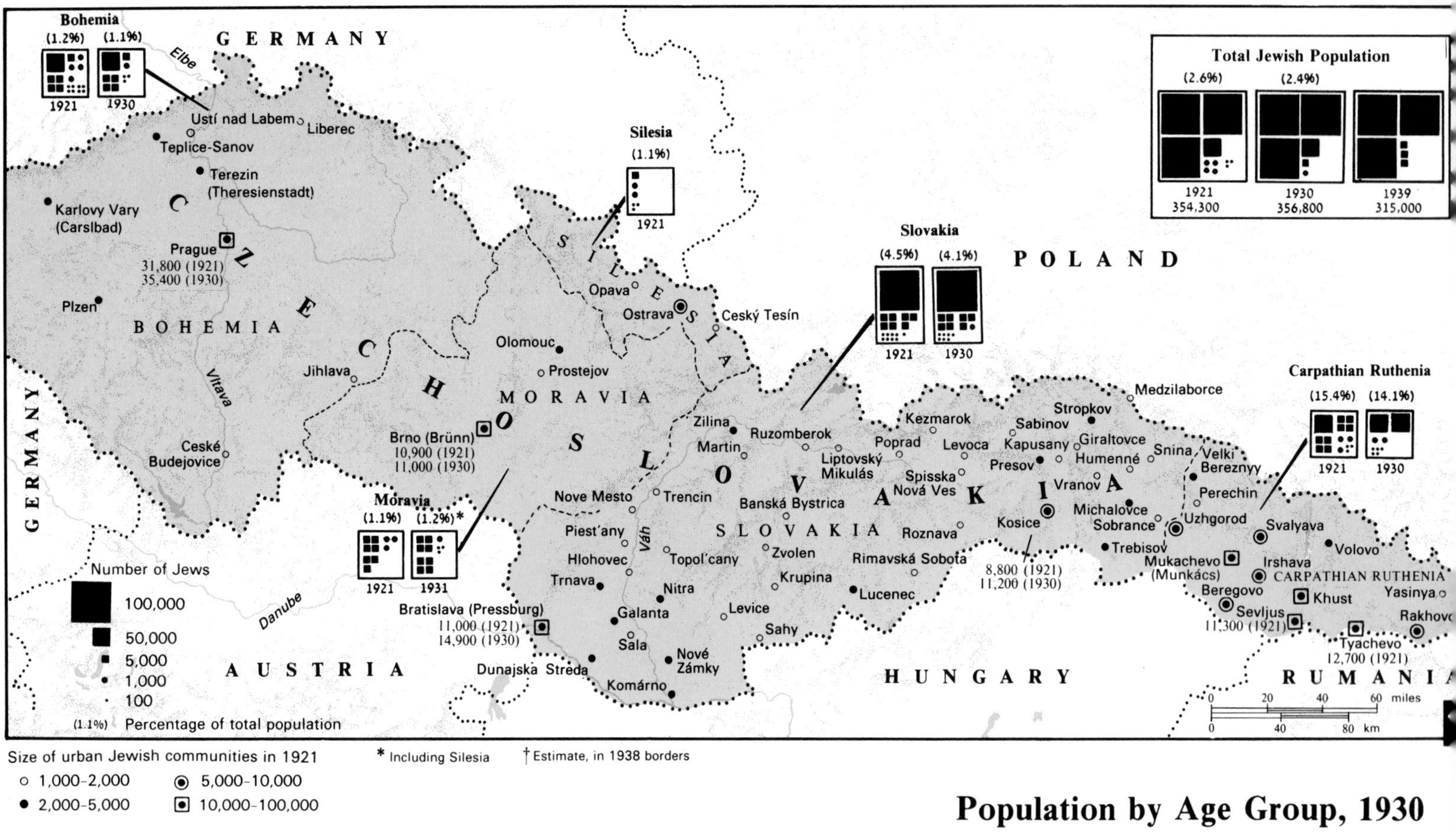


## Population by Age Group, 1930

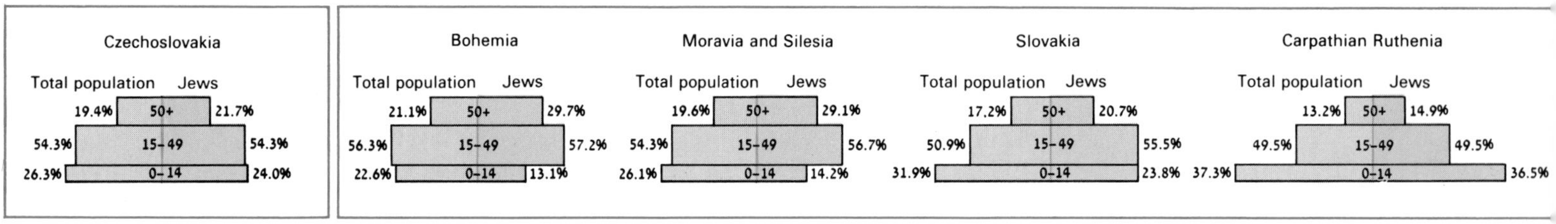


## Median Ages, 1921

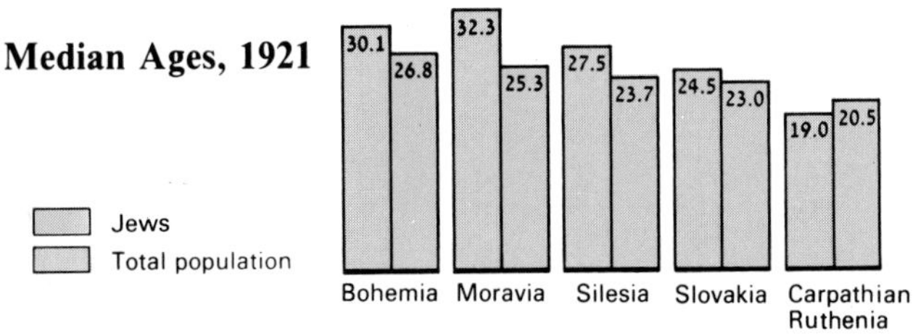


## "Nationality" Identification of Czechoslovakian Jews, 1921

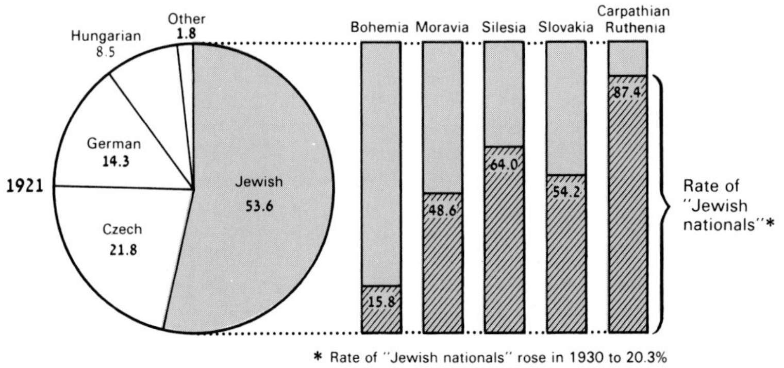


* Rate of "Jewish nationals" rose in 1930 to 20.3% in Bohemia and 51.7% in Moravia and Silesia

As formed after World War I, Czechoslovakia was a mosaic of various national groups living in five regions. There were old Jewish communities in all parts of the new state. Because of the diversity of general cultural influences, there were profound differences between the Jews in the western regions (Bohemia, Moravia, Silesia), which had belonged to the Austro-German part of the Hapsburg Empire, and the Jews in the eastern regions (Slovakia and Sub-Carpathian Ruthenia), which had belonged to the Hungarian part of the empire. The western Jews were urban; those in the eastern regions lived in villages or small towns. Additional differences were related to patterns of acculturation, religious tendencies, socioeconomic structure, and demographic trends. For example, while the Jewish population in the eastern part of the country was still growing, the Jews in the western part were experiencing the demographic problems characteristic of Western Jewry in general—no numerical growth and gradual aging.

The Czechoslovakian state scrupulously respected the national rights of its different groups, including the Jews. But there were severe tensions among the nationalities themselves. Since the Jews were not territorially concentrated but lived among other nationalities, they were accused by the Czechs of being representatives of German culture, or by the Slovaks of propagating Hungarian influences. In fact, between 1921 and 1930, there was an increase in the number of Jews who defined themselves as Czech nationals. Furthermore, fewer Jews regarded themselves as Germans or Hungarians, and relatively more defined themselves as Jewish nationals.

Czechoslovakia was conquered by the Germans in the spring of 1938. Many Jews left the country before the start of World War II. Of those who remained, about 85 percent (according to the 1938 borders) were exterminated during the Holocaust.

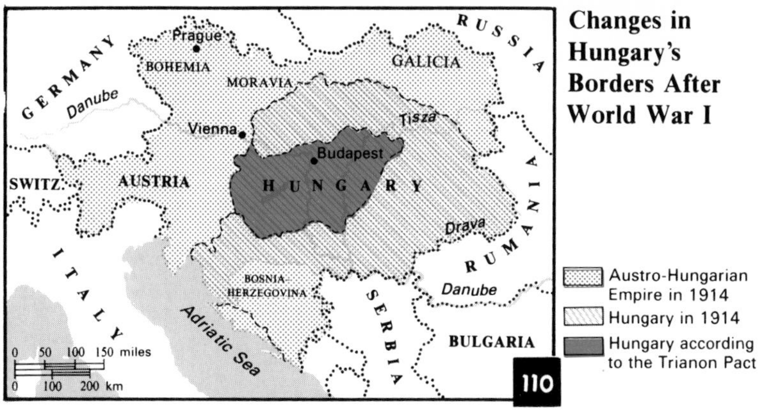


## Changes in Hungary's Borders After World War I

# The Jews in Hungary in the Interwar Years

Hungary as reconstituted after the Trianon Treaty of 1920 was a much smaller country than it had been in 1914. All the national minorities that had lived in Hungary were incorporated into other states, together with several million Hungarians—including hundreds of thousands of Jews (mainly in Czechoslovakia and Rumania). In theory, the Jews were full citizens, and since Hungary was a country of only one nationality, they were recognized as a religious group. In practice, antisemitism was rampant; Hungary was the only European country besides Germany to adopt explicit antisemitic laws before World War II (1938–1939).

Hungarian Jewry decreased in the interwar period, from 473,400 in 1920 to about 400,000 in 1939—mainly because of a low fertility rate and emigration. About 45 percent of Hungarian Jews lived in the capital, Budapest, which was one of the major Jewish centers in Europe at the time. Although their percentage in the city's population was decreasing (23.2 percent in 1920, to 18.9 percent in 1935), the Jews remained an important element in Budapest's cultural and economic life. In 1930, 55.1 percent of the lawyers in Budapest were Jews, as were 40.2 percent of the doctors and 36.1 percent of the journalists. Similar percentages obtained in the country as a whole: in 1920, 50.6 percent of the Hungarian lawyers, 59.9 percent of the doctors, and 34.3 percent of the journalists and editors were Jews. Budapest was Hungary's only large Jewish center. A significant part of the Jewish population lived in dozens of relatively small communities in the northeastern part of the country.

Hungarian Jewry suffered heavy losses in the Holocaust. About 75 percent of the Jews who lived within the borders of Trianon Hungary perished, most of them in 1943 and 1944.

## Population by Age Group, 1930

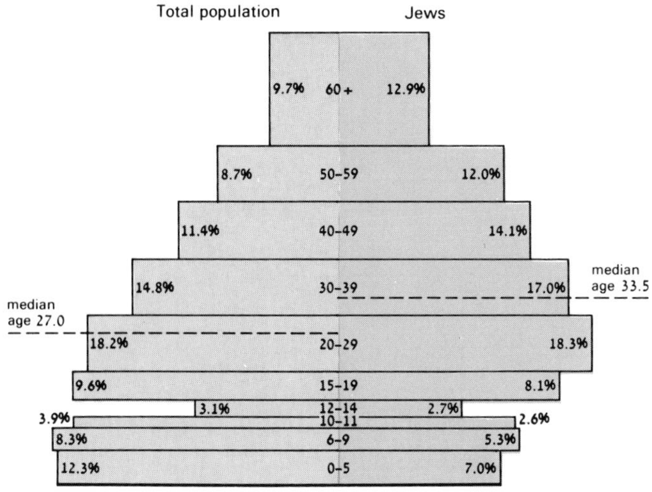


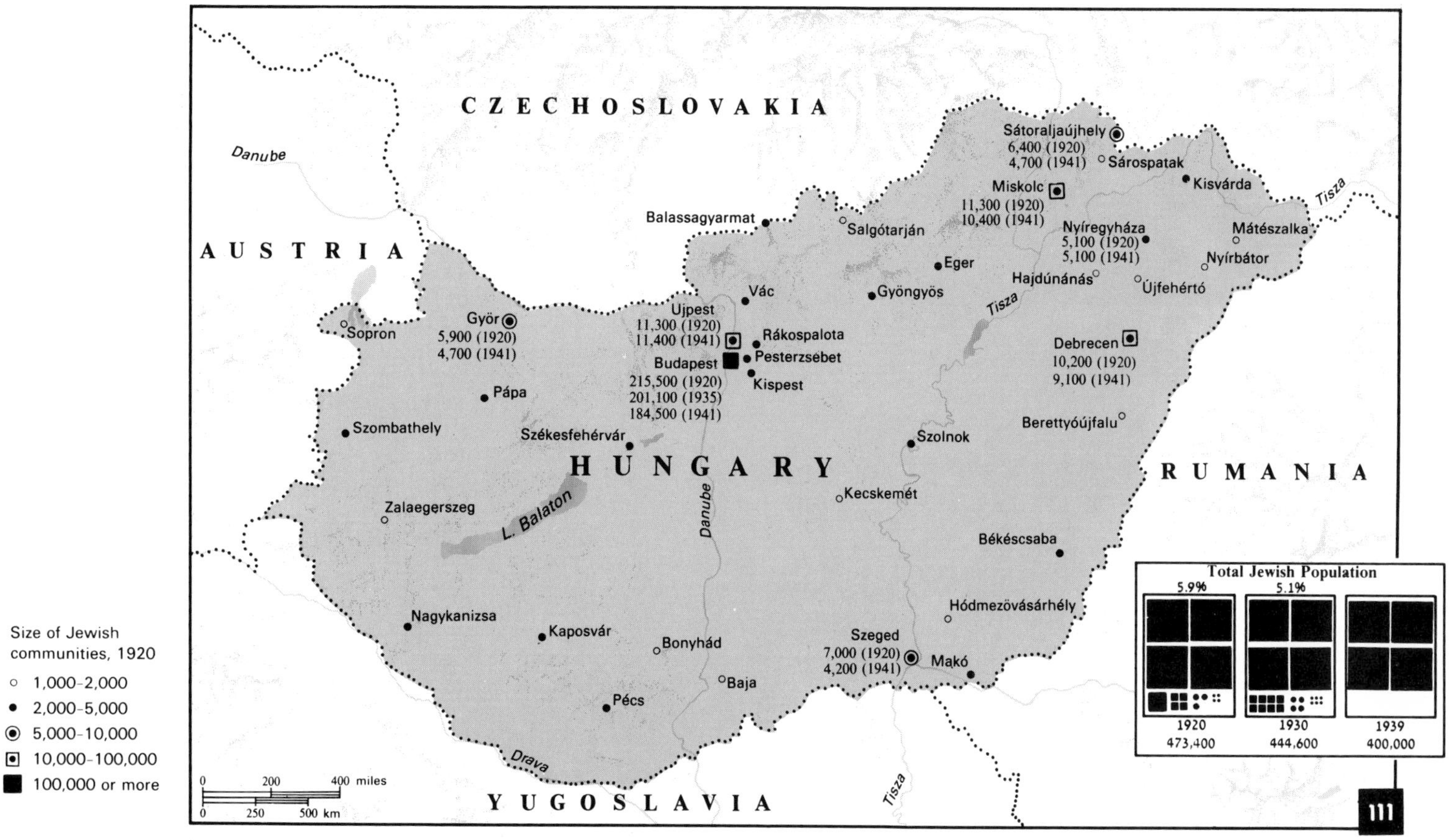


## Jewish University Students

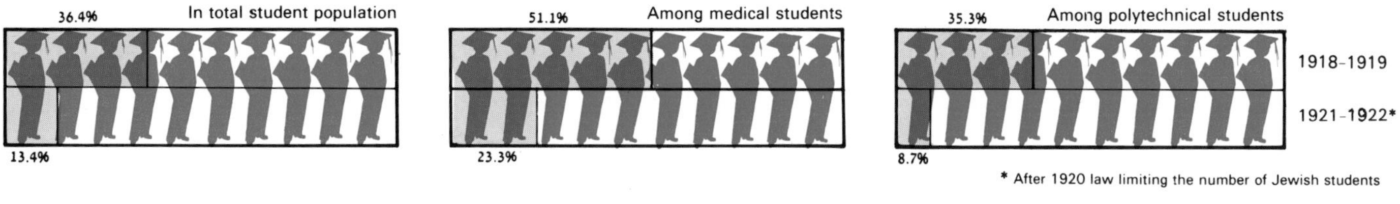

# The Jews in Rumania: Late Nineteenth Century

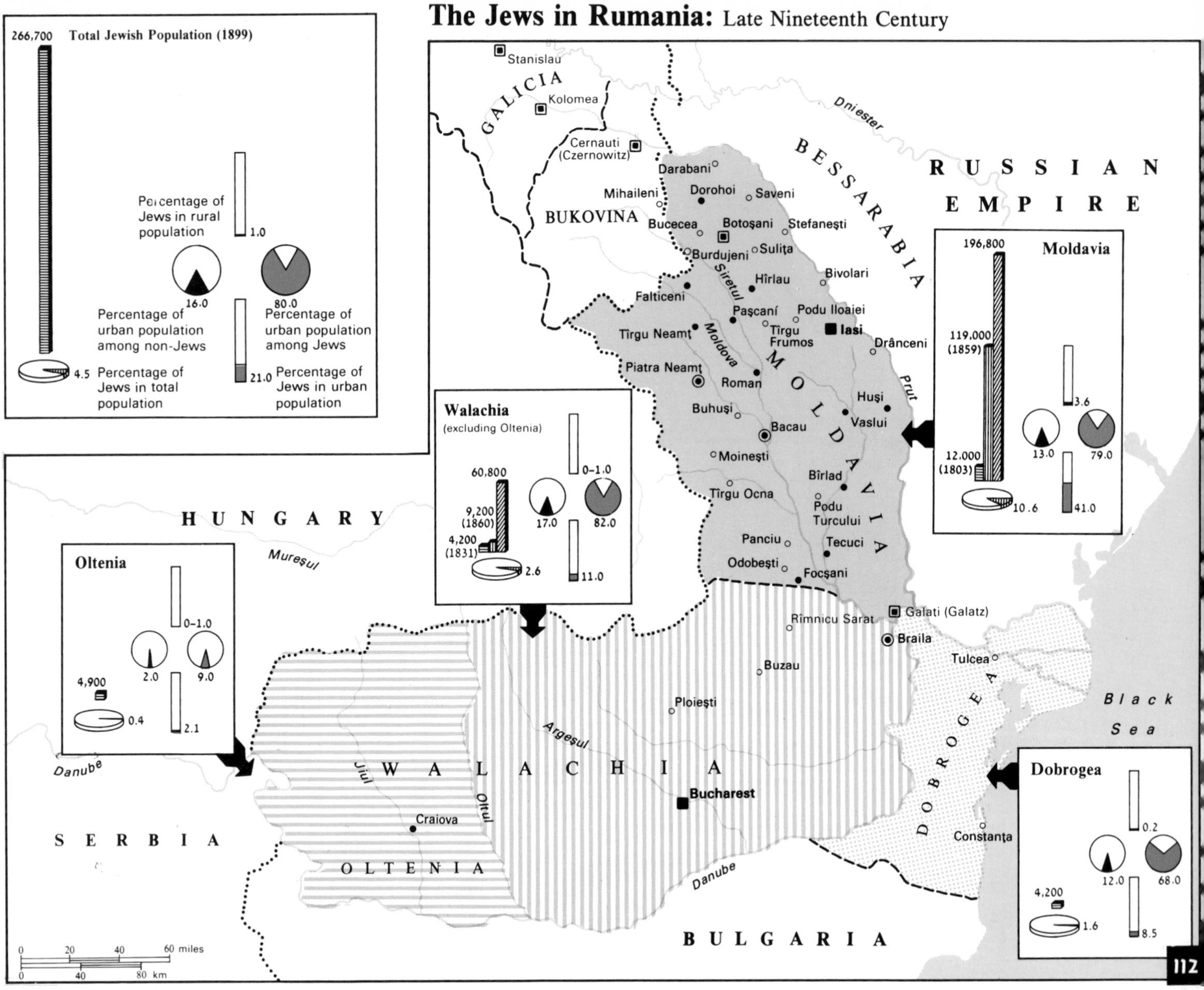


- ○ Community of 1,000–2,500 Jews
- • Community of 2,500–7,000 Jews
- ◉ Community of 8,000–10,000 Jews
- ▣ Community of 14,000–17,000 Jews
- ■ Community of about 40,000 Jews

The data from 1803 and 1859 are based on declarations made for tax purposes and tend to the low side. The data of 1899 are based on an official census.

**Birth and Death Rates, 1899** (per 1,000 population)

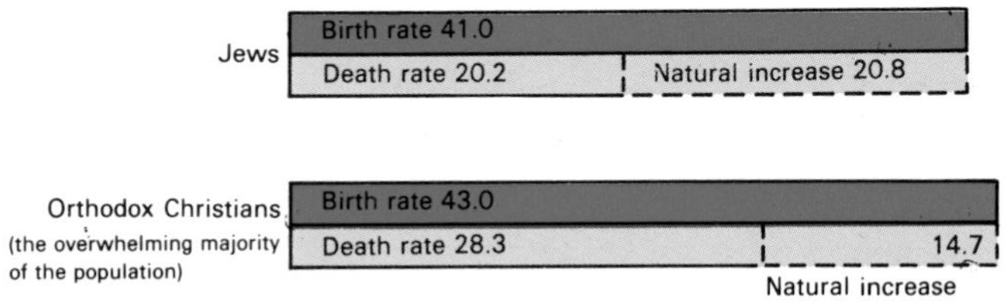


The Rumanian state was formed in 1859 through the unification of the principalities of Moldavia and Walachia (or Muntenia), which included the western region of Oltenia. The kingdom received international recognition after the Berlin Conference in 1878, when northern Dobrogea (Dobruja) was added to it. After World War I, these regions were called the Regat, or Old Kingdom. Some Jews had lived in the principalities (especially Moldavia) since the Middle Ages. In the nineteenth century, their numbers grew; Jews arrived from the north (Poland, Galicia) and from the east (the Russian Empire) to settle in the Regat. The Jewish population in Moldavia increased from 15,000 in 1803 to 196,800 in 1899; in Walachia, from 4,200 in 1831 to 60,800 in 1899, about 60 percent of Jews living in the capital, Bucharest. In the nineteenth century, the Jews were the second largest religious group in the kingdom, after the Orthodox Christians. They constituted 4.5 percent of the total population, but 10.4 percent of the population in Moldavia, where about 75 percent of the Rumanian Jews lived. In general, they were an urban population: 20.2 percent in the thirty-two regional capitals, and 40 percent of the city dwellers in Moldavia.

The question of the civil rights of Rumanian Jews occupied Jewish public opinion in Western Europe since the formation of the kingdom. The Berlin Conference of 1878 had established that all inhabitants of Rumania should receive full civil rights, regardless of religious affiliation. But anti-Jewish sentiment ran high among all sectors of the general population, and the Rumanian government circumvented the 1878 decision by declaring most Jews to be aliens. In 1899, the country had only about 10,000 Jews, or 4 percent of the Jewish population, of any nationality, only 4,000 of whom were Rumanian citizens. All the others—96 percent of the Jewish population—remained without civil and political rights. The combination of civil disabilities and economic difficulties impelled many Jews to emigrate in the 1880s: to Western Europe, the United States, and Palestine. From 1881 to 1914, 75,000 Rumanian Jews entered the United States, representing 80 to 90 percent of the Rumanian emigrants. In the early twentieth century, the rate of natural increase among Rumanian Jews dropped sharply. This, together with the high emigration rate, resulted in a decline in Rumania's Jewish population from 266,700 to 240,000 between 1899 and 1912, and a drop in the proportion of Jews in the total population from 4.5 to 3.3 percent.

# The Jews in Rumania in the Interwar Years

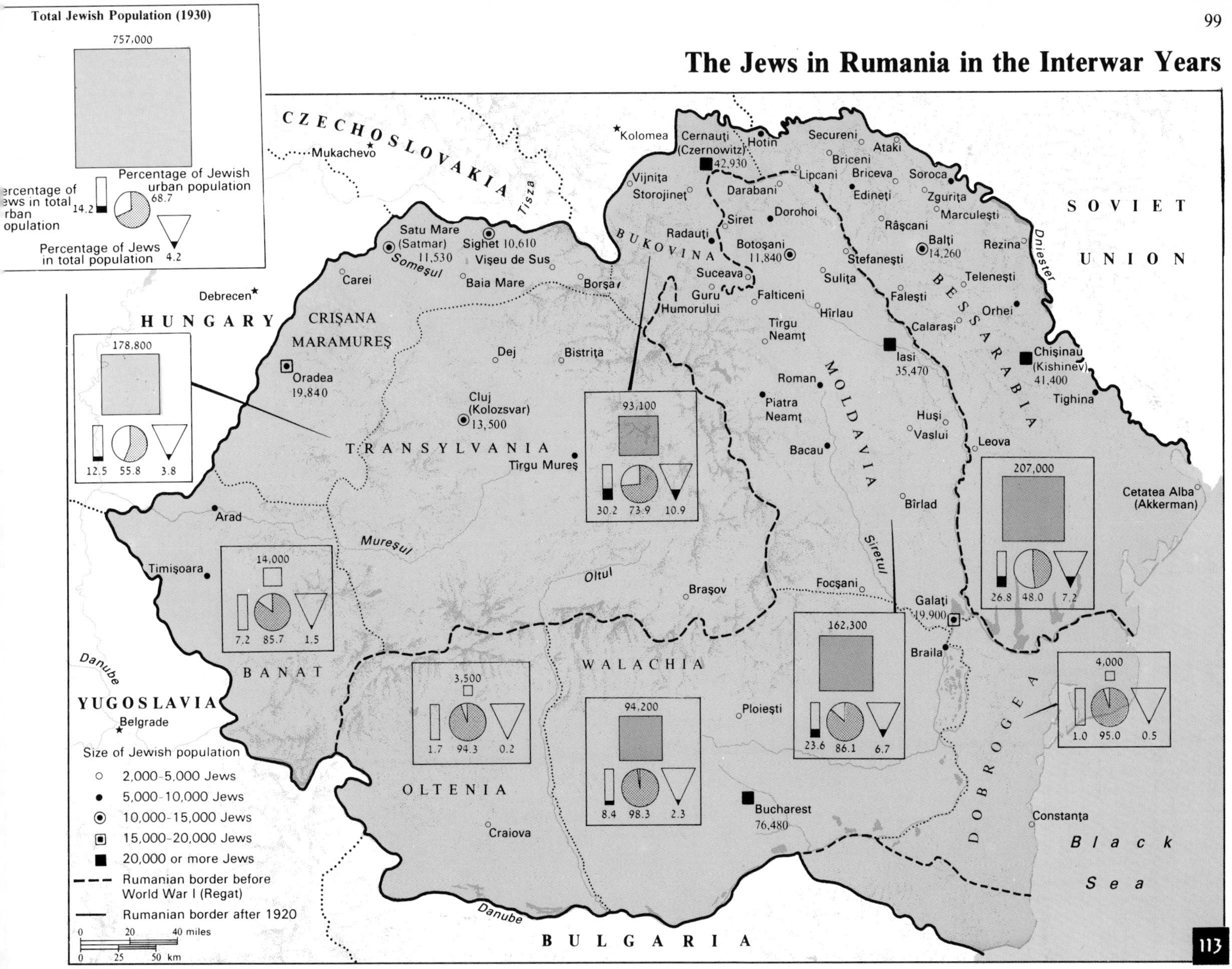


As a result of World War I, Rumania became a multinational state: Transylvania in the west (formerly Hungarian), Dobrogea (Dobruja) in the south (from Bulgaria), Russian Bessarabia in the east, and Austrian Bukovina in the north became part of the new Rumania. Many of these territories contained large Jewish communities. According to records, Rumania's Jewish population had risen by 1930 to 757,000. But there are many indications that its actual, undeclared number was about 20 percent higher. Culturally, these Jewries continued to belong to their historical groups, only the Jews of the Regat (the Old Kingdom) coming under Rumanian cultural influence.

Seventy percent of Rumanian Jews lived in cities, as compared with 20 percent of the general population. Their urban character found expression in their occupational structure: in 1930, 73.2 percent of the general population lived from agriculture, while only 6.5 percent of Jews did so; the rest were concentrated in commerce, crafts, and industry.

The legal situation of Rumanian Jews remained problematic in the enlarged state. At the Paris Peace Conference, Rumania had pledged to grant full citizenship to all the inhabitants of its new lands. Where the Jews were concerned, however, only those of the Regat became citizens, while difficulties were created regarding all the others. Antisemitism, a serious problem even before 1919, became worse in the interwar period: antisemitic parties were organized, and the Jews were subjected to pogroms and economic pressure. This resulted in a sizable Jewish emigration.

Rumania, which fought in World War II on the German side, underwent several territorial changes during the war that affected its large Jewish population. The Jews in Bukovina, Bessarabia, and Transylvania suffered considerably, under either a German or a Rumanian military presence, with many sent to extermination camps. In the Old Kingdom, despite Rumanian antisemitism, the Jews fared better. About half of the Jews living within the country's 1939 borders perished during the war.

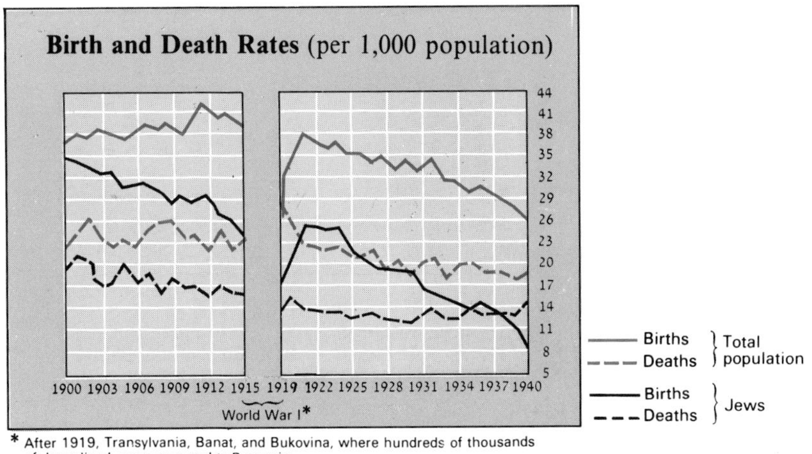


* After 1919, Transylvania, Banat, and Bukovina, where hundreds of thousands of Jews lived, were annexed to Rumania.

## Occupations, 1930

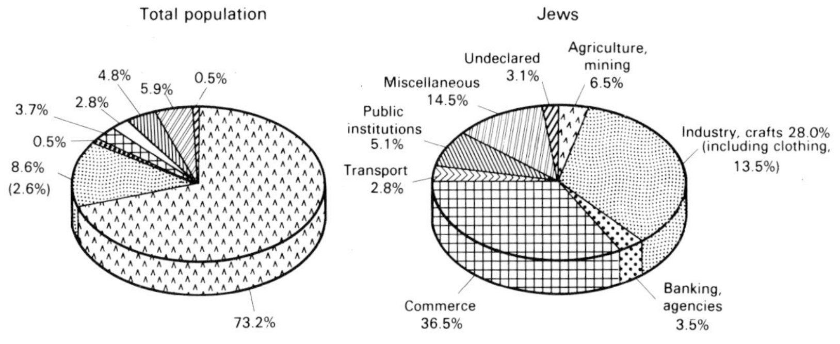

# The Jews in Southeastern Europe:
Early Twentieth Century

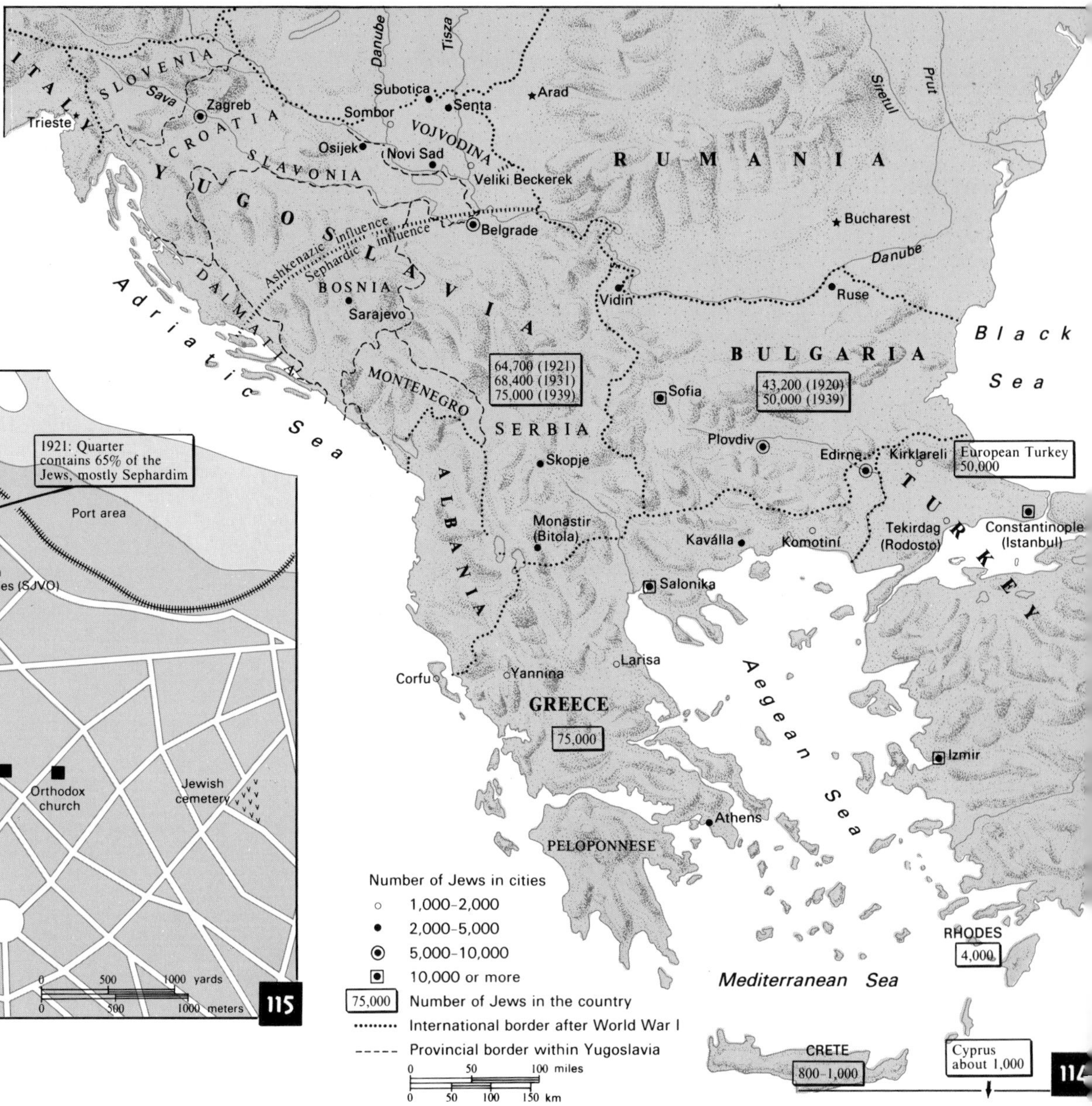


# The Jews in Belgrade

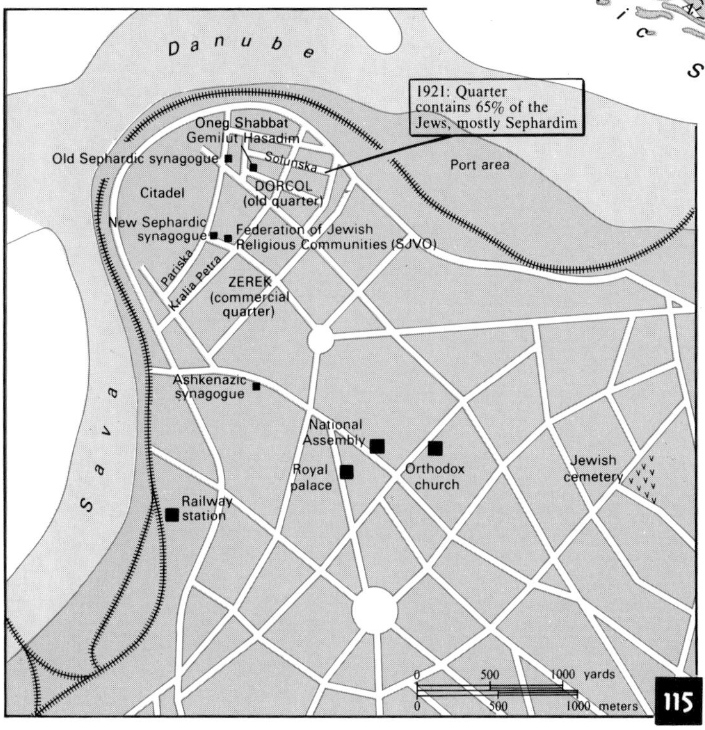


Four countries in southeastern Europe (the Balkans) contained important Jewish communities: Yugoslavia, Bulgaria, Greece, and European Turkey. Before World War II, the Jews numbered about 250,000, about 100,000 of whom lived in two cities that were Jewish centers of great historical significance: Salonika (which after 1913 belonged to Greece) and Constantinople.

Sixty percent of the Jews in these countries were Sephardim, descendants of Jews expelled from Spain and Portugal at the end of the fifteenth century. They had gradually settled in the Ottoman Empire, where they had been well received, prospered, and created influential Jewish centers. Parts of southeastern Europe were under Turkish domination until the nineteenth century, and Jews had settled there, too.

In the twentieth century, the Jewish communities in southeastern Europe were very different from one another. The Jews of Sofia, the capital of Bulgaria, and of Salonika were organized in a more unified structure than were those of Constantinople (Istanbul), who were divided into many independent communities. In Yugoslavia, Jewish groups of various historical roots found themselves living in the same state as a result of World War I. An imaginary line divided the Ashkenazic and Sephardic spheres of Jewish influence in Yugoslavia, evident also in the country's three major Jewish centers: Zagreb, Sarajevo, and Belgrade. In Sarajevo, in Bosnia, the Sephardic community was more influential, while in Zagreb, the capital of Croatia, the Ashkenazic element was dominant. Belgrade, in Serbia, was on the line dividing the two spheres: the community had originally been Sephardic, but in the nineteenth century there was a large Ashkenazic influx. In the interwar period, the two groups were equally represented.

The Jews in all four countries were well integrated into and acculturated to the general society. But unlike those in Western Europe, the Jewish communities in the Balkans maintained distinct social patterns. Assimilation and out-marriage were relatively low.

In World War II, Bulgaria allied itself with the Germans. Yet in spite of many antisemitic measures, the Bulgarian government refused (after some vacillation) to hand over its Jewish citizens to the Germans. Yugoslavia and Greece were occupied by the Italians and the Germans, and most of the Jews there were sent to extermination camps. About 86 percent of Greek Jews and about 80 percent of Yugoslavian Jews perished in the Holocaust.

## Occupations of Yugoslavian Jews, 1938

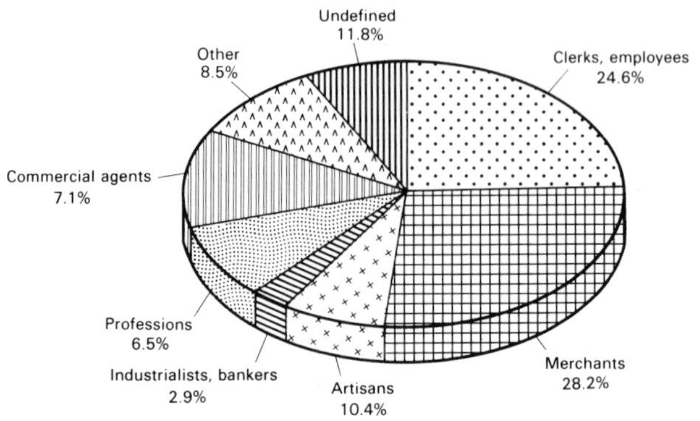

# The Jews in Western Europe in the 1930s

Almost 1.7 million Jews lived in Western Europe in the 1930s, 70 percent of them in Germany, the United Kingdom, and France. Most lived in cities, especially in the capitals. Half were concentrated in six large centers: Berlin, London, Paris, Amsterdam, Antwerp, and Vienna. In a few countries, about 50 percent or more of the Jews lived in the capital: Austria (91 percent), the Netherlands (56 percent), France (46 percent), and the United Kingdom (67 percent). The same applied to several countries with smaller Jewish populations.

West European Jewry in the interwar period was very much the product of the large Jewish immigration from Eastern Europe that began in the second half of the nineteenth century. Between 1897 and 1939, the Jewish population of France trebled, and that of Great Britain grew four- or fivefold. The West European Jewries may be said to have been "East European" in some of their basic characteristics, even if the second and third generations underwent rapid and far-reaching acculturation to the societies into which they were born. An additional Jewish group in almost all the countries were the refugees from Germany, who arrived after 1933.

British Jewry underwent two basic transformations in the modern era. At its beginnings, in the seventeenth century, its composition was mainly Spanish–Portuguese. Toward the end of the eighteenth century, Ashkenazic Jews, mostly from Central Europe, settled in England. And from the mid-nineteenth century, British Jewry gradually became predominantly East European. From the start, most Jews who settled in the United Kingdom were attracted to London. Although from the late eighteenth century, Jewish communities were established in other English cities, they remained much smaller than the London center. The second largest community in England was in Manchester, which in the 1930s had fewer than 40,000 Jews.

The Jewish community in the Netherlands was the fourth largest in Western Europe. Its development was similar in certain respects to that in Britain: the Spanish–Portuguese origins, the Ashkenazic newcomers in the late seventeenth and the eighteenth centuries, and the East European immigrants in the second half of the nineteenth century. In 1909, only 6,600 Sephardic Jews lived in Holland, 6 percent of the Jewish population. Dutch Jewry numbered 104,000 in 1899, a figure that remained stable until 1940.

In the interwar years, the internal life of most West European Jewish communities was marked by serious demographic problems. Whatever numerical increase there was in these communities resulted entirely from Jewish immigration, while the older segments of the Jewish populations showed a negative demographic balance, because of low birth rates, a growing rate of out-marriage, and conversion. In some countries (such as Switzerland, Italy, and Germany before 1933), not even the arrival of Jewish immigrants could compensate for the losses due to the other factors. Most of the West European Jewries were not organic Jewish communities in the sense of developing stable patterns of Jewish life accepted by most members. The extensive acculturation of the older element of Jewish society, and the differences between it and Jewish newcomers with very different characteristics, created a situation in which the diverse segments of Jewish society in each country had very little in common. Consequently, there was insufficient collaboration between the older Jewish strata and the newcomers, even problems that posed serious threats to all Jews, such as the growing menace of modern antisemitism.

**Jnited Kingdom**

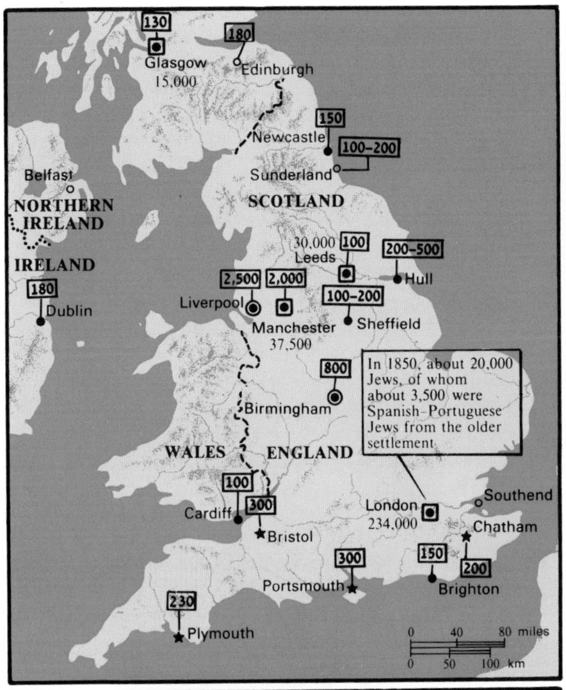


First communities outside London in the 19th century and number of Jews

umber of Jews in ties, 1930s

1,000–2,000

2,000–5,000

5,000–10,000

10,000 or more

**Holland and Belgium**

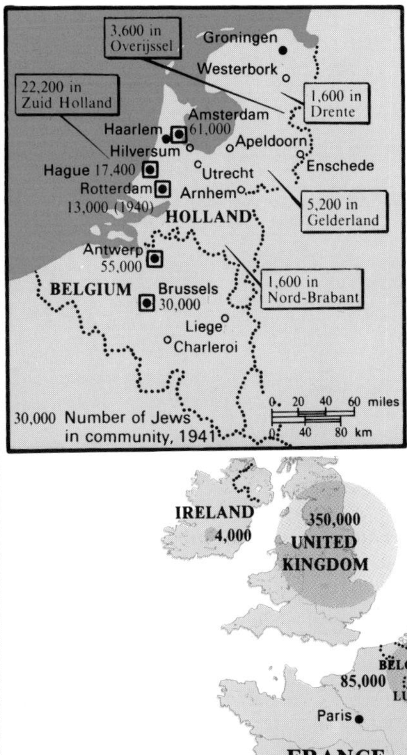


**France**

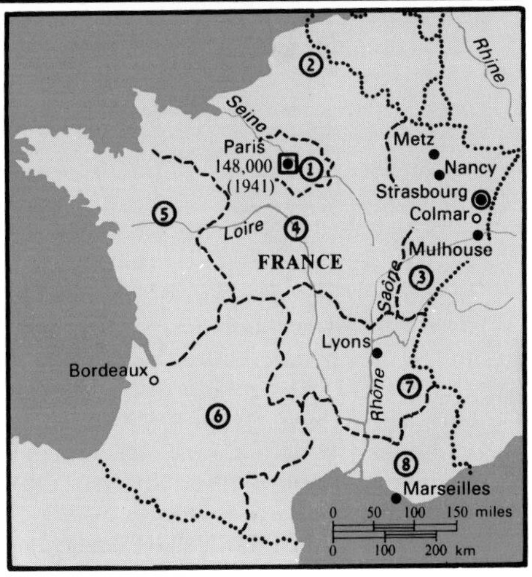


| Region | 1897 | 1941 |
|---|---|---|
| ʾaris and suburbs | 45,600 | 155,000 |
| North | 3,200 | 400 |
| East | 42,200 | 33,700 |
| ʾaris basin | *1 | 27,700 |
| West | *2 | 23,400 |
| Southwest | 4,800 | 22,300 |
| Southeast | 2,600 | 11,900 |
| Mediterranean | 5,300 | 43,200 |
| Total | 103,700* | 317,600† |

ata from 1897 divided among regions 2, 3, 5

ata from 1897 included in region 6

cludes 32,500 Jews in Alsace-Lorraine, en part of Germany

cludes 30,000 Jews in Alsace-Lorraine 936 census)

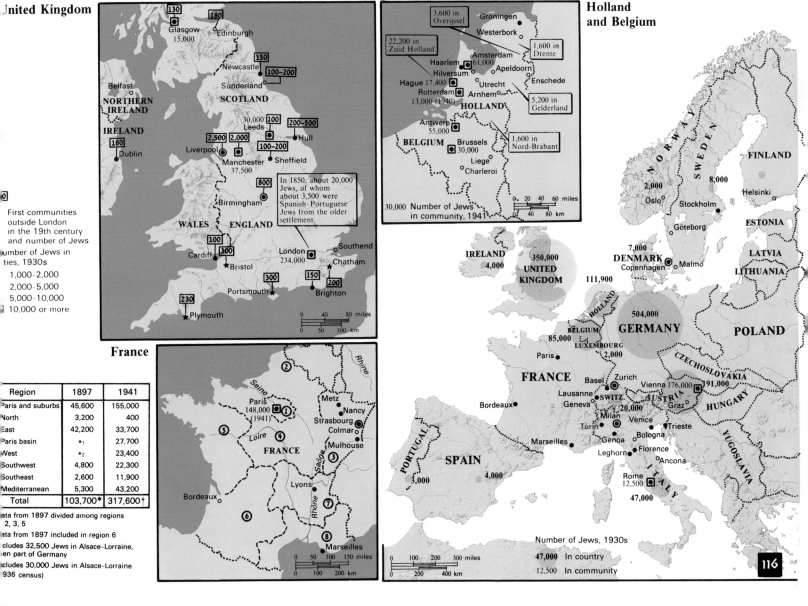

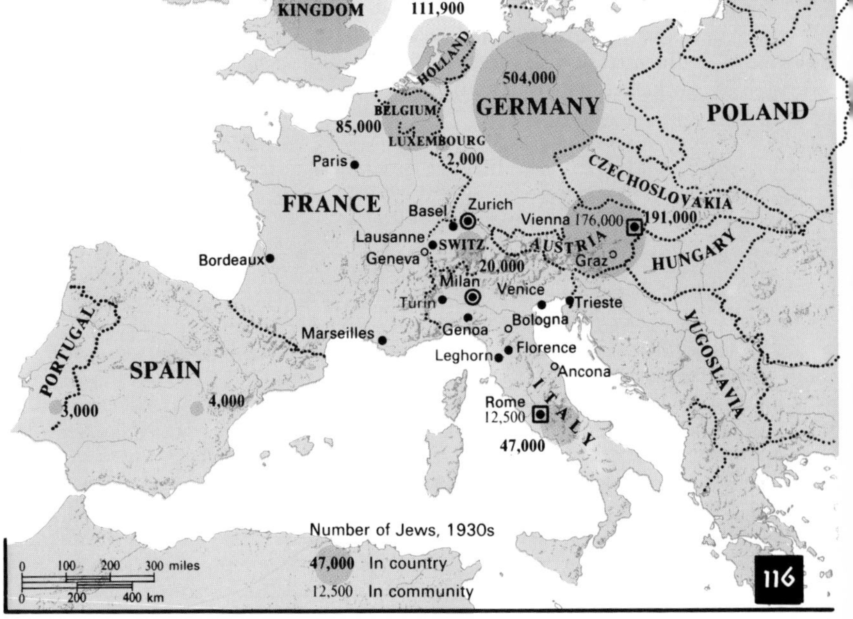


116

# The Jews in Prussia, 1871

○ Community of 1,000–1,500 Jews
● Community of 1,500–2,000 Jews
◉ Community of 3,000–4,000 Jews
▣ Community of 7,000 Jews or more
7,300 Number of Jews in large community
14.7 Jewish population in Prussian regions (in thousands)
12.0 Jewish population in other German states (in thousands)
Prussia, 1871
Border of German Reich, 1871

All the data are according to 1871 borders (Jewish population noted only in states where Jews numbered more than 3,000).

*In 1870, the region was conquered from France. In 1918, it was returned to France.

## Jewish Population Growth

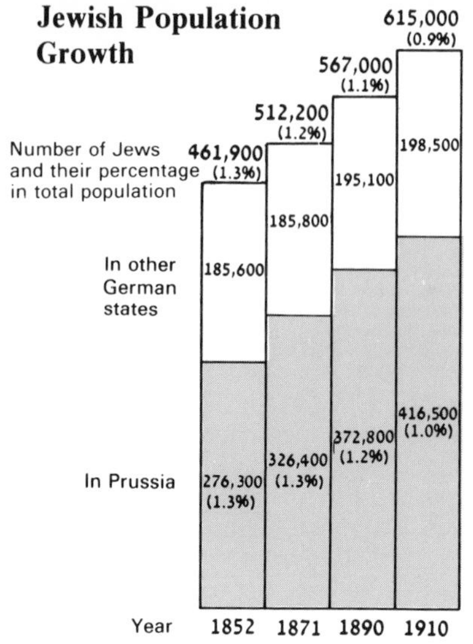


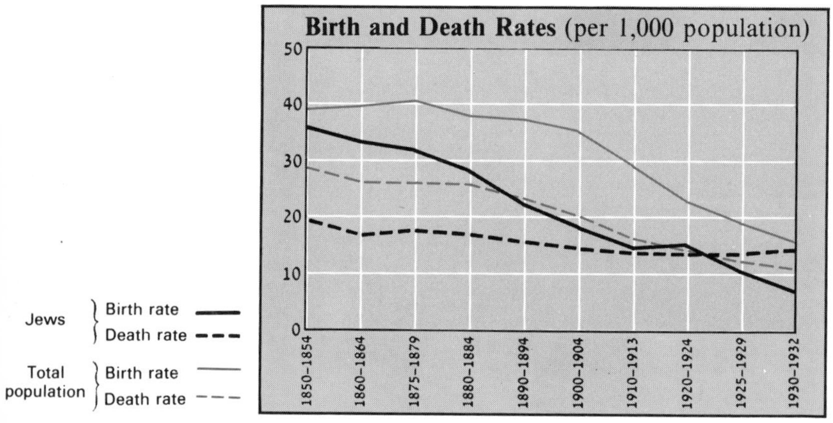


## Occupational Composition (percent)

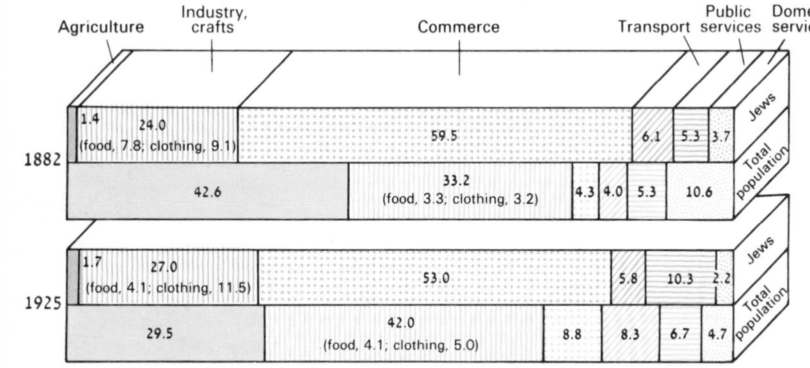


When Germany was unified in 1871, almost two-thirds of all German Jews lived in Prussia. In modern times, Jewish life in Prussia dates from the second half of the seventeenth century, when a group of wealthy Jewish families, from among the Jews expelled from Vienna in 1670, were permitted to settle in the Margravate of Brandenburg, whose capital was Berlin. The Jewish population of Prussia grew rapidly in the eighteenth century, after the conquests or annexations of Silesia (1742), Posen (1772), and other former Polish territories. In the eighteenth century, the official policy toward the Jews changed: from 1730, and especially from 1750, royal edicts were issued to limit their numbers. But the social reforms in Prussia in the early nineteenth century resulted in a better attitude toward the Jewish population: the Hardenberg Law of 1812 granted the Jews important civil rights. As a result of the revolution of 1848, Jews were recognized as full citizens, a status reaffirmed in 1869, on the eve of the establishment of the unified German state. Nevertheless, a wide gap remained between theory and practice regarding the social and civil status of Prussian Jewry.

In the 1850s, Prussia, with 276,000 Jews, had the third largest Jewry in the world, after the Russian and the Austro-Hungarian empires. Until the 1870s, natural increase among Prussian Jews was very high, but then it decreased sharply. In 1852, the Jews made up 1.3 percent of the total population, but only 1 percent in 1910.

Many of the cultural and spiritual trends in modern Judaism were born and developed in Prussia, and from there spread to other countries. Berlin had been one of the main centers of the Jewish enlightenment since the end of the eighteenth century, and in the 1820s, the “Science of Judaism” cultural movement also developed there. It was in Prussia that the religious Reform movement arose and evolved.

Outside Prussia, in 1871, 10 percent of all German Jews lived in Bavaria. Their social structure was somewhat different from that of Prussian Jewry; as in other South German states (Württemberg, Baden, and farther north, Hesse), a significant number of Jews lived in villages and small towns, as middlemen and cattle dealers. The Jewry of Alsace–Lorraine, which was part of Germany from 1871 to 1918, was older than the other German Jewries and different in character. Different, too, were the Jews of Hamburg (a state in its own right), who, from 1671 to 1811, had been organized in one communal structure with the Jews of Altona and Wandsbeck. In Hamburg, an important Spanish–Portuguese community had been established in the seventeenth century. Ashkenazic Jews settled there only toward the end of that century.

# The Jews in Germany, 1925

*The Fasanenstrasse Liberal synagogue in Charlottenburg, Berlin. Burned down in November 1938*

- ○ Community with 1,000–1,500 Jews
- • Community with 1,500–2,500 Jews
- ⦿ Community with 2,500–4,000 Jews
- ⊡ Community with 4,000–5,000 Jews
- ■ Large community and number of Jews

Year 1871 / Year 1925 — Jewish population by states (*Laender*) (in thousands)

* Assigned to France in 1919

More than 500,000 Jews lived in Germany when the Second Reich was founded in 1871. German Jews, like all the country's inhabitants, became full citizens, but since the German states retained considerable internal autonomy, the status of the local Jewish communities varied from place to place. Between 1871 and 1933, German Jewry concentrated in larger cities, mostly in Prussia, Saxony, and Hamburg. In other German states, the number of Jews decreased. The urban and middle-class character of the Jewish population was reflected in its occupational structure: concentration in commerce, industry, and the professions.

Negative demographic tendencies began to characterize German Jewry in the 1880s: a falling birth rate, fewer marriages, aging, and more out-marriage. The arrival of Jewish immigrants from Posen province and from Eastern Europe (the *Ostjuden*) compensated somewhat for the losses among the older Jewish population. In 1900, 7 percent of all German Jews were foreign-born; by 1933, the percentage had risen to 20 percent.

In spite of its demographic problems, German Jewry was one of the most active Jewries in modern times. German Jews had a high degree of self-awareness and defined themselves in a rich spectrum of ideological and religious positions. They were a good example of West European Jewry in general: socially and culturally integrated into the general society, many of them also wished to preserve some form of Jewish identity. In this respect, there were three main ideological options: the integrationist position, Zionism, and Orthodoxy. The integrationists, who usually belonged to the Liberal religious tendency, were the majority of German Jewry. They considered themselves German citizens in the political, national, and cultural senses, but stressed their religious particularism. Some defined Jewish religion very narrowly, favored far-reaching religious reforms, and sometimes adopted an extreme German nationalistic position. Others were more aware of the deeper meanings and implications of Judaism. The Zionists, especially many of their leaders, were as integrated into German life as the integrationists. Their integration, however, led

## Age Distribution in Berlin, 1871 and 1925

(percent)

## Median Age in Germany, 1925

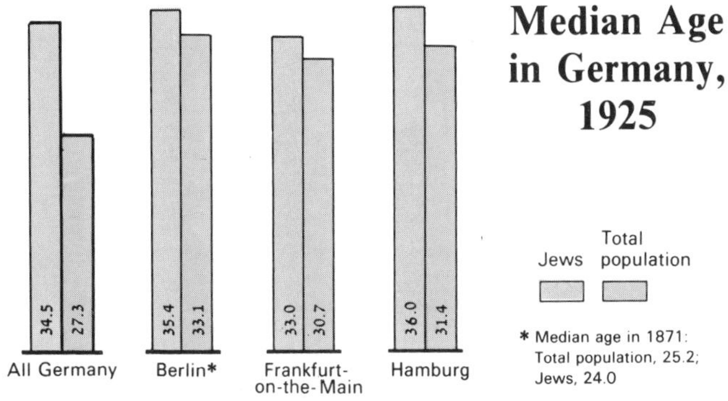

them to a totally opposite conclusion: German Jews could not become completely German and were, in fact, a different people.

Among the Orthodox, the most articulate were the neo-Orthodox. They strove to be exemplary German citizens, blending full cultural integration into the general society with uncompromising observance of Jewish religious law, the *Halakhah*. Although they were a small group, there was almost no assimilation among them. They kept apart from other German Jews, opposing both the Liberal religious trend and the Zionist position. In time, however, part of German Orthodoxy came to support religious Zionism.

Many German Jews were Socialists or Communists, some occupying leading positions in their parties. Since they believed that the solution to the problems of German Jewry was to be found in the economic and political change of German society as a whole, most of them remained aloof from the Jewish community. Finally, there were the foreign-born East European Jews. Many continued to cling to their religious and cultural traditions, and their relations with the established part of German Jewry were often problematic.

The extreme self-consciousness of German Jewry and the elaborate formulations of German Jewish intellectuals in their efforts to explain their German and Jewish attachments were, in part, a reflection of the uncertain relationship between the Jews and the Germans. In the end, they achieved almost nothing. Most Germans neither understood nor cared about the hair-splitting distinctions drawn by German Jews between their German and their Jewish loyalties. The negative attitude of many Germans was not evoked by this or that interpretation of Judaism, but by Judaism per se. In this respect, too, German Jewry symbolized many of the tensions between Jews and non-Jews in other parts of Europe.

## The Jewish Population in Germany by Years

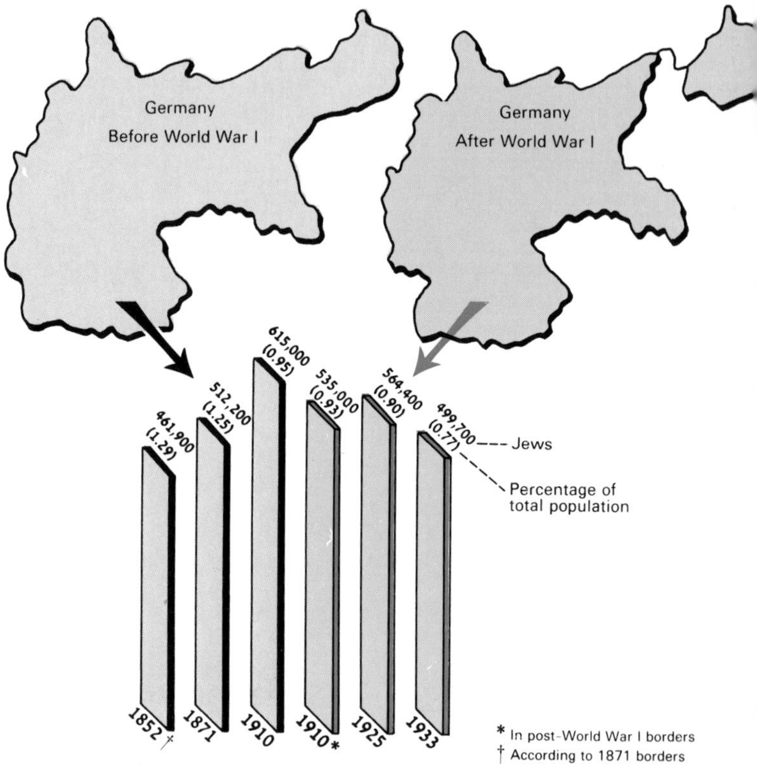


## Natural Increase

(per 1,000)

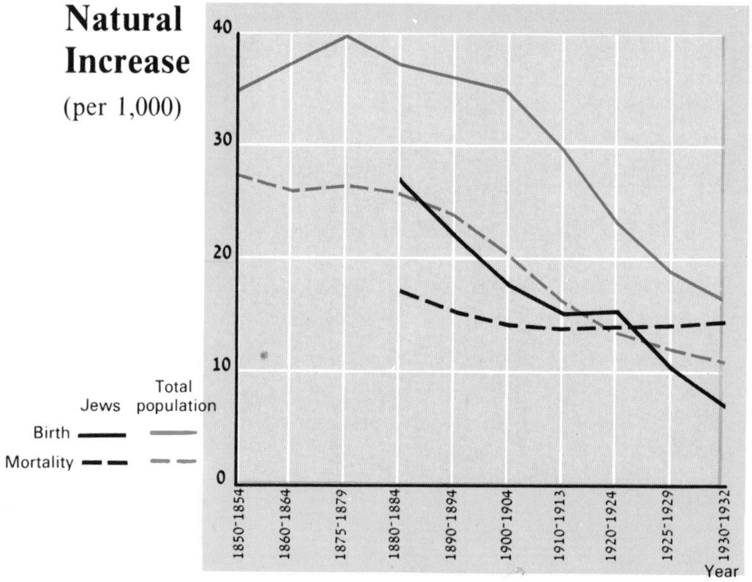


## Urban and Rural Population (percent)

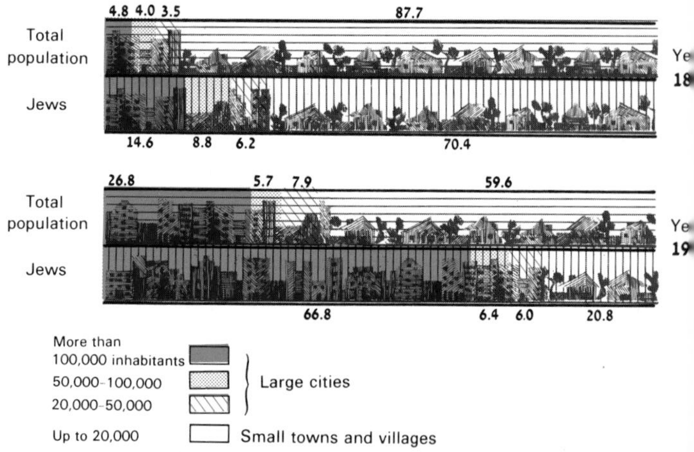


## Rate of Out-Marriages

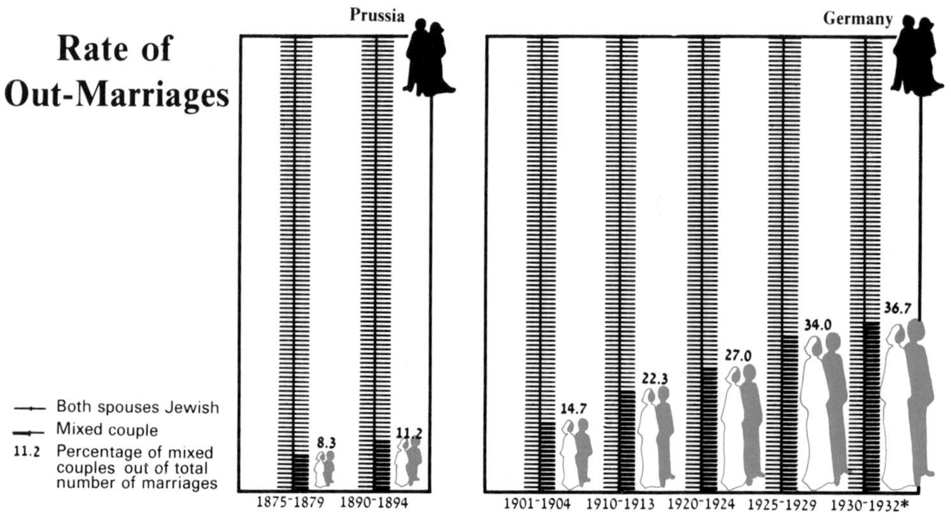


* In 1930 to 1932, 22.5% of single Jews married a non-Jewish spouse.

## Occupations in Greater Berlin, 1907 and 1933 (excluding agriculture)

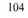

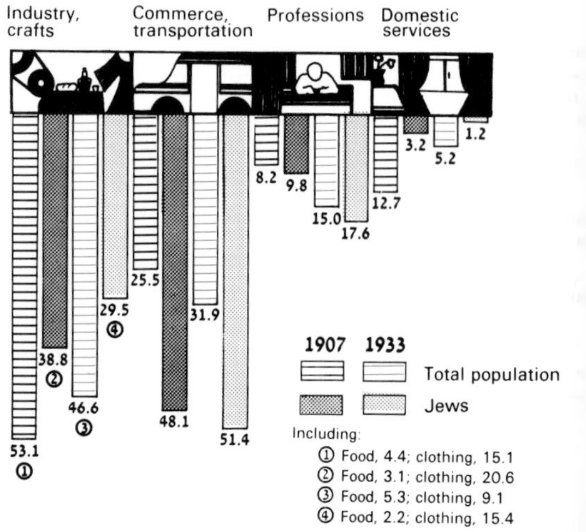


The Jews made up 1.5% of the total population of Greater Berlin in 1910, and 3.2% in 1933.

## The Jews in Berlin, 1925

The economic and cultural opportunities of the Prussian and (from 1871) German capital attracted a large Jewish population. About 36,000 Jews lived in Berlin in 1871, and about 172,700 in 1925. Jews moved to Berlin from the eastern German provinces (especially Posen), the smaller German towns, and Eastern Europe. In 1925, about 25 percent of Berlin's Jewish inhabitants were foreigners; by 1933, 30 percent were.

From the end of the eighteenth century, Berlin was the main cultural center of West European Jewry. Various movements sprouted and flourished there, such as the Jewish enlightenment (Moses Mendelssohn and his circle, in the late eighteenth century), the "Science of Judaism" (from the 1820s), and the religious Reform. From the end of the nineteenth century, and especially during the Weimar Republic, Jews occupied a prominent place in the city's cultural and professional life. Jews were strongly represented among Berlin's physicians, lawyers, journalists, and intellectuals. In the 1920s, Berlin was also an important center of Jewish cultural and public activity, and a meeting place for Jewish intellectuals from Western and Eastern Europe. The central institutions of the World Zionist Organization had their seat in Berlin from 1911 to 1919, and all the major German Jewish organizations had their national headquarters there. In the 1920s, one-third of all Jews in Germany lived in Berlin.

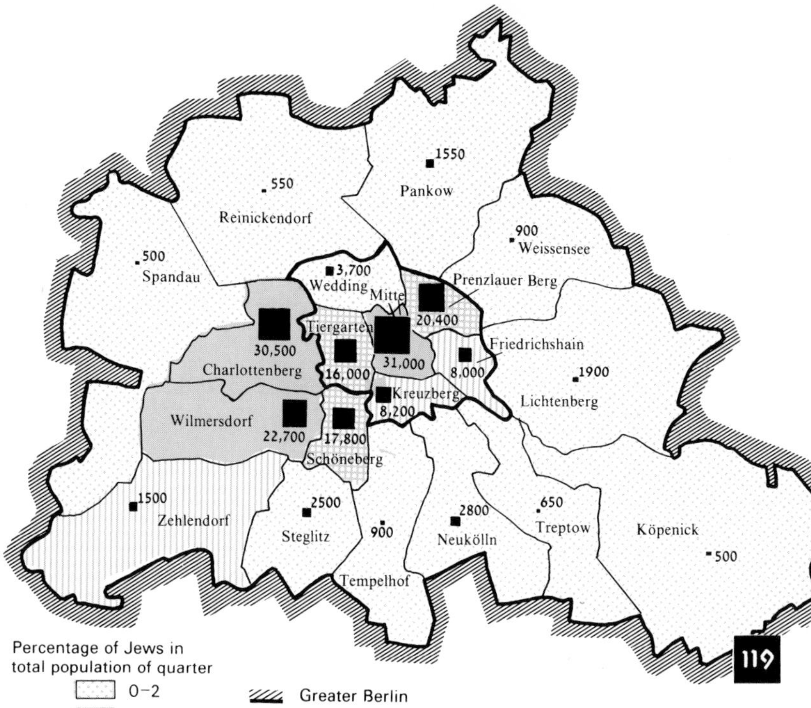


## Jewish Population in Berlin

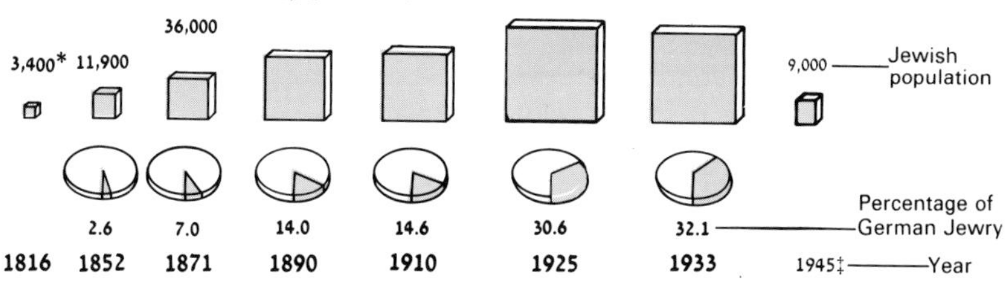


* Estimate
† Including suburbs: 144,000 Jews (23.4% of German Jewry)
‡ 1980: 6,000 (17.4% of Jews in both Germanies)

## Jewish Emigration from Germany During the Nazi Period

The appointment of Adolf Hitler as German chancellor in January 1933 marked the first step toward the ultimate disaster for not only the Jews of Germany, but also those of most of Europe. In the first part of the Nazi regime (1933–November 1938), the general aims of its Jewish policy were to strip the Jews of their civil rights (Nuremberg Laws, from September 1935) and remove them from German professional, social, and cultural life in order to force them to emigrate. In the next phase (November 1938–October 1941), the pressure on the Jews intensified and their institutions were closed. After October 1941, Jewish emigration from Germany was forbidden, and most German Jews were sent to concentration and extermination camps in Poland.

About 500,000 Jews lived in Germany in 1933. By the end of 1937, about 130,000 had left the country. By October 1941, another 300,000 had escaped or were deported.

In 1933, the leaders of the major German Jewish organizations established a central institution, the Reichsvertretung der Juden in Deutschland (National Representation of the Jews in Germany), headed by Leo Baeck. Its aim was to assist German Jews under the Nazi regime. It provided information on emigration and vocational retraining, and organized social, educational, and cultural activities. After the *Kristallnacht* pogrom (November 9/10, 1938), the authorities closed the Reichsvertretung.

### …ti-Jewish Laws and Actions

| | |
|---|---|
| …ril 1, 1933 | Boycott of Jewish-owned businesses |
| …3 | Jews expelled from public service. Number of Jews in universities restricted |
| …ptember 15, 1935 | First Nuremberg Laws: Being member of German race prerequisite for German citizenship |
| …rch 28, 1938 | Legal status of communities abolished |
| …tober 27/28, 1938 | 15,000–17,000 Polish Jews expelled across the Polish border |
| …vember 9/10, …8 | *Kristallnacht*: Synagogues burned and businesses destroyed throughout the country; about 26,000 Jews sent to concentration camps; Jewish community ordered to pay fine of 1 billion marks |
| …tober 1941 | About 164,000 Jews still in Germany |

### Jewish Emigration from Germany

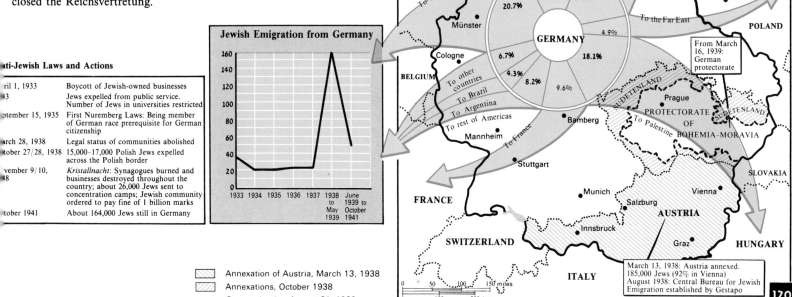

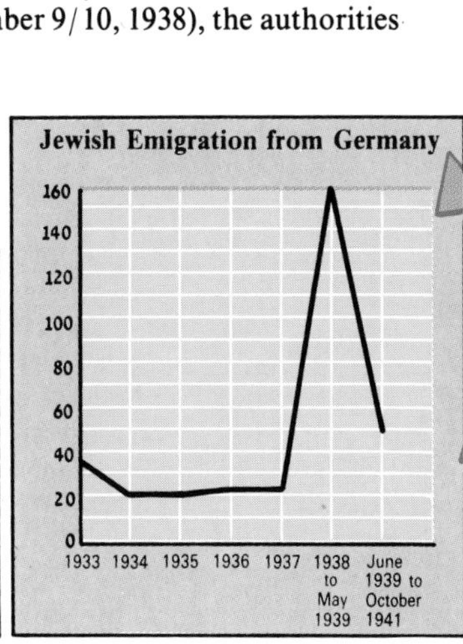

Annexation of Austria, March 13, 1938
Annexations, October 1938
German border, August 31, 1939

# The Holocaust, 1939–1945

The years 1939 to 1945 are inscribed in the chronicles of the Jewish people as the time of one of the worst calamities in its multimillennial history. More than one-third of the Jews of the world were exterminated by the Germans in Europe during World War II.

Beyond the horrors involved in the actual killing of the Jews, what made the Holocaust so uniquely terrible was its being based on the concept that it was necessary, for the good of the German nation and all mankind, to exterminate the Jewish people. As evil and perverted as this idea may seem, it gripped the minds and hearts of so advanced a people as the Germans, and directed their actions with terrifying consistency.

The resolution to exterminate the Jews had deep roots: the age-old tension between Christians and Jews in Europe, which was expressed over the centuries in Christian society's anti-Jewish hatred. In the ideological conditions of nineteenth-century Europe, that historical hatred developed into modern antisemitism. The more extreme antisemites began to preach the "removal" of Jews and Judaism from European culture and society. Against the background of Europe's (particularly, Germany's) interwar political and social troubles, political groups of the extreme right incorporated antisemitism into their platforms. In January 1933, the National Socialist Party came to power when its leader, Adolf Hitler, was nominated German chancellor. The way was now paved for the ultimate catastrophe of European Jewry.

Although there is much evidence that Nazi ideology considered the "solution" of the "Jewish problem" a major aim of its political program, the plans to implement it took time to mature. In the first period, from 1933 to 1939, Nazi policy aimed to exclude the Jews from German society and force them to emigrate. Jews were expelled from the public service (1933); they were stripped of their German citizenship and reduced to the status of German subjects (1935); they were gradually excluded from all cultural life and educational institutions; those with Polish citizenship were expelled to Poland (1938). After the annexation of Austria in March 1938, these measures and laws were immediately applied to the Jews in Vienna. During the *Kristallnacht* of November 9/10, 1938, all the synagogues in Germany were burned and Jewish businesses were damaged. But until September 1941, Jews could still emigrate from Germany or German-dominated countries—if they found a country willing to accept them.

The next phase started in September 1939 with the German conquest of Poland, which had a large Jewish population. At first the Jews were concentrated in several large ghettos. Many died or were killed during this phase. With the German invasion of the Soviet Union in June 1941, the large-scale killing of Jews began.

### *Einsatzgruppen*

The *Einsatzgruppen* were German paramilitary units formed in preparation for the invasion of the Soviet Union. Their task was to deal with "dangerous" elements in the conquered territories, such as Communists and Jews. They were organized into 4 main groups of about 800 members each, each main group subdivided into smaller units that were assisted by Ukrainian and Lithuanian militiamen. Although they worked in coordination with and received logistical support from the German army, the *Einsatzgruppen* were under the command of the German Security Services (Sicherheitsdienst and SS). They entered a region as soon as it was occupied by the army, rounded up the Jews who had not managed to escape, and killed them, generally by shooting, alongside large burial pits, which in many instances had been dug by the victims themselves. The *Einsatzgruppen* were especially active from the middle of 1941 until the end of 1942. In that time, they killed between 900,000 and 1.3 million people, about 90 percent of whom were Jews.

*Memorial at Yad Vashem, Jerusalem, to the victims of the concentration and extermination camps (sculptor Nandor Glid)*

### Concentration and Extermination Camps

Concentration camps existed in Germany since the beginning of the Nazi regime, for political prisoners (Communists, socialists, liberals, and others), Jews, and, after the start of World War II, prisoners of war, political prisoners from the conquered countries, forced laborers, and Gypsies. During the war, there were hundreds of such camps throughout Europe. Conditions were, in general, very harsh, but there was a clear difference between the camps for Russian prisoners

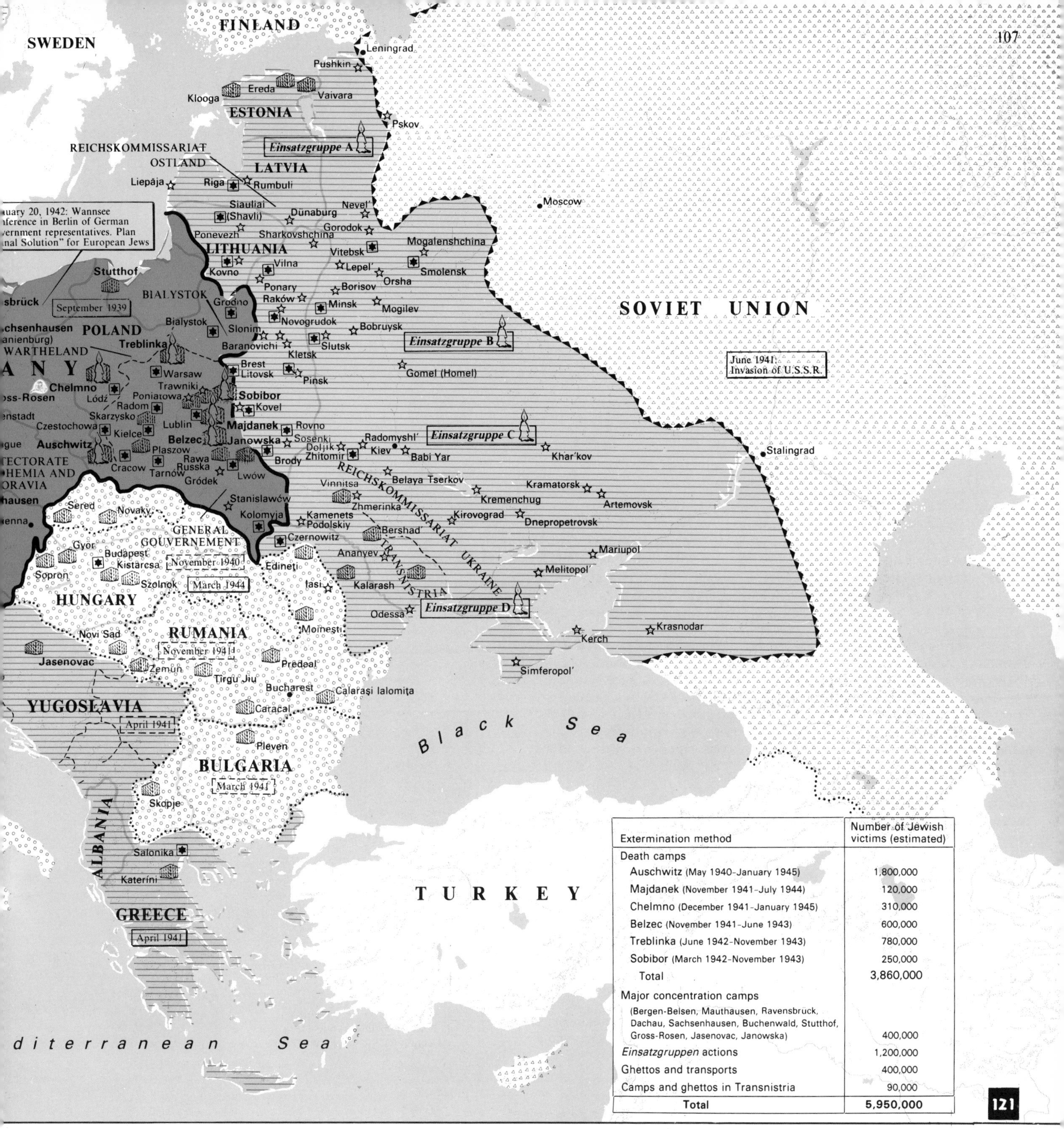


| Extermination method | Number of Jewish victims (estimated) |
|---|---|
| Death camps | |
| Auschwitz (May 1940-January 1945) | 1,800,000 |
| Majdanek (November 1941-July 1944) | 120,000 |
| Chelmno (December 1941-January 1945) | 310,000 |
| Belzec (November 1941-June 1943) | 600,000 |
| Treblinka (June 1942-November 1943) | 780,000 |
| Sobibor (March 1942-November 1943) | 250,000 |
| Total | 3,860,000 |
| Major concentration camps (Bergen-Belsen, Mauthausen, Ravensbruck, Dachau, Sachsenhausen, Buchenwald, Stutthof, Gross-Rosen, Jasenovac, Janowska) | 400,000 |
| *Einsatzgruppen* actions | 1,200,000 |
| Ghettos and transports | 400,000 |
| Camps and ghettos in Transnistria | 90,000 |
| **Total** | **5,950,000** |

of war (which were terrible) and those for prisoners from the Western Allies. Many camps also served as transit points for Jews sent to Eastern Europe. On the way, many Jews perished from hunger, disease, and torture.

A unique type of camp—indeed, a uniquely modern creation—was the extermination camp, six of which functioned in Poland from 1941 until the beginning of 1945: Auschwitz, Treblinka, Majdanek, Chelmno, Belzec, and Sobibor. Auschwitz and Majdanek had non-Jewish inmates as well. Some of them were also used as workers' camps, serving nearby factories. Few Jewish prisoners were sent to work in the factories; in the end, those workers, too, were killed. Killing was done by gas poisoning, and the corpses were burned in huge crematoria especially devised for that purpose. At the peak of its operation, the extermination process reached a horrifying level of "efficiency": a Jew who arrived in the morning would be dead by evening, his corpse burned and his belongings (clothes, as well as gold dental fillings and hair) sorted and prepared for shipment to Germany. In three and a half years, between 3 and 4 million Jews perished in the extermination camps.

The combined result of the operations of the *Einsatzgruppen*, the slaughter in the concentration and extermination camps, and the conditions in the ghettos in Eastern Europe was that 80 percent of the Jews in the German-dominated parts of Europe perished. The Jewish people survived, but decades later the Holocaust still defied evaluation. It destroyed some of the oldest and most vibrant centers of Jews and Judaism. It terminated a relationship between Jews and non-Jews that, for better or for worse, had existed for centuries. It created the need for new patterns of interaction between Jewish and general society. And it raised questions about the nature of man and civilization that seem unanswerable.

# Jewish Reactions and Resistance

The Jews of Europe coped with the Nazi onslaught in various ways. In retrospect, the best solution would have been to leave Europe, but too few did so. At first, the Jews were oblivious to the looming dangers, and later the escape routes were closed. Once they fell under German domination, the Jews tried to conduct their private, family, social, and communal lives as normally as possible. In every occupied community, the Germans forced the Jews to form a Jewish council (Judenrat), whose task was to govern Jewish communal life and carry out German orders. In principle, the councils were in keeping with the Jewish tradition of self-help, and up to a point they performed services that were both positive and necessary. But when their leaders were ordered to help organize the deportation of Jews to "the East" (the extermination camps)—which today we know meant collaborating in the killing of Jews rather than maintaining Jewish life—the councils found themselves in an impossible position. The behavior of some of their leaders later aroused fierce controversy. But even if some serious mistakes were committed, the outcome would have been no less tragic if the leaders had acted differently. Moreover, no Jewish council identified itself with Nazi ideology, supported German aims, or desired a German victory.

Resistance against the Germans erupted in several ghettos and concentration camps. In all instances, the Germans reacted swiftly and ruthlessly, executing the rebels who were caught. Those who escaped from the ghettos, the camps, or the *Einsatzgruppen* hid in the forests and swamps of Poland and western Russia. Some joined resistance groups. In Western Europe, Jews fought in the general resistance movement. In Eastern Europe, they fought alongside non-Jews or formed Jewish partisan units. Escaping Jews faced an additional handicap: having managed to elude the Germans, they now faced a hostile rural population in Eastern Europe. This hostility sometimes manifested itself also in the general resistance groups in which Jews participated. Nevertheless, here and there non-Jews—"Righteous Gentiles"—risked their lives to help Jews, even in Eastern Europe.

Tens of thousands of Jews participated in the resistance against the Germans in the occupied countries. In Poland and other East European countries, 15,000 to 20,000 Jews fought in general or in Jewish partisan units, or in resistance groups in ghettos and camps.

# The Warsaw Ghetto Uprising

About 400,000 Jews lived in Warsaw on the eve of the German invasion of Poland in September 1939. In November 1940, the Germans declared the Jewish ghetto a closed area, concentrating all the Jews of the city and its suburbs there, and bringing in tens of thousands of Jews from outside. A Jewish council was established.

In July 1942, the Germans began to send Jews from Warsaw to death camps. The head of the Jewish council, Adam Czerniakow, committed suicide, to avoid carrying out the German orders. About 300,000 Jews were sent from Warsaw to extermination camps, mainly Treblinka. Tens of thousands died or were killed in the ghetto itself. About 70,000 Jews remained in the ghetto in the autumn of 1942, and about 55,000 in the spring of 1943.

In the second half of 1942, resistance groups began to organize in the ghetto, affiliated with Zionist youth movements or Jewish political parties. With immense difficulty, arms were smuggled in and workshops were set up to make weapons and bombs. The first armed clashes with the Germans took place in January 1943. In the coming months, the Jewish resistance groups united to form the Jewish Fighting Organization (ZOB), headed by Mordechai Anielewicz. The revolt began on April 19, 1943. After suffering initial losses, the Germans brought in reinforcements and heavy guns, and started burning the ghetto, house by house. The fighting continued until the fall of the Jewish headquarters, at 18 Mila Street, on May 8, 1943, with Anielewicz among those killed. To mark the suppression of the uprising, the German commander, General Stroop, blew up the Warsaw Great Synagogue, which was located outside the ghetto. The ghetto itself was razed. About 50,000 Jews perished in the revolt.

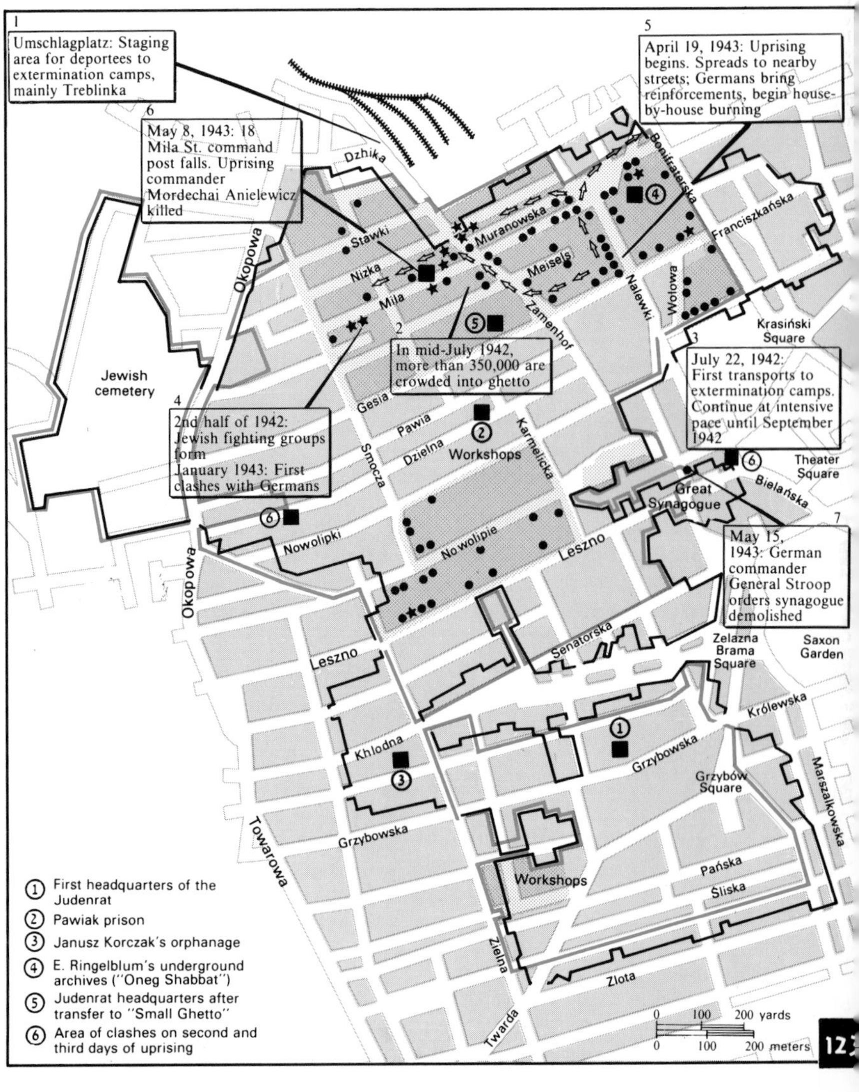

**Extermination Installation 2**
(photographed on August 25, 1944)

·matorium and machine room, installations ·nd 3 (photographed by SS construction ·ervisor in Auschwitz)

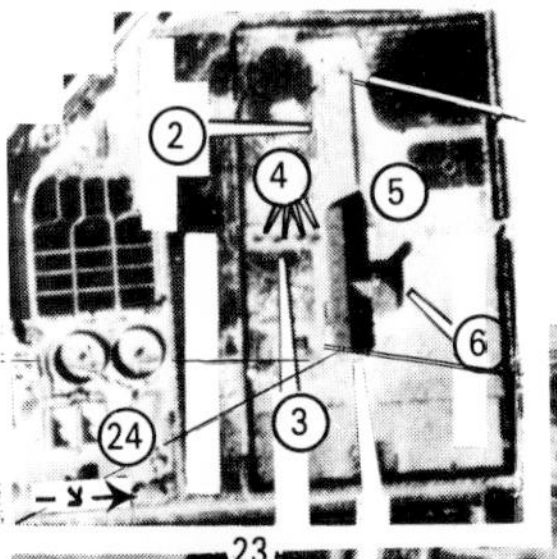


# Auschwitz
(aerial photographs taken by the U.S. Army Air Force, 1944)

## uschwitz 2, or Birkenau
ıain extermination camp)
hotographed on September 13, 1944)

Extermination installation 2
Underground chamber where inmates left their clothes
Underground gas chamber
Four openings for throwing in gas pellets
Crematorium: 15 ovens
Machine room
Extermination installation 3
Main entrance to the camp (through main guard building)
Train station and "selection" place (some for work, most to gas chambers)
"Sauna": Area for washing and disinfecting new inmates
"Canada": Barracks for sorting inmates' effects
Electrified barbed-wire fences
Hospital for inmates and laboratory for medical experiments
Gypsies' barracks
Kitchens
Main men's section
Punishment block
Section for Jewish women from Hungary in 1944
Section for Jewish families from Theresienstadt
Men's isolation section
Women's punishment block
"Mexico": Additional barracks whose construction was not finished
Electrified barbed-wire fences and watchtowers around the camp
Installation for processing feces for agricultural use
Main road

mp dimensions: 0.6 × 1.2 miles (1 × 2 km)
mensions of each block: 131 × 29.5 feet (40 × 9 m)

Auschwitz differed from the other extermination camps in size and in the sophistication of its death machinery. It began to function in May 1940, and was closed by the Germans in January 1945. About 1.8 million people were killed there in that period, close to 90 percent of them Jews. At the peak of its operations, in the summer of 1944, thousands of human beings were gassed every day and their bodies cremated.

Auschwitz was a complex of about forty camps, divided into three groups. *Auschwitz 1*: the main camp, containing the commandant's headquarters, the central administration of all the camps, and about 20,000 to 25,000 prisoners. *Auschwitz 2*, or *Birkenau*: the main extermination camp, more than a mile from Auschwitz 1. At its peak it contained about 146,000 prisoners, although planned for 250,000. *Auschwitz 3*, or *Buna*: a complex of labor camps for industrial production, built on the sites of villages close to Auschwitz 2. About 20 percent of the inmates of Auschwitz 2 worked in these factories. It is these inmates who had a number tattooed on their arms. Of the approximately 405,000 prisoners who worked in the factories at one time or another, about 30,000 survived.

## Auschwitz 1 (main camp) (photographed on August 25, 1944)

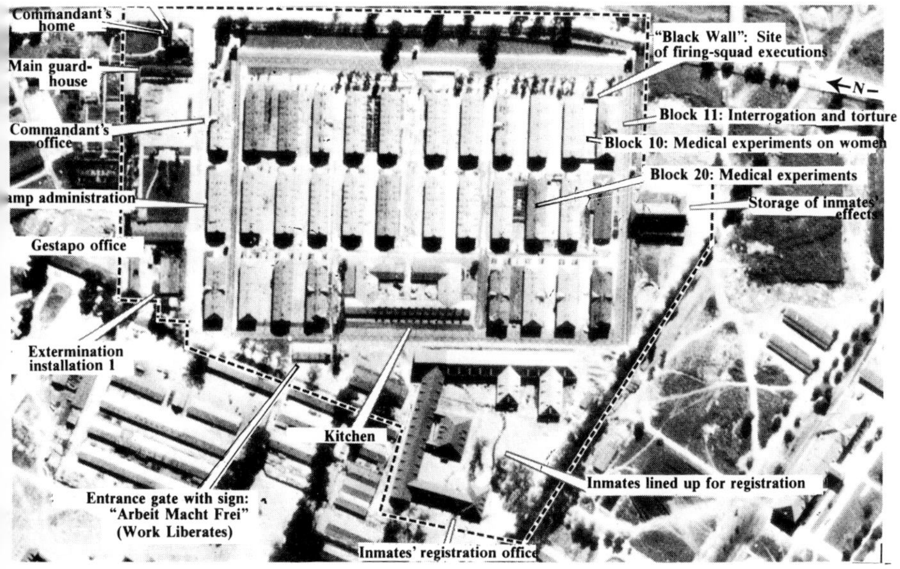


## Auschwitz Area (photographed on June 26, 1944)

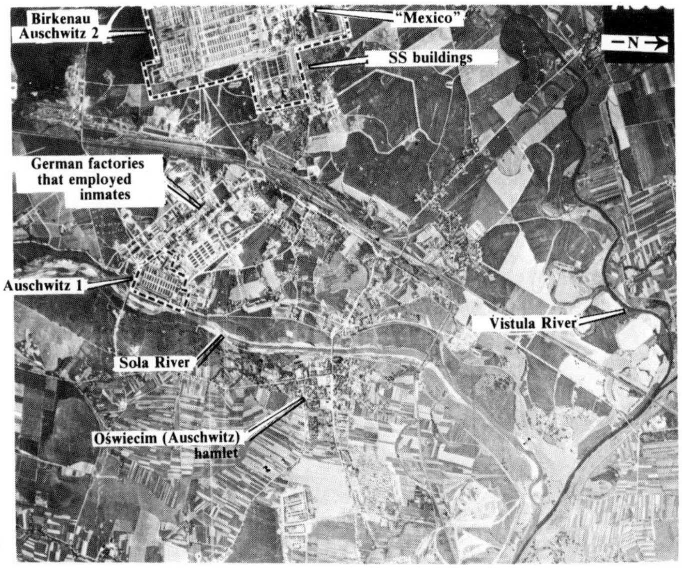

# Political Efforts to Help European Jewry

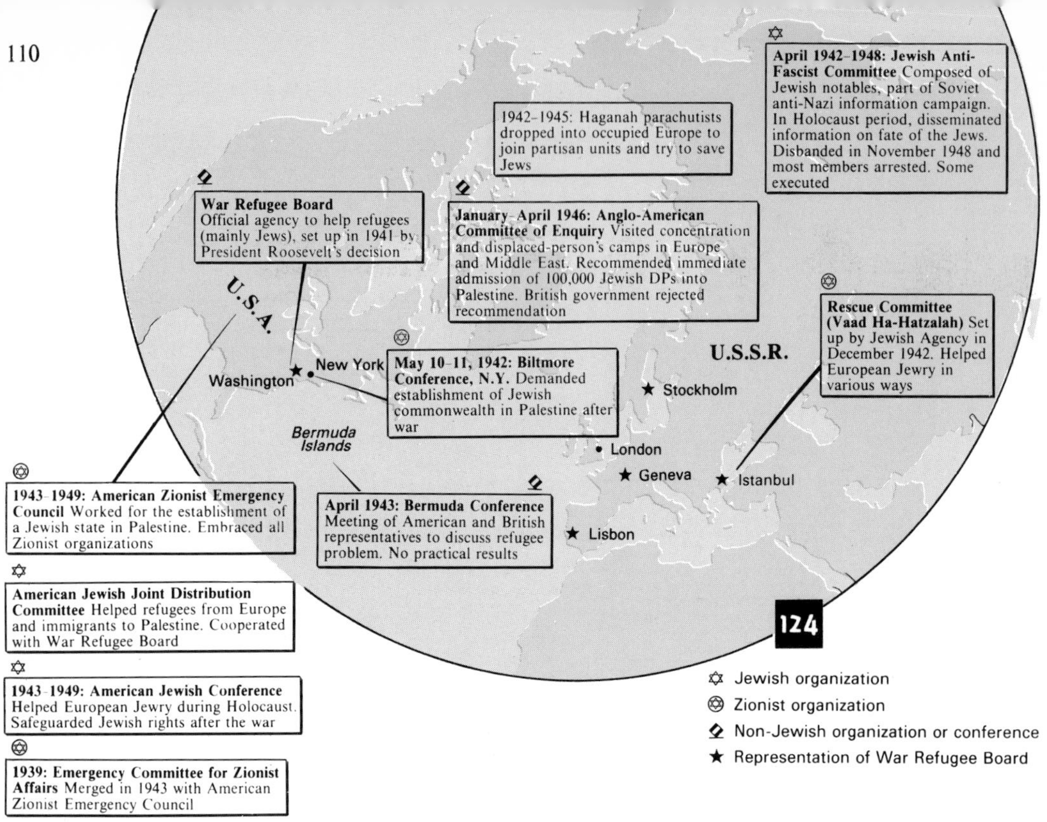


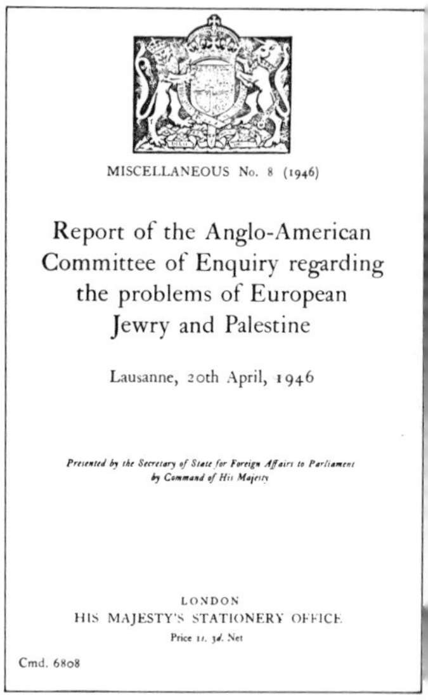

MISCELLANEOUS No. 8 (1946)

Report of the Anglo-American Committee of Enquiry regarding the problems of European Jewry and Palestine

Lausanne, 20th April, 1946

*Presented by the Secretary of State for Foreign Affairs to Parliament by Command of His Majesty*

LONDON
HIS MAJESTY'S STATIONERY OFFICE
Price 1s. 3d. Net

Cmd. 6808

## The Escape from Europe (*Briha*)

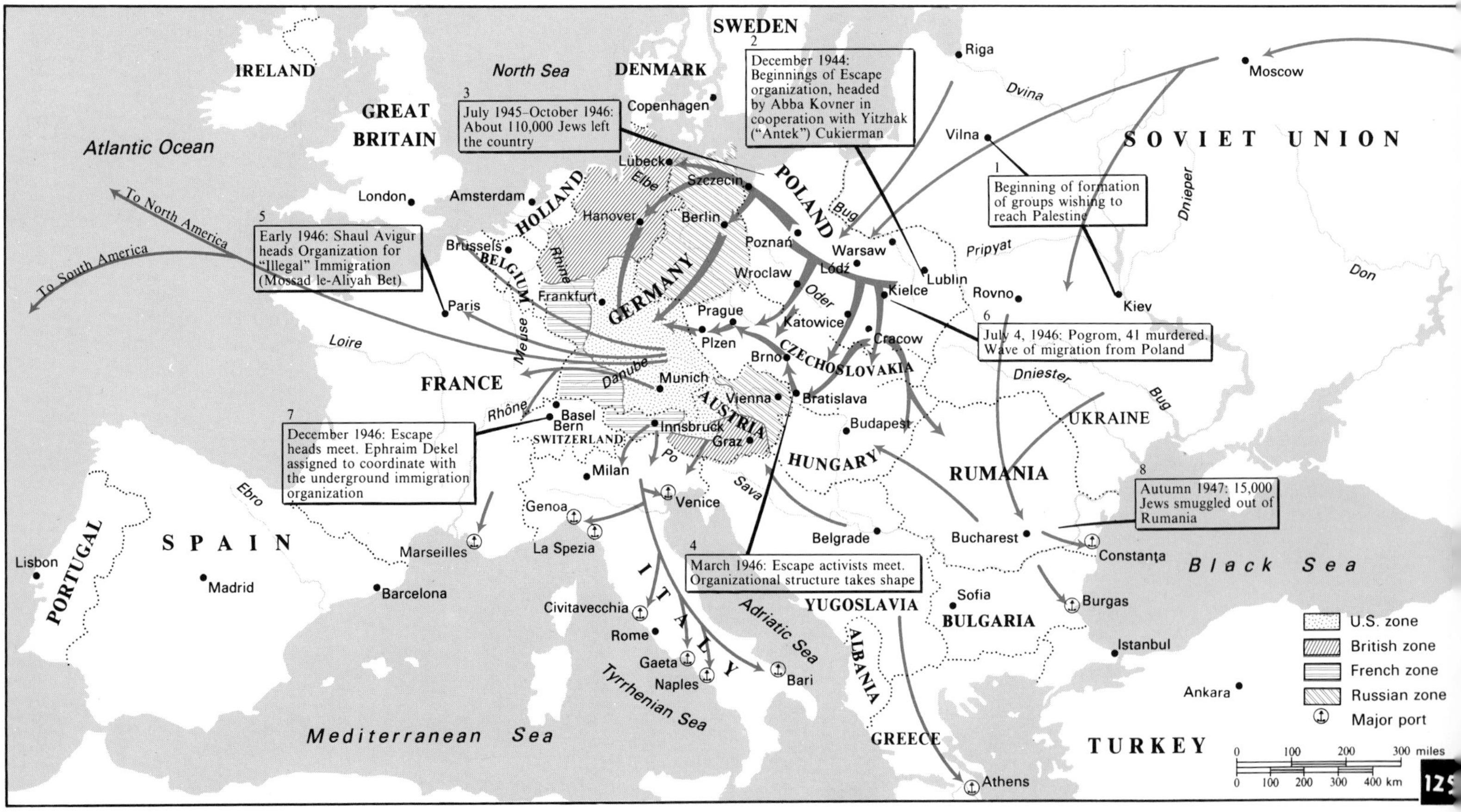


About 250,000 Jews, survivors of the Holocaust and refugees, left Europe toward the end of and after the war (1944–1948). This movement, called *Briha* (Escape), was characterized by the fears and despair of the survivors. They wanted to leave Europe, that gigantic graveyard of their families and friends, and try to erase from their memory what they had seen and experienced. The anti-Jewish pogroms in Europe, even after the Holocaust (Kielce, Poland, in July 1946), strengthened their determination to flee the continent, and they went to various countries. Most wished to migrate to Palestine. The escape routes were strewn with obstacles: the frontiers were gradually sealed—not only between Eastern and Western Europe, but also between the occupied regions of Germany and Austria, and the passages to Italy, Rumania, and Yugoslavia.

Emissaries from Palestine and representatives of American Jewish aid organizations prepared transit camps for the refugees in the American-occupied zone in southern Germany and Austria, from where they were sent to Mediterranean ports en route to Palestine. The Jewish refugee problem had worldwide repercussions, and various political groups, especially in the United States, sought to solve it.

## The Extermination of European Jews, by Countries

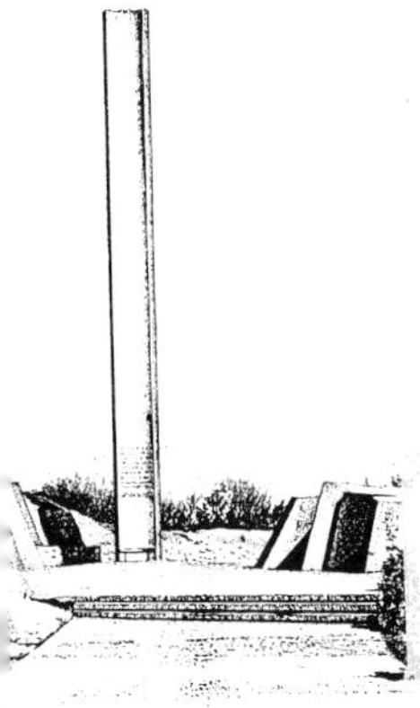

*Pillar of Heroism at Yad Vashem (sculptor Buky Schwartz)*

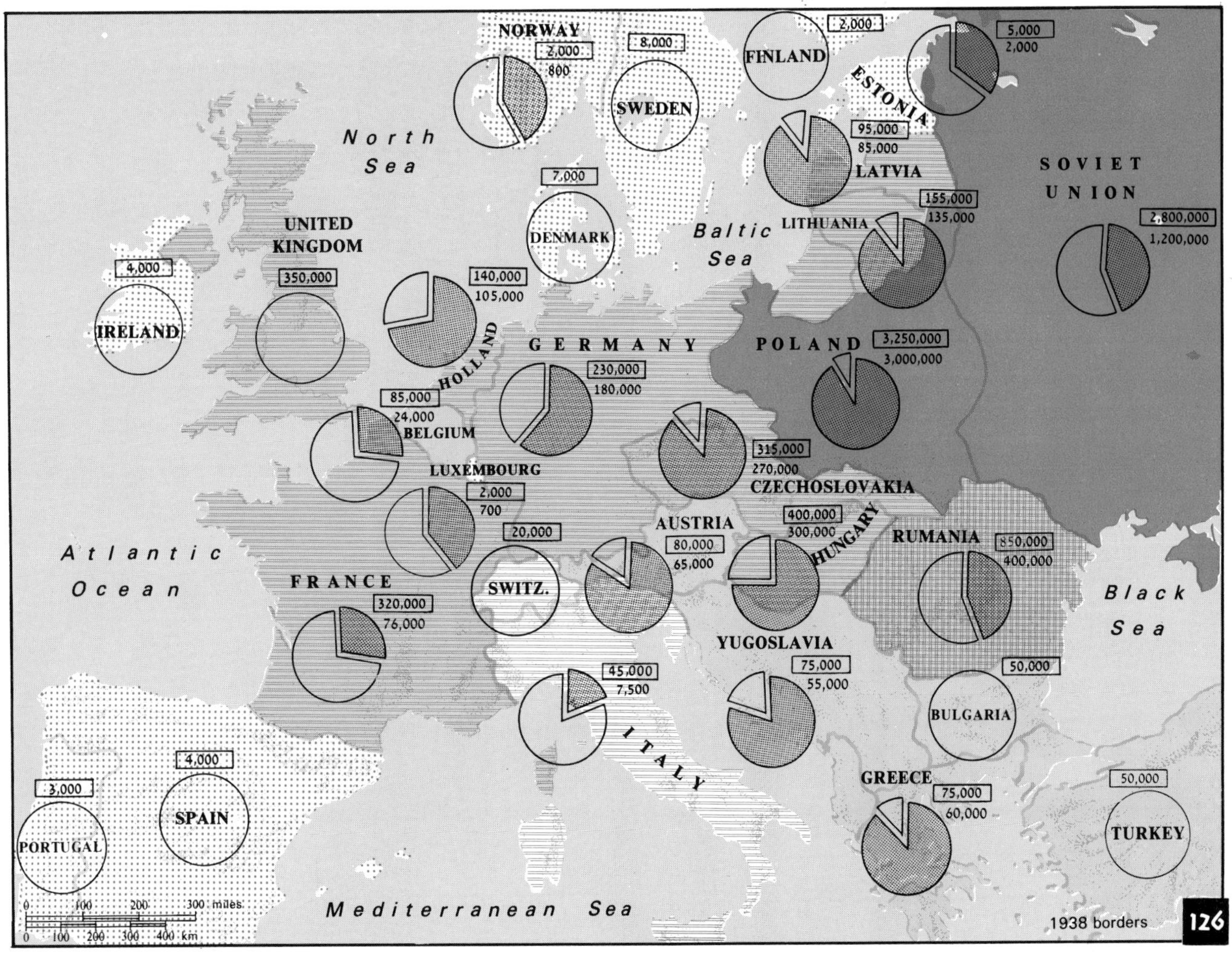

## Outcome of the Holocaust, 1951

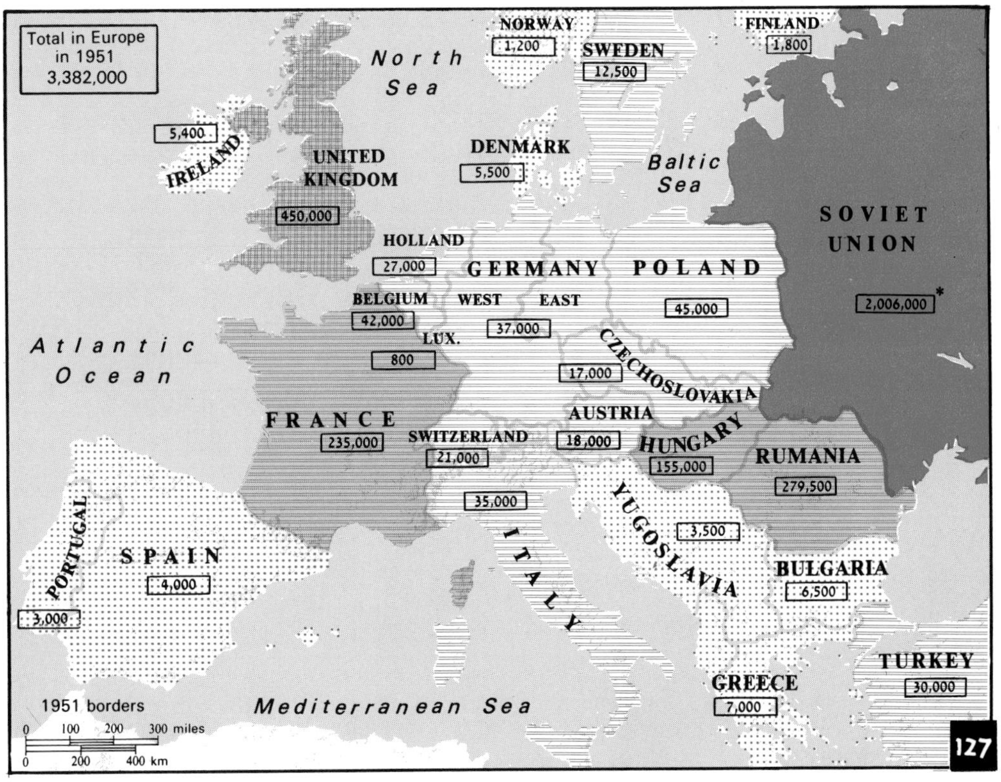


Number of Jews in the country
- Up to 10,000
- 10,000–50,000
- 50,000–100,000
- 100,000–400,000
- 400,000–800,000
- 2,000,000–4,000,000

* According to the 1959 census. The calculation was based on the assumption that in 1951 about 10% of the Jews of the Russian Republic—R.S.F.S.R. (about 88,000 Jews)—lived in the Asiatic part of the republic.

The Holocaust completely changed the demographic composition of the Jewish people. Sixty percent of all Jews lived in Europe in 1939, but only 30 percent in 1951. Worst hit were the large Jewish communities in Eastern Europe that had played such a significant role in the development of modern Jewry. Ninety percent of Polish Jewry—more than 3 million—perished; 90 percent of Lithuanian and Latvian Jewry; 85 percent of Czechoslovakian Jewry; 75 percent of Hungarian Jewry. In Western Europe, German Jewry disappeared, although not all the Jews were killed; many had left the country in the 1930s. More than 100,000 Dutch Jews, 75 percent of the total, were exterminated.

## Natural Increase
(annual average per 1,000 population)

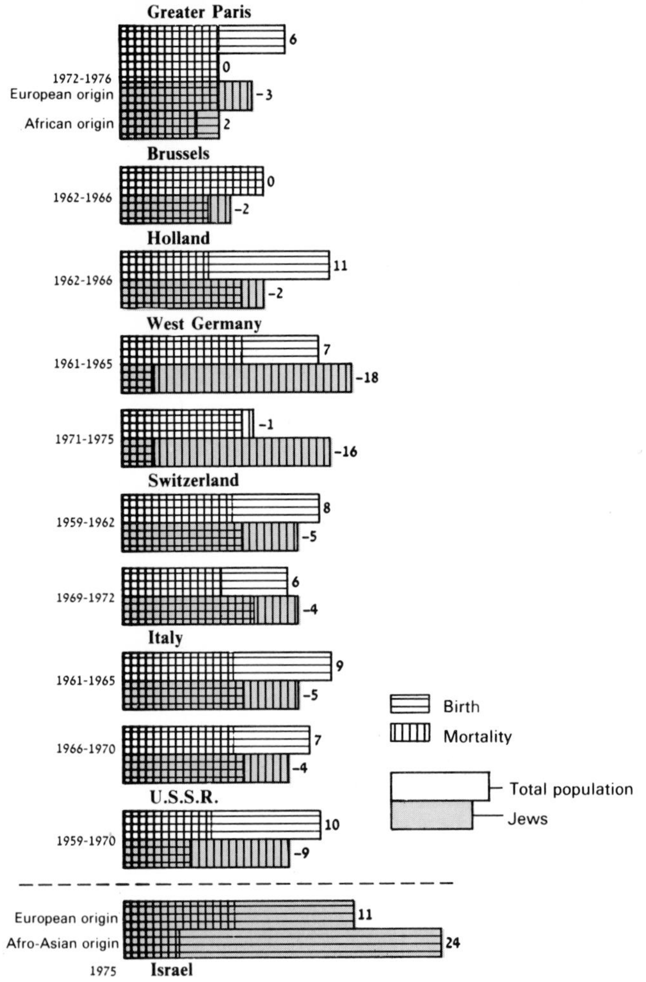


# European Jewry:
Late Twentieth Century

Number of Jews in community
- ○ Up to 2,000
- ● 2,000-5,000
- ◉ 5,000-10,000
- ▣ 10,000 or more
- 12,000 Number of Jews in large community, 1980s

The demographic configuration of European Jewry in the 1970s a 1980s was clearly a product of the Holocaust. Although some Jew centers did not suffer directly under Hitler, and although Jewish l was rebuilt in all the communities on the continent, the Holocaust h a long-range destructive effect on the social and cultural structu of European Jewry, the full significance of which only gradua became evident. The demographic characteristics of European Jew which were problematic before World War II, deteriorated afterwa due to emigration as well as to the Holocaust. In the thirty ye following the war, European Jewry gradually dwindled (especia in Eastern Europe), in spite of the influx, in the 1950s and 196 of hundreds of thousands of Jews, mainly from Muslim countri Between 1951 and 1986, the Jewish population in Europe decrea by 20.6 percent; and its age composition indicated an additio decrease of 36.4 percent by the end of the century.

## Population by Age Group (percent)

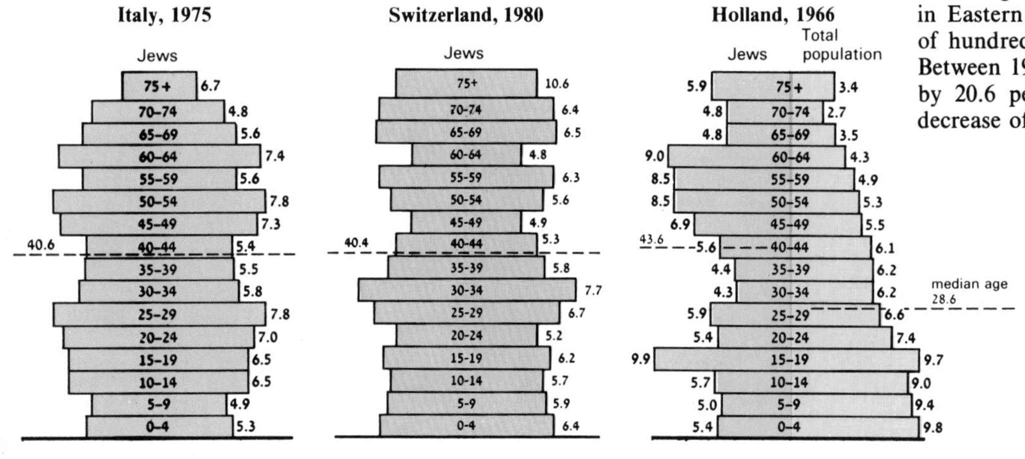


### Median Ages

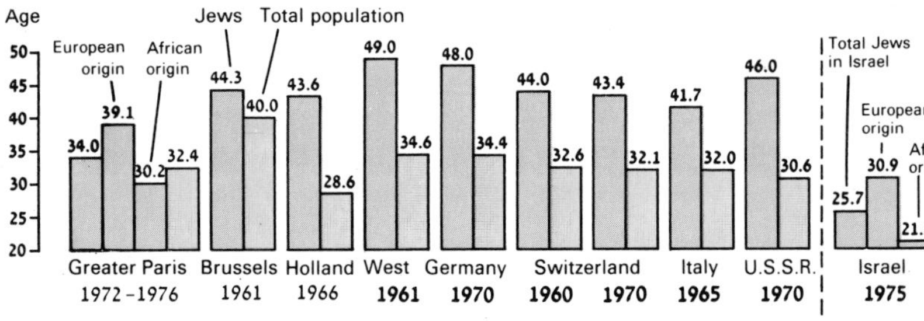


## Out-Marriages*, 1980s
(percent)

| Country | Out-Marriages | |
|---|---|---|
| | Per 100 Jewish individuals marrying | Per 100 couples with at least one Jewish spouse |
| West Germany[1], Eastern Europe (excluding U.S.S.R.)[4] | 65-74 | 79-85 |
| Scandinavia[3], Switzerland[1], Austria[1] | 55-64 | 71-78 |
| Netherlands[3] | 45-54 | 62-70 |
| Italy[2], France[2], Belgium[4] | 36-44 | 53-61 |
| U.S.S.R.[3] | 33-35 | 49-52 |
| United Kingdom[4] | 28-32 | 44-48 |

* Recent marriages in which no conversion of a non-Jewish-born spouse took place

The following rating of data quality was adopted:
[1] Recent and reliable statistical data
[2] Partial or less recent data of sufficient quality
[3] Rather out-dated or very incomplete data
[4] Conjectural

## The Jews in France, 1970

France was the only European country whose Jewish population increased significantly in the second half of the twentieth century. Hundreds of thousands of Jews migrated from Algeria (where most Jews held French citizenship), Morocco, Tunisia, and Egypt. After Soviet Jewry, French Jewry was the largest in Europe (about 530,000 in the mid-1980s), but it was divided into very different communities. The Jews of North African origin adapted very rapidly to French demographic and cultural patterns.

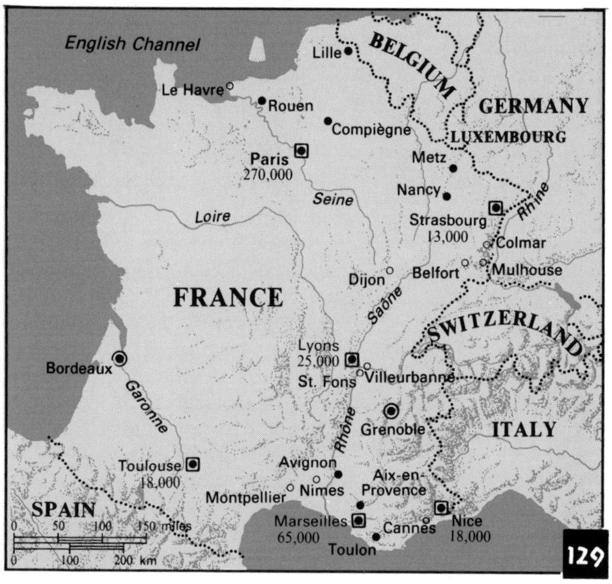


Number of Jews in city
- ○ 1,000–2,000
- • 2,000–5,000
- ◉ 5,000–10,000
- ▣ 10,000 or more

## Jewish Immigration to Paris, 1880–1939

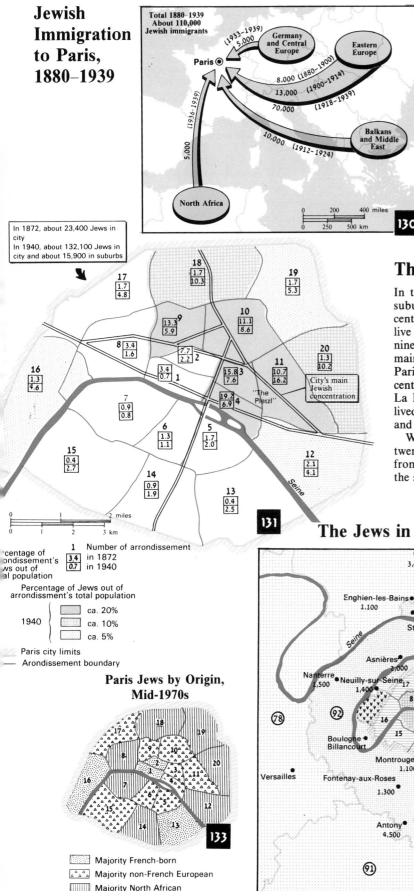

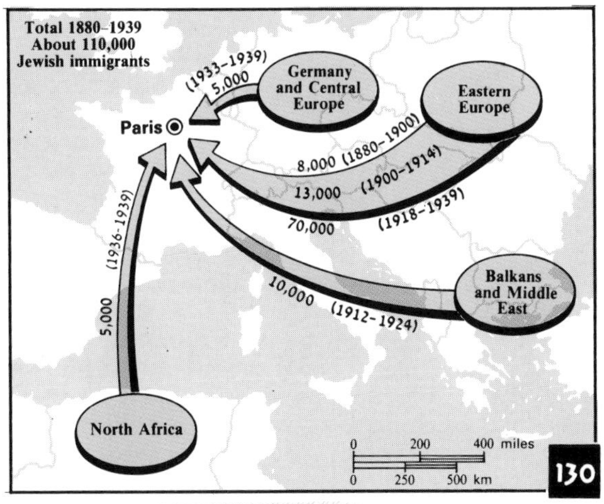


In 1872, about 23,400 Jews in city
In 1940, about 132,100 Jews in city and about 15,900 in suburbs

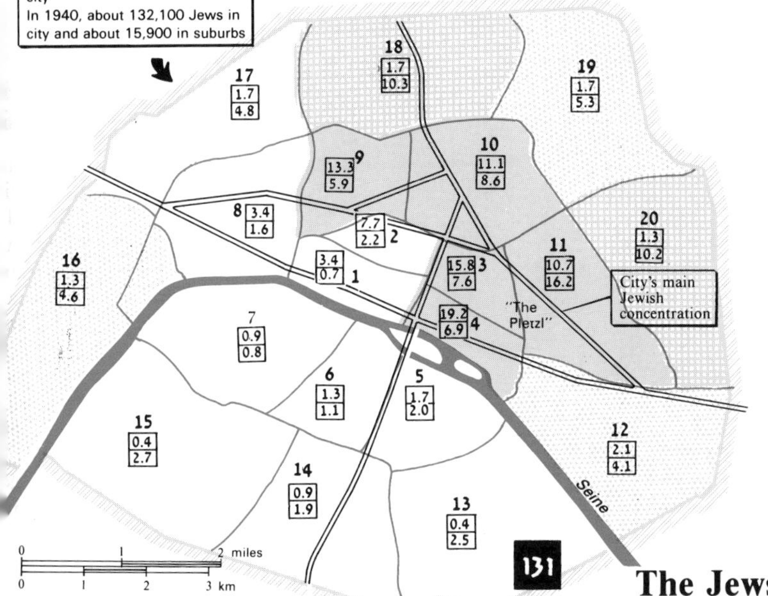


1 — Number of arrondissement
3.4 — in 1872
0.7 — in 1940
[Per]centage of [arr]ondissement's [Je]ws out of [tot]al population

Percentage of Jews out of arrondissment's total population

1940: ca. 20% / ca. 10% / ca. 5%

Paris city limits
Arondissement boundary

## The Jews in Paris, 1872–1970

In the 1970s, about half of all French Jews lived in Paris and its suburbs. The Jewish community in Paris began in the late eighteenth century; before the French Revolution, Jews were not permitted to live in the city. Jews from Alsace-Lorraine settled in Paris in the nineteenth century, and later immigrants came from various countries, mainly from Eastern Europe. In 1880, there were about 40,000 Jews in Paris, 80 percent of the country's Jewish population. In the nineteenth century, the well-known Jewish quarter, the "Pletzl," developed in the La Roquette neighborhood (Eleventh Arrondissement). Many Jews lived also in the city's Eighteenth and Twentieth arrondissements, and in other neighborhoods.

When suburban Paris began to expand in the second half of the twentieth century, many Jews settled there, too, especially newcomers from North Africa. In the 1970s, 44 percent of Parisian Jews lived in the suburbs, as compared with 72 percent of the total population.

## The Jews in Paris and Its Suburbs, 1970s

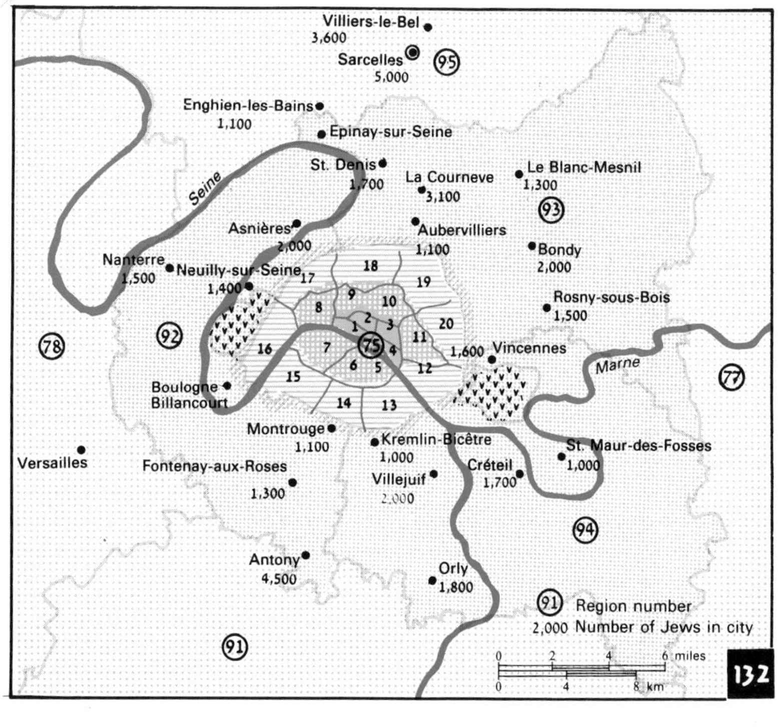


### The Jews in Paris and Its Suburbs by Regions

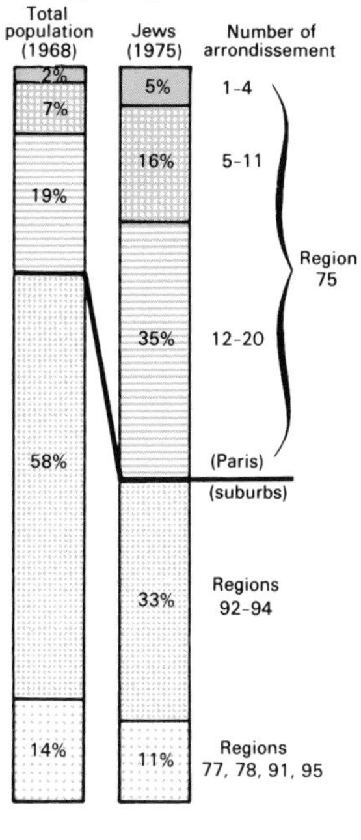


## Paris Jews by Origin, Mid-1970s

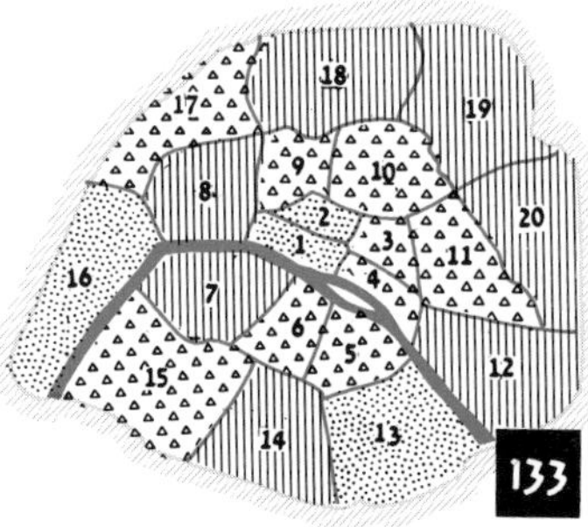


- Majority French-born
- Majority non-French European
- Majority North African

# The Jews in the United Kingdom:

## Late Twentieth Century

In the 1980s, Britain had the third largest Jewish community in Europe after the Soviet Union and France, numbering 326,000 in 1986. In spite of some immigration (mainly from Commonwealth countries), British Jewry had decreased since the 1950s, when estimates (probably too high) had set the figure at 450,000 Jews. About 61 percent of British Jews lived in Greater London throughout the twentieth century.

## The Jews in London's East End, 190

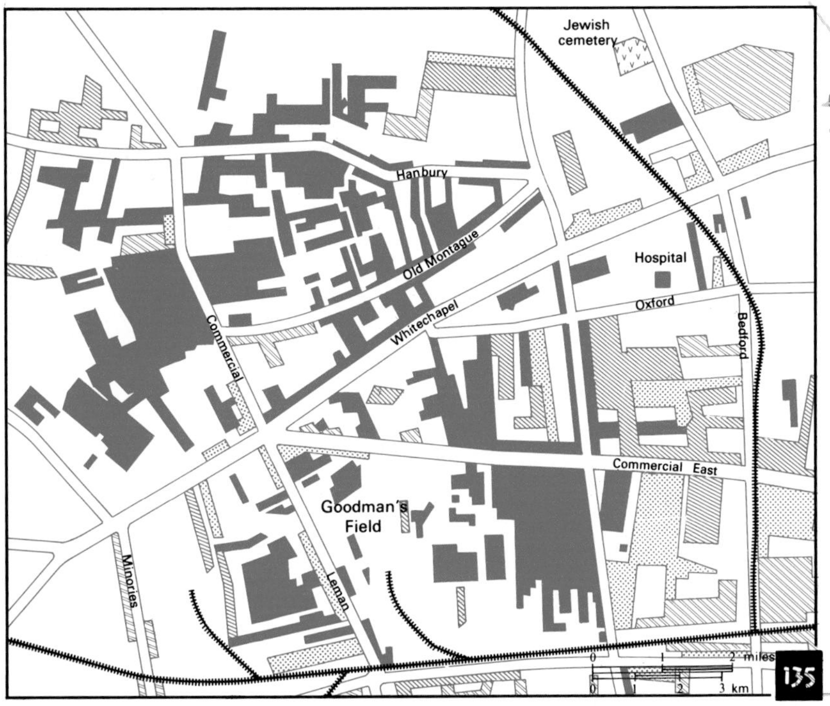


Percentage of Jews out of area's total population
- 75–100
- 50–75
- 25–50
- Less than 25

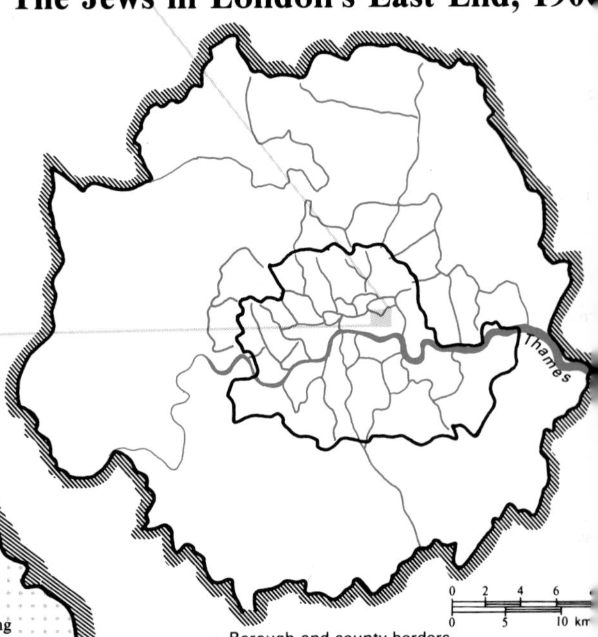

Percentage of Jews out of total population
- 10 or more
- 7–9.9
- 3–6.9
- 0.6–2.9
- Up to 0.5

9,600 Number of Jews in borough, 1984

**The Jewish Population in Greater London**

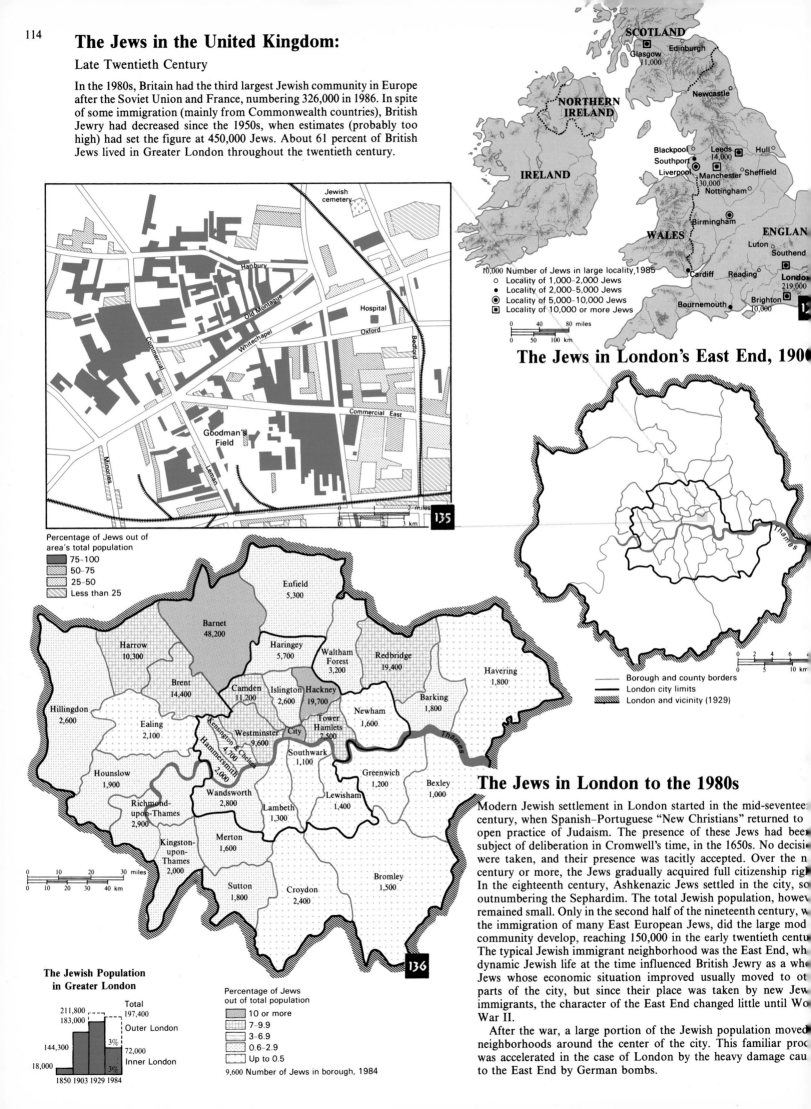

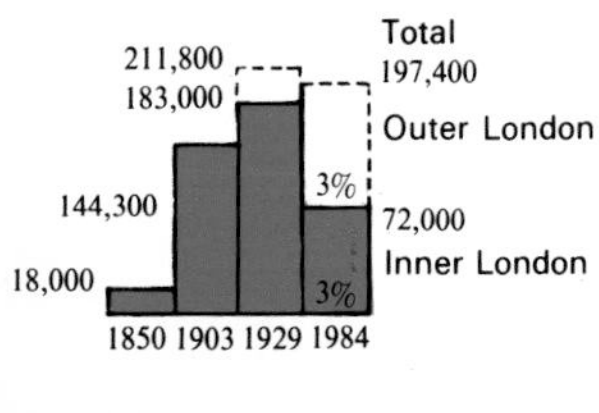


## The Jews in London to the 1980s

Modern Jewish settlement in London started in the mid-seventee century, when Spanish–Portuguese "New Christians" returned to open practice of Judaism. The presence of these Jews had bee subject of deliberation in Cromwell's time, in the 1650s. No decisi were taken, and their presence was tacitly accepted. Over the n century or more, the Jews gradually acquired full citizenship rig In the eighteenth century, Ashkenazic Jews settled in the city, so outnumbering the Sephardim. The total Jewish population, howe remained small. Only in the second half of the nineteenth century, w the immigration of many East European Jews, did the large mod community develop, reaching 150,000 in the early twentieth centu The typical Jewish immigrant neighborhood was the East End, wh dynamic Jewish life at the time influenced British Jewry as a wh Jews whose economic situation improved usually moved to ot parts of the city, but since their place was taken by new Jew immigrants, the character of the East End changed little until Wo War II.

After the war, a large portion of the Jewish population moved neighborhoods around the center of the city. This familiar proc was accelerated in the case of London by the heavy damage cau to the East End by German bombs.

# Jewish Centers in the Soviet Union, 1920s and 1930s

World War I and the 1917 revolutions caused drastic changes in the situation of Russian Jewry. Large areas in western Russia, with large Jewish populations, became independent countries (Poland, the Baltic States) or were incorporated into other states (Bessarabia, in Rumania). About half of the Jews of 1897 Russia now lived outside the Soviet Union. In 1926, the Soviet Union was politically and administratively reorganized into eleven republics, and 95 percent of its Jews were concentrated in three of them: the Russian Republic (Russian Socialist Federal Soviet Republic), the Ukraine, and Belorussia.

After 1917, all Russians became citizens with full political and civil rights, and the right to national self-definition. The Jews, too, were recognized as a national group, although many of their national rights could be exercised only in districts or towns where they were the majority of the population. In the 1930s, there were about 200 Jewish councils in locales with Jewish majorities.

The abolition of the Pale of Settlement and the economic and political changes in the Soviet Union radically transformed the demography of Jewish society. Jews moved from the Pale outward to the interior of the country, or into cities that had been barred to them. In 1897, 6 percent of all Jews had lived outside the Pale, 26 percent in 1926, and 37 percent in 1939. Jews entered new occupations: many became public servants, and others learned a trade or profession or acquired a higher education. The number of Jews in agriculture increased (especially in southern Russia and the Crimea), although this was only a temporary trend. All together, these changes in Jewish life created a new class of acculturated Jews who came to occupy positions of influence in Soviet political, cultural, and economic life.

Many Soviet Jews were among the victims of the purges in Russia in the late 1930s. Later, after the German invasion, hundreds of thousands were exterminated by the German *Einsatzgruppen*.

## Occupational Structure

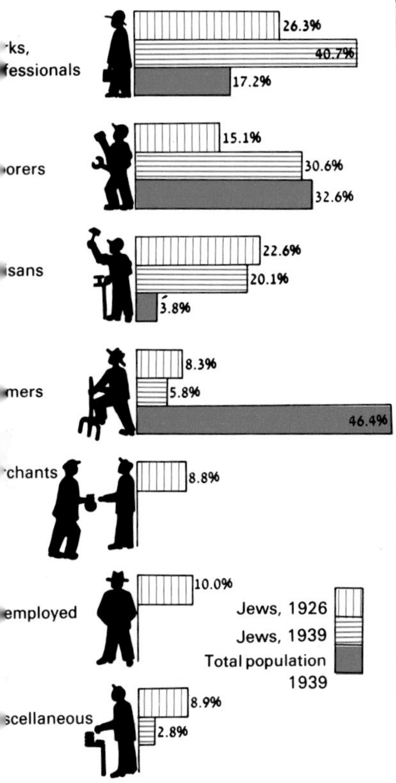


## Urbanization Among the Jews

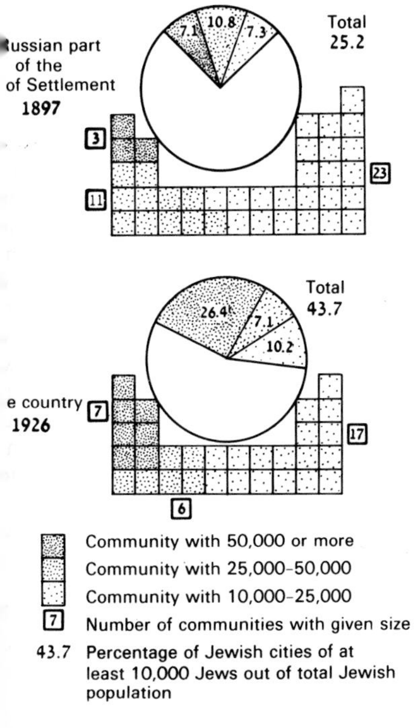


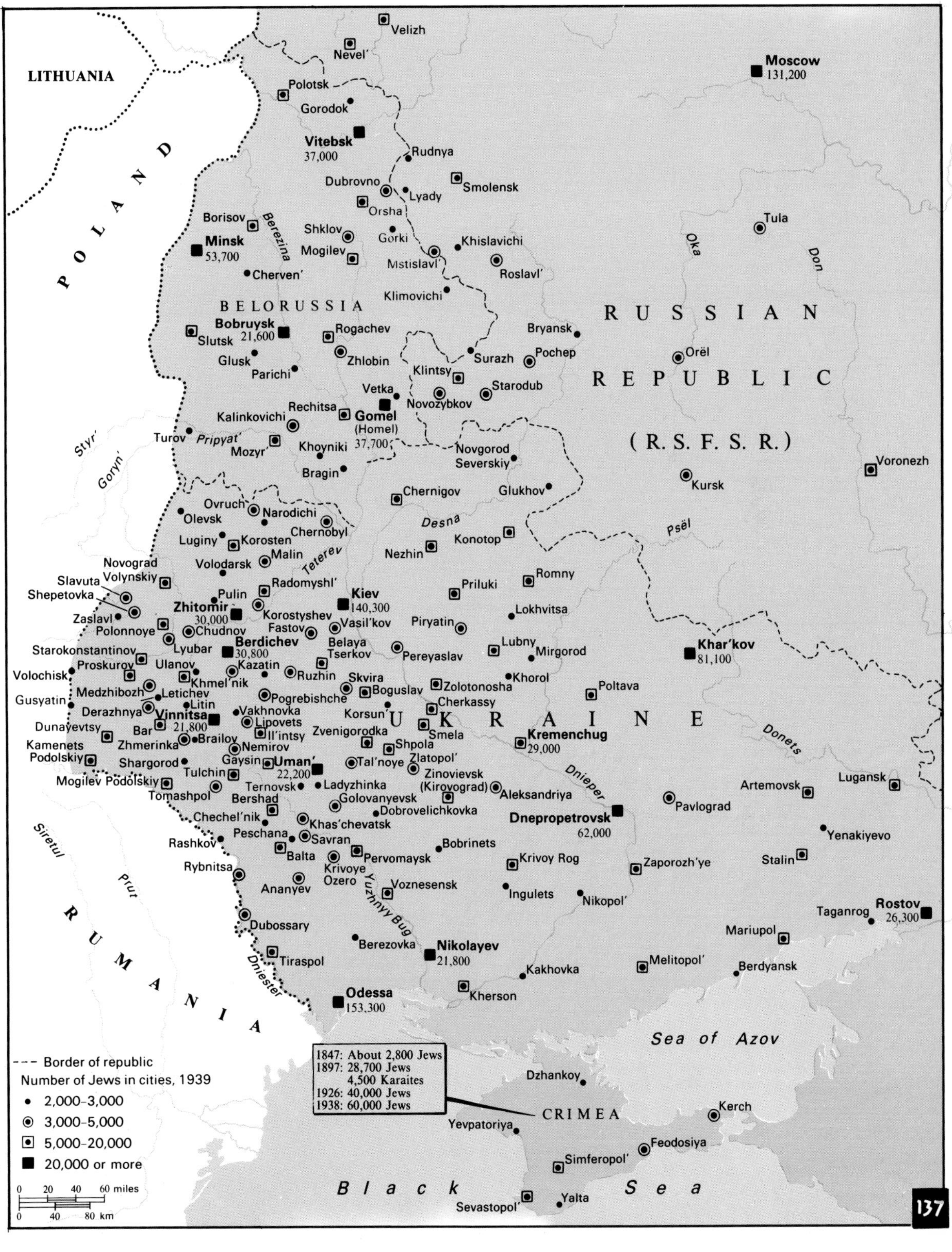

# The Jews in the Soviet Union in the Interwar Years

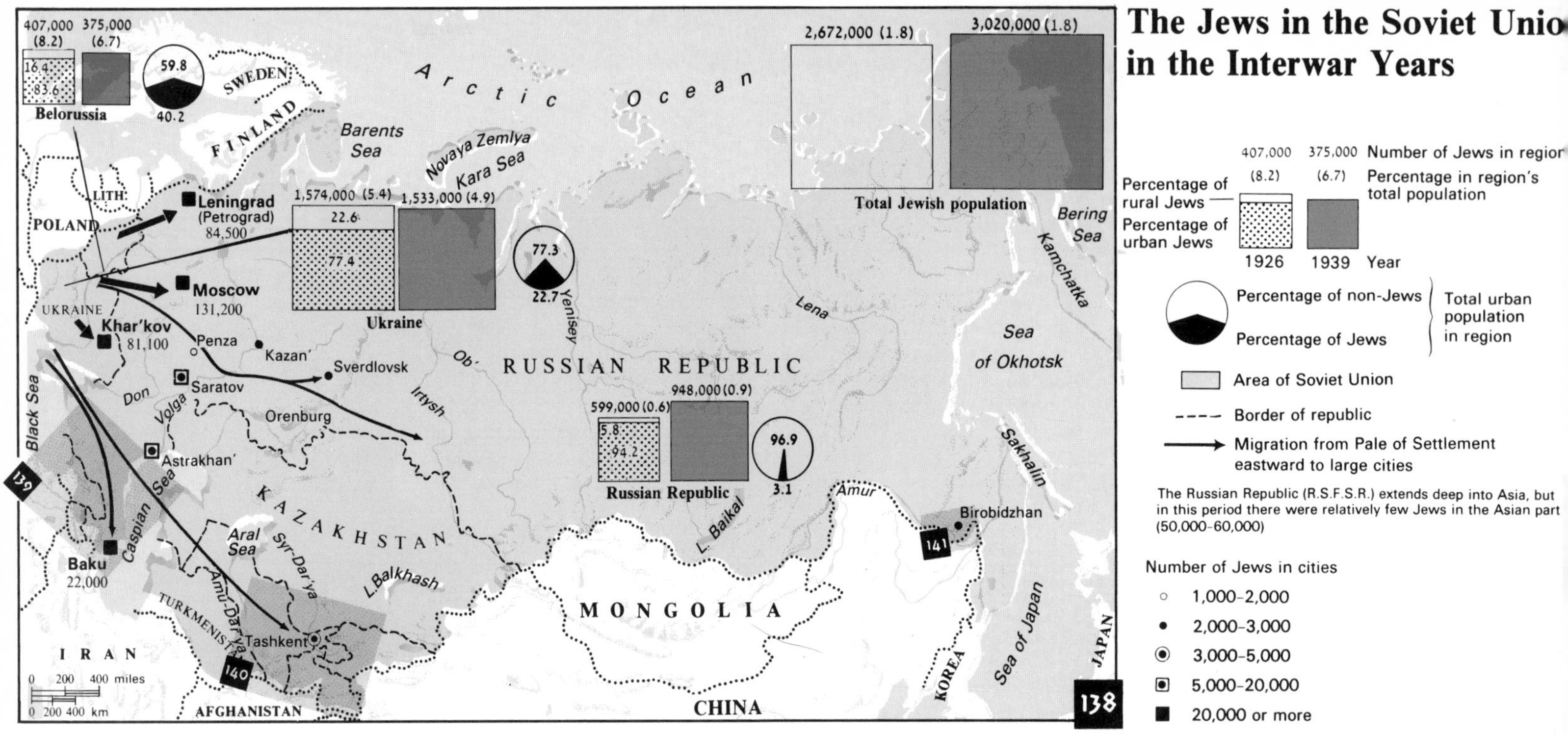


## The Caucasian "Mountain Jews" and the Jews in Georgia

In the Caucasus Mountains, mainly in the Dagestan region and in northern Azerbaijan, there lived for many generations the "Mountain Jews," who spoke their own Tatic language and had no contact with other Jews until the Russians conquered the region in the early nineteenth century. In the twentieth century, due to tensions with the Muslims, many Mountain Jews moved to the cities, especially to Derbent. During World War II, many Jewish refugees from the German-occupied parts of western Russia settled in the Caucasus.

Another Caucasian group were the Jews of Georgia. In the early nineteenth century, when the Russians occupied the region, these Jews lived in villages and towns and were so integrated into their society that the Russian authorities did not distinguish between them and the general population and did not apply to them the special laws promulgated for Jews in other parts of Russia. In the nineteenth century, "European" Russian Jews settled in Georgia, as did Karaites.

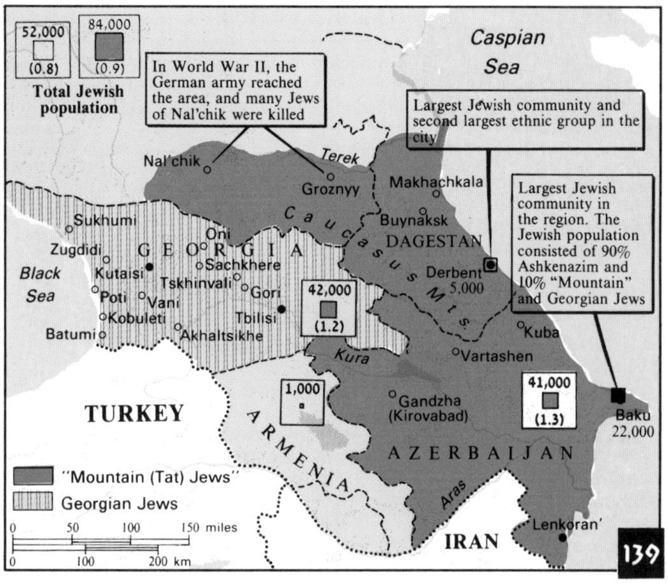

## The Jews in Bukhara

The Jews in the large Bukharan region (which included parts of Uzbekistan, Turkmenistan and Kazakhstan) were influenced by Persian Jewry, but developed their own Jewish life and spoke a specific dialect, Tajik. After the anti-Jewish riots in the nineteenth century in Meshed (Persia), many Jews emigrated from there to Bukhara. With the Russian conquest, from the mid-nineteenth century, many moved from the Muslim to the Russian parts, mainly to the cities of Samarkand and Kokand.

Bukharan Jews began to emigrate to Palestine toward the end the nineteenth century, without any connection with European Zionism. In 1892, the Bukharan Quarter was established in Jerusalem.

## The Jewish Autonomous Region in Birobidzhan

Birobidzhan was part of Khabarovsk territory in the Soviet Far East. The Russian authorities decided to establish an autonomous Jewish region there, to fortify the frontier with China, win over Jewish public opinion in the West, and create a Jewish national territory. Jewish settlement began in 1928, and six years later the Jewish autonomous region was officially founded. The Jewish population grew from 3,500 to about 20,000 in the 1930s, and to 30,000 in 1948. In the late 1940s, many Jews left the region. In 1959, there were 14,300 Jews in Birobidzhan (only 8.8 percent of the total population), 84 percent of whom lived in cities. In 1970, there were 11,500 Jews, 6.6 percent of the total population.

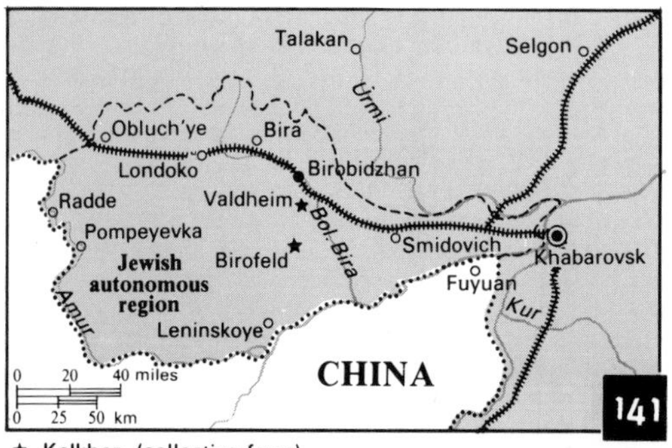


★ Kolkhoz (collective farm)

**The Jewish Population in Birobidzhan, 1936–1970**

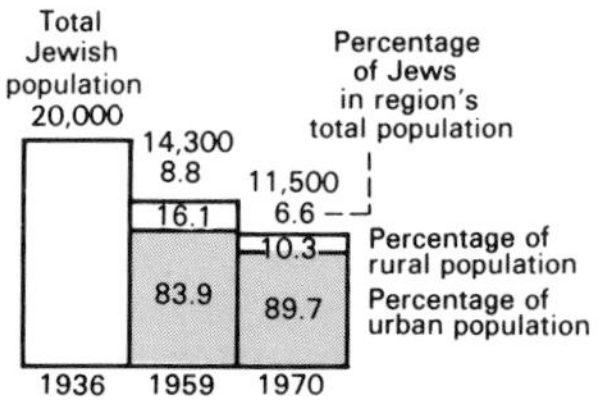

# he Jews in the Soviet Union:
## ate Twentieth Century

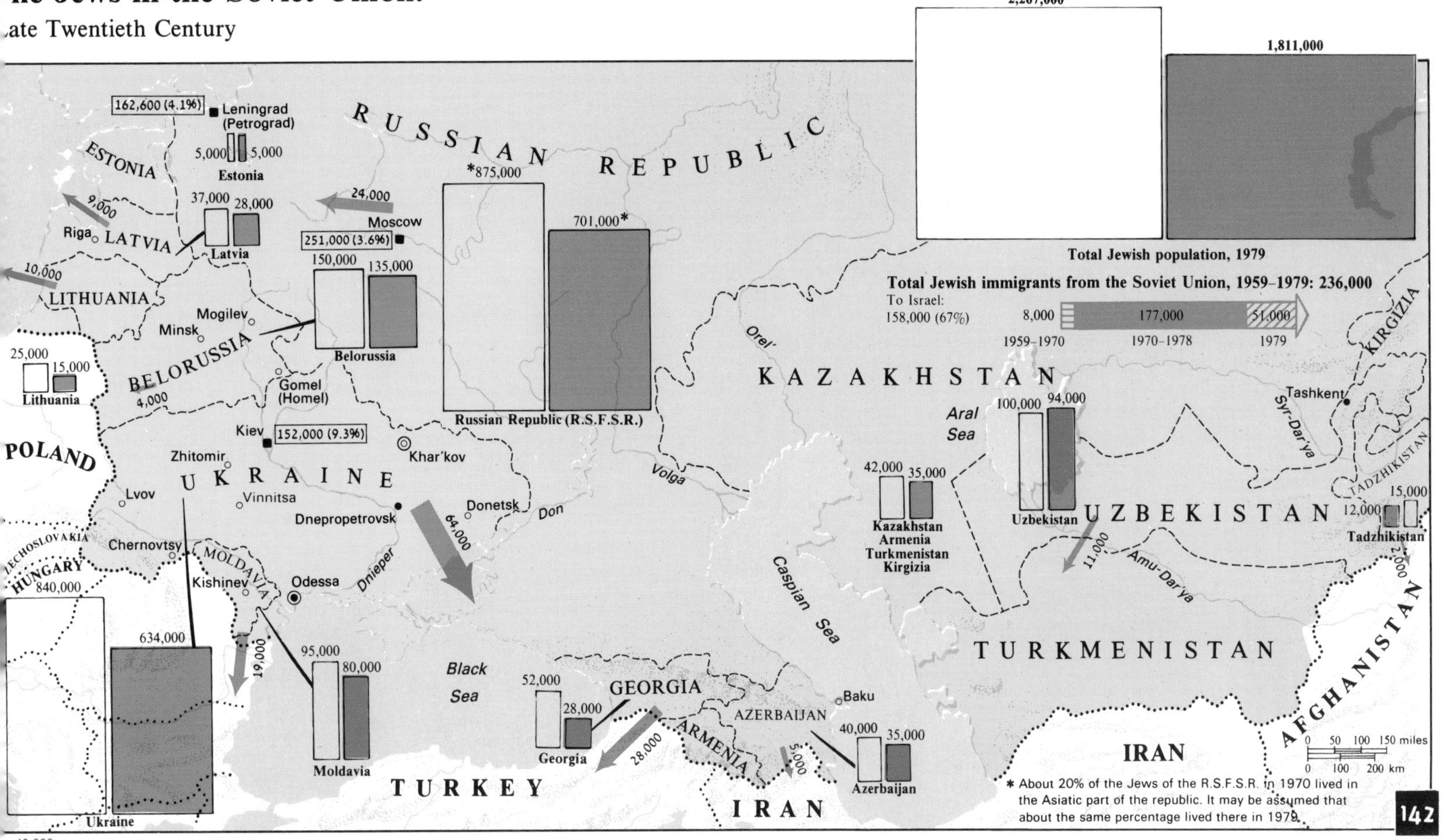


* About 20% of the Jews of the R.S.F.S.R. in 1970 lived in the Asiatic part of the republic. It may be assumed that about the same percentage lived there in 1979.

142

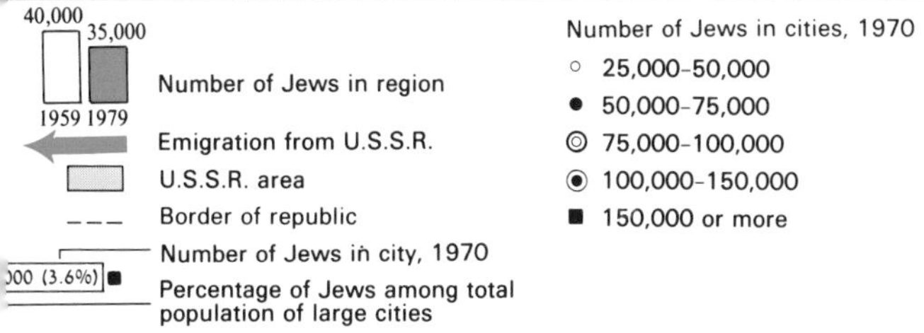


Two interrelated demographic trends characterized Soviet Jewry in the second half of the twentieth century: almost total urbanization and numerical decline. In 1979, the Soviet Union had 16 percent fewer Jews than it had had in 1959. Furthermore, estimates in the mid-1980s put the figure at only 1,515,000 Jews, or 13 percent fewer than in 1979. That year, about 75 percent of Soviet Jews lived in two republics: the Ukraine and the Russian Republic (RSFSR).

Demographically, Soviet Jewry shared the traits and problems that characterized the Jews of Western Europe and America: concentration in large cities, out-marriage, and very low natural increase. The birth rate in the years 1959 to 1970 was 8.9 per 1,000, while the death rate was 15.5 per 1,000, meaning a negative population growth combined with an aging Jewish population. Although 98 percent of the Jews lived in cities, their proportion there, too, was declining: the Jews made up 4.7 percent of Moscow's population in 1959, and only 3.6 percent in 1970. The restrictions on Jewish cultural and religious self-expression in the Soviet Union certainly contributed to the growing assimilation of the Jewish population.

Between 1959 and 1979, 236,000 Jews left the Soviet Union, the majority settling in Israel, and the rest in the United States and other countries.

### Population by Age Group, 1970 (percent)

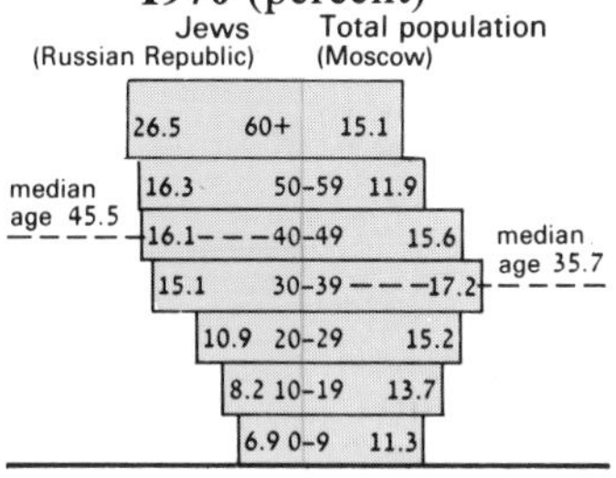


### Yiddish Speakers in the Ukraine* (percent)

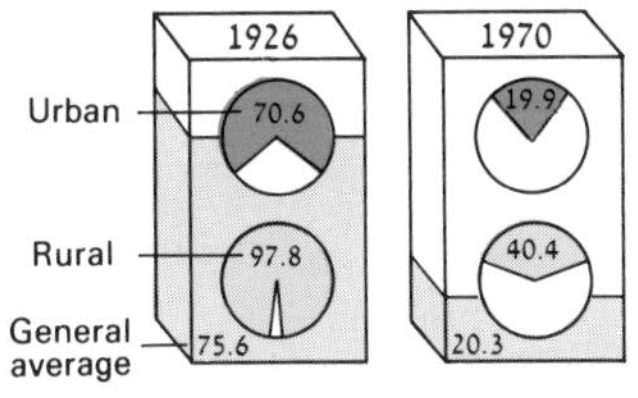


* In 1897, Yiddish was the first language of 97% of Ukrainian Jews.

### Urbanization Among the Jews

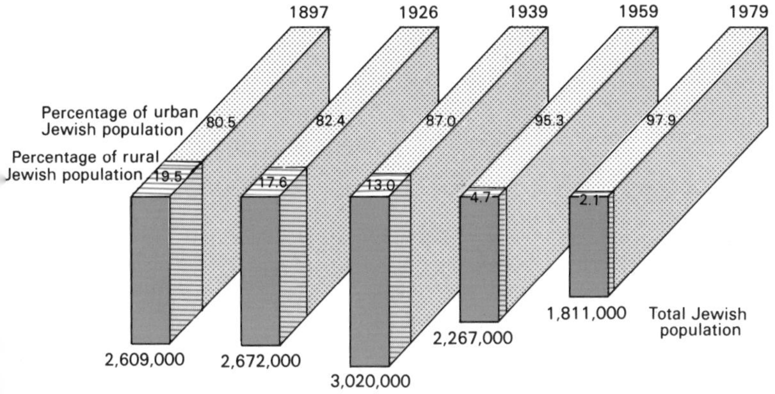


### Demographic Changes, 1897–1979*

| | | 1897 | 1926 | 1939 | 1959 | 1979 |
|---|---|---|---|---|---|---|
| U.S.S.R. | Percentage of Jews in total population | | 1.8 | 1.8 | 1.1 | 0.7 |
| | Number of Jews | 2,609,000 | 2,672,000 | 3,020,000 | 2,267,000 | 1,811,000 |
| Ukraine | Percentage of Jews in total population | 9.7 | 5.4 | 4.9 | 2.0 | 1.3 |
| | Percentage of Jews in total Jewish population | 27.3 | 59.0 | 50.8 | 37.1 | 35.0 |
| | Number of Jews | | 1,574,000 | 1,533,000 | 840,000 | 634,000 |
| Belorussia | Percentage of Jews in total population | 13.6 | 8.2 | 6.7 | 1.9 | 1.4 |
| | Percentage of Jews in total Jewish population | 13.9 | 15.2 | 12.4 | 6.6 | 7.5 |
| | Number of Jews | | 407,000 | 375,000 | 150,000 | 135,000 |

* The 1897 data are according to U.S.S.R. area in 1926. The Ukrainian and Belorussian data are according to 1897 borders. The other data are according to borders of year stated. The 1897 urbanization data are according to borders of Pale of Settlement (not including Poland and Bessarabia). The urbanization data for other years are according to borders of year stated.

# Palestine in the Nineteenth Century

In Ottoman times, Palestine was not a separate administrative unit, but divided between different provinces. About 6,700 Jews lived in the country in the early nineteenth century, mostly in the four "Holy Cities": Jerusalem, Safed, Tiberias, and Hebron. The majority were Sephardim, although several groups of Ashkenazim had arrived in the eighteenth century: Rabbi Judah Hehasid and his followers in 1700, and groups of Hasidim in 1764 and 1777.

The Egyptian conquest (1832–1840) launched a new period. A combination of political and religious circumstances generated a growing interest in the Holy Land among Europeans. The powers opened consulates and extended protection to the increasing activities of the Christian churches, under the terms of the Capitulations. The country's economic development was much enhanced.

Among the Jews, too, there was a revival of interest in the country and its Jewish population, an expression of the traditional Jewish attachment to the Holy Land. Jewish individuals and institutions became active in Palestine, some before the founding of the Zionist movement. The most important of these did not even have nationalistic aspirations: the Alliance Israélite Universelle, Baron Edmond de Rothschild, the German-Jewish Hilfsverein, and the Jewish Colonization Association.

The Jewish population in Palestine grew rapidly, from about 27,000 in 1880 to between 85,000 and 90,000 in 1914. Between 1890 and 1914, the Jewish population grew by 104 percent, and the non-Jewish population by 22.2 percent. Although most Jews lived in cities before World War I (86.3 percent in 1914), there were already about 12,000 Jews in forty agricultural villages, most of them established after 1881.

The gradual development of the Zionist movement from the 1880s added a most important dimension to the Jewish community in Palestine. Although the movement's practical work was still very modest (until World War I, the non-Zionists did much more), it gave ideological meaning and purpose to the Jewish presence in Palestine and influenced its character. A Zionist school system was established, and children spoke Hebrew in Palestine even before 1914. In 1908, the Palestine Zionist Office, headed by Arthur Ruppin, was opened in Jaffa. Other Zionist institutions followed.

**Jews and institutions that helped the Jewish community (Yishuv) in Palestine**

| | |
|---|---|
| 1827–1875 | Moses Montefiore visits Palestine 7 times, helps, buys land, builds Mishkenot Sha'ananim neighborhood. Concentrates activity in Jerusalem (Maskeret Moses Montefiore Fund) |
| From 1870 | Alliance Israélite schools in different cities; 12 educational institutions in 1912 |
| From 1870s | German Jews help Yishuv through Palestine Society headed by Rabbi Azriel Hildesheimer |
| From 1883 | Baron Edmond de Rothschild, help to colonies |
| From 1896 | Jewish Colonization Association (ICA) |
| 1901 | Rothschild transfers to ICA the colonies under his patronage (from 1923: PICA—Palestine Jewish Colonization Association) |
| From 1903 | Esra (Hilfsverein) educational institutions established; 20 institutions in 1912–1913 |

## Urban and Rural Populations in Palestine

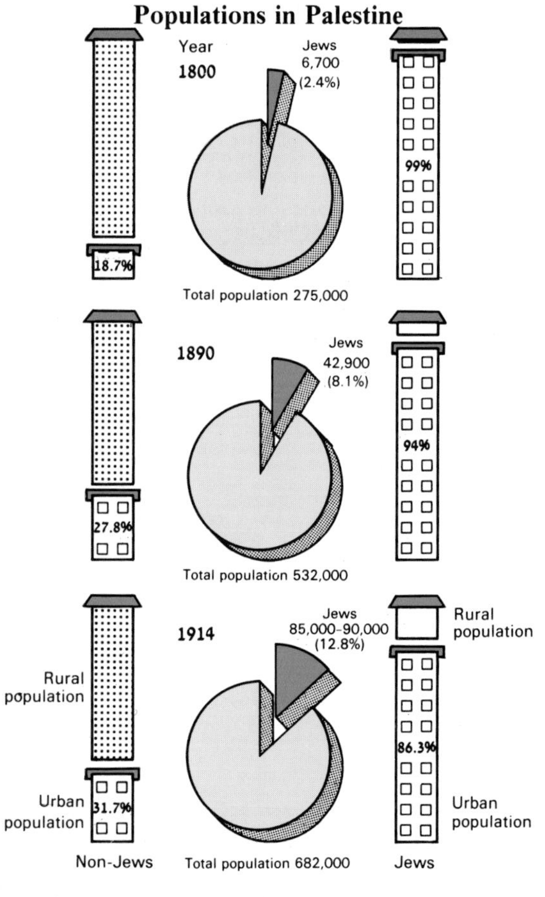


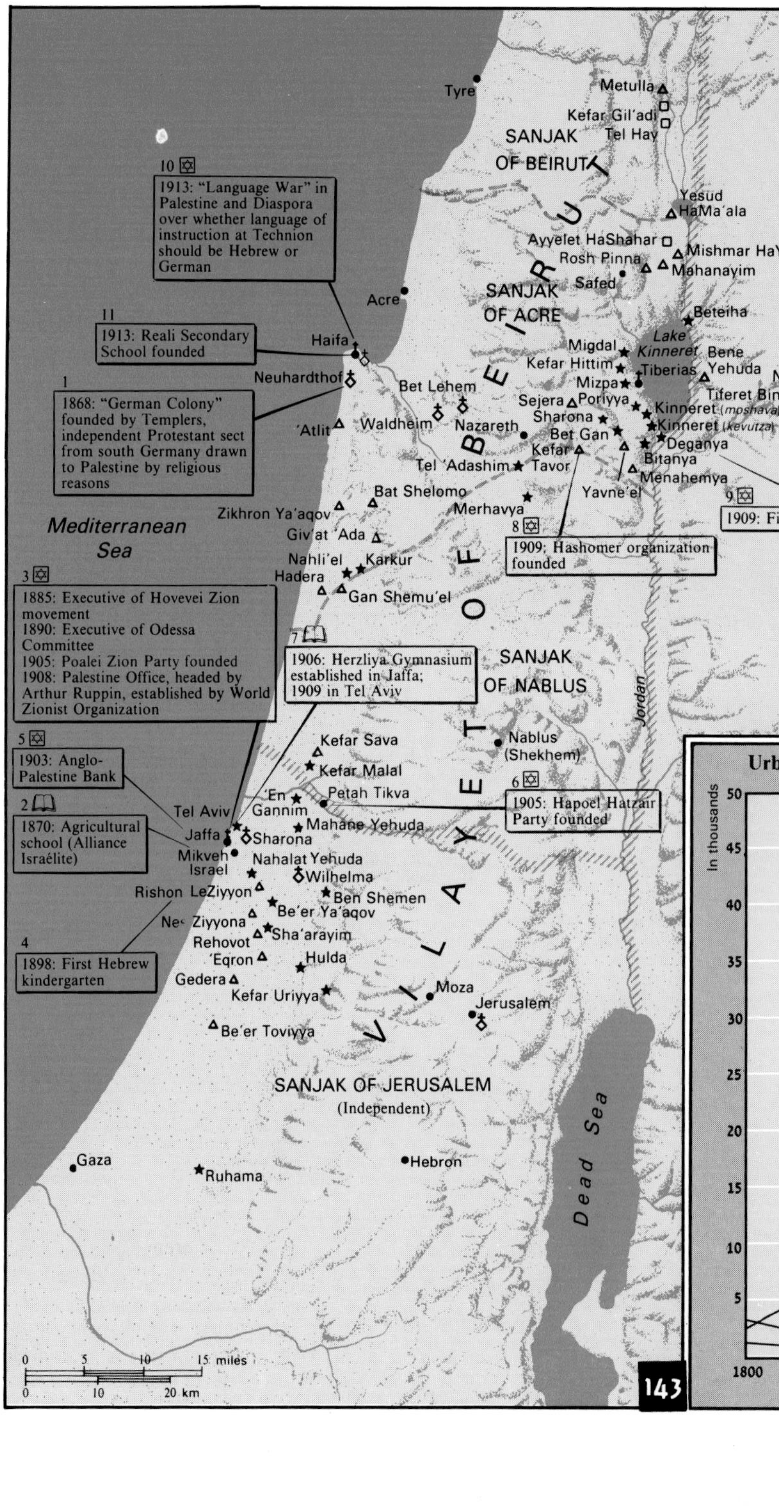


- • Settlement in existence in 1881
- △ Settlement founded 1882–1903
- ★ Settlement founded 1904–1914
- □ Settlement founded during World War I
- Zionist activity
- General Jewish activity
- Jewish educational institutions established
- Christian institutions established from 1851
- Templer colonies, 1868–1907
- Vilayet boundary
- Sanjak boundary

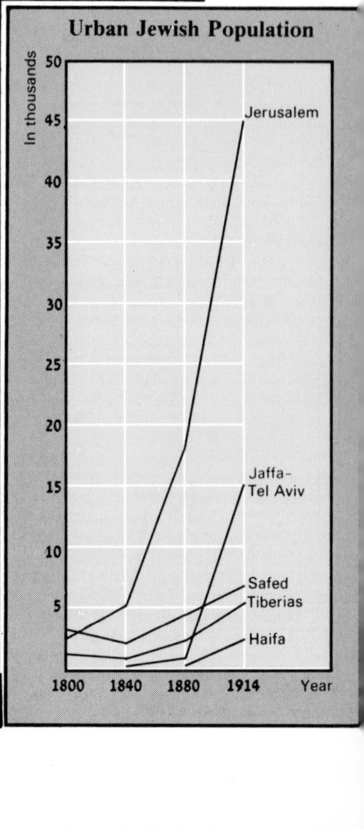

# Early Jewish Immigrations (*Aliyot*) to Palestine

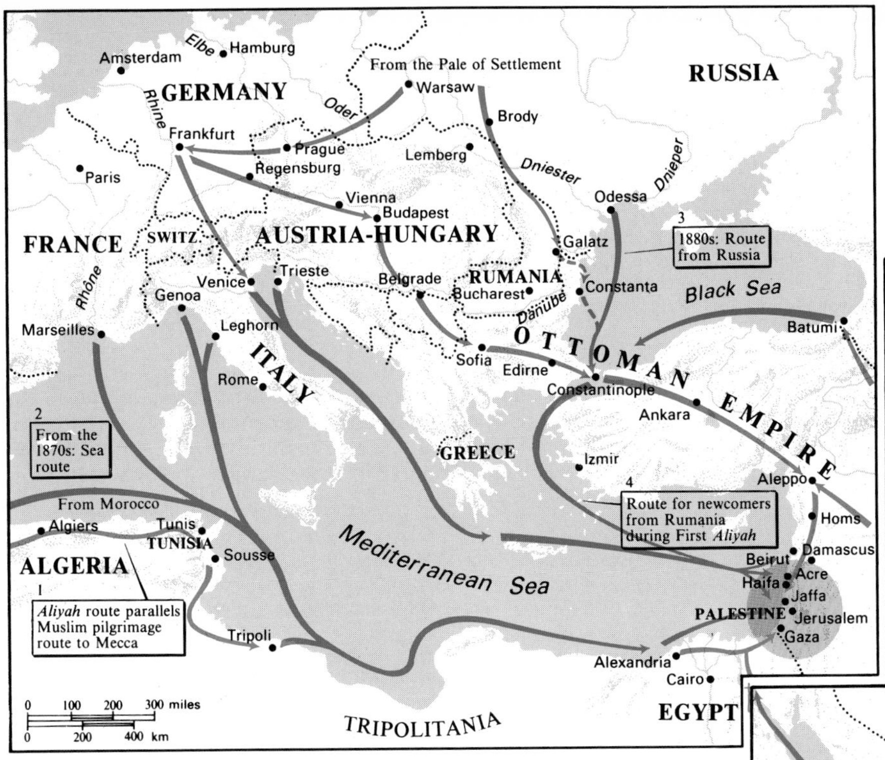


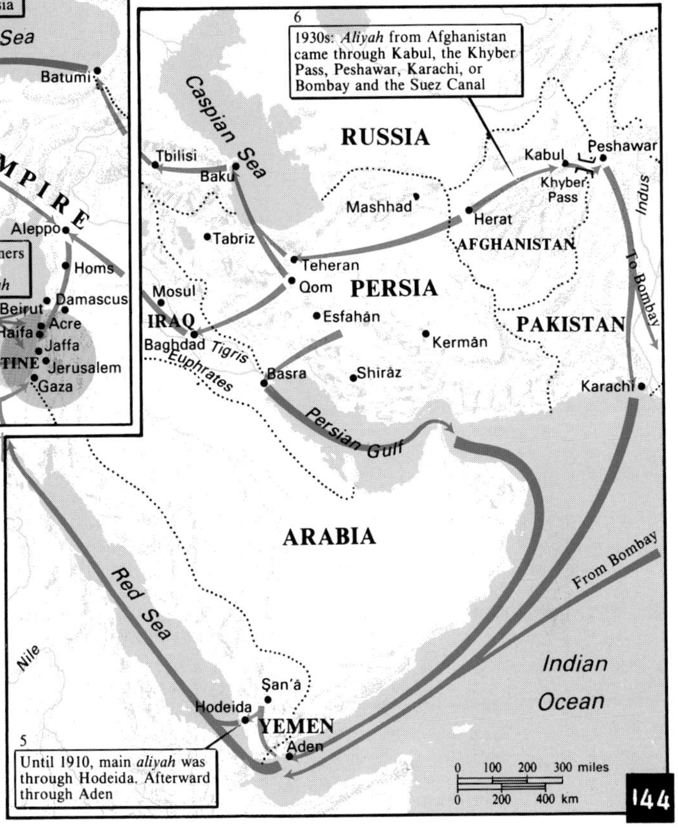


One of the expressions of the historical bond between the Jewish people and the land of Israel was *aliyah*, immigration (in Hebrew, "ascension") to Palestine. The *aliyah* continued throughout the centuries of Jewish dispersion, although at times it was only a trickle. It gradually increased in the nineteenth century (especially in the second half), long before the development of the Zionist movement. Jewish settlers came from all parts of the Diaspora: Morocco, Yemen, Bukhara, Kurdistan, and, from the 1880s, Rumania and Russia. Some of the historical *aliyah* routes were reopened in the twentieth century, during the development of the Zionist undertaking in Palestine.

# Jewish Immigration (*Aliyah*) to Israel After 1948

**Law of Return, 1950, 1954, 1970 (combined)**

1. Every Jew is entitled to enter Israel to live.
2. (a) The *aliyah* shall be implemented according to an *aliyah* permit.
   (b) The *aliyah* permit shall be granted to every Jew who has expressed a desire to settle in Israel. ...
3. Every Jew who settled in Israel before this law took effect, and every Jew born in the country before or since the law took effect, shall be considered as having entered the country under this law.

## By Origin

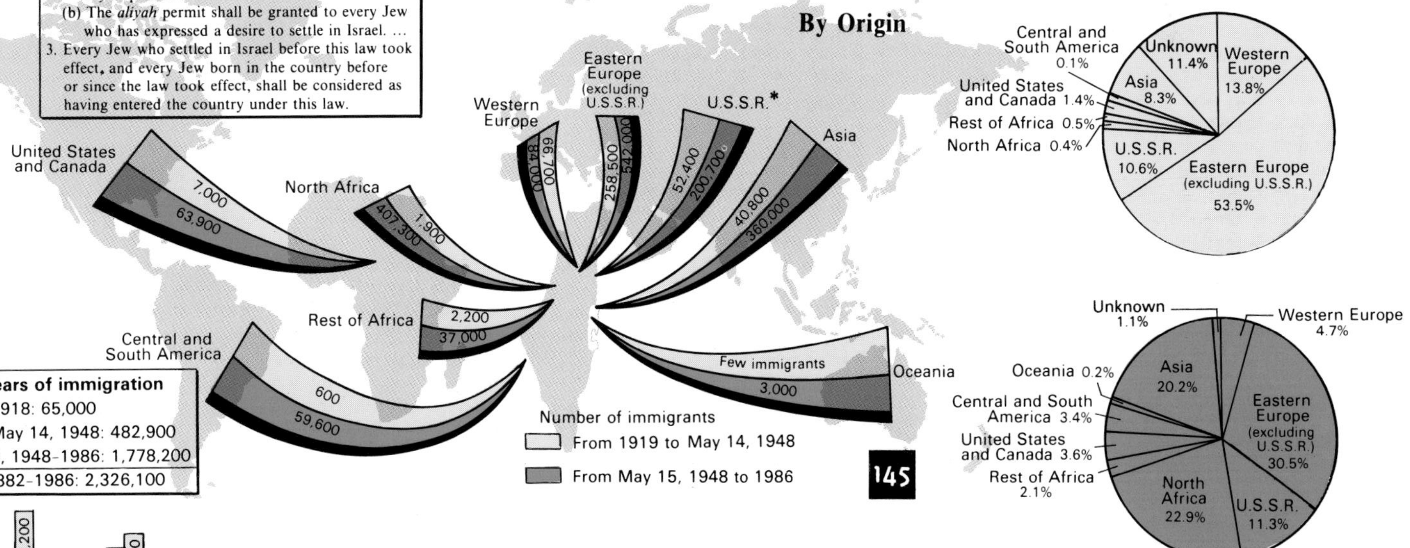


**100 years of immigration**

| | |
|---|---|
| 1882–1918: | 65,000 |
| 1919–May 14, 1948: | 482,900 |
| May 15, 1948–1986: | 1,778,200 |
| Total 1882–1986: | 2,326,100 |

## By Years †

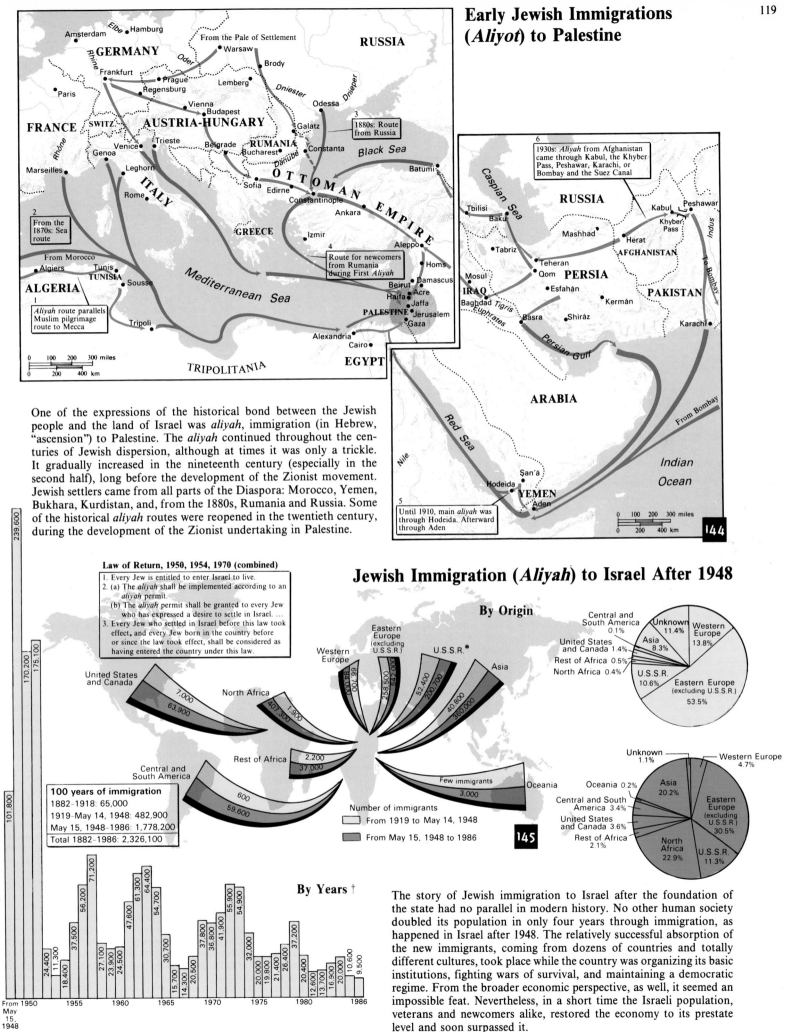

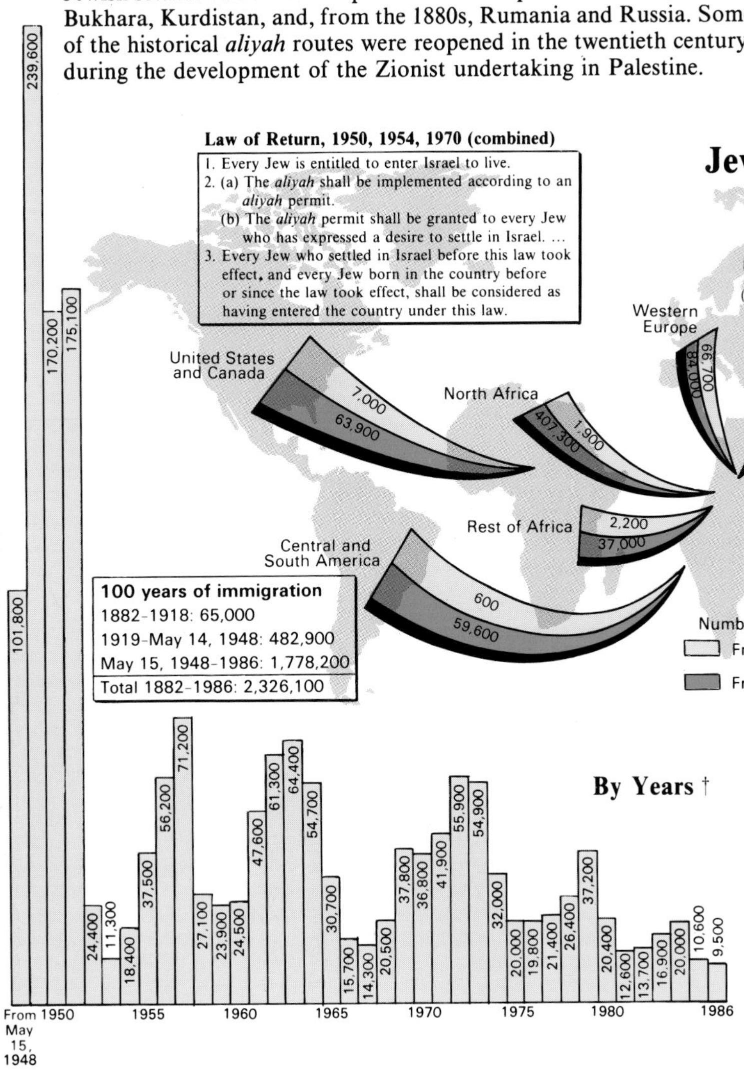


* Including areas in Asia and the Baltic states

† From 1969, includes data on "potential immigrants," Jews who spend at least 3 months in Israel. From 1969 to 1986, they constituted about 30% of the immigrants.

The story of Jewish immigration to Israel after the foundation of the state had no parallel in modern history. No other human society doubled its population in only four years through immigration, as happened in Israel after 1948. The relatively successful absorption of the new immigrants, coming from dozens of countries and totally different cultures, took place while the country was organizing its basic institutions, fighting wars of survival, and maintaining a democratic regime. From the broader economic perspective, as well, it seemed an impossible feat. Nevertheless, in a short time the Israeli population, veterans and newcomers alike, restored the economy to its prestate level and soon surpassed it.

The *aliyah* to Israel and the rapid absorption of the newcomers into the social fabric of Israeli society should be regarded as one of the great expressions of the constructive power of the Zionist idea.

# The Boundaries of Palestine

The frontiers of Palestine were fixed only in the twentieth century. In 1906, a southern boundary was established between Great Britain (Egypt) and the Ottoman Empire—from Rafah to Aqaba—giving the British administrative control over the Sinai Desert. The Sykes-Picot Agreement (May 1916) rather arbitrarily defined the territory of "Palestine." With some modifications, these lines became in 1920 the northern and northeastern frontiers of Palestine, although they included much less than the Zionists had hoped and asked for in 1919.

The British had intended to include the territory east of the Jordan River in an Arab state to be established under the Emir Faisal. After Faisal's expulsion from Damascus by the French in July 1921, the British decided to include the lands east of the Jordan in the Palestine Mandate, but not in the territory of the Jewish national home. Thus Transjordan was born, and the Palestinian frontier remained on the Jordan River, continuing south on that line to Aqaba.

Later, when plans were considered for the partition of the country between Jews and Arabs, new boundary lines were drawn, first in 1937 (Peel Commission Report), and again in 1947 (United Nations Special Commission on Palestine [UNSCOP] Report).

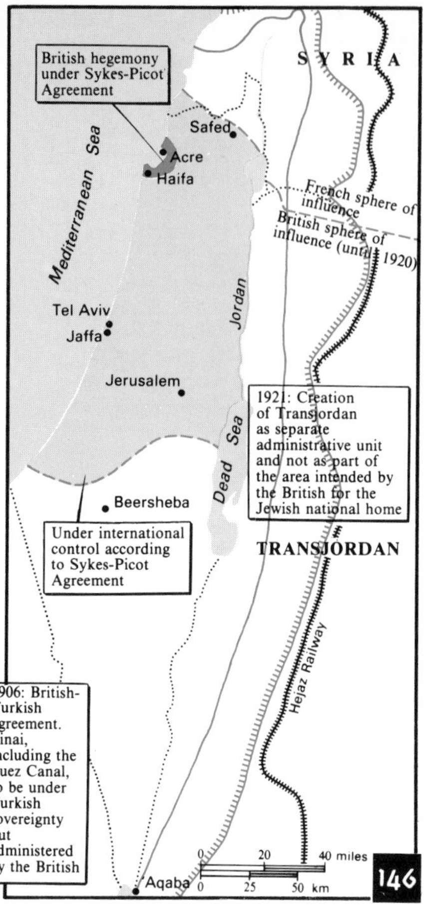


## United Nations Decision Regarding Partition of Palestine, November 29, 1947

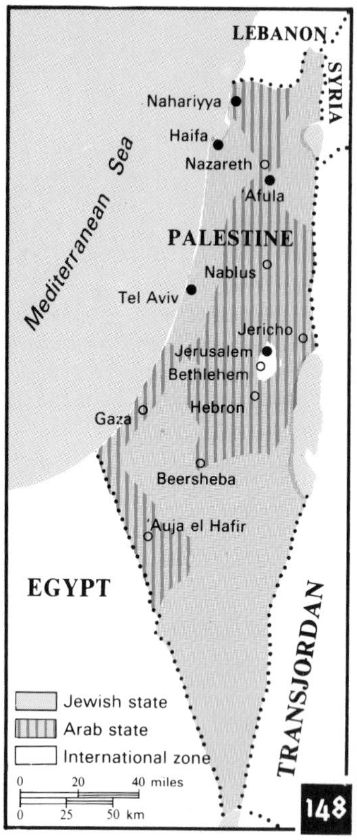


| | The British | The Arabs |
|---|---|---|
| 1917–1922<br>Definition and redefinition of British policy | **November 2, 1917** Balfour Declaration: "His Majesty's Government view with favour the establishment in Palestine of a national home for the Jewish people, and will use their best endeavours to facilitate the achievement of that object. ..."<br>**1917–1918** British conquest of Palestine; military administration<br>**April 1920** San Remo Conference: Mandate on Palestine to Great Britain; civil administration, Herbert Samuel as High Commissioner<br>**June 3, 1922** Churchill Memorandum: The principle of British dual obligation in Palestine, to Jews and Arabs<br>**July 24, 1922** British Mandate on Palestine approved by League of Nations | **April 1920** Riots in Jerusalem<br>**December 1920** Third Palestinian Arab Congress, in Haifa: Opposition to Zionism and Balfour Declaration; demand for Arab national government in Palestine; formation of Palestine Arab Executive<br>**May 1921** Riots in Jaffa and other cities<br>**August 1921** Arab delegation in London<br>**1921** Formation of Supreme Muslim Council, headed by Amin el-Husseini |
| 1922–1928<br>Period of calm | | |
| 1928–1931<br>Redefinition of British policy | **March 1930** Shaw Report: Zionist co-responsibility for Palestine disturbances<br>**October 1930** Hope-Simpson Report: No room in Palestine for further Jewish settlement<br>**October 1930** Passfield White Paper: Limitations on Jewish immigration and land acquisition<br>**February 13, 1931** MacDonald Letter: Practical nullification of the Passfield White Paper | **August 1929** Riots start in Jerusalem, spread to other cities |
| 1936–1938<br>Arab revolt | **July 1937** Peel Commission Report: Partition of Palestine between Jews and Arabs<br>**October 1938** Woodhead Commission: Rejection of partition plan | **1936** Formation of Supreme Arab Executive, headed by Amin el-Husseini, with representation of all Arab parties<br>**April 1936** General strike; beginning of Arab revolt, until end of 1938 |
| 1939<br>Redefinition of British policy and of Zionist policy | **May 13, 1939** MacDonald White Paper: Limitations on Jewish immigration and land acquisition; independent state (with Arab majority) in ten years | |

**David Ben-Gurion, at Twenty-first Congress (August 1939):** "The 'White Paper' has created a vacuum in the Mandate. For us, the 'White Paper' does not exist in any form, in any condition, under any interpretation. For us there is only that vacuum created in the Mandate, and it is up to us to fill this vacuum, by ourselves alone. ... We ourselves shall have to act as if we were the state in Palestine, and we have to act that way until we shall become and in order that we shall become the state in Palestine."

## Peel Commission Proposal for the Partition of Palestine, 1937

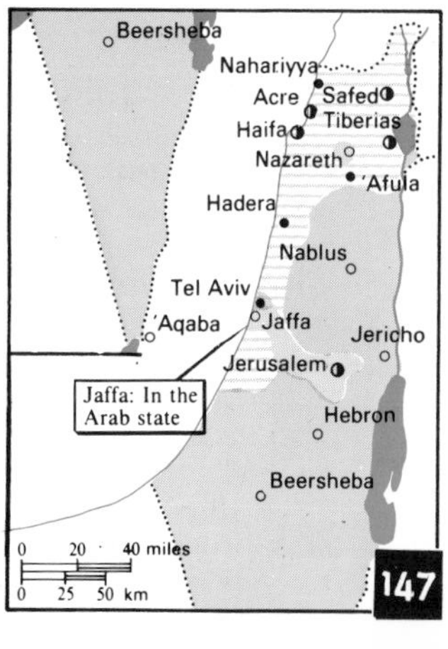


● Jewish town
○ Arab town
◑ Mixed town (to remain under Mandate for certain period)

Jewish state
Arab state
British Mandate area

## The Jews, British, and Arabs in Palestine, 1918–1939

British policy regarding Zionist aspirations in Palestine was guided by two main political documents issued at almost the same time: the Mandate, approved by the Council of the League of Nations in July 1922, and the Churchill Memorandum of a month earlier. In principle, the terms of the Mandate were more important, since it was an international document guaranteed by the League of Nations, which was responsible for Palestine. Its terms could be regarded as a continuation of those of the Balfour Declaration, and it established a framework for the development of a Jewish national home in Palestine. The Churchill Memorandum (actually conceived by Herbert Samuel) reaffirmed the right of the Jews to a national home in Palestine, but opposed the idea of a Jewish state there and enunciated the principle of the "double obligation" of the British to the Jews and to the Arabs in Palestine. It was a British document, without international standing. The Arabs rejected both documents.

From 1922 to 1939, the British gradually withdrew their support for the creation of a Jewish national home. This reflected a change in British political conceptions and the influence of Arab opposition to Zionism. The Passfield White Paper (1930) sought to slow the Zionists' plans, but it was revoked (in practice) in 1931. A royal commission headed by Lord Peel visited Palestine in 1936, and concluded that the continuing tension between Jews and Arabs made the partition of Palestine between both peoples the only solution. The Zionist reaction was hesitant, and that of the Arabs, negative. In the end, the British retreated from this position as well. In 1939, the MacDonald White Paper was issued, marking the end of British obligations regarding Zionist aspirations. It severely curtailed Jewish immigration, prohibited the purchase of land by Jews, and spoke of an independent nation in ten years—a country with an Arab majority and a Jewish minority (one-third of the population).

The White Paper of 1939 forced the Yishuv (the organized Jewish community in Palestine) and the Zionist movement to reevaluate the situation and their relations with Great Britain. The result was a new and more militant Zionist policy, which in 1948 led to Jewish independence.

# The Political Organization of the Jewish Community in Palestine, 1905–1948

The political structure of the organized Jewish community in Palestine (the Yishuv) began to take shape in the first decade of the twentieth century. Later, it expanded according to various ideological tendencies or political interests: left, right, religious, local interests, and so on. Nevertheless, from the 1920s the political initiative was in the hands of the leftist Labor parties (Hapoel Hatzair, Poalei Zion), which had been the first to organize. Their first steps had been slow and difficult; the Turkish authorities did not permit political organizations, and the political experience brought from the Diaspora did not suit the conditions in Palestine. They started with activities whose political aims were camouflaged as social, cultural, and economic projects. Their objective aim was "constructive action"—the building of a national home according to socialist theory.

The other political groups were much slower to formulate their own conceptions about the future character of the Yishuv. When the first Assembly of Representatives (Asefat Hanivharim) was elected in 1920, the smaller, but much better organized workers' parties offered a far clearer picture of the political work to be done in Palestine. Thus was established the political hegemony of the Zionist Labor parties in Palestine, which was to continue for many years. But since they did not win an outright majority, the Labor parties were forced to form coalitions with the "general" parties or with the religious Zionists. The ideological fervor characteristic of those years caused the various political parties to alternately unify and split again and again.

The parties became the basis for all activity connected with the building of the Jewish national home: culture, economy, education, and semilegal defense, the Haganah. The Zionist Labor movement founded the Histadrut (General Federation of Jewish Workers in Palestine), and was connected with the settlement movements (kibbutz and *moshav*). On the other ideological side, the nationalist Revisionist movement (in opposition) established in the 1930s its own underground military organization, the Irgun (Irgun Zva'i Leumi).

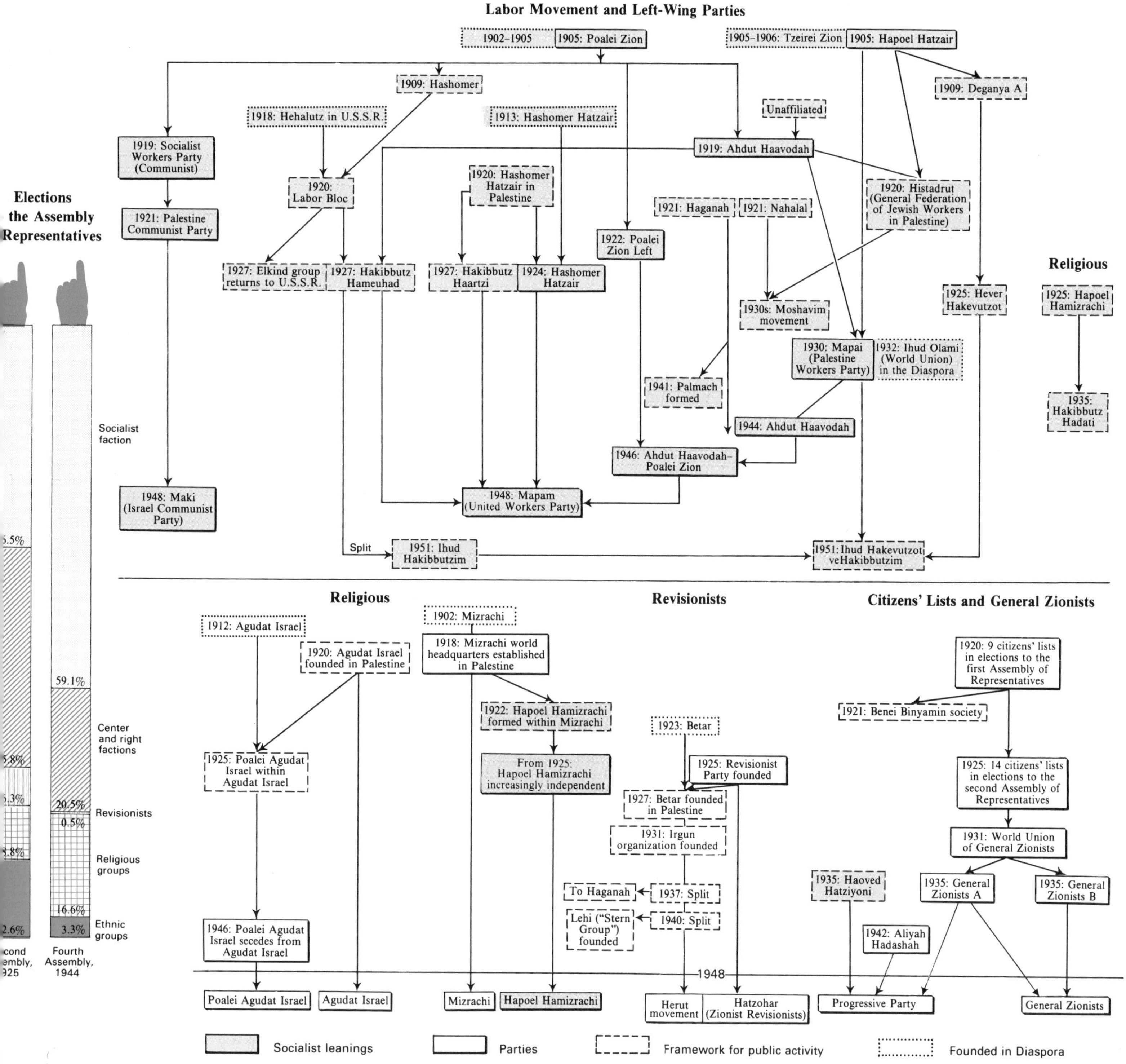

# Toward the Establishment of the Jewish State in Palestine, 1940–1948

Zionist policy in the 1940s had two conflicting aims: helping Great Britain in the war against Germany, and fighting the British because of the MacDonald White Paper of 1939. The extermination of European Jewry added another factor to the political considerations of the Zionist leaders. During the war, there was a measure of collaboration between the British and the Zionists. After 1945, however, relations between the two gradually deteriorated.

The Biltmore Conference, held in New York in May 1942, proclaimed that the aim of the Zionist movement was to create a Jewish "commonwealth" in Palestine after the war. When the war was over, the Zionists organized a large-scale escape movement of Jews from Europe to Palestine.

In addition to the recognized resistance organizations—the Haganah and the Palmach—two anti-British resistance groups arose in Palestine, unconnected with the official institutions of the Yishuv: the Irgun and the Stern Group. A growing number of actions against the British by the Haganah, the Irgun, and the Stern Group, sometimes by all three together, triggered equally violent reactions by the British. The British refusal to comply with the recommendation of the Anglo-American Committee of Enquiry (April 1946) and admit 100,000 Jews into Palestine brought the tension to new heights.

In February 1947, the British government presented the problem of Palestine to the United Nations. The United Nations Special Commission on Palestine (UNSCOP) was formed, and its recommendations were the basis of the United Nations decision of November 29, 1947, to partition Palestine between Jews and Arabs and create two states. The Zionists accepted the decision, and the Arabs rejected it, which is the main reason why an Arab state was not established in part of Palestine. Large-scale fighting between Arabs and Jews began shortly thereafter, developing into the War of Independence.

On May 14, 1948, the state of Israel was proclaimed.

THE PALESTINE POST

JERUSALEM SUNDAY, MAY 14, 1948

CARL MARX

Lighting, Heating, Cooking, Refrigeration

8 PRINCESS MARY AVE., JERUSALEM

# STATE OF ISRAEL IS BORN

The first independent Jewish State in 19 centuries was born in Tel Aviv as the British Mandate over Palestine came to an end at midnight on Friday, and it was immediately subjected to the test of fire. As "Medinat Yisrael" (State of Israel) was proclaimed, the battle for Jerusalem raged, with most of the city falling to the Jews. At the same time, President Truman announced that the United States would accord recognition to the new State. A few hours later, Palestine was invaded by Moslem armies from the south, east and north, and Tel Aviv was raided from the air. On Friday the United Nations Special Assembly adjourned after adopting a resolution to appoint a mediator but without taking any action on the Partition Resolution of November 29.

Yesterday the battle for the Jerusalem-Tel Aviv road was still under way, and two Arab villages were taken. In the north, Acre town was captured, and the Jewish Army consolidated its positions in Western Galilee.

*Headline of May 14, 1948.* Yom Hamedinah (Day of the State), *issued jointly by all of Israel's newspapers*

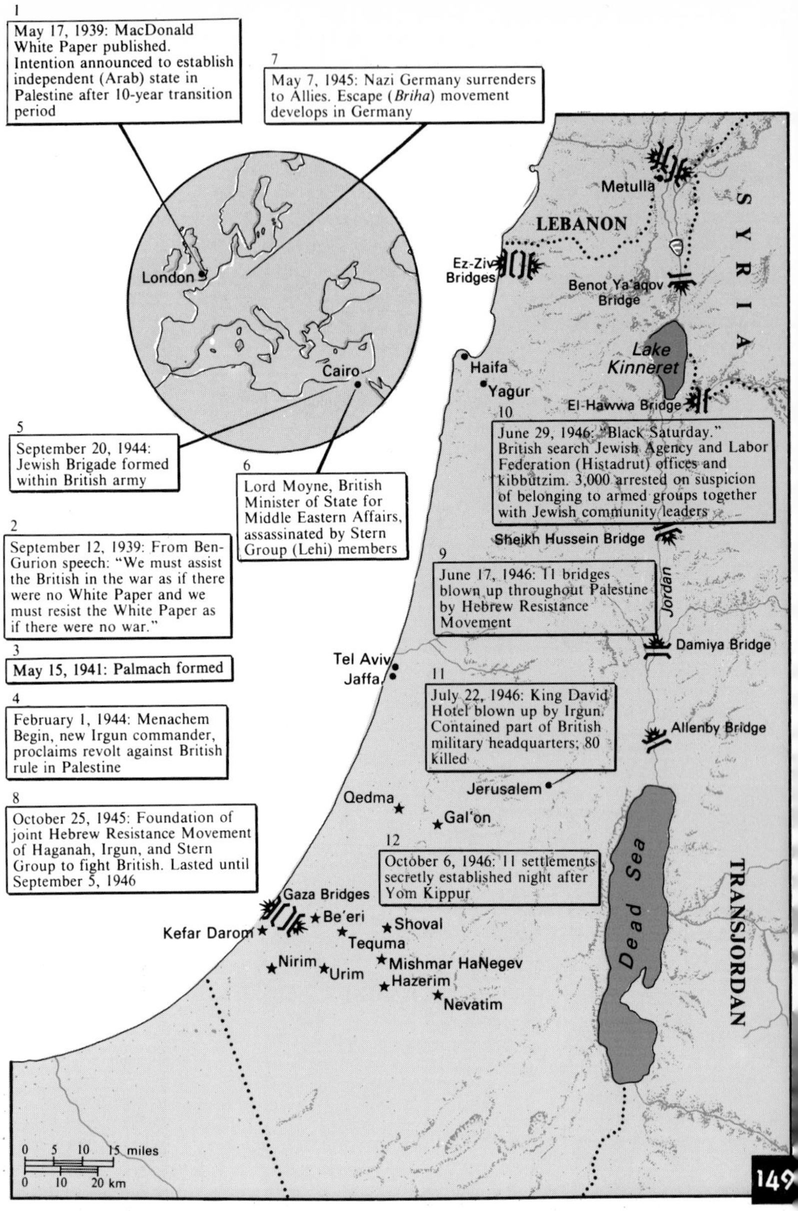




# The "Illegal" Immigration to Palestine, 1945–1948

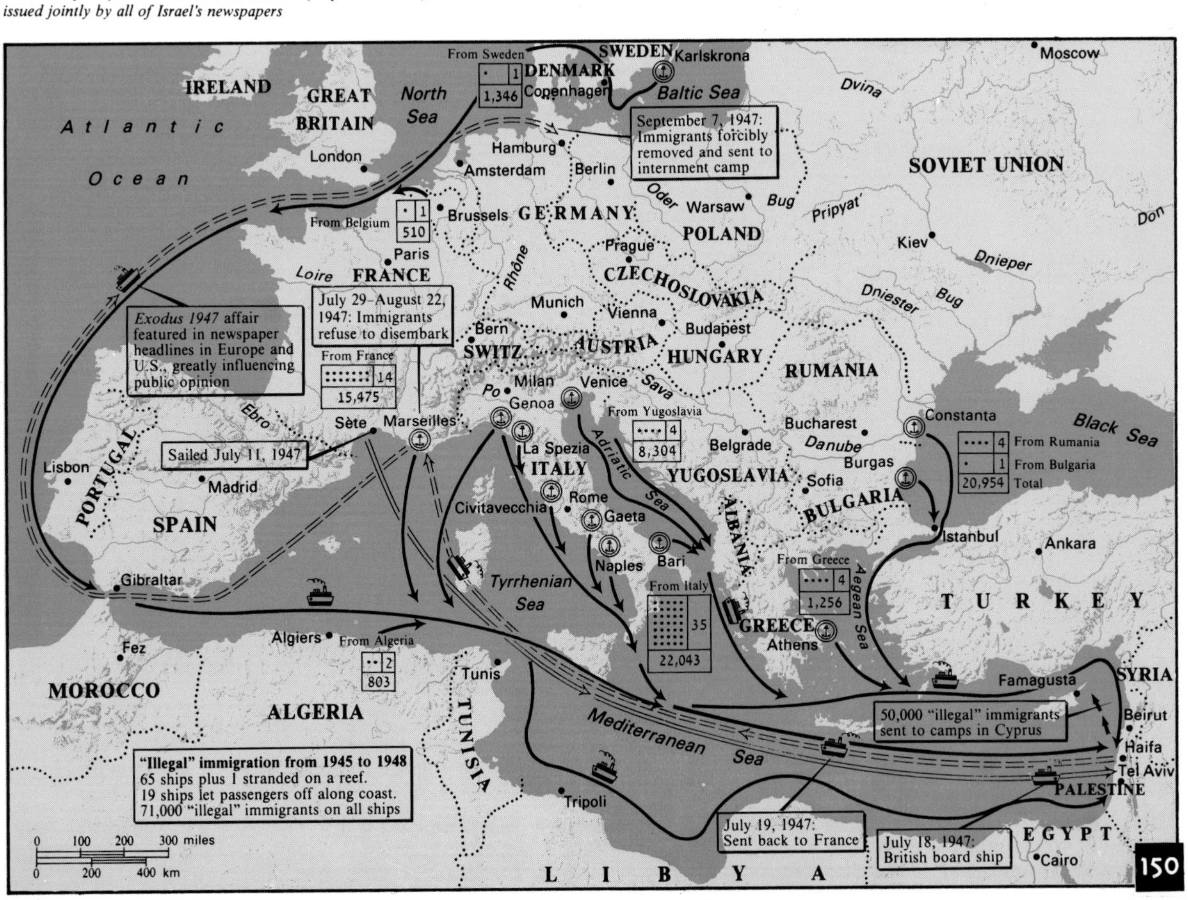




*Exodus 1947*

Route to Palestine

Expulsion route

Major port of departure

Immigration route

Number of ships

Number of immigrants

# he Wars Fought by Israel

## War of dependence, 1948–1949

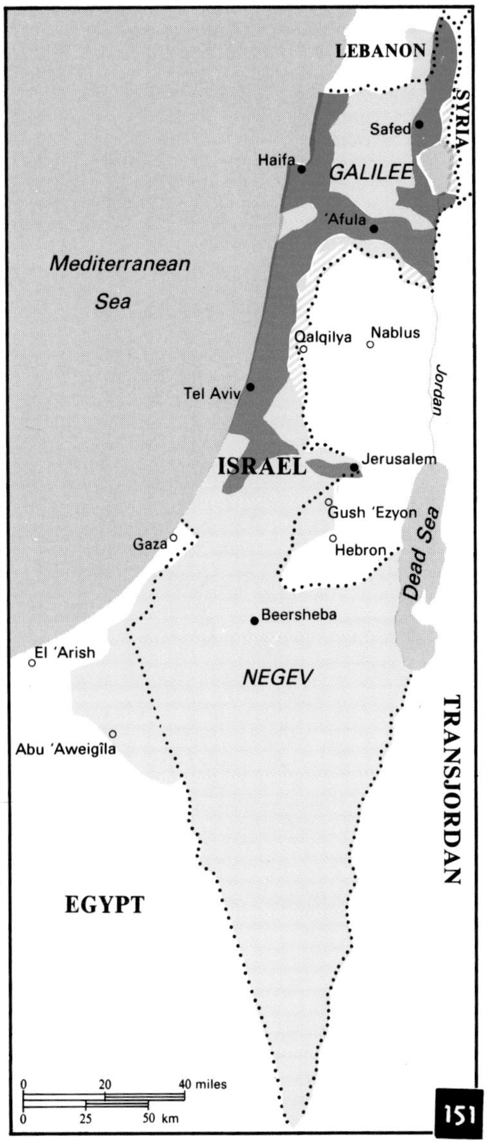


## Operation Kadesh ("Sinai Campaign"), 1956

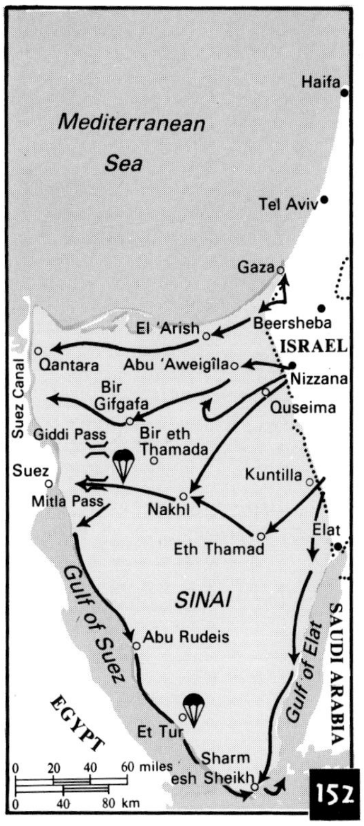


## Six-Day War, 1967

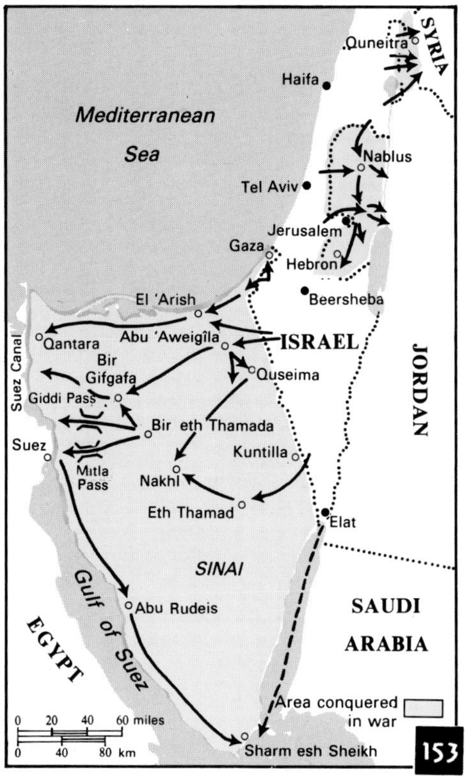


- Area under Jewish control at time of proclamation of state
- Area conquered in the war
- Area added to Israel under armistice agreement
- ........ 1949 armistice line

## Peace Treaty with Egypt, 1979

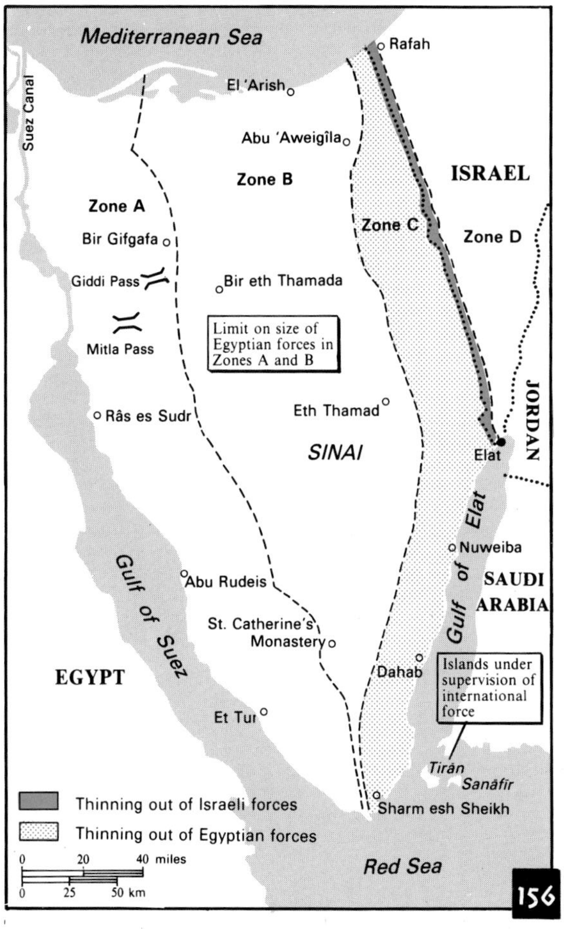


## Yom Kippur War, 1973

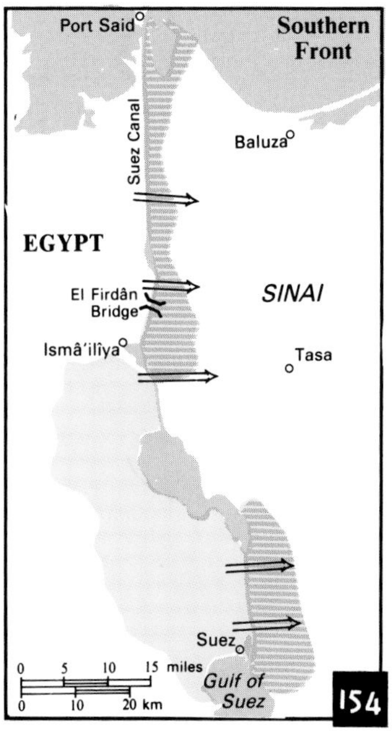


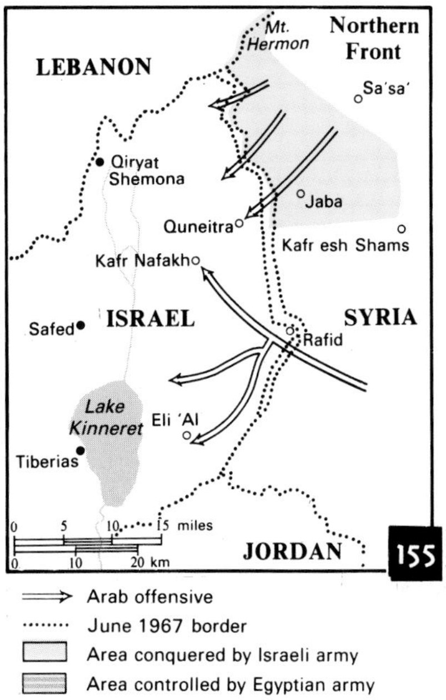


- ⟹ Arab offensive
- ........ June 1967 border
- Area conquered by Israeli army
- Area controlled by Egyptian army

After its establishment in 1948 (and even before), Israel was repeatedly forced to defend its existence against Arab threats. The Arab world would not accept the existence of a Jewish state in the Middle East. The Arabs also thwarted the implementation of the United Nations proposal of November 1947 for the creation of an Arab state in part of Palestine. The Arab–Israeli conflict took political, economic, diplomatic, and, periodically, military forms. The most difficult of these wars was the War of Independence, which continued through 1948 and part of 1949. Six thousand Jews were killed (4,000 soldiers and 2,000 civilians). During the Six-Day War of June 1967, Israel seized the Sinai Peninsula and Gaza Strip from Egypt, the West Bank from Jordan, and the Golan Heights from Syria. In October 1973, Israel was surprised by an Egyptian–Syrian attack (the Yom Kippur War) but managed to repel it. After the peace treaty with Egypt (1979), Israel withdrew from Sinai. New proposals for peace between Israel and its neighbors were considered periodically through the 1970s and 1980s.

# Jewish Settlement Before the Creation of Israel

## Economic Development

Domestic and Per Capita Product*

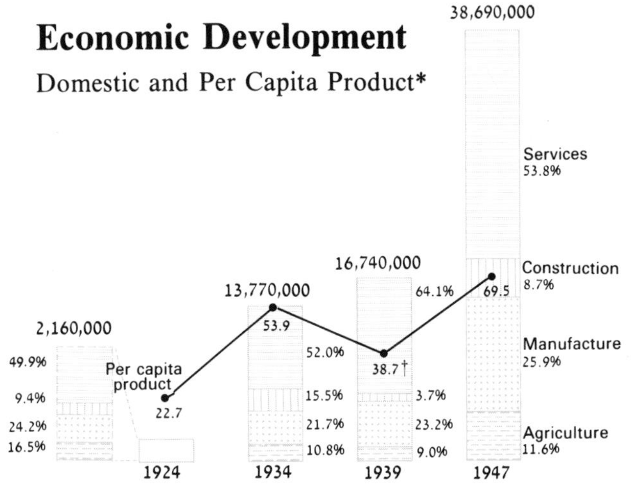


* In Palestine pounds according to the 1936 index, taking into account the net domestic product as against the gross, including amortization of equipment and buildings.

† The decline in per capita product in 1939 reflects the fact that the domestic product was being shared by a growing number of Jewish inhabitants.

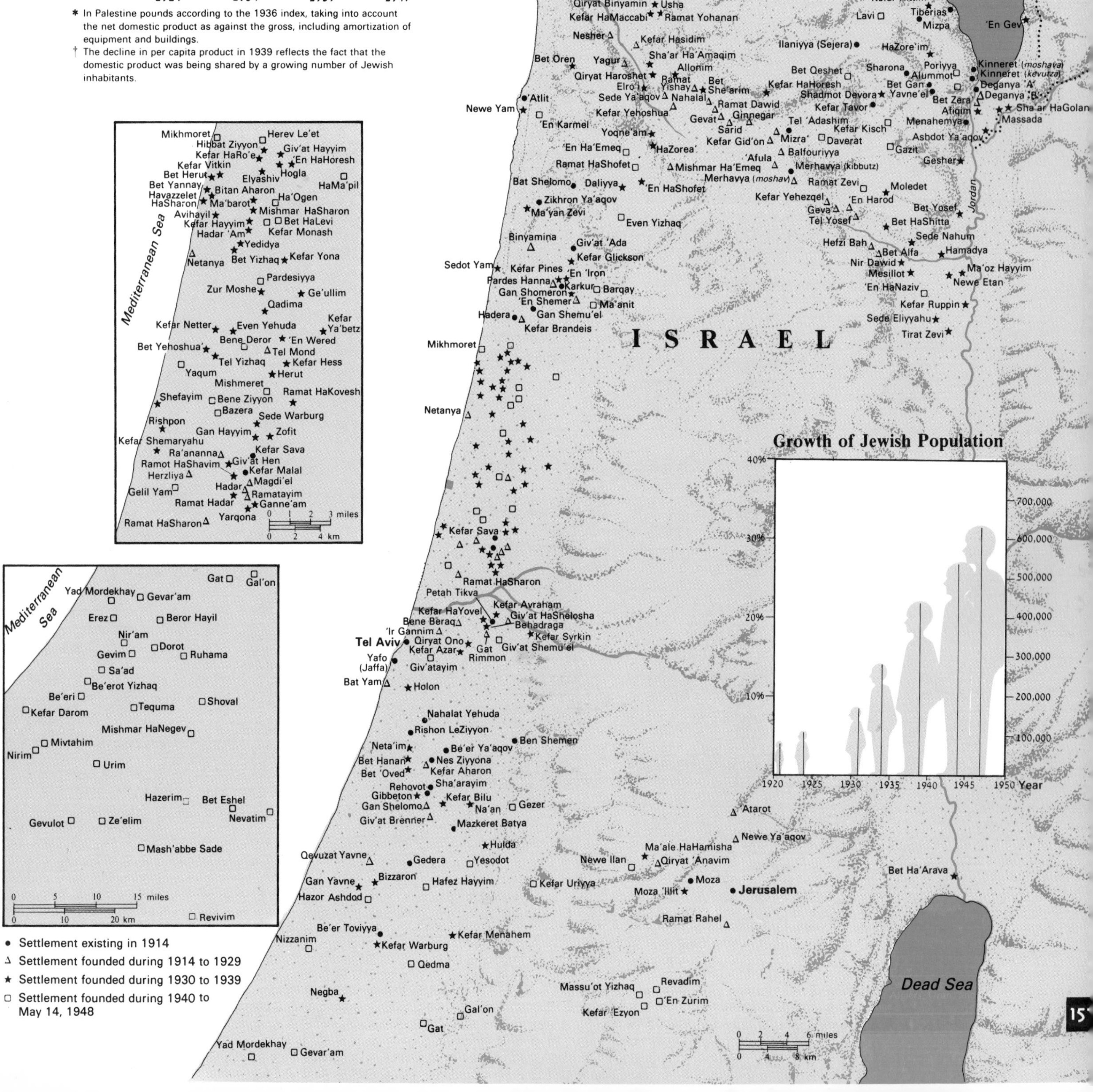


- ● Settlement existing in 1914
- △ Settlement founded during 1914 to 1929
- ★ Settlement founded during 1930 to 1939
- □ Settlement founded during 1940 to May 14, 1948

# State of Israel: Establishment of Jewish Localities, 1948–1980s

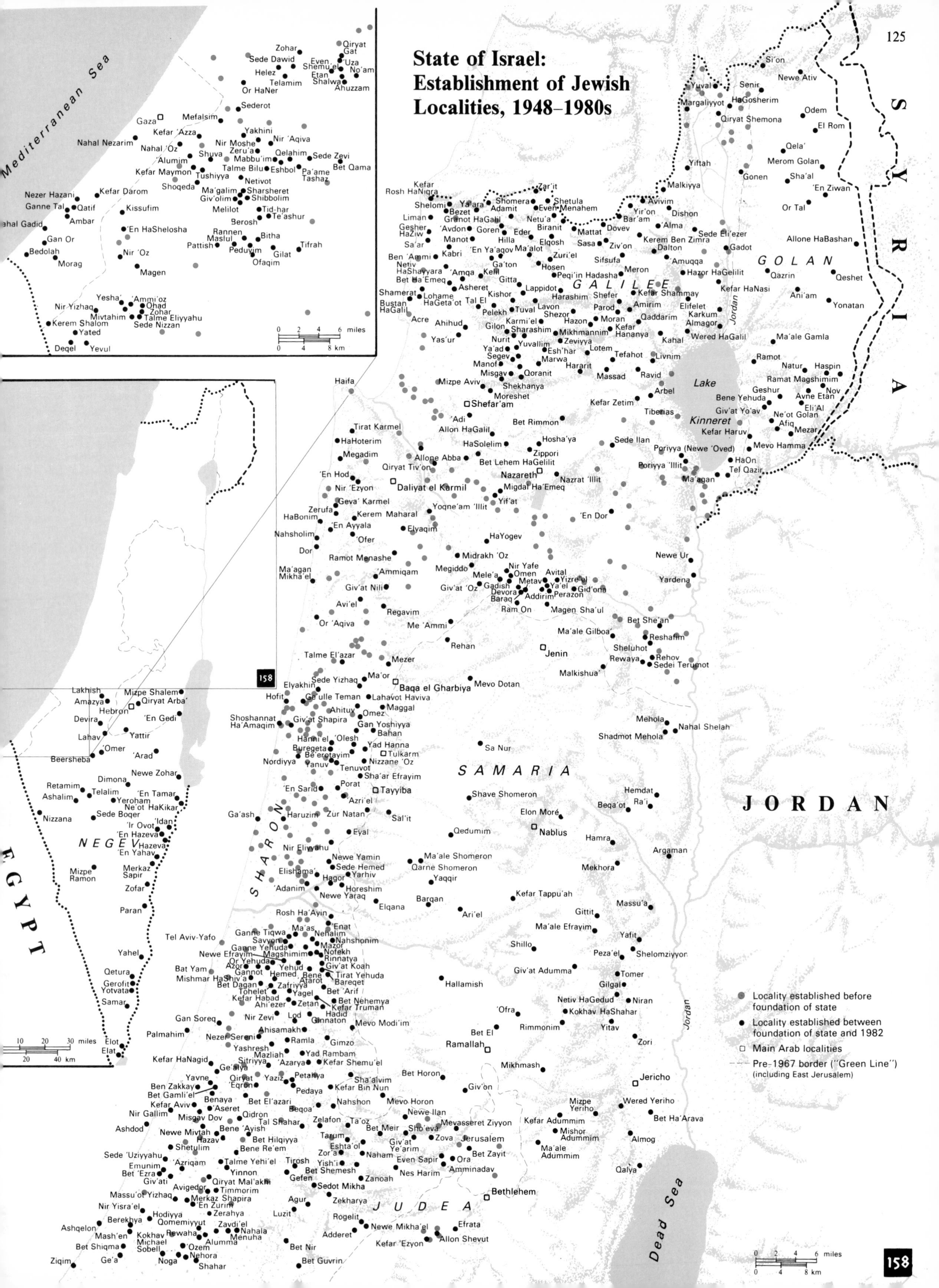

# The Population of Israel: Composition, Religions, and Median Ages

## The Population of Palestine/Israel, by Religion

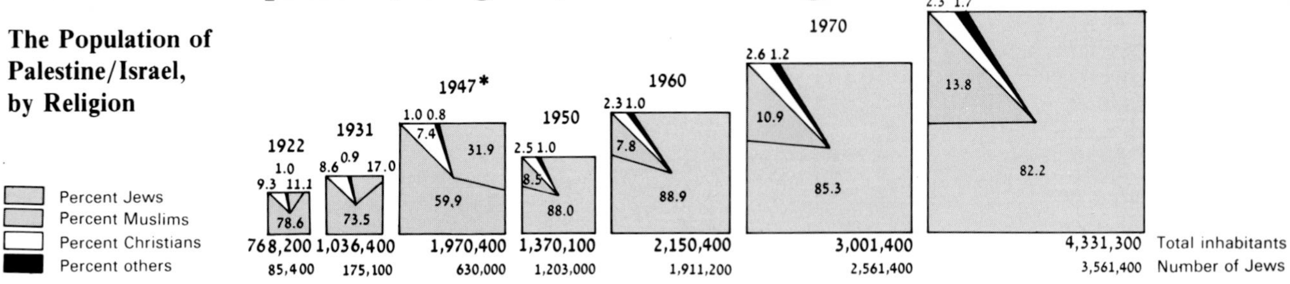


* On May 14, 1948, there were 649,600 Jews in the country

On the eve of the establishment of Israel, the Jews were about one-third of the country's population, as compared with one-sixth in 1922. After the War of Independence, the proportion of Jews to non-Jews in the state of Israel changed radically: in the 1950s, the Jews constituted almost 90 percent of the population. About 650,000 Arabs left Palestine during the war. Some settled in Arab countries around Israel, many in refugee camps. Others emigrated to far-away countries. Another wave of refugees left Palestine during or after the Six-Day War: 100,000 to 150,000 Arabs emigrated from the West Bank between 1967 and 1980. There was also a certain measure of migration among Israeli Arabs: from 1950 to 1972, about 20,000 left Israel and about 12,000 arrived, mostly under the family-reunification program.

Between 1948 and 1977, 745,000 Jews arrived in Israel from Muslim countries. Most came in massive waves, since the situation in their native countries had become untenable. Both waves—the departing Arabs and the arriving Jews—added up to a population exchange that, although unplanned, had a logic of its own.

In the years 1960 to 1986, the proportion of non-Jews in Israel rose again, reaching about 18 percent (Judea, Samaria, and the Gaza Region not included). This was a result of the slowing down of Jewish immigration (*aliyah*) and of the very high natural increase rate of Israeli Arabs.

### Median Ages in the Israeli Population

The median age of the Jewish population in Palestine, and later in Israel, was low, indicating a large number of young people. The median age in the small Arab Christian community was even lower, and that in the larger Arab Muslim population of Israel lower still. The Arab Muslim rate of increase was among the highest in the world, although the trend to urbanization and modernization among Israeli Arabs began to express itself in smaller families.

## Median Ages in Palestine/Israel

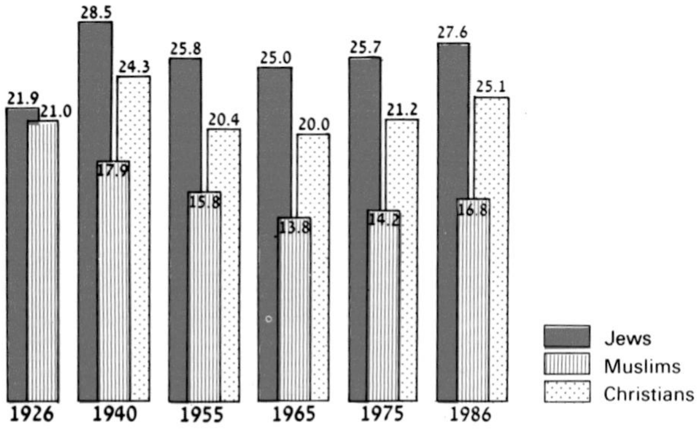


### Origins of Israeli Jews

More than any other country, Israel had a high percentage of people (Jews) born abroad. In the newborn to fourteen-year-old age group, however, which due to the age composition of the Jewish population was very large, more than 90 percent were born in Israel.

### Jewish Emigration (*Yeridah*) from Israel

As usual in lands of immigration, some Jews who came to Israel did not adapt to the country and emigrated again. There were also Israel-born Jews who decided to leave. Most settled in the United States, and others in Canada, South America, and Europe. The number of Israelis living outside Israel in the early 1980s was 350,000 to 400,000, including children born abroad. This meant that about 10 percent of what may be called "Israeli Jews" lived abroad in 1980—a high percentage compared with the nationals of other countries who live abroad. But when considered in the context of the increase in Israel's Jewish population, the proportion of *yordim* (Jews who left Israel) had actually decreased. From 1948 to 1960, six out of every 1,000 Israelis left the country annually; from 1977 to 1982 only 3 out of 1,000 did so.

## Jewish Emigration from Israel

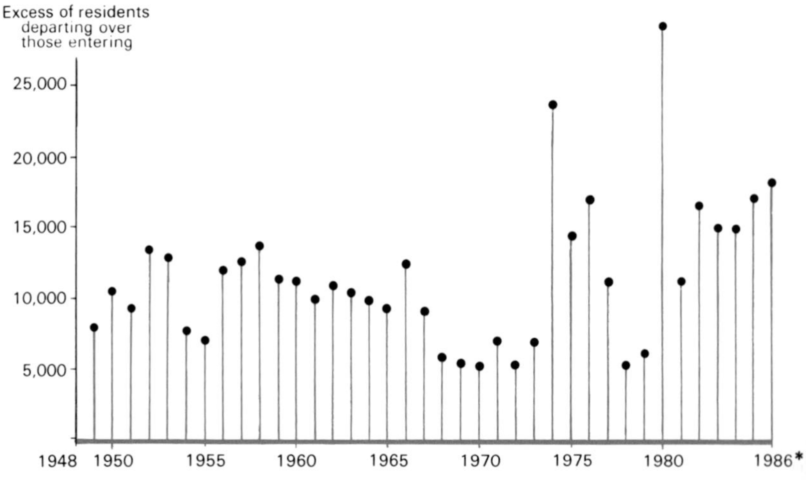


* 1983-1986: Estimates

## Jews in Israel by Place of Origin and Age, 1986

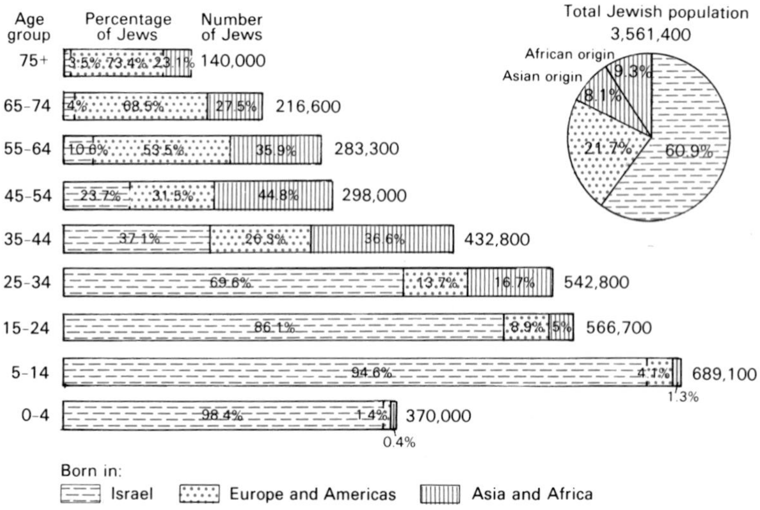

## Parties in the Knesset, 1949–1988

| Parties | Grouping | First Knesset January 25, 1949 | Seventh Knesset October 28, 1969 | Ninth Knesset May 17, 1977 | Twelfth Knesset November 1, 1988 |
|---|---|---|---|---|---|
| Mapai | Labor / Labor Alignment | 46 | | | |
| Ahdut Haavodah | Labor / Labor Alignment | | 56 | 32 | 39 |
| Rafi | Labor Alignment | | | | |
| Mapam | Labor Alignment | 19 | | | 3 |
| National Religious Party (NRP) | (religious) | | 12 | 12 | 5 |
| Agudat Israel | (religious) | 16 | 4 | 4 | 5 |
| Poalei Agudat Israel | (religious) | | 2 | 1 | |
| Progressives (Independent Liberals) | | 5 | 4 | 1 | |
| General Zionists (Liberals) | Gahal / Likud | 7 | | | |
| Herut | Gahal / Likud | 14 | 26 | 43 | 40 |
| Free Center | Likud | | 2 | | |
| State List | Likud | | 4 | | |
| Maki | Communist Party | 4 | 1 | | |
| Rakah (Hadash) | Communist Party | | 3 | 5 | 4 |
| Minorities lists | | 2 | 4 | 1 | 1 |
| Democratic Movement for Change (liberal) | | | | 15 | |
| Citizens' Rights Movement (liberal, left) | | | | 1 | 5 |
| Shas (religious, Sephardic) | | | | | 6 |
| Tehiya (extreme nationalist) | | | | | 3 |
| Shinui (liberal) | | | | | 2 |
| Tzomet (extreme nationalist) | | | | | 2 |
| Moledet (extreme nationalist) | | | | | 2 |
| Degel Hatorah (religious) | | | | | 2 |
| Other lists * | | 7 | 2 | 5 | 1 |

3 Number of Knesset members

* Lists with 1 representative each

## The Government of Israel

The state of Israel is a democratic republic founded on universal suffrage. Its system of government is parliamentary, with a largely ceremonial president, a prime minister and a Cabinet, and a unicameral legislature—the Knesset. Elections are held every four years.

The Knesset has 120 seats that are distributed by proportional representation. Each party offers a list of candidates, and the number of seats is determined by the percentage of votes the party wins.

Since no one party has yet held an absolute majority of the seats in the Knesset, all governments have been coalitions. Israeli politics have been dominated by two major blocs: socialist (Labor) and nationalist (Likud). Until 1977, the Labor Party led the government, generally supported by the National Religious Party and an assortment of smaller parties and independents. In May 1977, the leadership was passed to the Likud Party. In the 1980s, both blocs joined to form a national unity government.

## Urban and Rural Population in Israel

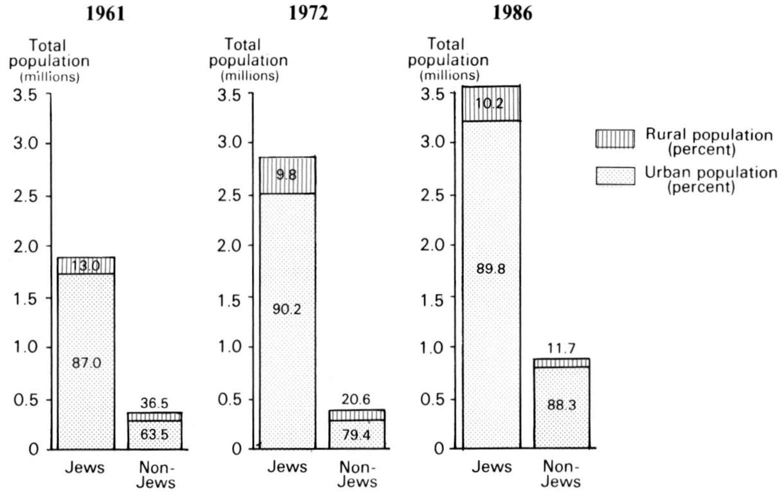


## Marriage Between Jews of Diverse Origins*

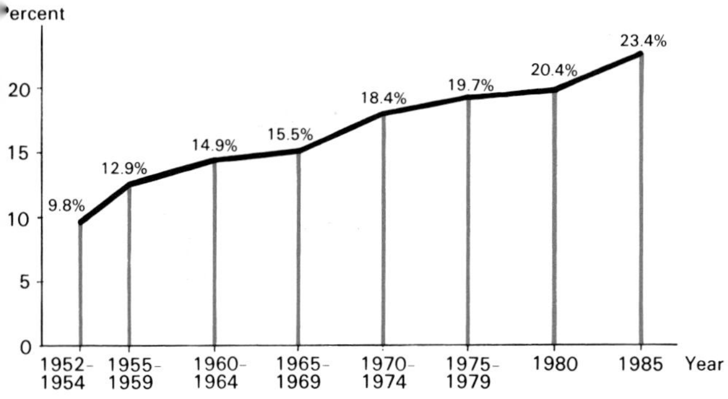


* Jews migrated to Israel from around the world. Marriage between Jews of diverse origins is a fair indicator of Jewish integration in Israel. Israeli population is here divided in the broadest cultural way possible: of European–American and of African–Asian origin, born there or first-generation Israeli. Not indicated are marriages between members of the diverse subgroups inside each of the two broad groups. Latest data (1985) are losing accuracy: about 20 percent of marriages were excluded, being of third or later generation Israelis. It seems apparent that they increased the trend toward integration of the diverse groups.

## Population in the Main Cities, by Religion

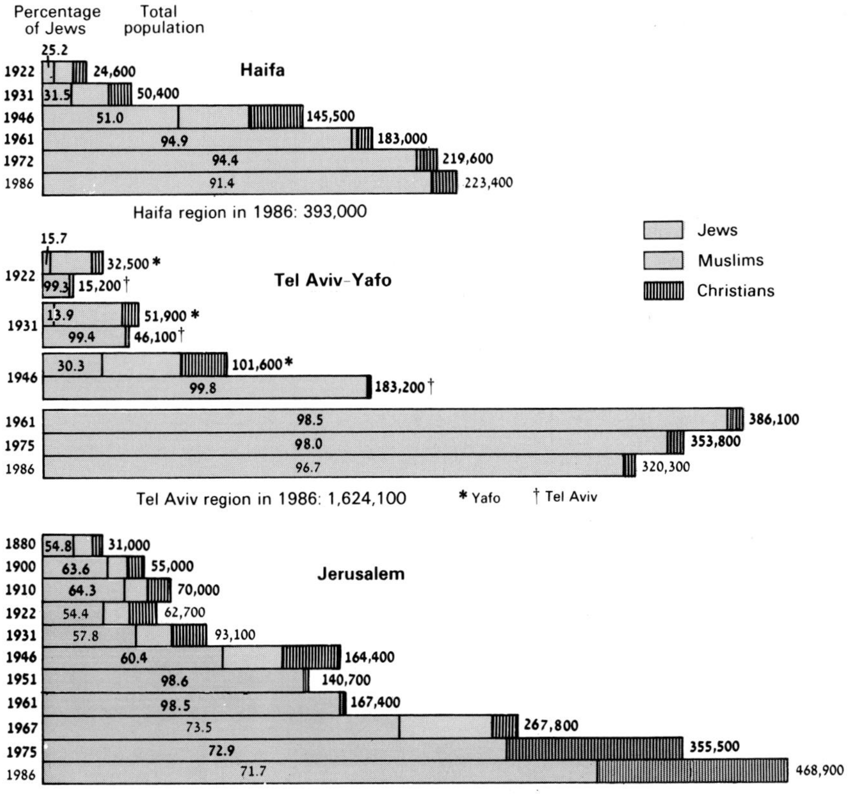

# Jerusalem:

## Nineteenth and Twentieth Centuries

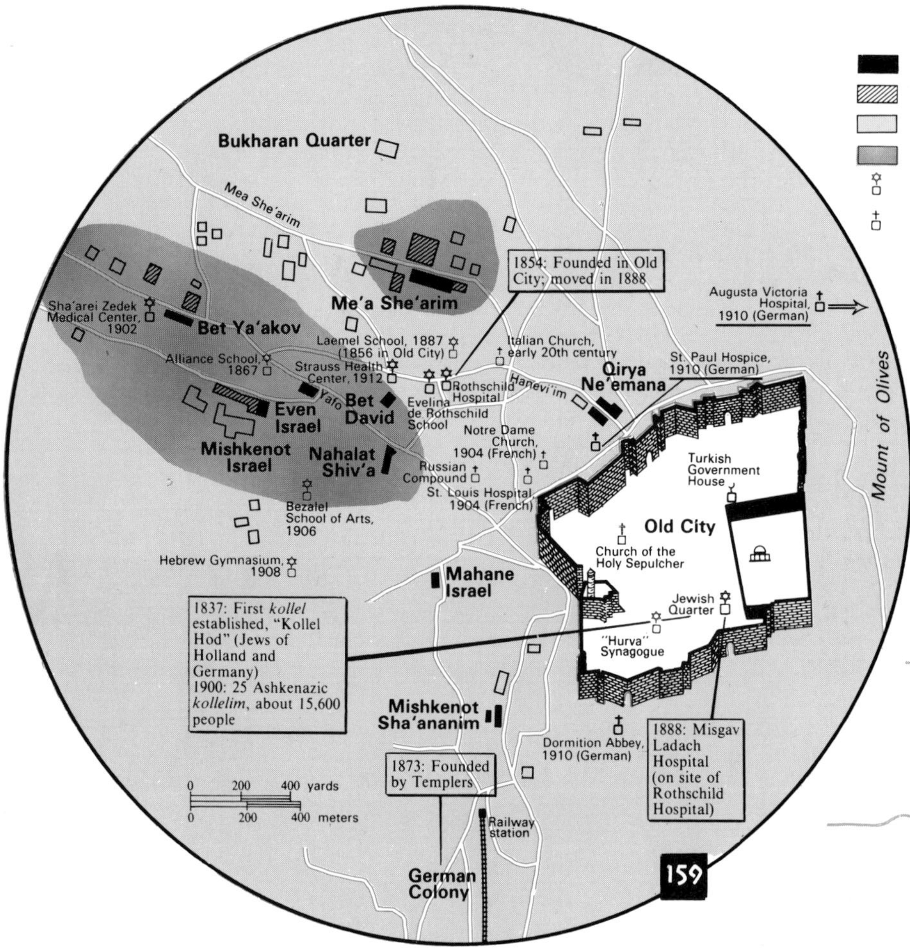


First Jewish neighborhoods outside the walls, 1860–1882
Neighborhood built, 1883–1890
Neighborhood built, 1891–1914
Main settlement area outside the walls
Jewish institution and year of establishment
Christian institution and year of establishment

| Opening of Consulates |
|---|
| 1839: Britain |
| 1842: Prussia |
| 1843: France |
| 1844: U.S. |
| 1849: Austria |
| 1858: Russia |
| 1877: Italy (formerly Sardinia) |

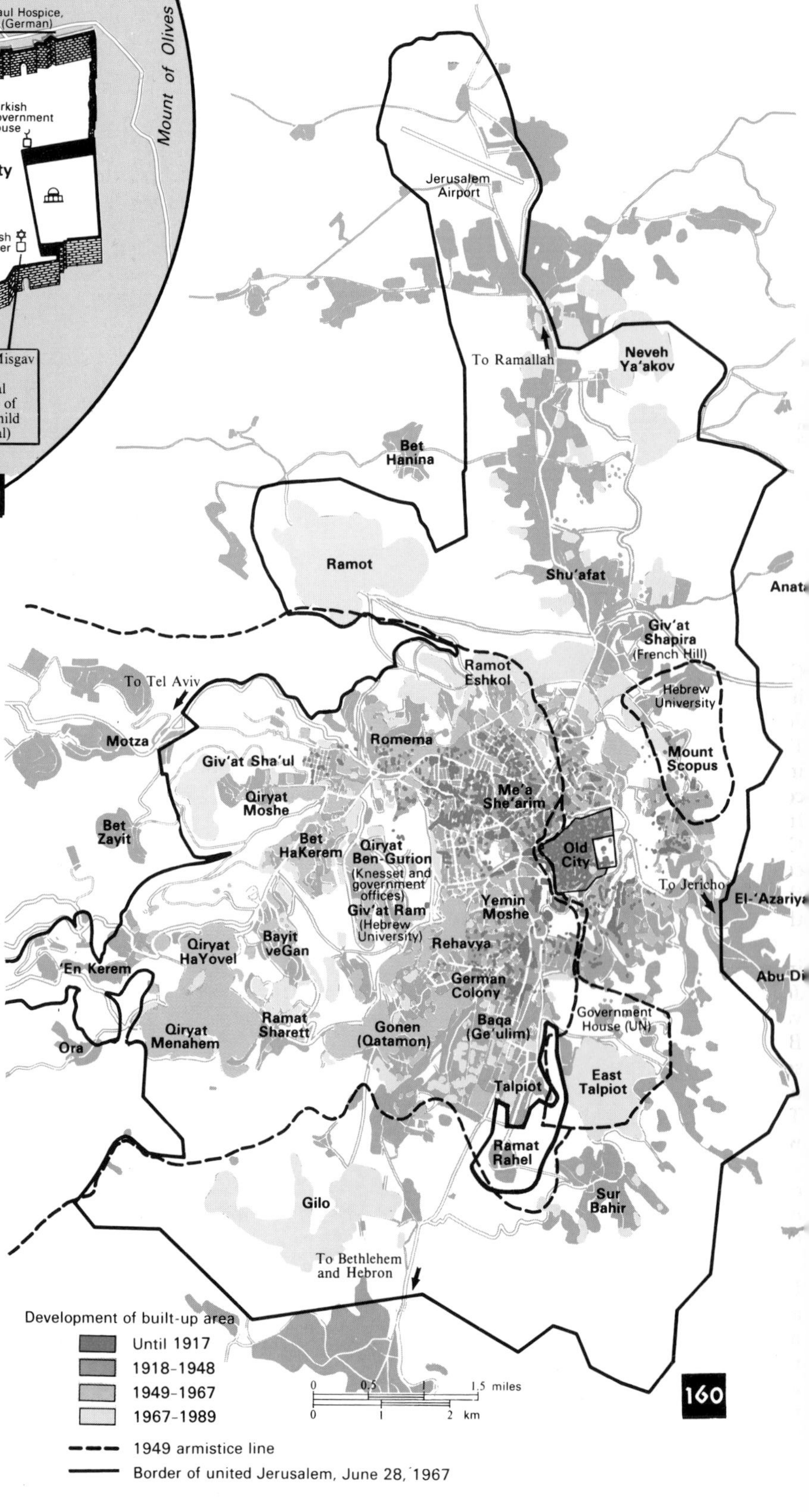


In the nineteenth century, a large part of non-Jewish endeavor in Palestine (as well as of Jewish non-national activities) was centered in Jerusalem. The European consulates and the Christian missions, with their religious, health, and educational work, brought prosperity to the city and attracted additional inhabitants. In the late nineteenth century, the Jews were already a majority of the total population: 60 percent in 1890, and 64 percent in 1910. In 1914, half of the country's Jewish population lived in the city.

The Jews of Jerusalem, mostly Orthodox, were organized according to their various liturgies and places of origin. The basic social structure of each group was the *kollel*, supported by money from abroad. Toward the end of the century, there were twenty-five *kollelim* in Jerusalem, varying in size and economic situation. The Jews also had their own institutions, such as schools (some of them modern) and hospitals. In 1860, the first Jewish neighborhood outside the walls of the Old City, Mishkenot Sha'ananim, was built with the help of Moses Montefiore of England and Judah Touro of the United States. Other Jewish neighborhoods followed. After World War I, under the British administration, Jewish settlement developed in all directions.

After the establishment of Israel, Jerusalem became the capital of the Jewish state. It had a checkered development. As a result of the battles of the War of Independence, the city was divided between Israel and Jordan. In the 1967 Six-Day War, Israel conquered the eastern part and annexed it. Before 1967, non-Jews had constituted 1.6 percent of Jerusalem's population. After the war, the proportion grew to 26.5 percent. Unified, Jerusalem was developed and improved, and the Jewish population grew rapidly, through internal immigration and natural increase. The non-Jewish population also grew. At the end of 1986, the city had 468,900 inhabitants, 71.7 percent of whom were Jews.

# The Jews in Canada: Twentieth Century

### Division of Male Jews by Occupational Branch, 1971
(percent)

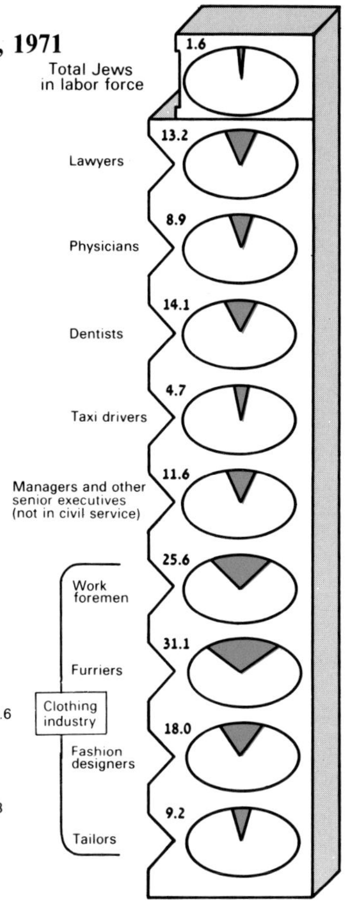


### Occupational Structure, 1971
(males; percent)

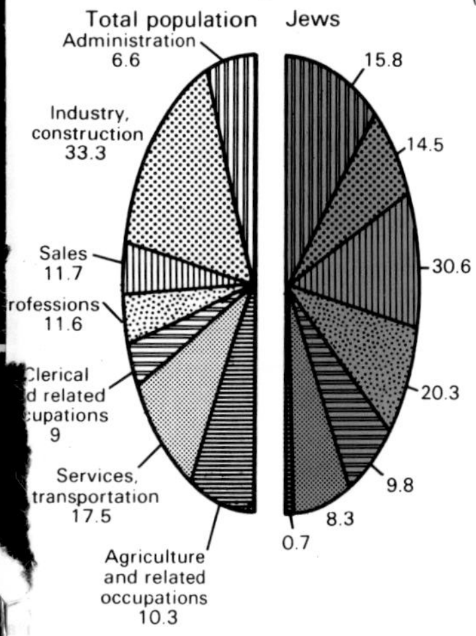


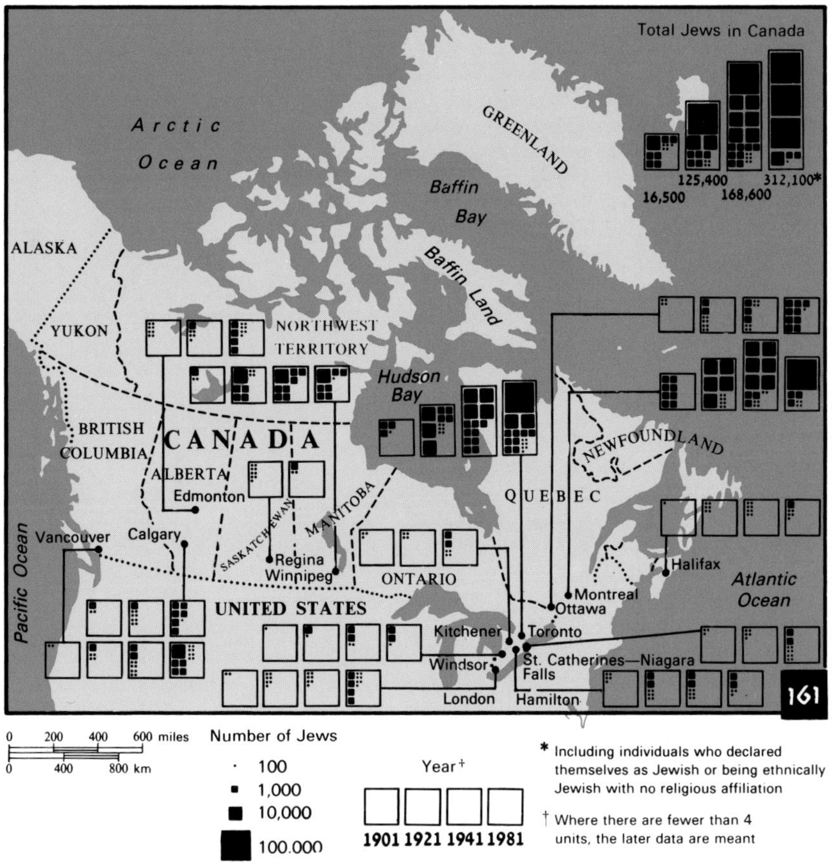


### Natural Increase
(per 1,000 population)

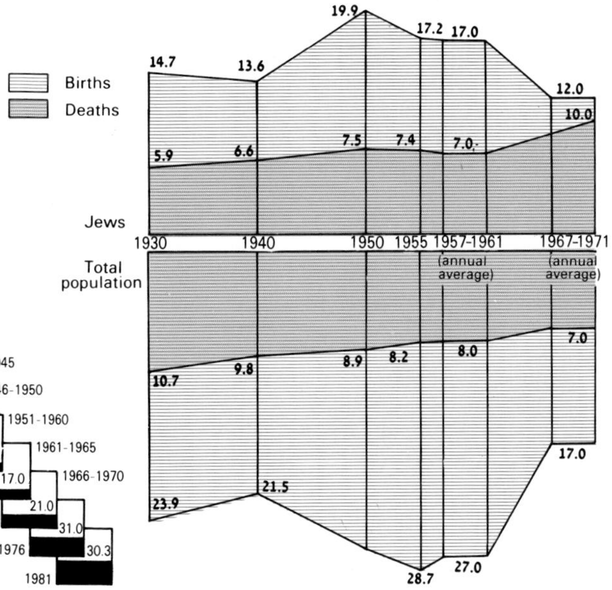


### Out-Marriages by Couples
(percent)

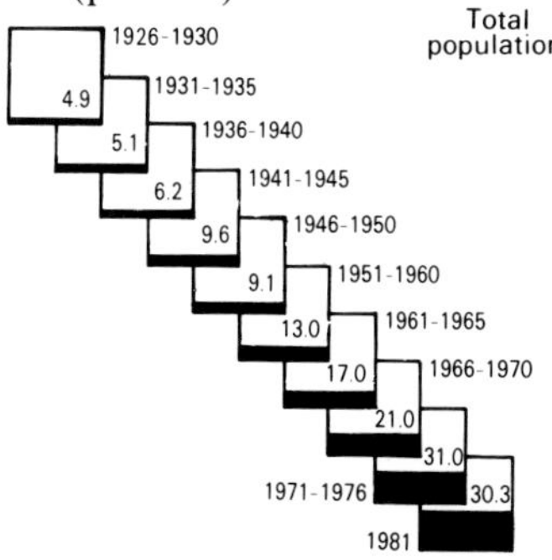

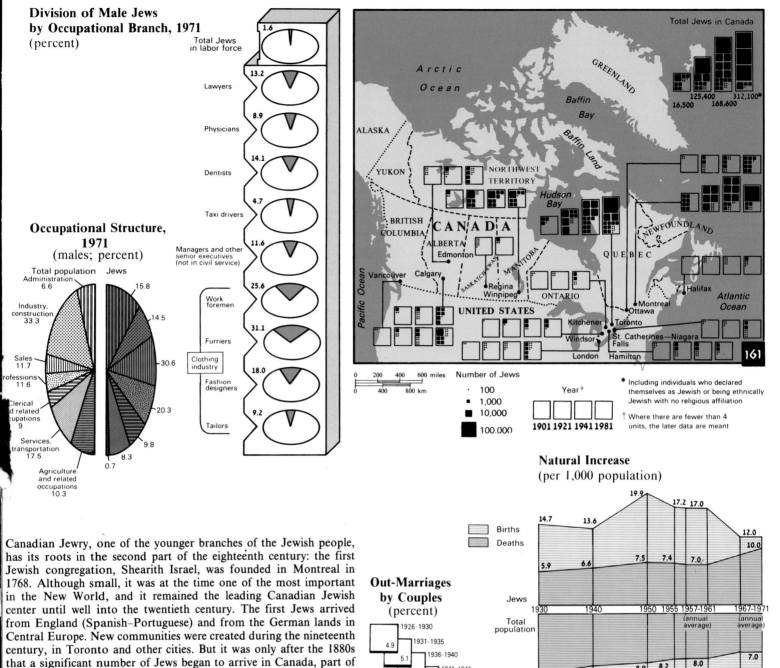

Canadian Jewry, one of the younger branches of the Jewish people, has its roots in the second part of the eighteenth century: the first Jewish congregation, Shearith Israel, was founded in Montreal in 1768. Although small, it was at the time one of the most important in the New World, and it remained the leading Canadian Jewish center until well into the twentieth century. The first Jews arrived from England (Spanish–Portuguese) and from the German lands in Central Europe. New communities were created during the nineteenth century, in Toronto and other cities. But it was only after the 1880s that a significant number of Jews began to arrive in Canada, part of the mass emigration from the Old World.

Although Canadian Jewry was connected with United States Jewry in many ways, it had distinct features. It shared with American Jewry the presence of three major religious trends (Reform, Conservative, and Orthodox) as well as many demographic characteristics. But Canadian Jewry defined itself differently vis-à-vis the general society. In principle, Canada was a binational country, with two officially recognized cultures and languages, English and French. This opened broad possibilities for the self-definition of other groups with a historical, cultural, or national identity, including the Jews. Combined with the fact that most Jews lived in the two major Jewish centers, Toronto and Montreal, this influenced the patterns of Jewish organization: Jewish institutions in Canada were more centralized than those in the United States.

In 1981, the Jews made up only about 1.4 percent of the population. Nevertheless, they were a noticeable element in Canadian life, since about 75 percent of them lived in Toronto and Montreal (each with more than 100,000 Jews), were concentrated in the middle and upper middle classes, and were prominent in the professions, commerce, and industry. Their proportion in several occupations far outstripped their proportion in the general population—a phenomenon found also among Jews in other countries.

### Age Distribution (percent)

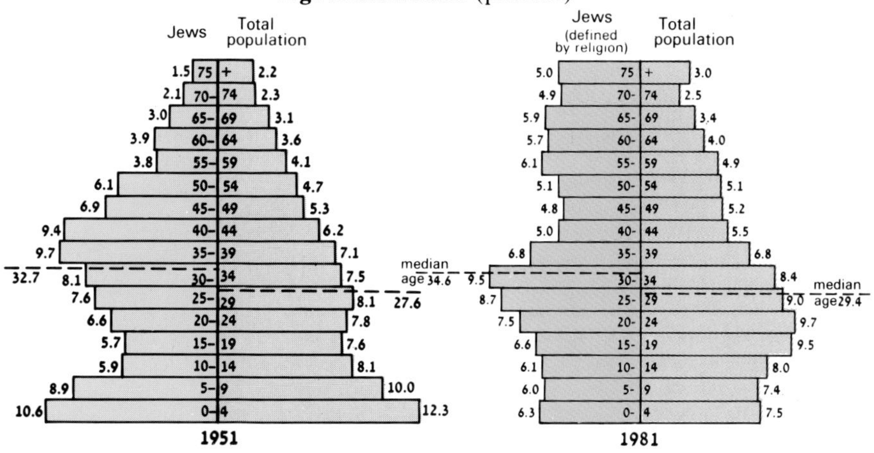

# The Development of American Jewry, 1878–1986

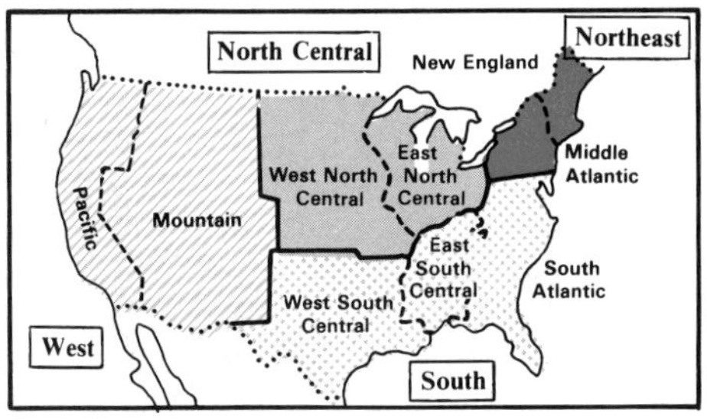


104,300 Number of Jews in subregion
(45.5) Percentage of total American Jews
0.5 Percentage of total population

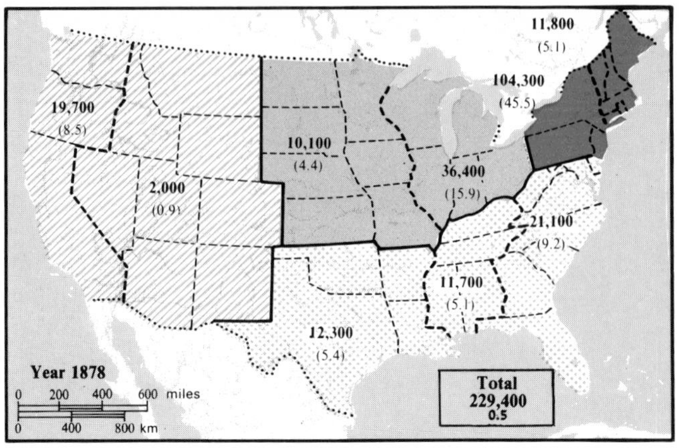


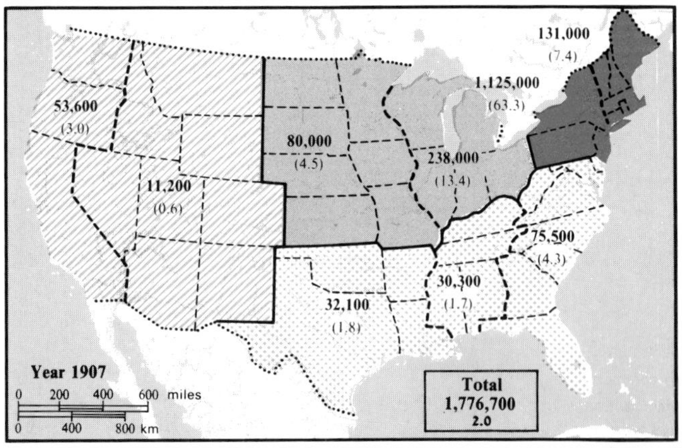


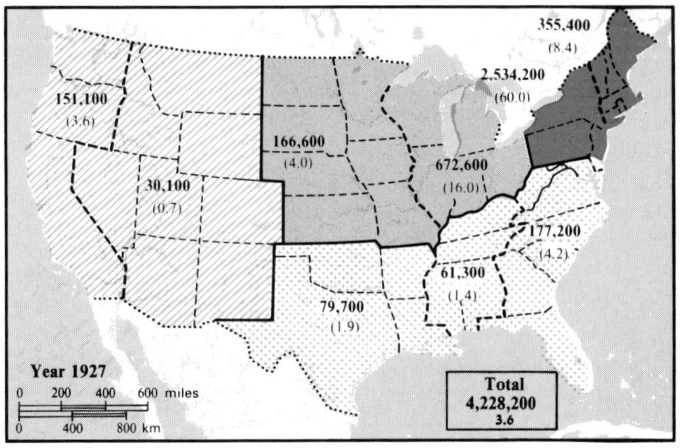


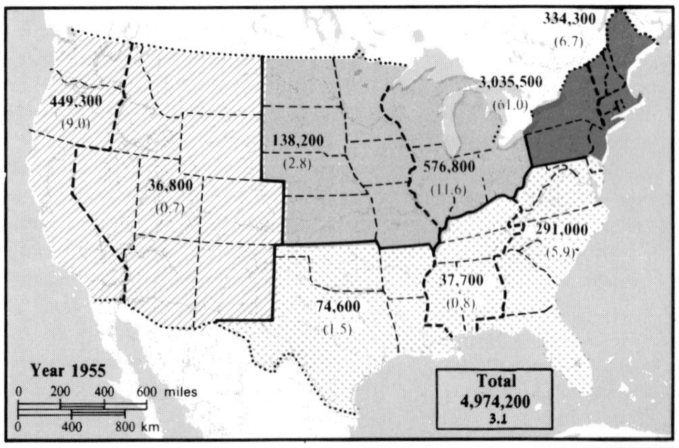


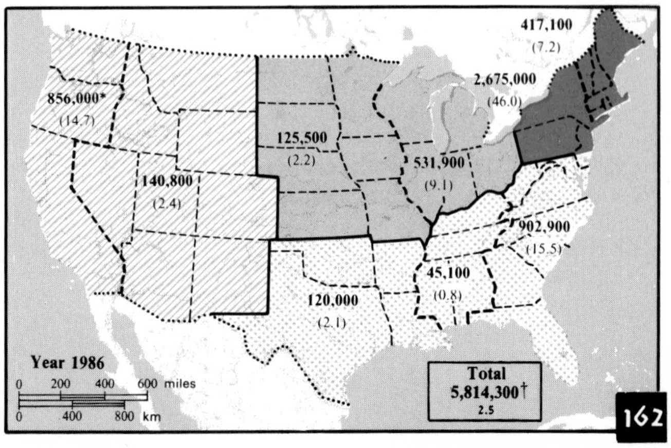


In the 1980s, the largest segment of the Jewish people lived in the United States: 43.9 percent of all Jews, 60.6 percent of all Diaspora Jews. Although the Jews were called "the third religious group in the United States" (after Protestants and Catholics), their proportion in the total population was small and getting smaller: 3.6 percent in 1927 (the high point), and 2.5 percent in 1986. Their numerical weight was larger in some areas: in 1986, 6.3 percent of the population of the northeastern United States (New England and Middle Atlantic regions) were Jews, as were 10.8 percent of the total population of New York State.

Social and geographical mobility were two of the main characteristics of American Jewry in the modern era. Most Jewish immigrants settled in the Jewish quarters that sprouted in most large American cities, especially on the northeastern Atlantic coast. Later, they moved to better neighborhoods, and still later, from the cities to the suburbs. In the 1960s, they began to leave the northeastern United States. Hundreds of thousands of Jews, many elderly, went southward, mostly to Florida. An equally large stream of Jews, usually younger, went westward, especially to California.

New large Jewish centers were created (or existing ones enlarged) in the second half of the twentieth century in the western part of the country: Los Angeles, Phoenix, Houston, San Francisco (whose Jewish community dates to the mid-nineteenth century). This process continued through the 1980s. In 1907, 3.6 percent of all American Jews lived in the West; in 1986, 17.1 percent. Nevertheless, in 1986, more than 50 percent of American Jews still lived in the Northeast. Furthermore, some Jews also returned to the area. In 1986, about 30 percent of American Jews lived in New York City and vicinity. New York continued to be the heart of American Jewry.

In the 1980s, American Jewry was influential in many sectors of American life, and in the life of the Jewish people in general. One century after the start of the large Jewish immigration from Eastern Europe, the Jews had integrated into the land and its culture, done extremely well economically and socially, and created their own patterns of Jewish life and consciousness. American Jewry suffered from the demographic problems characteristic of most Western Jewries in the twentieth century: low rate of fertility, out-marriage, and assimilation. But its large size and relative vitality made it better able to deal with these problems than most other modern Diaspora Jewries.

*Ellis Island: Site of entry to the United States, where millions of immigrants were processed between its opening in 1892 and closing in 1943*

* Including Hawaii and Alaska

† This total is slightly higher than the one indicated on other maps (5,700,000) because it includes non-Jews (less than 2%) living in Jewish households.

## The Jews in the Unites States, 1878

One community / Five communities — By states
Major concentration of Jews, with number
Year of admission to union after 1890

American Jewry as we know it emerged only in the second half of the nineteenth century. There were only 2,000 to 2,500 Jews in the United States at the beginning of the century, in about a dozen communities. By mid-century, the number had risen to 50,000, and by 1880, to about 250,000. Many of the later characteristics of American Jewry were already evident in 1880. There were nearly 300 communities across the land; 50 percent of all American Jews lived in the Northeast; and 64 percent lived in 16 large cities, 30 percent in New York and Brooklyn (a separate city until 1898).

In the 1870s, American Jewry comprised two main types: a small stratum of Sephardim and a much larger group of Ashkenazim from German lands. Jews of Spanish–Portuguese origin had lived in the country since at least the eighteenth century; they were, in general, prosperous and well integrated. The nineteenth-century immigrants from Germany were on their way to prosperity and social adaptation. There was already a large number of East European Jews. Some integrated into "German" congregations; others formed their own synagogues.

In the 1880s, a new period began for American Jewry, with the mass immigration of the "Russians," the Jews from Eastern Europe.

## The Jewish Population in the United States, 1878

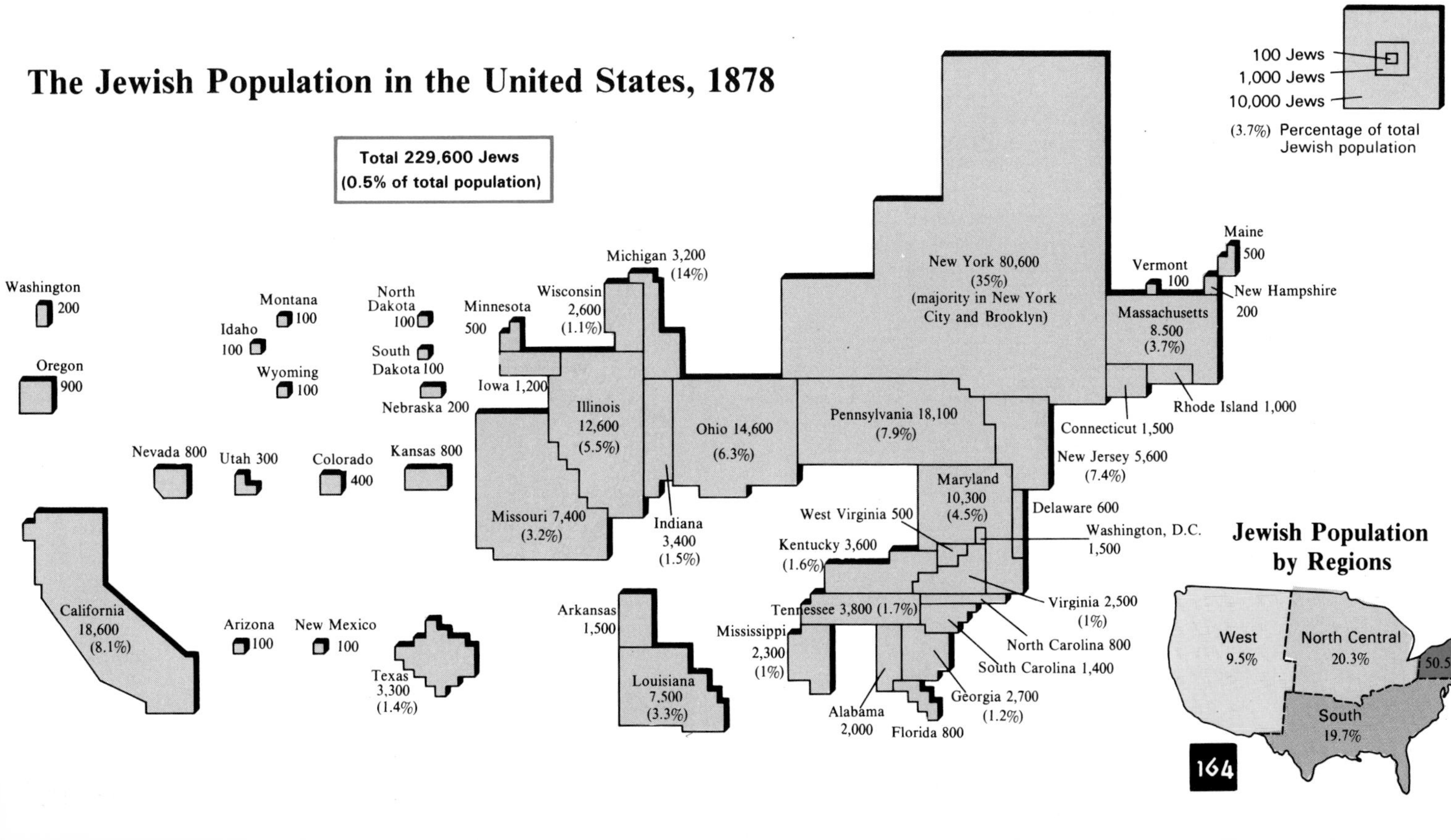

# Jewish Immigration to the United States: Nineteenth and Twentieth Centuries

The mass immigration of Jews to the United States, which started in the latter part of the nineteenth century, was one of the most important developments in modern Jewish history. The Jews were part of an enormous migratory movement, the largest in human history, which in the nineteenth and twentieth centuries brought tens of millions of Europeans to countries throughout the world, especially the United States. Its causes were the population growth in Europe in the nineteenth century, which exceeded the continent's economic capacity and forced people to look for homes in other countries; the development of large steamships, which made sea travel safer, cheaper, and quicker; and the attraction of America, that wide-open country, rich in resources and opportunities.

For the Jews, there were also the specific problems of East European Jewry, such as the oppressive policies of the Russian and Rumanian governments. The semiurban character of the Jews made it easier for them to adapt to conditions in the growing cities of the industrializing countries of the Western world. The relative number of Jews emigrating from East European countries was much higher than that of non-Jews. They settled in Western Europe and in different countries in the Americas, primarily the United States.

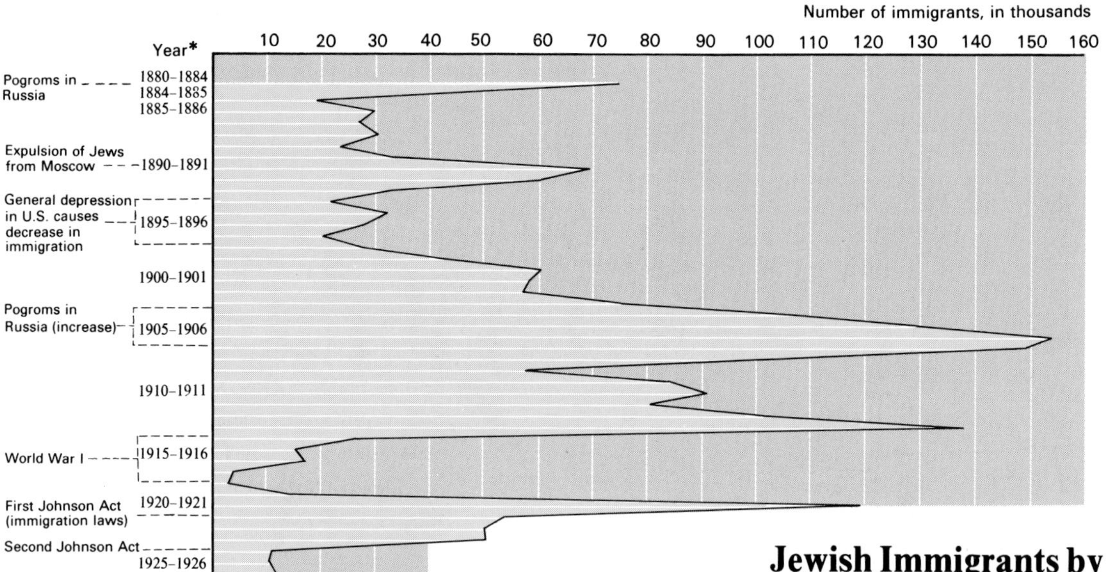
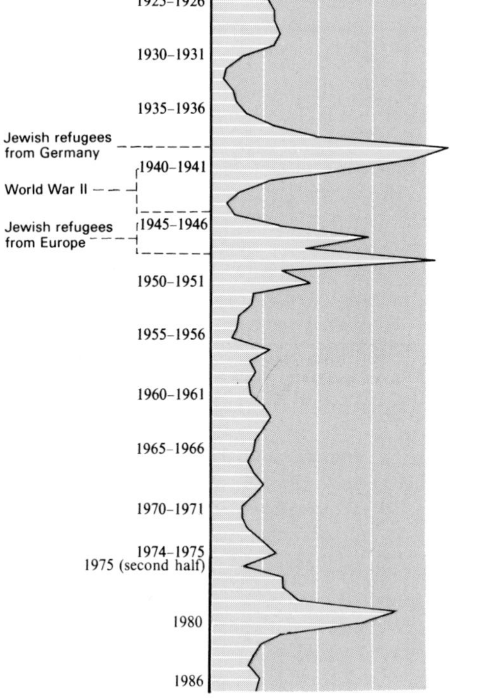


## Jewish Immigration, 1880–1986

**Total of 3,120,000 Jewish immigrants**

* U.S. fiscal year begins July 1 and ends June 30. Data since 1975 by calendar year Data from late 1960s onward included also non-Jewish members of Jewish households, who represented a significant proportion in Jewish families immigrating from the U.S.S.R.

## Jewish Immigrants by Country of Origin, 1899–19

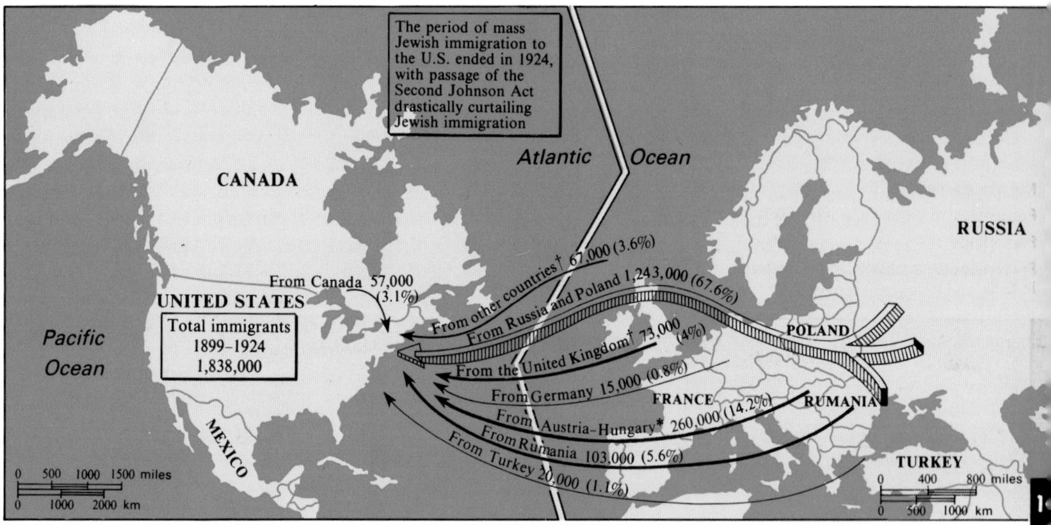


* Including countries that belonged to the empire before World War I, except Galicia after its annexation to Poland in 1919

† Most immigrants from these countries were there only for transition periods and were actually from Eastern Europe

## American Jewry in the 1920s

By 1927, the Jewish population of the United States had grown to more than 4 million and had become the largest Jewish community in the world. In the 1920s, American Jewry comprised two major historical groups: the smaller "German" segment, descendants of nineteenth-century immigrants who had become fully Americanized and achieved confortable social status and economic security; and the larger "Russian" group, immigrants from the various East European countries who had arrived mainly since the 1880s. Many were still newcomers, undergoing the difficult process of economic, social, and cultural adaptation to America. Another sector consisted of second-generation Americans. There were also smaller groups, such as the Jewish immigrants from Muslim countries. The oldest stratum of American Jewry, the Sephardim, had almost disappeared. The second Johnson Act (1924) practically shut the gates of the United States to Jewish immigration from Eastern Europe. About 120,000 Jews entered the United States in 1920 and 1921, only about 12,000 in 1925 and 1926.

In the 1920s, American Jewry underwent great organizational growth. The Jews had brought with them from Europe a rich tradition of communal organization, which developed unhindered in the free atmosphere of the New World. Every possible type of Jewish organization—religious, social, cultural, political—thrived in America. *Landsmanshaftn* (associations of Jews from the same town or region in Europe), fraternal orders, Zionist associations, labor organizations, cultural enterprises, synagogues of every type—all could operate freely in the United States. The number of Jewish organizations ran into the thousands, some of them operating on a national scale, with tens of thousands of members, others on a smaller, local scale.

The synagogue gradually became the center of Jewish communal life, with all the other institutions—educational, social, or political—structured around it. In 1927, there were about 3,000 synagogues in the United States, belonging to three main religious trends: Reform, Conservative, and Orthodox.

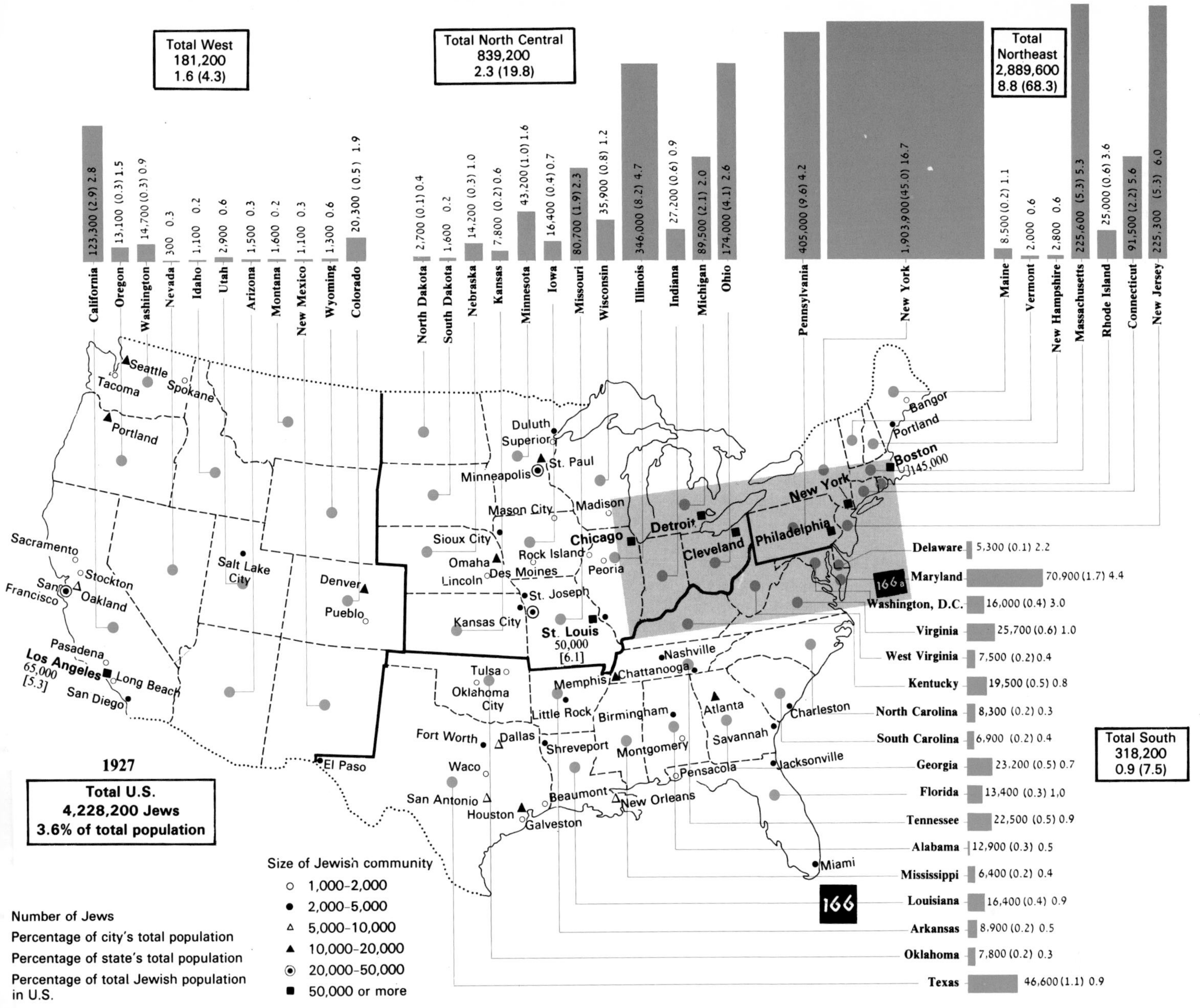
Total West
181,200
1.6 (4.3)
Total North Central
839,200
2.3 (19.8)
Total Northeast
2,889,600
8.8 (68.3)
Total South
318,200
0.9 (7.5)
California 123,300 (2.9) 2.8
Oregon 13,100 (0.3) 1.5
Washington 14,700 (0.3) 0.9
Nevada 300 0.3
Idaho 1,100 0.2
Utah 2,900 0.6
Arizona 1,500 0.3
Montana 1,600 0.2
New Mexico 1,100 0.3
Wyoming 1,300 0.6
Colorado 20,300 (0.5) 1.9
North Dakota 2,700 (0.1) 0.4
South Dakota 1,600 0.2
Nebraska 14,200 (0.3) 1.0
Kansas 7,800 (0.2) 0.6
Minnesota 43,200 (1.0) 1.6
Iowa 16,400 (0.4) 0.7
Missouri 80,700 (1.9) 2.3
Wisconsin 35,900 (0.8) 1.2
Illinois 346,000 (8.2) 4.7
Indiana 27,200 (0.6) 0.9
Michigan 89,500 (2.1) 2.0
Ohio 174,000 (4.1) 2.6
Pennsylvania 405,000 (9.6) 4.2
New York 1,903,900 (45.0) 16.7
Maine 8,500 (0.2) 1.1
Vermont 2,000 0.6
New Hampshire 2,800 0.6
Massachusetts 225,600 (5.3) 5.3
Rhode Island 25,000 (0.6) 3.6
Connecticut 91,500 (2.2) 5.6
New Jersey 225,300 (5.3) 6.0
Delaware 5,300 (0.1) 2.2
Maryland 70,900 (1.7) 4.4
Washington, D.C. 16,000 (0.4) 3.0
Virginia 25,700 (0.6) 1.0
West Virginia 7,500 (0.2) 0.4
Kentucky 19,500 (0.5) 0.8
North Carolina 8,300 (0.2) 0.3
South Carolina 6,900 (0.2) 0.4
Georgia 23,200 (0.5) 0.7
Florida 13,400 (0.3) 1.0
Tennessee 22,500 (0.5) 0.9
Alabama 12,900 (0.3) 0.5
Mississippi 6,400 (0.2) 0.4
Louisiana 16,400 (0.4) 0.9
Arkansas 8,900 (0.2) 0.5
Oklahoma 7,800 (0.2) 0.3
Texas 46,600 (1.1) 0.9
Seattle
Tacoma
Spokane
Portland
Sacramento
Stockton
San Francisco
Oakland
Salt Lake City
Denver
Pueblo
Pasadena
Los Angeles
65,000
[5.3]
Long Beach
San Diego
El Paso
Duluth
Superior
Minneapolis
St. Paul
Mason City
Madison
Sioux City
Omaha
Lincoln
Des Moines
Rock Island
Chicago
Peoria
St. Joseph
Kansas City
St. Louis
50,000
[6.1]
Detroit
Cleveland
New York
Philadelphia
Boston
145,000
Bangor
Portland
Tulsa
Oklahoma City
Memphis
Nashville
Chattanooga
Little Rock
Birmingham
Atlanta
Charleston
Fort Worth
Dallas
Shreveport
Montgomery
Savannah
Waco
Pensacola
Jacksonville
San Antonio
Houston
Beaumont
Galveston
New Orleans
Miami
166a
166
1927
Total U.S.
4,228,200 Jews
3.6% of total population
Size of Jewish community
1,000-2,000
2,000-5,000
5,000-10,000
10,000-20,000
20,000-50,000
50,000 or more
Number of Jews
Percentage of city's total population
Percentage of state's total population
Percentage of total Jewish population in U.S.

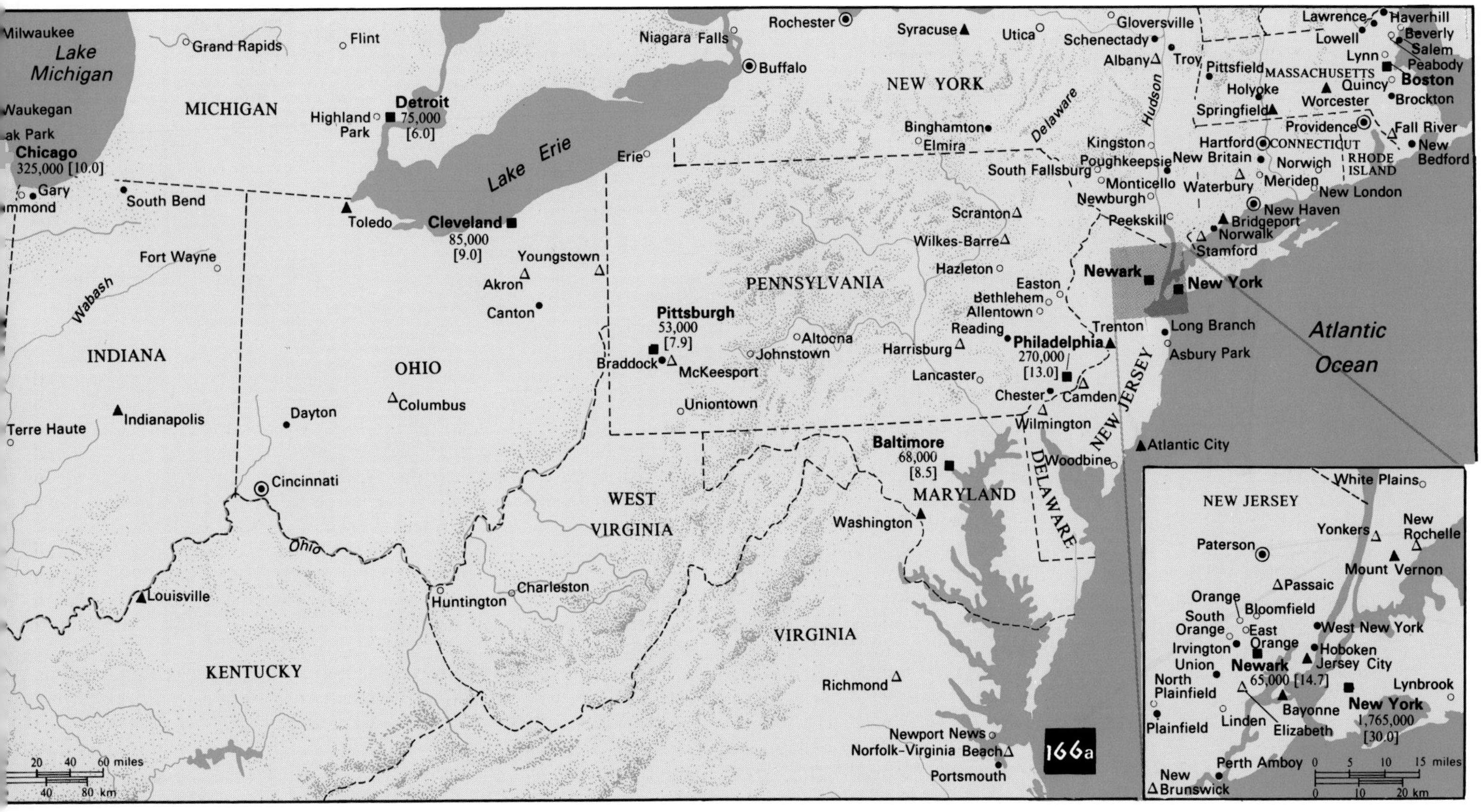
Milwaukee
Lake Michigan
Waukegan
Chicago
325,000 [10.0]
Gary
Grand Rapids
Flint
MICHIGAN
Highland Park
Detroit
75,000
[6.0]
South Bend
Toledo
Fort Wayne
Wabash
INDIANA
Indianapolis
Terre Haute
Lake Erie
Erie
Cleveland
85,000
[9.0]
Youngstown
Akron
Canton
OHIO
Dayton
Columbus
Cincinnati
Ohio
Louisville
KENTUCKY
Niagara Falls
Rochester
Buffalo
Syracuse
Utica
Gloversville
Schenectady
Albany
Troy
NEW YORK
Binghamton
Elmira
Delaware
Hudson
Kingston
Poughkeepsie
South Fallsburg
Monticello
Newburgh
Peekskill
Scranton
Wilkes-Barre
Hazleton
PENNSYLVANIA
Pittsburgh
53,000
[7.9]
Braddock
McKeesport
Uniontown
Altoona
Johnstown
Harrisburg
Easton
Bethlehem
Allentown
Reading
Lancaster
Philadelphia
270,000
[13.0]
Chester
Camden
Wilmington
Trenton
Newark
New York
Long Branch
Asbury Park
NEW JERSEY
Atlantic City
Atlantic Ocean
Woodbine
DELAWARE
Baltimore
68,000
[8.5]
MARYLAND
Washington
WEST VIRGINIA
Huntington
Charleston
VIRGINIA
Richmond
Newport News
Norfolk-Virginia Beach
Portsmouth
166a
Lawrence
Haverhill
Lowell
Beverly
Salem
Lynn
Peabody
Boston
Quincy
Brockton
Pittsfield
MASSACHUSETTS
Holyoke
Worcester
Springfield
Providence
Fall River
New Bedford
Hartford
CONNECTICUT
RHODE ISLAND
New Britain
Norwich
Waterbury
Meriden
New London
New Haven
Bridgeport
Norwalk
Stamford
20 40 60 miles
40 80 km
NEW JERSEY
White Plains
Yonkers
New Rochelle
Mount Vernon
Paterson
Passaic
Orange
Bloomfield
South Orange
East Orange
West New York
Irvington
Hoboken
Union
Jersey City
Newark
65,000 [14.7]
North Plainfield
Bayonne
New York
1,765,000
[30.0]
Lynbrook
Plainfield
Linden
Elizabeth
Perth Amboy
New Brunswick
0 5 10 15 miles
0 10 20 km

# Characteristics of Jewish Immigration to the United States

Between 1899 and 1924, 1,838,000 Jewish immigrants arrived in the United States, 10.4 percent of the total immigration from Europe. More than 90 percent of the Jewish immigrants came from Eastern Europe: 67.7 percent from Russia–Poland, 14.2 percent from Austria-Hungary (mainly Galicia), and 5.6 percent from Rumania. Many of those from other countries were actually of East European origin.

From 1908 to 1924, the Jews were the second largest group of immigrants, after the Italians (whose number was twice as large). But for every 100 Italians who entered the United States in that period, 54.7 left; among the Jews, only 5.2 out of 100 left. This meant that the Jews were in fact the largest group of newcomers, since their net immigration (13.5 percent of the total) was slightly higher than that of the Italians. The Jewish immigration was also more balanced in its composition: 44 percent of immigrants were women (1899–1924), as compared with the overall immigrant average of 31.7 percent; 24.4 percent of the Jews were under fourteen years of age—the overall percentage of children (Jews included) was 12.4. Thus the data show that Jewish immigration was more family oriented and evenly distributed regarding sex and age than was the totality of immigration. It was also more "definitive": the Jews came to the United States to stay.

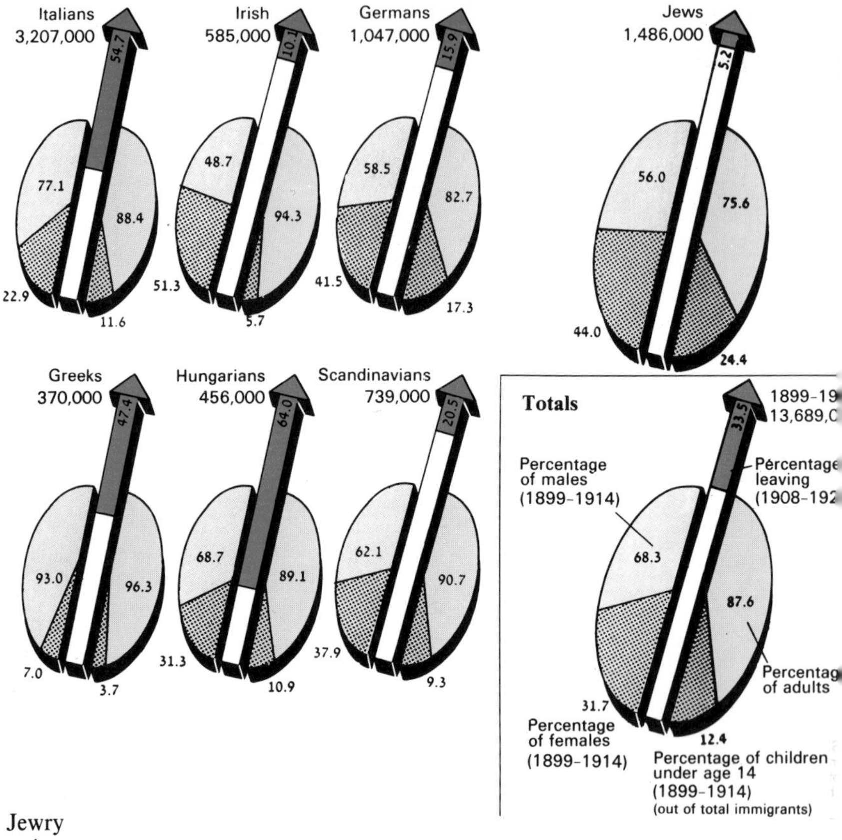


# The Socioeconomic Development of American Jewry

The occupational structure and social status of American Jewry changed profoundly over the generations. Many first-generation American Jews (born in Europe and arrived in the United States as adults) worked as laborers (usually in the garment industry). Later, they or their children went into commerce, mostly small businesses. Some entered occupations requiring a higher education, such as school teaching. A typical figure among the first- or second-generation Jews (born in America, or born in Europe and arrived as small children) was the salesman. In the third and fourth generations, the outstanding phenomenon was the increase of Jews with a university education and prominent in the professions. Parallel to this, Jews developed from small shopkeepers to big businessmen, industrial entrepreneurs, and major providers of services.

The occupational structure of American Jewry differed considerably from that of the general American society, even of whites. Furthermore, their socioeconomic dynamics were unique: rapid development from a largely working- and lower-middle-class group to a predominantly middle- and upper-middle-class one.

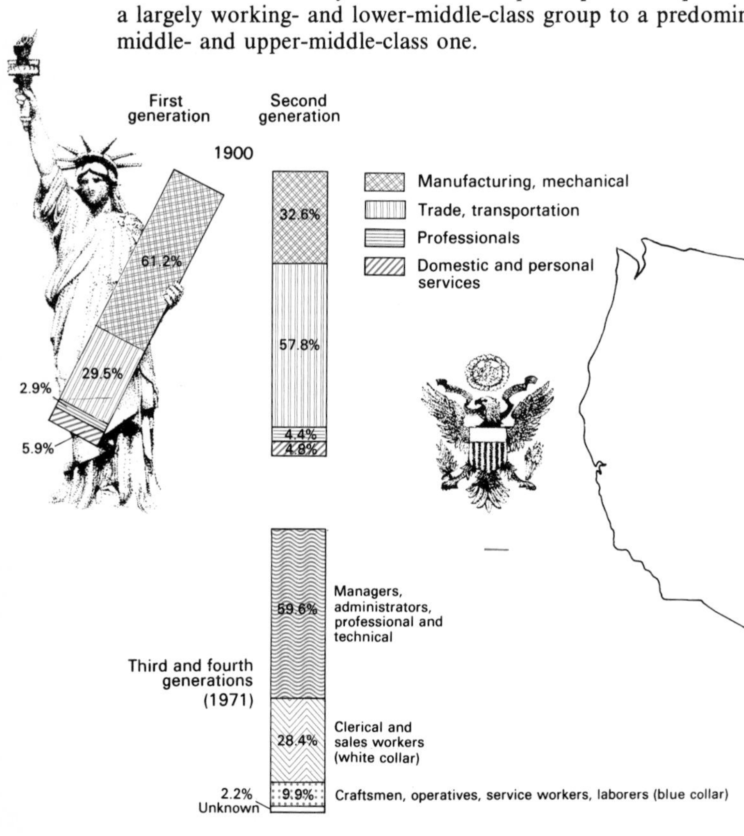


# Occupations of Jews in the United States

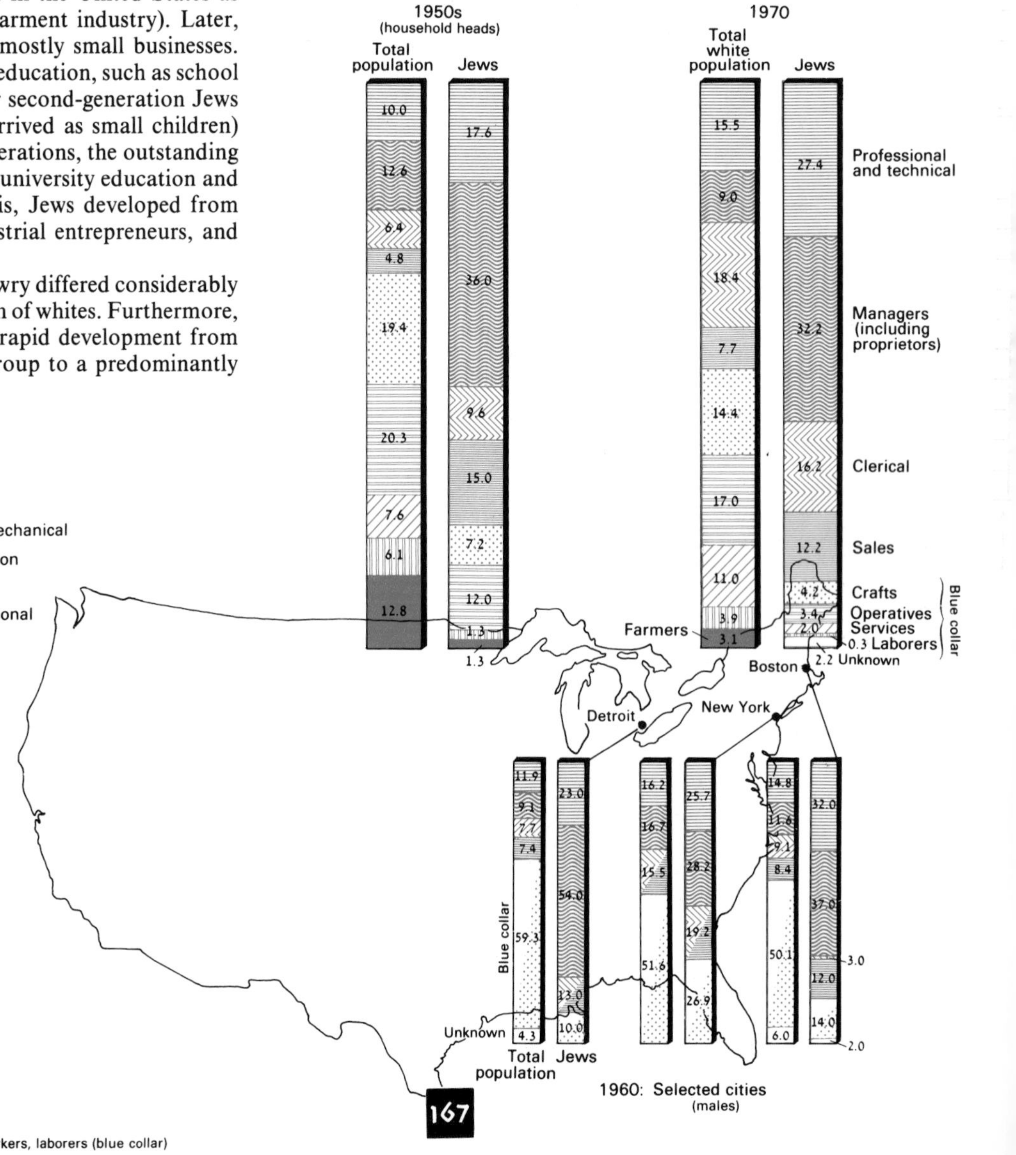

## The Jewish Labor Movement in the United States

Many of the Jewish immigrants who arrived in the United States beginning in the 1880s began their life in the country as workers, mostly in the various branches of the garment industry. A Jewish working class, with a highly cultivated political and social consciousness, developed in the large cities, especially New York. The arrival in America of Jewish political activists, many associated with the Bund, who left Russia after the failure of the first Russian revolution (1904–1906), provided the American Jewish labor movement with a cadre of experienced political leaders.

The Jewish workers formed a sophisticated organizational network and participated in the establishment and development of the general American labor movement, in which they played an important part. Through negotiations and strikes, they improved working conditions. But they also created social and cultural frameworks that were Jewish in language (Yiddish) and content.

In the 1920s, the labor organizations, especially those with a strong Jewish membership, were racked by the struggle between socialists and Communists. On the whole, the socialists had the upper hand. These struggles, together with the gradual de-proletarianization of the Jewish immigrants after their entry into middle-class occupations, considerably diminished the importance of the working sector in American Jewry.

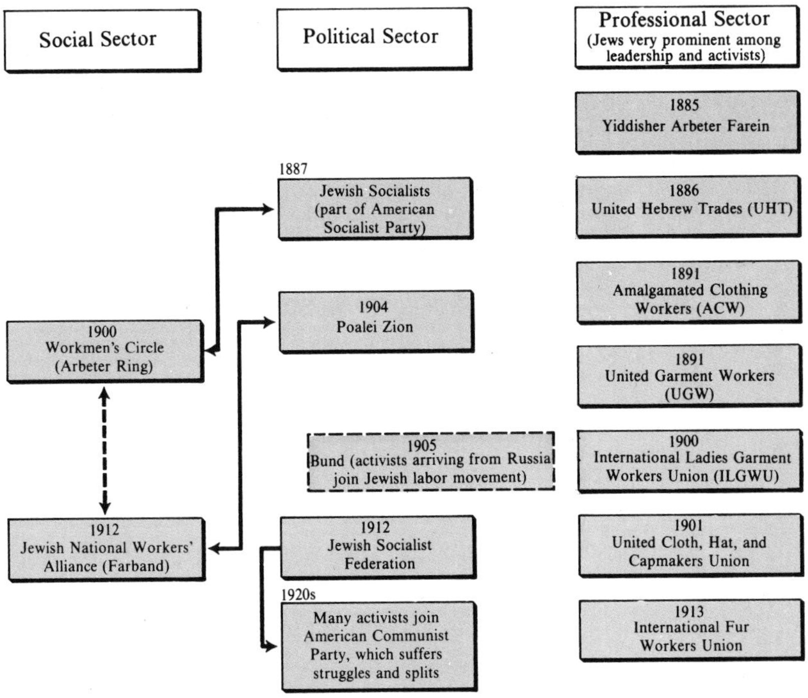


Since 1971, there has been no nationwide research on out-marriage among American Jews, but there is an accumulation of local data indicating a continuation of the tendencies in the accompanying diagram.

| Community | Year of Marriage | Out-Marriage (percent; individuals) |
|---|---|---|
| Canada* | 1981 | 28 |
| U.S.: St. Louis† | 1975-1984 | 25 |
| Kansas City | 1975-1984 | 46 |
| Boston | 1985 | 29 |

| Community | Year of Marriage | Percentage by Age Group 18-29 (individuals) |
|---|---|---|
| Los Angeles | 1979 | 33 |
| Cleveland | 1980 | 24 |
| Chicago | 1981 | 16 |
| Milwaukee | 1983 | 28 |
| Phoenix | 1983 | 40 |
| Washington‡ | 1983 | 28 |
| Philadelphia | 1983-1984 | 34 |
| Pittsburgh | 1984 | 29 |
| Richmond† | 1984 | 44 |
| Baltimore | 1985 | 24 |

* Official vital statistics, excluding Quebec
† Including persons converted to Judaism
‡ Ages 18 to 24

## Out-Marriage Among American Jews

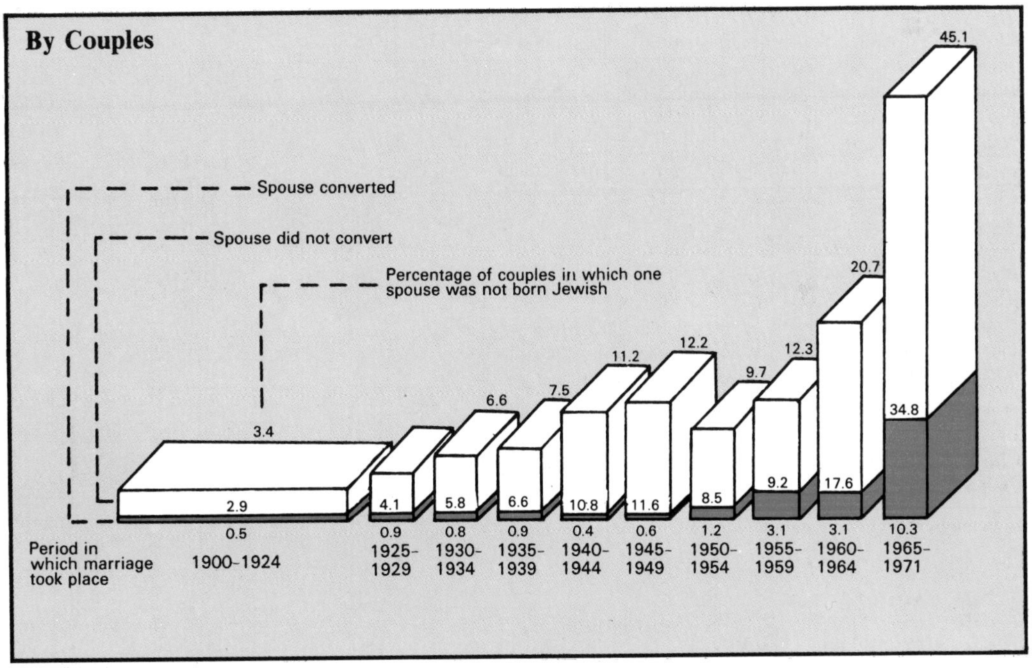


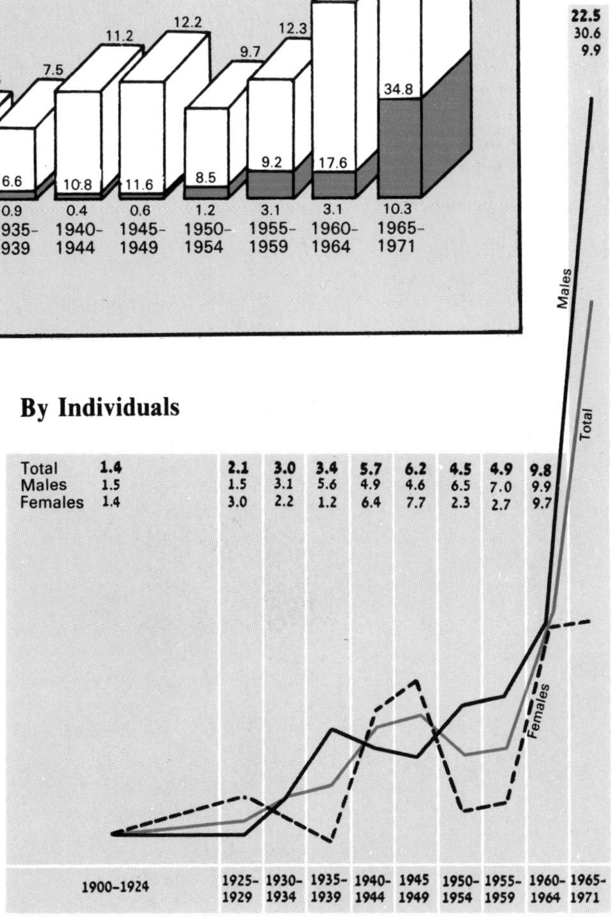


In 1971, the spouses of 8.1 percent of married American Jews were born non-Jews (1.3 percent of whom had converted). Calculated by couples, 15 percent of couples had one partner who was not born Jewish. But if we consider only the years 1965 to 1971, 29.2 percent of Jews who married did so to spouses who were not born Jewish (6.7 percent of whom had converted). There was a non-Jewish partner in 34.8 percent of all couples, deducting conversions; if we take into account all those born non-Jewish (even if converted later), 45.1 percent of marriages between 1965 and 1971 involving a Jew were to a spouse who was not born Jewish. Additional research in several American Jewish communities showed an even greater tendency to out-marriage in later years.

In the past, Jewish men had out-married much more than Jewish women. But about 25 percent of non-Jewish women who married Jews converted, while few non-Jewish men marrying Jewish women did so; 49 percent of the children of out-marriages born before 1971 were Jewish (by their parents' definition). Between 1965 and 1971, however, only 25 percent of the children born of out-marriages were Jewish.

# American Jewry, 1986

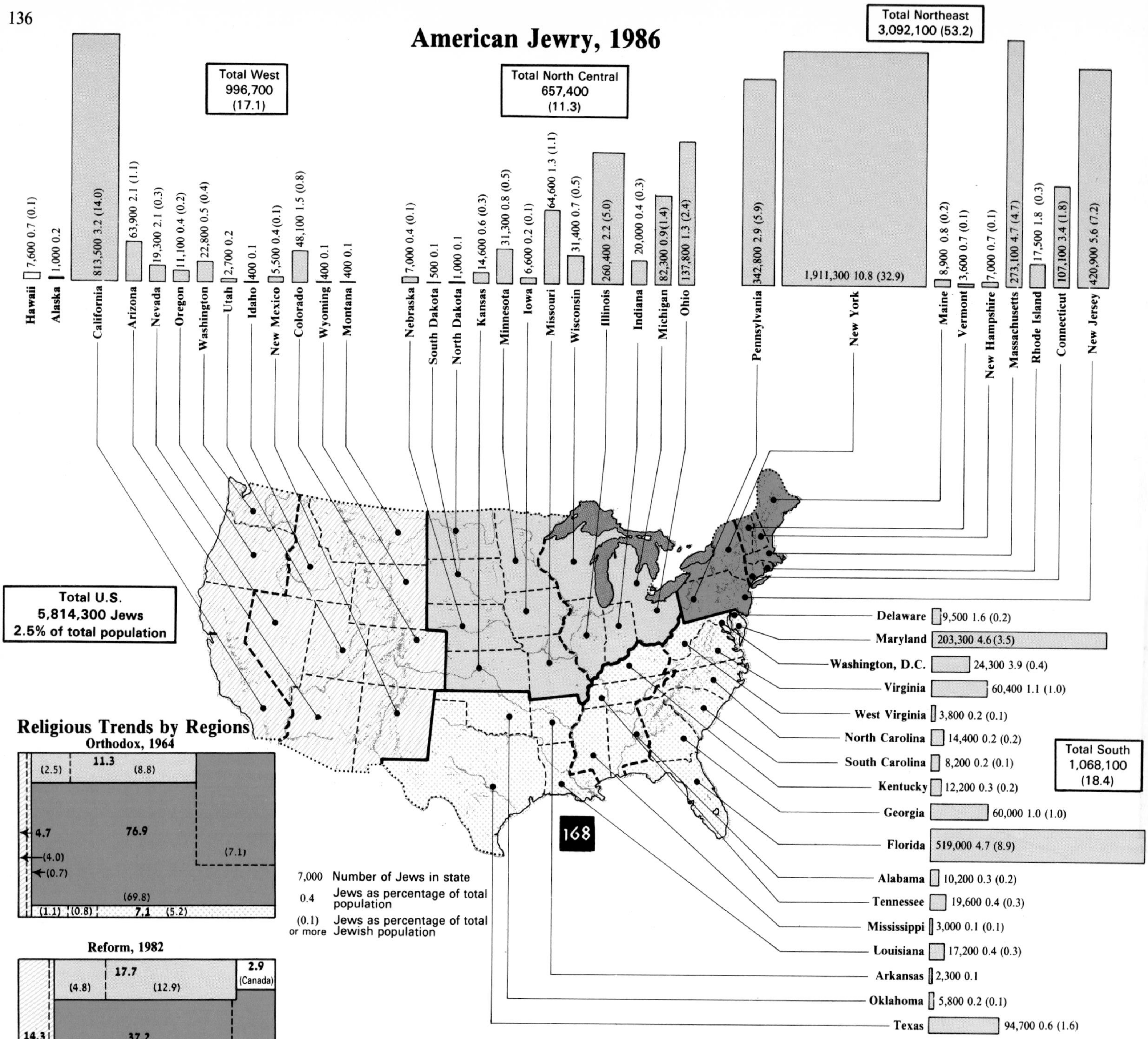


## Religious Trends by Regions

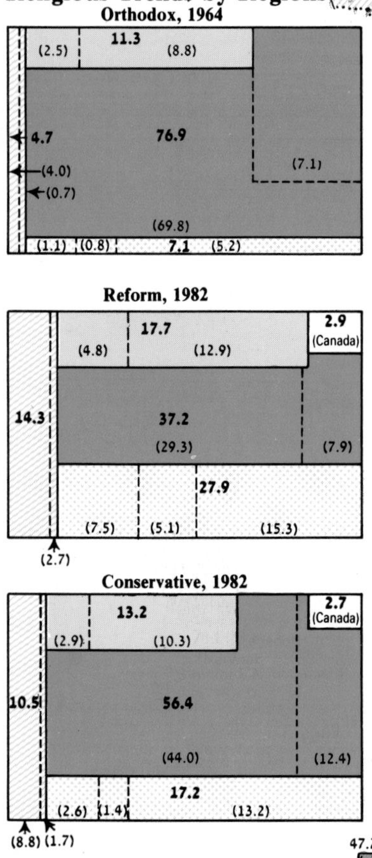


## Religious Affiliation*, 1970s

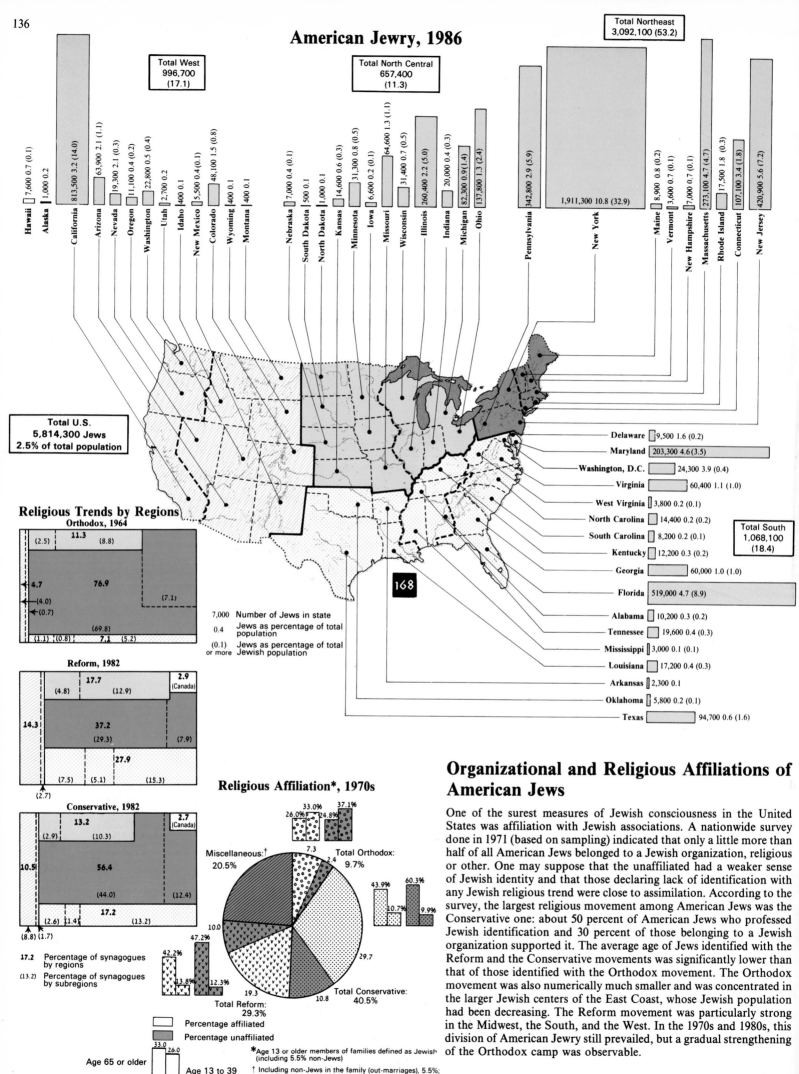

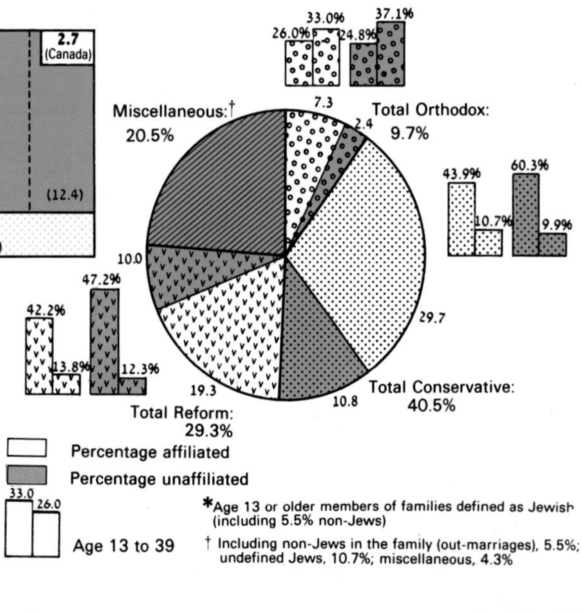


*Age 13 or older members of families defined as Jewish (including 5.5% non-Jews)

† Including non-Jews in the family (out-marriages), 5.5%; undefined Jews, 10.7%; miscellaneous, 4.3%

## Organizational and Religious Affiliations of American Jews

One of the surest measures of Jewish consciousness in the United States was affiliation with Jewish associations. A nationwide survey done in 1971 (based on sampling) indicated that only a little more than half of all American Jews belonged to a Jewish organization, religious or other. One may suppose that the unaffiliated had a weaker sense of Jewish identity and that those declaring lack of identification with any Jewish religious trend were close to assimilation. According to the survey, the largest religious movement among American Jews was the Conservative one: about 50 percent of American Jews who professed Jewish identification and 30 percent of those belonging to a Jewish organization supported it. The average age of Jews identified with the Reform and the Conservative movements was significantly lower than that of those identified with the Orthodox movement. The Orthodox movement was also numerically much smaller and was concentrated in the larger Jewish centers of the East Coast, whose Jewish population had been decreasing. The Reform movement was particularly strong in the Midwest, the South, and the West. In the 1970s and 1980s, this division of American Jewry still prevailed, but a gradual strengthening of the Orthodox camp was observable.

# ewish Centers in the United States, 1986

The urbanization trend in the U.S. and the concentration of Jews in the suburbs resulted in 2 new demographic phenomena: (1) urban communities, including smaller cities, that appeared separately on the 1927 map; (2) combining suburbs in a particular county into a single concentration of an urban character also embracing communities that appeared separately on the 1927 map. For example, the Oakland, California, community is included in the designation "Alameda and Contra Costa counties."

Number of Jews in city/in concentration of communities in county

- ○ ⊙ 1,000–2,000
- • ⊙ 2,000–5,000
- △ △ 5,000–10,000
- ▲ ▲ 10,000–20,000
- ◉ ◉ 20,000–50,000
- ■ ■ 50,000 or more
- 92,000 Number of Jews in city

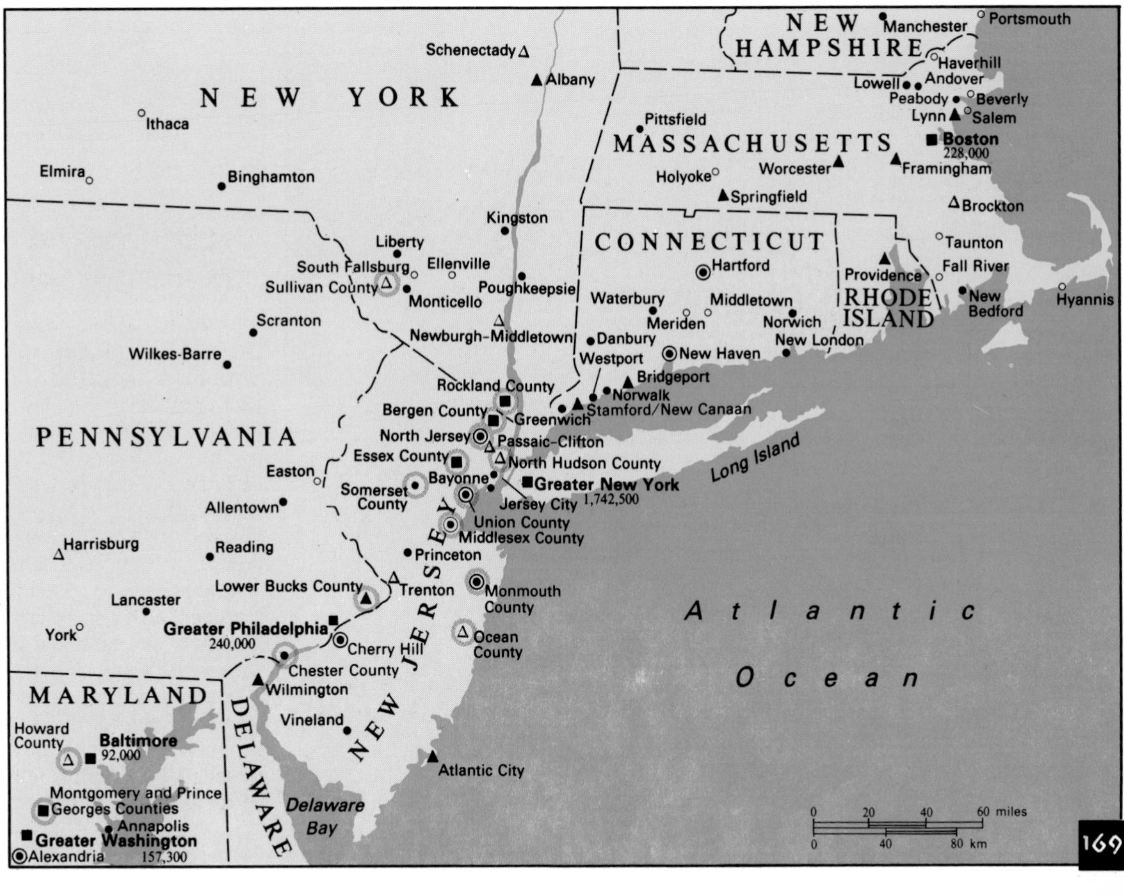


## ducational Level in the United States

(age 25 and older)

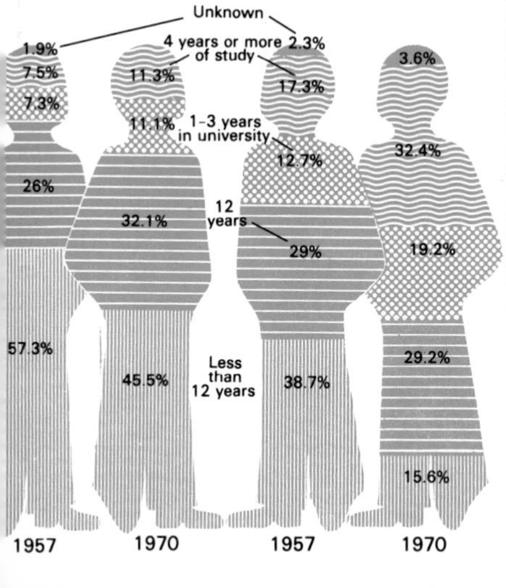

# The Jews in New York City

## Jewish Institutions in Manhattan Until 1914

1. 1695: Beaver Street
2. 1729–1860: Mill Street
6. 1860–1883: Crosby Street
11. 1883–1897: Nineteenth Street
29. From 1897: Seventieth Street and Central Park West

} Shearith Israel Congregation (Sephardic)

4. 1827–1849: Elm Street
7. 1850–1865: Greene Street
19. 1865–1884: Thirty-fourth Street
28. 1885–1917: Madison Avenue

} B'nai Jeshurun Congregation (first Ashenazic synagogue)

5. 1847–1854: Chrystie Street
9. 1854–1867: Twelfth Street
22. 1867–1929: Forty-third Street

} Temple Emanu-El

27. Rodeph Shalom Congregation (1847)
23. Central Synagogue (1872)
30. Temple Beth El
31. Sha'arei Tephillah Synagogue
59. Ohab Tzedek Synagogue

37. Chatham Square cemetery (1680s)
8. Eleventh Street cemetery
12. Twenty-first Street cemetery

35. Mount Sinai Hospital (1853)
45. Beth Israel Hospital (1890)
55. Jewish Maternity Hospital

34. Montefiore Home (1884)
33. Hebrew Benevolent and Orphan Asylum
55. Home for the Aged
55. Hebrew Sheltering House
13. Hebrew Charities Building
55. Hebrew Immigrant Aid Society (HIAS)
17. Federation of Jewish Philanthropies
56. Young Men's Benevolent Association

51. Educational Alliance (1893)
61. Educational Alliance, branch A
64. Hebrew Technical Institute for Boys
55. Hebrew Technical School for Girls
26. Baron de Hirsch Trade School
44. Rabbi Isaac Elchanan Yeshiva
53. Machzike Talmud Torah
57. Beth Hamidrash Hagadol
32. Jewish Theological Seminary of America (1902)

24. Independent Order B'nai B'rith (1843)
42. Independent Order B'nai B'rith, branch
62. Independent Order B'rith Abraham (1887)
36. Young Men's Hebrew Association (1901)
60. Independent Order B'rith Shalom (1905)
14. The *Kehillah* of New York (1909)
25. Intercollegiate Menorah Association (1913)
10. American Jewish Committee (1906)
18. Various Jewish social associations
21. Harmonie Club
63. Cooper Union
20. Federation of American Zionists (1898)
43. Federation of American Zionists (1914)

15. *American Hebrew* (1879)
3. *Hebrew Standard* (1883)
46. *Der Morgen Journal* (1901)
50. *Der Tog* (1914)
39. *Der Tegliche Herold* (1891)
47. *Die Yiddishe Welt* (1902)
48. *Forverts* (1897)
49. *Tageblat* (1885)

38. Windsor Theater
40. Yiddish Rialto (theater)
41. Grand Theater
58. People's Theater

54. Henry Street Settlement and Clinton Hall
16. Madison Square Garden

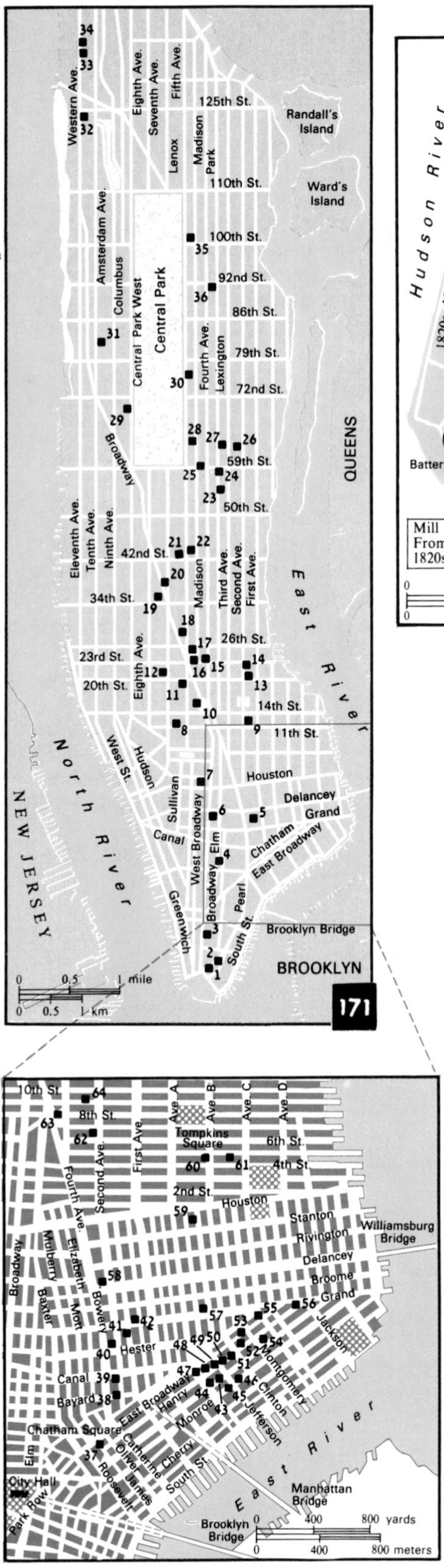


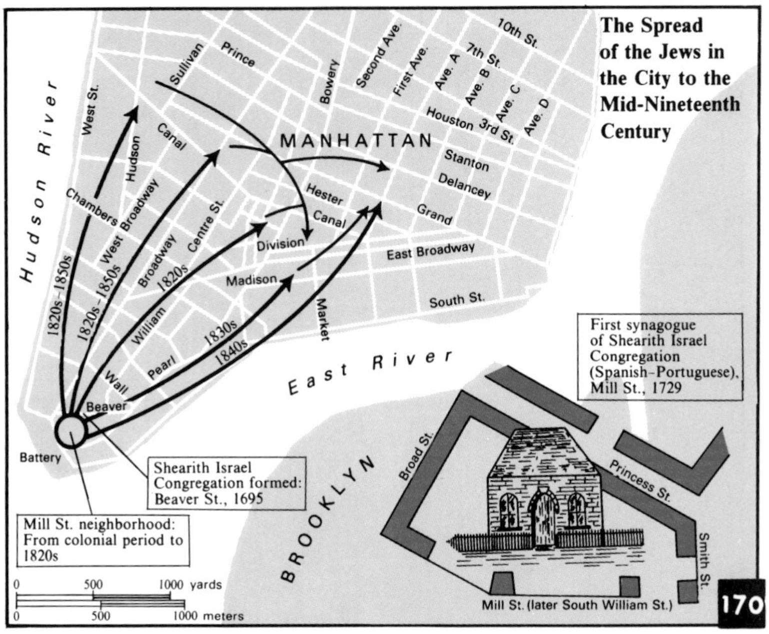


## The Jewish Population in New York City, 1917

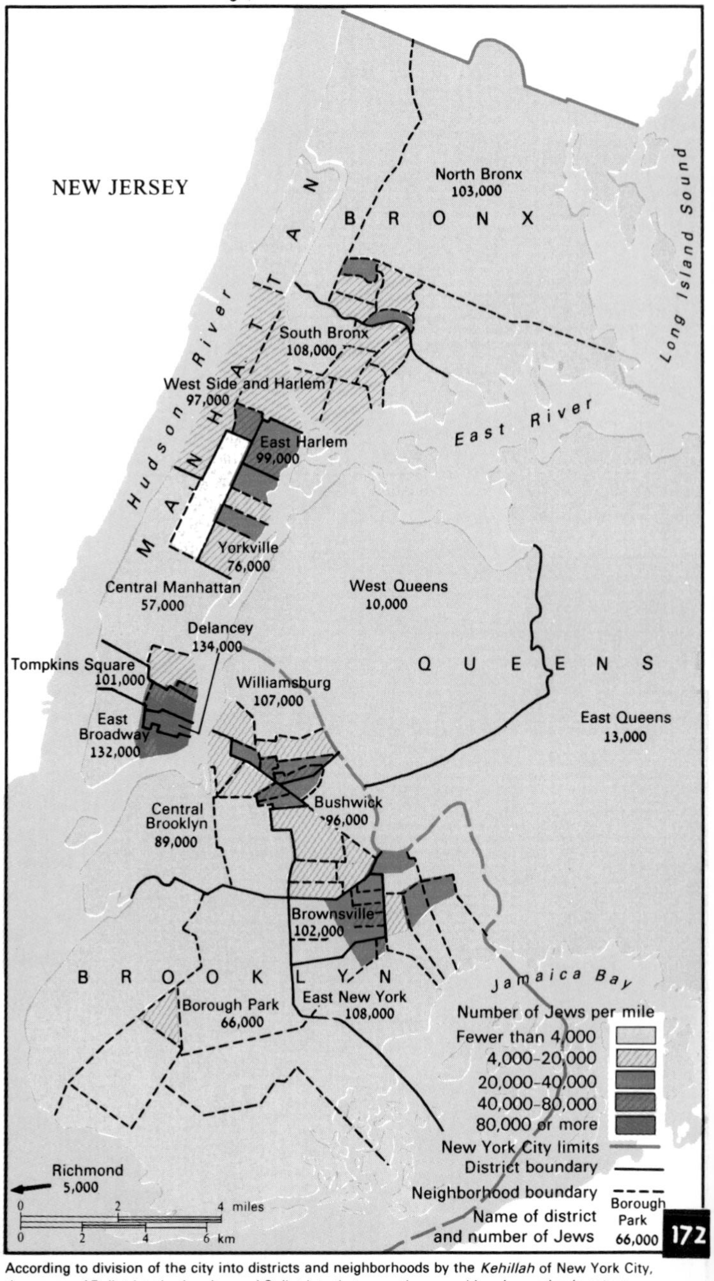


According to division of the city into districts and neighborhoods by the *Kehillah* of New York City, there were 15 districts in the city, and 3 districts that were then considered counties (western Queens, eastern Queens, and Richmond)

New York City was, in the twentieth century, the largest center in the history of the Jewish people. In 1957, 2,580,000 Jews lived in the city and its suburbs, 45 percent of American Jewry. New York was a vibrant city in which most American Jewish institutions had their headquarters.

The beginnings of Jewish New York date to 1654, when a ship with about twenty Spanish–Portuguese refugees arrived from Recife, Brazil. The settlement, founded in 1626 as New Amsterdam, was under Dutch domination. In 1664, the English took it over and changed its name to New York. The first known Jewish institution was the Jewish cemetery off Chatham Square, established in the 1680s. The first Jewish congregation, Shearith Israel, must have started at the same

# The Jewish Population in New York City, 1957



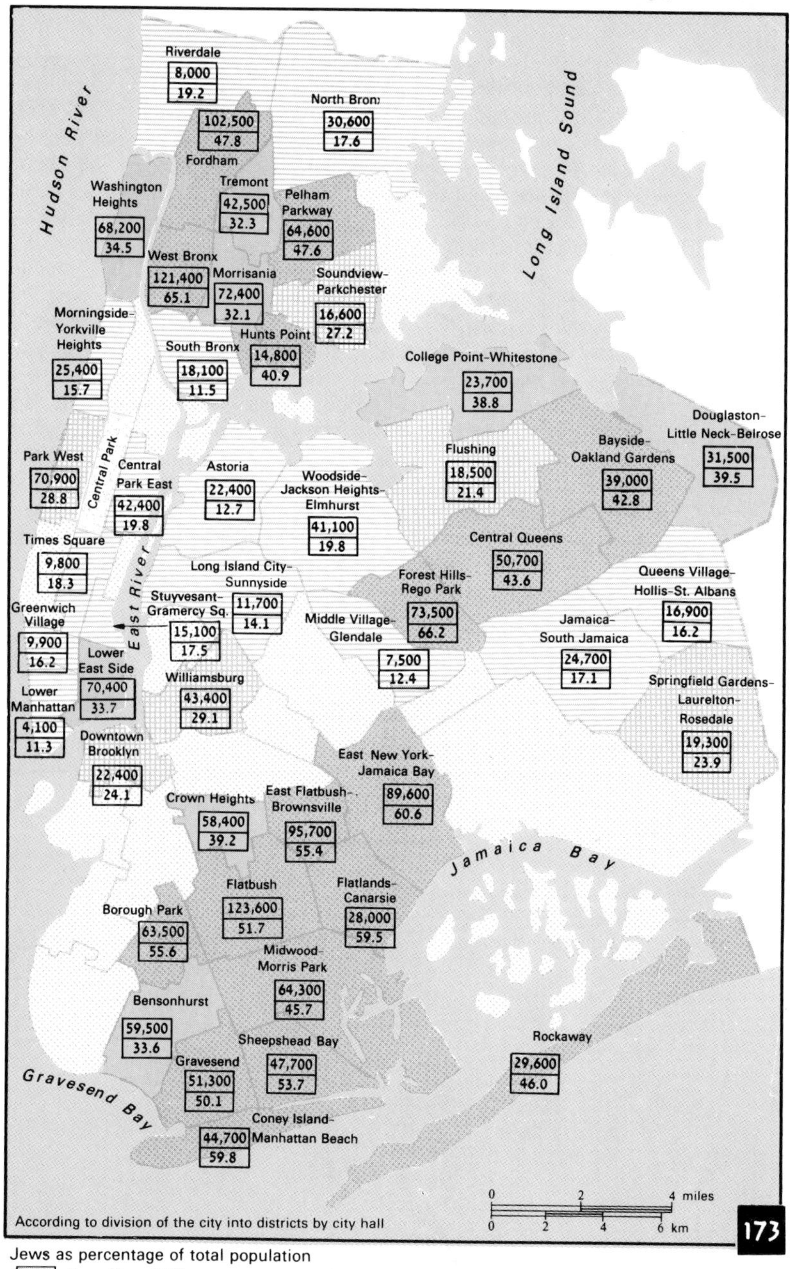


Jews as percentage of total population

- Less than 10%
- 10–20%
- 20–30%
- 30–40%
- 40% or more

New York City limits
District boundary
4,100 Number of Jews in district
11.3 or more Jewish percentage of total population

## The Jews in the New York Metropolitan Area, 1980s

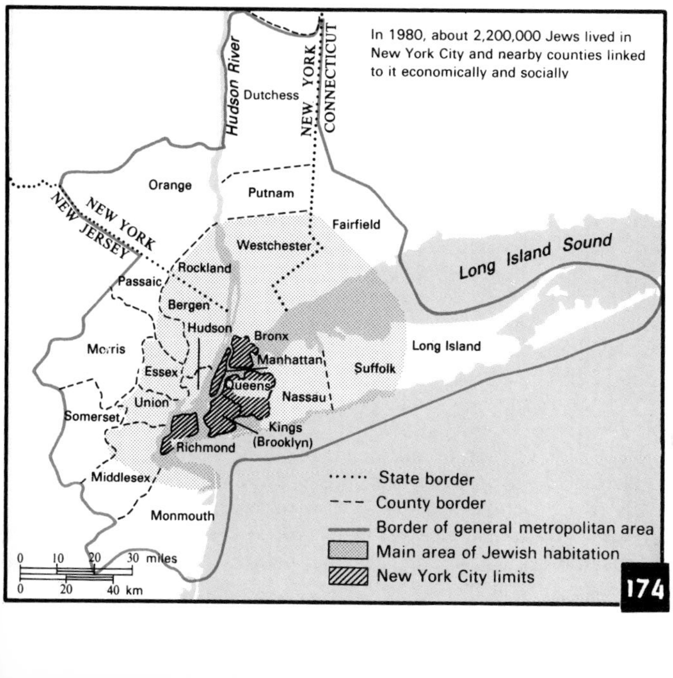


time. The congregation was Sephardic, and remained the most important Jewish institution of New York until the mid-nineteenth century.

Estimates are that 10,000 Jews lived in New York in 1850. By 1880, their number had grown to 60,000, with another 13,000 in neighboring Brooklyn. New York City was the gateway to America for millions of new immigrants who arrived beginning in the second half of the nineteenth century, including more than 2 million Jews. Most of the Jewish newcomers settled in the famous Lower East Side, where conditions were poor and crowded, but life was highly interesting. Orthodox Jews, socialists, and Zionists worked alongside and against one another. Most Jewish organizations, hundreds of synagogues, the editorial offices of Jewish newspapers, theaters, famous coffee houses, sweat shops, and hundreds of thousands of immigrants—mostly Jews, but also non-Jews—filled every nook and cranny of the Lower East Side. As Jews improved their economic situation, they moved out—up to Central Park, upper Manhattan, and Harlem; northward to the Bronx; eastward to Brooklyn; and, still later, to Queens. Synagogues and other Jewish institutions moved too. Famous congregations, such as Shearith Israel and Temple Emanu-El, moved three or more times, following their congregants.

In a sense, Jewish New York reached its high point in the 1950s. The social and economic crisis that in the 1960s and 1970s hit most northeastern cities struck New York with particular intensity. About 1 million Jews left New York City between 1957 and 1986. Many settled in the suburbs; many of the elderly went south to Florida; and many of the younger people went west to California. Neighborhoods that had been densely populated by Jews changed in character. In 1957, for example, about 500,000 Jews lived in the Bronx, more than in pre–World War II Warsaw, the second largest Jewish center in modern times. Fewer than 100,000 Jews remained in the Bronx in the early 1980s, mostly elderly people: in 1971, the median age of the Jewish population there was 56.5 years.

In spite of all this, in the 1980s New York City remained the great center of American Jewry. About 2.2 million Jews lived in the New York metropolitan area, including the suburbs (and nearby New Jersey), although the number of Jews in the city's five boroughs had decreased to about 1 million.

## Jewish Population Growth in New York to 1986

Until 1910

| | |
|---|---|
| 1790 | 385 |
| 1846 | 10,000 |
| 1880 | 73,000* |
| 1900 | 350,000 |
| 1910 | 900,000 |

| | 1917 | 1930 | | 1950 | | 1957 | | 1970 | 1986 | | % change |
|---|---|---|---|---|---|---|---|---|---|---|---|
| | Number | % | Number | % | Number | % | Number | Number | % | Number | 1957-1986 |
| **Greater N.Y.: 8 counties** | | | | | | 25.9 | 2,580,000 | 1,998,000 | 16 | 1,670,700 | –35.3 |
| **N.Y.C.: 5 boroughs** | 1,503,000 | 26.4 | 1,825,000 | 25.3 | 1,997,000 | 27.1 | 2,115,000 | 1,228,000 | 16 | 1,133,100 | –46.4 |
| Bronx | 211,000 | 46.2 | 585,000 | 35.7 | 519,000 | 34.6 | 493,000 | 143,000 | 8 | 95,800 | –80.6 |
| Brooklyn | 568,000 | 33.3 | 851,000 | 33.6 | 920,000 | 32.8 | 854,000 | 514,000 | 19 | 412,900 | –51.7 |
| Manhattan | 696,000 | 16.0 | 297,000 | 16.9 | 331,000 | 18.9 | 339,000 | 171,000 | 19 | 276,300 | –18.5 |
| Queens | 23,000 | 8.1 | 88,000 | 14.4 | 223,000 | 24 | 423,000 | 379,000 | 17 | 317,100 | –25 |
| Staten Island | 5,000 | 2.4 | 4,000 | 3.2 | 4,000 | 2.6 | 6,000 | 21,000 | 9 | 31,000 | 416.6 |
| **3 counties** | | | | | | 21.5 | 465,000 | 770,000 | 15 | 537,600 | 15.6 |
| Nassau | | | | | | 27.9 | 329,000 | 454,000 | 23 | 308,300 | –6.3 |
| Suffolk | | | | | | 3.8 | 20,000 | 151,000 | 8 | 106,200 | 431 |
| Westchester | | | | | | 15.5 | 116,000 | 165,000 | 14 | 123,100 | 6.1 |

25.9 Jews as percentage of total population

* Including 13,000 Jews in Brooklyn, then a separate city

## Median Ages

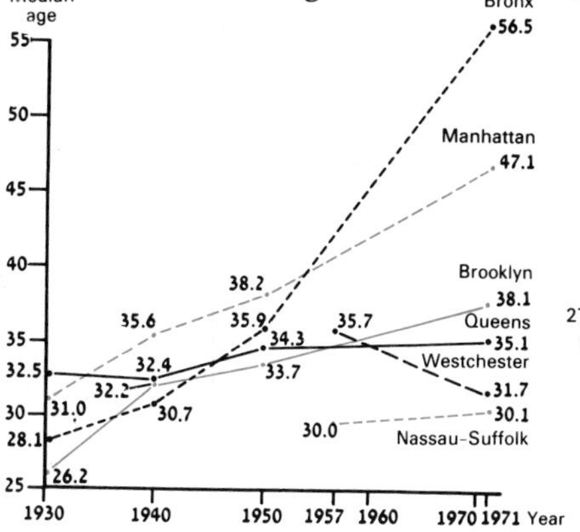


## Age Distribution of New York City Jews
(percent)

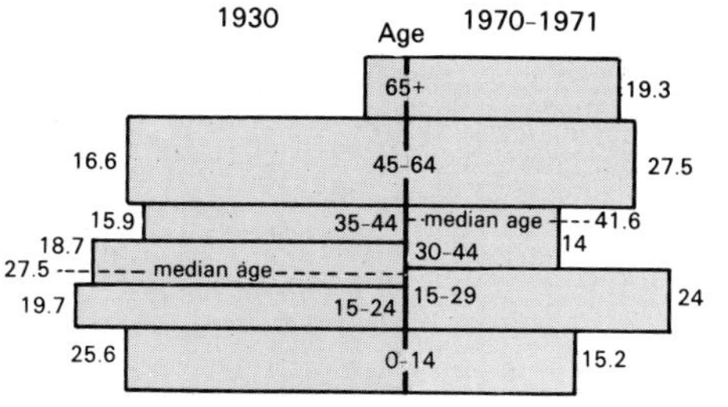

# The Jews in Chicago

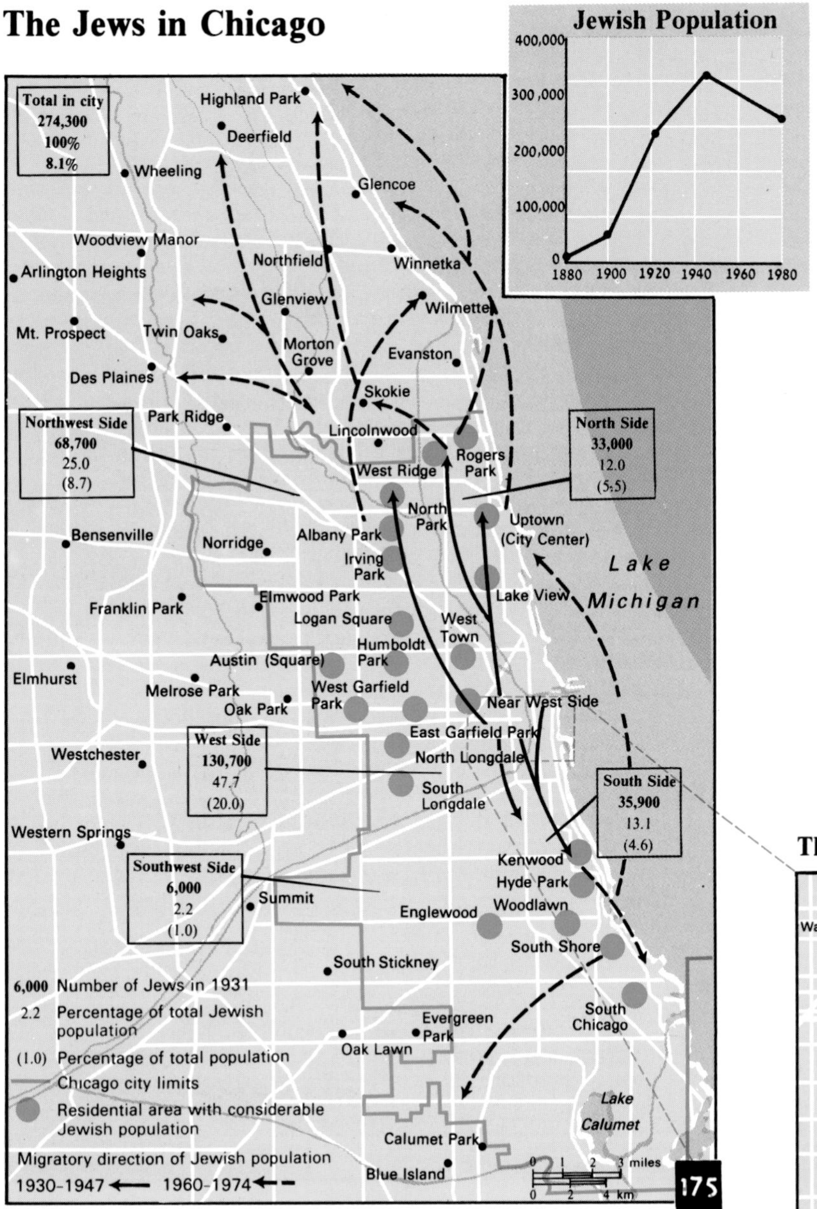



In the 1930s and 1940s, Chicago was the second largest Jewish center in the United States, and the main Jewish community in the Midwest. In the late 1940s, Chicago Jewry reached its greatest number: about 333,000. Later, many Jews left the city and settled in the suburbs or in other parts of the United States. In 1986, Chicago was the third largest community in the country, with about 250,000 Jews.

Jews, mostly of German origin, came to Chicago beginning in the mid-nineteenth century. They settled in what was then the eastern part of the city, east of the Chicago River, on the shore of Lake Michigan. Following the great fires of 1871 and 1874, which destroyed the Jewish neighborhood along with much of the city, Jews began to settle on the western side of the river. At the time, East European Jewish immigrants began to arrive in Chicago, and gradually the Jewish neighborhood, the West Side, developed. The most typical Jewish quarter on the West Side was North Lawndale, where the proportion of Jews in the total population reached 67.2 percent in the 1930s, and even more than 90 percent in certain streets. The heart of the Jewish quarter was Maxwell Street.

Chicago was known for its independent Jewish life. All major trends in American Jewry were strongly represented. Chicago was one of the birthplaces of the Reform movement, as represented by Congregation Sinai, founded in 1861, whose rabbi was the famous Bernard Felsenthal. Later, a strong branch of the Jewish labor movement developed in the city. A semi-independent branch of the American Zionist movement was active in Chicago for many years, the Knights of Zion Order.

From the 1970s, prosperity and the growing problems of the inner city caused many Jews to move to the north and south of Chicago, along the lake shore, beyond the municipal boundaries, and to the northwest.

## The West Side (Ghetto) Until the 1930s

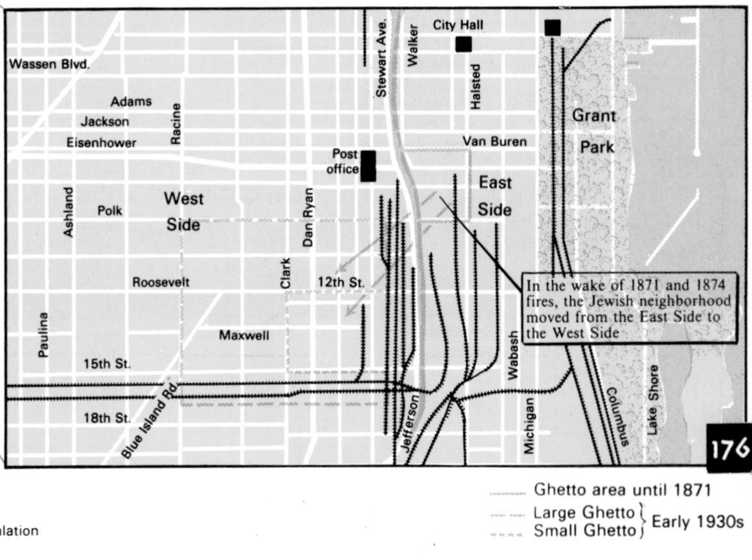

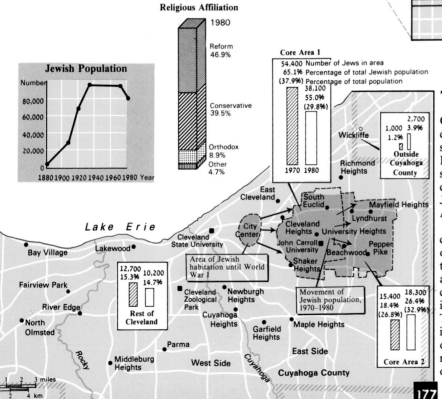

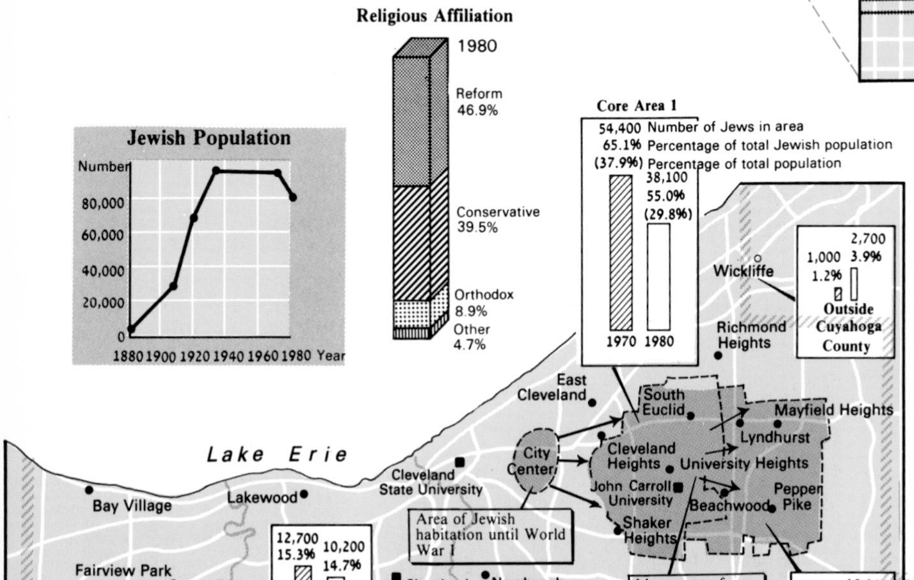




# The Jews in Cleveland

Cleveland Jewry was a typical medium-to-large American Jewish community. In the mid-nineteenth century, Jews from Central Europe settled in the city, followed by many immigrants from Eastern Europe. Both groups created their own communal institutions, and lived rather separately for the next generation or two. In the early twentieth century, all the main religious and ideological movements of American Jewry were found in Cleveland. One of the outstanding leaders of American Jewry in the 1940s, Rabbi Abba Hillel Silver, lived there.

Until World War II, most Jews lived in the inner part of the city, the downtown area. In the 1950s and 1960s, prosperity, on the one hand, and the growing social problems of the inner city, on the other, led most Jews to move to the eastern part of Cleveland and to the suburbs. In the second half of the twentieth century, the city's Jewish community showed typical demographic characteristics: in 1981, 17.5 percent of married Jews were married to non-Jews. The size of the average Jewish family decreased from 3.1 members in 1971 to 2.8 members in 1980. Between 1970 and 1980, the number of Jews in Cleveland decreased by 16 percent, reflecting the low rate of natural increase and, mainly, the move to the city's suburbs or to other parts of the country.

# The Jews in Boston



As in other American Jewish centers in the eastern United States, Jews started settling in Boston in the eighteenth century. The first community of "German" Jews was founded in the nineteenth century, and toward the end of the century, masses of "Russian" Jewish immigrants formed the large Jewish settlement in the city. In the second half of the twentieth century, Boston Jewry experienced the problems and developments of other Jewish communities in the northeastern United States: the Jewish population in the inner city decreased as Jews moved to the suburbs or to other states.

Nevertheless, Boston was the only northeastern Jewish center where between 1965 and 1985 the Jewish population became younger. In the late 1970s, there were fewer Jews in Boston, but the decrease was relatively moderate, since the city attracted many young Jews. The changing composition of the Jewish population was also reflected in its religious tendencies: fewer Jews declared affiliation with the Orthodox position; fewer were Conservatives; more were connected with the Reform movement or declared themselves religiously unaffiliated. There were indications that in the mid-1980s, more younger Jews were moving into Boston.

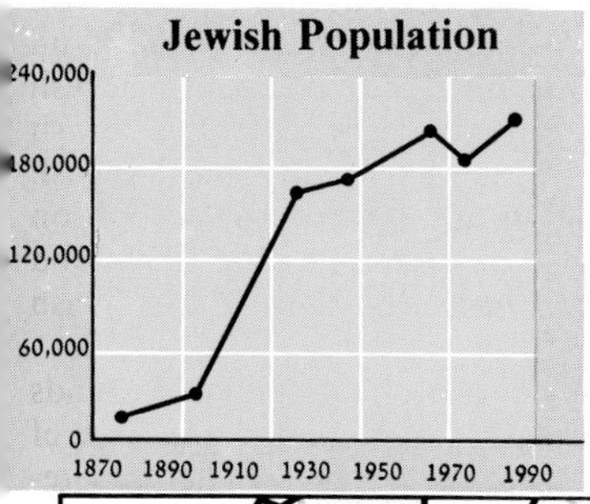


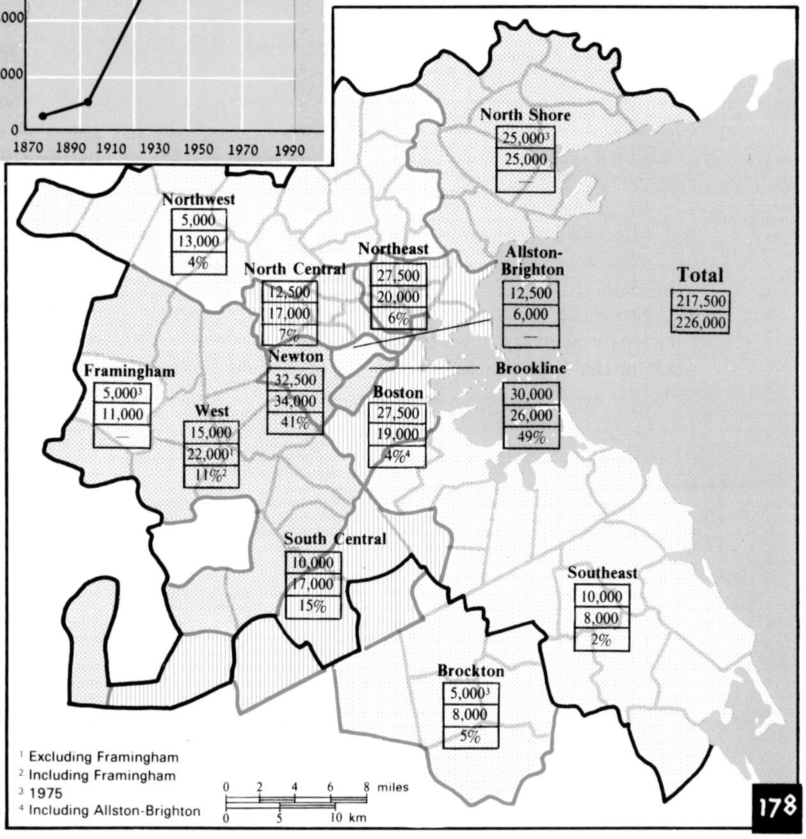


| | |
|---|---|
| 27,500 | Number of Jews in 1965 |
| 20,000 | Number of Jews in 1985 |
| 6% | Percentage of Jews in total population, 1985 |
| | 25,000 or more Jews |
| | 17,000–22,000 Jews |
| | Fewer than 15,000 Jews |

Border of Boston Standard Metropolitan Statistical Area (SMSA)

Community boundary

## Demographic Characteristics of Jews Over Age 18

### Denominational Preference*

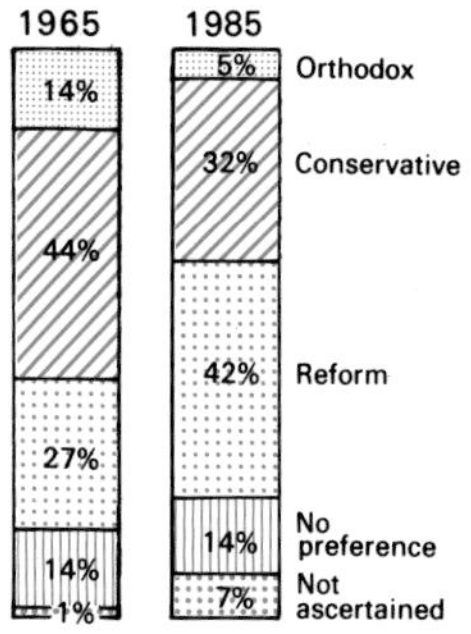


* Preference does not mean actual affiliation. In 1985, 72% of Jewish adults (84% of whom were in the 18 to 39 age group) were not members of any Jewish organization.

### Occupations, 1985

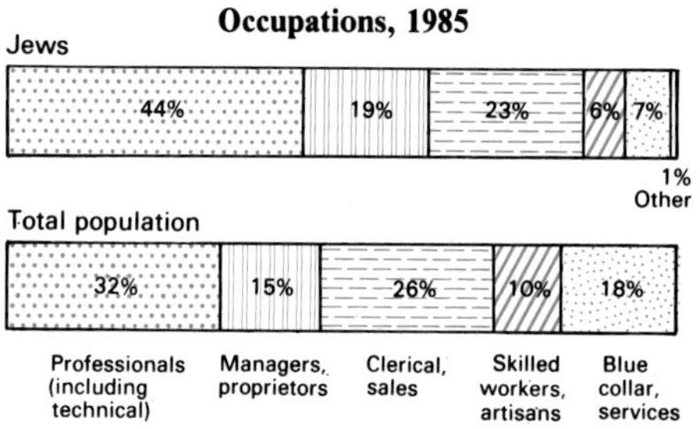


### Mixed Marriages*: Non-Jewish Spouses (percent)

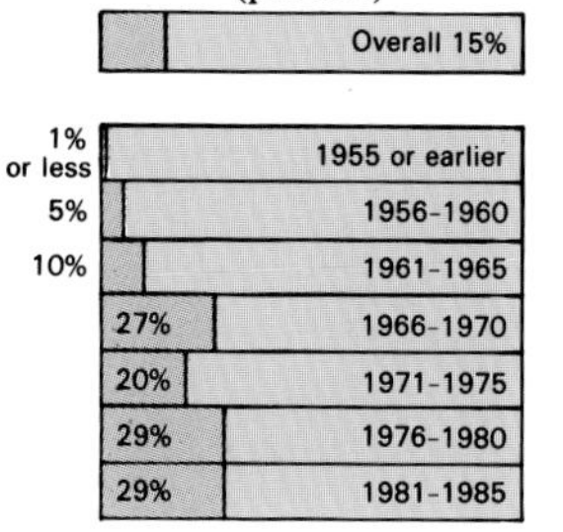


* Married only once and currently married

### Age Distribution of Jews

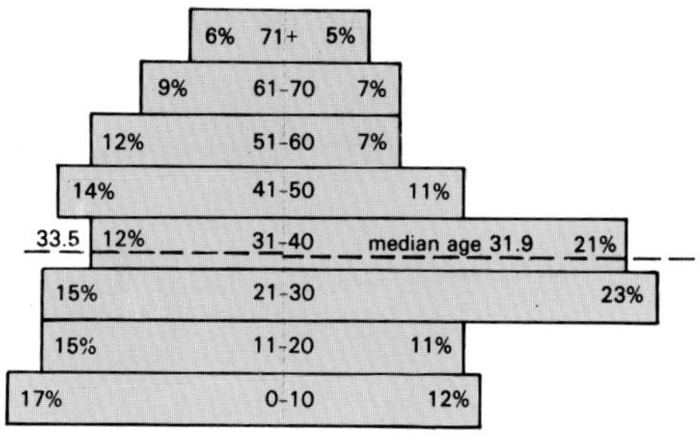


* Including non-Jews in Jewish households; no information, 3%.

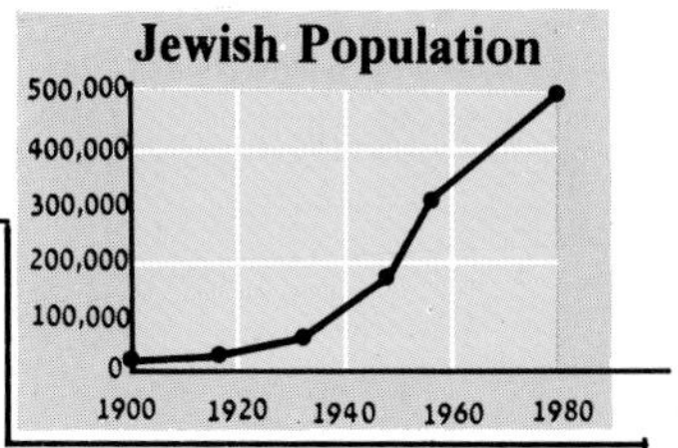


# The Jews in Los Angeles

Los Angeles Jewry represented a new kind of communal experience. There were about 500,000 Jews in Los Angeles in 1986, the second largest Jewish population in the United States. Jews had been living in the city since the end of the nineteenth century, and the Jewish population had reached about 100,000 before World War II. It was only after the war, however, that hundreds of thousands of Jews moved to the city, from all parts of the United States.

Most of the familiar demographic trends in other Jewish centers did not apply to Los Angeles, since its development was not based on a nucleus of Jewish settlement, from which the Jews moved to other parts of the city. The first Jews in Los Angeles settled there in several scattered groups simultaneously, and created Jewish institutions in the areas in which they lived. That process, and the size of the city, made it exceedingly difficult to consider the Jewish population as a broad community. Nevertheless, umbrella institutions were formed in order to bring together Jewish organizations in the various parts of the city.

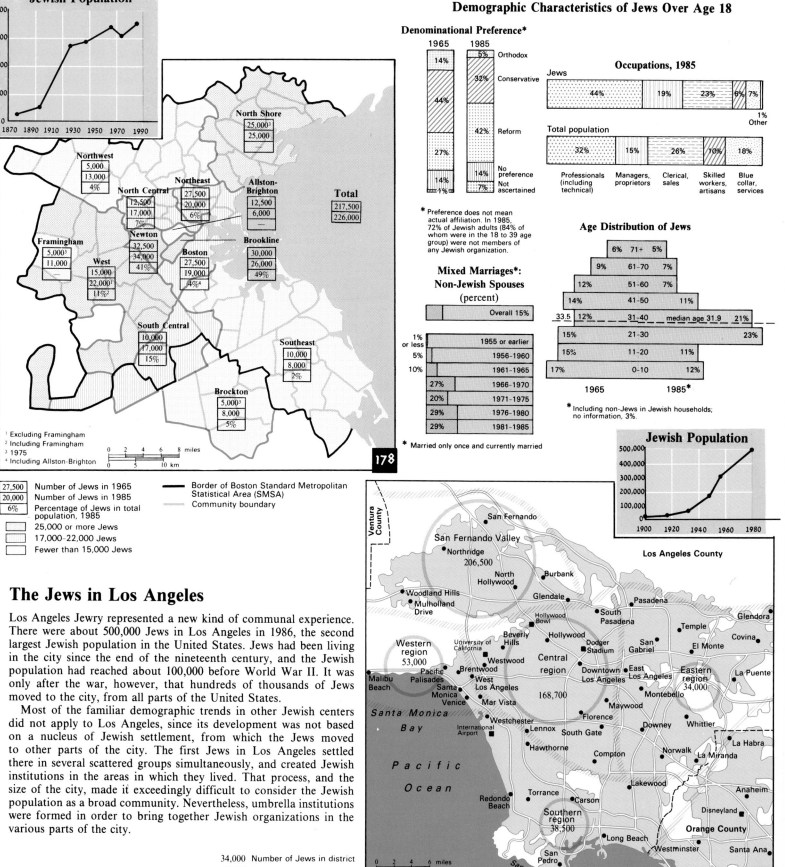

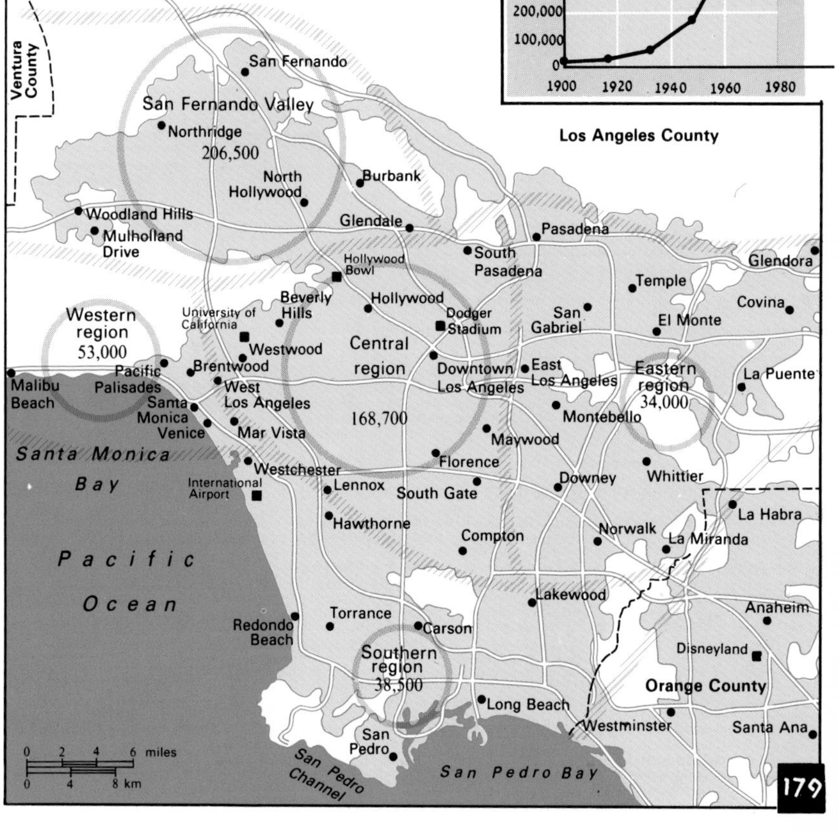


34,000 Number of Jews in district

District border

County border

# The Jews in Latin America: Nineteenth and Twentieth Centuries

Until the nineteenth century, the Inquisition laws forbade the presence of Jews in Spanish and Portuguese colonies. Jewish Sephardic communities were established in Recife, Brazil, during the short Dutch domination (1630–1654), and in the seventeenth and eighteenth centuries on the islands of the Caribbean Sea under Dutch, English, or French domination. Only in the late nineteenth century did Jews arrive in significant numbers in such countries as Uruguay, Argentina, and Brazil, which had become independent. These republics, in spite of their Catholic character, adopted liberal constitutions, and almost without exception Jews could live there freely.

From the early twentieth century until the outbreak of World War II, the Latin American countries absorbed hundreds of thousands of Jewish immigrants, mostly from Eastern Europe, but also from the Muslim countries and, in the 1930s, from Germany. Most Jews adapted well, prospered, integrated socially and culturally into the general society, and organized Jewish institutions. But the social unrest and political problems in many Latin American nations during the second half of the twentieth century affected the Jews, who left some countries, such as Cuba, for good and others, such as Chile and Argentina, for extended periods. Some emigrated to more stable neighboring countries, such as Brazil, Venezuela, and Colombia.

Brazilian Jewry was the second largest in Latin America. Most Jews lived in São Paulo and Rio de Janeiro, well accepted by the general population and with relatively well-organized Jewish institutions. The small Jewish community of Belém, in northern Brazil, established by Moroccan Jews in the nineteenth century, had its own very distinct characteristics.

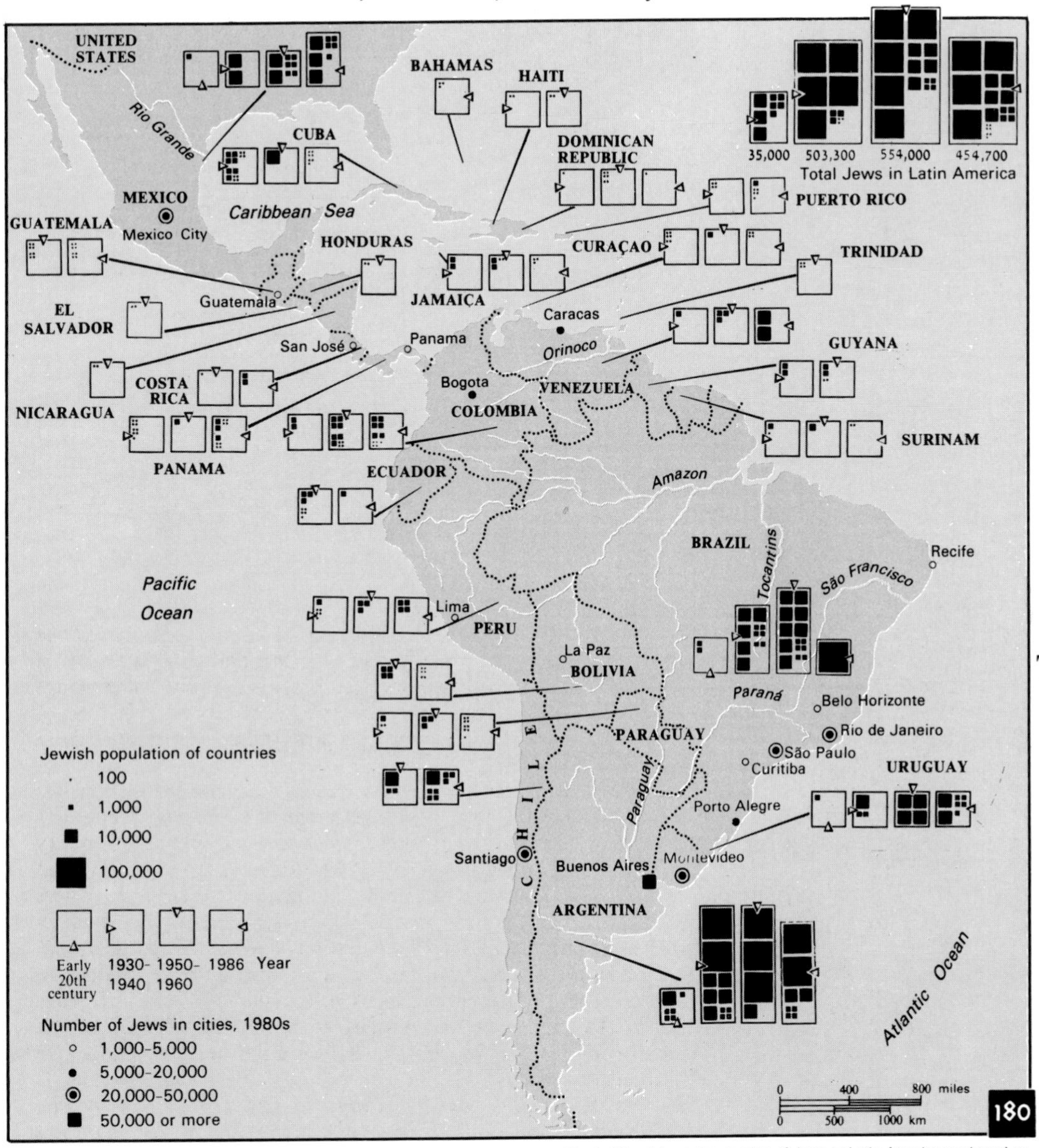


Most of the data on the number of Jews in Latin America are based on estimates. The data for the 1950s appear to be too high, especially for countries with larger Jewish populations.

## Occupations of Jews (percent)

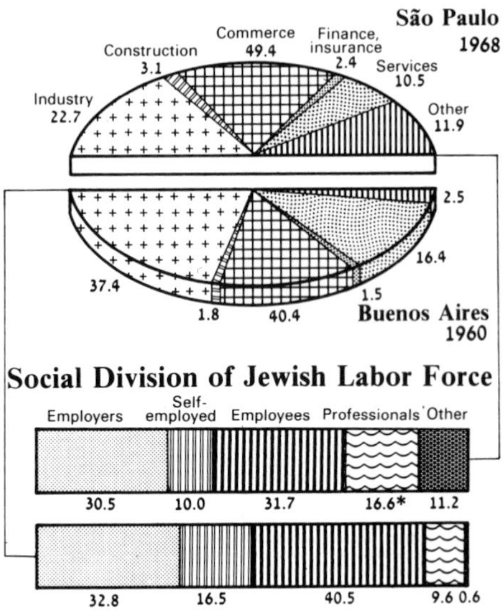


*Of whom 23% are engineers and 21%, physicians

## The Jews in Brazil by States, 1984

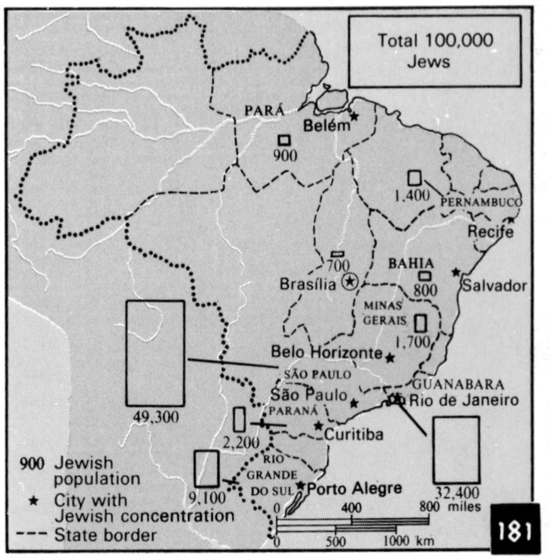


## Jewish Migration to Argentina

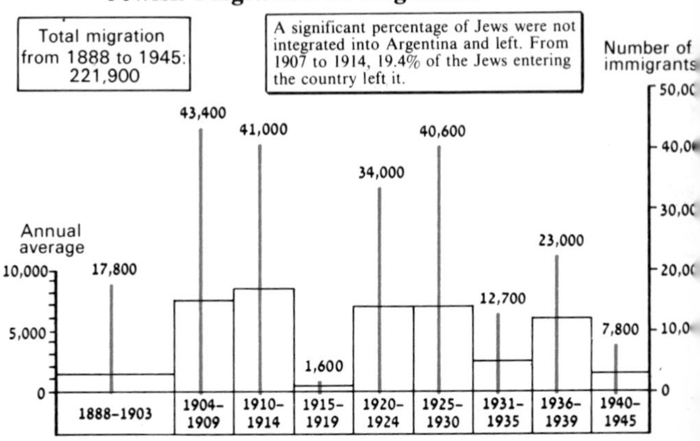


## The Jews in Argentina

The settlement of Jews in Argentina was stimulated by the activities of the Jewish Colonization Association (ICA), founded in 1891. ICA established agricultural colonies, mostly in the provinces of Entre Ríos and Santa Fé. Although in the 1930s, there were only 20,000 to 30,000 Jewish farmers, the ICA initiative brought many Jewish immigrants to Argentina; they settled in cities, especially in the capital, Buenos Aires. Gradually, Buenos Aires attracted most Argentinian Jews, including those living in the provincial cities or in the colonies. In the early twentieth century, two-thirds of Argentinian Jews lived in the provinces, especially Entre Ríos; by 1960, four-fifths lived in Greater Buenos Aires. In 1964, only about 800 Jewish families were engaged in agriculture, in the colonies.

Although in principle, the Jews were citizens with full rights, in practice there was a strong antisemitic movement in Argentina, influenced by European traditions. There were anti-Jewish riots in 1919 and problems in later years as well, reflecting the country's internal tensions.

The organization of Argentinian Jewry was strongly influenced (and dominated) by the Buenos Aires community. The Jews established two umbrella organizations. One was the Delegación de Asociaciones Israelitas Argentinas (DAIA), founded in 1933, whose purpose was to fight antisemitism and represent the community before the authorities. The other, Va'ad ha-Kehillot, organized in 1952, was based on the Ashkenazic community of Buenos Aires, the Asociación Mutual Israelita Argentina (AMIA). Va'ad ha-Kehillot became responsible for a broad spectrum of Jewish activities of a social, educational, religious, and cultural character. The Zionists had considerable influence in both bodies, and their representation was along the lines of the Zionist party structure.

From the 1960s, Argentina underwent much political and social unrest. This affected the Jewish community. The number of Jews in the country decreased significantly in the second half of the century, in part because of their low birth rate, and in part because of emigration.

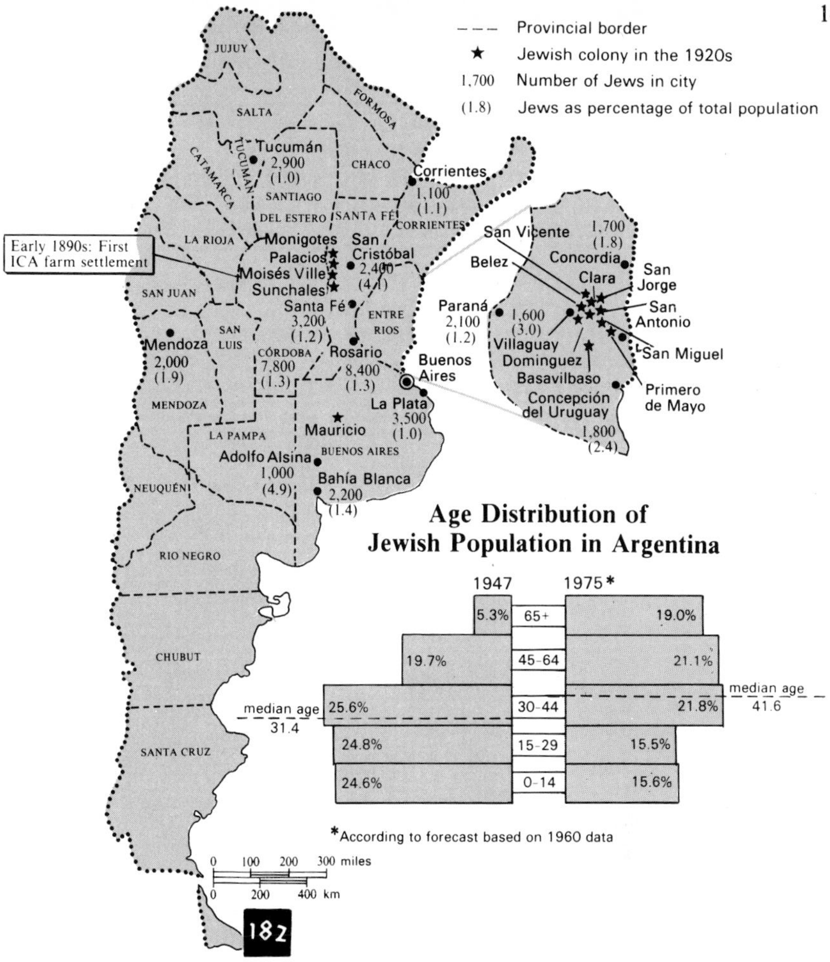


## The Jews in Buenos Aires

In the second half of the twentieth century, Buenos Aires was the largest Jewish center in Latin America. Its development was similar to that of many other Jewish communities in the New World: beginnings in the nineteenth century, but real growth only toward the end of the century, with the immigration of a large number of Jews from Eastern Europe.

The way the united (Ashkenazic) Jewish community of Buenos Aires (AMIA) came into being, although it had precedents, was curious in twentieth-century conditions: it grew out of a burial society (*hevra kadisha*) formed in the mid-1890s that over the years assumed a wide range of other Jewish communal functions, to the point where it performed nearly *all* of them in the city. The result was a much tighter centralization of Jewish institutions under one umbrella than occurred in most other twentieth-century Jewish centers. Since in the 1960s, about 80 percent of all Argentinian Jews lived in Buenos Aires, AMIA influenced the Jewish life of the majority of the country's Jews. The Sephardic community of Buenos Aires had separate Jewish institutions.

Buenos Aires Jewry was known for its rich Jewish cultural life. Although the Zionists dominated AMIA, there was an important group of Yiddish intellectuals, many of whom were associated with the Bund.

The size of Buenos Aires Jewry reached its peak in 1960. Thereafter, the number decreased steadily. Nevertheless, it remained a most important Jewish center through the 1980s.

## Year 1960

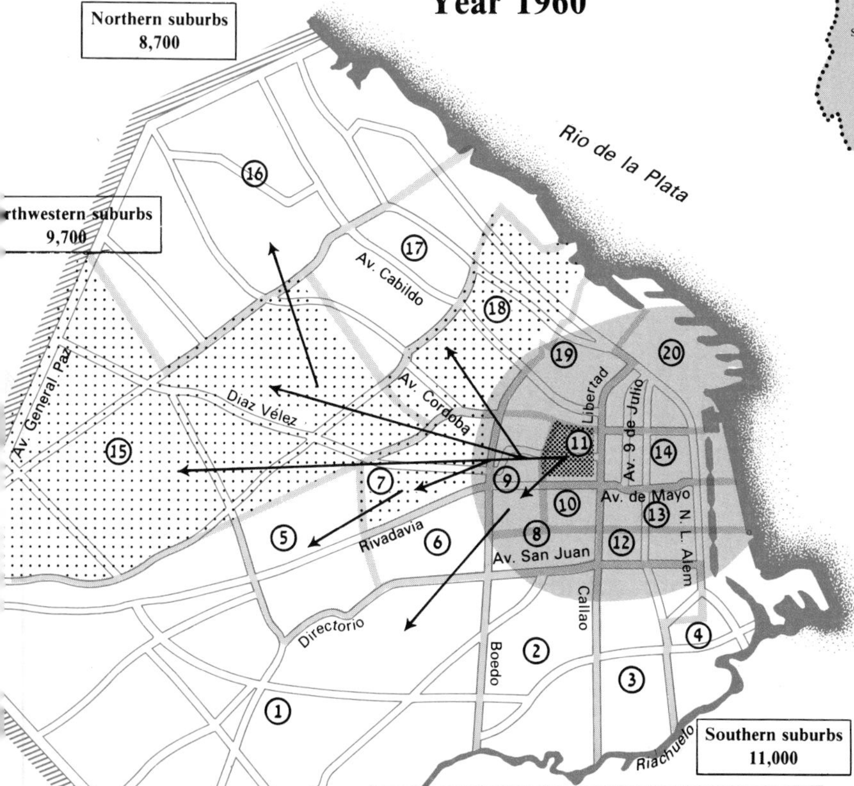


| | Quarter | Number of Jews | Percentage of total Jews | Percentage of total population |
|---|---|---|---|---|
| 1 | Vélez Sàrsfield | 15,600 | 6.7 | 3.0 |
| 2 | San Cristobàl Sur | 1,700 | 0.7 | 2.0 |
| 3 | Santa Lucía | 2,900 | 1.2 | 2.7 |
| 4 | San Juan Evangelista | 1,600 | 0.7 | 2.3 |
| 5 | Flores | 11,300 | 5.1 | 7.8 |
| 6 | San Carlos Sur | 4,400 | 1.9 | 3.8 |
| 7 | San Carlos Norte | 11,200 | 4.8 | 11.6 |
| 8 | San Cristobàl Norte | 2,300 | 1.0 | 3.3 |
| 9 | Balvanera Oeste | 12,800 | 5.5 | 14.4 |
| 10 | Balvanera Sur | 1,900 | 0.8 | 4.1 |
| 11 | Balvanera Norte | 13,400 | 5.8 | 24.5 |
| 12 | Concepción | 2,200 | 1.0 | 3.0 |
| 13 | Monserrat | 2,000 | 0.8 | 2.5 |
| 14 | San Nicolàs | 2,800 | 1.2 | 4.3 |
| 15 | San Bernardo | 61,000 | 26.3 | 11.8 |
| 16 | Belgrano | 13,400 | 5.8 | 4.1 |
| 17 | Palermo | 7,100 | 3.1 | 5.1 |
| 18 | Las Heras | 16,800 | 7.2 | 11.4 |
| 19 | Pilar | 6,900 | 3.0 | 5.1 |
| 20 | Socorro | 2,500 | 1.1 | 3.0 |
| | Total in city limits | 193,800 | 83.7 | 6.5 |
| | Southern suburbs | 11,000 | 4.6 | 0.7 |
| | Western suburbs | 8,800 | 3.8 | 1.0 |
| | Northwestern suburbs | 9,700 | 4.2 | 1.3 |
| | Northern suburbs | 8,700 | 3.7 | 1.4 |
| | Total suburbs | 38,200 | 16.3 | 1.0 |
| | **Total metropolitan Buenos Aires, 1960** | **232,000** | **100** | **3.4** |

### Concentration of Argentinian Jews in Buenos Aires

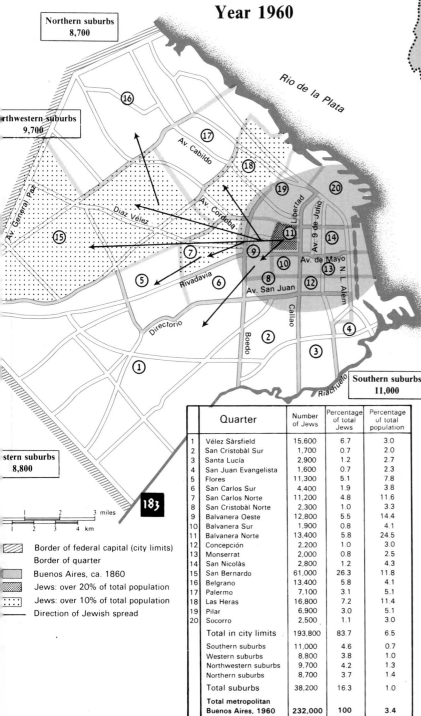

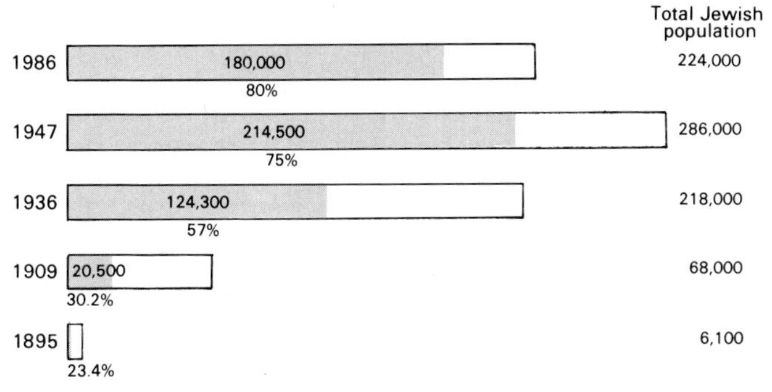

# The Jews in South Africa

Jews arrived in the land that became South Africa as early as the seventeenth century. But only in the nineteenth century did the country's economic development (after the discovery of gold and diamonds) attract a large number of Jews, mostly from Eastern Europe. They settled mainly in the Transvaal and the Cape, in the two main cities, Johannesburg and Cape Town. In 1980, over 95 percent of South African Jews lived in cities, about 57 percent in Johannesburg and 23 percent in Cape Town.

In the nineteenth century, the legal status of the Jews varied according to region; Jews living among the English were better off than those residing among the Dutch (Boers), for religious reasons. With the formation of the South African state (1902–1910), the Jews were granted full civil rights, but the rigid ethnic structure of the white population continued to leave its mark. In the larger cities, Jews tended to concentrate in certain neighborhoods, such as Glenhazel and Killarney in Johannesburg, where the Jews made up over half of the local population.

Compared with other modern Jewries, South African Jews were well organized and had a well-developed Jewish consciousness. Zionist ideology and party organization were very influential. South African Jewry was headed by the South African Jewish Board of Deputies, formed in 1912, and modeled on the British pattern of Jewish organization.

**Occupational Structure in South Africa, 1970**

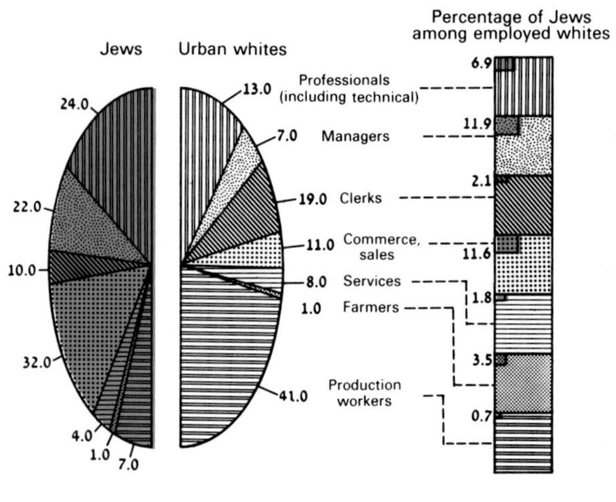


18% of all white males were in public service (5.8% of all Jews)

**Age Distribution, 1980**
(percent)

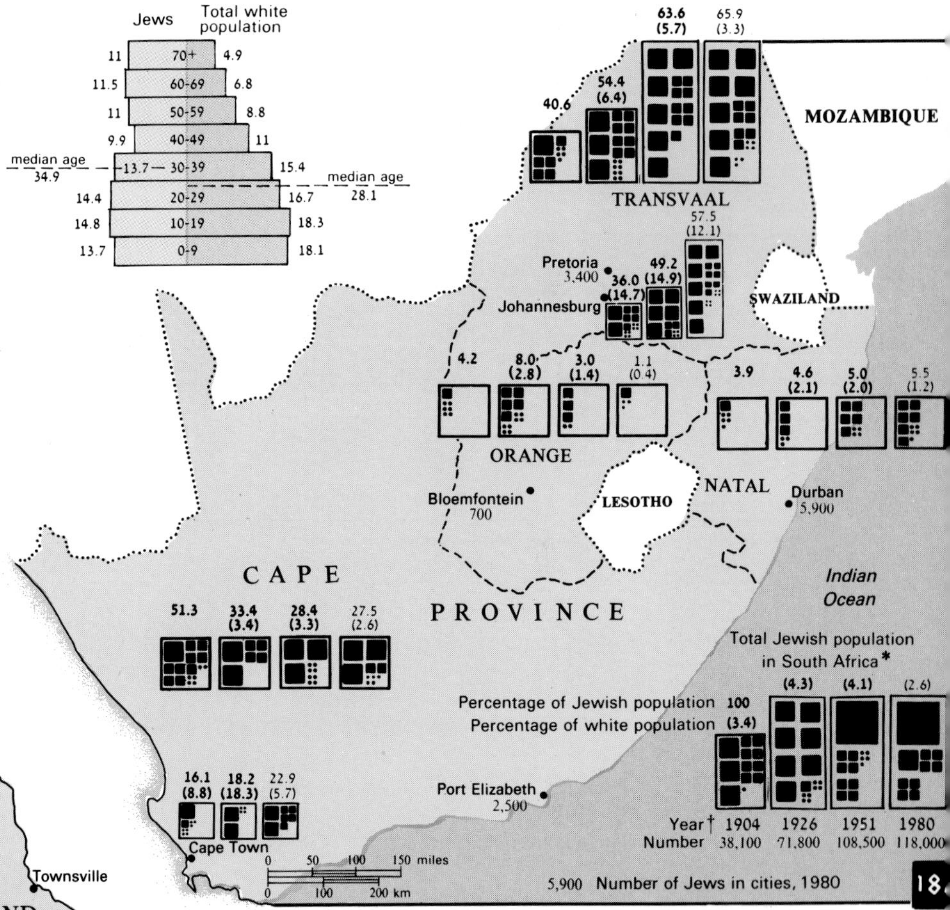


* As indicated elsewhere, the estimated Jewish population for 1986 was 115,000 (2.3%

† Where there are fewer than 4 units, the later data are meant

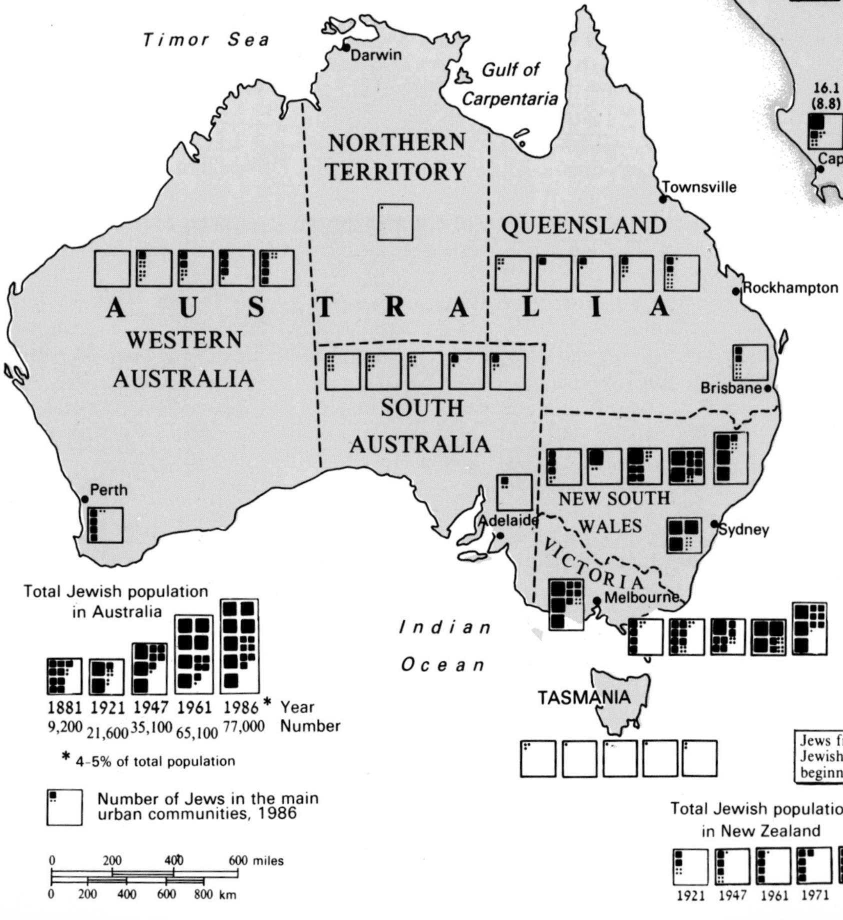


# The Jews in Australia and New Zealand

Jews began to arrive in Australia in the nineteenth century. It was only in the twentieth century, however, that the Jewish communities took shape, after several waves of immigration from Europe, mainly from Eastern Europe. Eighty to 90 percent of the Jews lived in the two main Jewish centers, Melbourne and Sydney. In 1986, there were about 77,000 Jews in Australia, and about 4,000 in New Zealand.

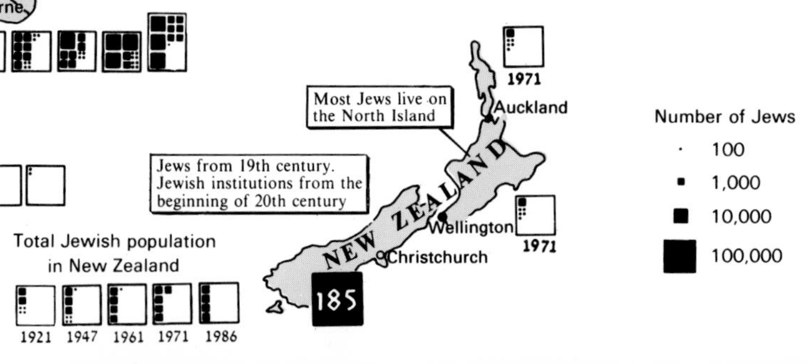

# BIBLIOGRAPHY

This bibliography lists selected works, relevant to the preparation of maps and diagrams.

### Abbreviations

*AJYB* *American Jewish Year Book*
*JPS* *Jewish Population Studies*
*LBIYB* *Leo Baeck Institute Year Book*
*PJD* *Papers in Jewish Demography*
*SJD* *Studies in Jewish Demography*
*ZfDSJ* *Zeitschrift fuer Demographie und Statistik der Juden*


## Atlases

*Andrees Allgemeiner Handatlas.* Edited by Konrad Frenzel. Bielefeld and Leipzig, 1914.
*Atlas général Vidal-Lablache, Histoire et Géographie.* Paris, 1928.
*Atlas of Israel.* Jerusalem and Amsterdam, 1970.
*Grosser historischer Weltatlas.* 3d ed. Vol. 3. Edited by Joseph Engel. Munich, 1967.
*The Historical Atlas of Poland.* Edited by Władysław Czapliński and Tadeusz Ładogorski. Wrocław, 1986.
*The Oxford Atlas.* Edited by Clinton Lewis and J. D. Campbell. Oxford, 1952.
*The Times Atlas of the World.* London, 1985.
*Ukraine, a Historical Atlas.* Edited by Paul Robery Magocsi. Toronto, 1985.
*The World Atlas.* Moscow, 1967.

## Encyclopedias, Journals, Collections (articles are listed separately)

*American Jewish Yearbook.* Philadelphia and New York, 1899–.
*Bletter far Yiddisher Demografi, Statistik un Ekonomi* (Pages for Jewish demography, statistics and economy; in Yiddish). Vols. 1–5. Berlin, 1923–1925.
Central Bureau of Statistics. *Statistical Abstract of Israel.* Jerusalem, various years.
*Encyclopaedia Judaica.* Vols. 1–16. Jerusalem, 1971.
*Ha-entsiklopediya ha'ivrit* (The Hebrew encyclopedia; in Hebrew). Vols. 1–32. Jerusalem, 1949–1973.
*The Jewish Encyclopedia.* Vols. 1–12. New York, 1907.
*Jewish Population Studies.* Jerusalem, 1970–.
*Yevreyskaya Entsiklopediya.* Vols. 1–16. St. Petersburg, 1906–1913.
*Zeitschrift fuer Demographie und Statistik der Juden.* Vols. 1–19. Berlin, 1905–1927.

## General Jewish Demography and Historical Themes

Alfassi, Itzhak. *Hasidut* (Hasidism; in Hebrew). 2d ed. Tel Aviv, 1977.
Bauer, Yehuda. *Flight and Rescue: Brichah.* New York, 1970 (?).
Ben-Amos, Dan, and Jerome R. Mintz. *In Praise of the Baal Shem Tov* (translation of *Shivhei Habesht*). Bloomington, Ind., 1972.
Boehm, Adolph. *Die Zionistische Bewegung.* 2 vols. Tel Aviv, 1935–1937.
DellaPergola, Sergio. "Aliya and Other Jewish Migrations: Toward an Integrated Perspective." In *Studies in the Population of Israel in Honor of Roberto Bachi.* Edited by Uziel O. Schmelz and Gad Nathan. (Reprinted in *Scripta Hierosolymitana* 30 [1986]: 172–209).
DellaPergola, Sergio. "Jewish Urban Ecology in European Cities: A Comparative Approach." *PJD 1985* (1989): 303–336.
DellaPergola, Sergio. "Comparative Trends in World Jewish Fertility, 1830–1980." Paper delivered at the General Conference of the Union for the Scientific Study of the Population, Manila, 1981.
DellaPergola, Sergio. "Distribution residentièlle des juifs dans quelques villes europeénes et a Rome en particulier." *Revue des Etudes Juives* 148, no. 1–2 (1989): 95–119.
DellaPergola, Sergio. "L'effect de marriages mixtes sur la natalité dans une sous-population: quelques problèmes et resultats concernant la diaspora juive." *Demographie et destin des sous-populations* 1 (1983): 223–236.
DellaPergola, Sergio. "The Localization of Jewish Neighborhoods in European Cities" (on page 38). [Use of this material only with the permission of the author.]
DellaPergola, Sergio. *La trasformazione demografica della diaspora ebraica.* Turin, 1983.
Dubnov, Simon. *Toldot ha-hasidut* (History of Hasidism; in Hebrew). 3 vols. Tel Aviv, 1920–1931.
Fraenkel, Joseph. *The Jewish Press of the World.* London, 1967.
Graetz, Paul. "Organisatorische Daten zur Geschichte der zionistischen Studentenbewegung in Deutschland." MS. A/231, Central Zionist Archives, Jerusalem.
Gross, Nahum, ed. *Economic History of the Jews.* New York, 1975.
Gross, Walter. "The Zionist Students' Movement." *LBIYB* 4 (1959): 143–164.
Gutman, Yisrael, ed. *The Nazi Concentration Camps.* Jerusalem, 1984.
Hadari, Ze'ev, and Ze'ev Tzahor. *Oniot o medina* (Ships or state; in Hebrew). Tel Aviv, 1981.
Hersch, Liebmann. "International Migration of the Jews." *International Migrations* 2 (1931):471–520.
Hersch, Liebmann. "Jewish Migrations During the Last Hundred Years." *The Jewish People—Past and Present* 1 (1946):407–430.
Hilberg, Raul. *The Destruction of the European Jews.* Chicago, 1961.
Jacob Joseph Hacohen of Polna. *Toldot Ya'akov Yosef* (The life of Jacob Joseph; in Hebrew). Tel Aviv, 1969.
Janowsky, Oscar I. *The Jews and Minority Rights, 1898–1919.* New York, 1933.
Katz, Jacob. *From Prejudice to Destruction: Anti-Semitism, 1700–1933.* Cambridge, Mass., 1980.
Kraus, Ota, and Erich Kulka. *The Death Factory; Documents on Auschwitz.* Oxford, [1966].
Kraushar, Alexander. *Frank i Frankiści Polscy.* 2 vols. Cracow, 1895.
Kuznets, Simon. "Economic Structure and Life of the Jews." In *The Jews: Their History, Culture and Religion.* Edited by Louis Finkelstein, 2:1597–1666. New York, 1960.
Lestschinsky, Jakob. "Die Umsiedlung und Umschichtung des juedischen Volkes im Laufe des letztens Jahrhunderts." *Weltwirtschaftlicher Archiv* 32 (1930): 563–599.
Lestschinsky, Jakob. *Dos yiddishe folk in tsifern* (The Jewish people in numbers; in Yiddish). Berlin, 1922.
Mendes-Flor, Paul R., and Jehuda Reinharz, eds. *The Jew in the Modern World: A Documentary History.* New York and Oxford, 1980.
Meyer, Michael A. *Response to Modernity: A History of the Reform Movement in Judaism.* New York and Oxford, 1988.
Milman, Ivor I. "Data on Diaspora Jewish Population from Official Censuses." *SJD* (Survey for 1969–1971): 155–228. Jerusalem and London, 1975.
Milman, Ivor I. "Data on Diaspora Jewish Population from Official Censuses." *SJD* (Survey for 1972–1980): 33–120. Jerusalem and London, 1983.
Mishkinsky, Moshe. *Reshit tenu'at ha-po'alim ha-yehudit be-russia: megamot yessod* (The beginnings of the Jewish labor movement in Russia: basic trends; in Hebrew). Tel Aviv, 1981.
Pulzer, Peter G. J. *The Rise of Political Anti-Semitism in Germany and in Austria.* Rev. ed. London, 1988.
Reinharz, Jehuda. "The Origin and Development of the Bund Juedischer Corporationen." *Wiener Library Bulletin* 30 (1977): 2–7.
Ruppin, Arthur. "Die Gesamtzahl der Juden auf der Erde." *ZfDSJ* 1 (1905), no. 12: 1–8.
Ruppin, Arthur. *The Jewish Fate and Future.* London, 1940.

Salmon, Yosef. "Massoret ve-moderniut ba-mahshava ha-tzionit ha-datit be-reishita" (Tradition and modernization in early Zionist religious thought; in Hebrew). In *Ideological and Political Zionism: Collected Historical Studies.* Edited by Ben Zion Yehoshua and Aaron Kedar, 21–37. Jerusalem, 1977.

Salmon, Yosef. "The Rise of Jewish Nationalism on the Border of Eastern and Western Europe." In *Danzig Between East and West.* Edited by Isador Twersky, 121–137. Cambridge, Mass., 1985.

Schatzker, Chaim. "The Jewish Youth Movement in Germany in the Holocaust Period (I). Youth in Confrontation with a New Reality." *LBIYB* 32 (1987): 157–182.

Schmelz, Uziel O. "Jewish Survival: The Demographic Factors." *AJYB* 81 (1981): 61–117.

Schmelz, Uziel O. *World Jewish Population—Regional Estimates and Projections.* Jerusalem, 1981.

Schmelz, Uziel O., and Sergio DellaPergola. "World Jewish Population." *AJYB* 82 (1982): 277–290.

Schmelz, Uziel O., and Sergio DellaPergola. "World Jewish Population, 1984." *AJYB* 85 (1985): 350–364.

Silber, Michael. "Sabbateanism, Frankism, and the Beginnings of Hasidism" (map 46). [Use of this material only with the permission of the author.]

Slutzky, Yehuda. *Ha'itonut ha-yehudit-russit ba-me'a ha-tesha-'esrei* (The Jewish-Russian press in the nineteenth century; in Hebrew). Jerusalem, 1970.

World Zionist Organization and Jewish Agency. *Din ve-heshbon stenografi shel ha-kongress ha-tzioni: 16th, 21st* (Stenographic minutes of the 16th and 21st Zionist congresses, 1929 and 1939; in Hebrew). Jerusalem, 1930, 1940.

## Countries and Geographical Regions

### Africa, Asia, Oceania (excluding Muslim countries)

DellaPergola, Sergio, and Allie A. Dubb. "South African Jewry: A Sociodemographic Profile." *AJYB* 88 (1988): 59–140.

Dubb, Allie A., and Mervyn Cohen. "Some Socio-Economic Aspects of the South African Jewish Population According to the Official Census of 1970." *PJD 1973* (1977): 149–207.

### The Americas

Avni, Haim. *Mebitul ha-inquisitzia ve'ad "hok ha-shevut": toldot ha-hagira ha-yehudit le-argentina* (From the abolition of the Inquisition until the "Law of Return": a history of Jewish immigration to Argentina; in Hebrew). Jerusalem, 1982.

Davids, Leo. "Canadian Jewry: Some Recent Census Findings." *AJYB* 85 (1985): 191–201.

DellaPergola, Sergio. "Demographic Trends of Latin American Jewry." In *The Jewish Presence in Latin America.* Edited by Judith Laikin Elkin and Gilbert W. Merkx, 85–133. Boston, 1987.

Rosenberg, Louis, "The Demography of the Jewish Community in Canada." *Jewish Journal of Sociology* 1 (1959): 217–233.

Schmelz, Uziel O., and Sergio DellaPergola. "The Demography of Latin American Jewry." *AJYB* 85 (1985): 51–102.

### Europe: Hapsburg Empire, East Central, Balkans (excluding Russian Empire and Soviet Union, Poland)

*Aşezările Evreilor din România—Memento Statistic.* [Bucharest], 1947.

Boháč, Antonin. "Hlavni město Praha." *Československý Statistický Vestnik* 3–4 (1922–1923).

Freidenreich, Harriet P. *The Jews of Yugoslavia.* Philadelphia, 1979.

Freidmann, Frantisek. *Einige Zahlen ueber die tschechoslovakischen Juden.* Prague, 1933.

Haas, Theodor. *Die Juden in Maehren.* Bruenn, 1908.

Herman, Jan. "The Evolution of the Jewish Population in Prague, 1869–1939." *PJD 1977* (1980): 53–67.

Illyefalvi, I. Lajos. *A székesfőváros multja és jelene grafikus abrázolásban.* Budapest, 1933.

Kestenberg-Gladstein, Ruth. "Internal Migration of Jews in Nineteenth Century Bohemia." *The Field of Yiddish* 3 (1969): 305–309.

Kórösi, Jozsef, and Gustáv Thirring. *Budapest fővárosa az 1891-ik évben: A népleirás és népszamlálás eredményei.* 3 vols. Budapest, 1894–1898.

Kovács, Alajos. *A zsidóság térfoglalása.* Budapest, 1922.

László, Ernó. "Hungary's Jewry: A Demographic Overview, 1918–1945." In *Hungarian Jewish Studies.* Edited by Randolph L. Braham, 2:137–182. New York, 1969.

Lavi, Theodor, and Aviva Broshi, eds. *Rumania: Pinkas ha-kehillot* (Rumania: communities register; in Hebrew). Vol. 1. Jerusalem, 1970.

*Magyar Statisztikai Közlemények, 1930, Népszámlálas.* Budapest, 1941.

Mendelsohn, Ezra. *The Jews of East Central Europe Between the World Wars.* Bloomington, Ind., 1983.

Oxaal, Ivar, and Walter R. Weitzmann. "The Jews of Pre-1914 Vienna—An Exploration of Basic Sociological Dimensions." *LBIYB* 30 (1985): 395–432.

Peric, Marco. "Demographic Study of the Jewish Community of Yugoslavia, 1971–1972." *PJD 1973* (1977): 267–287.

*Populația Evrecască in Cifre—Memento Statistic.* [Bucharest], 1945.

*Population de la Lithuanie—donneés du recensement du 17 septembre 1923.* Kaunas, n.d.

*Recensământul General al Populației României din 29.XII.1930.* Vol. 9, *Structura Populației României.* [Bucharest], n.d.

Rosenfeld, Max. "Die juedische Bevoelkerung Galiziens von 1772–1867." *ZfDSJ* 10 (1914): 138–143.

Rozenblit, Marsha L. *The Jews of Vienna, 1867–1914: Assimilation and Identity.* Albany, 1983.

Ruppin, Arthur. *Die Juden in Rumaenien.* Berlin, 1908.

Schipper, Ignatz. "Die galizische Judenschaft in den Jahren 1772–1848 in wirtschaftsstatistischer Beleuchtung, 1772–1848." *Neue juedische Hefte* 2 (1917–1918): 223–233.

Sedlaczek, Stephan. *Die k.k. Reichshaupt- und Residenzstadt Wien: Ergebnisse der Volkszaehlung vom 31. Dezember 1880.* 3 vols. Vienna, 1887.

Silber, Michael K. "The Historical Experience of German Jewry and Its Impact on Haskalah and Reform in Hungary." In *Toward Modernity: The European Jewish Model.* Edited by Jacob Katz, 107–157. New Brunswick, N.J., and Oxford, 1985.

Steinherz, Samuel. *Die Juden in Prag.* Prague, 1927.

Thirring, Gusztáv. *Magyarország népessége II Józsefkorában.* Budapest, 1938.

Thon, Jakob. *Die Juden in Oesterreich.* Berlin, 1908.

*Troisième recensement de la population en Lettonie, en 1930.* Riga, 1933.

*Volkszaehlung in der Cechoslovakischen Republik, 15. Februar 1921.* Prague, 1924.

### Europe: Western and Central

Barkai, Avraham. "German-Jewish Migrations in the Nineteenth Century, 1830–1910." *LBIYB* 30 (1985): 301–318.

Bensimon-Donath, Doris. *Socio-demographie des juifs de France et d'Algerie: 1867–1907.* Paris, 1976.

Bensimon-Donath, Doris, and Sergio DellaPergola. *La population juive en France: socio-demographie et identité.* Jerusalem and Paris, 1984.

Berg, Roger, Chalom Chemouny, and Franklin Didi, eds. *Guide juif de France.* Paris, 1971.

Bloom, Herbert I. *The Economic Activities of the Jews of Amsterdam in the 17th and 18th Centuries.* New York, 1937.

DellaPergola, Sergio. *Anatomia dell'ebraismo italiano.* Assisi and Rome, 1976.

Kantorowitsch, Miron. "Estimate of the Jewish Population in London in 1928–1933." *Journal of the Royal Statistical Society* 99 (1936): 327–379.

Lipman, Vivian D. *Social History of the Jews in England.* London, 1954.

Reinharz, Jehuda. *Fatherland or Promised Land: The Dilemma of the German Jew, 1893–1914.* Ann Arbor, Mich., 1975.

Roblin, Michel. *Les juifs de Paris.* Paris, 1952.

Russel, Charles, and Harry S. Lewis. *The Jew in London.* London, 1900.

Schmelz, Uziel O. "Die demographische Entwicklung der Juden in Deutschland von der Mitte des 19. Jahrhunderts bis 1933." *Zeitschrift für Bevoelkerungswissenschaft* 8 (1982): 31–72.

Trachtenberg, H. L. "Estimate of the Jewish Population of London in 1929." *Journal of the Royal Statistical Society* 96 (1933): 87–100.

Waterman, Stanley, and Barry A. Kosmin. *British Jewry in the Eighties: A Statistical and Geographic Study.* London, 1986.

### Muslim Countries

Attal, Robert, and Claude Sitbon. *Regards sur les Juifs de Tunisie.* Paris, 1979.

Ben-Yaakov, Abraham. *Kehillot yehudei kurdistan* (The Jewish communities in Kurdistan; in Hebrew). Jerusalem, 1961.

Ben-Yaakov, Abraham. *Yehudei bavel* (The Jews of Iraq; in Hebrew). Jerusalem, 1965.

Cohen, Hayyim. *Ha-yehudim be-aratzot ha-mizrah ha-tikhon be-yamenu* (The Jews in the Middle Eastern countries in the present; in Hebrew). Tel Aviv, 1973.

Hirschberg, Hayyim Ze'ev. *Toldot ha-yehudim be-afrika ha-tzefonit* (History of the Jews in North Africa; in Hebrew). 2 vols. Tel Aviv, 1965.

Landau, Yaakov M. *Ha-yehudim be-mitzrayim ba-me'a ha-tesha-'esrei* (The Jews in Egypt in the nineteenth century; in Hebrew). Jerusalem, 1967.

Netzer, Amnon. *Yehudei iran be-yamenu* (Iranian Jews in our time; in Hebrew). Jerusalem, 1980.

Nini, Jehuda. *Teman ve-tzion* (Yemen and Zion; in Hebrew). Jerusalem, 1982.

Shaw, Stanford J., and Ezel Kural Shaw. *History of the Ottoman Empire and Modern Turkey.* Cambridge, 1977.

Tobi, Yosef. *Toldot yehudei teman me-kitveihem* (History of the Jews in Yemen, from their writings; in Hebrew). Jerusalem, 1980.

Tobi, Yosef, Yaakov Barnay, Shalom Bar-Asher, and Shmuel Ettinger, eds. *Toldot ha-yehudim be-aratzot ha-islam* (History of the Jews in the Muslim countries; in Hebrew). 3 vols. Jerusalem, 1981.

### Palestine and Israel

Bachi, Roberto. *The Population of Israel.* Jerusalem, 1977.

Ben-Amram, Baruch. *Miflagot u-zeramim politi'im be-tekufat ha-bayit ha-le'umi, 1918–1948* (Parties and political trends in the national home period, 1918–1948; in Hebrew). Jerusalem, 1978.

Ben-Arieh, Yehoshua. *Jerusalem in the 19th Century.* 2 vols. Jerusalem, 1984–1986.

DellaPergola, Sergio. "Emigration from Israel." *Encyclopaedia of Zionism.* Jerusalem, 1988.

Eliav, Mordechai. *Eretz Israel ve-yishuvah ba-me'a ha-yod-tet, 1777–1917* (Palestine and its Jewish community in the nineteenth century, 1777–1917; in Hebrew). Jerusalem, 1978.

Kark, Ruth. "Ha-kehillah ha-yehudit be-yafo be-sof tekufat ha-shilton ha-otomani" (The Jewish community in Jaffa at the end of the Ottoman period; in Hebrew). *Cathedra* 16 (1980): 13–24.

Schmelz, Uziel O. *Modern Jerusalem's Demographic Evolution.* Jerusalem, 1987.

*Statistical Handbook of Jewish Palestine.* Jerusalem, 1947.

### Poland

*Annuaire statistique de la République Polonaise, 1925/26.* Warsaw, 1927.

Bloch, Bronislaw. *A Demographic and Geostatistical History of the Jews in Warsaw.* Forthcoming.

Bloch, Bronislaw. "Spatial Evolution of the Jewish and General Population of Warsaw, 1792–1939." *PJD 1973* (1977): 209–234.

Bloch, Bronislaw. "Urban Ecology of the Jewish Population of Warsaw, 1897–1938." *PJD 1981* (1985): 381–399.

Bronszteyn, Szyja. "The Jewish Population of Poland in 1931." *Jewish Journal of Sociology* 6 (1964): 3–29.

*Deuxième recensement général de la population, du 9 decembre 1931.* Warsaw, 1937.

Dubnow, Simon, ed. *Pinkas medina, o pinkas va'ad ha-kehillot ha-rashiot be-medinat lita* (Land register, or minute-book of the administration of the main communities of Lithuania; in Hebrew). Jerusalem, 1969.

Gutman, Yisrael. *Yehudei varsha, 1939–1943; ghetto; mahteret; mered* (The Jews of Warsaw, 1939–1943: ghetto; underground; revolt; in Hebrew). Jerusalem, 1971.

Heilperin, Israel, ed. *Pinkas va'ad arba aratzot* (Minute-book of the administration of the Four Lands; in Hebrew). Jerusalem, 1945.

Lestschinsky, Jakob. "The Jews in the Cities of the Republic of Poland." *YIVO Annual of Jewish Social Science* 1 (1946): 156–177.

Mahler, Raphael. "Shemot yehudi'im shel mekomot be-polin ha-yeshana" (Jewish names of places in old Poland; in Hebrew). *Reshumot* 5 (1953): 147–161.

Mahler, Raphael. *Yidn in amolikn poiln in likht fun tsifern* (The Jews in old Poland according to numbers; in Yiddish). 2 vols. Warsaw, 1958.

*Le premier recensement général de la République Polonaise, du 30 septembre 1921.* Warsaw, 1927.

Shipper, J. "Rassielenye yevreyev v Polske y Litvye." *Istorya Yevreyskogo Naroda.* Vol. 11. Moscow, 1915.

Stampfer, Shaul. "The 1764 Census of Polish Jewry." *Bar-Ilan* 24–25 (1989): 41–147.

[Ulbricht, H.] *Statistisches Gemeindeverzeichniss des bisherigen polnischen Staates.* Berlin, 1939.

Ziemian, Joseph. *The Borders of the Warsaw Ghetto.* Jerusalem, 1971.

### Russian Empire, Soviet Union

Altshuler, Mordechai. *Ha-kibbutz ha-yehudi be-vrit ha-mo'atzot be-yamenu: nitu'ah sotzio-demografi* (The Jewish community in the Soviet Union in our times: a socio-demographic analysis; in Hebrew). Jerusalem, 1980.

*Evrei v SSSR: Materialy i isseldovoniia.* Vol. 4. Moscow, 1929.

Goldberg, Boris. "Die Juden unter der staedtischen Bevoelkerung Russlands." *ZfDSJ* 1, no. 10 (1905): 1–6.

Herlihy, Patricia. *Odessa: A History, 1794–1914.* Cambridge, Mass., 1986.

Kantor, Jacob. *Die yiddishe bafelkerung in Ukraine, loit der folkstsailung fun 1926 yor* (The Jewish population in the Ukraine, according to the 1926 census; in Yiddish). Kiev, 1929.

Lorimer, Frank. *The Population of the Soviet Union: History and Prospects.* Geneva, 1946.

Rowland, Richard H. "Geographical Patterns of the Jewish Population in the Pale of Settlement of Late Nineteenth Century Russia." *Jewish Social Studies* 48 (1986): 207–234.

Ruppin, Arthur. *Die sozialen Verhaeltnisse der Juden in Russland.* Berlin-Halensee, 1906.

Singer, Lev. *Dos banaite folk: Tsifern un faktn wegen di yidn in der FSSR* (The renewed people: numbers and facts about the Jews in the Russian Republic; in Yiddish). Moscow, 1941.

Singer, Lev, and B. Engel. *Yiddishe bafelkerung fun FSSR in tabeles un diagrames* (The Jewish population in the Russian Republic in tables and diagrams; in Yiddish). Moscow, 1930.

Zipperstein, Steven J. *The Jews of Odessa: A Cultural History, 1794–1881.* Palo Alto, Calif., 1985.

### United States

Board of Delegates of American Israelites. *Statistics of the Jews of the United States, 1880.* Philadelphia, 1880.

DellaPergola, Sergio, and Uziel O. Schmelz. "Demographic Transformations of American Jewry: Marriage and Mixed Marriage in the 1980s." In *Studies in Contemporary Jewry* 5. Forthcoming.

Diamond, Jack J. "A Reader in the Demography of American Jews." *AJYB* 77 (1977): 251–319.

Goldberg, Nathan. *Occupational Patterns of American Jewry.* New York, 1947.

Goldstein, Sidney. "Jews in the United States: Perspectives from Demography." In *Jewish Life in the United States: Perspectives from the Social Sciences.* Edited by Joseph B. Gittler, 31–102. New York, 1981.

Grinstein, Hyman B. *The Rise of the Jewish Community of New York, 1654–1860.* Philadelphia, 1945.

Herberg, Will. "The Jewish Labour Movement in the United States." *AJYB* 53 (1952): 3–74.

*HIAS: Annual Report, 1987.* New York, 1988.

Horowitz, Morris C., and Lawrence J. Kaplan. *The Jewish Population of the New York Area, 1900–1975.* New York, 1975.

Israel, Sherry, ed. *Boston's Jewish Community: The 1985 CJP Demographic Study.* Boston, 1987.

Jaret, Charles. "Recent Patterns of Chicago Jewish Residential Mobility." *Ethnicity* 6 (1979): 235–248.

*The Jewish Communal Register of New York City, 1917–1918.* 2d ed. New York, 1918.

Joseph, Samuel. *Jewish Immigration to the United States from 1881 to 1910.* New York, 1914.

Kahan, Arcadius. "Jewish Life in the United States: Perspectives from the Economics." In *Jewish Life in the United States: Perspectives from the Social Sciences.* Edited by Joseph B. Gittler, 237–269. New York, 1981.

Liebmann, Charles S. "Orthodoxy in American Jewish Life." *AJYB* 66 (1965): 21–97.

Linfield, Harry S. *The Communal Organization of the Jews in the United States, 1927.* New York, 1930.

Massarik, Fred. "Affiliation and Nonaffiliation in the United States Jewish Community: A Reconceptualization." *AJYB* 78 (1978): 262–274.

Massarik, Fred, and Alvin Chenkin. "United States National Jewish Population Study." *AJYB* 74 (1973): 264–315.

Phillips, Bruce. *Los Angeles Jewish Community Survey: Overview for Regional Planning.* Los Angeles, 1980.

Raphael, Marc Lee. *Profiles in American Judaism: The Reform, Conservative, Orthodox and Reconstructionist Traditions in Historical Perspective.* San Francisco, 1984.

Reich, Nathan. "Economic Status." In *The American Jew: A Reappraisal.* Edited by Oscar Janowsky, 53–74. Philadelphia, 1964.

Ritterband, Paul, and Steven M. Cohen. "Sample Design and Population Estimation: The Experience of the New York Jewish Population Study (1981–1984)." In *Perspectives in Jewish Population Research.* Edited by S. M. Cohen, J. S. Woocher, and B. A. Phillips, 81–95. Boulder, Colo., and London, 1984.

Rosenthal, Erich. "The Jewish Population of Chicago, Ill." In *The Chicago Pinkas.* Edited by Simon Rawidowicz, 9–112. Chicago, 1952.

Schmelz, Uziel O., and Sergio DellaPergola. *Basic Trends in U.S. Jewish Demography.* New York, 1988.

Sklare, Marshall. *America's Jews.* New York, 1971.

*Survey of Cleveland's Jewish Population, 1981.* Cleveland, 1982.

Tcherikower, Eliyahu, ed. *Geshikhte fun der yiddisher arbeter bawegung in di varainikte shtaten* (History of the Jewish workers' movement in the United States; in Yiddish). 2 vols. New York, 1943.

Tobin, Gary A., and Alvin Chenkin. "Recent Jewish Community Population Studies: A Roundup." *AJYB* 85 (1985): 154–178.

*Union of American Hebrew Congregations: 41st Annual Report (1915).* Cincinnati, 1916.

*Union of American Hebrew Congregations: 1982 Directory of Member Congregations.* New York, 1982.

U.S. Bureau of the Census. *Statistical Abstract of the United States.* Washington, D.C., annual.

Wirth, Louis. *The Ghetto.* Chicago, 1956.

# GENERAL INDEX

This index lists names except place names.
Numbers in roman type refer to page numbers.
Numbers in italic type refer to map numbers.

# INDEX OF GEOGRAPHICAL NAMES

This index lists selected place names and the relevant maps only in which they appear.

The figures after each entry refer to the map numbers.

The Arabic definite articles (al-, el-) are disregarded in the alphabetical listing.

## A



## B

## G



## H



## I



## J



## K

## L



## M

## Q



## R



## S

## T



## U



## V



## W